CONTENTS

Welcome to Rick Steves' Europe

Travel is intensified living—maximum thrills per minute and one of the last great sources of legal adventure. Travel is freedom. It's recess, and we need it.

I discovered a passion for European travel as a teen and have been sharing it ever since—through my bus tours, public television and radio shows, and travel guide-books. Over the years, I've taught millions of travelers how to best enjoy Europe's blockbuster sights—and experience "Back Door" discoveries that most tourists miss.

Written with my talented co-author, Steve Smith, this book offers a balanced mix of Provence and the Riviera's lively cities and cozy towns, from happening Nice to the romantic hill towns of the Luberon. It's selective: Rather than listing dozens of beach towns, we recommend only the best three (Villefranche-sur-Mer, Antibes, and Cassis). And it's in-depth: Our self-guided museum tours, city walks, and driving tours provide insight into the region's vibrant history and today's living, breathing culture.

We advocate traveling simply and smartly. Take advantage of our money- and time-saving tips on sight-seeing, transportation, and more. Try local, characteristic alternatives to expensive hotels and restaurants. In many ways, spending more money only builds a thicker wall between you and what you traveled so far to see.

We visit Provence and the Riviera to experience them—to become temporary locals. Thoughtful travel engages us with the world, as we learn to appreciate other cultures and new ways to measure quality of life.

Judging by the positive feedback we receive from readers, this book will help you enjoy a fun, affordable, and rewarding vacation—whether it's your first trip or your tenth.

Bon voyage! Happy travels!

Rick Steves

Rick Steves®

PROVENCE &
THE FRENCH RIVIERA

Rick Steves & Steve Smith

EDGARTOWN
𝕱𝖗𝖊𝖊 𝕻𝖚𝖇𝖑𝖎𝖈 𝕷𝖎𝖇𝖗𝖆𝖗𝖞

THERE IS NOT such a cradle of democracy
upon the earth as the Free Public Library,
this republic of letters, where neither rank, office,
nor wealth receives the slightest consideration.
— Andrew Carnegie

Presented by

26 West Tisbury Road
Edgartown, Mass. 02539

PROVENCE & THE FRENCH RIVIERA

Provence and the French Riviera are an intoxicating bouillabaisse of enjoyable cities, warm stone villages, Roman ruins, contemporary art, and breathtaking coastlines steaming with sunshine and stirred by the wind. There's something about the play of light in this region, where natural and man-made beauty mingle to dazzle the senses and nourish the soul. It all adds up to *une magnifique* vacation.

Provence and the Riviera stretch along France's southeast Mediterranean coast from the Camargue (south of Arles) to Monaco, and ramble north along the Rhône Valley into the Alps. The regions combined are about the same size as Massachusetts—you can take a train or drive from one end to the other in just three hours—yet they contain more sightseeing opportunities and let's-live-here villages than anywhere else in France. Marseille and Nice, the country's second- and fifth-largest cities, provide good transportation and an urban perspective to this otherwise laid-back region, where every day feels like Sunday.

As you travel through this splendid slice of France, slo-o-o-ow down. Take time to smell the *fougasse,* spend hours in cafés dawdling over *un café,* and make a habit of unplanned stops. Here in France, *l'art de vivre*—the art of living—is not just a pleasing expression; it's a building block for a sound life.

Entertainers and artists are drawn to the region's colorful variety.

With five weeks of paid vacation, plus every Catholic holiday ever invented, the French have become experts at living well. It's no accident that France is home to linger-longer pastimes like café lounging, fine dining, and barge cruising. The French insist on the highest-quality beverages and food (whether it's sparkling water, croissants, cheese, or even mustard). They don't rush lunch, and an evening's entertainment is usually no more than a lovingly prepared meal with friends.

While both Provence and the Riviera share a relaxed pace, each region has a distinct vibe. Provence feels older and more *español* (with paella on menus and bullfights on Sundays), while the Riviera feels downright Italian—with fresh-Parmesan-topped pasta and terra-cotta-colored buildings. For every Roman ruin in Provence, there's a modern art museum in the Riviera. Provence is famous for its wines and wind, while the bikini and ravioli were born on the Riviera.

Sunbaked and windswept, Provence has a rustic charm and feels more working-class and earthy. This area was the first "foreign" conquest as ancient Rome set about building its vast empire. Since it wasn't Rome proper, they called it *Provincia Romana* (province of Rome)—and the name stuck. The Romans left behind some remarkable examples of engineering in their first province, including the Pont du Gard, built around 19 BC, one of the most striking—and impressive—sights in

How to Shop in a French Market

To experience the tasty, fragrant wonders of southern France's edible diversity, head to a street market (*marché*). No "sightseeing" activity better connects you to the French preoccupation with fresh products and their strong ties to the soil.

Markets offer a mind-boggling array of choices brought by area farmers and artisans, from the perishable (produce, meats, cheeses, breads, and pastries) to the nonperishable (kitchenwares, linens, and pottery). But more than just a place to shop, markets give travelers a window into the art of French living.

Most markets take place weekly in the town's main square. Larger towns (such as Arles) may have two weekly markets—the biggest are usually on weekends. Markets typically begin at about 8:00 and end by 13:00— in time for lunch. Most perishable items are sold directly from the producers—no middlemen, no credit cards, just fresh produce (*du pays* means grown locally). You may meet a widow selling a dozen eggs, two rabbits, and a wad of herbs tied with string. Vendors often follow a weekly circuit, showing up in the same spot every week, year in and year out.

Generally, the rule is don't touch— point and let the vendor serve you. If self-service is allowed, the seller will hand you a biodegradable bag. Many vendors speak enough English to assist you in your selection.

The French shop every day to get food that's very fresh. Usually only the vendor touches the produce. Point to what you want, then say or indicate by gesture the quantity you'd like.

Displays shift with the seasons, from asparagus in early spring to winter's little black truffles (or big ones, depending on your wallet size). You'll see the same in-season items on restaurant menus. ▶▶▶

▶▶▶ For more immediate consumption in any season, try local cheeses. These range from very fresh (aged one day) to aged for weeks or months. The older the cheese, the more dried and shrunken it looks. Some are speckled with edible mold or sprinkled with herbs or spices.

Move on to the selection of sausages (many also rolled in herbs or spices). Try the boar (*sanglier*). Be on the lookout for locally produced wines and ciders (free tastings are standard) and samples of foie gras (usually available in take-it-home tins). When teamed with a crusty baguette, these items make perfect picnic fare.

Market day is as important socially as it is commercially—it's a weekly chance for locals to resume friendships and get the current gossip. Vendors chat up their customers and one another; neighbors catch up on Henri's barn renovation, see photos of Jacqueline's new grandchild, and relax over *un café*. Dogs are tethered to café tables while friends exchange kisses. Tether yourself to a table and observe. It's bad form to be in a hurry on market day. Allow the crowd to set your pace.

At the market, buy a chunk of cheese and a cured sausage for your picnic. Relax at a café like the French, who top off shopping with coffee and conviviality.

When you visit a French town, find out when market days are held and plan to be there. You'll feel the energy, and you'll enjoy the local push and shove. I can't imagine a richer French sightseeing experience—one that brings together an appealing ensemble of local ingredients, culture, pride, and people. ∎

all of Europe. In the ancient world, water-bearing aqueducts were like flags of stone that heralded the greatness of Rome. You'll find a variety of other Roman ruins in Provence, from entire towns to outdoor theaters and sports arenas where gladiators dueled.

Throughout Provence, gnarled sycamores line roads that twist their way through stone towns and between oceans of vineyards. In small squares in every Provençal village and city, you're likely to find the local gang playing *boules,* the horse-shoes of southern France (also called *pétanque*). Take time to watch old-timers while away the afternoon tossing shiny silver balls on earthy courts—and give it a try yourself.

France's Riviera conjures images of sea and money—it's populated by a yacht-happy crowd wondering where the next "scene" will be. The Riviera, called *la Côte d'Azur* by locals, was a remote backwater until the late 18th century, when it began gaining fame as a resort town among British aristocrats. In 1864 the first rail service made Nice and the Riviera more accessible, drawing the likes of Czar Alexander II of Russia and Queen Victoria. By the early 20th century, the area's sunny glow had attracted painters such as Henri Matisse, Pablo Picasso, and Auguste Renoir. In towns all along the Riviera, graceful buildings from the turn-of-the-last-century line the sea—reminders of the belle époque. It was literally the "beau-

Try playing boules, *a popular sport at parks. Stroll through streets bordered by Roman ruins.*

Climb up Nice's Castle Hill for a French Riviera view. Browse the market for a new look.

tiful age," when the world seemed to revolve around the upper class and frivolous indulgence was a lifestyle.

The Riviera's most dramatic scenery hides inland. There you'll find cozy hill towns with panoramic views (Vence, St-Paul-de-Vence, and sky-high Eze-le-Village)—along with art galleries, boutiques, and *parfumeries.*

While in Provence and the French Riviera, you can marvel at ancient monuments, take a canoe trip along the meandering rivers, savor seaside hikes with drop-dead views, and settle into a shaded café on a made-for-movies square. Enjoy tasty yet affordable wines while feasting on a healthy cuisine bursting with olives, tomatoes, and herbs. Claim your favorite beach to call home, and at day's end dive headfirst into a southern France sunset. You'll experience the best this lovely region has to offer.

Provence and the French Riviera's Top Destinations

Oh là là! There's so much to see in this compact and fascinating part of France. To help you decide where to spend your time, we've rated both regions' top destinations and suggested a minimum number of days to allow in each.

If you build your trip around the top-rated ▲▲▲ sights, you'll get an unforgettable introduction to the best of Provence and the French Riviera.

Depending on your time and interests, weave any of the lower-ranked sights (▲ and ▲▲) into your trip. It's easy to add some destinations based on proximity; if you're going to Nice, Antibes is next door.

ITALY

25 Kilometers
25 Miles

NEAR AVIGNON:
NIMES, PONT DU GARD & UZES

COTES DU RHONE

FRENCH RIVIERA

EAST OF NICE:
VILLEFRANCHE, CAP FERRAT & EZE-LE-VILLAGE

AVIGNON

HILL TOWNS OF THE LUBERON

MONACO

NICE

ARLES

P R O V E N C E

INLAND RIVIERA

NEAR ARLES:
LES BAUX, ST-REMY & CAMARGUE

ANTIBES & NEARBY:
CANNES & ST-TROPEZ

MARSEILLE & NEARBY:
CASSIS & AIX-EN-PROVENCE

Mediterranean Sea

PLACES COVERED IN THIS BOOK

▲▲▲ Must See
▲▲ Try Hard to See
▲ Worthwhile

PROVENCE

Most choose Arles or Avignon as a home base. Drivers have more options (St-Rémy-de-Provence or the more remote Vaison-la-Romaine or Roussillon).

If you're short on time, I'd prioritize Arles, take day trips to Pont du Gard and Les Baux, spend a night or two in a Côtes du Rhône village, and see the ▲▲▲ sights in the French Riviera (described in the next section).

▲▲▲Arles (allow 1-2 days)

This once-important Roman outpost is now a bustling town, famous for its market days, an ancient amphitheater still used for summer "bullgames," and Vincent van Gogh sights. The town's engaging museums cover ancient history, Van Gogh-inspired works, and modern art.

▲▲▲Near Avignon (1 day)

Three worthy destinations combine well for a memorable (if busy) day trip from Avignon: the stunning Pont du Gard aqueduct; thriving Nîmes, with world-class Roman monuments; and pedestrian-friendly Uzès, a refreshing break from power monuments and busy cities.

▲▲▲The Côtes du Rhône (2 days)

Charming Vaison-la-Romaine makes a good home base for exploring the Côtes du Rhône region, with its sunbaked sunny wine road winding through picturesque villages and fields of lavender. There's a vibrant outdoor market somewhere nearby every day of the week. The overlooked town of Orange hosts a remarkably intact Roman theater and a lively town center.

A bullgame in Arles (bulls survive it); Pont du Gard aqueduct; Roman theater at Orange—still hosting events; Côtes du Rhône village (Gigondas)

▲▲Near Arles (1 day)

Several compelling sights are within a stone's throw of Arles: the cliff-topping castle ruins at Les Baux; St-Rémy with Roman ruins and a mental hospital that treated Van Gogh; and the Camargue—a nature lover's refuge, with flamingos, bulls, and white horses.

▲▲Hill Towns of the Luberon (1 day)

The windswept Luberon region features crumbled castles and cliffhanging villages, ochre canyons, and meditative abbeys; the watery market town of Isle-sur-la-Sorgue; and the delightful rock-top villages of Roussillon, Lacoste, and Ménerbes.

Medieval castle fun at Les Baux; red rock cliffs of Roussillon; river-straddling town of Isle-sur-la-Sorgue

Provence and the French Riviera's Top Destinations

▲▲Marseille and Nearby (2 days)
The photogenic port of Marseille has a gritty charm; the even more photogenic beach town of Cassis is home to the *calanques* (Mediterranean fjords); and inland is the genteel city of Aix-en-Provence, famous for its market-filled squares.

▲Avignon (half-day)
Fourteenth-century residence of the popes, today's youthful city hosts atmospheric cafés, lively squares and pedestrian areas, and a famous broken bridge.

Marseille's harbor viewpoint; market day in Aix-en-Provence; historic Palace of the Popes in Avignon

THE FRENCH RIVIERA

For a home base, choose among Nice, Villefranche-sur-Mer, or Antibes.

▲▲▲Nice (2 days)
The Riviera's metropolis, with a sun-drenched promenade, is a delightful Franco-Italian mashup featuring a lively old city, the finest Russian Cathedral outside Russia, plus museums dedicated to Chagall and Matisse.

▲▲▲East of Nice (1 day)
The small, romantic beach town of Villefranche-sur-Mer, ritzy but woodsy Cap Ferrat, and little cliff-topping Eze-le-Village are linked by the panoramic roads known as the Three Corniches.

▲▲▲Monaco (half-day)
Run as part of France, this tiny independent principality is known for its glamorous history, Grand Prix car race, and classy casino.

▲▲Inland Riviera (1-2 days)
To really do this region justice, head inland to the perfectly perched hill towns of Vence and St-Paul-de-Vence (France's most-visited village), the perfume capital of Grasse, and the spectacular Grand Canyon du Verdon.

▲Antibes and Nearby (1 day)
The Riviera's west stars laid-back Antibes, with a medieval old town wrapped around a sharp Picasso Museum; glamorous Cannes, with sandy beaches and movie stars; and the luxurious port town of St-Tropez.

Provence and the French Riviera's Top Destinations

Coastal Villefranche-sur-Mer; beach at Antibes; Grand Canyon du Verdon; Monaco's elegant glitz

Planning Your Trip

To plan your trip, you'll need to design your itinerary—choosing where and when to go, how you'll travel, and how many days to spend at each destination. For my best general advice on sightseeing, accommodations, restaurants, and more, see the Practicalities chapter.

DESIGNING AN ITINERARY

As you read this book and learn your options...

Choose your top destinations.

My recommended itineraries (see the sidebars) give you an idea of how much you can reasonably see in 14 days, but you can adapt them to fit your own interests and time frame.

Focus on Provence if Roman ruins are a priority (Arles, Pont du Gard, Nîmes, Orange, St-Rémy, and more). Wine lovers savor the Côtes du Rhône wine road and pop corks at the famous Châteauneuf-du-Pape. For meandering exploration, the hilly Luberon satisfies drivers, hikers, and hardy bikers.

The Riviera has the beaches and colorful harbors, of course. Nightlife is best in Nice, but it's a sure bet that gamblers head for Monaco.

Both regions have museums for art lovers, hill towns for connoisseurs (Provence has more), and scads of scenic beauty. Nature lovers seek out Provence's Camargue for wildlife, beach town Cassis for *calanques,* the inland Riviera's Grand Canyon du Verdon for dramatic scenery, and the wooded Cap Ferrat and Cap d'Antibes for coastal hikes with Mediterranean views. Foodies and photographers want to go everywhere.

Decide when to go.

With more than 300 days of sunshine per year, Provence and the Riviera enjoy France's sunniest weather. Spring and fall are best, with generally comfortable weather—though crowds can be a problem, particularly during holiday weekends and major events (May is worst). April can be a bit damp, and any month can be windy (mistral winds are infamous in Provence). Don't be fooled by sunny forecasts in shoulder season (April and October)—if the wind is blowing it can be chilly.

Summer means festivals, lavender (late June through July), sunflowers, steamy weather, long hours at sights, and longer lines of cars along the Riviera. Europeans vacation in July and August, jamming the Riviera, the Grand Canyon du Verdon (Gorges du Verdon), and the Ardèche (worst from mid-July through mid-Aug), but leaving the rest of this region relatively

Nightlife in Nice; wine—the lifeblood of France; hiking views over peninsular Cap Ferrat

Best Two-Week Trip of Provence & the French Riviera by Car

While this trip is doable in 14 days, most will appreciate adding an extra day here and there to rest their engine.

Day	Plan	Sleep
1	Arrive, stroll the Promenade des Anglais	Nice
2	Explore Vieux Nice, visit a museum or two, have dinner on the beach	Nice
3	Train or bus to Villefranche-sur-Mer, seaside walk in Cap Ferrat or boat cruise from Nice's port, afternoon or evening in Monaco	Nice
4	Pick up car, drive north to Vence or Grasse, continue to Grand Canyon du Verdon, then Aiguines or Moustiers-Ste-Marie	Aiguines or Moustiers-Ste-Marie
5	Drive into Luberon, explore villages of Provençal heartland	In or near Roussillon
6	Drive to Côtes du Rhône. If late June-late July, drive via Sault to see lavender fields (Mon arrival ideal for Tue market day in Vaison-la-Romaine)	In or near Vaison-la-Romaine
7	Explore Vaison-la-Romaine, drive Côtes du Rhône wine road, tour Crestet, and walk above Gigondas	In or near Vaison-la-Romaine
8	Tour Roman theater in Orange; quick stop in Châteauneuf-du-Pape. Self-guided walks and dinner in Avignon	Avignon
9	Explore Nîmes (Roman amphitheater) then Pont du Gard (if weather's good, bring swimsuit and float under aqueduct)	Avignon
10	Early morning visit to Les Baux and Carrières de Lumières. Wind up in Arles	Arles

calm. Though many French businesses close in August, the traveler hardly notices.

September brings the grape harvest, when small wineries are off-limits to taste-seeking travelers (though good options exist). Late fall delivers beautiful foliage and a return to tranquility.

Winter travel is OK in Nice, Aix-en-Provence, and Avignon, but you'll find smaller cities and villages buttoned up tight. Sights and tourist information offices keep shorter hours,

11	Spend all day in Arles. Possible late afternoon joyride through the Camargue (best in spring)	Arles
12	Drive to Cassis with lunch and visit to Aix-en-Provence or Marseille en route (Marseille is dicier by car). Watch the sun set from the old port and enjoy a bouillabaisse dinner in Cassis	Cassis
13	Enjoy *la vie douce* in Cassis. Boat trip or hike to the *calanques*, play or watch *pétanque*, and end day with a drive up Cap Canaille	Cassis
14	Fly out of Marseille or, if leaving from Nice, drive to Antibes and spend day and evening there	

and some tourist activities (such as English-language tours) vanish altogether.

Thanks to Provence's temperate climate, fields of flowers greet the traveler much of the year:

May: Wild red poppies *(coquelicots)* sprout.

June: Lavender begins to bloom in the lower hills of Provence, generally during the last week of the month.

July: Lavender is in full swing in Provence, and sunflowers are awakening. If you can find adjacent fields with lavender and sunflowers, celebrate! Cities, towns, and villages everywhere overflow with carefully tended flowers.

August-September: Sunflowers flourish.

October: In the latter half of the month, the countryside glistens with fall colors (most trees are deciduous). Vineyards go for the gold.

For weather specifics, see the climate chart in the appendix.

Connect the dots.

Link your destinations into a logical route. Determine which cities you'll fly into and out of (Lyon, Nice, and Marseille all work well). Begin your search for transatlantic flights at Kayak.com.

Decide if you'll travel by car or public transportation, or a combination. A car is invaluable for exploring the Côtes du Rhône or Luberon (where public transportation is sparse) but is useless in big cities and a nightmare in Monaco. Trains link cities and many towns easily, while buses reach some places that trains don't. Minibus tours are handy for regional sightseeing.

Distances are short in this region (for example, one of the longer trips—connecting Arles and Nice—takes only 2.5 hours by car or 4 hours by train). To determine approximate travel times between destinations, study the driving map in the Practicalities chapter or check Google Maps; visit Bahn. com for train schedules. Compare the cost of any long train ride in Europe with a budget flight; check Skyscanner.com for intra-European flights.

Write out a day-by-day itinerary.

Figure out how many destinations you can comfortably fit in your time frame. Don't overdo it—few travelers wish they'd hurried more. Allow enough days per stop (see estimates in "Provence and the French Riviera's Top Destinations," earlier). Minimize one-night stands. It can be worth taking a late-afternoon drive or train ride to settle into a town for two consecutive nights—and gain a full uninterrupted day for sightseeing. Include sufficient time for transportation between destinations.

Staying in a home base (like Arles) and making day trips can be more time-efficient than changing locations and hotels

Best Two-Week Trip of Provence & the French Riviera by Train and Bus

Note that on Sundays, fewer trains run, and buses often disappear.

Day	Plan
1	Fly into **Nice;** stroll the Promenade des Anglais **(4 nights)**
2	Explore Vieux Nice, visit museums, have dinner on the beach
3	Train or bus to Villefranche-sur-Mer, seaside walk in Cap Ferrat or boat cruise from Nice's port, afternoon or evening in Monaco
4	Bus to Vence and St-Paul-de-Vence or Grasse for sightseeing
5	Train to **Isle-sur-la-Sorgue.** Canoe ride down Sorgue River **(1 night)**
6	Morning market (Thu or Sun), then train to **Avignon** for self-guided walks and dinner **(2 nights)**
7	Train to Nîmes (Roman amphitheater), then bus to Pont du Gard
8	Short morning train to Orange, then bus to **Vaison-la-Romaine;** arrive Mon for Tue market **(2 nights)**
9	Visit a wine village, take a minivan tour of the wine road, bike to Séguret and Gigondas, or hike to Crestet for lunch (taxi back)
10	Morning bus to Orange, visit Roman theater, then train to **Arles (2 nights)**
11	Minivan tour or taxi (or, in summer, bus) to Les Baux. Return to Arles by taxi or bus; or taxi to St-Rémy, explore, then bus back to Arles
12	Train to Marseille, check bags at station, and take my walking tour of ancient center. Train to **Cassis,** then watch sunset from old port **(2 nights)**
13	Explore Cassis. Take boat trip or hike to *calanques*, then watch *pétanque* balls fly
14	Fly out of **Marseille** or train to **Nice (1 night)**

Train-hopping the French Riviera

(though I would not do it at the cost of an overnight in a peaceful village).

Take sight closures into account. Avoid visiting a town on the one day a week its must-see sights are closed. Check if any holidays or festivals fall during your trip—these attract crowds and can close sights (for the latest, visit France's tourist website, Us.france.fr).

Give yourself some slack. Every trip, and every traveler, needs downtime for doing laundry, picnic shopping, people-watching, and so on. Pace yourself. Assume you will return.

Luberon hill town of Gordes; driving in Provence; enjoying Arles—a good home base

Trip Costs Per Person

Run a reality check on your dream trip. You'll have major transportation costs in addition to daily expenses.

Flight: A round-trip flight from the US to Nice or Paris costs about $900-1,500, depending on where you fly from and when.

Public Transportation: Allow $10 per day per person for public transportation (trams, buses, and taxis). Nondrivers should allow $100 per week for trains and buses between towns.

Car Rental: $350-500 per week (booked well in advance), not including tolls, gas, parking, and insurance. If you need the car for three weeks or more, leasing is cheaper.

AVERAGE DAILY EXPENSES PER PERSON

$185
Applies to cities, figure on less for towns

Lodging
Based on two people splitting the cost of a $150 double room
$75

Meals
$15 for breakfast, $20 for lunch, and $35 for dinner
$70

City Transit
Buses and Métro
$10

Sights and Entertainment
This daily average works for most people.
$30

Budget Tips

To cut your daily expenses, take advantage of the deals you'll find throughout Provence and the Riviera and mentioned in this book.

Some businesses—especially hotels and walking-tour companies—offer discounts to my readers (look for the RS% symbol in the listings in this book).

Reserve your rooms directly with the hotel. Some hotels offer a discount if you pay in cash and/or stay three or more nights (check online or ask). Rooms can cost less outside of peak season (May-Sept). And even seniors can sleep cheaply in hostels (most have private rooms) for about $30 per ▶▶▶

▶▶▶ person. Or check Airbnb-type sites for deals.

It's no hardship to eat inexpensively in Provence or the Riviera. You can get tasty, affordable meals at delis, bars, cafés, and bakeries. Cultivate the art of picnicking in atmospheric settings.

Avid sightseers buy combo-tickets or passes that cover multiple museums, such as the Pass Liberté in Arles that covers the city's key sights. If a town doesn't offer deals, visit only the sights you most want to see, and seek out free sights and experiences (people-watching counts).

When you splurge, choose an experience you'll always remember, such as a food-tasting tour, hot-air balloon flight, or sleeping in a medieval castle-hotel. Minimize souvenir shopping; focus instead on collecting wonderful memories. ▮

To save money, picnic and sightsee smartly, but splurge for experiences (like a food-tasting tour).

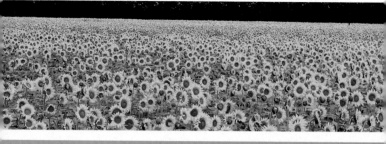

BEFORE YOU GO

You'll have a smoother trip if you tackle a few things ahead of time. For more details on these topics, see the Practicalities chapter and RickSteves.com, which has helpful travel-tip articles and videos.

Make sure your travel documents are valid. If your passport is due to expire within six months of your ticketed date of return, you need to renew it. Allow six weeks or more to renew or get a passport (www.travel.state.gov). Check for current Covid-19 entry requirements, such as proof of vaccination or a negative Covid test result.

Arrange your transportation. Book your international flights. Overall, Kayak.com is the best place to start searching for flights. Figure out your transportation options: It's worth thinking about renting a car or buying train tickets online in advance. (You can wing it once you're there, but it may cost more.)

Purchasing a rail pass or booking flights within Europe only makes sense if you are traveling beyond Provence and the Riviera, as distances are short and point-to-point fares are reasonable.

Note that all high-speed trains (TGVs) in France require a seat reservation; book as early as possible, as these trains fill fast. If you're using a rail pass, book even earlier—there's a tight limit on seat reservations for passholders. Most trains between Marseille and Nice and between Paris and Avignon are TGV—book well ahead for these.

Book rooms well in advance, especially if your trip falls during peak season or any major holidays or festivals.

Hire guides in advance. Popular guides can get booked up. If you want a specific guide, reserve by email as far ahead as possible.

Consider travel insurance. Compare the cost of insurance to the cost of your potential loss. Check whether your existing insurance (health, homeowners, or renters) covers you and your possessions overseas.

Call your bank. Alert your bank that you'll be using your debit and credit cards in Europe. Ask about transaction fees, and, if you don't already have one, get a "contactless" credit card (request your card PIN too). You don't need to bring euros for your trip; you can withdraw euros from cash machines in Europe or use your credit card for virtually all purchases as you do at home.

Use your smartphone smartly. Sign up for an international service plan to reduce your costs, or rely on Wi-Fi in Europe instead. Download any apps you'll want on the road, such as maps, translators, transit schedules, and Rick Steves Audio Europe (see sidebar).

Pack light. You'll walk with your luggage more than you think, even if you're driving. I travel for weeks with a single carry-on bag and a day pack. Use the packing checklist in the appendix as a guide.

Rick's Free Video Clips and Audio Tours

Travel smarter with these free, fun resources:

Rick Steves Classroom Europe, a powerful tool for teachers, is also useful for travelers. This video library contains about 500 short clips excerpted from my public television series. Enjoy these videos as you sort through options for your trip and to better understand what you'll see in Europe. Check it out at Classroom.RickSteves.com (just enter a topic to find everything I've filmed on a subject).

The **Rick Steves Audio Europe** app makes it easy to download audio content to enhance your trip. Use the app to listen to audio tours of Europe's top sights, plus interviews (organized by country) from my public radio show with experts from Europe and around the globe. Find it in your app store or at RickSteves.com/ AudioEurope.

Travel Smart

If you have a positive attitude, equip yourself with good information (this book), and expect to travel smart, you will.

Read—and reread—this book. To have an "A" trip, be an "A" student. Note opening hours of sights, closed days, crowd-beating tips, and whether reservations are required or advisable. Check the latest at RickSteves.com/update.

Be your own tour guide. As you travel, get up-to-date info on sights, reserve tickets and tours, reconfirm hotels and travel arrangements, and check transit connections. Visit local tourist information offices (TIs). Upon arrival in a new town, lay the groundwork for a smooth departure; confirm the train, bus, or road you'll take when you leave (TIs and hotel staff can help with updated road information).

Outsmart thieves. Pickpockets abound in crowded places where tourists congregate. Treat commotions as smokescreens for theft. Keep your cash, credit cards, and passport secure in a money belt tucked under your clothes; carry only a day's spending money in your front pocket or wallet. Don't set valu-

The Language Barrier and That French Attitude

You may have heard that French people are cold and refuse to speak English. In my experience, the French are as friendly as other people (though a bit more formal) and many speak English well. But be reasonable in your expectations: French waiters are paid to be efficient, not chatty.

The best advice? Slow down. Impatient travelers unaware of the joys of people-watching from a café often misinterpret French attitudes. With five weeks of paid vacation and a shorter work week than ours, the French don't understand why anyone would rush through their time off.

The French view formality as being polite and prefer to avoid eye contact with strangers. When tourists stroll down the street grinning and blurting *"Bonjour!"* to everyone, the French find it odd rather than friendly.

You'll get better reactions if you use the pleasantries. Learn these five phrases: *bonjour* (good day), *pardon* (pardon me), *s'il vous plaît* (please), *merci* (thank you), and *au revoir* (goodbye). Begin every encounter (for instance, when entering a shop) with *"Bonjour, madame (or monsieur),"* and end every encounter with *"Au revoir, madame (or monsieur)."*

*It's très French: At sidewalk cafés, people take their time. At small shops (like this bakery), say, "*Bonjour, madame (or monsieur)."*

The French take language seriously. To ask a French person to speak English, say, *"Bonjour, madame (or monsieur). Parlez-vous anglais?"* They may say *"non"* (because they don't speak English fluently), but you may soon find out they speak more English than you speak French.

Practice French survival phrases (see the appendix), and have a phrase book or translator app handy. In transactions, a notepad and pen can help; have vendors write down the price. ◼

able items down on counters or café tabletops, where they can be quickly stolen or easily forgotten.

Minimize potential loss. Keep expensive gear to a minimum. Bring copies or take photos of important documents (passport and cards) to aid in replacement if they're lost or stolen. Back up photos and files frequently.

Beat the summer heat. If you wilt easily, choose a hotel with air-conditioning, start your day early, take a midday siesta, and resume your sightseeing later. Churches offer a cool haven (modest attire is appreciated). Take frequent breaks and drink lots of liquids.

Guard your time and energy. If you're exhausted, take a taxi across town instead of figuring out the bus system. And a regional minibus tour can be a good value if it spares you long waits for cheap and time-consuming buses on a hot day. Use

Canoeing at the ancient Pont du Gard; chilling in a cool, medieval church

the tips throughout this book to organize your sightseeing efficiently.

Be flexible. Even if you have a well-planned itinerary, expect changes, strikes, closures, sore feet, bad weather, and so on. Your Plan B could turn out to be even better.

Attempt the language. Many French—especially in the tourist trade and in cities—speak English, but if you learn some French, even just a few pleasantries, you'll get more smiles and make more friends. Apps such as Google Translate work for on-the-go translation help, but you can get a head start by practicing the survival phrases near the end of this book.

Connect with the culture. Interacting with locals carbonates your experience. Enjoy the friendliness of the French people. Ask questions; most locals are happy to point you in their idea of the right direction. Cheer for your favorite bowler at a *boules* match, leave no chair unturned in your quest for the best café, find that perfect hill-town view, and make friends with a waiter (it happens). When an opportunity pops up, make it a habit to say "yes."

Your next stop...Provence and the French Riviera!

PROVENCE

PROVENCE

"There are treasures to carry away in this land, which has not found a spokesman worthy of the riches it offers."

—Paul Cézanne

The magnificent region of Provence is shaped like a giant wedge of quiche. From its sunburned crust, fanning out along the Mediterranean coast from the Camargue to Marseille, it stretches north along the Rhône Valley to Orange. The Romans were here in force and left lots of ruins—some of the best anywhere (the region's name comes from its status as the first Roman province). Seven popes, artists such as Vincent van Gogh and Paul Cézanne, Nostradamus, and author Peter Mayle all enjoyed their years in Provence. This region features a splendid recipe of arid climate, oceans of vineyards, stunning scenery, lively cities, and adorable hill-capping villages.

Explore the ghost town that is ancient Les Baux, and see France's greatest Roman ruins—the Pont du Gard aqueduct, the theater in Orange, and the arena in Nîmes. Admire the skill of ball-tossing *boules* players in small squares in every Provençal village and city. Spend a few Van Gogh-inspired starry, starry nights in Arles. Youthful but classy Avignon bustles in the shadow of its brooding Palace of the Popes. Stylish and self-confident Aix-en-Provence lies 30 minutes from the sea and feels more Mediterranean. It's a short hop from Arles or Avignon into the splendid scenery and villages of the Côtes du Rhône and Luberon regions. To properly understand southern France, day-trip into gritty Marseille. If you prefer a perfectly Provençal beach fix, linger in Cassis, just to the east.

PROVENCE

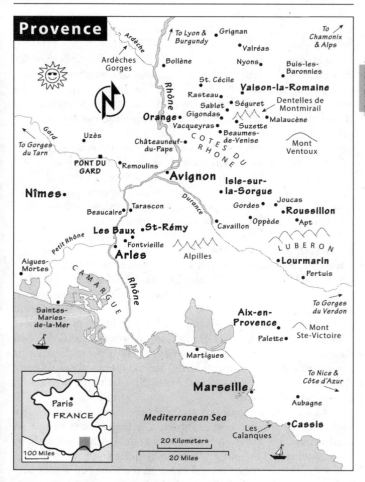

Provence

To Lyon & Burgundy • Grignan
• Valréas
Ardèche
Ardèches Gorges • Bollène
Nyons•
Buis-les-Baronnies
St. Cécile
Rasteau• **Vaison-la-Romaine**
Sablet• •Séguret
Gard •Séguret Dentelles de Montmirail
To Gorges du Tarn
Uzès• **Orange**• Gigondas• Suzette• Malaucène
Vacqueyras• Beaumes-de-Venise
Châteauneuf-du-Pape• Mont Ventoux
PONT DU GARD •Remoulins
Nîmes•
Avignon Isle-sur-la-Sorgue
Durance Joucas
Beaucaire• Tarascon Gordes• •**Roussillon**
Les Baux •**St-Rémy** Oppède• •Apt
•Fontvieille Cavaillon
Arles Alpilles L U B E R O N
Aigues-Mortes •**Lourmarin**
Pertuis•
C A M A R G U E
Rhône To Gorges du Verdon
Saintes-Maries-de-la-Mer **Aix-en-Provence**• Mont Ste-Victoire
Palette•
Martigues•
To Nice & Côte d'Azur
Marseille•
Paris Aubagne•
FRANCE _Mediterranean Sea_ •**Cassis**
Les Calanques
100 Miles 20 Kilometers
20 Miles

CHOOSING A HOME BASE

With limited time, make Arles or Avignon your sightseeing base—particularly without a car. Italophiles prefer compact Arles, while poodles pick sophisticated Avignon. Many enjoy nights in both cities. (With a car, head for St-Rémy or the hill towns.)

Arles has a blue-collar quality; the entire city feels like Van Gogh's bedroom. It also has this region's best-value hotels and is handy to Les Baux, St-Rémy, and the Camargue.

Avignon—double the size of Arles—feels more upscale and classy, with more nightlife and shopping. Avignon makes a good base for nondrivers thanks to its convenient public-transit options. Within an hour or so, you can reach Pont du Gard, Uzès, and St-Rémy by bus, or Marseille and Aix-en-Provence by TGV train or shuttle bus. Within a half-hour, you can reach Arles, Isle-sur-la-Sorgue, and Nîmes by regional train (TER).

For drivers who prefer a smaller-town base, **St-Rémy-de-Provence** works well. It offers a nice range of hotels with free and easy parking, good restaurants, and a few sights of its own. The towns of **Vaison-la-Romaine** (in the Côtes du Rhône region) and **Roussillon** (in the Luberon) are two appealing but remote hill-town options.

Aix-en-Provence works well as a base for Provence sights east of Arles and Avignon, with easy access to Marseille, Cassis, and some Luberon villages. About halfway between Arles and Nice, Aix-en-Provence also makes a convenient stopover, and if you're flying in or out of Marseille, Aix has quick access to the airport, making it a convenient first- or last-day stop.

PLANNING YOUR TIME

The bare minimum you should spend in Provence is three days: one day for sightseeing in Arles and Les Baux (Arles is best on Wed or Sat, when it's market day); a day for Pont du Gard and Nîmes; and a full day for Orange and the Côtes du Rhône villages. Add two more days to explore Avignon, Uzès or St-Rémy, and more Provençal villages (such as Roussillon). Allow an additional two days in Cassis, using one of them for a day trip to Marseille or Aix-en-Provence (or both). Ideally, see the cities—Arles, Nîmes, Avignon, Aix-en-Provence, and Marseille—by train, then rent a car for the countryside.

To measure the pulse of rural Provence, spend at least a few nights in the smaller towns. Provençal villages come to life on market days, but are dead on Sundays and Mondays when shops are shuttered tight—and are terminally quiet from mid-October to Easter. I've described several towns in the Côtes du Rhône and Luberon. The Côtes du Rhône is ideal for wine connoisseurs and an easy stop for those heading to or from the north. The Luberon was made for hill-town lovers and works well for travelers heading east, toward Aix-en-Provence or the Riviera. Avoid speeding through these areas. Provençal village evenings are what books are written about—spend a night, or two, or...

The small port town of Cassis is a marvelous Mediterranean meander between Provence and the Riviera (and more appealing than most Riviera resorts). It has easy day-trip connections to Marseille and Aix-en-Provence.

Depending on the length of your trip, here are my recommended priorities for Provence:

4 days:	Arles and Les Baux; Pont du Gard and Nîmes; and Orange and Côtes du Rhône villages
5-6 days, add:	Cassis, Marseille, and Aix-en-Provence

7-8 days, add: Luberon hill towns
9-10 days, add: Avignon and either St-Rémy or Uzès

HELPFUL HINTS

Resources: Imagine Tours (near Avignon) offers free assistance to travelers. They can help you plan your itinerary, book hotels, or deal with travel problems (for contact information, see listing under "Tours in Provence," later).

Cruise-Ship Sightseeing: Cruise lines that visit Provence call at either Marseille or La Seyne-sur-Mer/Toulon (about 40 miles east of Marseille). Public-transit options are limited—with a short day, only Marseille, Cassis, and Aix-en-Provence are do-able. (It's possible to visit Avignon or Arles from Marseille—but only with a long day in port.) To journey beyond the immediate area and/or connect several sights in one busy day, join a cruise-line excursion, hire a driver or guide, or rent a car. For in-depth coverage, consider my guidebook, *Rick Steves Mediterranean Cruise Ports.*

GETTING AROUND PROVENCE

By Bus or Train: Public transit is good between cities and decent to some towns, but marginal at best to the smaller villages. Frequent trains link Avignon, Arles, and Nîmes (no more than an hour between each). Avignon has good train connections with Orange and adequate service to Isle-sur-la-Sorgue. Marseille is well connected to all cities in Provence, with frequent service to Cassis (25 minutes) and Aix-en-Provence (45 minutes).

Buses connect many smaller towns, though service can be sporadic. From Arles you can catch a bus to Les Baux (in summer), Stes-Maries-de-la-Mer (in the Camargue), or St-Rémy. From Avignon, you can bus to Pont du Gard, St-Rémy, Uzès, Isle-sur-la-Sorgue, and to some Côtes du Rhône villages. St-Rémy, Isle-sur-la-Sorgue, and Uzès are the most accessible and interesting small towns. Vaison-la-Romaine—my favorite town—is a manageable bus ride from Orange (with fast and frequent train connections to Avignon). A visit here works well with a tour of Orange's Roman Theater.

While a tour of the Côtes du Rhône or Luberon is best on your own by car, a variety of minivan tours and basic bus excursions are available. (TIs in Arles and Avignon also have information on bus excursions to regional sights that are hard to reach *sans* car; see "Tours in Provence," later.)

By Car: The region is made to order for a car, though travel time between some sights will surprise you—thanks, in part, to narrow roads and endless roundabouts (for example, figure an hour from Les Baux to Pont du Gard, and almost two hours from Arles to Vaison-la-Romaine). Michelin map #527 (1:275,000 scale) covers this area perfectly. Michelin maps #332 (Luberon and Côtes du Rhône) and #340 (Arles area) are also worth considering. I've described key sights and a variety of full-day drives deep into the countryside. Be wary of thieves: Park only in well-monitored spaces and leave nothing valuable in your car. Drivers are smart to offload bags at hotels before sightseeing.

Avignon is a headache for drivers. Arles is easier but still challenging. Les Baux and St-Rémy work well from Arles or Avignon (or vice versa). Nîmes and Pont du Gard are a short hop west of Avignon. The town of Orange ties in tidily with a trip to the Côtes du Rhône villages and with destinations farther north. If you're heading north from Provence, consider a half-day detour through the spectacular Ardèche Gorges. The Luberon villages are about halfway between Arles or Avignon and Aix-en-Provence (little Lourmarin works as a base for day trips to Aix-en-Provence). And if you're continuing on to the Riviera, joyride through the Grand Canyon du Verdon (see the Inland Riviera chapter). Drivers will prefer exploring con-

gested Marseille on foot—take the train from Cassis or Aix-en-Provence (both towns have parking at their train stations with frequent trains and buses to the center of Marseille).

Note that metered parking is strictly monitored. For tips on parking in France, see the "Driving" section in the Practicalities chapter.

By Bike: Wind, heat, and hilly terrain make this region a challenge for many to bike. I list bike rental options in most cities (including electric bikes). **Telecycles** will deliver your bike to hotels within about 12 miles of St-Rémy (+33 6 11 64 04 69, www.telecycles-location.com). Check also with **Sun-e-Bike** for handy electric bike rentals throughout Provence (www.sun-e-bike.com).

TOURS IN PROVENCE

Towns with a lot of tourism generally have English-speaking guides available for private hire (about €130 for a 3-hour guided walk). It's also possible to take half-day or full-day excursions to most of the sights in Provence. TIs have wads of brochures on day trips and can help you make a reservation. Excursions are best from Avignon, where most tours can pick you up at your hotel, the TI, or

Top 10 Provençal Towns and Villages

1. **Roussillon,** a beautiful hill town sitting atop a huge ochre deposit, giving it a red-rock appeal, popular with American tourists; see page 221.

2. **Uzès,** a chic town with manicured pedestrian streets, popular with European tourists; see page 164.

3. **Joucas,** an adorable little village where flowers and stones are lovingly maintained, a magnet for artists; see page 229.

4. **Brantes,** a spectacularly situated cliff village literally at the end of the road, with few tourists; see page 206.

5. **Vaison-la-Romaine,** a bustling midsize town that spans both sides of a river and has Roman ruins, popular with tourists; see page 179.

6. **Lourmarin,** a lovely upscale village, busy during the day but quiet at night; see page 243.

7. **Crestet,** an overlooked village with a sensational hilltop location and one commercial enterprise; see page 196.

8. **Séguret,** a linear hillside village with memorable views, many day-trippers, but few overnighters; see page 193.

9. **Gigondas,** a world-famous wine village with a nice balance of commercial activity and quiet; see page 201.

10. **Nyons,** an overlooked midsize town with a few pedestrian streets, famous for its olive oil and ideal climate; see page 205.

at either of the city's train stations. Here are several good options to consider:

Tours with a Wine Focus
Wine Safari
Dutchman Mike Rijken runs a one-man show, taking travelers through the region he adopted 25 years ago. His English is fluent, and though his focus is on wine and wine villages, Mike knows the region thoroughly and is a good teacher of its history (per person: €80/half-day, €140/day, 2-6-person groups; pickups possible in Arles, Avignon, Lyon, Marseille, or Aix-en-Provence; +33 4 32 70 10 15, mobile +33 6 19 29 50 81, www.winesafari.net, mikeswinesafari@orange.fr).

Le Vin à la Bouche
Charming Céline Viany—a sommelier and easy-to-be-with tour guide—is an expert on her region and its chief product (from €250/half-day or €320/day for 2 people, price depends on pickup location and number of clients, +33 4 90 46 90 80, mobile +33 6 76 59 56 30, www.levinalabouche.com, contact@degustation-levinalabouche.com).

Wine Uncovered

Passionate Englishman Olivier Hickman takes small groups on focused tours of selected wineries in Châteauneuf-du-Pape and in the villages near Vaison-la-Romaine. Olivier knows his subject matter inside and out. His in-depth tastings include a half-day tour of two or three wineries (€40-75/person for half-day to full-day tours, prices subject to minimum tour fees, +33 6 75 10 10 01, www.wine-uncovered.com, olivier.hickman@orange.fr).

Travel in Provence

Sophie Bergeron is native to the Côtes du Rhône region. She can help you organize your trip and guide you from monuments to villages to vineyards (travelinprovence@yahoo.com).

Tours du Rhône

Low-key but wine smart American Doug Graves, who owns a small wine *domaine* in the Côtes du Rhône, runs custom tours of Châteauneuf-du-Pape, the villages of the Côtes du Rhône, and the Luberon Valley (per person: €155/day, up to 4 people, includes lunch; +33 6 37 16 04 56, www.toursdurhone.com, doug@masdelalionne.com).

Winery Plus Tours

This company offers small group tours centered on wine and food with a good dose of history and local culture. Experienced guide and wine connoisseur Joe McLean leads tours focusing on the wines of Uzès, Châteauneuf-du-Pape, and the Côtes du Rhône (per person: about €70-95/half-day, €130-160/day, prices include pickup from Uzès hotels; fully private tours available—add €30/person, custom tours possible from Arles and Avignon, no tours on Sun, +33 6 73 08 23 97, www.wineryplustours.com, contact@wineryplustours.com).

Provence & Wine

Sommelier Romain Gouvernet is a young and sincere wine guide concentrating on Châteauneuf-du-Pape and the Luberon. Ask about his evening wine tours (per person: €95/half-day, €150/day; +33 6 86 49 56 76, www.provenceandwine.com, provenceandwine@gmail.com).

Avignon Wine Tour

For a playful perspective on wines of the Côtes du Rhône region, contact François Marcou (€130/person for all-day wine tours that include 4 tastings, +33 6 28 05 33 84, www.avignon-wine-tour.com, contact@avignon-wine-tour.com).

Plane Trees

Stately old plane trees line boulevards such as Cours Mirabeau in Aix-en-Provence and provide canopies of shade for roads

and town squares all over southern France. These trees are a part of the local scene.

The plane tree is a hybrid of the Asian and American sycamores—created accidentally in a 16th-century Oxford botanical garden. The result was the perfect city tree: fast-growing, resistant to Industrial Age pollution, and hearty (it can survive with little water and lousy soil). The plane tree was imported to southern France in the 19th century to replace traditional elm trees. Napoleon had thousands of them planted along roads in southern France to give his soldiers shade for their long marches. Plane trees were used to leaf up grand boulevards as towns throughout France—including Aix-en-Provence—built their Champs-Elysées wannabes. Sadly, a modern disease is taking its toll and many trees are dying.

Cultural and Historical Tours
Imagine Tours

This organization offers personalized cultural excursions that highlight the "true heart of Provence and Occitania." Itineraries are adapted to your interests, and your guide can meet you at your hotel or the departure point of your choice (€190/half-day, €315/day, prices for up to 4 people starting from near Avignon or Arles, +33 6 89 22 19 87, www.imagine-tours.net, imagine.tours@gmail.com). They can also help plan your itinerary, book hotel rooms, or address other travel issues.

Local Guide

Catherine D'Antuono is a smart, capable, licensed guide for Aix-en-Provence and the region. She guides tours as far west as Pont du Gard and as far east as St-Tropez (€540/day for 2 people, €20 extra for each additional person, 8-person maximum, +33 6 17 94 69 61, www.provence-travel.com, tour.designer@provence-travel.com).

Discover Provence

Discover Provence was founded by English-born Sarah Pernet, who has lived in Aix-en-Provence for more than 20 years. She and her small team offer a variety of well-organized, easygoing, small-group tours throughout Provence (from €170/person for half-day,

Top 10 Roman Sights in Provence

1. Pont du Gard aqueduct and its museum
2. Roman Theater in Orange
3. Maison Carrée in Nîmes
4. Roman History Museum (and Arena) in Nîmes
5. Ancient History Museum in Arles
6. Arena in Arles
7. Roman city of Glanum (in St-Rémy)
8. Ruined aqueduct near Fontvieille
9. Roman city of Vaison-la-Romaine
10. Julien Bridge (near Roussillon)

+33 6 16 86 40 24, www.discover-provence.net, sarah@discover-provence.net).

THE ROMANS IN PROVENCE

Provence is littered with Roman ruins. Many scholars claim the best-preserved ancient Roman buildings are not in Italy, but in France. These ancient stones will be an important part of your sightseeing agenda in this region, so it's worth learning about how they came to be.

Classical Rome endured from about 500 BC through AD 500—spending about 500 years growing, 200 years peaking, and 300 years declining. Julius Caesar conquered Gaul—which included Provence—during the Gallic Wars (58-51 BC), then crossed the Rubicon River in 49 BC to incite civil war within the Roman Republic. He erected a temple to Jupiter on the future site of Paris' Notre-Dame Cathedral.

The concept of one-man rule lived on with his grandnephew, Octavian (whom he had also adopted as his son). Octavian killed Brutus, eliminated his rivals (Mark Antony and Cleopatra), and united Rome's warring factions. He took the title "Augustus" and became the first in a line of emperors who would control Rome for the next 500 years—ruling like a king, with the backing of the army and the rubber-stamp approval of the Senate. Rome morphed from a republic into an empire: a collection of many diverse territories ruled by a single man.

Augustus' reign marked the start of 200 years of peace, prosperity, and expansion known as the *Pax Romana*. At its peak (c. AD 117), the Roman Empire had 54 million people and stretched from Scotland in the north to Egypt in the south, as far west as Spain and as far east as modern-day Iraq. To the northeast, Rome was bounded by the Rhine and Danube rivers. On Roman maps, the Mediterranean was labeled *Mare Nostrum* ("Our Sea"). At its peak, "Rome" didn't just refer to the city, but to the entire civilized Western world.

The Romans were successful not only because they were good soldiers, but also because they were smart administrators and businessmen. People in conquered territories knew they had joined the winning team and that political stability would replace barbarian invasions. Trade thrived. Conquered peoples were welcomed into the fold of prosperity, linked by roads, education, common laws and gods, and the Latin language.

Provence, with its strategic location, benefited greatly from Rome's global economy and grew to become an important part of its worldwide empire. After Julius Caesar conquered Gaul, Emperor Augustus set out to Romanize it, building and renovating cities in the image of Rome. Most cities had a theater (some had several), baths, and aqueducts; the most important cities had  sports arenas. The Romans also erected an elaborate infrastructure of roads, post offices, schools (teaching in Latin), police stations, and water-supply systems.

With a standard language and currency, Roman merchants were able to trade wine, salt, and olive oil for foreign goods. The empire invested heavily in cities that were strategically important for trade. For example, the Roman-built city of Arles was a crucial link in the trade route from Italy to Spain, so they built a bridge across the Rhône River and fortified the town.

A typical Roman city (such as Nîmes, Arles, Orange, or Vaison-la-Romaine) was a garrison town, laid out on a grid plan with two main roads: one running north-south (the *cardus*), the other east-west (the *decumanus*). Approaching the city on your chariot, you'd pass by the cemetery, which was located outside of town for hygienic reasons. You'd enter the main gate and wheel past warehouses and apartment houses to the town square (forum). Facing the square were the most important temples, dedicated to the patron gods of the city. Nearby, you'd find bathhouses; like today's fitness clubs, these served the almost sacred dedication to personal vigor. Also close by were businesses that catered to the citizens' needs: the marketplace, bakeries, banks, and brothels.

Aqueducts brought fresh water for drinking, filling the baths, and delighting the citizens with bubbling fountains. Men flocked to the stadiums in Arles and Nîmes to bet on gladiator games; eager couples attended elaborate plays at theaters in Orange, Arles, and Vaison-la-Romaine. Marketplaces brimmed with exotic fruits, vegetables, and animals from the far reaches of the empire. Some cities in Provence were more urban 2,000 years ago than they are today. For instance, experts believe that Roman Arles had a population of between 70,000 and 100,000—almost double today's size. Think about that when you visit.

You'll come across rounded arches throughout Provence. These were constructed by piling two stacks of heavy stone blocks, connecting them with an arch (supported with wooden scaffolding), then inserting an inverted keystone where the stacks met. *Voilà!* The heavy stones were able to support not only themselves, but also a great deal of weight above the arch. The Romans didn't invent the rounded arch, but they exploited it better than their predecessors, stacking arches to build arenas and theaters, stringing them side by side for aqueducts, stretching out their legs to create barrel-vaulted ceilings, and building freestanding "triumphal" arches to celebrate conquering generals.

When it came to construction, the Romans eventually discovered a magic building ingredient: concrete. A mixture of volcanic ash, lime, water, and small rocks, concrete—easier to work than stone and longer-lasting than wood—served as flooring, roofing, filler, glue, and support. Builders would start with a foundation of brick, then fill it in with poured concrete. They would then cover important structures, such as basilicas, in sheets of expensive marble (held on with nails), or decorate floors and walls with mosaics—proving just how talented the Romans were at turning the functional into art.

PROVENCE'S CUISINE SCENE

Provence has been called France's "garden market," featuring farm-fresh food (vegetables, fruits, and meats) prepared in a simple way, and meant to be savored with family and friends. Grilled foods are common, as are dishes prepared by lengthy simmering—in part a reflection of long days spent in the fields. Colorful and lively, Provençal cuisine hammers the senses with an extravagant use (by French standards) of garlic, olive oil, and herbs. Order anything *à la provençale,* and you'll be rewarded with aromatic food heightened by rich and pungent sauces. Thanks to the proximity of the Riviera, many seafood dishes show up on Provençal menus (see "The Riviera's Cuisine Scene" on page 310).

Unlike other French regional cuisines, the food of Provence is inviting for nibblers. Appetizers (hors d'oeuvres) often consist of bowls of olives (try the plump, full-flavored black *tanche* or the green, buttery *picholine*), as well as plates of fresh vegetables served with lusty sauces ready for dipping. These same sauces adorn dishes of hard-boiled eggs, fish, or meat. Look for tapenade, a paste of pureed olives, capers, anchovies, herbs, and sometimes tuna. True anchovy lovers dig into *anchoïade* (a spread of garlic, anchovy, and parsley) or *bagna cauda* (a warm sauce of anchovies and melted butter or olive oil).

Aioli—a rich, garlicky mayonnaise spread over vegetables, potatoes, fish, or whatever—is another Provençal favorite, often served with the main course. In the summertime, entire village festivals celebrate this sauce. Watch for signs announcing *aioli monstre* ("monster aioli") and, for a few euros, dive into a deeply French eating experience.

Despite the heat, soup is popular in Provence. *Soupe au pistou* is a thin yet flavorful vegetable soup with a sauce (called *pistou*) of basil, garlic, and cheese—pesto minus the pine nuts. Or try *soupe à l'ail* (garlic soup, called *aigo bouido* in the Provençal dialect).

Provençal main courses venerate fresh vegetables and meats. (Eat seafood on the Riviera and meat in Provence.) Ratatouille is a mixture of Provençal vegetables (eggplant, zucchini, onions, and peppers are the usual suspects) in a thick, herb-flavored tomato sauce. It's readily found in charcuteries and often served at room temperature, making it the perfect picnic food. Ratatouille veggies also show up on their own, stuffed and served in spicy sauces. Look for *aubergines* (eggplants), *tomates* (tomatoes), *poivrons* (sweet peppers), and *courgettes* (zucchini—especially *fleurs de courgettes*, stuffed and batter-fried zucchini flowers). *Tians* are gratin-like vegetable dishes named for the deep terra-cotta dish in which they are cooked and served. *Artichauts à la barigoule* are stuffed artichokes flavored with garlic, ham, and herbs (*barigoule* is from the Provençal word for thyme, *farigoule*). Also look for *riz de Camargue*—the reddish, chewy, nutty-tasting rice that has taken over the Camargue area, a marshy region that is otherwise useless for agriculture.

The famous herbs of Provence influence food long before it's cooked. The locally renowned lambs of the *garrigue* (shrub-covered hills), as well as rabbits and other small edible beasts in Provence, dine on wild herbs and spicy shrubs—preseasoning their delicate

PROVENCE

meat. Regional specialties include lamb (*agneau,* most often leg of lamb, *gigot d'agneau*), grilled and served no-frills, or the delicious *lapin à la provençale*—rabbit served with garlic, mustard, tomatoes, and herbs in white wine. Locals have a curious passion for quail *(caille)*. These tiny, bony birds can be grilled and served with any variety of sauces, including those sweetened with Provençal cherries or honey and lavender. *Daube,* named for the traditional cooking vessel *daubière,* is generally beef simmered in wine with spices and herbs—and perhaps a touch of orange zest—until it is spoon-tender; it's then served with noodles or the local rice. *Taureau* (bull's meat), usually raised in the marshy Camargue, melts in your mouth.

By American standards, the French undercook meats: *bleu* (bluh) is virtually raw (just flame-kissed); *saignant* (sehn-yahn) is close to raw; *à point* (ah pwahn)—their version of "medium"—is rare; and *bien cuit* (bee-yehn kwee, "well cooked") is medium. (Because French cows are raised on grass rather than corn, the beef is leaner than in the US, so limiting the cooking time keeps the meat tender.)

You may want to steer clear of these dishes: *Pieds et paquets* is a scary dish of sheep's feet and tripe (no amount of Provençal sauce can hide this flavor). *Tourte de blettes* is a confused "pie" made with Swiss chard; both savory and sweet, it can't decide whether it should be a first course or dessert (it shows up as both).

Eat goat cheese *(fromage de chèvre)* in Provence. Look for *banon de banon* or *banon à la feuille* (dipped in *eau-de-vie* brandy to kill bad mold, then wrapped in a chestnut leaf), spicy *picodon* (the name means "spicy" in the old language), or the fresh, creamy *brousse du Rove* (often served mixed with cream and sugar for dessert). On Provençal cheese platters, you'll find small rounds of bite-size chèvres, each flavored with a different herb or spice—and some even rolled in chopped garlic.

Desserts tend to be light and fruit-filled, or traditionally French. Treat yourself to fresh tarts made with seasonal fruit, regional Cavaillon melons (cantaloupes, served cut in half with a trickle of the sweet Rhône wine Beaumes-de-Venise), and ice cream or sorbet sweetened with honey and flavored with various herbs such as lavender, thyme, or rosemary. Don't miss the region's delicious cherries and apricots, which are often turned into jams and candied fruits.

Remember, most restaurants serve only during lunch (12:00-14:00) and dinner (19:00-21:00, later in bigger cities), but some cafés serve food throughout the day. For details on dining in France's restaurants, cafés, and brasseries, getting takeout, and assembling a picnic—as well as a rundown of French cuisine—see the "Eating" section in the Practicalities chapter.

WINES OF PROVENCE

For many, a highlight of a visit to Provence is tasting its lovely wines. Enjoying a glass of Rhône wine—especially when poured by someone whose family name has been on the label for two centuries—is a memorably rich, and quintessentially Provençal, experience.

The American wine-tasting experience (I'm thinking Napa Valley) is generally informal, chatty, and entrepreneurial (logo-adorned baseball caps and golf shirts). Although Provençal vintners are welcoming and more easygoing than in other parts of France, it's still a serious, wine-focused experience. Your hosts are not there to make small talk, and they're likely to be "all business." Still, Provence's shorts-and-T-shirt climate and abundance of hearty, reasonably priced wines make for an enjoyable experience, particularly if you're patient and willing to learn. See the "French Wine-Tasting 101" sidebar later in this chapter for the basics.

Provence saw the first grapes planted in France, in about 600 BC, by the Greeks. Romans built on what the Greeks started, realizing 2,000 years ago that Provence had an ideal climate for producing wine: mild winters and long, warm summers—but not too hot, thanks to the cooling winds. This sunbaked, wine-happy region offers Americans a chance to sample wines blended from several grapes—resulting in rich, delicious flavors.

In France, wine production is strictly controlled by the government to preserve the overall quality. This ensures that vintners use specified grapes that grow best in that region and follow certain grape-growing procedures. The *Appellation d'Origine Contrôlée* (AOC) label found on many bottles is the government's seal of approval, indicating that a wine has met various requirements. The type and percentages of grapes used, vinification methods, and taste are all controlled and verified.

Provençal vintners can blend wines using a maximum of 13 different types of grapes (5 white and 8 red)—unique in France. Only in Châteauneuf-du-Pape are all 13 grapes used; most vintners blend 4 or 5 types of grapes. (In Burgundy and Alsace, only one grape variety is used for each wine—so pinot noir, chardonnay, Riesling, Tokay, and pinot gris are each 100 percent from that grape.) This blending allows Provençal winemakers great range in personalizing their wine. The most common red grapes used are grenache, mourvèdre, syrah, carignan, and cinsault. The white grapes include grenache blanc, roussanne, marsanne, bourboulenc, and clairette.

There are three primary growing areas in Provence: Côtes du Rhône, Côtes de Provence, and Côteaux d'Aix-en-Provence. A few wines are also made along the Provençal Mediterranean coast. All regions produce rich, fruity reds and dry, fresh rosés. Only about 5 percent of wine produced here is white (the best of which comes from Cassis and Châteauneuf-du-Pape). Most Provençal whites are light, tart, with plenty of citrus and minerals, and work best as a predinner drink or in a *kir*.

In Provence, I often drink rosé instead of white. French rosé is generally crisp and fruity, a perfect match to the hot days and Mediterranean cuisine. Rosé wines are made from red grapes. After the grapes are crushed, their clear juice is left in contact with their dark-red skins just long enough to produce the pinkish color (no more than 24 hours). Rosés from Tavel (20 minutes northwest of Avignon) are the darkest in color and considered among the best in Provence, but you'll find many good producers at affordable prices in other areas as well. If you're unaccustomed to drinking rosés, try one here.

Provençal wines are also reasonably priced in grocery stores (€5-10/bottle on average). Look for wines from Gigondas, Rasteau, Cairanne, Beaumes-de-Venise, Vacqueyras, and Châteauneuf-du-Pape. For the cheapest but still tasty wines, look for labels showing Côtes du Rhône Villages or Côtes de Provence. For reds, splurge for Châteauneuf-du-Pape or Gigondas, and for a fine aperitif wine or a dessert wine, try the Muscat from Beaumes-de-Venise.

Here's some terminology to help you decipher what you'll see on bottles:

appellation: area in which a wine's grapes are grown

bouquet: bouquet (the fragrance when first opened)

cave: cellar (or wine shop)

cépage: grape variety (syrah, chardonnay, etc.)

côte, côteaux: hillside or slope

domaine: wine estate

étiquette: label

fût, tonneau: wine barrel

grand vin: excellent wine

millésimé: wine from a given year

mis en bouteille au château/au domaine: estate-bottled (bottled where it was made)

vin de table: house wine (can be a blend of several wines)

vin de pays: wine from a given area (a step up from *vin de table*)

Côtes du Rhône Wines

The king of Provençal wines hails from the Côtes du Rhône, the area along the Rhône River from just south of Lyon to near Avignon. My focus is on the southern section, roughly from Vaison-la-Romaine to Avignon (though wine lovers should also try the big, complex reds found in the northern Rhône wines of St-Joseph, Crozes-Hermitage, and Cornas, as well as the tasty whites of Condrieu). The wines of the southern Rhône are consistently good, sometimes exceptional, and usually inexpensive. The reds are full-bodied, rosés are dry and fruity, and whites are dry and fragrant. (For more on this wine region, including a self-guided driving tour of the area's villages and vintners, see the Côtes du Rhône chapter.)

Many subareas of the southern Côtes du Rhône are recognized for producing outstandingly good wines and have been awarded their own *appellations* (like Châteauneuf-du-Pape, Gigondas, Beaumes-de-Venise, Côtes de Ventoux, Tavel, and Côtes du Luberon). Wines often are named for the villages that produce them. The "Côtes du Rhône Villages" *appellation* is less prestigious, as grapes could come from any of the 20 villages on the eastern side of the Côtes du Rhône, including Séguret, Sablet, Rasteau, and Cairanne. Strict guidelines govern the production of these wines (called *appellation controllée*).

Here's a summary of what you might find on a Côtes du Rhône *carte des vins* (wine list):

Châteauneuf-du-Pape: Almost all wines from this famous village are reds (often blends; the most dominant grapes are grenache, mourvèdre, and syrah). These wines have a velvety quality and can be spicy, with flavors of licorice and prunes. A few delicious whites are made here and worth sampling. Châteauneuf-du-Pape red wines merit lengthy aging. Château de Beaucastel, Le Vieux Télégraphe, Clos des Papes, and Château la Nerthe are traditionally considered among the best producers. Domaine Roger Sabon and Domaine Durieu are up-and-coming producers. You should find most of these wines in North America.

Gigondas: These wines have many of the same qualities as Châteauneuf-du-Pape, but are lesser known and usually cheaper. Gigondas red wines are spicy, meaty, and often tannic. Again, aging is necessary to bring out the full qualities of the wine. Near Gigondas look for Domaine du Terme, Domaine Les Goubert, or Château de Montmirail. The following places also make fine Gigondas—and are more scenically set along my Côtes du Rhône wine road tour: Domaines de Coyeux and Cassan (both near La Fare), or Domaine de la Garance in Suzette.

Beaumes-de-Venise: While this village produces reds that are rich and flavorful, Beaumes-de-Venise is most famous for its Muscat—a sweet, fragrant wine usually served as an aperitif or with dessert. It often has flavors of apricots and peaches, and it should be consumed within two years of bottling. Try Domaine de

PROVENCE

French Wine-Tasting 101

France is peppered with wineries and wine-tasting opportunities. For some, trying to make sense of the vast range of French wines can be overwhelming, particularly when faced with a no-nonsense winemaker or sommelier. Do your best to follow my tips, and don't linger if you don't feel welcome.

Visit several private wineries or stop by a *cave coopérative* or a *caveau* to taste wines from a number of local vintners in a single, less intimidating setting. (In this book, I try to identify which vineyards are most accepting of wine novices.) At wineries, you'll have a better experience if you call ahead to let them know you're coming (even if it's open all day; ask your hotelier for help). Avoid  visiting places between noon and 14:00: Many wineries close midday, and those that don't are staffed by people who would rather be at lunch.

Winemakers and sommeliers are usually happy to work with you, but it helps to know what you like (drier or sweeter, lighter or full-bodied, fruity or more tannic, and so on). The people serving you may know those words in English, but you're wise to learn the key words in French.

French wines usually have a lower alcohol level than American or Australian wines. While Americans might like a big, full-bodied wine, most French prefer subtler flavors. They judge a wine by how well it pairs with a meal. The French enjoy sampling younger wines and divining how they will taste in a few years, allowing them to buy bottles at cheaper prices and stash them in their cellars. Americans want it now—for today's picnic.

At tastings, vintners and wine shops are hoping you'll buy a bottle or two (otherwise you may be asked to pay a small tasting fee). They understand that North Americans can't take much wine with them, but they hope you'll look for their wines when you're back home. Some places will ship wine—ask.

Coyeux, Domaine de Durban, and Château Redortier, or visit the *cave coopérative* in Beaumes-de-Venise.

Rasteau: This village sits across the valley from Gigondas and shares many of its qualities—at lower prices. Rasteau makes fine rosés, robust (at times "rough") and fruity reds, and a naturally sweet wine (Vin Doux Naturel). Their Côtes du Rhône Villages can be excellent. The cooperative in Rasteau is good, as are the wines from Domaine des Girasols and Domaine de Beaurenard.

PROVENCE

Here are some phrases to get you started when wine-tasting:
Hello, madam/sir.
Bonjour, madame/monsieur.
(bohn-zhoor, mah-dahm/muhs-yuh)

We would like to taste a few wines.
Nous voudrions déguster quelques vins.
(noo voo-dree-ohn day-gew-stay kehl-kuh van)

We would like a wine that is ____ and ____.
Nous voudrions un vin ____ et ____.
(noo voo-dree-ohn uhn van ____ ay ____)

Fill in the blanks with your favorites from this list:

English	French
red	*rouge* (roozh)
white	*blanc* (blahn)
rosé	*rosé* (roh-zay)
light	*léger* (lay-zhay)
full-bodied	*robuste* (roh-bewst)
fruity	*fruité* (frwee-tay)
sweet	*doux* (doo)
tannic	*tannique* (tah-neek)
fine	*fin, avec finesse* (fan, ah-vehk fee-nehs)
ready to drink (mature)	*prêt à boire* (preh ah bwar)
not ready to drink	*fermé* (fair-may)
oaky or woody	*boisé* (bwah-zay)
from old vines	*de vieilles vignes* (duh vee-yay-ee veen-yuh)
sparkling	*pétillant* (pay-tee-yahn)

Sablet: This village lies down in the valley below Gigondas and makes decent, fruity, and inexpensive reds and rosés.

Tavel: The queen of French rosés comes from this area 20 minutes north and west of Avignon, close to Pont du Gard. Tavel produces a rosé that is dry, crisp, higher in alcohol, darker, and more full-bodied than other rosés from the region. Look for any rosé from Tavel.

The Rules of *Boules*

The game of *boules*—also called *pétanque*—is the horseshoes of France. Invented here in the early 1900s, it's a social yet serious sport and endlessly entertaining to watch—even more so if you understand the rules.

The game is played with heavy metal balls and a small wooden target ball called a *cochonnet* (piglet). Whoever gets his *boule* closest to the *cochonnet* is awarded points. Teams commonly have specialist players: a *pointeur* and a *tireur*. The *pointeur*'s goal is to lob his balls as close to the target as he can. The *tireur*'s job is to blast away opponents' *boules*.

In teams of two, each player gets three *boules*. The starting team traces a small circle in the dirt (in which players must stand when launching their *boules*), and tosses the *cochonnet* about 30 feet to establish the target. The *boule* must be thrown underhand and can be rolled, launched sky-high, or rocketed at its target. The first *pointeur* shoots, then the opposing pointeur shoots until his *boule* gets closer. Once the second team lands a *boule* nearest the *cochonnet*, the first team goes again. If the other team's *boule* is very near the *cochonnet*, the *tireur* will likely attempt to knock it away.

Once all *boules* have been launched, the tally is taken. The team with a *boule* closest to the *cochonnet* wins the round, and they receive a point for each *boule* closer to the target than their opponents' nearest *boule*. The first team to get to 13 points wins. A regulation *boules* field is 10 feet by 43 feet, but the game is played everywhere—just scratch a throwing circle in the sand, toss the *cochonnet,* and you're off.

Côtes de Provence Wines

The lesser-known vineyards of the Côtes de Provence run east from Aix-en-Provence almost to St-Tropez. Typical grapes are cinsault, mourvèdre, grenache, carignan, and a little cabernet sauvignon and syrah. The wines are commonly full-bodied and fruity and are meant to be drunk when they're young. They cost less than Côtes du Rhônes wines and have similar characteristics. But the region is most famous for its "big" rosés that can be served with meat and garlic dishes (rosé accounts for 60 percent of production).

For one-stop shopping, make it a point to find the superb **La Maison des Vins Côtes de Provence** on RN-7 in Les Arcs-sur-Argens (a few minutes north of the A-8 autoroute, about halfway between Aix-en-Provence and Nice). This English-speaking wine shop and tasting center represents hundreds of producers, selling bottles at vineyard prices and offering good and free tastings (daily 10:00-19:00, Oct-March Mon-Sat 10:00-12:30 & 14:00-18:00, closed Sun, +33 4 94 99 50 20, www.maison-des-vins.fr).

Côteaux d'Aix-en-Provence Wines

This large growing region, between Les Baux and Aix-en-Provence, produces some interesting reds, whites, and rosés. Commonly used grapes are the same as in Côtes de Provence, though several producers (mainly around Les Baux) use a higher concentration of cabernet sauvignon, which helps distinguish their wines. The vintners around Les Baux produce some exceptionally good wines, and many of their vineyards are organic. The tiny wine-producing area of Palette houses only three wineries, all of which make exceptional rosés; one (Château Simone) also makes a delicious white wine. The Côtes de Provence-Sainte-Victoire wineries, with their beautiful views of Mont Ste-Victoire (famously painted by Cézanne), also produce some excellent rosés.

Provençal Mediterranean Wines

Barely east of Marseille, Cassis and Bandol sit side by side, overlooking the Mediterranean. Though very close together, they are designated as separate wine-growing areas because of the distinctive nature of their wines. Cassis is one of France's smallest wine regions and is known for its strong, fresh, and very dry whites (made with the Marsanne grape)—arguably the best white wine in Provence. Bandol is known for its luscious, velvety reds. This wine, aged in old oak and made primarily from the mourvèdre grape, is one of your author's favorites.

ARLES

Arles (pronounced "arl") is a down to earth slice of urban Provence, with evocative Roman ruins, an eclectic assortment of museums, made-for-ice-cream pedestrian zones, and squares that play hide-and-seek with visitors.

Back in Roman times, the city earned the imperial nod by helping Julius Caesar defeat his archrival Pompey at Marseille and grew into an important port. Site of the first bridge over the Rhône River, Arles was a key stop on the Roman road from Italy to Spain, the Via Domitia. After reigning as the seat of an important archbishop and as a trading center for centuries, the city became a sleepy afterthought of little importance in the 1700s. Vincent van Gogh settled here in the late 1800s, but left only a chunk of his ear. American bombers destroyed much of Arles in World War II as the townsfolk hid out in its underground Roman galleries.

Until recently, Arles felt like a backwater. A city in search of an economy, workaday Arles seemed unpolished and a touch gritty compared to nearby Avignon and Nîmes. While that aspect remains part of Arles' charm, it's impressive to see how this city is transforming itself. The LUMA Foundation and Frank Gehry notoriety seem to have sparked some investors to fix up old hotels and fire up trendy cafés and bistros that in turn are drawing

renewed interest to the city. On top of that, the city has all but eliminated cars from the historic center and created new pedestrian-only lanes, making Arles a joy to stroll. And so far, this "progress" has not happened at the expense of the city's down-to-earth character. Locals still display a genuine joie de vivre that's hard to sense in Arles' larger, more cosmopolitan neighbors.

PLANNING YOUR TIME

For a helpful overview to your Arles sightseeing, start at the Ancient History Museum (at the edge of town, closed Tue), then enjoy the city-center sights, linked by my Arles City Walk. Following the walk, visit the Arlaten Folk Museum. For cost-efficient sightseeing, get one of the city's sightseeing passes, which cover the ancient monuments and the Ancient History Museum.

Orientation to Arles

Arles turns its back on Paris and embraces its slow paced, southern roots. And although the town is built along the Rhône, it largely ignores the river. Landmarks hide in Arles' medieval tangle of narrow, winding streets. Hotels have good, free city maps, and helpful street-corner signs point you toward sights and hotels.

TOURIST INFORMATION

The TI is on the ring road Boulevard des Lices, at Esplanade Charles de Gaulle (daily 9:00-18:00; off-season Mon-Sat until 17:00, Sun 10:00-13:00; +33 4 90 18 41 20, www.arlestourisme. com). Ask about the worthwhile city sightseeing passes (see "Helpful Hints," later) and find out if "bullgames" are scheduled in Arles or nearby (Provence's more humane version of bullfights—see "Experiences in Arles," later).

ARRIVAL IN ARLES

By Train: The train station is on the river, a 10-minute walk from the town center. There are two good options for baggage storage (see "Helpful Hints," later).

To reach the town center **on foot** from the train station, turn left out of the station and walk a level 15 minutes. Or you can hire a **pedicab** to the center for €5 (see "Helpful Hints," later). **Taxis** usually wait in front of the station (if there's not a taxi waiting, call +33 4 84 84 58 58 or ask the train info desk staff to call for you). Though the rides are short, allow €12 to any of my recommended hotels. Uber is not very present in Arles.

By Bus: There are two key bus stops in Arles: at the train station and near the TI on Boulevard Georges Clemenceau. For destinations served by each stop, see "Arles Connections," later.

By Car: I'd avoid driving in Arles' historic center. Enter on foot after stowing your car at Arles' only parking garage, **Parking des Lices,** near the TI on Boulevard des Lices (about €2/hour, €5/overnight—arrive after 20:00 and leave by 8:00, €18/24 hours). All of my recommended hotels are within a 10-minute walk of this garage. Some hotels have parking deals for a nearby lot (ask before you arrive).

Lots and curbside parking spots in Arles center are metered 9:00-19:00 every day May-Sept (some limited to 2.5 hours). You'll find metered lots along the city wall at Place Lamartine (except Tue night, when it is restricted). To find these, first follow signs to *Centre-Ville*, then *Gare SNCF* (train station) until you come to the roundabout with a Monoprix department store to the right. The hotels I list are no more than a 15-minute walk from here.

ARLES

HELPFUL HINTS

Sightseeing Tips: Arles has a smart ticket-and-hours plan for its sightseeing. Ancient monuments, such as the Roman Arena and Classical Theater, share the **same hours** (daily 9:00-19:00, April and Oct until 18:00, Nov-March 10:00-17:00).

A €9 entry fee gets you access to all of Arles' monuments (but not its museums). The good-value **Pass Liberté** (€12) covers any four monuments and one museum of your choice (I recommend the Ancient History Museum). The **Pass Avantage** (€16) covers all monuments and most museums and is worthwhile if you plan to visit two or more eligible museums. (Note that the Arlaten Folk Museum is not covered by either pass.) You can buy passes at the TI or any included sight.

While only the Ancient History Museum, Roman Arena, and Arlaten Folk Museum are important to enter, a pass makes the city fun to explore, as you can pop into nearly everything, even for just a couple of minutes.

Van Gogh Trail: The TI has placed helpful "Van Gogh easels" around town marking points where Vincent set up his easel and painted. Many (but not all) are incorporated into my "Arles City Walk."

Market Days: The big markets are on Wednesdays and Saturdays (see the Shopping chapter for more on French markets).

Crowds: An international photo event jams hotels the second weekend of July. The let-'er-rip, twice-yearly Féria draws crowds over Easter and in mid-September (described under "Experiences in Arles," later).

Baggage Storage/Bike Rental/Pedicabs: Taco & Co stores luggage, rents bikes, and offers pedal-cab (pedicab) service into the city center; it's located straight across from the train station, at the main bus stop (€5/bag for 24 hours, bike rental-€10/day, pedicab to the center-€5; daily 9:00-18:00, until 17:00 and closed Sun off-season; +33 4 82 75 73 45, www.tacoandco.fr). The recommended **Hôtel Régence** will store your bags and

Arles at a Glance

▲▲**Roman Arena** This big amphitheater, once used by gladiators, today hosts concerts, summer "bullgames," and occasional bullfights. **Hours:** Daily 9:00-19:00, April and Oct until 18:00, Nov-March 10:00-17:00. See page 63.

▲▲**St. Trophime Church** Church with exquisite Romanesque entrance. **Hours:** Church—daily 9:00-12:00 & 14:00-18:00. See page 67.

▲▲**Arlaten Folk Museum** Leading museum in Provence for traditional culture and folklore. **Hours:** Tue-Sun 10:00-18:00, closed Mon. See page 74.

▲▲**Ancient History Museum** Filled with models and sculptures, this museum takes you back to Arles' Roman days. **Hours:** Wed-Mon 10:00-18:00, closed Tue. See page 75.

▲**Fondation Van Gogh** Small gallery with works by major contemporary artists paying homage to Van Gogh. **Hours:** Daily 10:00-19:00, until 18:00 and closed Mon off-season. See page 71.

▲**Forum Square** Lively, café-crammed square that was once the Roman forum. See page 71.

▲**Réattu Museum** Decent, mostly modern art collection in a fine 15th-century mansion. **Hours:** Tue-Sun 10:00-18:00, Nov-Feb until 17:00, closed Mon year-round. See page 74.

▲**Frank Gehry Tower and LUMA Arles** Climbable Gehry-designed tower overseeing LUMA Arles art exhibit space. **Hours:** Tower open Wed-Mon 10:00-18:00, closed Tue. See page 79.

ARLES

rents bikes (one-way rentals within Provence possible, daily 7:30-22:00, closed in winter, 5 Rue Marius Jouveau).

Laundry: The best launderette in Arles is at 17 Rue Gambetta (open long hours daily).

Car Rental: Europcar and **Hertz** are downtown (Europcar is at 61 Avenue de Stalingrad, +33 4 90 93 23 24; Hertz is closer to Place Voltaire at 10 Boulevard Emile Combes, +33 4 90 96 75 23).

Local Guides: Charming **Agnes Barrier** knows Arles and nearby sights intimately. Her tours cover Van Gogh and Roman history (€160/3 hours, +33 6 11 23 03 73, agnes.barrier@hotmail.fr).

ARLES

Arles

Arles City Walk

1. The Yellow House (Easel)
2. Starry Night over the Rhône (Easel)
3. Rue Voltaire
4. Old Town
5. Arena (Easel)
6. Roman Arena
7. Alpilles Mountains View
8. L'Entrée du Jardin Public (Easel)
9. Classical Theater
10. Republic Square
11. Cryptoporticos
12. St. Trophime Church
13. St. Trophime Cloisters
14. Rue de la République
15. Espace Van Gogh (Easel)
16. Fondation Van Gogh
17. Rue du Docteur Fanton
18. Place du Forum & Café Terrace at Night (Easel)

Other

19. Bag Storage/Bike Rental
20. Bag Storage/Bike Rental/Pedicab
21. Launderette
22. To Europcar Car Rental
23. Hertz Car Rental

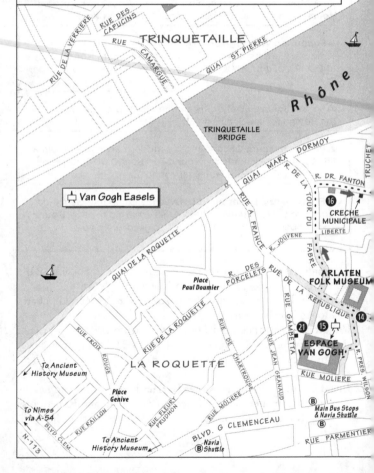

ARLES

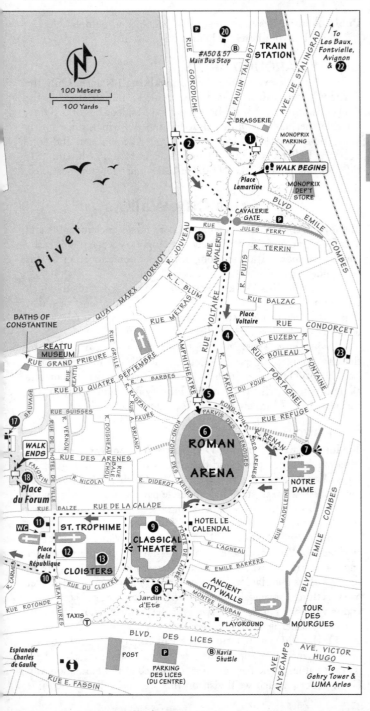

Public Pools: Arles has three pools (indoor and outdoor). Ask at the TI or your hotel for hours and locations.

GETTING AROUND ARLES

In this flat city, everything's within **walking** distance. Only the Ancient History Museum (a direct, scenic 25-minute stroll on the riverside promenade) is far enough out to consider a bus or taxi ride. Or ride the **Navia minibus shuttle** (line A), which runs mostly along Boulevards des Lices and Georges Clemenceau, and connects the LUMA complex, TI, and Ancient History Museum (€1/ride, 3-4/hour, daily 7:45-19:00, see "Arles" map for stop locations).

Arles City Walk

The joy of Arles is how its compact core mixes ancient sights and Van Gogh memories with a lively contemporary scene that is easily covered on foot. All dimensions of the city come together in this self-guided walk.

Length of This Walk: If you enter the sights described (which I recommend, even if briefly), this walk will take most of a day. If the walk seems long, split it into two half-days. To follow this walk, see the "Arles" map, earlier.

Sightseeing Tips: Most sights on this walk are covered by the city's sightseeing passes—sold at the TI and included sights (see "Helpful Hints," earlier). To better understand the ancient sites along this route, visit the Ancient History Museum before taking this walk (see "More Sights in Arles," later).

BACKGROUND

The life and artistic times of Dutch artist **Vincent van Gogh** form a big part of Arles' draw, and the city does a fine job of highlighting its Van Gogh connection with its Van Gogh Trail: Throughout town, about a dozen steel-and-concrete panels, or "easels," provide then-and-now comparisons, depicting the artist's paintings alongside the current view of that painting's subject.

In the dead of winter in 1888, 35-year-old Van Gogh left big-city Paris for Provence, hoping to jump-start his floundering career and social life. He was as inspired as he was lonely. Coming from the gray skies and flat lands of the north, Vincent was bowled over by everything Provençal—the sun, bright colors, rugged landscape, and raw people. For the next two years he painted furiously, cranking out a masterpiece every few days.

Of the 200-plus paintings that Van Gogh made in the south, none permanently resides in the city that so moved him. (But there is always at least one here on loan, displayed at the Fondation Van Gogh gallery, which we'll visit on this stroll.) Walking the same

streets he knew and seeing the places he painted, you can understand how Arles inspired him.

⊙ SELF-GUIDED WALK

*• Start on Place Lamartine, across the big roundabout from the medieval
gate, and stand with the big Monoprix store across the street to your
right. A four-foot-tall easel shows Van Gogh's painting.*

❶ The Yellow House Easel

Vincent arrived in Arles on February 20, 1888 to a foot of snow.
He rented a small house here on the north side of Place Lamartine.

The house was destroyed
in 1944 by an errant
bridge-seeking bomb, but
the four-story building behind it still stands (find it
in the painting). The house
(which stood where the
street runs today) had four
rooms, including a small
studio and the cramped
trapezoid-shaped bedroom made famous in his paintings. It was
painted yellow inside and out, and Vincent named it..."The Yellow House." In the distance, the painting shows the same bridges
you see today, as well as a steam train—which was a rather recent
invention in France, allowing people like Vincent to travel greater
distances and be jarred by new experiences. (Today's TGV system
continues that trend.)

Arles, so cold in the winter, was buttoned up tight when Vincent arrived, so he was forced to work
inside, where he painted still lifes and
self-portraits—anything to flex his
artistic spirit. In late March, spring
finally arrived. In those days, a short
walk from Place Lamartine led to
open fields. Donning his straw hat,
Vincent set up his easel outdoors and
painted quickly, capturing what he saw
and felt—the blossoming fruit trees,
gnarled olive trees, peasants sowing
and reaping, jagged peaks, and windblown fields, all lit by a brilliant sun
that drove him to use ever-brighter

paints. "I'm as happy as a cicada," he wrote. Everywhere he turned
seemed to radiate vivid color.

• With your back to the Monoprix store, walk to the river.

As you walk, you'll pass: on the right, an eight-foot tall stone monument in honor of two WWII American pilots killed in action during the liberation of Arles (erected in 2002 as a post-9/11 sign of solidarity with Americans); a post celebrating Arles' nine sister cities (left); and a big concrete high school and tour bus parking lot (right).

At the river, find the easel in the wall where ramps lead down. The Roman bridge stood here (look for a few stones directly across), and just upstream are the remains of a modern bridge bombed by the Allies in World War II. This is the busier-than-ever cruise port, which brings crowds into the city throughout the season. River cruise ships tie up at the big rust brown pilings. The success of river cruising has provided a huge economic boost to the city of Arles. Looking downstream, notice the embankment (designed to tame floods).

• *Now, turn your attention to the...*

❼ Starry Night over the Rhône Easel

One night, Vincent set up his easel along the river and painted the stars boiling above the city skyline. Vincent looked to the night sky for the divine and was the first to paint outside after dark, adapting his straw hat to hold candles (which must have blown the minds of locals back then). As his paintings progressed, the stars became larger and more animated (like Vincent himself). The lone couple in the painting pops up again and again in his

work. Experts say that Vincent was desperate for a close relationship...someone to stroll the riverbank with under a star-filled sky. (Note: This painting is not the *Starry Night* you're probably thinking of—that one was painted later, in St-Rémy.)

To his sister Wilhelmina, Vincent wrote, "At present I absolutely want to paint a starry sky. It often seems to me that night is still more richly colored than the day; having hues of the most intense violets, blues, and greens. If only you pay attention to it, you will see that certain stars are lemon-yellow, others pink or a green, blue, and forget-me-not brilliance." Standing here in the evening, it's fun to match his painting with the contemporary scene.

• *With your back to the river, angle right through the scruffy park of plane trees (a kind of sycamore), where the old boys occasionally gather for pétanque. Observe the action. If you're inclined (and charming), you may be invited to give it a try. Continue into town through the park and between the stumpy 14th-century stone towers where the city gates once stood. Walk a block up Rue de la Cavalerie to the decorative (if dry) fountain with the colorful old mosaic.*

❸ Rue Voltaire

Van Gogh first walked into town down this street in 1888. When he saw this fountain, it was just a year old. Its mosaic celebrates the high culture of Provence (she's the winged woman who obviously loves music and reading). But this neighborhood was Arles' 19th-century red light district, and the far-from-home Dutchman spent many lonely nights in its bars and brothels. Though it's no longer the rough area it was in Van Gogh's day, this street still has a certain raw local color with humble shops, bars, and bakeries.

• Stay left and keep walking to Place Voltaire, a center of this working-class neighborhood (the local Communist Party headquarters is across the square on the left). Arles is famously red; its communist mayor is in his third term and quite popular. Stop at the top end of the square under the plane tree in front of Brasserie le Pitchounet.

❹ Old Town

Take a slow 360-degree spin tour to enjoy the rough elegance of this setting. Pretend you're a one-eared painter looking for a place to set up your easel. You've left the bombed-out part of town and entered the old town. The stony white arches of the ancient Roman Arena ahead mark your destination. As you hike up Rue Voltaire, notice the shutters, which add so much to Arles' character. The old town is strictly protected: These traditional shutters come in a variety of styles and cannot be changed. But the owners can personalize their homes with vibrant colors.

• Keep straight up Rue Voltaire, climb to the Roman Arena, and find the Arena easel at the top of the stairs, to the right.

❺ Arena Easel

All summer long, fueled by sun and alcohol, Vincent painted the town. He loved the bullfights in the arena and sketched the colorful surge of the crowds, spending more time studying the people than watching the bullfights (notice how the bull is barely visible). Vincent had little interest in Arles' antiquity—it was people and nature that fascinated him.

• At this point you can take a break from your town walk and visit the Roman Arena, or read about it as you circle clockwise to the left.

❻ Roman Arena (Amphithéâtre)

This well-preserved arena is worth ▲▲ and is still in use today. Nearly 2,000 years ago, gladiators fought wild animals to the delight of 20,000 screaming fans. Now local daredevils still fight wild animals here—"bullgame" posters around the arena advertise up-

ARLES

coming spectacles (see "Experiences in Arles," later). Don't miss the tower climb for fantastic views over Arles, the arena, and the Rhône River.

Cost and Hours: €9 combo-ticket with Classical Theater; daily 9:00-19:00, April and Oct until 18:00, Nov-March 10:00-17:00, Rond-point des Arènes, +33 4 90 49 36 86, www.arenes-arles.com.

Visiting the Arena: After passing the ticket kiosk, find the helpful English display under the second arch, where you can read about the arena's history and renovation. Then climb the steps under the next arch and find your stone seat in the theater.

Thirty-four rows of stone bleachers extended all the way to the top of those vacant **arches** that circle the arena. All arches were numbered to help fans find their seats. The many passageways you'll see (called *vomitoires*) allowed for rapid dispersal after the games—fights would break out among frenzied fans if they couldn't leave quickly.

The arena takes its name from the central **floor** where the action took place—"arena" derives from the Latin word for sand, which was spread across the floor to absorb the blood. Wild animals were caged in passages and storage areas underneath the floor and hoisted up on an elevator to make surprise appearances. (While Rome could afford exotic beasts, places like Arles made do with snarling local fauna...bulls, bears, and lots of boars.) The standard fight was as real as professional wrestling is today—mostly just crowd-pleasing.

The arena is a fine example of Roman engineering...and propaganda. In the spirit of "give them bread and circuses," games were free—sponsored by city bigwigs. The idea was to create a populace that was thoroughly Roman—enjoying the same activities, entertainment, and thoughts (something like how US television contributes to the psyche of the American masses).

After Rome fell and stability was replaced by Dark Ages chaos, this huge structure was put to good use: Throughout medieval times and until the early 1800s, the stadium became a fortified town with towers added, arches bricked up, and 200 humble homes crammed within its circular defenses. Parts of three of the medieval **towers** survive.

Find your way to the outside corridor that circles the top level of the arena. As you stroll, savor the fine stonework and views. Above the arena entry is access to one of the medieval towers. It's well worth the climb, leading to magnificent **views** over Arles and the arena.

• *Exit at street level and turn right. A quarter of the way around, turn left (where the metal fence ends). Start up the cute stepped lane to the left (Rue Renan). Take three steps and turn around to study the arena. (You can lean on the bollard, put there by yours truly for your sightseeing convenience.)*

The big stones are Roman; the little medieval stones—more like rubble—filling the two upper-level archways are a reminder of the arena's time as a fortified town in the Middle Ages. You can even see rooflines and beam holes where the Roman structure provided a solid foundation to lean on.

• *Hike up the pretty, stepped lane through the parking lot, keeping to the left of the stark and stony church to the highest point in Arles. Take in the countryside view.*

❼ Alpilles Mountains View

This view pretty much matches what Vincent van Gogh, an avid walker, would have seen. Imagine him hauling his easel into those fields under intense sun, leaning against a ferocious wind, struggling to keep his hat on. He trekked into the countryside many times during his stay in Arles, just to paint the farm workers. Vincent venerated but didn't deify peasants. Wanting to accurately show their lives and their struggles, he reproached Renoir and Monet for glorifying common people in their works.

Vincent carried his easel as far as the medieval Abbey of Montmajour, that bulky structure on the hill in the distance. The St. Paul Hospital, where he was eventually treated in St-Rémy, is on the other side of the Alpilles mountains (which look more like hills to me), several miles beyond Montmajour.

• *Cross in front of the church to return to the arena and continue circling it clockwise. At the high point (where the arena was rebuilt after WWII bombing), turn left and walk out Rue de Porte de Laure. If you're ready for a break, the recommended **Hôtel Le Calendal** (on the left) has a handy self-service bar with drinks, great little sandwiches, and a welcoming garden out back. (You'll also pass the ancient Classical Theater on your right, which we'll visit later.) After a couple of charming blocks, go right, down the curved staircase into the park. At the bottom of the stairs continue toward the busy street. Take the second right (through the gate and into the park) and find the...*

❽ L'Entrée du Jardin Public Easel

Vincent spent many a sunny day painting in the leafy Jardin d'Eté. In another letter to his sister, Vincent wrote, "I don't know whether you can understand that one may make a poem by arranging colors...In a similar manner, the bizarre lines, purposely selected and multiplied, meandering all through the picture may not present a literal image of the garden, but they may present it to our minds as if in a dream."

• *Hike through the park and uphill toward the three-story surviving tower of the ancient Classical Theater. On the right in the grass is a monument that reads "to 1.5 million Armenian victims of the 1915 Genocide." (French law makes it a crime to deny the Ottoman Empire's genocide of Armenians, causing tension with today's Turkey.) At the ancient tower, follow the white metal fence to the left, enjoying peeks at "le jardin" of stone—a collection of ancient carved bits of a once-grand Roman theater. Go up four steps and around to the right to the corner of the fence for a fine view of the...*

❾ Classical Theater (Théâtre Antique)

This first-century BC Roman theater once seated 10,000...just like the theater in nearby Orange. But unlike Orange, here in Arles there was no hillside to provide structural support. Instead, this elegant, three-level structure had 27 buttress arches radiating out behind the seats.

Cost and Hours: €9 combo-ticket with Roman Arena, same hours as arena.

Visiting the Theater: Start with the 10-minute video, which provides background information that makes it easier to imagine the scattered stones back in place (you may need to crouch in front to make out the small English subtitles).

Then walk into the theater and pull up a stone seat in a center aisle. (For more context, read the description of Orange's Roman theater on page 171 while you rest—this theater was the same size.) Imagine that for 500 years, ancient Romans gathered here for entertainment. The original structure was much higher, with 33 rows of seats covering three levels to accommodate demand. During the Middle Ages, the old theater became a convenient town quarry—much of St. Trophime Church was built from theater rubble. Precious little of the original theater survives—though it still is used for events, with seating for 2,000 spectators.

Two lonely Corinthian columns are all that remain of a three-story stage wall that once featured more than 100 columns and statues painted in vibrant colors (a model in the Ancient History Museum shows the complete theater). Principal actors entered through the central arch, over which a grandiose statue of Caesar Augustus stood (it's now on display at the Ancient History Museum). Bit players entered through side arches. The orchestra section is defined by a semicircular pattern in the stone in front of you. Stepping up onto the left side of the stage, look down to the slender channel that allowed the brilliant-red curtain to disappear below, like magic. The stage, which was built of wood, was about 160 feet across and 20 feet deep. The actors' changing rooms are backstage, down the steps.

• *From the theater, walk a long block downhill on Rue de la Calade. As you stroll, enjoy the fine facades of 17th and 18th century mansions. Take the first left into a big square.*

❿ Republic Square (Place de la République)

This square used to be called "Place Royale"...until the French Revolution. The obelisk was the former centerpiece of Arles' Roman Circus (outside of town). The lions at its base are the symbol of the city, whose slogan is (roughly) "the gentle lion." Observe the age-old scene: tourists, peasants, shoppers, pilgrims, children, and street musicians. The City Hall (Hôtel de Ville) has a stately facade, built in the same generation as Versailles. Where there's a City Hall, there's always a free WC (if you win the Revolution, you can pee for free at the mayor's home). Notice the flags: The yellow-and-red of Provence is the same as the yellow-and-red of Catalunya, its linguistic cousin in Spain.

• *Today's City Hall sits upon an ancient city center. Inside, admire the engineering of the ceiling and find the entrance to an ancient cryptoportico (foundation).*

⓫ Cryptoporticos (Cryptoportiques)

This dark, drippy underworld of Roman arches was constructed to support the upper half of Forum Square (necessary for a big, level square in a town built on a slope). Two thousand years ago, most of this gallery of arches was at or above street level; modern Arles has buried about 20 feet of its history over the millennia. Through the tiny windows high up you would have seen the sandals of Romans on their way to the forum. Other than dark arches and broken bits of forum littering the dirt floor, there's not much down here beyond ancient memories (€4.50, same hours as arena).

• *The highlight of Place de la République is...*

⓬ St. Trophime Church

Named after a third-century bishop of Arles, this church, worth ▲▲, sports the finest Romanesque main entrance I've seen anywhere. The Romanesque and Gothic interior—with tapestries, relics, and a rare painting from the French Revolution when this was a "Temple of Reason"—is worth a visit.

Cost and Hours: Free, daily 9:00-12:00 & 14:00-18:00.

Exterior: Like a Roman triumphal arch, the church **facade**

trumpets the promise of Judg-ment Day. The tympanum (the semicircular area above the door) is filled with Christian symbolism. Christ sits in majes-ty, surrounded by symbols of the four evangelists: Matthew (the winged man), Mark (the winged lion), Luke (the ox), and John (the eagle). The 12 apostles are

lined up below Jesus. It's Judgment Day...some are saved and others aren't. Notice the condemned (on the right)—a chain gang doing a sad bunny-hop over the fires of hell. For them, the tune trum-peted by the three angels above Christ is not a happy one. Below the chain gang, St. Stephen is being stoned to death, with his soul leaving through his mouth and instantly being welcomed by angels. Study the exquisite detail. In an illiterate world, long before the vivid images of our Technicolor time, this was colorfully painted, like a neon billboard over the town square. It's full of meaning, and a medieval pilgrim understood it all.

Interior: Just inside the door on the right wall, the chart in the large glass frame locates the interior highlights and helps explain the carvings you just saw on the tympanum. The tall 12th-century Romanesque nave is decorated by a set of tapestries (typical in the Middle Ages) showing scenes from the life of Mary (17th century, from the French town of Aubusson). Walk down the nave. About halfway to the altar, find and enter the side chapel on the right.

The **Chapel of Baptism** has a statue of St. John Paul II under the window (with a relic of his blood adjacent). Facing the win-

dow, look to the right wall where you'll see a faded painting of a triangle with a sunburst from 1789. The French Revolution secularized the country and made churches "Temples of Reason." This painting is the only example I've seen of church decor from this age.

Amble counterclockwise around the ambulatory toward the **Gothic apse.** Choose which chapel you need or want: If you have the plague or cholera, visit the second chapel. It's devoted to St. Roch—notice the testimonial plaques of gratitude on the wall. Some spaces are still available... if you hurry.

Two-thirds of the way around, behind the ornate wrought iron gate is the **relic chapel**, with fine golden boxes that hold the long-venerated bones of obscure saints. These relics generated lots of money for the church from pilgrims through the ages. Pop in a coin to share some light. The next chapel houses the skull of St. Anthony of the Desert.

Nearing the exit, look for two black columns and an early-Christian **sarcophagus** from Roman Arles (dated about AD 300). You'll see Christians wearing togas and praying like evangelicals do today—hands raised. The heads were likely lopped off during the French Revolution.

For 800 years, this church has been a stop on the ancient pilgrimage route to Santiago de Compostela in northwest Spain...and it still is today. You may notice the modern-day pilgrimages advertised on the far right near the church's entry.

• *To reach the adjacent peaceful cloister, leave the church, turn left, then left again through a courtyard.*

ARLES

⓭ St. Trophime Cloisters

Worth seeing if you have an Arles sightseeing pass (otherwise €5.50, same hours as arena), the cloisters' many small columns were scavenged from the ancient Roman theater and used to create an oasis of peace in Arles' center. Enjoy the delicate, sculpted capitals, the rounded Romanesque arches (12th century), and the pointed Gothic ones (14th century). The pretty vaulted hall exhibits 17th-century tapestries showing scenes from the First Crusade to the Holy Land. There's an instructive video and a chance to walk outside along an angled rooftop designed to catch rainwater: Notice the slanted gutter that channeled the water into a cistern and the heavy roof slabs covering the tapestry hall below.

• *From Place de la République, exit on the far corner (opposite the church and kitty-corner from where you entered) and turn right to stroll a delightful pedestrian street.*

⓮ Rue de la République

Rue de la République is Arles' primary shopping street. Walk downhill, enjoying the scene and popping into shops that catch your interest.

Near the top of the street is **Maison Soulier Bakery** (not to be confused with the nearby tearoom of the same name). Inside you'll be tempted by *fougasse* (bread studded with herbs, olives, and bacon bits), *sablés Provençal* (cookies made with honey and almonds), *tarte lavande* (a sweet almond lavender tart), and big crispy meringues (the egg-white-and-sugar answer to cotton candy—a cheap favorite of local kids). They also have sandwiches and salads if you feel like a picnic on the square. A few doors down is **Restaurant Les Maisons Rabanel** (around the corner, with two prized Michelin stars), **L'Occitane en Provence** (local perfumes), **Puyricard Choc-**

olate (with enticing €1 treats and *calisson*, a sweet almond delight), as well as local design and antique shops. The fragile spiral columns on the left (just before the tourist-pleasing Lavender Boutique on the corner) show what 400 years of weather can do to decorative stonework. The big **Arlaten Folk Museum** is up on the right and is well worth a visit now or later (see listing later, under "More Sights in Arles").

• *Take the first left onto Rue Président Wilson. (Wilson was honored by the French for his noble efforts to create the League of Nations—a proto-UN—after World War I.) Just after the butcher shop (Chez Mère Grand, with local pork-and-bull sausages hanging above a counter filled with precooked dishes to take home and heat up), turn right to find the* **Hôtel Dieu***, a hospital made famous by one of its patients: Vincent van Gogh.*

⓯ Espace Van Gogh Easel

In December 1888, shortly after his famous ear-cutting incident (see *Café Terrace at Night* easel, described later), Vincent was ad-

mitted into the local hospital— today's Espace Van Gogh cultural center. The Espace—with its exhibit space, classrooms, and library—is free (there's a handy WC inside). It surrounds a flowery courtyard (open to the public) that the artist loved and painted when he was being treated for blood loss, hallucina-

tions, and severe depression that left him bedridden for a month. The citizens of Arles circulated a petition demanding that the mad Dutchman be kept under medical supervision. Félix Rey, Vincent's kind doctor, worked out a compromise: The artist could leave during the day so that he could continue painting, but he had to sleep at the hospital at night. Look through the postcards sold in the courtyard to enjoy a tour of Arles through the eyes of Vincent. Find a painting of Vincent's ward—that's right here—showing nuns attending to patients in a gray hall.

• *Return to Rue de la République. Take a left and continue two blocks downhill. Take the second right up Rue Tour de Fabre and follow signs to* Fondation Van Gogh. *After a few steps, you'll pass* **La Main Qui Pense** *(The Hand That Thinks) pottery shop and workshop, where sincere Cécile Cayrol is busy creating and teaching (open afternoons only).*

Back on Rue Tour de Fabre, a couple blocks farther down, turn right onto Rue du Docteur Fanton. On your immediate right is the...

⑯ Fondation Van Gogh

This art foundation, worth ▲, delivers a refreshing stop for modern-art lovers and Van Gogh fans, with temporary exhibits in which contemporary artists pay homage to Vincent with thought-provoking interpretations of his works. You'll also see at least one original work by Van Gogh (more during big events in Arles, such as the Féria) painted during his time in the region. The gift shop has a variety of souvenirs, prints, and postcards.

Cost and Hours: €10, €12 combo-ticket with Réattu Museum; daily 10:00-19:00, until 18:00 and closed Mon off-season—check website for current hours and what's on; audioguide may be available-€4, 35 Rue du Docteur Fanton, +33 4 90 49 94 04, www.fondation-vincentvangogh-arles.org.

• *Continue on Rue du Docteur Fanton.*

⑰ Rue du Docteur Fanton

A few recommended restaurants line this pleasing street. On the right is the **Crèche Municipale.** Open workdays, this is a free government-funded daycare where parents can drop off their infants up to two years old. The notion: No worker should face financial hardship in order to receive quality childcare. At the next corner is the recommended **Soleileïs,** Arles' top ice cream shop.

After the ice cream shop, turn right and step into **Bar El Paseo** at 4 Rue des Thermes. This little restaurant is run by the Leal family, famous for its "dynasty" of bullfighters and proud of its bullfighting lore. They've lovingly wallpapered the place with photos and bullfighting memorabilia. The main museum-like room is full of bull—including the mounted heads of three big ones who died in the local arena and a big black-and-white photo of Arles' arena packed to capacity. You're welcome to look around...and even more welcome to buy a glass of Spanish Rioja wine or sangria.

• *A few steps farther is...*

⑱ Forum Square (Place du Forum) and Café Terrace at Night Easel

Named for the Roman forum that once stood here, **Forum Square,** worth ▲, was the political and religious center of Roman Arles. Still lively, this café-crammed square is a local watering hole and popular for a *pastis* (anise-based aperitif). The bistros on the square can put together a passable salad or

plat du jour—and when you sprinkle on the ambience, that's €14 well spent.

At the corner of Grand Hôtel Nord-Pinus, a plaque shows how the Romans built a foundation of galleries to make the main square level and compensate for Arles' slope down to the river. The two columns are all that survive from the upper story of the entry to the forum (you'll see other forum fragments at the Arlaten Folk Museum).

The statue on the square is of **Frédéric Mistral** (1830-1914). This popular poet, who wrote in the local dialect rather than in French, was a champion of Provençal culture. After receiving the Nobel Prize in Literature in 1904, Mistral used his prize money to preserve and display the folk identity of Provence. He founded a regional folk museum (the Arlaten Folk Museum) at a time when France was rapidly centralizing and regions like Provence were losing their unique identities. (The local mistral wind—literally "master"—has nothing to do with his name.)

• *Facing the brightly painted yellow café, find your final Van Gogh painting reproduced on the café's exterior; or walk a few steps left to find the easel*—**Café Terrace at Night.**

In October 1888, lonely Vincent—who dreamed of making Arles a magnet for fellow artists—persuaded his friend Paul Gauguin to come. He decorated Gauguin's room with several humble canvases of sunflowers (now some of the world's priciest paintings), knowing that Gauguin had admired a similar painting he'd done in Paris. Their plan was for Gauguin to be the "dean" of a new art school in Arles, and Vincent its instructor-in-chief. At first, the two got along well. They spent days side by side, rendering the same subjects in their two distinct styles. At night they hit the bars and brothels. Van Gogh's well-known *Café Terrace at Night* captures the glow of an absinthe buzz at Café la Nuit on Place du Forum.

After two months together, the two artists clashed over art and personality differences (Vincent was a slob around the house, whereas Gauguin was meticulous). The night of December 23, they were drinking absinthe at the café when Vincent suddenly went ballistic. He threw his glass at Gauguin. Gauguin left. Walking through Place Victor Hugo, Gauguin heard footsteps behind him and turned to see Vincent coming at him, brandishing a razor. Gauguin quickly fled town. The local paper reported what happened next: "At 11:30 p.m., Vincent van Gogh, painter from Holland, appeared at the brothel at no. 1, asked for Rachel, and gave her his cut-off earlobe, saying, 'Treasure this precious object.' Then he vanished." He woke up the next morning at home with his head wrapped in a bloody towel and his earlobe missing. Was Vincent emulating a successful matador, whose prize is cutting off the bull's ear?

The **bright-yellow café**—called Café la Nuit—was the subject of one of Vincent van Gogh's most famous works in Arles. Although his painting showed the café in a brilliant yellow from the glow of gas lamps, the facade was bare limestone, just like the other cafés on this square. The café is now a tourist trap that its current owners painted to match Van Gogh's version...and to cash in on the Vincent-crazed hordes who pay too much to eat or drink here.

In spring 1889, the bipolar genius (a modern diagnosis) checked himself into the St. Paul Monastery and Hospital in St-Rémy-de-Provence (see page 101). He spent a year there, thriving in the care of nurturing doctors and nuns. Painting was part of his therapy, so they gave him a studio to work in, and he produced more than 100 paintings. Alcohol-free and institutionalized, he did some of his wildest work. With thick, swirling brushstrokes and surreal colors, he made his placid surroundings throb with restless energy. Today, at the hospital in St-Rémy, you can see a replica of his room and his studio, plus several scenes he painted in situ like these in Arles—the courtyard, the plane trees, the view out the upstairs window of nearby fields, and the rugged Alpilles mountains.

Eventually, Vincent's torment became unbearable. In the spring of 1890, he left Provence to be cared for by a sympathetic doctor in Auvers-sur-Oise, just north of Paris. On July 27, he wandered into a field and shot himself. He died two days later.

• *With this walk, you have seen the best of Arles. The colorful Roquette District, the Arlaten Folk Museum, and the Réattu Museum are each a short walk away (all described next). Or enjoy a drink on the Place du Forum and savor the joy of experiencing the essence of Provence.*

More Sights in Arles

IN THE CENTER

Many of Arles' city-center sights (such as the Roman Arena and St. Trophime church) are covered on my self-guided walk. The important sights listed below will add to your understanding of Arles' history and contemporary life.

▲▲Arlaten Folk Museum (Museon Arlaten)

Set in a 15th-century manor home, the Arlaten is the leading museum in Provence for traditional culture and folklore. Following an 11-year wait for renovations to be completed, the museum is finally open again—and it does not disappoint.

Cost and Hours: €8, not covered by sightseeing passes; Tue-Sun 10:00-18:00, closed Mon; +33 4 13 31 51 99, www.museonarlaten.fr/en.

Visiting the Museum: After entering the four-floor museum through the courtyard, you'll find well-devised displays of every aspect of life in Provence, mostly from the 18th century to present. Excellent English explanations, presented through touchpad screens and short videos, provide more info than you probably have time for.

Climb the glassy stairway above exposed ruins from the Roman forum (or take the elevator) and find rooms with life-size mannequins showing slice-of-life scenes, traditional dress, tools, musical instruments (including a hurdy gurdy), and more. You'll discover the importance of the Rhône River and the Camargue to the area's economy and culture, and learn about major celebrations and legends—such as the 15th-century tale of the tarasque, a turtle-like monster (I know, weird) that lived on the riverbank and terrorized locals. It was eventually vanquished by a woman, and is now celebrated at an annual festival. The museum ends with a look at the challenges that face Provence today.

La Roquette District

To escape the tourist beat in Arles, take a detour into Arles' little-visited western fringe. Find Rue des Porcelets near the Trinquetaille Bridge and stroll several blocks into pleasing Place Paul Doumer, where you'll find a lively assortment of cafés, bakeries, and bistros catering to locals (see "Eating in Arles," later, for my suggestions). Continue along Rue de la Roquette and turn right on charming Rue Croix Rouge to reach the river. Those walking to or from the Ancient History Museum can use this appealing stroll as a shortcut.

▲Réattu Museum (Musée Réattu)

Housed in the former Grand Priory of the Knights of Malta, this modern-art collection, while always changing, is a stimulating and well-lit mix of new and old. Picasso loved Arles and came here regularly for the bullfights. At the end of his life in 1973, he gave the city a series of his paintings, some of which are always on display here. The permanent collection usually includes a series of works by homegrown Neoclassical artist Jacques Réattu.

Cost and Hours: €6, €12 combo-ticket with Fondation Van Gogh; Tue-Sun 10:00-18:00, Nov-Feb until 17:00, closed Mon

year-round; 10 Rue du Grand Prieuré, +33 4 90 49 37 58, www.
museereattu.arles.fr.

Baths of Constantine (Thermes de Constantin)

These partly intact Roman baths were built in the early fourth century when Emperor Constantine declared Arles an imperial residence. Roman cities such as Arles had several public baths like this,
fed by aqueducts and used as much for exercising, networking, and
chatting with friends as for bathing (like today's athletic clubs).
These baths were located near the Rhône River for easy water dis-
posal. You'll get a pretty good look at the baths through the fence.
If you enter, you'll walk elevated metal corridors at the original
floor level. Imagine the elaborate engineering: the hypocaust system for heating the floor and big tubs with various temperatures—
hot, tepid, and cold—next to a sauna and steam room heated by
slave-stoked, wood-burning ovens.

Cost and Hours: €4, daily 9:00-19:00, April and Oct until
18:00, Nov-March 10:00-17:00, near the Réattu Museum.

ON THE OUTSKIRTS

▲▲Ancient History Museum (Musée Départemental Arles Antique)

This museum, just west of central Arles along the river, provides
valuable background on Arles' Roman history: Visit it before the
other city sights if you can (drivers should consider stopping on the
way into town).

Located on the site of the Roman chariot racecourse (the arc of
which defines today's parking lot), this manageable, one-floor museum is filled with models
and original sculptures
that re-create the Roman
city, making workaday life
and culture easier to imagine. While the museum's
posted descriptions of most
of its treasures are only in
French, the audioguide
does a fine job describing

the exhibits in English. For a deeper understanding of Provence's
ancient roots, read "The Romans in Provence" on page 42.

Cost and Hours: €8, includes audioguide, free first Sun of
the month; open Wed-Mon 10:00-18:00, closed Tue; Presqu'île du
Cirque Romain, +33 4 13 31 51 03, www.arlesantique.fr/en.

Getting There: Drivers will see signs for the museum at the
city's western end. To reach the museum from the city center *sans*
car, take the €1 **Navia minibus shuttle** (line A, 3-4/hour, see

A Day in the Life of an Arles Citizen in the Roman Era

Ancient Rome's wealth made a lifestyle possible that was the envy of the known world. Let's look at a typical well-to-do Arles citizen and his family in the era of Roman rule over the course of a day.

In the morning, Nebulus reviews the finances of the country farm with his caretaker/accountant/slave. He's interrupted by a "client," one of many poorer people dependent upon him for favors. The client, a shoemaker, wants permission from the government to open a new shop. He asks Nebulus to cut through the red tape. Nebulus promises to consult a lawyer friend in the basilica, or legal building.

Hungry, Nebulus stops at Burger Emp to grab a typical fast-food lunch. Most city dwellers don't cook in their cramped, wooden apartments because of the fire hazard. After a siesta, he walks to the baths for a work-out and a little business networking. He discusses plans for donating money to build a new aqueduct for the city.

The children, Raucous and Ubiquitous, say goodbye to the pet dog and head off to school in the Forum. Nothing funny happens on the way. At school, it's down to business. They learn the basic three Rs. When they get older, they'll study literature, Greek, and public speaking. (The saving grace of this dreary education is that they don't have to take Latin.)

Work done, Nebulus heads for the stadium. The public is

"Getting Around Arles," earlier). The museum is about a 25-minute **walk** from the city center: Turn left at the river and take the riverside promenade under two bridges to the big, modern blue building (or better, stroll through Arles' enjoyable La Roquette neighborhood, described earlier). As you approach the museum, you'll pass the verdant Hortus Garden—designed to recall the Roman circus and chariot racecourse that were located here. A **taxi** ride costs about €13 (the museum can call a taxi for your return).

Visiting the Museum: The permanent collection is housed in a large hall flooded with natural light. Highlights include models of the ancient city and its major landmarks, a 2,000-year-old Roman boat, statues, mosaics, and sarcophagi. Here's what you'll see:

A wall **map** of the region during the Roman era greets visitors and shows the geographic importance of Arles: Three important

crazy about the chariot races. There are 12 per day, 240 days a year. Four teams dominate the competition (Reds, Whites, Blues, and Greens), and Nebulus has always been a die-hard Blue.

Back home, Nebulus' wife, Lucida, tends to the household affairs. She pauses in the bedroom to offer a prayer to her personal goddess for good weather for tonight. Meanwhile, the servants clean the house and send clothing to the laundry. A typical outfit is a simple woolen tunic: two pieces of cloth, front and back, sewn together at the sides. But tonight they'll dress up for a dinner party. She'll wear silk, with a wreath of flowers, and Nebulus will wear his best toga, a 20-foot-long white cloth. It's heavy and hard to put on, but it's all the rage. Nebulus dons his phallic-shaped necklace, which serves as an amulet against the evil eye and as a symbol of good luck in health, business, and bed.

At the dinner party, Lucida marvels over the chef's creation: ham soaked with honey, pasted in flour and baked. The guests toast each other with clay goblets bearing inscriptions like "Fill me up," and "Love me, baby!" Reclining on a couch, waited on by slaves, Nebulus orders a bowl of larks' tongues and a roast pig stuffed with live birds, then washes it down with wine. He calls for a feather, vomits, and starts all over. He catches the eye of a dark-skinned slave dancer from Egypt, and he takes her to the bedroom just down the hall...

...Or so went the stories. In fact, the legendary Roman orgy was just that—legendary. Romans advocated moderation and fidelity. Stuffiness and business sense were the rule. The family unit was considered sacred. If anything, the decadence of Roman life was confined to the upper classes in the later years of the empire.

Roman trade routes—vias Domitia, Grippa, and Aurelia—all converged on or near Arles.

After a small exhibit on pre-Roman Arles (including a pueblo-like structure that looks like something out of present-day New Mexico, but dates from 3,000 BC), you'll come to fascinating **models of the Roman city** and impressive Roman structures in (and near) Arles. The models breathe life into the buildings, showing how they looked 2,000 years ago.

Start with the **model of Roman Arles** and ponder the city's splendor when Arles' population was almost double that of today. Look at the space Romans devoted to their arena and huge racecourse—a reminder that a passion for sports is not unique to modern civilizations (the museum you're in is at the far end of the racecourse). The model also illustrates how little Arles' core has changed over two millennia, with its houses still clustered around the city center, and warehouses still located on the opposite side of the river. Find the forum—it's still the center of town, although only two columns survive (the smaller section of the forum is where today's Place du Forum is built; you can also get a glimpse of the forum ruins at the Arlaten Folk Museum). The next model shows the grandeur of the forum in greater detail.

At the museum's center stands the original **statue of Julius Caesar,** which once graced Arles' ancient theater's magnificent

stage wall. To the left of Julius, find a **model of Arles' theater** and its wall, as well as models of the ancient town's other major buildings. Farther to the left, find models of the floating wooden bridge over the widest, slowest part of the river—giving Arles a strategic advantage; moving clockwise, see the hy-draulic mill of Barbegal with its 16 waterwheels cascading water down a hillside (the remains of which you can visit; see page 98), and the **arena** with its moveable cover to shelter spectators from sun or rain.

Step down into the hall to Julius's right and find the large model of the **chariot racecourse.** Part of the original racecourse was just outside the windows, and although long gone, it likely re-sembled Rome's Circus Maximus. The rest of this hall is dedicated to the museum's most exciting exhibit: a **Gallo-Roman vessel** and much of its cargo (helpful English translations on wall panels). This almost-100-foot-long Roman barge was hauled out of the Rhône in 2010, along with some 280 amphorae and 3,000 ceramic arti-facts. It was typical of flat-bottomed barges used to shuttle goods between Arles and ports along the Mediterranean (vessels were manually towed upriver). This one hauled limestone slabs and big rocks—no wonder it sank. A worthwhile 20-minute video about the barge's recovery (with English subtitles) plays continuously in a tiny theater at the end of the hall.

Elsewhere in the museum, you'll see displays of pottery, jewelry, metal, and glass artifacts. You'll also see well-crafted mosaic floors that illustrate how Roman Arles was a city of art and culture. The many **statues** are all original, except for the greatest—the *Venus of Arles,* which Louis XIV took a liking to and had moved to Versailles. It's now in the Louvre—and, as locals say, "When it's in Paris...bye-bye."

The final section is dedicated to expertly carved pagan and early Christian **sarcophagi** (from the second to fifth century AD). These would have lined the Via Aurelia outside the town wall. In the early days of the Church, Jesus was often portrayed beardless and as the good shepherd, with a lamb over his shoulder.

▲Frank Gehry Tower and LUMA Arles

A ten-minute walk east of the TI, a striking Frank Gehry-designed aluminum tower rises up 180 feet over Arles. It's the centerpiece of the LUMA Arles complex, which provides space for independent artists with a vast park and warehouses converted to exhibition halls and cafés. The LUMA Foundation supports artists of all kinds, from sculptors to photographers to writers.

The tower and art complex are located in Arles' once thriving railyard quarter, which struggled to recover after the bombings of World War II. But this formerly neglected neighborhood is finally enjoying a futuristic facelift and economic resurgence thanks to this far-out development. It's easy, free, and well worth the time to visit the tower (with views and exhibits) and the pleasing park at its base.

Cost and Hours: Tower—free, Wed-Mon 10:00-18:00, closed Tue, last entry at 16:30, 35 Avenue Victor Hugo; park—free, daily 7:00-20:30, Chemin des Minimes; +33 4 90 47 76 17, www.luma-arles.org. The tower and park are served by the Navia minibus shuttle (line A, stop: Victor Hugo).

Visiting the Tower: Upon entering, the helpful staff will get you oriented with a good English handout that describes each floor. Two short but worthwhile videos play at the entry: one features Maja Hoffmann, founder of the LUMA Foundation; the other (more interesting) video features an interview with architect Frank Gehry, in which he describes his tower design and its influences (including the swirling objects in Van Gogh's paintings). Then take the elevator to the top floor (notice the salt bricks that line the wall—Camargue salt is a big export item here). Enjoy amazing views from the outside terraces, then drop down to any floor with an exhibit that interests you. Admire the interlocking spiral stairways near the bottom, and take a ride down two floors on the tube slide.

Experiences in Arles

▲▲Markets

On Wednesday and Saturday mornings, Arles' ring road erupts into an open-air festival of fish, flowers, produce...and everything Provençal. The main event is on Saturday, with vendors jamming the ring road from Boulevard Emile Combes to the east, along Boulevard des Lices near the TI (the heart of the market), and continuing down Boulevard Georges Clemenceau to the west. The south (TI) side of the market is all about produce and food stands serving local treats, while the north side features clothing, sunglasses, baskets, and such. Wednesday's market runs only along Boulevard Emile Combes, between Place Lamartine and Avenue Victor Hugo; the segment nearest Place Lamartine is filled with produce and other food stuffs, and the upper half features clothing, tablecloths, purses, and so on. On the first Wednesday of the month, a flea market doubles the size of the usual Wednesday market along Boulevard des Lices near the TI.

Part of the market has a North African feel, thanks to the many Algerians and Moroccans who live in Arles. As with immigrants in any rich country, they came to do the lowly city jobs that locals didn't want, and now they mostly do the region's labor-intensive agricultural jobs (picking olives, harvesting fruit, and working in local greenhouses).

Both markets are open until about 12:30. Dive in: Buy some flowers for your hotelier, try the olives, sample some wine, swat a pickpocket, and stop by a fish stand to sample the local tellines clams (sautéed in garlic).

▲▲Bullgames (Courses Camarguaises)

Provençal "bullgames" are held in Arles and in neighboring towns. Those in Arles occupy the same seats that fans have used for nearly 2,000 years and deliver the city's most memorable experience— the *courses camarguaises* in the ancient arena. The nonviolent bullgames are more sporting than bloody bullfights (though traditional Spanish-style bullfights still take place on occasion). The bulls of Arles (who, locals insist, "die of old age") are

promoted in posters even more boldly than their human foes. In the bullgame, a ribbon *(cocarde)* is laced between the bull's horns. The *razeteur,* dressed in white and carrying a special hook, has 15 minutes to snare the ribbon. Local businessmen encourage a *razeteur* by shouting out how much money they'll pay for the *cocarde.* If the bull pulls a good stunt, the band plays the famous "Toreador" song from *Carmen.* The following day, newspapers report on the games, including how many *Carmens* the bull earned.

Three classes of bullgames—determined by the experience of the *razeteurs*—are advertised in posters: The *Course de Protection* is for rookies. The *Trophée de l'Avenir* comes with more experience. And the *Trophée des As* features top professionals. During Easter *(Féria de Pâques)* and the fall rice-harvest festival *(Féria du Riz),* the arena hosts traditional Spanish bullfights (look for *corrida)* with outfits, swords, spikes, and the whole gory shebang. (Nearby villages stage *courses camarguaises* in small wooden bullrings nearly every weekend; TIs have the latest schedule.)

Bullgame tickets usually run €11-20; bullfights are pricier (€36-250). Schedules for bullgames vary (usually July-Aug on Wed and Fri)—ask at the TI or check www.arenes-arles.com.

Easter and Fall Fairs (Féria de Pâques and Féria du Riz)

For 150 years, Arles has thrown citywide parties to celebrate the arrival of spring and fall. During the four days that each event lasts, more than 500,000 people pile into Arles for bullfights, street concerts, piles of paella, and parties (*Feria de Pâques* is Fri-Mon of Easter weekend, and *Feria du Riz* is Fri-Mon on the second weekend of Sept). The Easter event kicks off the bullfighting season, while the September event celebrates the land and traditions of Arles. Only during these fairs are bulls killed in the bullfights and only during these events does Arles feel overrun.

Sleeping in Arles

Hotels are a great value here—most are air-conditioned, though few have elevators. The Calendal, Musée, and Régence hotels offer exceptional value.

I rank accommodations from **$** budget to **$$$$** splurge. For the best deal, contact smaller hotels directly by phone or email. When you book direct, the owner avoids a commission and may be able to offer a discount. Book well in advance for peak season or if your trip coincides with a major holiday or festival (see the appendix). For more details on reservations, short-term rentals, and more, see the "Sleeping" section in the Practicalities chapter.

$$ Hôtel le Calendal*** is a service-with-a-smile place ideally located between the Roman Arena and Classical Theater. The hotel opens to the street with airy lounges and a palm-shaded courtyard, providing an enjoyable refuge. You'll find snacks and drinks in the café/sandwich bar (daily 8:00-20:00). The soothing rooms show a modern flair with creations from  local artists (and explanations of their art). Rooms come in all shapes and sizes (some with balcony, family rooms, air-con, free spa for adults, ask about parking deals, just above arena at 5 Rue Porte de Laure, +33 4 90 96 11 89, www.lecalendal.com, contact@

lecalendal.com). They also run the nearby budget Hostel Arles City Center, described later.

$ Hôtel du Musée** is a quiet, affordable manor-home hideaway tucked deep in Arles (if driving, call the hotel from the street—they'll open the barrier so you can drive in to drop off your bags). This delightful place comes with 29 tasteful rooms, a flowery courtyard, and comfortable lounges. Lighthearted Claude and English-speaking Laurence are good hosts (family rooms, no elevator, rental bikes available, pay parking garage, follow *Réattu Museum* signs to 11 Rue du Grand Prieuré, +33 4 90 93 88 88, www.hoteldumusee.com, contact@hoteldumusee.com).

$ Hôtel de la Muette** is an intimate, good-value hotel located in a quiet corner of Arles, run by gentle Sylvie. Its sharp rooms and bathrooms come with tiled floors and stone walls (family rooms, no elevator, pay private garage, 15 Rue des Suisses, +33 4 90 96 15 39, www.hotel-muette.com, hotel.muette@wanadoo.fr).

$ Hôtel Acacias*** sits just off Place Lamartine and inside the old city walls. It's a modern hotel with small, clean, and comfortable rooms (double rooms only, air-con, pay parking garage, 2 Rue de la Cavalerie, +33 4 90 96 37 88, https://hotel-arles.brithotel.fr, arles@brithotel.fr).

¢ Hôtel Régence** is a top budget deal with a riverfront location, comfortable, Provençal rooms, and easy parking. Of all the hotels I list, this one is the closest to the train station—a 10-minute walk (RS%, family rooms, choose river-view or quieter courtyard rooms, no elevator; from Place Lamartine, turn right after passing between towers to reach 5 Rue Marius Jouveau; +33 4 90 96 39 85, www.hotel-regence.com, contact@hotel-regence.com). Gentle Valérie and Eric speak English.

¢ Hostel Arles City Center offers good four-bed dorm rooms, a shared kitchen, and homey living area. It's a great value for backpackers and those on a shoestring. Check in next door at the recommended Hôtel le Calendal (air-con, just above the Roman Arena at 26 Place Pomme, +33 6 99 71 11 89).

NEAR ARLES

Many drivers, particularly those with families, prefer staying outside Arles in the peaceful countryside, with easy access to the area's sights.

$$ Mas Petit Fourchon is a grand farmhouse with country-classy and spacious rooms on a sprawling property a few minutes from Arles. Adorable owner Pascale loves speaking English. Here you get the largest bathrooms I've seen in Provence and acres of room to roam—with two lovable dogs, a few alpaca, and several horses (includes good breakfast, some rooms with air-con, big heated pool, 1070 Chemin de Nadal in the Fourchon suburb; take exit 6 from N-113 toward *l'hôpital,* turn right just after passing the hospital and follow signs—see the "Near Arles" map on page 91; +33 4 90 96 16 35, www.petitfourchon.com, info@petitfourchon. com).

$ Domaine de Laforest, a few minutes' drive below Fontvie-ille, near the aqueduct of Barbegal, is a 320-acre spread engulfed by vineyards, rice fields, and swaying trees. The sweet owners (Syl-vie and mama Mariette) rent eight well-equipped and comfortable two-bedroom apartments with great weekly rates (may be rentable for fewer days, air-con, washing machines, pool, big lawn, swings, 1000 Route de l'Aqueduc Romain—see the "Near Arles" map on page 91, +33 6 23 73 44 59, www.domaine-laforest.com, contact@ domaine-laforest.com).

ARLES

Eating in Arles

You can dine well in Arles on a modest budget (most of my listings have *menus* for under €25). Monday is a quiet night for restaurants, though eateries on Place du Forum are open. For a portable snack, try Maison Soulier Bakery (see my "Arles City Walk," earlier), and for groceries, use the big Monoprix supermarket/department store on Place Lamartine (Mon-Sat 8:30-19:30, closed Sun).

I rank eateries from **$** budget to **$$$$** splurge. For more ad-vice on eating in Provence, including ordering, tipping, and French cuisine and beverages, see the "Eating" section of the Practicalities chapter.

FOR LUNCH OR A LIGHT DINNER

$ Cuisine de Comptoir is the Provençal answer to a pizzeria, of-fering light and cheap meals. For €13, you get a *tartine*—a cross between pizza and bruschetta with a fun array of toppings served on Poilâne bread—along with soup or salad. It's run by Vincent and his charming wife, and has both indoor and outdoor seating (closed Sun-Mon, off lower end of Place du Forum at 10 Rue de la Liberté, +33 4 90 96 86 28).

$ Café Factory République is a youthful, creative, and fun-loving place run by jovial Gilles. He's fun to talk with and serves sandwiches, hearty salads, and a wide variety of drinks. While not really a dinner place, he takes orders at least until 18:00 (Mon-Sat 8:00-19:00, closed Sun, 35 Rue de la République, +33 4 90 54 52 23, skinniest WC in France).

$ Le Comptoir du Calendal, in the recommended Hôtel le Calendal, serves light, seasonal fare curbside overlooking the theater, in its lovely courtyard, on the front terrace, or inside the café. They offer tasty and cheap little sandwiches and salads,

ARLES

Arles Hotels & Restaurants

Accommodations

1. Hôtel/Comptoir Le Calendal & Hostel Arles City Center
2. Hôtel du Musée
3. Hôtel de la Muette
4. Hôtel Acacias
5. Hôtel Régence
6. To Mas Petit Fourchon
7. To Domaine de Laforest

Eateries

8. Cuisine de Comptoir
9. Café Factory République
10. Maisons Rabanel & Greeniotage
11. Le Criquet
12. Volubilis
13. Le Mistral
14. Place du Forum Eateries
15. Rue du Dr. Fanton Eateries
16. Soleileïs Ice Cream
17. Pizza 22
18. Le Gibolin
19. Maison Soulier Bakery

RUE DES CAPUCINS

RUE DE LA VERRIERE

RUE CAMARGUE

R. ROBESPIERRE

TRINQUETAILLE

RUE

QUAI ST. PIERRE

Rhône

TRINQUETAILLE BRIDGE

QUAI MARX DORMOY

R. DE LA TOUR DU FABRE

R. DR. FANTON

FONDATION VAN GOGH

LIBERTE

RUE A. FRANCE

R. JOUVENE

QUAI DE LA ROQUETTE

RUE DE LA REPUBLIQUE

ARLATEN FOLK MUSE

Place Paul Doumier

R. DES PORCELETS

RUE DE LA ROQUETTE

RUE DE CHARTROUSE

RUE GAMBETTA

RUE JEAN GRANAUD

ESPACE VAN GOGH

RUE MOLIERE

RUE CROIX ROUGE

LA ROQUETTE

Place Genive

RUE MOLIERE

Main Bus Stops & Navia Shuttle

To Ancient History Museum

RUE FLEURY PRUDHON

RUE RAILLON

BLVD. CLEM.

N-113

To Nîmes via A-54

BLVD. G CLEMENCEAU

To Ancient History Museum

Navia Shuttle

RUE PARMENTI

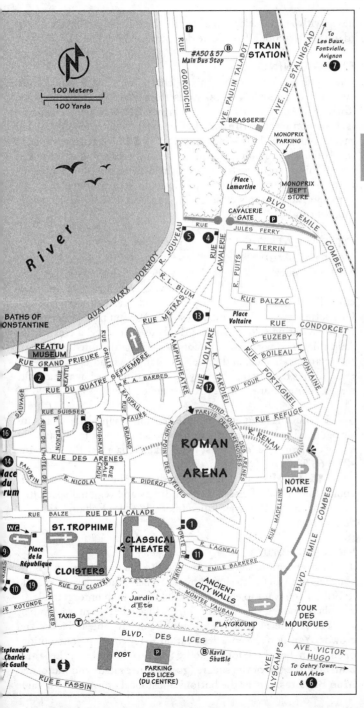

ARLES

To Les Baux, Fontvielle, Avignon & **7**

P

RUE GORODICHE

#A50 & 57 Main Bus Stop **B**

TRAIN STATION

RUE PAULIN TALABOT

AVE. DE STALINGRAD

BRASSERIE

AVE. DE STALINGRAD

MONOPRIX PARKING

Place Lamartine

MONOPRIX DEP'T STORE

BLVD. EMILE COMBES

River

CAVALERIE GATE

P

RUE **5** **4** JULES FERRY

R. TERRIN

RUE CAVALERIE

R. PUITS

R. JOUVEAU

QUAI MARX DORMOY

R. L. BLUM

RUE BALZAC

RUE METRAS

Place Voltaire

RUE CONDORCET

13

BATHS OF CONSTANTINE

REATTU MUSEUM

RUE GRILLE

L'AMPHITHEATRE

RUE VOLTAIRE

R. A. TARDIEU

R. EUZEBY

R. BOILEAU

RUE PORTAGNEL

R. LA FONTAINE

RUE GRAND PRIEURE **2**

RUE REATTU

RUE DU QUATRE SEPTEMBRE

R. A. BARBES

DU FOUR

12

RUE REFUGE

RUE SUISSES **3**

R. VERNON

R. DOISNEAU

R. KASPAIL

RUE R. BRIAND

R. FAURE

ROND-POINT DES ARENES

PARVIS DES ARENES

RUE DE L'HOTEL DE VILLE

16

FAVORIN

RUE DES ARENES

RUE NICOLAI

R. DIDEROT

R. BARBE CHOU

ROMAN ARENA

R. RENAN

14

Place du Forum

RUE BALZE

RUE DE LA CALADE

ROND-POINT DES ARENES

RUE MADELEINE

NOTRE DAME

BLVD. EMILE COMBES

WC

ST. TROPHIME

CLASSICAL THEATER

PORTE DE LAURE

1

R. L'AGNEAU

9

Place de la République

CLOISTERS

11

R. EMILE BARRERE

10 **19**

RUE DU CLOITRE

Jardin d'Ete

MONTEE VAUBAN

ANCIENT CITY WALLS

JEAN JAURES

RUE ROTONDE

TAXIS **T**

PLAYGROUND

TOUR DES MOURGUES

BLVD. DES LICES

AVE. VICTOR HUGO

Esplanade Charles de Gaulle

i

POST

P

PARKING DES LICES (DU CENTRE)

B Navia Shuttle

AVE. ALYSCAMPS

To Gehry Tower, LUMA Arles & **6**

RUE E. FASSIN

100 Meters

100 Yards

along with a small selection of *plats*—the salmon gratin is delicious (daily 8:00-20:00, 5 Rue Porte de Laure, +33 4 90 96 11 89).

FINER DINING

One of France's most recognized chefs, Jean-Luc Rabanel, runs two very different places 50 yards from Place de la République. They sit side by side at 7 Rue des Carmes. **$$$$ Maisons Rabanel** is a top end place with two Michelin stars (contemporary tasting menus only, €95-145). And next door is **$$$ Greeniotage,** with much the same quality, less pretense, and meals at a third of the price. This is an opportunity to sample the famous chef's talents with the €49 three-course *menu* (limited selection of wines by the glass, both restaurants closed Mon-Tue, +33 4 90 47 61 13, www.rabanel.com).

OTHER EATERIES
Near the Arena

$$ Le Criquet, possibly the best value in Arles, is a sweet little place two blocks above the arena, serving well-presented and delicious Provençal classics with joy at good prices. Sisters Lili and Charlotte serve while mama and son-in-law run the kitchen. Their mouth-watering €26 *bourride* is the house specialty: a creamy fish soup thickened with aioli and lots of garlic and stuffed with mussels, clams, calamari, and more. The octopus salad is a treat—but every dish is tasty here. They have a lovely dining room and a petite terrace (closed Sun-Mon, 21 Rue Porte de Laure, +33 4 90 96 80 51).

$ Volubilis is an endearing little spot serving Moroccan cuisine at good prices. The restaurant covers two floors inside and has a tiny deck outside (daily, just below the arena at 53 Rue Voltaire, +33 6 66 53 78 41).

$$$ Le Mistral, a few blocks below the arena, is a smart choice for a meal of classic French dishes and regional specialties served by hands-on owner Julien (daily, 18 Place Voltaire, +33 4 90 96 35 01).

Place du Forum

The most charming square in town is also the most touristy. While you feel sure Van Gogh sipped his *pastis* here, these days he'd avoid it. Still, if you want to enjoy forgettable food with unforgettable atmosphere under a starry, starry night, Place du Forum is a winner.

For Dinner: Circle the square to compare the ambience and crowds. You don't need a reservation here, so keep your options open. Your best bets for a good **$$** meal are probably **Le Tambourin** at the top of the square (good dinner salads and more) and **Mon Bar Brasserie** at the bottom (most local crowd, decent value plates; both places closed Sun). **La Taverne du Forum** always seems the liveliest with the least lively food. **Le Comptoir d'Italie** serves your basic Italian grub, pizzas, and salads. **Apostrophe Café** has a younger vibe, more modern food, and

smoothies. **Café La Nuit** may have the best street appeal, but it's a tourist trap designed to hook those with Vincent fantasies.

Before-Dinner Drink or Dessert: You can eat at a better restaurant elsewhere and enjoy the ambience of Place du Forum for an aperitif or dessert. Any bar can serve you a *pastis*—one of the most local rituals you can enjoy in Arles. This anise-based aperitif is served straight with ice, along with a carafe of water—dilute to taste. And the ice cream shop on the square has a handful of tables, giving you a front-row seat to the Provençal ambience.

While here, immerse yourself in Arles' lore with a drink at **The Grand Hôtel Nord-Pinus Bar**, a once popular watering hole for toreadors and greats from Ernest Hemingway to Jean Cocteau to Ingrid Bergman (14 Place du Forum).

On Rue du Docteur Fanton

This pedestrian-friendly street—with a pleasing lineup of restaurants, all with good outside and inside dining—is a fine place to comparison-shop for dinner (reservations are smart on busy evenings). And, for your dessert pleasure, a good ice cream place is just across the street.

$$ Le Galoubet is a popular local spot, blending a warm interior, traditional French cuisine, and gregarious service, thanks to owner Frank. If it's cold, a roaring fire keeps you toasty (closed Sun-Mon, great fries and desserts, at #18, +33 4 90 93 18 11).

$$ Le Plaza la Paillotte buzzes with happy diners enjoying well-presented Provençal cuisine. Attentive owners Stéphane and Graziela (he cooks, she serves) welcome diners with a comfortable terrace and a Spanish feeling interior. The stuffed bull *(taureau estauffé),* more like a beef stew, is delectable (daily, at #28, +33 4 90 96 33 15).

Ice Cream: At **Soleileïs,** Marijtje scoops up fine ice cream made with organic milk, fresh fruit, all-natural ingredients, and creative flavors that fit the season. There's also a shelf of English books for exchange (daily 14:00-18:30, closed in winter, at #9).

In the La Roquette District

For a less-touristy-feeling dining experience, wander into the La Roquette neighborhood (described earlier, under "More Sights in Arles"). The neighborhood is more youthful with a foodie energy. Place Paul Doumer is the center of the action—a delightful square crowded with tables from a ring of fun eateries under shady plane trees.

$ Pizza 22 fires up the best pizza in Arles with inviting tables on Place Paul Doumer (closed Tue, 22 Place Paul Doumer, +33 4 86 63 65 60).

$$ Le Gibolin, is an intimate place for traditional French cuisine. Dine in a warm interior surrounded by wine bottles and locals, to whom the chef's talents are well known. Wife Alizon serves while husband Arnaud cooks (closed Sun-Mon, reservations a day ahead are smart, 13 Rue des Porcelets, +33 4 88 65 43 14).

Arles Connections

BY TRAIN

Note that Intercité trains in and out of Arles require a reservation. These include connections with Nice to the east and Bordeaux to the west (including intermediary stops). Ask at the station.

Compare train and bus schedules: For some nearby destinations, the bus may be the better choice, and it's usually cheaper.

From Arles by Train to: Paris (hourly, 4 hours, transfer in Avignon or Nîmes), **Avignon Centre-Ville** (hourly, 20 minutes), **Nîmes** (hourly, 30 minutes), **Orange** (6/day direct, 45 minutes, more with transfer in Avignon), **Aix-en-Provence Centre-Ville** (hourly, 2 hours, transfer in Marseille, train may separate midway—be sure your section is going to Aix-en-Provence), **Marseille** (1-2/hour, 1 hour), **Cassis** (hourly, 2 hours, transfer in Marseille), **Carcassonne** (4/day direct, 2.5 hours, more with transfer in Narbonne, direct trains may require reservations), **Beaune** (hourly, 4-5 hours, transfer in Lyon and Avignon or Nîmes), **Nice** (hourly, 4 hours, most require transfer in Marseille), **Barcelona** (3/day, 4.5 hours, transfer in Nîmes), **Italy** (3-8/day, transfer in Marseille and Nice; from Arles, it's 5 hours to Ventimiglia on the border, 8-10 hours to Milan, 10 hours to Cinque Terre, 11 hours to Florence, and 13 hours to Venice or Rome).

BY BUS

Travel by bus is a bargain here as most trips cost under €2. There are two key bus stops in Arles. The stop at the train station serves buses connecting Arles with destinations to the north and east, including Avignon, Les Baux, and St-Rémy-de-Provence. The stop on Boulevard Georges Clemenceau (see the "Arles" map) serves buses heading west and south to destinations such as Nîmes, Stes-Maries-de-la-Mer, and Aigues-Mortes. Some routes use both stops.

From Arles by Bus to Les Baux and St-Rémy: Verify Les Baux bus schedules at the TI. Cartreize bus #57 connects Arles to St-Rémy-de-Provence via Les Baux in summer only (6/day, daily July-Aug, none off-season; 35 minutes to Les Baux, 50 minutes to St-Rémy, then runs to Avignon). Bus #54 also goes to St-Rémy but not via Les Baux (5/day Mon-Fri, 3/day Sat, none on Sun, 1 hour, timetables at www.maregionsud.fr/transports).

By Bus to Other Destinations: Nîmes (#130, 8/day Mon-Fri, 2/day Sat-Sun, 1 hour), **Camargue/Stes-Maries-de-la-Mer** (Agglo bus #50, 6/day, 1 hour, www.tout-envia.com).

ARLES

NEAR ARLES

*Les Baux • St-Rémy •
The Camargue*

The diverse terrain around Arles harbors many worthwhile and easy day trips. The medieval ghost town of Les Baux haunts the eerie Alpilles mountains, while chic and compact St-Rémy-de-Provence awaits just over the hills, offering Roman ruins and memories of Vincent van Gogh. For an entirely different experience, the flat Camargue wetlands region knocks on Arles' southern door with sandy beaches, saltwater lakes, rice paddies, flamingos, wild horses, and wild black bulls.

PLANNING YOUR TIME

Because public transportation in this area is sparse, these sights are most convenient by car, taxi, or minivan tour. For a memorable one-day road trip from Arles or Avignon, spend the morning in Les Baux (before the crowds), have lunch in St-Rémy and explore its sights, then finish at the Roman aqueduct of Barbegal. Nondrivers can do the same day trip (cheaper without the aqueduct) by bus and taxi. If you have more time or are  a nature or bird-watching buff, head for the Camargue. A good market pops up on Tuesday mornings in little Eyguières (near Les Baux and St-Rémy) and fills the streets and squares of St-Rémy on Wednesdays.

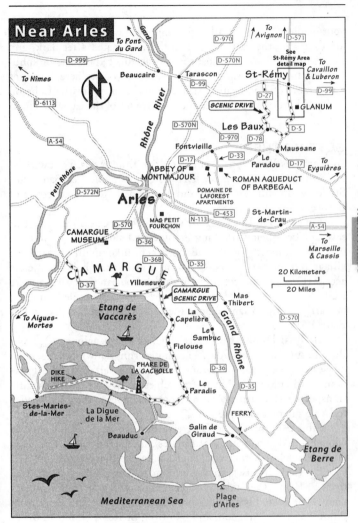

Les Baux

Tucked between Arles and Avignon, the hilltop town of Les Baux and its medieval citadel crown the rugged Alpilles (ahl-pee) mountains. Here, you can imagine the struggles of a strong community that lived a rough-and-tumble life—thankful more for their top-notch fortifications than for their dramatic views. It's mobbed with tourists most of the day, but Les Baux rewards those who arrive by 9:00 or after 17:30. (Although the hilltop citadel's entry closes at the end of the day, once you're inside, you're welcome to live out your medieval fantasies all night long, even with a picnic.) Sunsets are dramatic, the castle is brilliantly illuminated after dark, and nights in Les Baux are ghost town-peaceful. Expect lots of uphill walking to visit this sight. (If you like what you see here, but want a way more off-the-beaten-path experience, head for the Luberon and find Fort de Buoux—see the Hill Towns of the Luberon chapter.)

GETTING THERE

By Car: Les Baux is a 20-minute drive from Arles. Follow signs for *Avignon,* then *Les Baux.* Drivers can combine Les Baux with St-Rémy (15 minutes away) and the ruined Roman aqueduct of Barbegal.

On arrival in Les Baux, drivers pay to park near the village or several blocks below. Parking is squirreled along roads as you approach, and most spaces require a decent hike uphill to reach the village (€6 for two hours, €0.50/hour after that, half the meters accept coins, others accept credit cards). You can park a 15-minute walk away for free at the quarry-cave called Carrières de Lumières, but arrive early to land a spot (described later, under "Near Les Baux").

By Bus: From **Arles,** Cartreize bus #57 usually runs to Les Baux in summer only (6/day, 35 minutes, runs daily July-Aug, none off-season; via Abbey of Montmajour, Fontvieille, and Le Paradou; destination: St-Rémy, timetables at www.maregionsud.fr/transports). Make sure to confirm bus schedules at the TI as service to Les Baux may change.

From **Avignon,** ride Cartreize bus #57 to St-Rémy (hourly Mon-Fri, 6/day Sat-Sun, 45 minutes), then continue to Les Baux on the same bus. Otherwise, continue to Les Baux by taxi.

By Taxi: If buses aren't running to Les Baux, you can taxi from St-Rémy, then take another taxi to return to St-Rémy or to your home base. Figure €40 for a taxi one-way to Les Baux from Arles, €65 from Avignon, and €25 from St-Rémy (+33 6 13 07 55 00).

By Minivan Tour: The best option for many is a minivan tour, which can be both efficient and economical (easiest from Avignon; see page 119).

Orientation to Les Baux

Les Baux is actually two visits in one: castle ruins perched on an almost lunar landscape, and a medieval town below. Savor the castle, then tour—or blitz—the lower town's polished-stone gauntlet of boutiques. While the town, which lives entirely off tourism, is packed with shops, cafés, and tourist knickknacks, the castle above stays manageable as crowds are dispersed over a big area. The town's main drag leads directly to the castle—just keep going uphill (a 10-minute walk).

Tourist Information: The TI is immediately on the left as you enter the village (daily 9:00-18:00, shorter hours and closed Sun in off-season). The TI can call a cab.

Sights in and near Les Baux

CASTLE RUINS (CHATEAU DES BAUX)

The sun-bleached ruins of the stone fortress of Les Baux are carved into, out of, and on top of a rock 650 feet above the valley floor.

Many of the ancient walls of this striking castle still stand as a testament to the proud past of this once-feisty village. A visit here is worth ▲▲▲.

NEAR ARLES

Cost: €8, €18 Pass Baux-de-Provence combo-ticket with Carrières de Lumières, entry fees include excellent audioguide. You may be charged €2 extra on some summer days if there are special activities (see "Entertainment," below).

Hours: Daily 9:00-18:00, Oct-May 9:30-17:00, www. chateau-baux-provence.com. If you're inside the castle when the entry closes, you can stay as long as you like.

Entertainment: In summer, the castle presents medieval pageantry, tournaments, demonstrations of catapults and crossbows, and jousting matches. Pick up a schedule as you enter (or check online).

Picnicking: While no food or drink is sold inside the castle grounds, you're welcome to bring your own and use one of several picnic tables (the best view table is at the edge near the siege weaponry). Sunset dinner picnics are memorable.

Background: Imagine the importance of this citadel in the Middle Ages, when the Lords of Baux were notorious warriors (who could trace their lineage back to one of the "three kings" of Christmas-carol fame, Balthazar). In the 11th century, Les Baux was a powerhouse in southern France, controlling about 80 towns. The Lords of Baux fought the counts of Barcelona for control of Provence...and eventually lost. But while in power, these guys were mean. One ruler enjoyed forcing unransomed prisoners to jump off his castle walls.

In 1426, Les Baux was incorporated into Provence and France.

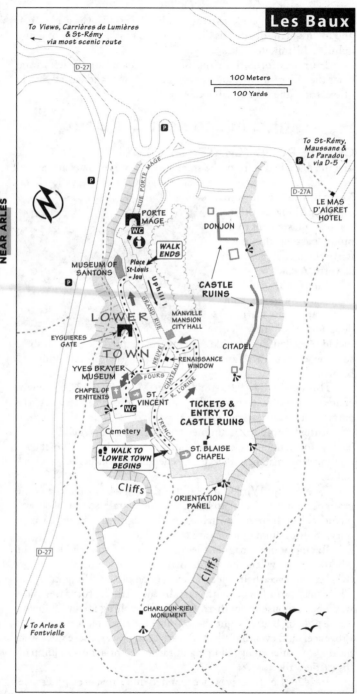

NEAR ARLES

Not accustomed to playing second fiddle, Les Baux struggled with the French king, who responded by destroying the fortress in 1483. Later, Les Baux regained some importance and emerged as a center of Protestantism. Arguing with Rome was a high-stakes game in the 17th century, and Les Baux's association with the Huguenots brought destruction again in 1632 when Cardinal Richelieu (under King Louis XIII) demolished the castle. Louis rubbed salt in the wound by billing Les Baux's residents for his demolition expenses. The once-powerful town of 4,000 was forever crushed.

Visiting the Castle: Before buying your ticket, get your bearings using the panel on the far side of the rocky plateau. This would be one dilly of a place to lay siege to, and wait—are those other castles in the distance growing out of the rocks?

Buy your ticket and pick up your included audioguide (or download the app on your phone). As you wander, key in the number for any of the 30 narrated stops that interest you.

The sight is exceptionally well presented. As you walk on the windblown spur (*baux* in French), you'll pass kid-thrilling medieval siege weaponry (go ahead, try the battering ram). Good displays in English and big paintings in key locations help reconstruct the place. Imagine 4,000 people living up here. Notice the water-catchment system (a slanted field that caught rainwater and drained it into cisterns—necessary during a siege) and find the reservoir cut into the rock below the castle's highest point. Look for post holes throughout the stone walls that reveal where beams once supported floors.

For the most sensational views, climb to the blustery top of the citadel—hold tight if the mistral wind is blowing.

The St. Blaise chapel across from the entry/exit runs videos with Provençal themes (plays continuously; just images and music, no words).

LOWER TOWN

After your castle visit, you can shop and eat your way back through the lower town (worth ▲). Or, escape some of the crowds by visiting these minor but worthwhile sights as you descend. I've linked the sights with walking directions.

• *Follow the main drag about 100 yards through the town and look for the flags marking...*

Manville Mansion City Hall

The 15th-century City Hall offers art exhibits under its cool vaults. It often flies the red-and-white flag of Monaco amid several others, a reminder that the Grimaldi family (longtime rulers of the tiny principality of Monaco) owned Les Baux until the French Revolution (1789). In fact, in 1982, Princess Grace Kelly and her royal husband, Prince Rainier Grimaldi, came to Les Baux to receive the key to the city.

Exit left and walk uphill 20 steps to the empty 1571 **Renaissance window frame.** This beautiful stone frame stands as a reminder of this town's Protestant history. This was probably a place of Huguenot worship—the words carved into the lintel, *Post tenebras lux,* were a popular Calvinist slogan: "After the shadow comes the light."

• *Continue walking uphill, and turn right on the first street to find the...*

Yves Brayer Museum (Musée Yves Brayer)

This enjoyable museum lets you peruse three small floors of luminous paintings (Van Gogh-like Expressionism) by Yves Brayer (1907-1990), who spent his final years here in Les Baux. Like Van Gogh, Brayer was inspired by all that surrounded him, and by his travels through Morocco, Spain, and the rest of the Mediterranean world. Ask about the English information sheet at the entry.

Cost and Hours: €8, less if you have the Pass Baux-de-Provence; daily 10:00-12:30 & 14:00-18:30, Oct-March Wed-Mon 11:00-12:30 & 14:00-17:00, closed Tue and all of Jan-Feb; +33 4 90 54 36 99, www.yvesbrayer.com.

• *Next door is...*

St. Vincent Church

This 12th-century Romanesque church was built short and wide to fit the terrain. The center chapel on the right (partially carved out of the rock) houses the town's traditional Provençal processional chariot. Each Christmas Eve, a ram pulls this cart—holding a lamb, symbolizing Jesus, and surrounded by candles—through town to the church.

• *As you leave the church, WCs are to the left (dug into the stone wall) and up the stairs. Directly in front of the church is a vast view, making clear the strategic value of this rocky bluff's natural fortifications. A few steps away is the...*

Chapel of Penitents

The elaborate Nativity scene painted by Yves Brayer covers the entire interior and illustrates the local legend that says Jesus was born in Les Baux.

• *As you leave the church, turn left and find the old town "laundry"—*

with a pig-snout faucet and 14th-century stone washing surface designed for short women.

Continue past the Yves Brayer Museum again, keep left, and curve down Rue de la Calade, passing view cafés, the town's fortified wall, and one of its two gates. At the end you'll run into the...

Museum of Santons

This free and fun "museum" displays a collection of *santons* ("little saints"), popular folk figurines that decorate local Christmas mangers. Notice how the Nativity scene "proves" once again that Jesus was born in Les Baux. These painted clay dolls show off local dress and traditions (with good English descriptions).

NEAR LES BAUX
▲▲Carrières de Lumières (Quarries of Light)

A 15-minute walk from Les Baux, this colossal quarry-cave with immense vertical walls offers a mesmerizing multimedia experience. Enter a darkened world filled with floor-to-ceiling images and booming music. Wander through a complex of cathedral-like aisles, transepts, and choirs (no seating provided) as you experience the spectacle. There's no storyline to follow, but information panels by the café give some background. The show lasts 40 minutes and runs continuously. If you'd like an intermission, you can exit the "show" into a part of the quarry that opens to the sky and take a break at the café before re-entering. Dress warmly, as the cave is cool.

Cost and Hours: €14.50, €18 Pass Baux-de-Provence combo-ticket with the castle, reservations recommended for non-passholders in high season; daily 9:30-19:30, Nov-March 10:00-18:00, last entry one hour before closing; +33 4 90 54 47 37, www.carrieres-lumieres.com.

Les Baux Views and St-Rémy Loop Drive

This loop drive to St-Rémy and back (35 minutes not including stops) comes with impressive views and access to walking trails (ask at TIs for info on hikes in the Alpilles; Les Baux to St-Rémy is a 2.5-hour hike).

From Les Baux, take D-27 toward Maillane (which passes the Carrière des Lumières). A half-mile beyond Les Baux, you'll come to dramatic views of the hill town. There are pullouts with great vistas, and cavernous caves in former limestone quarries dating back to the Middle Ages. (The limestone is easy to cut, but gets hard and nicely polished when exposed to the weather.) In 1821, the rocks and soil of this area were found to contain an important mineral for making aluminum. It was named after the town: bauxite.

For more sensational views over Les Baux, continue up D-27 to the top, turn right on the paved road (at the red road marker signed *Al.110*), and find a pullout among the rocks. You'll see walking trails nearby.

D-27 continues to St-Rémy. To complete the loop, return from St-Rémy to Les Baux via D-5.

BETWEEN LES BAUX AND ARLES

The following stops are worthwhile for drivers.

Abbey of Montmajour

This brooding hulk of a ruin, just a few minutes' drive from Arles toward Les Baux, was once a thriving abbey and a convenient papal retreat (c. AD 950). Today, the vacant abbey church is a massive example of Romanesque architecture that comes with great views from its tower. Film buffs will appreciate this sight as the setting for *The Lion in Winter,* where Eleanor of Aquitaine (played by Katharine Hepburn) battled with her husband, Henry II (Peter O'Toole). For more on abbeys, see the sidebar on page 232.

The surrounding fields were a favorite of Van Gogh, who walked here from Arles to paint his famous wheat fields.

Cost and Hours: €6, closed Mon Nov-March, +33 4 90 54 64 17.

▲Roman Aqueduct of Barbegal

To be all alone with evocative Roman ruins, drivers can take a quick detour to the crumbled arches of ancient Arles' principal aqueduct.

The aqueduct *(L'Aqueduc Romain)* is a few minutes south of Fontvieille on the D-82 (well signed off the D-17 between Font-vieille and Arles). Park at the dirt pullout (just after the *Los Pozos Blancos* sign, where the ruins of the aqueduct cross the road).

From the parking area, follow the dirt path through the olive grove and along the aqueduct ruins for 200 yards. Approaching the bluff with the grand view, you'll see that the water canal is split into two troughs: One takes a 90-degree right turn and heads for Arles; the other goes straight to the bluff and over, where it once sent water cascading down to power eight grinding mills. Romans grew wheat on the vast fields you see from here, then brought it down to the mega-watermill of Barbegal. Historians figure that this mill produced enough flour each day to feed 12,000 hungry Romans. If you saw the model of this eight-tiered mill in Arles' Ancient History Museum, the milling is easy to visualize—making a visit here quite an exciting experience.

Returning to your car, find the broken bit of aqueduct—it's positioned like a children's playground slide—and take a look at the waterproofing mortar that lined all Roman aqueducts.

NEAR ARLES

Sleeping and Eating in Les Baux

Sleeping: If you want to beat the crowds by arriving early or lingering later, consider **$$ Le Mas d'Aigret,***** a 10-minute walk east of Les Baux on the road to St-Rémy (D-27). From this comfy refuge, you can gaze up at the castle walls rising beyond the heated swimming pool or enjoy valley views from the groomed terraces. The rooms are tastefully appointed—10 have great

views and decks or terraces (convenient half-pension dinner and breakfast option, air-con, *pétanque* courts, +33 4 90 54 20 00, www.masdaigret.com, contact@masdaigret.com).

Eating: There are a few worthwhile places in the untouristed village of **Maussane,** a few scenic minutes' drive south of Les Baux (and 15 minutes from Arles). **Place de la Fontaine,** the town's central square, makes a good stop for café fare. **$ Pizza Brun** has tasty wood-fired pizza to take out or eat in with fun seating indoors and out (closed Mon-Tue, 1 Rue Edouard Foscalina; with your back to Place de la Fontaine, walk to the right for about 10 minutes and look for colored tables in an alleyway; +33 4 90 54 40 73).

St-Rémy-de-Provence

Sophisticated and sassy, St-Rémy (sahn ray-mee) gave birth to Nostradamus and cared for a distraught artist. Today, it caters to

shoppers and Van Gogh fans. A few minutes from the town center, you can visit the once-thriving Roman city called Glanum and the psychiatric ward where Vincent van Gogh was sent after lopping off his earlobe. Best of all is the chance to elbow your way through St-Rémy's raucous Wednesday morning market. A ring road hems in a fun-filled pedestrian-friendly center that's fully loaded with fine foods, beauticians, art galleries, and the latest Provençal fashions.

Popular and well-situated St-Rémy

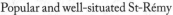

offers fine hotel options and makes a good base for day trips to Arles, Avignon, Les Baux, and the Luberon.

GETTING THERE

By Car: From Les Baux, St-Rémy is a spectacular 15-minute drive over the hills and through the woods. Roads D-5 and D-27 each provide scenic routes between these towns, making a loop drive between them worthwhile (the most scenic approach is on D-27; see "Les Baux Views and St-Rémy Loop Drive" listing, earlier).

Parking in St-Rémy is tricky; it's easiest at the pay lot by the TI. You can park for free but less centrally by the cemetery (see the "St-Rémy Area" map).

By Bus: From **Arles** you can take bus #54 (3-5/day Mon-Sat, none on Sun, 1 hour) or bus #57 (6/day, daily July-Aug, Sat-Sun only in early May-June and Sept, none in off-season, 50 minutes). It's 45 minutes from **Avignon** via bus #57 (hourly Mon-Fri, 6/day Sat-Sun). If arriving in St-Rémy by bus, get off on the ring road at the République stop. The TI is a few blocks away (take a left off the bus then turn right on Avenue Durand Maillane).

By Taxi: From Les Baux, allow €30 one-way; from Arles figure €70, and from Avignon, count on €60 (+33 6 14 81 34 85 or +33 6 25 17 00 73). St-Rémy's four taxis park on Place de la République, next to the bus stop, but it's best to have the TI call for you.

By Bike: Rent all types of bikes (including electric bikes) at **Sun-e-Bike** (2 Rue Camille Pelletan, +33 4 32 62 08 39, www.sun-e-bike.com, stremy@sun-e-bike.com).

Orientation to St-Rémy-de-Provence

From St-Rémy's circular center, it's a 20-minute walk along a busy road with no sidewalk to Glanum and the St. Paul Monastery (Van Gogh's psychiatric hospital).

Tourist Information: The TI is two blocks toward Les Baux from the ring road (Mon-Sat 9:00-18:30, Sun 10:00-12:30, closed for lunch and on Sun in off-season, +33 4 90 92 05 22, www.alpillesenprovence.com). Pick up bus schedules, hiking trail maps, and a town map that includes Van Gogh's favorite painting locations with easels showing copies of the paintings he produced (the *Starry Night* panel is just outside the TI).

Helpful Hints: St-Rémy's Wednesday **market** swallows Place de République with clothing, fabric, and bric-a-brac, and spreads along the town's traffic-free lanes selling anything Provençal. You'll find produce on picturesque Place Pelisser (by City Hall). The market wraps up by about 12:30.

Each year during the last week of September, St-Rémy celebrates *les fêtes votives*, a tradition in the Camargue region honoring the town's patron saint. The carnival-like festivities include bullfights, parades, and *boules* competitions.

Sights in St-Rémy-de-Provence

St-Rémy's key sights—the ruins at Glanum and the hospital where Vincent van Gogh was treated—are an unappealing 20-minute walk south of the TI. If you're driving, you can park free at the St. Paul Monastery (coming from Les Baux, it's the first right after Glanum) and walk a few minutes on a footpath to Glanum from there (or pay to park at Glanum; leave nothing of value in your car). Nearby paths lead to concrete easels with copies of Van Gogh paintings.

▲St. Paul Monastery and Hospital
(Le Monastère St. Paul de Mausole)

The still-functioning psychiatric hospital (Clinique St. Paul) that treated Vincent van Gogh from 1889 to 1890 is a popular pilgrimage for Van Gogh fans (the 2017 film *Loving Vincent* amped up interest). Here you'll enter Vincent's temporarily peaceful world: a small chapel, intimate cloisters, a re-creation of his room, and a small lavender field with several large displays featuring copies of his paintings. There's also a display about sculptor Camille Claudel, who sought solace in St-Rémy following a tumultuous affair with Auguste Rodin. Plans are afoot to expand the sight with more displays designed to re-create Vincent's experience here.

Cost and Hours: €7; daily 9:30-18:30, Oct-March 10:15-12:00 & 13:00-17:15, closed Jan-mid-Feb; +33 4 90 92 77 00, www.saintpauldemausole.fr.

Background: Amazingly, in his 53 weeks here Van Gogh completed 143 paintings and more than 100 drawings (for more on Vincent van Gogh's time in this region, see the Arles chapter). The contrast between the utter simplicity of his room (and his life) and the multimillion-dollar value of his paintings today is jarring.

"I wanted you to know that I think I've done well to come here, first, in seeing the reality of life for the diverse mad or crazy people in this menagerie, I'm losing the vague dread, the fear of the thing. And little by little I can consider my madness as being an illness like any other. And the change of surroundings is doing me good, I imagine. The idea of the duty to work comes back to me a lot."

—Vincent van Gogh's letter to brother Theo, May 9, 1889

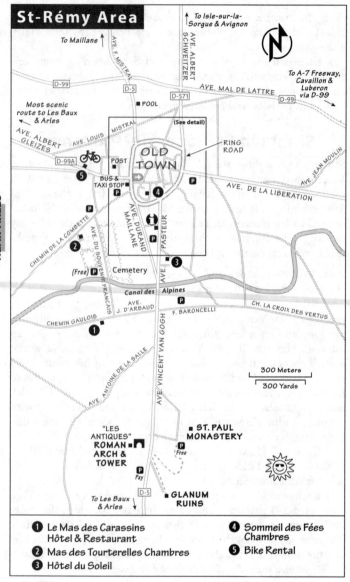

St-Rémy Area

To Maillane

To Isle-sur-la-Sorgue & Avignon

To A-7 Freeway, Cavaillon & Luberon via D-99

Most scenic route to Les Baux & Arles

POOL

(See detail)

RING ROAD

OLD TOWN

POST

BUS & TAXI STOP

Cemetery

(Free)

Canal des Alpines

300 Meters
300 Yards

"LES ANTIQUES" ROMAN ARCH & TOWER

ST. PAUL MONASTERY

Free

Pay

GLANUM RUINS

To Les Baux & Arles

AVE. F. MISTRAL
AVE. ALBERT SCHWEITZER
AVE. MAL DE LATTRE
AVE. ALBERT GLEIZES
AVE. LOUIS MISTRAL
AVE. JEAN MOULIN
AVE. DE LA LIBERATION
AVE. DURAND MAILLANE
AVE. PASTEUR
CHEMIN DE LA COMBETTE
AVE. DU SOUVENIR FRANÇAIS
AVE. J. D'ARBAUD
CHEMIN GAULOIS
F. BARONCELLI
CH. LA CROIX DES VERTUS
AVE. ANTOINE DE LA SALLE
AVE. VINCENT VAN GOGH

1 Le Mas des Carassins Hôtel & Restaurant
2 Mas des Tourterelles Chambres
3 Hôtel du Soleil
4 Sommeil des Fées Chambres
5 Bike Rental

In the spring of 1890, Vincent left St-Rémy and traveled to Auvers-sur-Oise near Paris to enter the care of Dr. Paul Gachet, whom he hoped could help stabilize his mental condition. Gachet advised the artist to throw himself into his work as a remedy for his illness, which he did—Vincent spent the last 70 days of his life knocking out a painting a day. On July 27, 1890, Vincent wandered into the famous Auvers wheat field and shot himself, dying of his injuries two days later.

Visiting the Hospital: Inside, read the thoughtful English explanations about Vincent's tortured life. In and around the complex, you'll see copies of Vincent's works—some positioned right where he painted them. Several are located through the gift shop in a lavender garden. Stand among flame-like cypress trees, gazing over the Alpilles mountains, and realize you're in the midst of some of Van Gogh's most famous works.

While at Monastère St. Paul de Mausole, you'll also find memories of another troubled artist, Camille Claudel (1864-1943), whose parents had her committed to a nearby mental ward after her anguished affair with sculptor Auguste Rodin. *Camille Claudel 1915*, a film about her life starring Juliette Binoche, was shot here using real patients from the clinic. Watch for a re-creation of her kitchen and see a short video about her life.

▲Glanum Ruins

These crumbling stones are the foundations of a Roman market town, located at the crossroads of two ancient trade routes between Italy and Spain. While the ruins are, well...ruined, their setting at the base of the rocky Alpilles is splendid. It's also unshaded and can be very hot (making it easier to enjoy early or late).

A stubby Roman arch and tall tower stand across the road from the site as proud reminders of the town's glory days. These lonely monuments marked the entry to Glanum 2,000 years ago. The plump triumphal arch, now missing its upper level, was designed to impress visitors with scenes of Rome's power—and by association, Glanum's prestige. The three-level tower was built as a mausoleum by one of Glanum's most distinguished families. The battle scene relief on the lowest level is dripping with intensity: The Romans were not just good builders, but skilled artists as well.

Cost and Hours: €8; daily 9:30-18:00, Oct-March Tue-Sun 10:00-17:00, closed Mon; parking-€3/day, +33 4 90 92 23 79.

Visiting the Ruins: Start at the helpful little museum at the entrance, with good English explanations of key buildings and the excavation process, as well as a model of Glanum in its prime. The free English handout and information panels scattered about the site provide more context to the ruins you'll see. Serious students of ancient Rome will want to spring for the well-done *Itineraries* book (€7).

The Roman site was founded in 27 BC and occupied for about 30 years. About 2,500 people lived in Glanum at its zenith (the Roman city was about seven times bigger than the ruins you see today). And though this was an important town, with grand villas, temples, a basilica, a forum, a wooden dam, and aqueducts, it was not important enough to justify an arena or a theater (such as those in Arles, Nîmes, and Orange). Locals had to charter buses to reach events in those cities.

Stroll up Glanum's main street and see remains of a market hall, a forum, thermal baths, reservoirs, and more. The view from the belvedere justifies the uphill effort. These ruins highlight the range and prosperity of the Roman Empire. Taken together with other Roman monuments in Provence, they paint a more complete picture of Roman life.

Sleeping in St-Rémy-de-Provence

Unless otherwise noted, the following hotels have easy parking and air-conditioning. For locations, see the "St-Rémy Area" map, earlier.

$$ Le Mas des Carassins,*** a 15-minute walk from the center, is well run by Michel and Pierre. Luxury is affordable here, with two generously sized pools, ample outdoor lounging spaces, big gardens, and everything just so. The 22 rooms are split between the more traditional main building (which I prefer) and the newer annex, which comes with larger rooms and more modern decor (American-style breakfast, table tennis, great dinner option—see next page, 1 Chemin Gaulois, +33 4 90 92 15 48, www.masdescarassins.com, info@masdescarassins.com).

$ Mas des Tourterelles Chambres, a Provençal farmhouse in a pleasant neighborhood, is a 10-minute walk from the town center. While the garden could use a little TLC, it's a fine getaway with six spotless and bright rooms and three apartments. There's also a pool and small garden with outdoor picnic facilities including a fridge (2-night minimum in high season, air-con in top-floor rooms—others don't need it, 21 Chemin de la Combette, +33 9 54 64 83 30 or mobile +33 6 15 87 24 55, www.masdestourterelles.com, contact@masdestourterelles.com). Turn right at the top of Place de la République onto Chemin de la Combette; after 400 yards look for the brown sign down a lane on the left (just after the second speed bump).

$ Hôtel du Soleil,** a 10-minute walk from St-Rémy's center, is a sharp hotel, with fresh white stone and beige decor throughout.

Food Lovers' Guide to St-Rémy

Wednesday is market day in St-Rémy, but you don't have to fast until then. Foodies will appreciate these shops clustered around the ring road in St-Rémy, near the turnoff to Les Baux.

L'Epicerie du Calanquet, in the same family for five generations, is where locals buy olive oil. The shop encourages you to sample olives, tapenades, and jams (daily, in the town center at 8 Rue de la Commune).

Le Petit Duc offers a remarkable introduction to traditional cookies (daily, 7 Boulevard Victor Hugo, +33 4 90 92 08 31).

Just one whiff from **Joel Durand Chocolates** will lure chocoholics inside. Ask for a sample and learn the letter-coded system. The lavender is surprisingly good (daily, a few doors down from Le Petit Duc at 3 Boulevard Victor Hugo, +33 4 90 92 38 25).

NEAR ARLES

Its spotless rooms cluster around a courtyard/parking area and pool (five rooms have small terraces, a block above the TI at 35 Avenue Pasteur, +33 4 90 92 00 63, www.hotelsoleil.com, info@hotelsoleil.com).

¢ **Sommeil des Fées Chambres** rents five simple, clean, and comfortable rooms in the center of St-Rémy. They also run a good restaurant, La Cuisine des Anges, described later (4 Rue du 8 Mai 1945, +33 4 90 92 17 66, mobile +33 6 98 01 98 98, www.angesetfees-stremy.com).

Eating in St-Rémy-de-Provence

The town is packed with restaurants, each trying to outdo the other. Join the evening strollers and compare.

$$$ Le Mas des Carassins offers a four-course food experience worth booking ahead. One *menu* is prepared each night and served in a country-classy setting inside or out. Service is friendly, kids are welcome, and the cuisine is utterly delicious. Review their website to see what's cooking before booking a table (see listing on previous page; for location see the "St-Rémy Area" map, earlier).

$$ Bar-Tabac des Alpilles is a great choice for lunch or dinner thanks to a fun-loving staff, good ambience inside and out, and delicious food. It's popular with locals, and serves the best leg of lamb I've tasted. The menu offers just enough choice, including good salads and several choices of *plats*. Dinner has two seatings, at about 19:15 and 20:45; it's best to book at least a day ahead (daily except closed Tue-Wed for dinner, 21 Boulevard Victor Hugo, +33 4 90 92 02 17).

NEAR ARLES

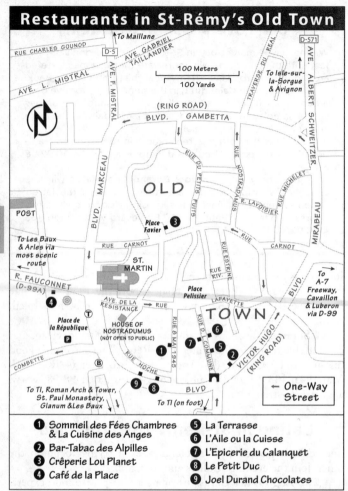

Restaurants in St-Rémy's Old Town

1 Sommeil des Fées Chambres & La Cuisine des Anges
2 Bar-Tabac des Alpilles
3 Crêperie Lou Planet
4 Café de la Place
5 La Terrasse
6 L'Aile ou la Cuisse
7 L'Epicerie du Calanquet
8 Le Petit Duc
9 Joel Durand Chocolates

$ Crêperie Lou Planet, on lovely Place Favier, is welcoming, cheap, and peaceful, with outdoor seating in summer, tasty crêpes, nice salads, and inexpensive, good house wine (daily April-Sept, behind Hôtel de Ville at Place Favier, next to Musée des Alpilles).

$$ Café de la Place, on Place de la République behind the parking lot, is a hit with St-Rémy's young people (as well as aging travel writers). Come for a coffee, a drink, or a good meal of classic café fare (big *terrasse*, open daily, +33 4 90 92 02 13).

$$ La Cuisine des Anges is a low-key place serving home-made dishes with a Mediterranean accent in a charming courtyard or simple dining room (closed Thu, 4 Rue du 8 Mai 1945, +33 4 90 92 17 66).

$ La Terrasse is a cheery spot that's all about tasty wood-fired pizza (closed Mon-Tue, 11 Rue de la Commune, +33 4 90 90 26 49).

$$$ L'Aile ou la Cuisse is St-Rémy's vintage bistro, with a snazzy interior and a tradition of serving fine cuisine (closed Mon-Tue, 5 Rue de la Commune, +33 4 32 62 00 25).

The Camargue

The Camargue region, occupying the vast delta of the Rhône River, is one of Europe's most important wetlands. This marshy area exists where the Rhône splits into two branches (big and little), just before it flows into the Mediterranean. Over the millennia, a steady flow of sediment has been deposited at the mouth of the rivers—thoroughly land-locking villages that once faced the sea.

Since World War II, farmers have converted large northern tracts of the Camargue to rice fields, making the delta a major producer of France's rice. Salt is the other key industry in the Camargue: You can see vast salt marshes and evaporation beds around the town of Salin de Giraud. Because the salt marshes were long considered useless, the land has remained relatively untouched, leaving it a popular nature destination today.

Today the Camargue Regional Nature Park is a protected "wild" area, where pink flamingos, wild bulls, nasty boars, nastier mosquitoes (in every season but winter—come prepared), and the famous white horses wander freely through lagoons and tall grass. The dark bulls are harder to spot than the white horses and flamingos, so go slow and make use of the viewing platforms. For more on these animals, see the sidebar.

The Camargue's subtle wetlands beauty makes it a worthwhile joyride for naturalists. The Everglades-like scenery is a birder's paradise, and occasional bulls and wild horses add to the enjoyment. But for avid city sightseers, this can feel like a big swamp—interesting to drive through, but where's the excitement? The best time to visit is in spring, when the flamingos are out in full force; the worst time to visit is in summer, when birds are fewest and mosquitoes are everywhere.

If you have children, a picnic on the long sandy beach at Plage

Wildlife of the Camargue

In the nature reserve of the Camargue, amusing flamingos and countless other bird species flourish—attracting birdwatchers from all over the world. Once an endangered species, flamingos flock here because of all that salt—which is why they come to the Camargue rather than to, say, the sandy beaches of the Riviera. Ten thousand flamingos leave here each fall, heading to warmer climates, and then return in March to pink up the Camargue (a visit here in the spring reaps big, pink rewards). To see a formation of these long, clumsy-looking birds in flight is an experience you won't soon forget.

The black bulls are raised for bullfights (by local cowboys called *gardians*) and eventually end up on plates in Arles' restaurants (you may have met one already). The *gardians,* who have patrolled the Camargue on local horses for centuries, give the area a Wild West aura. The region's unique small horses—born brown or black, later turning light gray or white—are one of the oldest breeds in the world, and may have existed in the area since prehistoric times.

With the continual loss of wetlands throughout the world, it's critical that places like this remain preserved and that we understand their significance.

d'Arles may be just what the doctor ordered. Also called Plage de Piémanson, this public beach is six miles (10 kilometers) after Salin de Giraud. Bring everything you might need, as there are no vendors. Skinny dippers will appreciate the nudist beach at the extreme eastern end.

GETTING THERE

If you don't have a car, there are several ways to experience the Camargue: horseback, mountain bikes, and jeep safaris. All three options are available in Stes-Maries-de-la-Mer, and jeep safaris are also offered from Arles (ask at TI). Hiking is not good in the Camargue, as there are few decent trails. The best biking is across the Digue (dike) to Phare de la Gacholle.

By Scenic Drive

There are two primary driving routes from Arles through the Camargue: to Stes-Maries-de-la-Mer, and toward Salin de Giraud.

My favorite route is toward **Salin de Giraud** (see the "Near Arles" map at the start of this chapter): Leave Arles driving clockwise on its ring road, then find signs to *Stes-Maries-de-la-Mer* and join D-570. Skip the D-36 turnoff to Salin de Giraud (you'll return along this route). After about 6 kilometers, enthusiasts can consider a stop at the **Camargue Museum** (described later). Next, continue along D-570 past swampy rice fields, then turn left on D-37 and follow it as it skirts the Étang de Vaccarès lagoon, with opportunities to get out of the car for views and to smell the marshes (look for viewing stands, but any dirt turnoff works). Turn right off D-37 onto the tiny road at Villeneuve, following signs for C-134 to *La Capelière* and *La Fiélouse* (poorly marked—it's where D-36b leads back to Arles). The drive along C-134 is the highlight of the Camargue for me.

Make time for a stop at **La Capelière** (headquarters for Camargue birders), where you can pick up a good map, ask the staff questions, and enjoy an exhibit (small fee) and worthwhile one-mile walking trail with some English information posted (daily 9:30-13:00 & 14:00-17:30, Oct-March until 16:30 and closed Tue). Birders can check the register to see what birds have been spotted recently (observations in English are in red), and can buy the Camargue booklet in English.

The best part of this drive (particularly in spring) is the next stretch to and around **La Digue de la Mer,** about six scenic miles past La Capelière. You'll most likely see flamingos along this section and witness the memorable sight of platoons of flamingos in flight (best at La Digue de la Mer, though tides will affect their location). At La Digue de la Mer, get out of your car and walk a few hundred yards past the pavement's end, where the dirt road curves left, to reach a good spot. This is a critical reproduction area for flamingos (about 13,000 couples produce 5,000 offspring annually). If you rented a mountain bike, now would be the right time to use it: It's about eight bumpy but engaging miles between water and sand dunes to Stes-Maries-de-la-Mer.

From here, most will want to retrace their route back to Villeneuve, then continue straight onto D-36b, which leads back to Arles.

By Bus

Buses serve the Camargue (stopping at the Camargue Museum and Stes-Maries-de-la-Mer) from Arles' bus or train station (Agglo bus #50, 6/day, 1 hour, departs from both the bus and train station, www.tout-envia.com). Buses and trains also serve **Aigues-Mortes** (best from Nîmes).

Sights and Towns in the Camargue

Camargue Museum (Musée de la Camargue)

Located in a traditional Camargue barn on the road to Stes-Maries-de-la-Mer, this well-designed folk museum does a good job of describing the natural features and cultural traditions of the Camargue. The costumes, tools, and helpful exhibits come with some English explanations (look for handouts and small screens). A two-mile nature trail, picnic tables, and a WC round out the amenities.

Cost and Hours: €5; daily 10:00-17:00; 8 miles from Arles on D-570 toward Stes-Maries-de-la-Mer, at Mas du Pont de Rousty farmhouse; +33 4 90 97 10 82, www.museedelacamargue.com.

Stes-Maries-de-la-Mer

At the western end of the Camargue lies this whitewashed, Spanish-feeling seafront town with acres of flamingos, bulls, and horses at its doorstep. From the bus stop, walk to the church (10 minutes) to get oriented. The place is so popular that it's best avoided on weekends and during holidays. It's a French Coney Island—a trinket-selling, perennially windy place.

The town is also famous as a mecca for the Roma (Gypsies). Every May, Roma from all over Europe pile in their caravans and migrate to Stes-Maries-de-la-Mer to venerate the town's statue of Saint Sarah. Legend has it that Mary Magdalene made landfall here in a boat with no oars after an epic journey across the Mediterranean from Egypt. Fleeing persecution for practicing the new and unpopular Christian faith, she was accompanied by two other "Stes-Maries": Mary of Clopas, the mother of the apostle James the Less, and Mary Salome, the mother of the apostles James the Great and John. Also in the boat was "Black Sarah," an Egyptian servant. Sarah collected alms for the poor; over time, her request for handouts became associated with the Roma people, who embrace her as their patron saint (the name Gypsy comes from the label Europeans gave those who came across from Egypt—*Gyptians*). Today's impressive spectacle to honor Sarah is like a sprawling flea market spilling out from the town for two weeks.

Tourist Information: Stes-Maries-de-la-Mer's TI is located along its waterfront promenade (daily 9:00-19:00, shorter hours in off-season, 5 Avenue Van Gogh, +33 4 90 97 82 55, www.saintesmaries.com).

Sights and Activities: Outside of May, the town of Stes-Maries-de-la-Mer has little to offer except its beachfront promenade, bullring, and towering five-belled fortified church. The **church** interior is worth a look for its unusual decorations and artifacts, including the statue of Saint Sarah (small fee to climb to roof for Camargue and sea views). Avoid the women with flowers and the assertive palm readers, who often cluster near the church.

Most tourists come to take a horse, a Jeep, or a bike into the Camargue—and there's no lack of outfits ready to take you for a ride. The TIs in Arles and Stes-Maries-de-la-Mer have long lists. Rental **bikes** (for the ride out to La Digue de la Mer) and advice on the best routes are available at Le Vélo Saintois (€20/day, 19 Rue de

NEAR ARLES

la République in Stes-Maries-de-la-Mer, +33 4 90 97 74 56, www. levelosaintois.com).

Jerry Perkins offers **Jeep excursions** at Nature et Découverte (2-hour trips from €40, pickup in Stes-Maries-de-la-Mer, mobile +33 6 12 44 64 74, www.visite-camargue.com), and **Camargue Alpilles Safaris** runs top Jeep tours from Stes-Maries-de-la-Mer (from €52/half-day, +33 4 90 97 89 33, www.camargue.com, info@ camargue.com). **Les Cabanes de Cacharel** gives horseback tours (€25 for one-hour ride, Route de Cacharel near Stes-Maries-de-la-Mer, +33 4 90 97 84 10, www.cabanesdecacharel.com, info@ camargueacheval.com).

Aigues-Mortes

This curiously situated walled city, on the western edge of the Camargue (20 miles from Nîmes or from Stes-Maries-de-la-Mer), was built by Louis IX as a jumping-off point for his Crusades to the Holy Land. Although Aigues-Mortes was designed as a strategically situated royal port city, it was actually never near the sea. Ships reached it via canals that were dug through an immense lagoon—a lagoon that silted up before long, making the port aspect of Aigues-Mortes a losing proposition. The name Aigues-Mortes means "dead waters."

Today its tall towers and thick fortifications seem oddly out of place, surrounded by nothing but salt marshes and flamingos. Still it provides the easiest glimpse into the Camargue thanks to good train and bus service (best from Nîmes; I'd skip this place on weekends and in high season unless you need more souvenirs and crowded streets). The entire length of its mighty rampart walls can be walked in an hour (€9 entry); the walls offer good views into the Camargue and salt fields that generate hills of salt.

Getting There: Drivers going between Nîmes and Arles can detour to Aigues-Mortes for a quick and easy taste of the Camargue. Aigues-Mortes and Nîmes are linked by bus (#132, 6/day, 50 minutes) and train (summer: 6/day Mon-Fri, 2/day Sat-Sun; off-season: 2/day, 45 minutes).

AVIGNON

Famous for its nursery rhyme, medieval bridge, and brooding Palace of the Popes, contemporary Avignon (ah-veen-yohn) bustles and prospers behind its mighty walls. For nearly 100 years (1309-1403) Avignon was the capital of Christendom, home to seven popes. (And, for a difficult period after that—during the Great Schism when there were two competing popes—Avignon was "the other Rome.") During this time, it grew from a quiet village into a thriving city. Today, with its large student population and fashionable shops, Avignon is an intriguing blend of medieval history, youthful energy, and urban sophistication. Street performers entertain international throngs who fill Avignon's ubiquitous cafés and trendy boutiques. And each July the city goes pedal to the metal during its huge theater festival (with about 2,000 performances, big crowds, higher prices, and hotels booked up long in advance). Clean, lively, and popular with tourists, Avignon is more impressive for its outdoor ambience than for its museums and monuments.

Orientation to Avignon

Cours Jean Jaurès, which turns into Rue de la République, runs straight from the Centre-Ville train station to Place de l'Horloge and the Palace of the Popes, splitting Avignon in two. The larger eastern half is where the action is. Climb to the Jardin du Rochers des Doms for the town's best view, tour the pope's immense palace, lose yourself in Avignon's back streets (following my self-guided "Discovering Avignon's Back Streets Walk"), and go organic in its vibrant market hall.

TOURIST INFORMATION

The TI is located on the main street linking the Centre-Ville train station to the old town (Mon-Sat 9:00-18:00, Sun 10:00-17:00, shorter weekend hours in winter, 41 Cours Jean Jaurès, +33 4 32 74 32 74, www.avignon-tourisme.com).

At the TI, pick up a map with several good (but tricky to follow) walking tours and ask about guided English tours on varying themes (from €10, listed on their website).

Also ask about the Baladine and City Zen minibuses that loop through the old city (see "Helpful Hints," later) and get bike maps for good rides in the area, including the Ile de la Barthelasse.

ARRIVAL IN AVIGNON
By Train

Avignon has two train stations: Centre-Ville and TGV (linked to downtown by shuttle trains). Some TGV trains stop at Centre-Ville—verify your station in advance.

The **Centre-Ville station** *(Gare Avignon Centre-Ville)* gets all non-TGV trains (and a few TGV trains). To reach the town center, cross the busy street in front of the station and walk through the city walls onto Cours Jean Jaurès. Baggage storage is close by (see "Helpful Hints," later).

The **TGV station** *(Gare TGV)*, on the outskirts of town, has easy car rental, but no baggage storage (see "Helpful Hints," later, for options). Car rental, buses, and taxis are outside the north exit *(sortie nord)*. To reach the city center, take the **shuttle train** from platform A or B to the Centre-Ville station (€1.70, included with rail pass, 2/hour, 5 minutes, buy ticket from machine on platform or at *billeterie* in main hall). A **taxi** ride between the TGV station and downtown Avignon costs about €20 (more at night and on Sun). **Buses** to nearby towns stop in front of the station across from the car rental offices.

By Bus

The efficient bus station *(gare routière)* is 100 yards to the right as you exit the Centre-Ville train station, beyond and below Hôtel Ibis (helpful info desk open Mon-Sat 7:00-19:30, closed Sun, +33 4 90 82 07 35).

Avignon

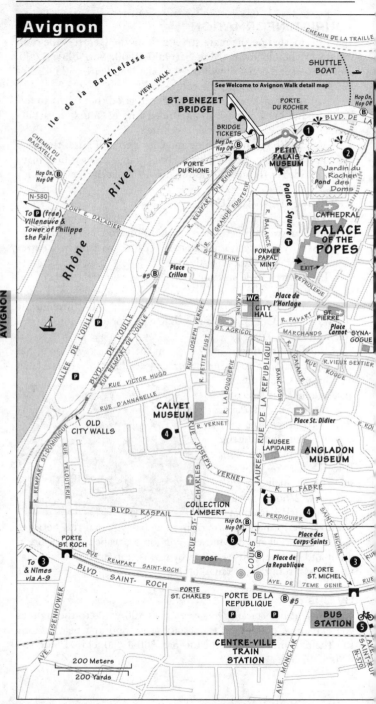

CHEMIN DE LA TRAILLE

SHUTTLE BOAT

Île de la Barthelasse

VIEW WALK

ST. BENEZET BRIDGE

PORTE DU ROCHER

Hop On, Hop Off

BLVD. DE LA

BRIDGE TICKETS
Hop On, Hop Off

PORTE DU RHONE

PETIT PALAIS MUSEUM

Jardin du Rocher
Pond des Doms

CHEMIN DU BAGATELLE

Hop On, Hop Off

River

N-580

To P (free), Villeneuve & Tower of Philippe the Fair

PONT E. DALADIER

Palace Square

See Welcome to Avignon Walk detail map

CATHEDRAL

PALACE OF THE POPES

Rhône

R. REMPART DU RHONE

R. GRANDE FUSTERIE

R. ST. ETIENNE

FORMER PAPAL MINT

R. BALANCE

EXIT

PEYROLERIE

#5 B

Place Crillon

RACINE

WC CITY HALL

Place de l'Horloge

ST. PIERRE

ALLEE DE L'OULLE

BLVD. DE L'OULLE

RUE REMPART DE L'OULLE

ST. AGRICOL

R. FAVART

Place Carnot

MARCHANDS

SYNAGOGUE

RUE VICTOR HUGO

RUE JOSEPH VERNET

R. PETITE FUST.

R. LA BOUQUERIE

RUE DE LA REPUBLIQUE

R. BANCASSE

R. GALANTE

R. VIEUX SEXTIER

RUE ROUGE

OLD CITY WALLS

RUE D'ANNANELLE

CALVET MUSEUM

R. VERNET

Place St. Didier

R. ROI

RUE VELOUTERIE

RUE JOSEPH VERNET

MUSEE LAPIDAIRE

ANGLADON MUSEUM

R. REMPART ST-DOMINIQUE

RUE ST. DOMINIQUE

BLVD. RASPAIL

COLLECTION LAMBERT

RUE ST. CHARLES

R. H. FABRE

R. PERDIGUIER

RUE SAINT MICHEL

PORTE ST. ROCH

Hop On, Hop Off

COURS J.

Place des Corps-Saints

To Nîmes via A-9

RUE REMPART SAINT-ROCH

POST

Place de la République

PORTE ST. MICHEL

BLVD. SAINT-ROCH

PORTE ST. CHARLES

PORTE DE LA REPUBLIQUE

7EME GENIE

AVE. EISENHOWER

P

P

B #5

AVE. MONCLAR

BUS STATION

N-570

AVE. SAINT-RUF

CENTRE-VILLE TRAIN STATION

200 Meters

200 Yards

AVIGNON

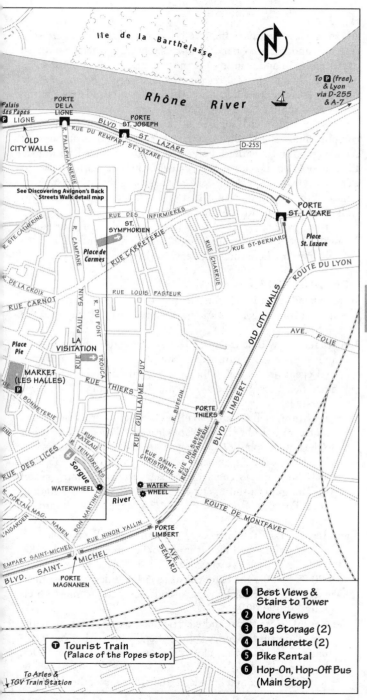

AVIGNON

Ile de la Barthelasse

Rhône River

To **P** (free),
& Lyon
via D-255
& A-7

Palais
des Papes
P LIGNE

PORTE
DE LA
LIGNE

PORTE
ST. JOSEPH

BLVD.   ST. LAZARE

R. PALAPHARNERIE

RUE DU REMPART ST. LAZARE

D-255

OLD
CITY WALLS

See Discovering Avignon's Back
Streets Walk detail map

RUE DES INFIRMIERES

ST.
SYMPHORIEN

R. STE CATHERINE

R. CAMPANE

Place
de
Carmes

RUE CARRETERIE

RUE CHARRUE

RUE ST-BERNARD

PORTE
ST. LAZARE

Place
St. Lazare

ROUTE DU LYON

R. DE LA CROIX

RUE LOUIS PASTEUR

RUE CARNOT

R. DU PONT

OLD CITY WALLS

AVE.   FOLIE

Place
Pie

LA
VISITATION

RUE TROUCAS

LIMBERT

MARKET
(LES HALLES)

P

RUE PAUL SAIN

RUE THIERS

RUE GUILLAUME PUY

R. BUFFON

PORTE
THIERS

BLVD.

R. BONNETERIE

RUE
RATEAU

RUE
TEINTURIERS

RUE SAINT
CHRISTOPHE

RUE DU 58EME
REG. D'INFANTERIE

RUE DES LICES

Sorgue

WATERWHEEL

WATER-
WHEEL

River

ROUTE DE MONTFAVET

R. PORTAIL MAG.

NANEN

BON MARTINE

RUE NINON VALLIN

PORTE
LIMBERT

L'AIGARDER

EMPART SAINT-MICHEL

SAINT-   MICHEL

AVE.
SEMARD

BLVD.

PORTE
MAGNANEN

T Tourist Train
(Palace of the Popes stop)

To Arles &
TGV Train Station

1 Best Views &
Stairs to Tower
2 More Views
3 Bag Storage (2)
4 Launderette (2)
5 Bike Rental
6 Hop-On, Hop-Off Bus
(Main Stop)

By Car

Avignon is essentially traffic-free in the old center. There are several safe underground parking lots clearly signposted. For those day-tripping in and wanting the most central garage, follow signs to *Centre*, then to the *Centre Historique* and then *P Palais des Papes* (from where, after parking, you'll climb the stairs and arrive at the pope's doorstep, €12 half-day, €20/24 hours).

You can also park for free at the edge of town at lots with complimentary shuttle buses to the center (no shuttles on Sunday; see "Avignon" map, earlier). Follow *P Gratuit* signs for **Parking Ile Piot**, across Pont Daladier on Ile de la Barthelasse, with shuttles to Place Crillon; or to **Parking des Italiens**, along the river east of the Palace of the Popes, with shuttles to Place Pie (allow 30 minutes to walk from either parking lot to the center).

Street parking is €1-3/hour for a maximum of four hours Mon-Sat 9:00-19:00 (free 19:00-9:00 and all day Sunday).

No matter where you park, leave nothing of value in your car.

HELPFUL HINTS

Book Ahead for July: During the July theater festival, rooms are almost impossible to come by—reserve early, or stay in Arles or St-Rémy.

Local Help: David at **Imagine Tours,** a nonprofit group to promote this region, can help with hotel emergencies and special-event tickets (+33 6 89 22 19 87, www.imagine-tours.net, imagine.tours@gmail.com). If you don't get an answer, leave a message.

Baggage Storage: There are two places located on either side of the Centre-Ville train station. **Conciergerie-Bagagerie** is closer to the bus station (€4/day, daily 8:00-20:00, shorter hours and closed for lunch in off-season, 35 Rue St. Michel, +33 6 29 21 31 36, www.bs-conciergerie-bagagerie-avignon.fr). **Hôtel Ibis Budget** is a short walk from the west side of the station, across Porte St. Roch (€2/day, 24/7 storage, 8 Boulevard St. Dominique).

Laundry: At **La Blanchisseuse,** you can drop off your laundry in the morning and pick it up later the same day (daily 7:00-21:00, several blocks west of the TI at 24 Rue Lanterne, +33 4 90 85 58 80). The launderette at 66 Place des Corps-Saints, where Rue Agricol Perdiguier ends, is handy to most hotels (daily 7:00-20:00).

Bike Rental: Rent pedal and electric bikes and scooters near the train station at **Provence Bike** (generally open Mon-Sat 9:00-18:00, closed Sun, also closed midday in April and Sept-Oct, closed in winter, 7 Avenue St. Ruf, +33 4 90 27 92 61, www.provence-bike.com), or ask at the TI about other options.

You'll enjoy riding on the Ile de la Barthelasse (the TI has bike maps), but biking is better in and around Isle-sur-la-Sorgue (described in the Hill Towns of the Luberon chapter) and Vaison-la-Romaine (consider taking a bike on the train to Bédarrides, biking from there to Châteauneuf-du-Pape and on to Orange, then taking it on the train back to Avignon; see the Côtes du Rhône chapter).

Taxi: Dial +33 4 90 82 20 20 to get a cab.

Car Rental: The TGV station has counters for all the big companies.

Shuttle Vans: Wave down a **Baladine** electric minivan along its loop route through Avignon, or use **City Zen** minibuses with fixed stops (€0.50, 4/hour for either). City Zen minibuses also link remote parking lots with the city center. The TI has route maps.

Shuttle Boat: A free shuttle boat, the *Navette Fluviale,* plies back and forth across the river (as it did in the days when the town had no functioning bridge) from near St. Bénezet Bridge (3/hour, daily April-June and Sept 10:00-12:15 & 14:00-18:00, July-Aug 11:00-20:45; Oct-March weekends and Wed afternoons only). It drops you on the peaceful Ile de la Barthelasse, with its recommended riverside restaurant, grassy walks, and bike rides with memorable city views. If you stay on the island for dinner, check the schedule for the last return boat—or be prepared for a taxi ride or a 30-minute walk back to town.

Commanding City Views: For great views of Avignon and the river, walk or drive across Daladier Bridge, or ferry across the Rhône on the *Navette Fluviale* (described above). I'd take the boat across the river, walk the view path to Daladier Bridge, and then cross back over the bridge (45-minute walk). You can enjoy other impressive vistas from the top of the Jardin du Rochers des Doms, from the  tower in the Palace of the Popes, from the end of the famous, broken St. Bénezet Bridge, and from the entrance to Fort St. André, across the river in Villeneuve-lès-Avignon.

Sound-and-Light Show: During the month of August, the main monuments are beautifully lit at night on Place du Palais, Place de l'Horloge, Place Pie, and more; ask at the TI about the *Hélios* show (daily 21:30-23:30).

Festival d'Avignon

Three weeks each July, Avignon hosts a massive theater festival with contemporary theater groups from throughout Europe. The festival has more than 1,500 official performances, along with countless unofficial events: The entire city becomes a stage, with mimes, fire-breathers, singers, and musicians filling the streets, creating a Mardi Gras-like atmosphere.

Every possible venue is in action—20 in all—from actual theater spaces to small chapels to the inner courtyard of the Palace of the Popes, which seats 800. While many performances book up well in advance, many more are available the same day (tickets generally €20). There's also a "fringe festival," called Avignon-Off, which adds another 100 sites and numerous performances, as well as a children's theater festival, with storytellers, dance, musicals, and marionettes. Most productions are in French, but some are in English, and the dance performances don't require language at all (www.festival-avignon.com and www.avignonleoff.com).

Tours in Avignon

Local Guides

Isabelle Magny is a fine local guide for the city and region (€160/half-day, €330/day, no car, +33 6 11 82 17 92, isabellemagny@sfr.fr). **Nina Seffusatti** is equally talented (same prices as Isabelle, +33 6 14 80 30 37, nina.seffusatti@wanadoo.fr).

Food Tour

The **Avignon Gourmet Walking Tour** is a terrific experience if you like to eat. Avignon native Julien meets small groups at the TI for a well-designed three-hour, eight-stop walk (Tue-Sat at 9:00 and 15:30). His tours are filled with information and tastes of top-quality local foods and drinks. His morning tour finishes in the market hall while his afternoon tour highlights Avignon sweets (€49-65/person, 2-10 people per group, +33 6 62 89 55 44, www.avignongourmetours.com). Book in advance online, and inquire about customized food tours.

Tourist Train

The little train leaves regularly (generally on the half hour) from in front of the Palace of the Popes and offers a decent overview of the city, including the Jardin du Rochers des Doms and St. Bénezet Bridge (€9.50, cash only, 2/hour, 45 minutes, recorded English commentary, mid-March-Oct daily 10:00-18:00, July-Aug until 20:00).

Avignon at a Glance

▲▲**Scenic Squares** Numerous hide-and-seek squares ideal for postcard-writing and people-watching—pick your favorite: Place des Corps-Saints, Place St. Pierre, Place des Châtaignes (adjacent to Place St. Pierre), Place Crillon, touristy Place de l'Horloge, and the big Place Pie (see map on page 114).

▲▲**Palace of the Popes** Fourteenth-century Gothic palace built by the popes who made Avignon their home. **Hours:** Daily 10:00-18:00, July-Aug 9:30-19:00, Nov-March 10:00-17:00. See page 125.

▲**Jardin du Rochers des Doms** Park and ramparts at the hilltop where Avignon was first settled, with great views of the Rhône River Valley and the famous broken bridge. **Hours:** Daily 7:30-20:00, June-July until 22:00, Oct-March until 18:00. See page 123.

▲**St. Bénezet Bridge** The "Pont d'Avignon" of nursery-rhyme fame, once connecting the pope's territory to France. **Hours:** Daily 10:00-18:00, July-Aug until 19:00, Nov-March until 17:00. See page 124.

▲**Tower of Philip the Fair** Massive tower across St. Bénezet Bridge, featuring the best view over Avignon and the Rhône basin. **Hours:** Tue-Sun 10:00-12:30 & 14:00-18:00, Nov-April 14:00-17:00 only, closed all of Dec-Jan and Mon year-round. See page 131.

AVIGNON

Hop-On, Hop-Off B

Visite Avignon's one-hour loop on an open-top double-decker crosses the river onto Ile de la Barthelasse, travels into Villeneuve-les-Avignon, and goes around the old city. One of the five stops gets you to within a 10-minute walk of the Tower of Philip the Fair (€12, departs hourly April-Sept, main stop near the TI at 40 Cours Jean Jaurès, www.visiteavignon.com). This bus offers city views and access to the Barthelasse island and Villeneuve-les-Avignon.

Minivan Excursions from Avignon

Several minivan tour companies based in Avignon offer transportation to destinations described in this book, including Pont du Gard, the Luberon, and the Camargue (see "Tours in Provence" on page 38).

Walks in Avignon

For an excellent city overview, combine these two self-guided walks. "Welcome to Avignon" covers the major sights, while "Discovering Avignon's Back Streets" leads you along the lanes less taken, delving beyond the surface of this historic city.

WELCOME TO AVIGNON WALK

Start this ▲▲ tour where the Romans did, on Place de l'Horloge, in front of City Hall (Hôtel de Ville).

❶ Place de l'Horloge

In ancient Roman times this was the forum, and in medieval times it was the market square. The square is named for the clock tower (now hiding behind the more recently built City Hall) that, in its day, was a humanist statement. In medieval France, the only bells in town rang from the church tower to indicate not the hours but the calls to prayer. With the dawn of the modern age, secular clock towers like this rang out the hours as people organized their lives independent of the Church.

Taking humanism a step further, the City Hall, built after the French Revolution, obstructed the view of the old clock tower while celebrating a new era. The slogan "liberty, equality, and brotherhood" is a reminder that the people supersede the king and the Church. And today, judging from the square's jammed cafés and restaurants, it is indeed the people who rule.

The square's present popularity arrived with the trains in 1854. Facing City Hall, look left down the main drag, Rue de la République. When the trains came to Avignon, proud city fathers wanted a direct, impressive way to link the new station to the heart of the city—so they destroyed existing homes to create Rue de la République and widened Place de l'Horloge. This main drag's Parisian feel is intentional—it was designed in the Haussmann style that gives Paris its distinctive character (broad, straight boulevards lined with stately buildings). Today, this Champs-Elysées of Avignon is lined with department stores and banks. And locals see the Place de l'Horloge as the intersection of high culture, city government, and the populace.

• *Walk slightly uphill past the neo-Renaissance facade of the theater and the carousel (public WCs behind). Look back to see the late Gothic bell tower. Then veer right at the Palace of the Popes and continue into...*

❷ Palace Square (Place du Palais)

Pull up a concrete stump just past the café. These bollards effectively keep cars from double-parking in areas designed for people.

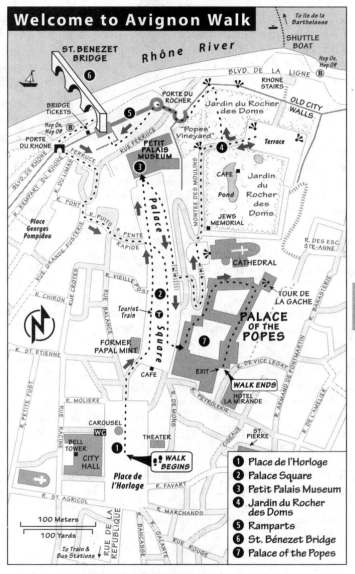

Welcome to Avignon Walk

To Île de la Barthelasse

SHUTTLE BOAT

ST. BENEZET BRIDGE

Rhône River

BLVD. DE LA LIGNE (B)

Hop On, Hop Off

⑥

BRIDGE TICKETS

Hop On, Hop Off (B)

PORTE DU RHONE

BLVD. DE RHONE

R. REMPART DU RHONE

R. DU LIMAS

RUE FERRUCE

R. PONT

R. PUITS

R. PENTE RAPIDE

R. GRANDE FUSTERIE

Place Georges Pompidou

R. CROIES

RUE BALANCE

R. VIEILLE POST

R. CHIRON

R. ST. ETIENNE

Tourist Train Ⓣ

FORMER PAPAL MINT

CAFE

R. MOLIERE

R. PETITE FUST.

RUE RACINE

BELL TOWER

CITY HALL

CAROUSEL

WC

THEATER

⚕

R. ST. AGRICOL

Place de l'Horloge

100 Meters

100 Yards

To Train & Bus Stations

RUE DE LA REPUBLIQUE

R. FAVART

R. MARCHANDS

RUE DE LA BANCASSE

GALANTE

RUE ROUGE

R. DE MONS

① WALK BEGINS

ST. PIERRE

R. CISEAUX

R. PEYROLERIE

HOTEL LA MIRANDE

WALK ENDS

EXIT → R. DE VICE LEGAT

R. ARMAND DE PONTMARTIN

R. DE L'AVELIER

R. BANASTERIE

R. DES ESC. STE-ANNE

PALACE OF THE POPES

⑦

TOUR DE LA GACHE

CATHEDRAL ✝

JEWS MEMORIAL

Jardin du Rocher des Doms

CAFE Pond

"Popes' Vineyard"

Terrace

④

MONTEE DES MOULINS

Jardin du Rocher des Doms

RHONE STAIRS

OLD CITY WALLS

PORTE DU ROCHER

⑤

Palace Square

PETIT PALAIS MUSEUM

③

② Palace Square

Ⓣ

⑦

AVIGNON

① Place de l'Horloge
② Palace Square
③ Petit Palais Museum
④ Jardin du Rocher des Doms
⑤ Ramparts
⑥ St. Bénezet Bridge
⑦ Palace of the Popes

Many of the metal ones slide up and down by remote control to let privileged cars come and go.

Now take in the scene. This grand square is lined with the Palace of the Popes, the Petit Palais, and the cathedral. In the 1300s the entire headquarters of the Roman Catholic Church was moved to Avignon. The Church purchased the city of Avignon and gave it a complete makeover. Along with clearing out vast spaces like this square and building a three-acre palace, the Church erected more than three miles of protective wall (with 39 towers), "appropriate" housing for cardinals (read: mansions), and residences for its entire bureaucracy. The city was Europe's largest construction zone. Avignon's population grew from 6,000 to 25,000 in short order. (Today, only 13,000 people live within the walls.) The limits of pre-papal Avignon are outlined on your city map: Rues Joseph Vernet, Henri Fabre, des Lices, and Philonarde all follow the route of the city's earlier defensive wall (about half the diameter of today's wall).

The imposing facade behind you, across the square from the Palace of the Popes' main entry, was "the papal mint," which served as the finance department for the Holy See (today it's a hotel). The Petit Palais (Little Palace) seals the uphill end of the square and was built for a cardinal; today it houses medieval paintings.

Avignon's 12th-century Romanesque cathedral, just to the left of the Palace of the Popes, has been the seat of the local bishop for more than a thousand years. Predating the Church's purchase of Avignon by 200 years, its simplicity reflects Avignon's modest, pre-papal population. The gilded Mary was added in 1854, when the Vatican established the doctrine of her Immaculate Conception.

• *At this point, you could visit the massive **Palace of the Popes** (described later). However, it works better to visit it at the end of this walk, then continue directly to my "Discovering Avignon's Back Streets Walk."*

Now is a good time to take in the...

❸ Petit Palais Museum (Musée du Petit Palais)

This former cardinal's palace now displays the Church's collection of (mostly) art. Though there's no English information, a visit here before going to the Palace of the Popes helps furnish and populate that otherwise barren building. You'll see bits of statues and tombs—an inventory of the destruction of exquisite Church art that was wrought by the French Revolution (which tackled established French society with fervor). Then you'll see many rooms filled with religious Italian paintings, organized in chronological order from early Gothic to late Renaissance. Room 10 holds two paintings by Botticelli.

Cost and Hours: Free, Wed-Mon 10:00-13:00 & 14:00-18:00, closed Tue, at north end of Palace Square, +33 4 90 86 44 58, www.petit-palais.org.

• *From Palace Square, head up to the cathedral (enjoy the viewpoint overlooking the square from its front porch), fill your water bottle just past the gate, ponder the war memorial (World War I and World War II, as well as Algeria 1954-1962), then side-trip 20 yards to the left to pause at a memorial to the 300 Jews deported from here to concentration camps by the Nazis. Now climb the ramp (to the left of the memorial) to the top of a rocky hill, passing "the popes' vineyard," to where Avignon was first settled.*

❹ Jardin du Rocher des Doms

The Jardin du Rocher des Doms, worth ▲, is home to an inviting café, a pond, and fine views. At the far side (the top end with the green fence) is a view-point high above the river from where you can see Avignon's beloved broken bridge.

Enjoy the **view** from this bluff. On a clear day, the tallest peak you see (far to the right), with its white limestone cap, is Mont Ventoux ("Windy Mountain"). Below and just to the right, you'll spot free passenger ferries shuttling across the river, and—tucked amidst the trees on the far side of the river—the recommended restaurant, Le Bercail, a local favorite. The island in the river is the Ile de la Barthelasse, a lush nature preserve where Avignon can breathe. In the distance to the left is the TGV rail bridge.

Medieval Avignon was administered by the Vatican and independent of the rest of France. The Rhône River marked the border of Vatican territory in medieval times. Fort St. André—across the river on the hill—was in the kingdom of France. The fort was built in 1360, shortly after the pope moved to Avignon, to counter the papal incursion into this part of Europe. Avignon's famous bridge was a key border crossing, with towers on either end—one was French, and the other was the pope's. The French one, across the river, is the Tower of Philip the Fair (described later, under "More Sights in Avignon").

Cost and Hours: Free, park gates open daily 7:30-20:00, June-July until 22:00, Oct-March until 18:00.

• *Take the walkway down to the left (passing the popes' vineyard again) and find the stairs leading down to the tower. You'll catch glimpses of the...*

❺ Ramparts

The only bit of the rampart you can walk on is accessed from St. Bénezet Bridge (accessible only with your ticket to the bridge). Just after the papacy took control of Avignon, the walls were extended to take in the convents and monasteries that had been outside the city. What you see today was partially restored in the 19th century.

• *When you come out of the tower on street level, turn left to walk inside the city wall to the entry to the old bridge.*

❻ St. Bénezet Bridge (Pont St. Bénezet)

This bridge, whose construction and location were inspired by a shepherd's religious vision, is the "Pont d'Avignon" of nursery-rhyme fame (and worth ▲). The

ditty (which you've probably been humming all day) dates back to the 15th century: *Sur le Pont d'Avignon, on y danse, on y danse, sur le Pont d'Avignon, on y danse tous en rond* ("On the bridge of Avignon, we will dance, we will dance, on the bridge of Avignon, we will dance all in a circle").

And the bridge was a big deal even outside its kiddie-tune fame. Built between 1171 and 1185, it was strategic—one of only three bridges crossing the mighty Rhône in the Middle Ages, important to pilgrims, merchants, and armies. It was damaged several times by floods but always rebuilt. In the winter of 1668 most of it was knocked out for the last time by a disastrous icy flood. The townsfolk decided not to rebuild this time, and for more than a century, Avignon had no bridge across the Rhône. While only four arches survive today, the original bridge was huge: Imagine a 22-arch, half-mile-long bridge extending from Vatican territory across the island to the lonely Tower of Philip the Fair, which marked the beginning of France (see displays of the bridge's original length).

Cost and Hours: €5, includes audioguide, €14.50 combo-ticket with Palace of the Popes, €17 combo-ticket with Palace of the Popes and Papal Garden; daily 10:00-18:00, July-Aug until 19:00, Nov-March until 17:00, +33 4 90 27 51 16.

Useful App: Download the free "Avignon 3D" app before your visit to see what the bridge looked like in the 14th and 17th centuries (the bright Provençal sun makes it difficult to use the app on the bridge, so skip the €2 tablet).

Visiting the Bridge: The ticket booth is housed in what was a medieval hospital for the poor (funded by bridge tolls). Admission includes a small room that displays a 3-D reconstruction of the bridge and your only chance to walk a bit of the ramparts (enter both from the tower). Visit the exhibit room first and take time to enjoy the two instructive videos (one in a small theater and the other on a small monitor). These explain the building of a stone bridge in a river with medieval technology—one of the great engineering feats of 12th-century Europe.

Climbing out onto the bridge you'll pass a double chapel (a Romanesque chapel dedicated to St. Bénezet below and a Gothic chapel to St. Nicolas above). Though there's not much to see on the bridge, the audioguide tells a good enough story. It's also fun to be in the breezy middle of the river with a sweeping city view.

• *To get to the Palace of the Popes from here, walk away from the river and follow the signs to* Palais des Papes.

❼ Palace of the Popes (Palais des Papes)

In 1309 a French pope was elected (Pope Clément V). His Holiness decided that dangerous Italy was no place for a pope, so he

moved the whole operation to Avignon for a secure rule under a supportive French king. The Catholic Church literally bought Avignon (then a two-bit town) and built the Palace of the Popes, where the popes resided until 1403 and where a visit today is worth ▲▲. Eventually, Italians demanded a Roman pope, so from 1378 on, there were twin popes—one in Rome and one in Avignon—causing a schism in the Catholic Church that wasn't fully resolved until 1417.

Cost and Hours: €12, includes multimedia Histopad; €14.50 combo-ticket with St. Bénezet Bridge, €17 combo-ticket with bridge and Papal Garden (skippable); advance timed-entry reservations strongly recommended in June-Sept; daily 10:00-18:00, July-Aug 9:30-19:00, Nov-March 10:00-17:00, last entry one hour before closing; +33 4 90 27 50 00, www.palais-des-papes.com.

Light Show: A nighttime sound-and-light show projected on the walls of the inner courtyard may be discontinued but is worth asking about(€12, standing room only, mid-Aug-mid-Oct at 21:30).

Visiting the Palace: Visitors follow a tangled one-way route through mostly massive rooms equipped with an iPad they call "The Histopad"—an earnest effort to bring these old papal spaces to life. There's a lot of history here, but artifacts are sparse and wall frescos are faint: Without guiding help, it's mostly meaningless. Old-fashioned English language boards in each room provide a little info, but your visit becomes greatly enriched if you master the Histopad—the staff is happy to help you with it. Nine posts during the tour activate a time-tunnel effect, taking you back to the 14th century as you furnish the rooms by pointing your iPad. While in this mode, you can click on various points in the room for more info.

The palace was built stark and strong, before the popes knew how long they'd be staying (and before the affluence and fanciness of the Renaissance and Baroque ages). This was the most fortified palace of the time (remember, the pope left Rome to be more secure). With 10-foot-thick walls, it was a symbol of power. There are huge ceremonial rooms (rarely used) and more intimate living quarters. The bedroom comes with the original wall paintings, a decorated wooden ceiling, and a fine tiled floor. And there's one big "chapel" (twice the size of the adjacent cathedral), which while simple, is majestic in its pure French Gothic lines.

This largest surviving Gothic palace in Europe was built to accommodate 500 people as the administrative center of the Holy See and home of the pope.

Seven popes ruled from here, making this the center of Christianity for nearly 100 years. The last pope checked out in 1403, but the Church owned Avignon until the French Revolution in 1791. During this interim period, the palace still housed Church authorities. Avignon residents, many of whom had come from Rome, spoke Italian for a century after the pope left, making the town a cultural oddity within France.

The palace is pretty empty today—nothing portable survived both the pope's return to Rome and the French Revolution. In fact, Revolutionary leaders (who called the building "the Bastille of the South") decreed that it be demolished but lacked the money to carry out the destruction. With the Napoleonic age, the palace found a practical use, housing about 1,800 troops. It remained a barracks until 1906.

The artillery room is now a gift shop channeling all visitors on a full tour of knickknacks for sale. Just before the gift shop exit, you can climb the tower (Tour de la Gâche) for grand views..

• *You'll exit at the rear of the palace, where my next walk begins. Or, to return to Palace Square, make two rights after exiting the palace.*

DISCOVERING AVIGNON'S BACK STREETS WALK

This easy, level, 30-minute walk is worth ▲▲. We'll begin in the small square (Place de la Mirande) behind the Palace of the Popes. If you've toured the palace, this is where you exit. Otherwise, from

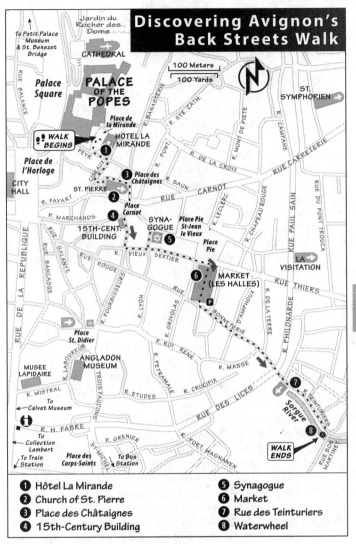

Discovering Avignon's Back Streets Walk

100 Meters
100 Yards

1. Hôtel La Mirande
2. Church of St. Pierre
3. Place des Châtaignes
4. 15th-Century Building
5. Synagogue
6. Market
7. Rue des Teinturiers
8. Waterwheel

the front of the palace, follow the narrow, cobbled Rue de la Peyrolerie—carved out of the rock—around the palace on the right side as you face it.

• *Our walk begins at the...*

❶ **Hôtel La Mirande:** Avignon's finest hotel welcomes visitors. Find the atrium lounge, check out the queenly garden, and consider a coffee break amid the understated luxury (€12 afternoon tea served daily 15:00-18:00, see listing under "Eating in Avignon," later).

• *Turn left out of the hotel and left again on Rue de la Peyrolerie (Coppersmiths Street), then take your first right on Rue des Ciseaux d'Or (Street of the Golden Scissors). On the small square ahead you'll find the...*

❷ **Church of St. Pierre:** The original walnut doors were carved in 1551, when tales of New World discoveries raced across Europe. (Notice the Native American headdress, top center of left-side door.) The fine Annunciation (eye level on right-side door) shows Gabriel giving Mary the exciting news in impressive Renaissance 3-D. The niches on the facade are empty except for one mismatched Mary and Child filling the center niche. (The original was ransacked by the Revolution.) Now take 10 steps back from the door and look way up. The tiny statue breaking the skyline of the church is a tiny, naked baby—that's Bacchus, the pagan god of wine, with oodles of grapes. What's he doing sitting atop a Christian church? No one knows. The church's interior—with its art amped up as a Counter-Reformation answer to the Protestant threat—holds a beautiful Baroque altar.

• *Facing the church door, turn left near the recommended L'Epicerie restaurant, then follow the alley, which was covered and turned into a tunnel during the town's population boom. It leads into...*

❸ **Place des Châtaignes:** The cloister of St. Pierre (with recommended eateries) is named for the chestnut *(châtaigne)* trees that once stood here (now replaced by plane trees). The practical atheists of the French Revolution destroyed the cloister, leaving only faint traces of the arches along the church side of the square.

• *Continue around the church and cross the busy street. At the start of little Rue des Fourbisseurs at the right corner, find the big...*

❹ **15th-Century Building:** With its original beamed eaves showing, this is a rare vestige from the Middle Ages. Notice how this building widens the higher it gets. A medieval loophole based taxes on ground-floor square footage—everything above was tax-free. Walking down Rue des Fourbisseurs ("Street of the Animal Furriers"), notice how the top floors almost touch. Fire was a constant danger in the Middle Ages, as flames leapt easily from one home to the next. In fact, the lookout guard's primary responsibility was watching for fires, not the enemy. Because of fires, this is the only 15th-century home surviving in town. After this period, buildings were made of fire-resistant stone, like those across the street.

• *Walk down Rue des Fourbisseurs past lots of shops and turn left onto the traffic-free Rue du Vieux Sextier ("Street of the Old Sexy People"); another left under the first arch leads in 10 yards to one of France's oldest synagogues.*

❺ **Synagogue:** Jews first arrived in Avignon with the Diaspora (exile after the Romans destroyed their great temple) in the first century. Avignon's Jews were nicknamed "the Pope's Jews" because of the protection that the Church offered to Jews expelled from France. Although the original synagogue dates from the 1220s, in the mid-19th century it was completely rebuilt in a Neoclassical Greek-temple style by a non-Jewish architect. This is the only synagogue under a rotunda. It's an intimate, classy place—where a community of 500 local Jews worships—dressed with white colonnades and walnut furnishings (free, Mon-Fri 10:00-12:00, ring doorbell, closed Sat-Sun and holidays, 2 Place Jerusalem).

· *Retrace your steps to Rue du Vieux Sextier and turn left. Continue to the big square (across the busy street) and find the big, boxy market building with the vertical (hydroponic) garden growing out its front wall.*

❻ **Market** (Les Halles): In 1970, the town's open-air market was replaced by this modern one (more efficient, with a parking

garage overhead, hoping to compete with supermarkets in the suburbs). The market's jungle-like hydroponic green wall reflects the changes of seasons and helps mitigate its otherwise stark exterior (Tue-Sun until 13:30, closed Mon). Step inside for a sensual experience of organic breads, olives, and festival-of-mold cheeses. Cheap cafés, bars, and good cheese shops are mostly on the right—the stinky fish stalls are on the left. This is a terrific place for lunch—especially if you'd fancy a big plate of mixed seafood with a glass of white wine (see "Eating in Avignon," later, for more about the market and several good lunch options).

· *Walk through the market and exit out the back door, then turn left on Rue de la Bonneterie (Street of Hosiery), which has recently transitioned from a busy street for cars to a more peaceful—and therefore more prosperous—pedestrian zone lined with triple-A shops (alternative, arty, and artisan). Track the street for five minutes to the plane trees, where it becomes...*

❼ **Rue des Teinturiers:** This "Street of the Dyers" is a bohemian-friendly, tree- and stream-lined lane, home to earthy cafés and galleries. This was the cloth industry's dyeing and textile center in the 1800s. The stream is a branch of the Sorgue River. Those stylish Provençal fabrics and patterns you see for sale everywhere were first made here, based on printed fabrics originally imported from India.

About three small bridges down, you'll pass the Grey Penitents chapel on the right. The upper facade shows the GPs, who dressed up in robes and pointy hoods to do their anonymous good deeds back in the 13th century. (While the American KKK dresses in hoods to hide their hateful racism, these hoods symbolized how all are equal in God's eyes.) As you stroll on, you'll see the work of amateur sculptors, who have carved whimsical car barriers out of limestone. Fun restaurants on this atmospheric street are recommended later, under "Eating in Avignon."

• *Farther down Rue des Teinturiers, you'll come to the...*

❽ **Waterwheel:** Standing here, imagine the Sorgue River—which hits the mighty Rhône in Avignon—being broken into several canals in order to turn 23 such wheels. Starting in about 1800, waterwheels powered the town's industries. The little cogwheel above the big one could be shoved into place, kicking another machine into gear behind the wall. (For more on the Sorgue River and its waterwheels, see my self-guided walk of Isle-sur-la-Sorgue on page 213.)

• *Our walk is done. To return to the center of town, double back on Rue des Teinturiers and turn left on Rue des Lices, which traces the first medieval wall. (A "lice" is the no-man's-land along a protective wall.) After a long block you'll pass a striking four-story building that was a home for the poor in the 1600s, an army barracks in the 1800s, a fine-arts school in the 1900s, and is a deluxe condominium today (much of this neighborhood is going high-class residential). Eventually you'll return to Rue de la République, Avignon's main drag.*

More Sights in Avignon

Most of Avignon's top sights are covered earlier by my self-guided walks. With more time, consider these options.

Angladon Museum (Musée Angladon)

Visiting this museum is like being invited into the elegant home of a rich and passionate art collector. It houses a small but enjoyable collection of art from Post-Impressionists to Cubists (including Paul Cézanne, Vincent van Gogh, Edgar Degas, and Pablo Picasso), with re-created art studios and furnishings from many periods. It's a quiet place with a few superb paintings and good temporary exhibits.

Cost and Hours: €8, Tue-Sun 13:00-18:00, closed Mon year-round and on Sun in winter, 5 Rue Laboureur, +33 4 90 82 29 03, www.angladon.com.

Calvet Museum (Musée Calvet)

This fine-arts museum, ignored by most, impressively displays a collection highlighting French Baroque works and Northern masters such as Hieronymus Bosch and Pieter Bruegel. You'll find a few gems upstairs: a painting each by Manet, Sisley, Géricault, and David. On the ground floor is a room dedicated to more modern artists, with works by Soutine, Bonnard, and Vlaminck. The Calvet Museum's antiquities collection, Le Musée Lapidaire, is hosted in a church a few blocks away at 27 Rue de la République.

Cost and Hours: Free, includes audioguide and Le Musée Lapidaire, Wed-Mon 10:00-13:00 & 14:00-18:00, closed Tue, in the western half of town at 65 Rue Joseph Vernet, +33 4 90 86 33 84, www.musee-calvet.org.

Collection Lambert

This modern art museum, situated in a grand 18th-century mansion, features works from the 1960s to the present. It came from the famous art dealer Yvon Lambert, who was determined to make well-known contemporary art accessible outside Paris. The recommended Le Violette restaurant in the courtyard is worth the visit alone (see page 137).

Cost and Hours: €10, July-Aug daily 11:00-19:00, Sept-June Tue-Sun 11:00-18:00, closed Mon, 5 Rue Violette, +33 4 90 16 56 21, www.collectionlambert.com.

NEAR AVIGNON
▲Tower of Philip the Fair (Tour Philippe-le-Bel)

Built to protect access to St. Bénezet Bridge in 1307, this hulking tower, located in nearby Villeneuve-lès-Avignon, offers a terrific view over Avignon and the Rhône basin.

Cost and Hours: €4; Tue-Sun 10:00-12:30 & 14:00-18:00, Nov-April 14:00-17:00, closed all of Dec-Jan and Mon year-round.

Getting There: To reach the tower from Avignon, drive five minutes (cross Daladier Bridge, follow signs to *Villeneuve-lès-Avignon*), or take bus #5 (3/hour, bus stops just outside Place Crillon at Porte De l'Oulle, or from close to the train station—for stop locations, see the "Avignon" map, earlier).

Sleeping in Avignon

Hotel values are better in Arles. Avignon is crazy during its July festival—you must book long ahead and pay inflated prices. Drivers should ask about parking discounts through hotels.

NEAR CENTRE-VILLE STATION

These listings are a 5- to 10-minute walk from the Centre-Ville train station.

$$ Hôtel Bristol**** is a big, professionally run place on the main drag, offering predictable "American" comforts at fair rates. Enjoy spacious public spaces, large rooms, big elevators, and a generous buffet breakfast (family rooms, 44 Cours Jean Jaurès, +33 4 90 16 48 48, www.bristol-avignon.com, contact@bristol-avignon.com).

$ Hôtel Ibis Centre Gare*** offers tight-but-tasteful comfort and quiet near the central train and bus stations (42 Boulevard St. Roch, +33 4 90 85 38 38, www.ibis.com, h0944@accor.com).

$ Hôtel Colbert** is on a quiet lane, with a dozen spacious rooms gathered on four floors around a skinny spiral staircase (no elevator). Patrice decorates each room as if it were his own, with a colorful (occasionally erotic) flair. There are warm public spaces and a sweet little patio (some tight bathrooms, rooms off the patio can be musty, closed Nov-March, 7 Rue Agricol Perdiguier, +33 4 90 86 20 20, www.lecolbert-hotel.com, contact@avignon-hotel-colbert.com).

$ At Hôtel Boquier,** helpful owner Frédéric offers 13 quiet, good-value, and homey rooms under wood beams in a central location (family rooms, steep and narrow stairways to some rooms, no elevator, pay parking nearby, near the TI at 6 Rue du Portail Boquier, +33 4 90 82 34 43, www.hotel-boquier.com, contact@hotel-boquier.com).

IN THE CENTER, NEAR PLACE DE L'HORLOGE

$$$$ Hôtel d'Europe,**** one of Avignon's most prestigious addresses, lets peasants sleep affordably—but only if they land one of the six reasonable *classique* rooms. With formal staff, spacious lounges, and a shady courtyard, the hotel is located on the handsome Place Crillon, near the river (pay garage parking, near Daladier Bridge at 12 Place Crillon, +33 4 90 14 76 76, www.heurope.com, reservations@heurope.com). Readers seeking top comfort should compare this hotel with Hôtel la Mirande, next.

$$$$ Hôtel la Mirande**** pampers its guests with traditional luxury in a quiet, central location behind the Palace of the Popes. The welcoming staff delivers service with a smile, public spaces are comfy, and the rooms are exquisitely decorated (4 Place de l'Amirande, +33 4 90 14 20 20, www.la-mirande.fr, mirande@la-mirande.fr). The hotel also houses a well-respected restaurant, listed later.

$$$ Hôtel Mercure Palais des Papes,**** about a block from the Palace of the Popes, has a modern exterior and 86 big, smartly designed rooms, many with small balconies (about half the rooms have views over Place de l'Horloge, others are quieter with views over the Palace of the Popes, 1 Rue Jean Vilar, +33 4 90 80 93 00, www.mercure.com, h1952@accor.com).

$$$ Hôtel Pont d'Avignon,**** just inside the walls near St. Bénezet Bridge, is part of the same chain as Hôtel Mercure Palais des Papes, with the same prices for its 87 rooms. There's an airy atrium breakfast room and small garden terrace (direct access to a garage makes parking easier than at the other Mercure hotel, parking deals, on Rue Ferruce, +33 4 90 80 93 93, www.mercure.com, h0549@accor.com).

$$ Hôtel de l'Horloge**** is as central as it gets—on Place de l'Horloge. It offers 66 comfortable rooms, some with terraces and views of the city and the Palace of the Popes (1 Rue Félicien David, +33 4 90 16 42 00, www.hotel-avignon-horloge.com, hotel.horloge@hoa-hotels.com).

$$ Autour du Petit Paradis Apartments and **Aux Augustins,***** run by Sabine and Patrick, offer 22 contemporary, well-furnished rooms and studios with kitchenettes spread over two locations. Autour du Petit Paradis, in a restored 17th-century mansion, is central and plenty comfortable (5 Rue Noël Biret, +33 4 90 81 00 42); Augustins is less central with larger rooms and a nicer courtyard with lovely stonework dating from its time as a medieval monastery (16 Rue Carreterie, +33 4 84 51 01 44). For a fee, either will pick you up at the TGV station or at the Marseille airport; neither has an elevator (www.autourdupetitparadis.com, contact@autourdupetitparadis.com).

$ Hôtel Médiéval,** burrowed deep in the old center a few blocks from the Church of St. Pierre, was built as a cardinal's home. This stone mansion's grand staircase leads to 34 comfortable, pastel rooms (no elevator, kitchenettes in some rooms, 5 blocks east of Place de l'Horloge, behind Church of St. Pierre at 15 Rue Petite Saunerie, +33 4 90 86 11 06, www.hotelmedieval.com, hotel.medieval@wanadoo.fr, run by Régis).

¢ Hôtel Mignon* is a sleepable, homey one-star place with tiny bathrooms (no elevator, 12 Rue Joseph Vernet, +33 9 70 35 37 67, www.hotel-mignon.com, contact@hotel-mignon.com).

ON THE OUTSKIRTS

Auberge Bagatelle offers dirt-cheap beds in two buildings—a **$** budget hotel and a **¢** youth hostel—and has a young and lively vibe, café, grocery store, launderette, great views of Avignon, and campers for neighbors (cheaper rooms with shared bath, family rooms, across Daladier Bridge on Ile de la Barthelasse, bus #5, +33 4 90 86 71 35, www.aubergebagatelle.com, auberge.bagatelle@wanadoo.fr).

Avignon Hotels & Restaurants

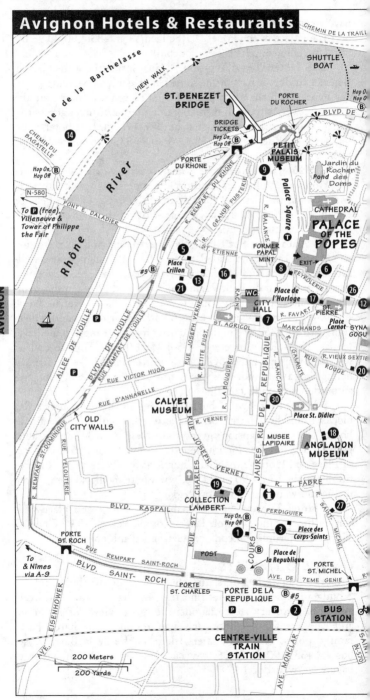

CHEMIN DE LA TRAILL

SHUTTLE BOAT

ILE de la Barthelasse

VIEW WALK

ST. BENEZET BRIDGE

PORTE DU ROCHER

Hop On Hop O

BRIDGE TICKETS
Hop On Hop Off

PETIT PALAIS MUSEUM

BLVD. DE L

PORTE DU RHONE

14

Hop On Hop Off

River

CHEMIN DU BAGATELLE

N-580

PONT E. DALADIER

To P (free), Villeneuve & Tower of Philippe the Fair

Rhône

9

Jardin du Rocher
Pond des Doms

CATHEDRAL

PALACE OF THE POPES

R. REMPART DU RHONE

R. GRANDE FUSTERIE

R. BALANCE

Palace Square

FORMER PAPAL MINT

5

Place Crillon

R. ST. ETIENNE

13

16

21

WG

CITY HALL

RACINE

ST. AGRICOL

7

Place de l'Horloge

8

EXIT

PEYROLERIE

6

17

ST. PIERRE

26

12

R. FAVART

MARCHANDS

Place Carnot

SYNA GOGU

RUE JOSEPH VERNET

RUE PETITE FUST.

R. GARANTE

RUE VIEUX SEXTIE

R. VIEUX ROUGE

20

RUE VICTOR HUGO

RUE D'ANNANELLE

CALVET MUSEUM

R. VERNET

R. LA BOUQUERIE

RUE DE LA REPUBLIQUE

R. BANCASS

30

Place St. Didier

ALLEE DE L'OULLE

BLVD. DE L'OULLE

RUE REMPART DE L'OULLE

P

P

R. REMPART ST-DOMINIQUE

RUE VELOUTERIE

OLD CITY WALLS

RUE JOSEPH VERNET

R. CHARLES

MUSEE LAPIDAIRE

ANGLADON MUSEUM

18

JAURES

R. H. FABRE

27

19

4

COLLECTION LAMBERT

BLVD. RASPAIL

PORTE ST. ROCH

RUE ST-CHARLES

R. PERDIGUIER

Hop On Hop Off

1

COURS J.

3

Place des Corps-Saints

SAINT MICHEL

To & Nîmes via A-9

RUE REMPART SAINT-ROCH

POST

Place de la Republique

PORTE ST. MICHEL

7EME GENIE

BLVD. SAINT- ROCH

PORTE ST. CHARLES

PORTE DE LA REPUBLIQUE

B #5

2

BUS STATION

AVE. DE

AVE. EISENHOWER

CENTRE-VILLE TRAIN STATION

AVE. MONCLAR

N-570

200 Meters

200 Yards

AVIGNON

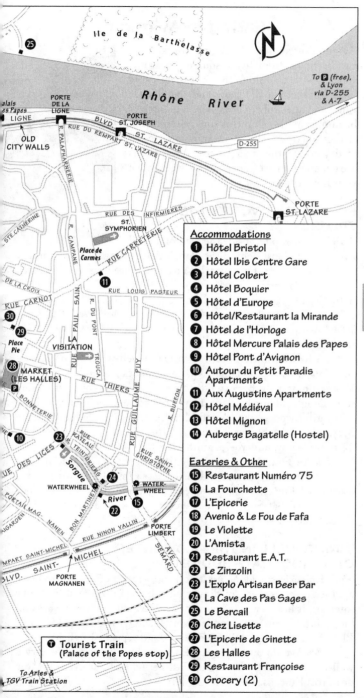

Ile de la Barthelasse

To **P** (free),
& Lyon
via D-255
& A-7

Rhône River

PORTE
DE LA
LIGNE

lais
es Papes
LIGNE

OLD
CITY WALLS

R. PALAPHARNERIE

BLVD.

RUE DU REMPART ST. LAZARE

PORTE
ST. JOSEPH

ST. LAZARE

D-255

PORTE
ST. LAZARE

RUE DES INFIRMIÈRES

STE CATHERINE

ST.
SYMPHORIEN

R. CAMPANE

Place de
Carmes

RUE CARRETERIE

DE LA CROIX

RUE LOUIS PASTEUR

RUE CARNOT

R. DU PONT

R. PAUL SAIN

LA
VISITATION

TROUCA

RUE GUILLAUME PUY

Place
Pie

MARKET
(LES HALLES)

RUE THIERS

R. BUFFON

BONNETERIE

RUE
RATEAU

RUE
TEINTURIERS

RUE SAINT-
CHRISTOPHE

RUE DES LICES

Sorgue

WATERWHEEL

PORTAIL MAG.

NANEN

BON MARTINE

River

WATER-
WHEEL

PORTE
LIMBERT

RUE NINON VALLIN

VIGARDEN

NANEN

AVE
SEMARD

MPART SAINT-MICHEL

SAINT-

MICHEL

BLVD.

PORTE
MAGNANEN

🚂 Tourist Train
(Palace of the Popes stop)

To Arles &
TGV Train Station

Accommodations
1. Hôtel Bristol
2. Hôtel Ibis Centre Gare
3. Hôtel Colbert
4. Hôtel Boquier
5. Hôtel d'Europe
6. Hôtel/Restaurant la Mirande
7. Hôtel de l'Horloge
8. Hôtel Mercure Palais des Papes
9. Hôtel Pont d'Avignon
10. Autour du Petit Paradis Apartments
11. Aux Augustins Apartments
12. Hôtel Médiéval
13. Hôtel Mignon
14. Auberge Bagatelle (Hostel)

Eateries & Other
15. Restaurant Numéro 75
16. La Fourchette
17. L'Epicerie
18. Avenio & Le Fou de Fafa
19. Le Violette
20. L'Amista
21. Restaurant E.A.T.
22. Le Zinzolin
23. L'Explo Artisan Beer Bar
24. La Cave des Pas Sages
25. Le Bercail
26. Chez Lisette
27. L'Epicerie de Ginette
28. Les Halles
29. Restaurant Françoise
30. Grocery (2)

Eating in Avignon

Avignon offers a good range of restaurants and settings, from lively squares to atmospheric streets. Skip the crowd-pleasing places on Place de l'Horloge and enjoy better value and atmosphere elsewhere. Avignon is brimming with delightful squares and back streets lined with little restaurants eager to feed you. At the finer places, reservations are generally smart (especially on weekends); your hotel can call for you.

FINE DINING WORTH THE SPLURGE

$$$$ La Mirande, inside the recommended five-star hotel just behind the Pope's Palace, transports you into a historic and aristocratic world. What was once a cardinal's palace today is a romantic oasis where you'll dine in 18th-century splendor with elegant service and presentation. Dress as nicely as you can (dine inside or in the queenly garden, closed Mon-Wed, €50 *plats*, set €150-190 *menus*, 4 Place de l'Amirande, +33 4 90 14 20 20, www.la-mirande.fr).

$$ Restaurant Numéro 75 fills the well-worn Pernod mansion (of *pastis* liquor fame) with a romantic, chandeliered, Old World dining hall that extends to a leafy, gravelly courtyard. They serve delightful lunch salads, fish is a forte, and the French cuisine is beautifully presented (closed Mon for dinner, Sat for lunch Sept-May, and all day Sun year-round, 75 Rue Guillaume Puy, +33 4 90 27 16 00, www.numero-75.com).

$$ La Fourchette is an inviting, dressy place graced with warm colors and spacious indoor-only seating. The cuisine mixes traditional French with Provençal. Book ahead for this popular place (closed Sat-Sun, 17 Rue Racine, +33 4 90 85 20 93, www.la-fourchette.net).

DINING WELL IN THE OLD CENTER ON A MODERATE BUDGET

$$ L'Epicerie sits alone under green awnings on romantic Place St. Pierre and is ideal for dinner outside (or in the small but cozy interior). It has an accessible menu with Mediterranean dishes and big, splittable *assiettes* (sample plates), each with a theme (daily, 10 Place St. Pierre, +33 4 90 82 74 22, Magda speaks English).

$$$ Avenio owns a sweet terrace and cozy interior and serves well-presented, delicious regional dishes (closed Sun-Mon, 19 Rue des Trois Faucons, +33 4 90 03 14 41).

$$ Le Fou de Fafa is a warm, spacious, 12-table dinner place where delightful Antonia serves while her husband cooks (by reservation only, closed Sun-Mon, 17 Rue des Trois Faucons, +33 4 32 76 35 13).

$$ Le Violette, in the peaceful courtyard of the Collection Lambert modern art museum, serves fresh modern cuisine and is gorgeous when lit by the museum rooms at night (July-Aug daily, Sept-June closed Sun-Mon, 5 Rue Violette, +33 4 90 85 36 42).

$$ L'Amista ("the spot to meet friends") is a cozy, youthful, and welcoming place on a quiet lane with indoor and outdoor seating. Run by Delphine, it offers a fun Provençal/Spanish-inspired menu that always includes vegetarian options. Tapas-style plates are great for sharing (closed Sun-Mon off-season, 23 Rue Bonneterie, +33 6 19 24 15 47).

$$ Restaurant E.A.T., whose name stands for "Estaminet, Arômes et Tentations" (a small restaurant with aroma and temptations), is just off Place Crillon. It's locally popular, serving eclectic and fun options in a modern interior (closed Wed and Sun, 8 Rue Mazan, +33 4 90 83 46 74, www.restaurant-eat.com).

BOHEMIAN CHIC, CANALSIDE ON RUE DES TEINTURIERS

Rue des Teinturiers' fun concentration of midrange, popular-with-the-locals eateries justifies the long walk on a balmy evening. (In bad weather, it's dead.) It's a trendy, youthful area, spiffed up but with little hint of tourism. You'll find wine bars, vegetarian options, and live music at rickety metal tables under shady trees along the canal. I'd walk the street's entire length to find the best ambience before making a choice. Note that the finer Restaurant Numéro 75, listed earlier, is just around the corner.

$$ Le Zinzolin is a big bohemian diner serving European cuisine with a few vegetarian options, including lots of salads in the summer. The atmosphere is good inside and out (daily, 22 Rue des Teinturiers, +33 4 90 82 41 55).

Drinks in the Rue des Teinturiers Quarter: For a break from sightseeing or a relaxing night spot for a drink, this pedestrian-only street has two particularly good watering holes: a craft beer place at the start and a laid-back hippie wine bar at the lazy waterwheel. **L'Explo Artisan Beer Bar** is like a beer lovers club on a canal. It's mod, minimal, and cheap, with a convivial terrace. They serve 10 craft beers (no bottles) all on tap, and sausage and cheese plates to help soak it up (closed Sun-Mon, 2 Rue des Teinturiers. +33 4 90 31 06 35). **La Cave des Pas Sages,** a down and dirty wine bar, is just right to linger with the locals over a cheap glass of regional wine or beer. Choose from the blackboard by the bar that lists all the open bottles, then join the gang outside by the canal (closed Sun, 41 Rue des Teinturiers, +33 4 32 74 25 86).

ACROSS THE RHONE

$$ Le Bercail offers a fun opportunity to cross the river, get out of town, and take in the country air with a terrific riverfront view of Avignon, all while enjoying big portions of Provençal cooking. Make a reservation before trekking out there (closed Mon-Tue in off-season, +33 4 90 82 20 22, www.restaurant-lebercail.fr). Take the free shuttle boat (located near St. Bénezet Bridge) to the Ile de la Barthelasse, turn right, and walk five minutes. As the boat usually stops running at about 18:00 (20:45 in July-Aug), you can either taxi back or walk 25 minutes along the pleasant riverside path and over Daladier Bridge.

GOOD BUDGET PLACES IN THE CENTER
Place des Châtaignes

This "square of the chestnut trees" (technically Place du Cloître Saint-Pierre) offers cheap meals and a fun commotion of tables.

$ Chez Lisette, a tiny bakery/deli with the best tables on the square, is great for salads, sandwiches, and daily *plats* (great *fougasse;* closed Sun, +33 4 86 65 80 62).

Place des Corps-Saints

This welcoming square offers the best feeling of a neighborhood dining, drinking, and simply living outdoors together. It's great for outdoor dining in Avignon, with several eateries in all price ranges sharing the same great setting under big plane trees. Survey the scene: tables crammed into every nook and cranny, there's standard café fare, Italian options, a pizza joint, a wine bar, and finer dining choices. **$ L'Epicerie de Ginette** serves salads, *tartines* (big slices of toast with a variety of toppings), and tasty desserts (daily, +33 4 90 85 58 70).

Les Halles and Place Pie

Avignon's youth make their home on Place Pie, a big square filled with cafés. At the south end of the square is Les Halles, Avignon's farmers market hall (described in my "Discovering Avignon's Back Streets Walk," earlier). Les Halles is an ideal lunch spot, with a handful of wonderfully characteristic and cheap places serving locals the freshest of food surrounded by all that market fun (Tue-Sun until 13:30, closed Mon). If picnicking, there are plenty of benches under the trees outside on the square.

Les Halles Orientation: Use the main aisle to orient yourself (enter under vertical garden). The third place on the left is **Comptoir du Sud** (fun sampling of edibles from the South); down the aisle on the right is a traditional café where you can BYOC (C for croissant); the mid-center aisle on the right is the "250 cheeses shop"; at the end of the center aisle on the right, behind the bakery, is **Cuisine Centr'Halles** (described below); the WC is in the far-left corner, and **fish bars** are in the two back corners. Either shop will assemble the plate of your fishy dreams at a painless price (€18 for an assortment for two). While the prices at both these places are about the same, the outfit in the far-left corner (**La Cabane d'Oleron**) has better quality and outdoor tables (open daily). For a real French market experience, purchase a fish filet from the fish-monger, then have Philippe at **ID Halles** cook it for you (€5, add market veggies to your fish for an extra €5).

$$ Cuisine Centr'Halles is where Jonathan Chiri (an American chef who landed here 20 years ago) serves tasting plates (land or sea) offering the best of the market in an elegant setting (about €20). He also runs two-hour market tours (€45, includes tapenade demo cooking and tasting with wine, Wed-Sat at 9:00, +33 6 46 89 85 33, www.jonathanchiri.com).

$ Restaurant Françoise is a fine deli-café a block off Place Pie, where fresh-baked tarts—savory and sweet—and a variety of salads and soups make a healthful meal, and vegetarian options are plentiful. Order at the counter and eat inside or out (closed Sun, 6 Rue Général Leclerc, +33 4 32 76 24 77).

Grocery Stores

Carrefour City is central (2 blocks from TI, toward Place de l'Horloge on Rue de la République). A second Carrefour City is near Les Halles at 19 Rue Florence (both open long hours daily).

Avignon Connections

BY TRAIN

There are two train stations in Avignon: the suburban TGV station and the Centre-Ville station in the city center (€1.60 shuttle trains connect the stations, buy ticket from machine on platforms or at a counter, included with rail pass, 2/hour, 5 minutes). TGV trains usually serve the TGV station only, though a few depart from Centre-Ville station (check your ticket). The TGV station has a broad choice of car rental agencies; only Avis is at Centre-Ville station. Some cities are served by slower local trains from Centre-Ville station as well as by faster TGV trains from the TGV station; I've listed the most convenient stations for each trip.

From Avignon's Centre-Ville Station to: Arles (roughly hourly, 20 minutes, less frequent in the afternoon), **Orange** (hourly, 20 minutes), **Nîmes** (hourly, 30 minutes), **Isle-sur-la-Sorgue** (10/day on weekdays, 7/day on weekends, 30 minutes), **Lyon**

(hourly, 2 hours; faster from TGV station), **Carcassonne** (8/day, 7 with transfer in Narbonne or Nîmes, 3 hours), **Barcelona** (2/day, 6 hours with changes).

From Avignon's TGV Station to: Nice (hourly, most by TGV, 4 hours, many require transfer in Marseille), **Marseille** (hourly, 35 minutes), **Cassis** (10/day, transfer in Marseille, 1.5 hours), **Aix-en-Provence TGV** (hourly, 20 minutes), **Lyon** (hourly, 70 minutes, slower from Centre-Ville station), **Paris' Gare de Lyon** (hourly direct, 2.5 hours), **Paris' Charles de Gaulle airport** (4/day direct, 3 hours, more with transfer in Lyon or Paris), **Barcelona** (1/day direct, 4 hours).

BY BUS

The bus station *(gare routière)* is just past and below Hôtel Ibis, to the right as you exit the train station. Nearly all buses leave from this station (a few leave from the ring road outside the station—ask, buy tickets on bus or at bus station). Service is reduced or nonexistent on Sundays and holidays. Check your departure time beforehand, and make sure to verify your destination with the driver. Buses are cheap in this region, figure €1.50-5 for most trips. When connecting big cities (like Avignon and Aix-en-Provence), check FlixBus and Blablabus schedules as well as the local lines listed next (see the "Transportation" section of the Practicalities chapter for more on these bus companies).

From Avignon to Pont du Gard: For details on taking the bus to the famous aqueduct, see the "Getting There" section for Pont du Gard on page 159 of the Near Avignon chapter. For a great day trip, see my suggested train/bus excursion that combines Nîmes and Pont du Gard (see "Planning Your Time," next chapter).

From Avignon by Bus to Other Regional Destinations: These lines all depart from Avignon's main bus station; **Nîmes** (8/day Mon-Fri, 3-4/day Sat-Sun, 1.5 hours, much faster by train); **Aix-en-Provence** (6/day Mon-Fri, 3/day Sat-Sun, 75 minutes, faster and easier than train); **Uzès** (5/day Mon-Fri, 3/day Sat-Sun, 1 hour, stops at Pont du Gard); **St-Rémy-de-Provence** (#57, hourly Mon-Fri, 6/day Sat-Sun, 45 minutes); **Orange** (hourly Mon-Fri, 8/day Sat, 2/day Sun, 1 hour faster by train); **Isle-sur-la-Sorgue** (#6, hourly Mon-Sat, 2/day Sun, 45 minutes, also possible by train). For the **Côtes du Rhône** area, buses leave from Orange to **Vaison-la-Romaine** and other towns (faster to take the train to Orange and transfer to a bus there; see "Orange Connections" on page 176 for details). Buses to the **Luberon** area are too infrequent to be workable.

ROUTE TIPS FOR DRIVERS

Arles is well signed from the TGV station. If driving to St-Ré-my-de-Provence, Les Baux, or the Luberon, leave the station following signs to *Avignon Sud,* then *La Rocade.* You'll soon see exits to Arles (follow those for St-Rémy and Les Baux) and Cavaillon (for Luberon villages).

NEAR AVIGNON

Nîmes • Pont du Gard • Uzès

Although Avignon lacks Roman monuments of its own, some of Europe's greatest Roman sights are an easy, breezy day trip away. (To get the most out of these sights, read "The Romans in Provence" on page 42 before you visit.) The Pont du Gard aqueduct is a magnificent structure to experience, as is Nîmes, the city it served 2,000 years ago. Nîmes wraps a handful of intriguing Roman monuments and a grand Roman World Museum in a mellow, bigger-city package. The pedestrian-friendly town of Uzès, between Nîmes and Pont du Gard, is a refreshing break from power monuments and busy cities. Combining these three sights makes a memorable (if busy) day trip into the Languedoc-Roussillon region. Traveling by car, you'll drive scenic roads between Uzès and Nîmes that show off the rugged *garrigue* landscape that has made this region famous.

PLANNING YOUR TIME

Dodge the crowds and spend a night in classy Nîmes or cozy Uzès; both beat Avignon for quick and easy access to Pont du Gard. If you're on a tight schedule, this region's sights are doable as day trips from Avignon, even without a car. From Avignon it's 30 minutes by car to Pont du Gard, and 45 minutes to Uzès or Nîmes. Allow 30 minutes between Nîmes and Pont du Gard or Uzès, and 15 minutes between Pont du Gard and Uzès.

Without a car, you have these options from Avignon:

Minivan Tour: Several reliable companies run day trips from Avignon to Pont du Gard, Uzès, and other popular destinations (see page 38). All day bus tours include Nîmes, Uzès, and Pont du Gard for about €90 per person (www.getyourguide.com). Avignon's TI can suggest other options.

Bus, Train, and/or Taxi: Buses take around 40 minutes from

Near Avignon

To Lyon

Vaison-la-Romaine

Orange

Malaucène

Uzès

PONT DU GARD

Châteauneuf-du-Pape

Carpentras

Avignon

TGV STN

Isle-sur-la-Sorgue

Roussillon

Nîmes

Apt

Cavaillon

St-Rémy

GLANUM

LUBERON

Les Baux

Note: In some cases regular train lines and TGV lines share the same track

To Marseille

Distance By Bus/Train From Avignon

Orange: 20 minutes by train; 60 minutes by bus

Isle-sur-la-Sorgue: 30 minutes by train; 45 minutes by bus

Nîmes: 30 minutes by train; 90 minutes by bus

Uzès: 60 minutes by bus only

Pont du Gard: 40 minutes by bus only

Arles: 20 minutes by train; 60 minutes by bus

St-Rémy-de-Provence: 45 minutes by bus only;
   Les Baux is 20 minutes more by bus (summers only)

Vaison-la-Romaine: 105 minutes by bus;
   faster via train to Orange, then bus

Avignon or Nîmes to Pont du Gard (for details, see the Pont du Gard's "Getting There" section, later). With few buses connecting Avignon with Pont du Gard and Uzès, plan carefully—particularly off-season when weekend service all but vanishes. Connecting Avignon and Nîmes is easy, with almost hourly trains that take 30 minutes. By taxi, allow €50 and 30 minutes for a one-way ride from Avignon or Nîmes to Pont du Gard.

Here are three day-trip plans to consider. The best morning buses usually depart Avignon for Pont du Gard at about 8:45 and 11:40. Double-check all departure times before you set out.

Day Trip to Pont du Gard Only: Take a morning bus from Avignon's bus station to Pont du Gard, tour the site, then hop on an afternoon bus back to Avignon. For more flexibility, catch a cab from Avignon, then ride the bus back.

> **Day Trip to Pont du Gard and Nîmes:** Take the first bus from Avignon to Pont du Gard, tour the site, then take an early-afternoon bus to Nîmes for more sightseeing. Return by train to Avignon.
>
> **Day Trip to Pont du Gard and Uzès:** Take the first bus from Avignon to Pont du Gard, tour the site, then catch a midday bus to Uzès and stroll the town. Catch the late-afternoon bus back to Avignon.

Nîmes

Most travelers make time in their schedules for Arles and Avignon but ignore Nîmes. Arles and Avignon may have more popular appeal, but Nîmes—which feels richer and surer of itself—is refreshingly lacking in overnight tourists. This thriving town of classy shops and serious businesses is studded with world-class Roman monuments and laced with traffic-free lanes. (And if you've visited the magnificent Pont du Gard, you must be curious where all that water went.)

Since the Middle Ages, Nîmes has exported a famous fabric: The word "denim" actually comes from here (*de Nîmes* = "from Nîmes"). Denim caught on in the United States in the 1800s, when a Bavarian immigrant, Levi Strauss, popularized its use in the American West.

Today, Nîmes is officially in the Languedoc-Roussillon region (for administrative purposes), yet historically the town has been a key player in the evolution of Provence. Only 30 minutes by train or car from Arles or Avignon, and three hours from Paris on the TGV, Nîmes is easy to reach. The city keeps its clean and tranquil old center a secret for its well-heeled residents. (Locals admit they don't need the tourism money as much as other Provençal towns.) While most visitors understandably prefer sleeping in Arles or Avignon, a night here provides a less touristic taste of this corner of France.

NEAR AVIGNON

Orientation to Nîmes

Nîmes ("neem") has no river or natural landmark to navigate by, so it's easy to become disoriented. For a quick visit, limit yourself to the manageable triangle within the ring of roads formed by boulevards Victor Hugo, Amiral Courbet, and Gambetta.

The town's landmarks are connected by 10-minute walks: It's 10 minutes from the train station to the arena and Roman World Museum, 10 minutes from the arena to the Roman temple of Maison Carrée, and 10 minutes from Maison Carrée to either the Castellum or the Fountain Garden. Apart from seeing a handful of museums and ancient monuments, appreciate the city's traffic-free old center—a delight for browsing, strolling, sipping coffee, and people-watching.

TOURIST INFORMATION

The TI is across the street from the arena (daily 9:00-19:00, shorter hours in off-season, 6 Boulevard des Arènes, +33 4 66 58 38 00, www.nimes-tourisme.com). Pick up the English-language pamphlet, which includes a map with a description of the city's sights and museums and a worthwhile Old City walk; inquire about sightseeing passes; and ask staff to start the English version of a 10-minute animated presentation giving a good overview of Nîmes' history and urban development.

ARRIVAL IN NIMES

By Train: There are two stations in Nîmes (the more important **Nîmes Centre** and the new **Nîmes Pont du Gard TGV station**). You want **Nîmes Centre station** for sightseeing and access to the bus station (handy if you're combining Pont du Gard with Nîmes, plus there's baggage storage nearby—see "Helpful Hints," later). **Nîmes Pont du Gard** has a misleading name, at 9 miles out of town and not close to the Pont du Gard. If you end up at Nîmes Pont du Gard, express bus #33 connects the two train stations (8 minutes by train or 30 minutes by bus).

By Bus: The bus station and bus information office are a block straight out the Nîmes Centre train station's back door (Mon-Fri 8:00-18:00, closed Sat-Sun). Buses relevant to sightseers use stalls 8 to 15 (coming from the train station, the shelters are to the right). Confirm your destination and pay the driver (use small bills or coins).

The ancient Roman arena is a pleasant 10-minute walk out the front of the train station. Head up the pedestrian parkway, go left at the big plaza, curve right, and you'll see the arena (to find its entrance, walk counterclockwise around it). To reach the TI, walk

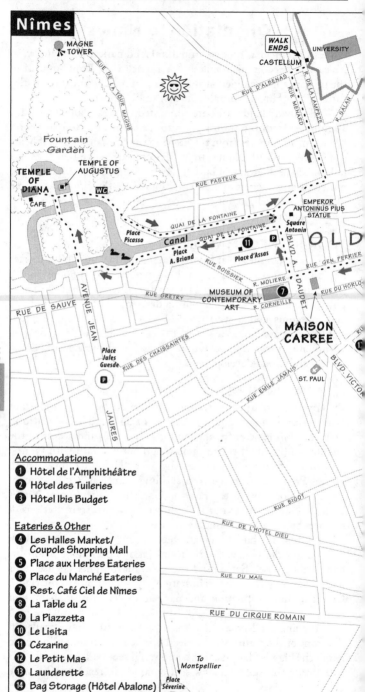

Nîmes

MAGNE TOWER

WALK ENDS

UNIVERSITY

CASTELLUM

RUE DE LA TOUR MAGNE

RUE D'ALBENAS

R. DE LA LAMPEZE

RUE MENARD

R. SALAN

Fountain Garden

TEMPLE OF AUGUSTUS

RUE PASTEUR

TEMPLE OF DIANA

WC

EMPEROR ANTONINUS PIUS STATUE

CAFE

Square Antonin

QUAI DE LA FONTAINE

OLD

Canal

Place Picasso

QUAI DE LA FONTAINE

Place A. Briand

BLVD A.

RUE BOISSIER

Place d'Assas

RUE GEN. PERRIER

R. MOLIERE

RUE GRETRY

MUSEUM OF CONTEMPORARY ART

R. CORNEILLE

RUE DU HORLO

AVENUE JEAN

RUE DE SAUVE

MAISON CARREE

BLVD. VICTOR

Place Jules Guesde

RUE DES CHAISSAINTES

RUE EMILE JAMAIS

ST. PAUL

JAURES

RUE BIGOT

RUE DE L'HOTEL DIEU

RUE DU MAIL

RUE DU CIRQUE ROMAIN

To Montpellier

Place Séverine

Accommodations
1. Hôtel de l'Amphithéâtre
2. Hôtel des Tuileries
3. Hôtel Ibis Budget

Eateries & Other
4. Les Halles Market/ Coupole Shopping Mall
5. Place aux Herbes Eateries
6. Place du Marché Eateries
7. Rest. Café Ciel de Nîmes
8. La Table du 2
9. La Piazzetta
10. Le Lisita
11. Cézarine
12. Le Petit Mas
13. Launderette
14. Bag Storage (Hôtel Abalone)

NEAR AVIGNON

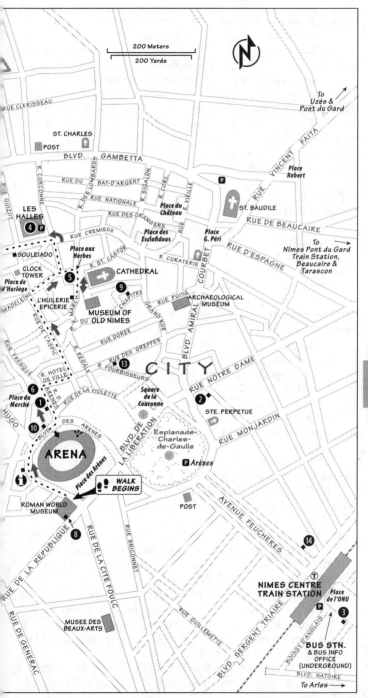

200 Meters
200 Yards

To
Uzès &
Pont du Gard

RUE CLÉRISSEAU

ST. CHARLES
POST

BLVD. GAMBETTA

R. CORCONNE

RUE DU BAT-D'ARGENT

RUE NATIONALE

RUE DES ORANGERS

RUE CRÉMIEUX

R. SIGALON

R. CORC.

R. E. VIEILLE

Place du Château

P

ST. BAUDILE

Place Robert

RUE VINCENT FAÏTA

RUE DE BEAUCAIRE

To
Nîmes Pont du Gard
Train Station,
Beaucaire &
Tarascon

LES HALLES
4 P

SOULEIADO

CLOCK TOWER
Place de l'Horloge

5

L'HUILERIE ÉPICERIE

Place aux Herbes

R. ST. CASTOR

R. MARCH

CATHEDRAL

9

R. CHAPITRE

MUSEUM OF OLD NIMES

RUE DORÉE

Place des Esclafidous

RUE DE L'ASPIC

MADELEINE

RUE FRESQUE

RUE GUIZOT

RUE DE L'ASPIC

R. HÔTEL DE VILLE

R. RÉGALE

R. BÉCALE

RUE DES GREFFES

R. FOURBISSEURS

13

CITY

Place G. Péri

RUE D'ESPAGNE

R. CURATERIE

ARCHAEOLOGICAL MUSEUM

GRAND RUE

RUE POISE

BLVD. AMIRAL COURBET

RUE NOTRE DAME

6

Place du Marché

1

10

HUGO

R. D.

RUE DE LA VIOLETTE

Square de la Couronne

2

STE. PERPÉTUE

RUE MONJARDIN

BLVD. DES ARÈNES

ARENA

Place des Arènes

Esplanade-Charles-de-Gaulle

P Arènes

WALK BEGINS

BLVD. DE LA LIBÉRATION

i

ROMAN WORLD MUSEUM

8

RUE DE LA RÉPUBLIQUE

RUE DE LA CITÉ FOULC

RUE BRICONNET

POST

AVENUE FEUCHÈRES

14

RUE DE GÉNÉRAC

MUSÉE DES BEAUX-ARTS

RUE GUILLEMETTE

BLVD. SERGENT TRIAIRE

NIMES CENTRE TRAIN STATION

T

Place de l'ONU

P

3

BOISSY D'ANGLAIS

BUS STN.
& BUS INFO OFFICE
(UNDERGROUND)

BLVD. NATOIRE

To Arles

clockwise around the arena. The Maison Carrée is a lovely stroll from the arena through Nîmes' traffic-free Old City.

By Car: The A-54 autoroute from Arles provides the easiest access to Nîmes. You can follow signs for *Centre-Ville* and *TI*, then *Arènes Parking*, and pay to park underneath the arena, or use Nîmes' efficient park-and-ride scheme. Simply leave A-54 at Nîmes-Centre exit #1 and follow signs to *Caissargues Tram Bus T1 P&R* (a few seconds from the off-ramp). There you can park for free and hop tram-bus T1 directly to the center (Arènes; see "Helpful Hints," below, for details). Use the same lot if you're coming from Montpelier or Avignon on the A-9 autoroute.

HELPFUL HINTS

Summer Thursdays: The "Jeudi de Nîmes" (Thursdays of Nîmes) tradition turns the entire old center of town into a festival of shops, street music, and liveliness on Thursday nights in July and August from 18:00 until late.

June Féria: Nîmes sheds its calm demeanor around Pentecost weekend for a weeklong Féria. You'll find bullfights in the Roman arena, cowboys and bulls from the Camargue parading in the streets, brass bands, and concerts.

Sightseeing Pass: The €17 **Romanity Pass** covers the arena, Maison Carrée, Magne Tower, and the Roman World Museum—a deal even if you just visit the arena and museum. If you're also visiting Orange, consider the €18.50 Nîmes-Orange Pass that covers the arena, Maison Carrée, Magne Tower, and the Orange Roman Theater (buy online, at the TI, or at sights; www.arenes-nimes.com).

Baggage Storage: The **Hôtel Abalone** stores bags. It's to your right as you exit the Nîmes Centre train station (€5/bag, daily 8:00-22:00, 23 Avenue Feuchères, +33 4 66 29 20 14).

Laundry: A launderette is near my recommended hotels at 1 Rue des Fourbisseurs (daily 7:00-21:00).

Taxi: Call +33 4 66 29 40 11 for a cab. It's about €50 to Pont du Gard.

Car Rental: Find **Avis** inside the Nîmes Centre train station (+33 4 34 14 80 15), **Europcar** (under the Nîmes Centre station, +33 4 66 29 07 94), and **Hertz** (by the recommended Hôtel Ibis Budget, +33 4 66 76 25 91).

Public Transit: Only one transit route matters here: the sleek tram-bus T1 which circles through the town center (€1.60, buy ticket from machines, runs every 7 minutes from the P&R Caissargues park-and-ride lot and stops near the arena, Maison Carrée, and Les Halles).

Local Guide: Delightful **Sylvie Pagnard**'s walking tours are top quality. She also does regional tours of Provence and Languedoc (€170/3 hours, €360/8 hours, extra if she drives, mobile +33 6 03 21 37 33, sylviepagnard@gmail.com).

Tourist Train: Nîmes' *petit train* leaves from the arena for a 40-minute circuit of town with recorded English commentary (€8, daily June-Sept, leaves nearly hourly 10:00-18:00, off-season 11:00-17:00 and no trains on Sun, no trains Nov-March).

Views: Don't miss the arena view from the green rooftop of the **Roman World Museum** (free access during museum hours) or its recommended restaurant **La Table du 2**. Or ride the glass elevator to the recommended, top-floor **Restaurant Café Ciel de Nîmes** at the Museum of Contemporary Art for a great view over the ancient Maison Carrée and a quiet break (Tue-Sun 10:00-18:00; also Thu-Sat 20:00-late in July-Aug; closed Mon).

Nîmes Walk

I've described Nîmes' best sights below in a logical order for a good daylong visit and have linked them with walking directions. You'll get your historic bearings next door to the arena at the...

Roman World Museum (Musée de la Romanité)

This worthwhile ▲▲ sight provides the city a museum to match its fine ancient ruins. The state-of-the-art building has a grassy rooftop terrace with views of the arena and a public lane passing through it to an archaeological park out back (both free during museum opening hours). Its airy design is meant to counter the heaviness of the ancient arena it faces.

Cost and Hours: €9, free first Sun of the month except July-Aug, covered by Romanity Pass; daily 10:00-19:00, Nov-March until 18:00; €3 audioguide, Boulevard des Arènes, +33 4 48 21 02 20, www.museedelaromanite.fr.

Visiting the Museum: While you'll find good information panels in English, most visitors find the audioguide worth the investment. Your visit starts on the first floor with an immersion in the pre-Roman and Roman world. With the help of high-tech interactive stations, the museum shows off 5,000 artifacts—the forte being a rich collection of Latin-inscribed stones and mosaics—some of which were discovered when digging the garage for the site.

Continue on the mezzanine floor covering the medieval history of the town, then return to the ground floor for its interesting display of Roman building models (scale 1:100) comparing, for example, the Colosseum in Rome and Nîmes' arena as they looked in the 19th century.

• *Next to the museum is the...*

Arena (Amphithéâtre)

Nîmes' arena, worth ▲▲, dates from about AD 100 and is more than 425 feet in diameter and 65 feet tall. Considered the best-preserved arena of the Roman world, it's a superb example of Roman engineering. The 24,000 seats could be filled and emptied in minutes (through 60 passageways called *vomitoires*). The games that were held here were free and designed to keep the populace entertained...and distracted from other concerns.

Since 1850, Nîmes' arena has been a venue for entertainment, including bullfights and rock concerts featuring musical gladiators from Sting to Santana.

Cost and Hours: €10, includes the necessary audioguide, covered by Romanity Pass; daily 9:00-18:30, June until 19:00, July-Aug until 20:00, closes earlier in winter. +33 4 66 21 82 56, www.arenes-nimes.com.

Visiting the Arena: You'll find helpful information panels in English as you tour the arena; these combine with the excellent audioguide to give a thorough and enjoyable history lesson. Don't miss the panels describing the different types of gladiators.

Climb to the very **top.** This is a rare opportunity to enjoy the view from a surviving high point—the nosebleed seats—of a

Roman arena. An amphitheater is literally a double theater: two theaters facing each other, designed so that twice the people could view a Dirty Harry spectacle—without the acoustics provided by the back wall of a theater stage. (You may think of this as a "colosseum," but that's not a generic term. Rome's Colosseum was a one-of-a-kind arena—named for a colossal statue of Nero that stood nearby.)

As at the arena in Arles and other Roman arenas, the floor here would have been covered in sand (to absorb blood). Underground were tunnels and rooms for storage. An elevator raised angry animals to the floor level to do battle with gladiators.

After Rome fell, the arena was bricked up and made into a fortress (as in Arles). In the 13th century, after the region was incorporated into France, the arena became a gated community hous-

---

Roman Nîmes

Born a Celtic city (about 500 BC), Nîmes joined the Roman Empire in the first century BC. Because it had a privileged status within the Roman Empire, Nîmes was never considered part of the conquered barbarian world. It rated highly enough to merit one of the longest protective walls in the Roman world and to have a 30-mile-long aqueduct (and its famous Pont du Gard) built to serve its growing population.

Today, the physical remains of Roman Nîmes testify to its former importance. The city's emblem—a crocodile tied to a palm tree—is a reminder that Nîmes was a favorite retirement home for Roman officers who had conquered Egypt. (The crocodile is Egypt, and the palm tree symbolizes victory.) All over town, little bronze croc-palm medallions shine on the sidewalks. In the City Hall, 400-year-old statues of crocodiles actually swing from the top of a monumental staircase (worth a look).

---

ing about 700 people—with streets, plumbing, and even gardens on the top level. Only in 1809 did Napoleon decide to scrape away the dwellings and make this a historic monument, thus letting the ancient grandeur of Roman Gaul shine.

The two exhibits at the end of your visit are small side-by-side "multimedia" rooms on the ground floor with puny offerings: one for bulls and the other for gladiators. To get the most out of these rooms, look for the audioguide numbers before entering the exhibits.

The **Bulls in Provençal Culture** exhibit *(Le Taureau dans l'Arène,* Room V104) shows the thrilling Camargue bullgames in action. Different from Spanish *corrida, La Course Camarquaise* is the crazy local "bullfight" where daredevil young men get chased into the seats by famous nimble bulls. The **Gladiators in the Arena** exhibit *(Vestiaire des Gladiateurs,* gladiators' locker room, Room V106) is a kid-friendly look at gladiator life. Monitors show the Hollywood-created image of gladiators.

• *From the arena, enter Nîmes' Old City.*

Old City

Those coming to Nîmes only for its famous Roman sights are enchanted by its carefully preserved old center (rated ▲▲). Here, you can study how elements from medieval and Renaissance times artfully survive in the buildings: Shop interiors incorporate medieval brick with stone arches, windows expose Gothic finery, and Renaissance staircases grace peaceful courtyards.

• *With your back to the arena's ticket office, angle right to follow Rue des Arènes one block into...*

Place du Marché

With an inviting café ambience, including a wispy palm-tree-and-crocodile fountain (Nîmes' emblem in Roman times—see sidebar), this fine square is ideal for lunch or a coffee break. Facing the fountain, the recommended **Courtois Café/Pâtisserie** (closed Wed) is the class act of the square—check out its old-time interior. Marie Manuelle can explain how it's been in her family since 1892. If you have a sweet tooth, sample the house specialty, a chocolate-dipped *nélusko;* it's like a cross between a cake and a cookie, and the oldest recipe of the house. Or try a Nîmes specialty, *caladon*—literally "cobble," like on the street—a hard honey-and-almond cookie.

• *Leave the square, passing the croc on your right (on Rue des Broquiers), then turn left on Rue de l'Aspic, the town's primary shopping spine. Follow Rue de l'Aspic straight past lots of shops several blocks to Place de l'Horloge (with its freestanding bell tower of the city government), marking the center of the Old City. From here pedestrian-friendly streets fan out in all directions, including directly to Maison Carrée. We'll take unsigned Rue de la Madeleine, the first street to the right as you enter Place de l'Horloge, to...*

Place aux Herbes

This inviting ▲ square is the site of Nîmes' oldest market. At the center of the Old City, it's a good hub for a bit of sightseeing and café lounging. The next three sights are on or near this square.

Nîmes Cathedral: While its Romanesque facade survives from the 12th century, the cathedral's interior—gutted over centuries of dynastic squabbles, Reformation, and Revolution—is unremarkable Neo-Romanesque, mostly from the 19th century.

Museum of Old Nîmes: Turn left as you leave the cathedral to see this humble museum inhabiting a 17th-century bishop's palace. You'll get a sense of how the bishop lived; see a room of fine, carved hutches (delicately carved with reliefs illustrating Bible stories); exquisite textile and silk work, and learn the story of indigo, 19th-century denim wear, and early Levi's. You'll even see a 200-year-old denim jacket (€5, Tue-Sun 10:00-18:00, closed Mon). A free English booklet describes the museum in general, but, sadly, exhibit information is in French only.

Old-Time Spice Shop: L'Huilerie is a charming time warp displaying spices and herbs, oils, and candy (Tue-Sat 9:00-12:30 & 14:30-19:00, closed Sun-Mon; 50 yards from the church, down the small lane by Le Petit Moka café, at 10 Rue des Marchands).

• *Return to the square. Standing with your back to the church door, leave the square at the far right corner and go one block down Rue des Halles.*

Across Rue Général Perrier on the left is the big, modern black-and-green market hall. Enter under the glassy facade a half-block to your left.

Les Halles Market/Coupole Shopping Mall

Les Halles de Nîmes looks modern on the outside with its glass entrance, but inside its ground floor is a thriving, traditional, colorful market, well worth exploring (Tue-Sun until 13:00, closed Mon). Within the market, Halles Auberge is a cheap and characteristic lunch-only spot (in the far-left corner) and Crèmerie de la Rue des Greffes is every local's favorite for Chantilly and strawberries (mid-market on the far right).

If it's hot, and/or you need to shop, walk straight through the produce market and into the air-conditioned Coupole shopping mall, where you'll find a FNAC department store and lots of mod French stores.

• *Leaving the market, take a right on Rue Général Perrier. On the corner opposite the market hall is* **Souleiado,** *a festival of fashion with dresses, shirts, scarves, and more all made locally of Provençal fabrics (closed Sun, 3 Rue Guizot). Then walk several blocks to the...*

Maison Carrée

This stunning ▲▲▲ temple rivals Rome's Pantheon as the most complete and splendid building that survives from the Roman Empire. Admire the original columns and Corinthian capitals. The temple survived in part because it's been in constant use for the last thousand years—as a church, a City Hall, a private stable, an archive during the Revolution, a people's art gallery after

the Revolution (like Paris' Louvre), and finally as the monument you visit today. It's a textbook example of a pseudo-peripteral temple (surrounded by columns, half of which support the roof over a porch, and half of which merely decorate the rest of the building) and a "six-column temple" (a standard proportion—if it's six columns wide, it must be eleven columns deep).

The lettering across the front is long gone, but the tiny surviving "nail holes" presented archaeologists with a fun challenge: Assuming each letter would leave a particular series of nail holes as evidence, derive the words. Archaeologists agree: This temple was built to honor Caius and Lucius, the grandsons of Emperor Augustus. And from this information, they date the temple to the year AD 4.

Maison Carrée ("Square House"—named before they had a word for "rectangle") was the centerpiece of a fancy colonnaded plaza surrounded by a U-shaped commercial, political, and religious forum. This marked the core of Roman Nîmes. As was the case in all Roman temples, only the priest went inside. Worshippers gathered for religious rituals at the foot of the steps. Climb the steps as a priest would—starting and ending with your right foot... *dexter* (from the Latin for "right") rather than *sinister* ("left"). Put your right foot forward for good karma.

Inside, a new multimedia system should be in place in 2023 to help you follow the evolution of this monument (€6, covered by Nîmes passes, daily 10:00-18:30, July-Aug 9:30-20:00, shorter hours in off-season).

Nearby: The modern building facing the temple is Nîmes' **Carré d'Art** ("Square of Art"), designed by British architect Lord Norman Foster. It's home to the city's Museum of Contemporary Art (Tue-Sun 10:00-18:00, closed Mon, WCs, recommended view café).

• *Next, facing the Museum of Contemporary Art, turn right and walk up the busy Boulevard Daudet one block to a statue of a Roman emperor. Emperor Antoninus Pius (who ruled after Hadrian in the second century AD, and whose mother was from Nîmes) seems to be enjoying a view of the canals leading to the ancient spring. Step across the street for a fine canal view. The force of the little waterfall gives an indication of the water gushing into town from the spring. Walk along the left side of the tree-lined canal until you reach...*

NEAR AVIGNON

Fountain Garden (Jardin de la Fontaine)

The grand Fountain Garden (worth ▲) is marked by a grand gate. Centuries before the Romans arrived in Nîmes, the Spring of Nemo was here (named, like the town itself, for a Celtic god). Rather than bulldoze the Nemo temple, the Romans built a shrine to Emperor Augustus around it and welcomed Nemo into their own pantheon (as was their "the-more-gods-the-merrier" tradition). Today, the spring remains, though the temple is gone.

Cost and Hours: Free, daily 7:30-22:00, shorter hours off-season.

Visiting the Garden: Walk into the center of the Fountain Garden to the statue of the goddess of the spring, which is sitting atop the ancient temple of Augustus. You can see the ancient stones and a band of carved reliefs down by the spring's water.

In the early 1700s, Nîmes needed a reliable source of water for its textile industry—to power its mills and provide water for the indigo dyes for the fabric *serge de Nîmes* (denim). About 1735, the city began a project to route a canal from this ancient spring through the city, and excavated clues to its ancient past. The city eventually agreed to fund a grander project that resulted in what you see today: a lavish Versailles-type park, complete with an ornate network of canals and boulevards. It was finished just 50 years after the construction of Versailles, and to the French, this place has a special significance: These were the first grand gardens not meant for a king, but for the public. The industrial canals built then still wind throughout the city.

• *Hiding behind trees in the back-left corner of Fountain Garden, find the...*

Temple of Diana

This first-century ▲ "temple," which modern archaeologists now believe was more likely a Roman library, has long been considered one of the best surviving examples of ancient stonework. Its roof—a round Roman barrel vault laced together with still-visible metal pegs (find the panel with a drawing of the temple before entering)—survived until it was hit by a blast in the 1500s, during the Catholic-Protestant Wars of Religion.

Cost and Hours: Free; same hours as Fountain Garden.

Visiting the Temple: As you explore the ruins, notice the graffiti carved artfully into the stones. It's actually part of the temple's story. For centuries, France had a highly esteemed guild of stone-, metal-, and woodworkers called the Compagnons, founded by Gothic-church builders in the Middle Ages. As part of their ritualistic training, these craftsmen would visit many buildings—including the great structures of antiquity (such as this one)—for inspiration. Walk through the side aisle (right side) for a close look at the razor-accurate stonework and the 17th-, 18th-, and 19th-century signatures of the Compagnon craftsmen inspired by this building. Notice how their signatures match their era—no-nonsense "Enlightened" chiseling of the 18th century gives way to ornate script in the Romantic 19th century.

Magne Tower (Tour Magne)

Overlooking the garden, capping the hill high above, is the ancient Magne Tower. Originally a Celtic lookout (450 BC), it was built grander by the Romans and is arguably the oldest structure in the city. If you wish, you can hike up there to climb the tight spiral staircase 140 steps to the tiny lookout at the top for a commanding view (€3.50, covered by Nîmes passes, skip the included headset). But if you're tired, you can just have a coffee at the inviting café adjacent to the Temple of Diana.

• *From the Temple of Diana, the next (worthwhile) sight is a 10-minute walk away. Angle back across the park, turning left at the canal (Quai de la Fontaine). You're walking back to the statue of the emperor but on the other side of the canal. If the old guys are out playing* pétanque, *drop in*

NEAR AVIGNON

and observe. (This is a popular way to spend your retirement in France.)
When you reach the emperor, continue straight another block. Just after
the tiny park, turn left onto tiny Rue Ménard. Follow it uphill for three
blocks, then head right on Rue d'Albenas, which ends at the...

Castellum

This small excavation site sitting next to the street is free, always
open, and worth ▲. It's the end of the grand, 30-mile-long Nîmes
aqueduct made famous by the
Pont du Gard. Two thousand
years ago this modest-looking
water tank distributed the water
brought in by the aqueduct to the
hot and thirsty city of Nîmes.

Discovered in the 1850s,
this is one of only two known
Roman distribution tanks (the
other is in Pompeii). The water
needs of Roman Nîmes had grown beyond the capacity of its local
springs and an aqueduct was needed to bring water in from farther
afield. Imagine the jubilation on the day in AD 50 that this system
was finally operational. Suddenly, the town had an abundance of
water—for basic needs as well as for cool extras like public fountains.

Notice the square hole marking the end of the aqueduct, a
pool, a lower water channel, and the water-distribution holes. The
lower channel, which runs under you, served top-priority needs,
providing water via stone and lead pipes to the public wells that
graced neighborhood squares. The higher holes—which got wet
only when the supply was plentiful—routed water to the homes
of the wealthy, to public baths, and to nonessential fountains. (For
more on this impressive example of Roman engineering, see the
"Pont du Gard" section, later.)

Sleeping in Nîmes

Hotels in Nîmes are a terrific value.

$ Hôtel de l'Amphithéâtre*** is ideally located on a pedestrian
street a spear's toss from the arena. Run by friendly Philippe, this is
a top Nîmes value, with quiet, spacious, and sharp rooms (RS% if
you book direct, no elevator, 4 Rue des Arènes, +33 4 66 67 28 51,
www.hoteldelamphitheatre.com, contact@hoteldelamphitheatre.
com).

$ Hôtel des Tuileries*** is a basic option, with helpful Eng-
lish hosts (Andrew and Caryn) and a central location 10 minutes
on foot from the train station. Rooms are large and modern, and

most have balconies (22 Rue de Roussy, +33 4 66 21 31 15, www.
hoteldestuileries.com, les-tuileries@wanadoo.fr).

¢ **Hôtel Ibis Budget,**** behind the train station, gives modern,
minimalist comfort for cheap (2 Avenue de la Méditerranée, +33 8
92 68 20 36, www.ibis.com, h7467@accor.com).

Eating in Nîmes

LUNCH

Enjoy the elegance of Nîmes by eating lunch in the market or on
one of its charming squares. These cafés serve lunch but many close
for dinner.

Les Halles Market/Coupole Shopping Mall: This thriving,
colorful market (described on my Nîmes Walk, earlier), is well
worth exploring (Tue-Sun until 13:00, closed Mon). **$ Halles Au-
berge,** in the far-left corner, is a convivial lunch-only spot serving
fresh French cuisine. While there are a few tables, the action is at
the bar. **Crèmerie de la Rue des Greffes** (mid-market on the far
right) is the traditional favorite for dessert to go—try the strawberries with Chantilly cream.

Place aux Herbes: This square, beautifully situated in the
shadow of the cathedral, boasts several popular bistros where you
can lunch for €10. All close daily at 19:00 and all day on Sundays.

Place du Marché: A block from the arena, this square is home
to several worthwhile eateries, including **$ Courtois Café/Pâtis-
serie,** with a fine *salade Nîmoise* (local pâté, tapenade, and *bran-
dade*) and trademark desserts (Thu-Tue until 19:00, closed Wed,
described under my self-guided walk).

Overlooking the Maison Carrée: Filling a terrace atop the
Museum of Contemporary Art, **$$ Restaurant Café Ciel de
Nîmes** offers great views of the Roman temple (Tue-Sun 10:00-
18:00, also open for dinner Thu-Sat in July-Aug, closed Mon, Place
de la Maison Carrée, +33 4 66 36 71 70).

DINNER

$$$ La Table du 2, on top of the Roman World Museum, serves
elaborate Provençal cuisine with a splendid view over the arena.
The €21 lunch *menu* is a deal, available every day but Sun (daily, 2
Rue de la République, +33 4 48 27 22 22).

$ La Piazzetta is a fun place to enjoy inexpensive pizza and
pasta on a lively, outdoor terrace (closed Sun, near Place aux Herbes at 2 Place du Chapitre, +33 4 66 84 93 15).

$$ Le Lisita, a dressy place a few steps from the arena, serves
serious French cuisine and has a smart interior with modern art and
terrific exterior seating. It feels formal and a bit pretentious (daily

July-Aug, otherwise closed Sun-Mon, 2 Boulevard des Arènes, +33 4 66 67 29 15, www.lelisita.com).

$$ Cézarine serves traditional Mediterranean cuisine and cocktails on a breezy square. It has fine terrace seating and a well-appointed interior with a big bar, open kitchen, and friendly service (daily except closed Wed in off-season, 6 Place d'Assas, +33 4 66 38 99 59).

$$ Le Petit Mas is a family-friendly place with an eclectic menu, salads and tapas at fair prices, and a great selection of local wines by the glass (closed Sun, 25 Rue de la Madeleine, +33 4 66 36 84 25).

Nîmes Connections

See "Arrival in Nîmes," earlier, for train and bus station information.

From Nîmes by Train to: Arles (hourly, 30 minutes, beware of gaps in the afternoon), **Avignon** (hourly, 30 minutes), **Aigues-Mortes** in the Camargue (summer: 6/day Mon-Fri, 2/day Sat-Sun; off-season: 2/day, 45 minutes), **Carcassonne** (8/day, 2.5 hours, transfer in Narbonne), **Paris** (10/day, 3 hours).

From Nîmes by Bus to: Aigues-Mortes in the Camargue (#132, 6/day, 50 minutes), **Arles** (#130, 8/day Mon-Fri, 2/day Sat-Sun, 1 hour). For reaching Pont du Gard, see "Getting There," below. For **Uzès,** see "Getting to Uzès" on page 164.

Pont du Gard

Throughout the ancient world, aqueducts were like flags of stone that heralded the greatness of Rome. A visit to this impressively preserved sight still works to proclaim the wonders of that age.

In the first century AD, the Romans built a 30-mile aqueduct that ran to Nîmes, one of ancient Europe's largest cities. While most of it ran on or below the ground, at Pont du Gard the aqueduct spans a canyon on a massive bridge over the Gardon River—one of the most remarkable surviving Roman ruins anywhere. The aqueduct supported a small canal that dropped one inch for every 350 feet, supplying the city of Nîmes with nine million gallons of water per day (about 100 gallons per second).

Allow about a full four hours for visiting Pont du Gard (including transportation time from Avignon).

GETTING THERE

The famous aqueduct is between Remoulins and Vers-Pont du Gard on D-981, 17 miles from Nîmes and 13 miles from Avignon.

By Car: Pont du Gard is a 30-minute drive due west of Avignon (follow N-100 from Avignon, tracking signs to *Nîmes* and *Remoulins,* then *Pont du Gard* and *Rive Gauche*), and 45 minutes northwest of Arles (via Tarascon on D-15). If going to Arles from Pont du Gard, follow signs to *Nîmes* (not *Avignon*), then D-15, or faster A-54 (autoroute) to Arles. At Pont du Gard, park on the Left Bank (Rive Gauche). Parking is €9.

By Bus: Buses run to Pont du Gard (on the Rive Gauche side) from Avignon, Nîmes, and Uzès. To reach Pont du Gard from **Avignon** or **Uzès,** take bus #115 along the Alès-Avignon line (5/day Mon-Fri, 3/day Sat-Sun, 40 minutes from Avignon, 20 minutes from Uzès; check schedules at Avignon's bus station, TI, or at https://lio.laregion.fr). From **Nîmes,** take bus #121 (6/day Mon-Fri, 2/day Sat-Sun, 40 minutes, about €2 one-way). You can also take a bus from **Nîmes Pont Du Gard** station (bus #126, runs 3/day in April-Oct). Combining Pont du Gard with Nîmes and/or Uzès makes a great day trip from Avignon and gives you plenty of bus options when leaving Pont du Gard.

Buses stop at the traffic roundabout 400 yards from the Pont du Gard entry (stop name: Rond Point Pont du Gard; see "Pont du Gard" map). From the bus stop it's about a 15-minute walk to the site. If leaving by bus, make sure you're waiting on the correct side of the traffic circle (stops have schedules posted), and wave your hand to signal the bus to stop for you—otherwise, it may drive on by. When taking any bus in any direction, arrive at stops at least five minutes early, pay the driver (coins or small bills), and verify your stop and direction with the driver.

By Taxi: From Avignon, it's about €60 for a taxi to Pont du Gard (+33 4 90 82 20 20). If you're staying in Avignon and only want to see the Pont du Gard (and not Nîmes or Uzès), consider splurging on a taxi to the aqueduct in the morning, then take the early-afternoon bus back.

ORIENTATION TO PONT DU GARD

There are two riversides at Pont du Gard: the Left Bank (Rive Gauche) and Right Bank (Rive Droite). On the Rive Gauche, you'll find the museums, ticket booth, TI, cafeteria, WCs, and shops—all built into a modern plaza. A restaurant and ice-cream

Pont du Gard

TRAIL ALONG CANAL

PONT DU GARD

Wow!

To Canal Ruins

CANAL TUNNEL

CAFE/ RESTAURANT

Gardon River

Garrigue Natural Area

P Rive Droite DON'T PARK HERE

To Remoulins & Nîmes

MEETING POINT FOR TOUR THROUGH THE AQUEDUCT

MUSEUM COMPLEX
CINEMA, LUDO (KIDS' SPACE), INFO, SHOP, WC & CAFETERIA

P Rive Gauche PARK HERE

To Avignon & Nîmes

B

D-981

To Uzès

D-981

B From Avignon & Nîmes

ROUNDABOUT

To Remoulins, Nîmes, Avignon, Arles & A-9 Freeway

Not to scale:
Roundabout to Museum is a 10-minute walk
Museum to Pont du Gard is a 5-minute walk

NEAR AVIGNON

kiosk are on the Rive Droite side. You'll see the aqueduct in two parts: first the informative museum complex, then the actual river gorge spanned by the ancient bridge.

Cost: €6.50, free for those under 18, includes access to the aqueduct, museum, film, and outdoor *garrigue* nature area; add €8.50 (€6 for those under 18) for tour that includes walking through the top channel of the aqueduct (see below).

Hours: The Pont du Gard site is generally open daily 9:00-21:00, summer months until 22:00 or later, winter months until 20:00. The museum is open Tue-Sun 9:00-18:30, Mon from 12:00, July-Aug until 19:30, shorter hours off-season. Check the website for specifics.

Information: +33 4 66 37 50 99, www.pontdugard.fr.

Pont du Gard After Hours: During summer months, the site is open late so that people can hike, enjoy a picnic or the riverside restaurant, and watch the light show projected on the monument. The parking lot is staffed and guarded until 24:00. Seeing Pont du Gard in the evening is dramatic. The light show is projected from the north, so those in the picnic area and at the restaurant enjoy a good view.

Walking Tour of the Pont Du Gard: This one-hour tour of the sight includes going through a small section of the 4-foot-wide, 6-foot-high, 900-foot-long water channel at the very top of the aqueduct, where you'll walk the route of the water high above the river below. Guides range in quality and lead groups of up to 30 people (English tours available, reserve online in advance). The massive calcium buildup lining the channel from more than 400 years of flowing water is impressive to see. Manhole-cover-like openings allow light in, though a flashlight is helpful to discern details.

Canoe Rental: Floating under Pont du Gard by canoe is an unforgettable experience. **Collias Canoes** will pick you up at Pont du Gard (or elsewhere, if prearranged) and shuttle you to the town of Collias. You'll float down the river to the nearby town of Remoulins, where they'll pick you up and take you back to Pont du Gard (€24, €13 for kids under 12, figure 2 hours—though you can take as long as you like, reserve the day before in July-Aug, +33 4 66 22 87 20, www.canoe-collias.com).

Plan Ahead for Swimming and Hiking: Pont du Gard is perhaps best enjoyed on your back and in the water—bring along a swimsuit and flip-flops for the rocks. (Local guides warn that the bridge can create whirlpools and be dangerous to swim under.) The best Pont du Gard viewpoints are up steep hills with uneven footing—bring good shoes, too.

SIGHTS AT PONT DU GARD

▲Museum

In this state-of-the-art museum (well presented in English), you'll enter to the sound of water and understand the critical role fresh water played in the Roman "art of living." You'll see copies of lead pipes, faucets, and siphons; walk through a mock rock quarry; and learn how they moved those huge rocks into place and how those massive arches were made. A wooden model shows how Roman engineers determined the proper slope. While actual artifacts from the aqueduct are few, the exhibit shows the immensity of the undertaking as well as the payoff. Imagine the jubilation when this extravagant supply of water finally tumbled into Nîmes. A relaxing highlight is the scenic video of a helicopter ride along the entire 30-mile course of the aqueduct, from its start at Uzès all the way to the Castellum in Nîmes.

Other Activities

Several additional attractions are designed to give the sight more meaning (but for most visitors, the museum is sufficient). Skip the 15-minute film showing aqueduct images with no captions or information (in the museum building). The nearby kids' museum, called *Ludo,* offers a scratch-and-sniff teaching experience (in English) of various aspects of Roman life and the importance of water. The extensive outdoor *garrigue* natural area, closer to the aqueduct, features historic crops and landscapes of the Mediterranean.

▲▲▲Viewing the Aqueduct

A broad walkway from the museum complex leads in 10 minutes to the aqueduct. Until a few years ago, this was an actual road—ad-

jacent to the aqueduct—that had spanned the river since 1743. Before crossing the bridge, walk to a terrific riverside viewpoint by continuing under the aqueduct on a stony path, then find two staircases about 50 yards apart leading down to an unobstructed view of the world's second-highest standing Roman structure. (Rome's Colosseum is only 6 feet taller.)

This was the biggest bridge in the whole 30-mile-long aqueduct. The arches are twice the width of standard aqueducts, and the main arch is the largest the Romans ever built—80 feet across (the width of the river). The bridge is about 160 feet high and was originally about 1,200 feet long.

Though the distance from the source (in Uzès, on the museum side of the site) to Nîmes was only 12 miles as the eagle flew, engineers chose the most economical route, winding and zigzagging 30 miles. The water made the trip in 24 hours with a drop of only 40 feet. Ninety percent of the aqueduct is on or under the ground, but a few river canyons like this required bridges. A stone lid hides a four-foot-wide, six-foot-tall chamber lined with waterproof mortar that carried the stream for more than 400 years. For 150 years, this system provided Nîmes with good drinking water. Expert as the Romans were, they miscalculated the backup caused by a downstream corner, and had to add the thin extra layer you can see just under the lid to make the channel deeper.

Walk back to the bridge and stand above the river. The bridge and the river below provide great fun for holiday-goers. While parents sunbathe on rocks, kids splash into the gorge from under the aqueduct. For the most refreshing view, float flat on your back underneath the structure (but beware of whirlpools, which can be dangerous).

The appearance of the entire gorge changed in 2002, when a huge flood flushed lots of greenery downstream. Those floodwaters put Roman provisions to the test. Notice the triangular-shaped buttresses at the lower level—designed to split and divert the force of any flood *around* the feet of the arches rather than *into* them. The

2002 floodwaters reached the top of those buttresses. Anxious park rangers winced at the sounds of trees crashing onto the ancient stones...but the arches stood strong.

The stones that jut out—giving the aqueduct a rough, unfinished appearance—supported the original scaffolding. The protuberances were left, rather than cut off, in anticipation of future repair needs. The lips under the arches supported wooden templates that allowed the stones in the round arches to rest on something until the all-important keystone was dropped into place. Each stone weighs from two to six tons. The structure stands with no mortar (except at the very top, where the water flowed)—taking full advantage of the innovative Roman arch, made strong by gravity.

Cross to the right bank for a closer look and the best views. Soon find steps leading up a short, steep trail (marked *View Point/ Belvédère*). You'll come to the point where the aqueduct meets a rock tunnel, which was built in the 1800s to try to reuse the aqueduct and provide water to Nîmes (it failed). Notice how the aqueduct curves left before the tunnel. Follow the short-but-

rugged trail with the river to your right to several superb lookouts above the aqueduct.

Back on the museum side, steps lead up to the top of the Rive Gauche side of the aqueduct, where tours meet to enter the water channel. From here you can follow the canal path along a trail (marked with red-and-white horizontal lines) to find remains of the Roman canal (spur trails off this path lead to more panoramic views). Hikers can continue along the path, following the red-and-white markings that lead through a forest, after which you'll come across more remains of the canal (much of which are covered by vegetation). There's not much left to see because of medieval cannibalization—frugal builders couldn't resist the precut stones as they constructed area churches. The path continues for about 15 miles, but there's little reason to go farther.

Uzès

Located near the source of the spring that fed the Pont du Gard aqueduct, this intriguing, less-trampled town is officially in Languedoc-Roussillon, not Provence. Uzès (oo-zehs) feels like it must have been important once—and it was, as a bishopric from the fifth century until 1789. Today Uzès offers a refreshing small-town break from serious sightseeing. If you sleep here, try to arrive on a Tuesday or Friday night to enjoy the next morning's market day.

GETTING TO UZES

Uzès is a short hop west of Pont du Gard. It can be reached easily by **bus** from Nîmes (buses #152 and #121, direction: Saint-Ambroix or Pont St-Esprit, both cost €1.60; #152 is much faster—7/day Mon-Fri, 3/day Sat, 1/day Sun, 40 minutes; #121—6/day Mon-Fri, 2/day Sat-Sun, 75 minutes; also #126 from Nîmes Pont du Gard train station—runs 3/day in April-Oct). From Avignon take bus #115, direction: Alès (5/day Mon-Fri, 3/day Sat-Sun, 1 hour, stops near Pont du Gard). Check LiO.LaRegion.fr or call +33 8 10 33 42 73 for schedules. The bus stop for Uzès is Esplanade.

By **car,** Uzès is 15 minutes from Pont du Gard and 45 minutes from Nîmes and Avignon. Drivers will circle the old town on the busy ring road. The TI and hotels that I list are on this ring road.

Orientation to Uzès

The **TI** sits at the top of the ring road on Place Albert I. Pick up the brief self-guided tour brochure in English, with a map of the town—usually available outside when the TI is closed (daily 9:30-18:00, shorter hours and closed Sun in off-season, +33 4 66 22 68 88, www.uzes-pontdugard.uk).

Sights in Uzès

Strolling the Town

The traffic-free, tastefully restored town itself is the sight. It's best seen slowly on foot, with a lingering coffee break in its arcaded and mellow main square, **Place aux Herbes** (not so mellow during the colorful Wed morning market and even bigger Sat market).

In spite of all those bishops, there are no important sights to

visit in Uzès. You can follow the TI's self-guided walking tour, but avoid the dull, overpriced Palace of the Duché de Uzès. The town's trendy boutiques are as numerous as its English-speaking visitors, which give the place an upscale, international feel. The unusual circular tower called Tour Fenestrelle is all that remains of a 12th-century cathedral.

Medieval Garden

Even if you're not a plant enthusiast, pop into the Medieval Garden, a "living herbarium" with plants thought to have curative qualities. The garden is at the foot of the King's and Bishop's towers. The entrance fee includes a little shot of lemongrass tea lovingly delivered by the volunteers who care for this sight.

Cost and Hours: €7; daily 10:30-13:00 & 14:00-18:00 in summer, daily 14:00-18:00 plus Sat-Sun 10:30-13:00 in off-season, closed Nov-March; English handout, Rue Port Royal, +33 4 66 22 38 21.

NEAR UZÈS

The **Musée du Bonbon** candy museum, a mile and a half below Uzès on the road to Avignon and Pont du Gard, explains the history and manufacturing process of Haribo (of Gummi Bears fame). It's interactive and makes a worthwhile detour for kids.

Cost and Hours: €10, kids 5-15-€8, kids under 5 free, daily 10:00-19:00 except closed Mon Sept-June, last entry one hour before closing, +33 4 66 22 74 39, www.museeharibo.fr.

Sleeping and Eating in Uzès

Sleeping: Hotels in Uzès mirror the upscale flavor of the town. Pale-green signs direct drivers to hotels from the ring road.

$$$$ La Maison d'Uzès,***** in the heart of the old town, is filled with modern luxury and nestled in the charm of a beautifully restored 17th-century building. In this boutique hotel, you'll find sumptuous lounges, a gastronomic restaurant, a spa complete with a waterfall Roman bath, and nine well-designed rooms (elevator serves half the rooms, 18 Rue du Docteur Blanchard, +33 4 66 20 07 00, www.lamaisonduzes.fr, contact@lamaisonduzes.fr).

$$ L'Hostellerie Provençale,*** a charming place with nine plush rooms and four *chambres d'hôte*, is just off the ring road, a few blocks after the TI. Breakfast and dinner can be served on their splendid rooftop terrace or downstairs in the cozy restaurant (pricey breakfast on terrace, breakfast included for the four B&B rooms, kitchenette, no elevator, pay parking, restaurant closed Sun-Mon, 1 Rue de la Grande Bourgade, +33 4 66 22 11 06, www. hostellerieprovencale.com, contact@hostellerieprovencale.com).

Eating: When the weather cooperates, it's hard to resist meals on Place aux Herbes, which is lined with appealing cafés. **$$ Terroirs** has inviting seats at a corner on the square and feels like dining inside a high-end épicerie surrounded by shelves of intriguing foods. It's ideal for enjoying small dishes of Provençal tapas, *tartines,* or salads with a glass of local wine (daily, closes at 18:00 in off-season, 5 Place aux Herbes, +33 4 66 03 41 90).

$ Le Zanelli Italian, dishing up pizzas and more, is located on the most prized, tucked-away terrace in the center of Uzès. Leave Place aux Herbes through the passage between #17 and #19 (closed Tue-Wed, 3 Rue Nicolas Froment, +33 4 66 03 01 93).

$ La Tomate Bleue is less central but serves the best pizza in town and has a lovely garden terrace (closed Mon-Wed, 12 Avenue de la Gare, +33 4 66 75 94 42).

$$ Restaurant TEN, located one street north of Place aux Herbes, serves international cuisine in an appealing historic building. Choose between dining under the arcades outside, the trendy but welcoming interior, or the peaceful interior courtyard (closed Mon-Tue, 10 Place Dampmartin, +33 4 66 22 10 93).

To dine well indoors or high above the town on their rooftop terrace, find **$$$ La Parenthèse** restaurant (daily, fixed-price *menu* only) in the recommended L'Hostellerie Provençale.

THE COTES DU RHONE

*Orange • Châteauneuf-du-Pape •
Vaison-la-Romaine • Best of the
Côtes du Rhône Villages •
Côtes du Rhône Drives*

The sunny Côtes du Rhône wine road—one of France's most engaging—starts at Avignon's doorstep and winds north along a mountainous landscape carpeted with vines, studded with warm stone villages, and wrapped in fields of fragrant lavender, all presided over by the wind-scarred Mont Ventoux. The wines of the Côtes du Rhône (grown on the *côtes*, or hillsides, of the Rhône River valley) are easy on the palate and on your budget, as are the area's good-value restaurants. But this hospitable area offers lots more than wine—its hill-capping villages inspire travel posters, its Roman ruins add historical perspective, and the locals seem as excited about their region as you are.

PLANNING YOUR TIME

If you're sleeping in this area, Vaison-la-Romaine is a handy home base, with reasonable bus connections to Avignon and Orange, bike rental, and a mini Pompeii in the town center. For more Roman ruins, visit the awe-inspiring Roman Theater in nearby Orange. Follow my driving tour to get off the beaten path and explore some of the region's most exceptional scenery. With more time, dig deeper into the Côtes du Rhône with a drive up Mont Ventoux, a spin around the Drôme Provençale, or a visit to the Ardèche Gorges (see the self-guided drives at the end of this chapter). Or pedal along peaceful roads to nearby towns. The vineyards' centerpiece, the Dentelles de Montmirail mountains, are laced with hiking trails.

To explore this area, allow two nights for a decent dabble. Drivers should head for the hills (read this chapter's self-guided driving tour before deciding where to stay). If you're without wheels, Vaison-la-Romaine or Orange make the only practical

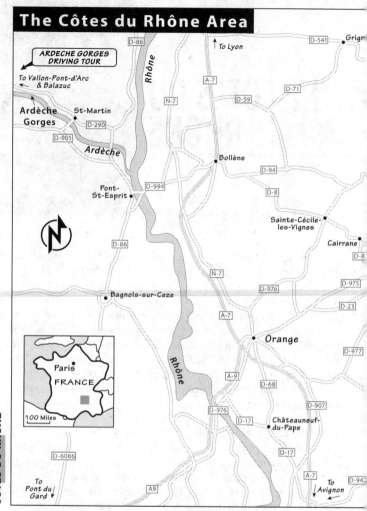

The Côtes du Rhône Area

home bases (good biking, hiking, and minivan tours are vailable from Vaison-la-Romaine).

GETTING AROUND THE COTES DU RHONE

By Car: Pick up Michelin maps #332 or #527. Landmarks like the Dentelles de Montmirail and Mont Ventoux help you get your bearings. I've described my favorite driving route in this region ("Côtes du Rhône Wine Road Drive") near the end of this chapter, along with other drives, including one that connects the Côtes du Rhône with the Luberon region via a scenic saunter over Mont Ventoux.

By Bus: Orange is the transit hub in this area. Buses run to

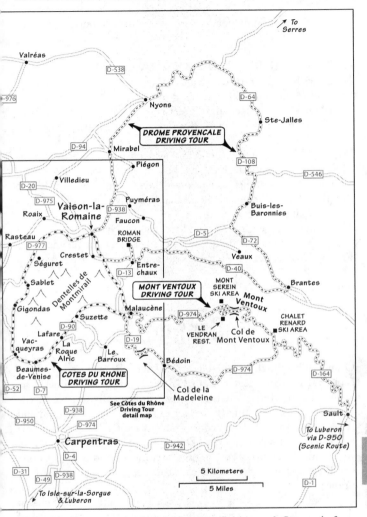

Vaison-la-Romaine (and neighboring Sablet and Séguret) from Avignon and Orange (8/day Mon-Sat, 2/day Sun). It's much faster to take the train to Orange, then transfer to the bus near the train station to reach these villages. A few buses also run from Orange to Châteauneuf-du-Pape, and there's scant service between Orange and several of the wine villages described in this chapter. All routes provide scenic rides through this area. For more details, see the Connections sections in this chapter.

By Train: Trains from Avignon (hourly, 20 minutes) will get you as far as Orange (and bus connections).

By Minivan Tour: There's no shortage of people willing to take you for a ride through this marvelous region—so buyer beware. For my recommendations on wine-focused tours, more general tours, and local guides, see "Tours in Provence" on page 38.

COTES DU RHONE MARKET DAYS

Monday: Bédoin (intimate market, between Vaison-la-Romaine and Mont Ventoux)

Tuesday: Vaison-la-Romaine (great market with produce and antiques/flea market) and Beaumes-de-Venise (smaller, more local market)

Wednesday: Malaucène (good and less touristy market with produce and antiques/flea market, near Vaison-la-Romaine), Buis-les-Baronnies (on recommended loop drive north into the Drôme Provençale), and Sault (handy if you're driving to the Luberon area)

Thursday: Orange (produce and local goods), Nyons (great market with produce and antiques/flea market), and Vacqueyras

Friday: Châteauneuf-du-Pape (small market) and Carpentras (big market)

Saturday: Sainte-Cécile-les-Vignes, near Vaison-la-Romaine

Orange

Orange (oh-rahnzh) is notable for its grand Roman arch and exceptional Roman Theater. Called "Arausio" in Roman times, Orange was a thriving city in those days—strategically situated on the Via Agrippa, connecting the important Roman cities of Lyon and Arles. It was founded as a comfortable place for Roman army officers to enjoy their retirement. Did the emperor want thousands of well-trained, relatively young guys hanging around Rome? I don't think so. What to do? "How about a nice place in the south of France...?"

Today's Orange is a busy, workaday city with a gritty charm that reminds me of Arles. Leafy café-lined squares, a handful of traffic-free streets, a fine Hôtel de Ville (City Hall), and that theater all give the town some serious street appeal. For some, Orange works well as a base, with its quick access to the Côtes du Rhône wine villages by car (slower but OK by bus) and quick rail access to Avignon (which even drivers should consider).

Orientation to Orange

TOURIST INFORMATION

The TI is located next to the fountain and parking area at 5 Cours Aristide Briand (Mon-Sat 9:00-12:30 & 14:00-18:00—no lunch break July-Aug, Sun 9:00-12:30; shorter hours and closed Sun in off-season; +33 4 90 34 70 88, www.orange-tourisme.fr).

Market Day: Thursday is market day, and it's a big deal here, with all the town's streets and squares crammed with produce and local goods for sale until 12:30. I like this market because it focuses on locals' needs and not touristy kitsch.

ARRIVAL IN ORANGE

By Train: Orange's train station is a level 15-minute walk from the Roman Theater (or an €8 taxi ride, +33 6 66 71 58 02). The recommended Logis Hôtel de Provence will store your bags (€5, across from the station) or try www.eelway.com/en/luggage-storage/orange. To walk into town from the station, head straight out of the station (down Avenue Frédéric Mistral), merge left onto Orange's main shopping street (Rue de la République), then turn left on Rue Caristie; you'll run into the Roman Theater's massive stage wall.

By Bus: All buses stop at Cours Pourtoules (at the *Théâtre* parking lot), two blocks from the Roman Theater; the bus to Vaison-la-Romaine also stops on Avenue Frédéric Mistral, a few blocks from the train station toward the center.

By Car: Follow *Centre-Ville* signs, then *Office du Tourisme* or *Théâtre Antique* signs; park as close to the Roman Theater's huge wall as you can. If coming from the autoroute take *sortie 21*, then park near the TI on Cours Aristide Briand. If coming from Avignon on D-907, park where you see *Parking Théâtre* signs. If arriving on a Thursday morning—market day—expect lots of traffic and scarce parking. Your best bets are to park along the road leading to the train station or near the Roman arch (both a 15-minute walk to the center). Parking by the Roman arch is free; all parking in Orange's center is metered (leave nothing visible in parked cars).

Sights in Orange

▲▲▲Roman Theater (Théâtre Antique)

Orange's ancient theater is the best preserved in existence and the only such theater in Europe with its (awesome) acoustic wall still standing. Built in the first century AD, the huge theater celebrated the glory of the empire and cemented Rome's presence in Provence. Strolling along the outside of its massive wall is an impressive experience today—imagine how it must have intimidated visitors 2,000 years ago.

Cost and Hours: €10, drops to €9 one hour before closing; includes good audioguide (not available within an hour of closing) and entry to the small museum across the street; if visiting the ancient sites in Nîmes, consider the €18.50 Nîmes-Orange

Pass, which also covers Nîmes' Roman arena, Maison Carrée, and Magne Tower, www.arenes-nimes.com; daily 9:00-18:00, June-Aug until 19:00, shorter hours Oct-March, closing times can change for evening performances or rehearsals; +33 4 90 51 17 60, www.theatre-antique.com.

Cheap Trick: Vagabonds wanting a partial but free view of the theater (or others wanting a bird's-eye view) can find it in the

Parc de la Colline St-Eutrope. Walk around to the left of the theater (see the "Orange" map, earlier), and find the steps to the right, just after the *tabac*. Climb the steps, keep left at the first fork, and continue for about 150 yards, then take the steps to the right to the top. From here, follow the *Point de Vue* sign to the right. Benches and grassy areas make this a good picnic spot (no WCs), and you can scamper about for views of the theater from different angles.

Eating: The café in the theater, La Grotte d'Auguste, has reasonably priced snacks and lunches plus views (closed Sun-Mon, +33 4 90 60 22 54). A shaded, café-filled square, Place de la République, is two blocks from the theater up Rue Segond-Weber.

Visiting the Theater: As you enter, to the right you'll see a huge dig devoted to the Temple to the Cult of the Emperor (English explanations posted). But we'll turn left, into the theater.

Climb the steep stairs to find a seat high up to appreciate the massive acoustical theater wall, one of the greatest surviving examples of Roman architecture. Imagine that 2,000 years ago, Orange residents enjoyed grand spectacles here, with high-tech sound and lighting effects—such as simulated thunder, lightning, and rain. If you've been to Arles' Ancient History Museum, conjure up the theater model there and visualize this place covered with brilliant white marble.

From the center of the acoustic wall, a grandiose **Caesar** overlooks everything, reminding attendees of who's in charge.

If it seems like you've seen this statue before, you probably have. Countless identical sculptures were mass-produced in Rome and shipped throughout the empire to grace buildings like this for propaganda purposes. To save money on shipping and handling, only the heads of these statues were changed with each new ruler. The permanent body wears a breastplate emblazoned with the imperial griffin (body of a lion, head and wings of an eagle) that only the emperor could wear. When a new emperor came to power, new heads were made in Rome and shipped off throughout the empire to replace the pop-off heads on these statues. (Imagine Donald Trump's head on Barack Obama's body—on second thought...)

Archaeologists believe that a puny, vanquished Celt was included at the knee of the emperor, touching his ruler's robe respectfully—a show of humble subservience to the emperor. It's interest-

COTES DU RHONE

ing to consider how an effective propaganda machine can con the masses into being impressed by their leader.

The horn has blown. It's time to find your **seat:** row 2, number 30. Sitting down, you're comforted by the "EQ GIII" carved into the seat (*Equitas Gradus* #3...three rows for the Equestrian order). You're not comforted by the hard limestone bench (thinking it'll probably last 2,000 years). The theater is filled with people. Thankfully, you mix only with your class, the nouveau riche—merchants, tradespeople, and city big shots. The people seated above you are the working class, and way up in the "chicken roost" section are slaves, beggars, and sex workers. Scanning the orchestra section (where the super-rich sit on real chairs), you notice the town dignitaries hosting some visiting VIPs.

OK, time to worship. Around the stage, they're parading a bust of the emperor from its sacred home in the adjacent temple. Next is the ritual animal sacrifice called *la pompa* (so fancy, future generations will use that word for anything full of such...pomp). Finally, you settle in for an all-day series of spectacles and dramatic entertainment. All eyes are on the big stage door in the middle—where the Emma Stones and Samuel L. Jacksons of the day will appear. (Lesser actors use the side doors.)

The play is good, but many spectators are here for the half-time shows—jugglers, acrobats, and striptease dancers. In Roman times, the theater was a festival of immorality. An ancient writer commented, "The vanquished take their revenge on us by giving us their vices through the theater."

With an audience of 10,000 and no amplification, **acoustics** were critical. A partial roof made of wood was originally suspended over the stage, somewhat like the glass and iron roof you see today (installed to protect the stage wall). The original was designed not to protect the stage from the weather but to project the voices of the actors into the crowd (see if you can eavesdrop on people by the stage). For further help, actors wore masks with leather caricature mouths that functioned as megaphones. The theater's side walls originally rose as high as the stage wall and supported a retractable awning (called a velarium) that gave the audience some protection from the sun or rain. (When you leave the theater, look up to the stage wall from the outside and notice the supports for poles that held the velarium in place, like the masts and sails of a ship.)

The Roman Theater was all part of the "give them bread and circuses" approach to winning the support of the masses. Its spectacles grew from 65 days of games per year when the theater was first built (and when Rome was at its height) to about 180 days each year by the time Rome finally fell.

In the fourth century (under Christian emperor Constantine), the Church forced many theaters to close their doors, and eventually this one was abandoned and forgotten. The entire seating area filled up with sand—effectively preserving it.

Later, during the barbarian invasions, the stage wall became a protective wall, essentially creating a secure zone for many residences. Amazingly, people squatted here until the 19th century, when the theater was finally dug out—in nearly perfect condition.

Nearby: Pop into the **Musée d'Art et d'Histoire** across the street (covered by theater ticket, otherwise €5.50, free audioguide, same hours as theater) to see a few theater details and a rare Roman land register, ordered by Emperor Vespasian in AD 79. Carved on marble, this was an official record of property ownership—each square represented a 120-acre plot of land. The fine mosaics and carvings displayed here humanize what are otherwise stony ancient ruins.

▲Roman "Arc de Triomphe"

This 60-foot-tall arch is in the center of a pleasant traffic circle, a level 15-minute walk north of the theater. Technically the only real Roman arches of triumph are in Rome's Forum—they were built to commemorate various emperors' victories. But this arch was the model for those in Rome, preceding the famous arches of Septimius Severus and Constantine. It was erected in about AD 19 to commemorate the Roman general Germanicus and one of the bloodiest battles in the conquest of Gaul. The facade is covered with reliefs of military exploits, including naval battles and Romans beating up on barbarians and those rude, nasty Gauls. (Around the arch, you'll find easy free parking and a picnic site.)

Hôtel de Ville

Orange owns a fine City Hall, worth the short detour to appreciate it (in the heart of the old town on Place Georges Clemenceau).

Sleeping and Eating in Orange

Sleeping: $ Hôtel le Glacier,*** across from the TI, is run by English-speaking and affable Philippe. It's a good value, with easy parking, a comfortable lobby with a bar, and well-designed rooms (book direct for a free upgrade when available, elevator, air-con, a few parking spaces, 46 Cours Aristide Briand, +33 4 90 34 02 01, www.le-glacier.com, info@le-glacier.com). The hotel also has a café-bistro with fair prices and a good selection.

¢ Logis Hôtel de Provence,** across from the train station, is a great value with simple but comfortable rooms, tight bathrooms, a pleasant café and restaurant, and a small pool (60 Avenue Frédéric Mistral, +33 4 90 60 58 63, www.logishotels.com, hoteldeprovence@orange.fr).

Eating: Orange has several inviting squares with ample eating

COTES DU RHONE

choices in all price ranges. A few cafés/restaurants are across from the **theater**; this is where I like to eat while gazing at the stage wall. You'll find more choices by wandering the lanes toward the Hôtel de Ville. For a more refined meal, **$$$ Au Petit Patio** delivers elegant dining and fine cuisine, which is best enjoyed on its lovely namesake patio (closed Wed-Thu for dinner and all day Sun, 58 Cours Aristide Briand, +33 4 90 29 69 27).

Orange Connections

From Orange by Train to: Avignon (hourly, 20 minutes), **Arles** (6/day direct, 45 minutes, more frequent with transfer in Avignon), **Lyon** (16/day, 2 hours, some require transfer).

By Bus to: Vaison-la-Romaine (bus #4, 8/day Mon-Sat, 2/day Sun, 1 hour; bus continues to **Sablet** and **Séguret**), **Avignon** (bus #2, hourly Mon-Fri, 8/day Sat, 2/day Sun, 1 hour), **Châteauneuf-du-Pape** (bus #23, 6/day Mon-Sat, none on Sun, 20 minutes). For all bus service, check www.rome2rio.com.

Buses to Vaison-la-Romaine and other wine villages depart from near the train station and from Cours Pourtoules (see "Orange" map, earlier). Because of occasional route changes, bus #4 to Vaison-la-Romaine may depart across from the bus shelter (look for blue bus icon or verify with any bus driver at the shelter).

Châteauneuf-du-Pape

This most famous of the Côtes du Rhône wine villages is busy with tourists eager to sample its famous product and navigate its climbing lanes. While I prefer the less famous wine villages farther north (described later, under "The Best of the Côtes du Rhône Villages"), this welcoming, wine-drenched town makes an easy day trip from Avignon and works well with a visit to nearby Orange.

Châteauneuf-du-Pape, meaning "New Castle of the Pope," is named for the pope's summer retreat—now a ruin capping the beautiful-to-see but little-to-do hill town (more interesting during the Friday market). Wine-loving popes planted the first vines here in the 1300s. The pope's crest is embossed on all bottles of this deservedly famous wine.

Approaching from Avignon, signs announce, *"Here start the vineyards of Châteauneuf-du-Pape."* Pull over and stroll into a vineyard with a view of the hill town. Notice the rocky soil—perfect for making a good wine grape. Those stones retain the sun's heat (plentiful here) and force the vines to struggle, resulting in a lean grape—lousy for eating but ideal for producing big wines (see "Côtes du Rhône Wines" on page 48). To make the local specialty, which has been strictly controlled for 80 years, a total of 13 different grapes may be blended, but vintners typically use just eight of those. Grenache dominates the blend, accounting for about 75 percent of the grapes grown. Syrah and mourvèdre are the next two most-used grapes, each contributing about 10 percent to the final blend. The most interesting white wines in Provence are also made here (a blend of up to five grapes), but the reds get all the attention. Most don't show their full flavor until at least five years after bottling. For more information on the area's wines, look for the Wine Museum (described later) at the start of the village as you come from Avignon.

Orientation to Châteauneuf-du-Pape

Arrival in Châteauneuf-du-Pape: If you're coming by **car,** park below the hill town, then walk following *Château* signs a few blocks up to the main square, Place du Portail, with its small fountain.

Tourist Information: The helpful TI by Place du Portail has a long list of wineries you can visit and good documentation on the area (Mon-Sat 9:30-18:00, closed Sun—except in July-Aug, shorter hours off-season, 3 Rue de la République, +33 4 90 83 71 08, www.chateauneuf-du-pape-tourisme.fr). Appealing streets fan out from here, most with cellars selling the famous wine.

Sights in Châteauneuf-du-Pape

Wine Museum (Musée du Vin)

Located at the Brotte Winery, this museum provides an excellent background for your Côtes du Rhône exploration. Use the audioguide for a 40-minute tour of the Côtes du Rhône exhibits, which explain the basics of grape growing, the winemaking process, and the work of a *vigneron*, after which you'll enjoy a tasting. The English-speaking staff are ready to help you make your choices, though it helps to tell them what you like. For a clear contrast, taste the "ready-to-drink" wine (*La Fiole du Pape*), which made the winery famous, then a wine "to keep" (*vin de garde*).

Cost and Hours: €6, includes three wines to taste, daily 9:00-13:00 & 14:00-19:00 (no lunch break June-mid-Sept), off-season 9:00-12:00 & 14:00-18:00, on Avenue Pierre de Luxembourg, at start of village if coming from Avignon, +33 4 90 83 59 44, www. brotte.com.

Wine Tasting

The town offers countless places to taste wine. If you have trouble deciding, try any of the following three.

Near the TI: These two cellars are central. With your back to the TI, find (on your left) **The Best Vintage** *cave,* a top place to sample Châteauneuf-du-Pape wines. Speaking fluent English and offering wines from 35 different producers, Stéphane provides a good introduction to area wines in the small shop he runs with business partner Danièle. They can arrange shipping back to the States—expensive but you're spared the VAT tax (daily 10:30-12:30 & 13:30-18:30, shorter hours Nov-Feb, near Place du Portail at 7 Rue de la République, +33 4 90 83 31 75, www.thebestvintage. fr). A basic WC is next door.

A few doors farther down this street and up the staircase, find **Vinadéa Maison des Vins,** where they sell more than 200 kinds of Châteauneuf-du-Pape appellation wines from 120 different producers and offer a free tasting selection every day. Thomas speaks English (daily 10:00-13:00 & 14:00-18:30, shorter hours Oct-May, 8 Rue Maréchal Foch, +33 4 90 83 70 69, www.vinadea. com).

Uphill from Place du Portail: Several blocks above Place du Portail is **Cave du Verger des Papes,** best suited for more serious tasters. Enter the glass door for tastings with friendly Claude-Richard and a look at underground ruins from Roman times (free, rotating selection of 3-4 wines, best to call ahead, Tue-Sun 10:00-18:30, 2 Rue Montée du Château, +33 4 90 83 58 08, www. caveduverger.com).

Sleeping and Eating in Châteauneuf-du-Pape

Sleeping: To bed down in Châteauneuf-du-Pape, try the traditional **$$ Hôtel-Restaurant La Garbure,** ideally located one door up the (mostly) pedestrian street from the TI (3 Rue Joseph Ducos, +33 4 90 83 75 08, www.la-garbure.com).

Eating: You'll find several appealing eateries around Place du Portail on Rue Joseph Ducos. It's well worth the time and energy to follow signs up the hill to **$$$ Le Verger des Papes,** a fine restaurant where you can feast both on the terrace views and on their traditional, sophisticated cuisine. Their €37 dinner *menu* is a great deal if you're hungry (closed Sun evenings and all day Mon, reservations smart, 4 Rue Montée du Château—drivers can follow

Château signs and park at the top to skip the climb, +33 4 90 83 50 40, www.vergerdespapes.com).

For **picnic** supplies, try one of the three cafés that surround the TI, all of which will make their sandwiches to go—or find the small grocery, **Le Cigalou,** halfway up Rue Joseph Ducos (daily 8:00-12:30, also Tue-Fri 15:30-19:30).

Vaison-la-Romaine

With quick access to vineyards, villages, and Mont Ventoux, this lively little town of 6,000 makes a good base for exploring the Côtes du Rhône region by car, by bike, or on foot. You get two villages for the price of one: Vaison-la-Romaine's "modern" lower city has Roman ruins, a lone pedestrian street, and the lively, café-lined main square—Place Montfort. The car-free medieval hill town looms above, with meandering cobbled lanes, a handful of cafés and art galleries, and a ruined castle. (Vaison-la-Romaine is also a good place to have your hair done, since there are more than 20 hairdressers in this small town.)

Orientation to Vaison-la-Romaine

The city is split in two by the Ouvèze River. A Roman-era bridge connects the lower town (Ville-Basse) with the hill-capping medieval upper town (Ville-Haute).

TOURIST INFORMATION

The TI is in the lower city, between the two Roman ruin sites, at Place du Chanoine Sautel (July-Aug daily 9:00-18:45 except closed midday on weekends; Sept-June Mon-Sat 9:30-12:00 & 14:00-17:45, Sun 9:30-12:00—except closed Sun mid-Oct-March; +33 4 90 36 02 11, www.vaison-ventoux-tourisme.com). Say *bonjour* to the *charmante* and ever-so-patient staff, use the free Wi-Fi, ask about

festivals and other events, and pick up information on walks and bike rides.

COTES DU RHONE

Vaison-la-Romaine

Accommodations
- ① Hôtel le Beffroi & Restaurant la Fontaine
- ② L'Evêché Chambres
- ③ Hôtel Burrhus
- ④ Les Tilleuls d'Elisée

Eateries, Nightlife & Other
- ⑤ La Table
- ⑥ Le Bistro Panoramique
- ⑦ Crêperie & Pizzeria
- ⑧ La Bartavelle
- ⑨ La Lyriste
- ⑩ O'Natur'elles
- ⑪ Brasserie l'Annexe
- ⑫ L'Arbre à Vins, Le Comptoir des Voconces & Grocery
- ⑬ Le Patio
- ⑭ To Auberge d'Anaïs & La Fleur Bleue
- ⑮ Launderette (2)
- ⑯ To Bike Rental

CÔTES DU RHÔNE

ARRIVAL IN VAISON-LA-ROMAINE

By Bus: For most, taking the train from Avignon to Orange and then the bus to Vaison-la-Romaine is the best way to get here. Bus stops are near the Cave la Romaine winery on the edge of the lower town. Tell the driver you want the stop for the Office de Tourisme. When you get off the bus, walk five minutes down Avenue Général de Gaulle to reach the TI and recommended hotels.

By Car: Follow signs to *Centre-Ville*, then *Office de Tourisme*, and park in or near the big lot across from the TI. Parking is free in Vaison-la-Romaine. If your hotel is the upper town—Ville-Haute—see "Sleeping in Vaison-la-Romaine" later in this chapter.

HELPFUL HINTS

Market Day: Sleep in Vaison-la-Romaine on Monday night, and you'll wake to an amazing Tuesday market. If you spend a Monday night, ask your hotelier where you can park—avoid parking at market sites and where signs indicate *Stationnement Interdit le Mardi*, or you won't find your car where you left it.

Supermarket: A handy **Casino** is on Place Montfort in the thick of the cafés (Mon-Sat until 19:00, closed Sun).

Laundry: The friendly owners at **Laverie la Lavandière** will do your laundry while you sightsee (Cours Taulignan, near Avenue Victor Hugo, Mon-Sat 9:00-12:00 & 15:00-18:00, closed Sun). The self-service **launderette** at the Super U store on Avenue Marcel Pagnol has longer hours.

Bike Rental: The TI has a list. **Sun-e-bike** is the most central, with electric and regular bikes (161 Avenue René Cassin, +33 9 54 94 99 14, www.sun-e-bike.com).

Taxi: Call +33 4 90 36 00 04 or +33 4 90 46 89 42.

Car Rental: You can rent cars by the day, though they must be returned to Vaison-la-Romaine and supply is limited; ask at the TI for locations. Better yet, rent a car more dependably in nearby Orange, where most major companies have offices.

Local Guide: Scottish by birth, attorney by profession, and yoga instructor by passion, **Janet Henderson** offers enthusiastic and educational walks of Vaison-la-Romaine that bring those Roman ruins and medieval buildings to life (€30/person, minimum 3 people or €120, allow 2.5 hours, +33 6 42 24 65 56, www.provencehistorytours.com).

Tourist Train: The **Petit Train** stops in front of the TI and does a 35-minute loop around the town (€5, free for kids under 12, daily July-Aug 10:00-17:00, Sept-June 14:00-17:00).

After-Dinner Fun: You won't party late in this quiet town, but there are a few fun places to consider. Place Montfort has most of the action: **Brasserie L'Annexe** has the warmest interior, **Le Comptoir des Voconces** is a happening hangout with a pub-like ambience, and **L'Arbre à Vins** draws wine-sipping types (all described later). Below the Roman bridge, **Le Patio** has cool wine-bar action at the back of its restaurant (closed Wed-Thu and Sun, 4 Rue de Ventoux).

Sights in Vaison-la-Romaine

Vaison's top sights are its Gallo-Roman ruins—Puymin and Villasse. Start your sightseeing day at the Puymin site, then follow my short self-guided walk to tie together Vaison's other sights. Pick up the detailed city map from the tourist office before you begin.

Roman Ruins

A modern road splits the town's Gallo-Roman ruins into two well-presented sites, Puymin and La Villasse. The Puymin side has more to see and gives a good introduction to these ruins, thanks to its small museum offering insight into life during the Roman Empire (see below). For helpful background about Roman civilization, read "The Romans in Provence" on page 42.

Cost and Hours: €9 ticket admits you to both sites; daily 9:30-18:00, Oct-March 9:30-12:00 & 14:00-17:00, closed Jan; good audioguide-€2, +33 4 90 36 50 48, www.vaison-la-romaine.com.

Visiting the Puymin Ruins: Near the entry are the modest ruins of a sprawling mansion. Find the faint remains of a colorful frescoed wall and mosaic floors, as well as a few wells, used before Vaison's two aqueducts were built. Climb the short hill to the good little **museum** (pick up your audioguide here; exhibits also well explained in an English loaner booklet). Artifacts include lead water pipes, well-preserved mosaic floors, and a few models of ancient buildings. Don't miss the 12-minute **film** (plays in English every other showing) that takes you inside the homes and daily life of wealthy Vaison residents some 2,000 years ago. A five-minute walk behind

the museum leads to a largely rebuilt (but still used) 6,000-seat **theater**—just enough seats for the whole town, then and now.

• *Exiting the Puymin site will deposit you just above the TI—and the start of my self-guided walk, next (see the "Vaison-la-Romaine" map).*

Self-Guided Walk from the Roman Ruins to the Roman Bridge

• *Allow 45 minutes for this level, crosstown ramble. We'll start at the back of the parking lot that's across from the TI, behind La Poste. Look for a railing overlooking the Villasse archaeological site.*

La Villasse Ruins: When the Romans took over Provence (second century BC), the people of Vaison-la-Romaine sided with their vanquishers, earning themselves a preferred "federated" relationship with Rome (rather than being a simple colony). Rome invested heavily in Vaison, and this, along with a healthy farming economy (olives and vineyards) and good weather, made it a most prosperous place...as a close look at these sprawling ruins demonstrates. Emperor Augustus, who ruled the empire at the time, worked to build cities in the image of Rome.

About 6,000 people called Vaison-la-Romaine home 2,000 years ago. The Roman town extended from where you're standing to the Ouvèze River (to the left, or south). The ancient forum (not excavated) lies between you and the river. At 172 acres, Vaison covered about the same area as Roman Arles (Nîmes was over double that size). And like Arles, Vaison was a river port, boasting aqueducts, a big theater, baths, a forum, busy shopping streets, and the trophy homes of wealthy businessmen. Trade thrived in Vaison-la-Romaine thanks to an extensive system of roads connecting it to other cities, a stable economy, and a common currency.

When the barbarians arrived in the fifth century AD, the Romans were booted out, and the townspeople fled from their unprotected neighborhoods—which had no defensive walls—into the hills (see "The Life of a Hill Town" sidebar, later). The town's population has only recently recovered from those barbaric times, with the number of residents again reaching Roman-era levels.

If you have a ticket, you can walk through the Villasse ruins, though you can see everything from the sidewalks that run along the perimeter—which is our plan. What you can see of both Puymin and Villasse is only about 10 percent of the Roman town's extent—most is still buried under today's city.

Make your way behind the post office to the corner and turn right (Rue Trogue Pompée). The ruins stretch behind the stone and green-metal fence that runs the length of this street. Stop in about 30 steps, before reaching the tall arch. Just uphill, spot the rusted wire mesh that covers parts of a Roman sewer that was used until the 1900s. Look up: That tall arch was the centerpiece of a public Roman bath and fitness center. Notice the public latrines next door. The stone channel in front of the toilets had running water that men used to rinse the public sponge (usually attached to a stick—before the invention of toilet paper). Hmmm.

The stone-paved street running perpendicularly below you was lined with shops. The columns and remnants on the left side are what's left of two mega-homes. The one-percenters needed plenty of room to house their extended families and slaves, to accommodate their own private baths, and to carry out public business. You won't see the homes of poorer folks, as they were built from cheap materials that didn't wear well.

Continue straight along the pedestrian walkway that hugs the ruins. Stop just after passing the terra-cotta roof structure. This was the Maison aux Animaux Sauvages, where wild animals were kept (as in a zoo) before doing battle with gladiators in Vaison's theater. Lean over the railing and peer right, just after the terra-cotta roof, to see a faded but original floor mosaic.

Continuing along, you'll pass scads of ruins waiting for someone to identify their purpose—imagine hair salons, bakeries, banks, and brothels. That proud statue across the ruins is of a Roman general—a gentle reminder for locals about who was in charge.

• *Turn left as you leave the ruins behind. You'll pass a lovely garden, then turn right at the first little path you come to. Stop when you reach the back of...*

Notre-Dame de Nazareth Cathedral: As you approach this medieval church, look at its base to find the stubs of Roman columns that form its foundation. This is a perfect example of how the traditions of the Roman Empire lived on through the Catholic Church (Latin became the language of the Mass; senators became bishops; emperors become popes; and Roman law courts—called basilicas—became churches like this). This church wasn't built until 600 years after the Romans left, due in large part to a lack of security in the lower town. The first church built over the Roman ruins was abandoned in the early Middle Ages, when residents fled to the relative safety of the upper town; the present building dates from the 11th to 12th century.

Walk left, then right, to view the church from its side. Appreciate the simple exterior. This is a fine example of Romanesque architecture: heavy arches, few windows, and little exterior decoration. Notice the intricate frieze under the eaves. You can enter the church through the side door in front of you. Find the ancient column from the preceding church. Inside, you'll see almost no art—just pure stonework and nothing to detract from the focus on God.

• *With your back to the church's side entrance, walk out to the street and turn left on Avenue Jules Ferry, then veer right (at the green house) onto Quai Louis Pasteur. After a long block, angle through the parking lot and find a spot above the river.*

Medieval Hill Town: During the Roman era, Vaison was

a port, and its river was navigable by flat-bottom boats with sails (hard to fathom today).

Look up to the medieval village. From the fourth century onward, Vaison-la-Romaine was ruled by a prince-bishop. When the sitting prince-bishop came under attack by the count of Toulouse in the 12th century, he built the abandoned castle you see on the top of this rocky outcrop (about 1195). Over time, the townspeople followed, vacating the lower town and building their homes behind the upper town's fortified wall—where they stayed until after the French Revolution. The castle housed the count of Toulouse who protected the town for a while, but the count was eventually chased out by the armies of a Cathar-hating pope and a land-grabbing French king. The bell tower, now crowned by a lovely 18th-century wrought-iron bell cage (beautiful at night), tolled to announce curfew, to warn of danger, or to signal important public events. The hill town was sealed tight after-hours.

• *Continue along the river to the corner of the parking area closest to the Roman bridge and find the information panel.*

Roman Bridge: The Romans cut this sturdy, no-nonsense vault into the canyon rock 2,000 years ago. Until the 20th century, this was the only way to cross the Ouvèze River. A vicious 1992 flood crested well above the bridge, and locals still talk of how water flowed through the windows and doors of the buildings on your left. The flood destroyed several other modern bridges downstream but couldn't budge the 55-foot Roman arch supporting the bridge.

• *Exit the parking lot, turning right, and make your way up to the bridge.*

Read the information panel on the left side of the bridge, then find the small dark plaque *(crue du 22 09 92)* on the wall to the right, showing the high-water mark of the record flood that killed 30 people. A 50-yard detour down the road (with the river to your right) leads to good views of the hill town's rock-hugging Catholic church (it replaced Notre-Dame de Nazareth when folks fled the lower town).

• *Our walk is over. From here, you have two choices: Explore the medieval lanes of the upper town, or meander the shops and main square of the lower town.*

Upper Town (Ville-Haute): To reach the upper town, hike across the Roman bridge and up to the right (passing a WWI memorial), looping around and through the medieval gate, under the lone tower. Although there's nothing of particular importance to see in the medieval town, the cobbled lanes and enchanting fountains make you want to break out a sketchpad. Look for occasional English information plaques as you meander. The château itself is closed, and the view from the steep, uneven trail to its base does not merit the effort.

Lower Town (Ville-Basse): To reach Place Montfort, the TI, and the main parking lots, from the Roman bridge do an about-face and walk up the pedestrian-only Grande Rue, Vaison's main shopping street. The modern town centers on café-friendly Place Montfort. Tables grab the north side of the square, conveniently sheltered from the prevailing mistral wind while enjoying the generous shade of the ubiquitous plane trees.

▲▲Market Day

In the 16th century, the pope gave Vaison-la-Romaine market-town status. Each Tuesday morning since then, the town has hosted a farmers market. Today merchants turn the main squares and streets in town into a festival of produce and Provençal products. This market is one of France's best, but it can challenge claustrophobes. Be warned that parking is a real headache unless you arrive early (see "Helpful Hints," earlier).

Wine Tasting

Cave la Romaine, a five-minute walk up Avenue Général de Gaulle from the TI, offers a big variety of good-value wines from nearby villages in a pleasant, well-organized tasting room (free tastes, Mon-Sat 9:00-12:30 & 14:00-18:30, Sun 9:00-12:00, Avenue St-Quenin, +33 4 90 36 55 90, www.cave-la-romaine.com).

▲Hiking and Biking

Stop at the TI for detailed information on hikes into the hills above Vaison-la-Romaine. Consider hiking one way and taking a taxi back (best to arrange pickup in advance—ask your hotelier). The TI also has details on several manageable bike routes, with good directions in English, as well as information on more mountain-biking trails (also available at bike shops).

It's about 1.5 hours to the quiet hill town of Crestet on foot and a fun mountain bike ride. To find the trail, bike, drive, or walk on Chemin des Bois Communaux, the road behind the castle in the upper town (with the rock base and castle on your left), continue onto Chemin des Fontaines (blue signs), and stay the course as far as you like (follow yellow *Crestet* signs). Cars are not allowed on the road after about a mile—during which you'll pass some homes but almost no cars.

You can hike the five-mile route to **Séguret,** but it is better by bike as it's on a paved lane (allow two hours on foot). Take the same road above Vaison-la-Romaine and look for a yellow sign *(Sablet/ Coste Belle)* to the right and stay straight. Bikers should loop back to Vaison via the D-88 and D-977. Walkers might consider doing the first half-mile for nice views over Vaison and its castle.

If the air's calm, the five-mile ride to cute little **Villedieu** is a delight. The bike route is signed along small roads; from Vaison-la-Romaine, find the road to Villedieu at the roundabout by Cave la Romaine (see "Vaison-la-Romaine" map).

Alternatively, get a good map and connect the following villages for an enjoyable 11-mile **loop ride**: Vaison-la-Romaine, St-Romain-en-Viennois, Puyméras, Faucon, and St-Marcellin-lès-Vaison.

Sleeping in Vaison-la-Romaine

Hotels in Vaison-la-Romaine are a good value and are split between the upper medieval village (with all the steps) and the lower main town (with all the services). Those in the upper village (Ville-Haute) are quieter, cozier, cooler, and give you the feeling of sleeping in a hill town (some come with views), with all the services of a real town just steps away. But they require a 10-minute walk down to the town center and Roman ruins. None of the hotels listed has an elevator, and few have air-conditioning.

If you have a car, consider staying in one of the Côtes du Rhône villages near Vaison-la-Romaine. I've listed a few nearby places here; for more suggestions see the "Côtes du Rhône Wine Road Drive," later.

IN THE UPPER TOWN

If staying in the upper village with a car, follow signs to *Cité Médiévale* and park just outside the upper village entry (driving into the Cité Médiévale itself is a challenge, with tiny lanes and nearly impossible parking).

$$ Hôtel le Beffroi*** hides deep in the upper town, just above a demonstrative bell tower (which stops demonstrating at 22:00). The hotel offers 16th-century red-tile-and-wood-beamed-cozy lodgings with nary a level surface. The rooms—split between two buildings a few doors apart—are Old World comfy, and some have views. You'll enjoy antique-filled public spaces, a view-filled garden, a small pool with more views, and a helpful staff at reception (several good family rooms, closed mid-Jan-March, Rue de l'Evêché, +33 4 90 36 04 71, www.le-beffroi.com, hotel@le-beffroi.com). The hotel has a **$$$ restaurant** with pleasant outdoor seating in fine weather (see "Eating in Vaison-la-Romaine," later).

$ L'Evêché Chambres, a few doors away from Hôtel le Beffroi, is a five-room melt-in-your-chair B&B. The charming own-ers (the Verdiers) have a fine sense of interior design and are pas-sionate about books, making this place feel like a cross between a library and an art gallery (the *solanum* suite is worth every euro). Expect many steps for some rooms and some tricky footing (Rue de l'Evêché, +33 4 90 36 13 46, eveche.free.fr, eveche@aol.com).

IN THE LOWER TOWN

$ Hôtel Burrhus**** is equal parts contemporary art gallery and funky-creaky hotel—but a good value. It's a central, laid-back place, with a broad, terrific terrace over Place Montfort and sur-prisingly big rooms (for maximum quiet, request a back room). Its floor plan will confound even the ablest navigator (air-con, 1 Place Montfort, +33 4 90 36 00 11, www.burrhus.com, info@burrhus. com).

$ Les Tilleuls d'Elisée is a terrific *chambres d'hôte* in a stone, blue-shuttered home in an orchard of olive and linden trees near the Notre-Dame de Nazareth Cathedral. Anne and Laurent Viau run this comfortable five-room place with grace and great rates. Relax in the garden with views to the upper town and sample the local product at their wine bar (includes breakfast, air-con, 1 Av-enue Jules Mazen, +33 4 90 35 63 04, www.vaisonchambres.info, anne.viau@vaisonchambres.info).

NEAR VAISON-LA-ROMAINE

$$ Auberge d'Anaïs, a short hop from Vaison-la-Romaine, is a peaceful seven-room hotel-restaurant and a good deal (see the res-taurant listing below). Rooms come with vineyards out your win-dow, a big pool, and a cool lounge (includes breakfast, +33 4 90 36 20 06, www.aubergeanais.com, auberge.anais@gmail.com). Head-ing east of Vaison-la-Romaine, follow signs to *Carpentras*, then *St-Marcellin-lès-Vaison*. Signs will guide you from there.

Eating in Vaison-la-Romaine

Vaison-la-Romaine offers a handful of good dining experiences—arrive by 19:30 in summer or reserve ahead, particularly on week-ends. And while you can eat very well on a moderate budget in Vaison, it's well worth venturing to nearby Côtes du Rhône villages to eat. I've listed three nearby places; for recommendations farther afield, see the "Côtes du Rhône Wine Road Drive," later. Wherever you dine, begin with a fresh glass of Muscat from the nearby village of Beaumes-de-Venise.

IN THE UPPER TOWN

$$$ Restaurant la Fontaine, located at the recommended **Hôtel le Beffroi,** serves traditional cuisine of average quality in the lovely hotel gardens when the weather agrees, and in the pleasant dining room when it doesn't. If they're serving in the garden, you won't find a better setting in Vaison (closed Wed, +33 4 90 36 04 71).

Les Maisons Du'O offers two refined dining experiences, each with fixed-price *menus* featuring creative and beautifully presented Franco-Provençal cuisine (book ahead, Rue Gaston Gévaudan, +33 4 90 28 84 08, www.maisonsduo.com). **$$$$ La Table** serves gastronomique cuisine in a refined, stone-arches-meet-wood-tables setting. Allow €90 for a five-course *menu* (open Thu-Sat only). Across a small lane, **$$$ Le Bistro Panoramique** is the more affordable of the two, with *menus* from about €40. Stylish yet relaxed, it hangs over the lower town with floor-to-ceiling windows (closed Sun-Mon).

$ You'll find a simple *crêperie* with a view deck and a decent **pizzeria** on the main street leading up to the old town. Both have indoor and outdoor seating, some views over the river, and cheap, basic food (good for families).

IN THE LOWER TOWN

$$ La Bartavelle, run by friendly Berangère, is a fine place to savor affordable and traditional French cuisine, with tourist-friendly mix-and-match choices of local options served in a stylish interior or at courtyard tables. The €31 *menu* gets you four courses, including a great cheese tray; the €24 *menu* offers top-end main-course selections and dessert (closed Mon year-round and Sun evening off-season, excellent foie gras and seafood plate—*assiette de pêcheur,* outside terrace, air-con, 15 Rue Camille Pelletan, +33 4 90 36 02 16, www.restaurant-bartavelle.com).

$$ La Lyriste is an unpretentious and intimate place to experience true Provençal cuisine, with Sandra taking your orders and her husband doing the cooking (closed Mon, 45 Cours Taulignan, +33 4 90 36 04 67).

$$ O'Natur'elles is a sweet little place for lunch. It's ideal for vegetarians but good for all persuasions, as the all-organic dishes can be served with or without meat. The cuisine is delicious, but the place is small (closed Mon, reservations smart, 38 Place Montfort, +33 4 90 65 81 67).

Cafés on Place Montfort: Come here for classic café fare and to observe the daily flow of life in Vaison-la-Romaine. Outdoor tables are ideal but can come with smokers. The popular **$$ Brasserie l'Annexe** is best, with a good selection of fine quality dishes ranging from big salads to tempting *plats du jour* (open daily).

$ L'Arbre à Vins is a cheery wine bar run by happy-go-lucky

CÔTES DU RHÔNE

Le Mistral

Provence lives with its vicious mistral winds, which blow 30-60 miles per hour, about 100 days out of the year. Locals say it blows in multiples of threes: three, six, or nine days in a row. The mistral clears people off the streets and turns lively cities into ghost towns. You'll likely spend a few hours or days taking refuge. The winds are strongest between noon and 15:00.

When the mistral blows, it's everywhere, and you can't escape. Author Peter Mayle said it could blow the ears off a donkey (I'd include the tail). According to the natives, it ruins crops, shutters, and roofs (look for stones holding tiles in place on many homes). They'll also tell you that this pernicious wind has driven many people crazy (including young Vincent van Gogh). A weak version of the wind is called a *mistralet*.

The mistral starts above the Alps and Massif Central mountains and gathers steam as it heads south, gaining momentum as it screams over the Rhône Valley (which acts like a funnel between the Alps and the Cévennes mountains) before exhausting itself when it hits the Mediterranean. And though this wind rattles shutters everywhere in the Riviera and Provence, it's strongest over the Rhône Valley...so Avignon, Arles, and the Côtes du Rhône villages bear its brunt. While wiping the dust from your eyes, remember the good news: The mistral brings clear skies.

Laurent and Matthieu, with a convivial setting inside and out. You'll find wines from throughout France with, *bien sûr*, a focus on ones from the region. There's a good selection of affordable wines by the glass and a small menu of fun dishes that can easily make a meal (closed Mon in Oct-April, +33 6 67 32 75 86).

NEAR VAISON-LA-ROMAINE

$$ Auberge d'Anaïs, at the end of a short dirt road 10 minutes from Vaison-la-Romaine, is a fun Provençal experience, ideal for a relaxing lunch or dinner *en plein air* (not worth it in bad weather). Outdoor tables gather under cheery lights with immediate vineyard views and classic Provençal cuisine. Ask for a table *sur la terrasse* (closed Mon, +33 4 90 36 20 06). Heading east from Vaison-la-Romaine, follow signs to *Carpentras*, then *St-Marcellin-lès-Vaison*. Signs will guide you from there.

$$ La Fleur Bleue is a find, serving fresh and local cuisine in a charming blue-shuttered farmhouse with wonderful outside and indoor seating. It's Dutch owned, so English is no issue (open for lunch and dinner Mon-Tue and Thu-Fri only, reservations smart, Chemin du Sublon, a mile from Crestet on the road toward Malaucène, +33 6 15 57 49 27, www.lafleurbleue.fr).

Vaison-la-Romaine Connections

The most central **bus stop** is a few blocks up Avenue Général de Gaulle from the TI near the main winery, Cave la Romaine. Buses to Orange and Avignon stop on the winery side. Buses to Nyons, Crestet, and Carpentras depart from the bus station farther east on that road. See the "Vaison-la-Romaine" map, earlier, for stop locations.

From Vaison-la-Romaine by Bus to: Avignon (#4 to Orange, transfer to #2, 8/day Mon-Sat, 2/day Sun, 1.5 hours—train from Orange is faster and bus stops at the train station), **Orange** (bus #4, 8/day Mon-Sat, 2/day Sun, 1 hour), **Nyons** (3-5/day, none on Sun, 25 minutes), **Crestet** (lower village below Crestet, bus #11, 5/day Mon-Sat, none on Sun, 5 minutes), **Carpentras** (bus #11, 5/day Mon-Sat, none on Sun, 1 hour).

Best of the Côtes du Rhône Villages

Officially, the Côtes du Rhône vineyards follow the Rhône River from just south of Lyon to Avignon. Our focus is the southern section of the Côtes du Rhône, centering on the small area between Châteauneuf-du-Pape and Vaison-la-Romaine.

Circling the rugged Dentelles de Montmirail mountain peaks, you'll experience all that's unique about this region: its natural beauty, glowing limestone villages, inviting wineries, and rolling hills of vineyards. One hundred million years ago, the Mediterranean Sea extended this far north, leaving behind a sandy soil base for today's farmers (the wine town of Sablet's name comes from the French word *sable,* meaning "sand").

PLANNING YOUR TIME

Although seeing the Côtes du Rhône is possible as a day trip by car from Arles or Avignon, you'll have a more enjoyable and intimate experience if you sleep in one of the villages (my favorite accommodations are listed under "Sleeping in Vaison-la-Romaine," earlier).

With a car, the best one-day plan is to do the "Côtes du Rhône Wine Road Drive" described later (allow an entire day from Avignon for the 80-mile round-trip; from Vaison-la-Romaine or nearby, you'll need a half-day for the 35-mile round-trip). For more tips, see "Planning Your Drive" on the next page.

COTES DU RHONE

GETTING AROUND THE CÔTES DU RHÔNE VILLAGES

This area is clearly easiest if you have four wheels (rentable in Orange or Avignon, and sometimes in Vaison-la-Romaine—ask at TI). Without a car, it's tougher, but a representative sampling is doable by **bike** (for ideas, see "Biking," earlier) or by **bus** (5-10 buses/day Mon-Sat stop at several Côtes du Rhône villages—bus #4 from Orange/Vaison-la-Romaine stops at Sablet and Séguret, bus #11 from Vaison-la-Romaine stops in Crestet and Malaucène.

For less effort and more expense, several of the local guides and minivan tour companies I list are happy to follow my route (see "Tours in Provence" on page 38).

Côtes du Rhône Wine Road Drive

SEGURET LOOP

This driving tour provides a crash course in Rhône Valley wine, an excuse to meet the locals who make the stuff, and breathtaking scenery—especially late in the day, when the famous Provençal sunlight causes colors to absolutely pop. Allow at least a half-day for this 35-mile loop drive, which starts in the village of Séguret, skirts Vaison-la-Romaine, and then winds clockwise around the Dentelles de Montmirail, visiting the mountaintop village of Crestet, adorable little Suzette, and the renowned wine villages of Beaumes-de-Venise and Gigondas. (You can, of course, start anywhere along this circular route.)

Even if wine isn't your thing, do this scenic drive. This region is not only about wine; you'll pass orchards of apricots, figs, and cherries, as well as fields of table grapes and lavender. As you drive, notice how some vineyards grow at angles—they're planted this way to compensate for the strong effect of the mistral wind.

Planning Your Drive: Our tour starts a bit south of Vaison-la-Romaine in little Séguret. Try to get the first two stops done before lunch (most wineries are closed 12:00-14:00; call ahead if possible), then complete the loop in the afternoon. Note that some wineries are closed on Sundays, holidays, and during the harvest (mid-Sept), so check ahead. This area is picnic-friendly, but there are few shops along the way—stock up before you leave.

By **bike**, or for a **more scenic drive** from Vaison-la-Romaine, cross to the Cité Médiévale side of the river, then follow D-977 signs downriver to Séguret (park in lots P-2 or P-3). Theft is a problem in this beautiful area—leave nothing in your car.

Alternatives on Foot: Hiking trails from above Vaison-la-

Romaine's castle lead to Séguret in five miles or Crestet in three miles (see "Hiking and Biking," earlier).

Wineries: Remember that the wineries you'll visit are serious about their wines—and they hope that you'll take them seriously, too. (Before you go, study up with "French Wine Tasting 101" on page 50.) At private wineries, tastings are not happy-go-lucky chances to knock back a few glasses and buy a T-shirt with the property's label on it. Show genuine interest in the wine, and buy some if you like it.

Eating: Drivers on this route can enjoy a wealth of country-Provençal dining opportunities in rustic settings (even within 15 minutes of Vaison-la-Romaine). It's a great opportunity to experience rural France. The restaurants listed have some outdoor seating and should be considered for lunch or dinner. Go French and make a relaxing lunch the centerpiece of your day.

➊ Séguret

Blending into the hillside with a smattering of shops, two cafés, made-to-stroll lanes, and a natural spring, this hamlet is understandably popular. Séguret makes for a good coffee or ice cream stop and has a good café-restaurant.

Séguret's name comes from the Latin word *securitas* (meaning "security"). The town's long, bulky entry arch came with a massive gate, which drilled in the message of the village's name. In the Middle Ages, Séguret was patrolled 24/7—they never took their *securitas* for granted. Find the drawing inside the arch of the medieval town with its high-flying castle. A castle once protected Séguret, but all that's left today is a tower that you can barely make out (though trails provide access).

Walk through the arch and up a block. To appreciate how the homes' outer walls provided security in those days, drop down the first passage on your right (near the fountain). These tunnel-like exit passages, or *poternes,* were needed in periods of peace to allow the town to expand below. Find **La Maison d'Eglantine** *salon de thé* tucked in here, serving delicious cakes, coffee, and tea in a cozy room with views.

Séguret's open washbasin *(lavoir)* lies ahead and was a hotbed of social activity and gossip over the ages. The basins behind the fountain (now planted) were reserved for washing animals, which outnumbered residents in the Middle Ages); the larger ones (on the left) were for laundry only. Public washbasins like this were used right up until World War II. Farther on, take a left at the fork. The community bread oven *(four banal)* was used for festivals and celebrations.

Moving along, you could follow Calade de l'Eglise up to the unusual 12th-century St. Denis church for views (the circular vil-

Côtes du Rhône Driving Tour

Legend:
- - - - Driving Loop
- 🚲 Bike Routes
- 🍷 Wine Tasting

To Nyons (Drôme Provençale Loop Drive)

Mirabel
Piégon
D-94
D-7
D-538
D-46

To Ardèche Gorges

L'ECOLE BUISSONIERE CHAMBRES
Villedieu
D-20
D-975

VILLEDIEU BIKE RIDE

Puyméras
Faucon

11 MILE BIKE LOOP

Roaix

Vaison-la-Romaine

St-Romain

Rasteau
D-977

To Cairanne
D-69

PATH

To Buis-les-Baronnies

St-Marcellin-lès-Vaison

DRIVING TOUR BEGINS

D-88

❷ 🍷

❶ **Séguret**

❸ **Crestet**

Entre-chaux

To Brantes (Drôme Provençale Loop Drive)

D-8
D-23
D-977
D-938
D-13

To Orange & Avignon

DOMAINE DE CABASSE

Sablet

D-977
D-7

Dentelles de Montmirail

Gigondas

❼ 🍷

HOTEL LES FLORETS

D-938
D-90

Malaucène

D-977
D-8

DOMAINE DE CASSAN

❹

❺ **Suzette**

LA FERME DEGOUTAUD

D-974

To Mont Ventoux

To Orange & A-7

D-7

❻ 🍷

La Fare

La Roque Alric

Le Barroux

D-19

To Mont Ventoux via Bédoin

Vacqueyras

D-90

D-938

D-52

Beaumes-de-Venise

To Carpentras

To Carpentras

D-7

5 Kilometers

5 Miles

❶ Séguret
❷ Domaine de Mourchon Winery
❸ Crestet
❹ Dentelles de Montmirail (Col de la Chaîne Mountain Pass)
❺ Suzette
❻ Domaine de Coyeux Winery
❼ Gigondas

lage you see below is Sablet). This rock-sculpted church is usually closed, but it's worth a look from the outside. We'll veer right and down instead, aiming for the **santon shop** (worth a peek for its displays). At Christmas, this entire village transforms itself into one big crèche scene—a Provençal tradition that has long since died out in other villages. From here, drop down and return to your car past the recommended **Restaurant/Café Côté Terrasse.**

Sleeping and Eating: Sure, it's a hotel, but winemaking is also part of the business at **$$ Domaine de Cabasse,***** a lovely spread flanked by vineyards at the foot of Séguret (with views and a walking path to the village). Each of the 23 rooms has tasteful decor, air-conditioning, and views over vines; all the first-floor rooms have balconies or decks (elevator, big heated pool, discount for 2-3 night stay if reserved directly with hotel; on D-23 between Sablet and Séguret, entry gate opens automatically...and slowly, +33 4 90 46 91 12, www.cabasse.fr, hotel@cabasse.fr). It's worth booking this place well ahead.

$$ Le Bouquet de Séguret Chambres d'Hôte is a perfectly Provençal refuge perched just below Séguret, with vineyard and village views. Outgoing Dutch owners Jos and Ingrid speak fluent English and spoil their guests with optional home-cooked dinners, wine tastings, pools, a *pétanque* court, and afternoon tea. They also rent several good apartments *(gîtes)* with full kitchens (3-5-night minimum). It's near Domaine de Cabasse (252 Route de Sablet, +33 4 90 28 13 83, www.lebouquetdeseguret.com, info@ lebouquetdeseguret.com).

With a terrific setting in the center of the village, **$$ Restaurant/Café Côté Terrasse** offers all-day café service as well as lunch and dinner. They deliver cheerful service and big portions of straightforward brasserie fare at reasonable prices, either on the terrace or in the modern interior (daily in high season from 10:00, Rue des Poternes, +33 4 90 28 03 48).

$$ Le Mesclun sits right next door, offering a step up in cuisine and prices, a terrific terrace, and three intimate dining rooms (closed Wed, +33 4 90 46 93 43).

• *Signs near Séguret's upper parking lots lead you up, up, and away for to our next stop, the nearby Domaine de Mourchon (leave bread crumbs or track your route up to find your way back down).*

❷ Domaine de Mourchon Winery

This high-flying winery blends state-of-the-art technology with traditional winemaking methods (a shiny ring of stainless-steel vats holds grapes grown on land plowed by horses). The wines have won the respect of international critics, yet the (Scottish) owners, Walter and daughter Kate, seem eager to help anyone understand Rhône Valley wines. Language is not an issue here, nor is a lack of stunning views.

COTES DU RHONE

The Life of a Hill Town in Provence

Heat-seeking northerners have made today's hill towns prosperous and worldly. But before the 1960s, few wanted to live in these sun-drenched, rock-top settings.

Like lost ships in search of safe harbor, locals have long been forced to seek refuge that hill towns provided. When the Romans settled Provence (125 BC), they brought stability to the warring locals, and hill-towners descended en masse to the Roman cities (such as Arles, Orange, Nîmes, and Vaison-la-Romaine). There they enjoyed theaters, fresh water from aqueducts, and commercial goods brought via the Roman road that stretched from Spain to Italy.

When Rome fell (AD 476), barbarians swept in, forcing residents back into the hills, where they'd stay for almost 1,000 years. These "Dark Ages" were when many of the villages we see today were established. Most grew up around castles, since peasants depended on their lord for security. The hill-towners gathered stones from nearby fields and built their homes side by side to form a defensive wall, terracing the hillsides to maximize the scarce arable land. But medieval life was not easy behind those walls—there were barbarians, plagues, crop failures, droughts, thieves, wars, and the everyday battle with gravity.

As the Renaissance approached, and Provence came under the protection of an increasingly centralized French nation, barbarian invasions dwindled. Just when the hill-towners thought the coast was clear to relocate below, France's religious wars (1500s) chased them back up. As Protestants and Catholics duked it out, hilltop villages prospered, welcoming refugees. Little Séguret (pop. 100 today) had almost 1,000 residents; the village of Mérindol (near Avignon) sprouted from nowhere; and Fort de Buoux

Take advantage of the amazing deal they've arranged to deliver wine stateside for nearly the same price you'd pay at the winery. Free and informative English tours of the vineyards are usually offered on Wednesdays at 17:00, followed by a tasting, though you're welcome to taste anytime they're open (Mon-Sat 9:00-18:00, Sun by appointment only; from Easter-Oct, call to verify; +33 4 90 46 70 30, www.domainedemourchon.com).

• *Next, drop back down to Séguret, head toward Vaison-la-Romaine, and once past the city follow signs for Carpentras/Malaucène. After passing through "lower" Crestet on the main highway, look for signs for a side road leading up to Le Village. Drivers can park at the second lot on the approach to the town, then hike up through the village on foot, or bypass the lower lots to keep climbing toward Place du Château at the top of town.*

(near Apt, nothing but ruins today) was an impregnable fortress. The turmoil of the Revolution (1789) continued to make the above-the-fray hill towns desirable.

Over the next century, hill towns slept peacefully as the rest of France modernized. Most of the hill towns you'll visit housed between 200 and 600 people and were self-sufficient. But 20th-century life down below required fewer stairs—and was closer to the convenience of trains, planes, and automobiles. So after World War I, down the hill-towners moved. To build in the flatlands, they pillaged the hill towns' stones, roof tiles—you name it, they took it—leaving those villages in ruins as virtual ghost towns.

Recent decades have brought a return to hill-town life. Real estate boomed as Parisians, northern Europeans, and (to a lesser extent) North Americans discovered its rustic charm. They invested huge sums—far more than most locals could afford. Provence's hill towns survive in part thanks to these outsiders' deep pockets.

Today, many villages have organizations to preserve their traditions and buildings. Made up of older residents, these groups raise money, sponsor festivals and dances, and even write collective histories of their villages. Many fear that younger folks won't have the motivation to carry on this tradition.

But hope springs eternal, as there may be a movement of locals back to these villages. Some northerners are finding hill-town life less romantic as they age, the popularity of organic produce is making it financially viable for hill-town farmers with smaller plots to make a living, and the internet age allows some hill-towners to telecommute. Could the cycle be restarting? Armed with laptops, smartphones, and tablets, will hill-towners once again prosper when the next wave of barbarians comes?

COTES DU RHONE

❸ Crestet

This quiet village—founded after the fall of the Roman Empire, when people banded together in high places like this for protection from marauding barbarians—followed the usual hill-town evolution (see sidebar). The outer walls of the village did double duty as ramparts and house walls. The castle above (from about 850) provided a final safe haven when the village was attacked.

The bishops of Vaison-la-Romaine were among the first occupants of this town, lending little Crestet a certain caché (they hid out here when things got too testy with the counts of Toulouse). With about 500 residents in 1200, Crestet was a big deal in this region, reaching its zenith in the mid-1500s, when 660 people called it home. Crestet's gradual decline started when the bishopric moved to Vaison-la-Romaine in the 1600s, though the population remained fairly stable until World War II. Today, about 35 people live within the walls year-round (about 55 during the summer boom).

Wander the peaceful lanes and appreciate the amount of work it took to put these stones in place. Notice the elaborate water channels. Crestet was served by 18 cisterns in the Middle Ages. Imagine hundreds of people living here with animals roaming everywhere. The bulky Romanesque church is built into the hillside; if it's open, peek in to see the unusual stained-glass window behind the altar.

Eating: The café-restaurant **$$ La Terrasse** (well signed) serves basic omelets, salads, crêpes, and *plats* from what must be Provence's greatest view tables. Stop for a coffee or drink and enjoy the panorama (daily, closed in bad weather and Dec-March, +33 4 90 28 76 42).

Nearby: A memorable lunch stop about a mile from Crestet is **$$ La Fleur Bleue** (see "Near Vaison-la-Romaine," earlier).

• *For those walking back to Vaison-la-Romaine, signs from the top of the village lead to a footpath. The trail leaves from Chemin de la Verrière at the very top of the village (by the intersection with the road from below). The brown sign indicates that it's 8.8 kilometers (about 5 miles) to Vaison-la-Romaine, but—in a few steps—turn right, following the yellow sign that shows it's 5.1 kilometers (3 miles) to Vaison-la-Romaine (via Chemin des Fontaines).*

Drivers should carry on and reconnect with the road below, following signs to Malaucène. Entering Malaucène, turn right on D-90 (direction: Suzette) just before the gas station. After a few minutes you'll approach a pass. After passing two scenic picnic areas, look for signs on the left to Col de la Chaîne (Chain Pass).

❹ Dentelles de Montmirail (Col de la Chaîne Mountain Pass)

Get out of your car at the pass (elevation: about 1,500 feet) and enjoy the breezy views. The peaks in the distance—thrusting up like the back of a stegosaurus or a bad haircut (you decide)—are the Dentelles de Montmirail, a small range running just nine miles basically north to south and reaching 2,400 feet in elevation. This region's land is constantly shifting. Those rocky tops were the result of a gradual uplifting of the land, which was then blown bald by the angry mistral wind. Below, pine and oak trees mix with the shrub Scotch broom, which blooms brilliant yellow in May and June. You may see rich yellow-to-reddish patches of land—the result of deposits of ochre located deep below. The village below the peaks is Suzette (you'll be there soon).

The scene is gorgeous and surprisingly undeveloped. You can thank the lack of water for the absence of more homes or farms in this area. Water is everything in this parched region, and if you don't have ready access to it, you can't build or cultivate the land. (Some farmers have drilled as far as 1,300 feet down to try to find water.) With no water at hand, farmers here lie awake at night wor-

Cicadas (*Cigales*)

In the countryside, listen for *les cigales*. They sing in the heat and are famous for announcing the arrival of summer. (Locals say their song also marks the coming of the tourists...and more money.) People here love these ugly, long-winged bugs, an integral part of Provençal life. You'll see souvenir cicadas made from every material possible. If you look closely—they are well camouflaged—you can find live specimens on tree trunks and branches. Cicadas live for about two years, all but the last two weeks of which are spent quietly underground as larvae. But when they go public, their chirping begins with each sunrise and goes nonstop until sunset.

rying about fire. Hot summers, dry pines, and windy days make a scary recipe for fast-traveling fires.

The Dentelles provide fertile ground for walking trails. Yellow-signed hiking-only trails lead from here to several destinations (the castle-topped village of Le Barroux is 3.5 miles away and mostly downhill).

Now turn around and face Mont Ventoux. Are there clouds on the horizon? You're looking into the eyes of the Alps (behind Ventoux), and those "foothills" help keep Provence sunny.

• *Time to push on. You'll pass more yellow trail signs along this drive. With the medieval castle of Le Barroux topping the horizon in the distance (off to the left) and lavender fields below, drive on to little...*

❺ Suzette

Tiny Suzette floats on its hilltop, with a small 12th-century chapel, wine tastings, a handful of residents, and the gaggle of houses where they live. Park in Suzette's lot, then find the big orientation board above the lot (Rome is 620 kilometers—385 miles—away). Look out to the broad shoulders of Mont Ventoux. At 6,000 feet, it always seems to have some clouds hanging around. If it's clear, the top looks like it's snow-covered; if you drive up there, you'll see it's actually white stone (see the Mont Ventoux drive later in this chapter). If it's very cloudy, the mountain takes on a dark, foreboding appearance.

Look to the village. A sign asks you to *Respectez son Calme* (respect its peace). Suzette's homes once lived in the shadow of an imposing castle, destroyed during the religious wars of the mid-1500s.

Back across the road from the orientation table is a simple tasting room for **Château Redortier** wines (unreliable hours, but well-explained wine list provided). Good picnic tables lie just past Suzette on our route.

A Wine-Growing Almanac

Phoenicians brought about five grape varieties with them to southern Europe approximately 3,000 years ago. Today there are more than 2,000 different grape varieties in the world, of which 150 are in France and 14 are in the Côtes du Rhône.

But some things have changed very little over the past three millennia: Today's Provençal farmers tend their grapes following much the same rhythm as did their Phoenician forerunners.

After a quiet winter, the plants begin waking up in March, pushing out new growth. By about mid-May, the plants are growing at a fast pace, requiring farmers to do their first pruning of the year. Often working by hand, they pull off sucker plants and prune back new shoots, focusing the plant's energy on four to five main stalks.

Over the next three months, the farmers plow the soil, encouraging moisture to reach the plants. Every few weeks they spray for mildew (not a big problem in this dry area).

Next comes the harvest. Its precise date is dictated by how much sun and warmth the vines absorbed through the spring and summer: The hotter and drier the weather, the earlier the harvest.

In France, the grape harvest starts in the south and rolls north, ending about six weeks later in the country's northernmost vineyards, in Champagne. During the harvest, grapes are picked from the vines—either by hand or by machine—then separated from their stems. Pressing comes 2 to 3 weeks later, and the winemaking process is under way.

In the fall, farmers are busy watching and tweaking their wines. By December it's time for heavy pruning, when the plants are cut way back for the winter hibernation. Farmers spend the winter months catching up on maintenance, reading..and sleeping.

Sleeping: $ La Ferme Dégoutaud is a splendidly situated, roomy, and utterly isolated *chambres d'hôte* about halfway between Malaucène and Suzette (well signed, a mile down a dirt road). Animated Véronique (speaks minimal English, her son Thibault more) rents three country-cozy rooms with many thoughtful touches, a view pool, table tennis, picnic-perfect tables, and a barbecue at your disposal (includes breakfast, apartments available by the week, 20-minute drive from Vaison-la-Romaine, +33 4 90 62 99 29, www.degoutaud.fr, le.degoutaud@wanadoo.fr).

• *But La Fare's best wine-tasting opportunity is back on our route, just after leaving the village, at...*

❻ Domaine de Coyeux Winery

A private road winds up and up to this impossibly beautiful setting, with the best views of the Dentelles I've found. Olive trees frame the final approach, and *Le Caveau* signs lead to a modern tasting room (you may need to ring the buzzer) within a big winery. The owners and staff are sincere and take your interest in their wines seriously—skip it if you only want a quick taste or are not interested in buying. These wines have earned their good reputation, and some are now available in the US (winery generally open daily 10:00-12:00 & 14:00-17:30, closed Sat off-season and no midday closure July-Aug; +33 4 90 12 42 42, www. domainedecoyeux.com, some English spoken). By the time you visit, their new bistro should be up and running.

A good stopping place for lunch or dinner is **$$ Côté Vignes,** just after the turnoff to Domaine de Coyeux. This light-hearted wood-fired-everything restaurant has outdoor tables, a fun interior dining atmosphere, and charming host Corinne. Try the Camembert cheese flambé with lettuce, potatoes, and ham (salads, good pizza and *plats*, closed Wed off-season, +33 4 90 65 07 16).

• *Drive on toward Beaumes-de-Venise. Navigate through Beaumes-de-Venise, following signs for Centre-Ville, then for Vacqueyras (a famous wine village with a Thursday market). At a big roundabout, you'll pass Beaumes-de-Venise's massive cave coopérative, which represents many growers in this area (big selection, but too slick for my taste); you'll see more modest coopératives showcasing local winemakers in other villages. Continue tracking signs for Vacqueyras, and then signs for Gigondas and Vaison par la route touristique (D-7). A small road leads right into Gigondas' town center.*

❼ Gigondas

This upscale village produces some of the region's best reds and is ideally situated for hiking, mountain biking, and driving into the mountains. Follow signs to the village center and park on the tree-shaded square or in the second lot just beyond the TI (the first lot is for locals). The TI has lists of wineries and *chambres d'hôtes*, and tips for good hikes or drives (Mon-Sat 10:00-12:30

COTES DU RHONE

& 14:30-18:00, closed Sun, 5 Rue du Portail, +33 4 90 65 85 46, www.gigondas-dm.com). **Caveau du Gigondas** is a good place to taste wines from over 75 producers (daily 10:00-12:00 & 14:00-18:30). Take a short walk up through the village lanes to find a good viewing platform over the heart of the Côtes du Rhône vineyards (leaving from Du Verre à l'Assiette restaurant, veer right just after the Nez Bar à Vins, then make a quick left uphill); you'll find even better views a little higher at the church.

Sleeping and Eating $ Nez Bar à Vins, with good ambience inside and out, is a cool-if-trendy place to enjoy a glass of wine and light appetizers; you'll find it along a pedestrian lane a block up from the main square (closed Sat-Sun, Place du Rouvis, +33 4 90 28 99 59).

$$ Hôtel les Florets,*** with tastefully designed rooms, is a half-mile above Gigondas, buried in the foothills of the Dentelles de Montmirail. It comes with an excellent restaurant, a vast terrace with views, a pool, and hiking trails into the mountains (no air-con, annex rooms by pool have front patios, +33 4 90 65 85 01, www.hotel-lesflorets.com, accueil@hotel-lesflorets.com). Their traditional, family-run **$$$ restaurant** is well worth the price—particularly if you dine on the magnificent terrace. Dinners blend classic French cuisine with Provençal accents, served with class by English-speaking Thierry. The weighty wine list is literally encyclopedic (closed Wed, also closed Thu for lunch, service can be slow).

• *From Gigondas, follow signs to the circular wine village of Sablet—with generally inexpensive wines (the TI and wine coopérative share a space in the town center)—then back to Séguret, where our tour ends.*

But if you haven't had your fill, consider adding a detour to...

Cairanne

About 10 miles west of Vaison-la-Romaine is this pleasant wine village, with one of the largest and most respected wine *coopératives* in this region. The **Cave de Cairanne** has been making wine for more than 80 years with grapes from more than 60 different farmers. Start with the free, museum-esque "sensory trail," which explores the five senses through interactive displays in English and French, preparing you to taste their large range of wines (free, daily wine tasting 9:00-18:00 but closes at lunchtime, museum closes at 17:00, lots of English spoken, on Route de Bollene on the outskirts of town on D-8—you can't miss the signs, +33 4 90 65 98 15, www.cave-cairanne.fr).

Eating: Consider a meal afterward at the nearby wine-bar/restaurant **$$ Le Tourne au Verre** (good value lunch *menu*, closed Sun evenings and all day Mon, Route de Sainte-Cécile, +33 4 90 30 72 18, www.letourneauverre.com).

More Côtes du Rhône Drives

For further explorations of the Côtes du Rhône region, consider these suggestions: a scenic mountaintop, an off-the-beaten-path countryside ramble, and an impressive gorge. You can trace the route of the first two drives on the "Côtes du Rhône Area" map at the beginning of this chapter.

▲MONT VENTOUX AND LAVENDER

The drive to Mont Ventoux is worth ▲▲▲ if the summit is open and skies are crystal-clear, or in any weather between late June and the end of July, when the lavender blooms. From Vaison-la-Romaine, allow a good hour to drive to the top of this 6,000-foot mountain, where you'll be greeted by cool temperatures, crowds of visitors, and acres of white stones. Most days you'll see any number of cyclists braving the long, grueling ascent, made famous by its annual inclusion in the Tour de France. This drive can also be extended to take you into the Luberon region (see details later).

Mont Ventoux is Provence's rooftop, referred to as the "Giant of Provence" or "the Bald Mountain," with astonishing Pyrenees-to-Alps views when it's really clear (it usually isn't). But even under hazy skies, it's an interesting place. The top combines a barren and surreal lunar landscape with souvenirs, bikers, and hikers. All that chalky mess you see was once the bottom of a sea. Miles of poles stuck in the rock identify the route.

Road Conditions: Before venturing out, confirm that the roads at the top are open, as they close annually from mid-November to mid-April (and sometimes later).

From Vaison-la-Romaine to Mont Ventoux: For the most direct route, drive to Malaucène (15 minutes on D-938), then wind up D-974 for another 45 minutes to the top. For a slightly longer but prettier route, from Malaucène you can drive around the base of the mountain, over the Col de la Madeleine (follow signs from Malaucène) and through the quaint village of Bédoin (good Mon-

Lavender

Whether or not you travel to Provence during the late-June and July lavender blossom, you'll see and smell examples of this particularly local product everywhere—in shops, on tables in restaurants, and in your hotel room. And if you come during lavender season, you'll experience one of Europe's great color events, where rich fields of purple lavender meet equally rich yellow fields of sunflowers. While lavender season is hot, you'll find the best fields in the cooler hills, because the flowers thrive at higher altitudes. The flowers

are harvested in full bloom (beginning in mid-July), then distilled to extract the oils for making soaps and perfume.

And though lavender seems like an indigenous part of the Provence scene, it wasn't cultivated here until about 1920, when it was imported by the local perfume-makers. Because lavender is not native to Provence, growing it successfully requires great care. Three kinds of lavender are grown in Provence: true lavender (traditionally used by perfume-makers), spike lavender, and lavandin (a cloned hybrid of the first two). Today, a majority of Provence lavender fields are lavandin—which is also mass-produced at factories, a trend that is threatening to put true lavender growers out of business.

Some of the best lavender fields bloom near Vaison-la-Romaine. Lavender blooms later the higher you go; the ones described here are listed from lowest to highest elevations. For an impressive display, drive north of Vaison-la-Romaine and ramble the tiny road between Valréas and Vinsobres (D-190 and D-46). You'll see more beautiful fields along D-538 between Nyons and Dieulefit, and still more if you climb Mont Ventoux to Sault (see Mont Ventoux drive below).

day market); from there the southern leg of D-974 leads to the top. For more driving and walking routes in the area, see the Routes de la Lavande website (www.routes-lavande.com).

Mont Ventoux Summit: Mont Ventoux has two small ski stations, both at 4,600 feet (about 4 miles from the top). Mont Serein station is on the north and Chalet Reynard station is on the south. The mountain pass (Col de Mont Ventoux) between these stations and the summit are inaccessible in winter months due to snow and ice. At the summit, you'll find an orientation board and **Le Vendran** restaurant (near the old observatory and Air Force control tower), whose snacks and meals come with commanding views.

Sault: Continuing on to Sault (pronounced "soh") is a worthwhile 45-minute detour (about 16 miles) when the lavender blooms (simply follow signs to *Sault*). Lavender fields forever surround this rock-top village, which produces 40 percent of France's lavender essence. A welcoming town in any season, Sault goes unnoticed by most hurried travelers. It's a slow-down-and-smell-the-lavender kind of place, with a sociable "mountain market" on Wednesdays.

There's no reason to sleep in Sault, but it's a fine place for lunch or *un café*. **La Promenade de Justin Sebastien** café has simple salads and grilled meats with territorial valley views (daily mid-April–mid-Sept, closed Tue off-season, +33 4 90 64 14 34). Or enjoy the same views with a picnic in the adjacent, tree-lined area, the "promenade."

From Mont Ventoux to the Luberon: Mont Ventoux provides a scenic connection between the Côtes du Rhône villages and the Luberon—and one of the most spectacular routes in Provence. From Sault, continue south toward Roussillon (start by following signs for *Gordes*, about 40 minutes, 20 miles). Along the way, you'll duck into and out of several climate zones and remarkably diverse landscapes. The scene alternates between limestone canyons, lush meadows, and wildflowers. On your way into the Luberon, you'll pass near St-Saturnin-lès-Apt (see page 238). If the summit is closed, skip the long alternate route through Bédoin; instead, zip to the Luberon on the autoroute via Orange and Cavaillon.

DROME PROVENCALE LOOP DRIVE

This meander north from Vaison-la-Romaine into the Drôme Provençale is overkill for many, as the scenery is only subtly different than what you'll see closer to your hotel. But if you haven't had your fill of pretty vistas, this 60-mile loop combines rugged scenery with overlooked towns and villages, away from popular tourist areas. I'd do it on a Thursday, when it's market day in Nyons, or on a Wednesday, when it's market day in Buis-les-Baronnies. Allow most of a day for this up-and-down, curve-filled drive, particularly if the market in Nyons is on. Or you can just do Nyons and call it a good day.

From Vaison-la-Romaine, drive to **Nyons,** an attractive mid-size town set along a river and against the hills. Here you'll find a Roman bridge with views, an olive mill, a lavender distillery, a handful of walking streets, and an arcaded square—all with few tourists. Nyons is famous for its rollicking Thursday market (until 12:30) and for producing France's best olives, which you can taste at its well-organized *coopérative* (Mon-Sat 9:00-12:30 & 14:00-

19:00, Sun until 18:00, shorter hours off-season, interesting museum about olives, on Place Olivier de Serres, +33 4 75 26 95 00).

From Nyons, head for the hills following signs to *Gap* on D-94, then follow signs to *Ste-Jalles* on D-64. Little **Ste-Jalles** hovers above the road, with a pretty Romanesque church (usually closed), two cafés (Bistrot des Lavandes overhangs the river, providing a fine backdrop for a drink, lunch, or a snack), and a small winery making crisp whites and easy reds (Domaine de Rieu Frais, daily 9:00-12:00 & 14:00-18:00, closed Sun in winter, +33 4 75 27 31 54, www.domaine-du-rieu-frais.com, best to call ahead and let them know you're coming).

From Ste-Jalles, cross the bridge following D-108 and *Buis-les-Baronnies* signs, and start your ascent over the rocky mountains. Prepare for miles of curves, territorial views, and no guardrails. Drop down (er, drive down) and meet the Ouvèze River, then follow it into bustling **Buis-les-Baronnies** (with all the services, including a slew of cafés and an attractive old town to stroll). Buis-les-Baronnies is the linden tree capital of France and hosts an earthy outdoor market on Wednesdays with produce and crafts.

From Buis-les-Baronnies, continue south on D-5, then turn left toward Eygaliers on D-72. Follow this slow, serpentine road along the back side of Mont Ventoux and go all the way to the jewel of this trip: **Brantes,** one of Provence's most spectacularly located villages. Stop here for some fresh air, a look at the local pottery, and lunch with a Ventoux view at **La Poterne de Pascale** (closed Wed and Nov-March, +33 4 75 28 29 13).

Finally, follow signs back to Vaison-la-Romaine along the faster, less curvy D-40. A few minutes before Vaison-la-Romaine, you'll pass through pleasing little Entrechaux.

▲ARDECHE GORGES (GORGES DE L'ARDECHE)

These gorges, which wow visitors with abrupt chalky-white cliffs, follow the Ardèche River through immense canyons and thick forests. To reach the gorges from Vaison-la-Romaine, drive west for 1.5 hours (about 50 miles), passing through Bollène and Pont Saint-Esprit to **Vallon-Pont-d'Arc** (the tourist hub of the Ardèche Gorges). From Vallon-Pont-d'Arc, you can canoe along the river through some of the canyon's most spectacular scenery and under the rock arch of Pont d'Arc (half-day, all-day, and 2-day trips possible; less appealing in summer, when the river is crowded and water levels are low). Otherwise, hiking trails will get you above it all (**TI** +33 4 28 91 24 10, www.pontdarc-ardeche.fr).

The Ardèche region is a hot destination, thanks to the recent opening of a replica of one of France's largest and most impressive prehistoric caves, the **Chauvet Pont-d'Arc,** just outside the village of Vallon-Pont-d'Arc. Not discovered until 1994, the cave holds the oldest and best preserved man-made images anywhere (some date back over 36,000 years). The original cave is closed to the public, but the full-scale replica reproduces its art and artifacts to create the same feeling that the original cave inspires (€17, includes audioguide, informative tours—including in English—run regularly, open daily generally 9:00-19:00, longer in summer, shorter in winter, last entry two hours before closing, +33 4 75 94 39 40, https://en.grottechauvet2ardeche.com).

If continuing north toward Lyon, connect Privas and Aubenas, then head back on the autoroute. Endearing little **Balazuc**—a village just north of the gorges, with narrow lanes, flowers, views, and a smattering of cafés and shops—makes a great stop.

HILL TOWNS OF THE LUBERON

France's Answer to Italy's Tuscany

Just 30 miles east of Avignon, the Luberon region hides some of France's most captivating hill towns and sensuous landscapes. Those intrigued by Peter Mayle's best-selling *A Year in Provence* love joyriding through the region, connecting I-could-live-here villages, crumbled castles, and meditative abbeys. Mayle's book describes the ruddy local culture from an Englishman's perspective as he buys a stone farmhouse, fixes it up, and adopts the region as his new home. *A Year in Provence* is a great read while you're here—or, better, get it as an audiobook and listen while you drive.

The Luberon terrain in general (much of which is a French regional natural park) is as enticing as its villages. Gnarled vineyards and wind-sculpted trees separate tidy stone structures from abandoned buildings—little more than rock piles—that challenge city slickers to fix them up. Mountains of limestone bend along vast ridges, while colorful hot-air balloons survey the scene from above. The wind is an integral part of life here. The infamous mistral wind, finishing its long ride in from Siberia, hits like a hammer (see the sidebar on page 190).

PLANNING YOUR TIME

There are no obligatory museums, monuments, or vineyards in the Luberon. Treat this area like a vacation from your vacation. Downshift your engine. Brake for views, and ditch your car to take a walk. Get on a first-name basis with a village café.

To enjoy the ambience of the Luberon, you'll want at least one night and a car (only Isle-sur-la-Sorgue is easily accessible by train and bus). Allow a half-day for Isle-sur-la-Sorgue if it's market day (less time if not). Add more time if you want to paddle the Sorgue River or pedal between villages. You'll also want at least a full day for the Luberon villages. Many find that two or three hill towns is the right dose to appreciate their sometimes subtle differences.

For the ultimate Luberon experience, drivers should base themselves in or near Roussillon or near Bonnieux. To lose all sight of tourists, set up in Oppède-le Vieux, St-Saturnin-lès-Apt, or Buoux.

If you lack wheels, prefer streams to hills, or like a little more action, stay in Isle-sur-la-Sorgue, located within striking distance of Avignon and on the edge of the Luberon. Adequate train service from Avignon and Marseille, and some bus service, connects Isle-sur-la-Sorgue with the real world. Level terrain, quiet, tree-lined roads, and nearby villages make Isle-sur-la-Sorgue good for biking.

The village of Lourmarin works as a southern base for visiting Luberon sights, as do Aix-en-Provence, Cassis, and Marseille. Patient travelers can take a bus from Aix-en-Provence to reach Lourmarin.

GETTING AROUND THE LUBERON

By Car: A car or bike (see next page) is essential to get a good feel for this beautiful area. Luberon roads are scenic and narrow. With no major landmarks, it's easy to get lost—but that's not a bad thing. Consider buying the Michelin map #332 or #527 to navigate, and look for free maps available at local TIs. Popular towns charge a small fee to park. Expect headaches parking in Isle-sur-la-Sorgue during its market days.

If connecting this region with the **Côtes du Rhône,** avoid driving through Carpentras (bad traffic, confusing signage). If you're in a hurry, use the autoroute between Cavaillon and Orange. If time is not an issue, drive via Mont Ventoux—one of Provence's most spectacular routes (see end of previous chapter).

By Bus: Isle-sur-la-Sorgue is connected with Avignon's town center by the Trans Vaucluse bus line #6 (hourly Mon-Sat, 2/day Sun, 45 minutes, central stop—called Robert Vasse—is near the post office in Isle-sur-la-Sorgue, ask for schedule at TI or download it at www.islesurlasorguetourisme.com). Buses also connect Isle-sur-la-Sorgue with the Marseille airport (4/day direct, 2 hours). Buses link Lourmarin with Aix-en-Provence (3/day Mon-Sat, 1/day Sun, 1.5 hours). Without a car or minivan tour, skip the more famous hill towns of the Luberon.

By Train: Trains get you to Isle-sur-la-Sorgue (station called L'Isle-Fontaine de Vaucluse) from Avignon (10/day on weekdays, 7/day on weekends, 30 minutes) or from Marseille (12/day, 1.5-3 hours). If you're day-tripping by train, check return times before leaving the station.

By Minivan Tour: I list several minivan tour companies and

local guides who can guide you through this marvelous region (see "Tours in Provence" on page 38).

By Taxi: Contact **Luberon Taxi** (based in Maubec off D-3, +33 6 08 49 40 57, www.luberontaxi.com).

By Bike: Isle-sur-la-Sorgue makes a good base for biking, with level terrain and good rental options. Hardy bikers can ride from Isle-sur-la-Sorgue to Gordes, then to Roussillon, connecting other villages in a full-day loop ride (30 miles round-trip to Roussillon and back, with lots of hills). Several appealing villages are closer to Isle-sur-la-Sorgue (see "Biking" under the "Near Isle-sur-la-Sorgue" section, later). **Luberon Biking** can help you plan a route and will deliver a rental bike anywhere in the Luberon (see "Helpful Hints" in the Isle-sur-la-Sorgue section). **Rentbike Luberon** is based in Bonnieux but delivers electric and road bikes (daily, 3 Rue Marceau, mobile +33 7 78 68 34 94, www.rentbikescooterluberon. com). **Sun-e-Bike** rents electric bikes and has a network of partners with spare batteries scattered across the Luberon, extending the range of your e-bike trip. They can also arrange bike tours and

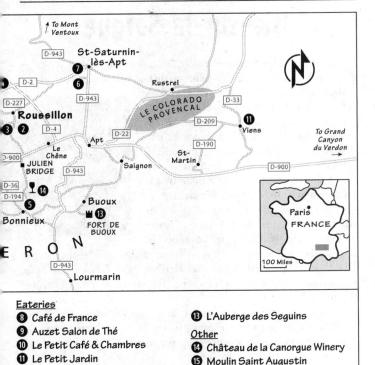

Eateries
- **8** Café de France
- **9** Auzet Salon de Thé
- **10** Le Petit Café & Chambres
- **11** Le Petit Jardin
- **12** Café de la Poste, La Bartavelle & La Terrasse

- **13** L'Auberge des Seguins

Other
- **14** Château de la Canorgue Winery
- **15** Moulin Saint Augustin
- **16** Musée des Boullions

shuttle your bags between hotels (1 Avenue Clovis Hugues in Bonnieux, +33 4 90 74 09 96, www.sun-e-bike.com).

LUBERON AREA MARKET DAYS

Monday: Cavaillon (produce and antiques/flea market)

Tuesday: Gordes, St-Saturnin-lès-Apt, and Lacoste (all small)

Wednesday: Sault (produce and antiques/flea market)

Thursday: Roussillon (cute) and Isle-sur-la-Sorgue (big, but still smaller than its Sunday market)

Friday: Lourmarin (very good) and Bonnieux (pretty good)

Saturday: Apt (huge produce and antiques/flea market)

Sunday: Isle-sur-la-Sorgue (granddaddy of them all, produce and antiques/flea market) and Coustellet (very local, filling a large parking lot)

LUBERON

Isle-sur-la-Sorgue

This sturdy market town—literally, "Island on the Sorgue River"—sits within a split in its crisp, happy little river at the foot of the Luberon. It's a workaday town that feels refreshingly real after so many adorable villages. It also makes a good base for exploring the Luberon (15 minutes by car, doable by hardy bikers) and Avignon (30 minutes by car or train) and can work for exploring the Côtes du Rhône by car (allow an hour to Vaison-la-Romaine).

After the arid cities and villages elsewhere in Provence, the presence of water at every turn is a welcome change. In Isle-sur-la-Sorgue—called the "Venice of Provence"—the Sorgue River's extraordinarily clear and shallow flow divides like cells, producing water, water everywhere. The river has long nourished the region's economy. The fresh spring water of the Sorgue's many branches has provided ample fish, irrigation for crops, and power for local industries for centuries. Today, antique shops power the town's economy—every other shop seems to sell some kind of antique.

Orientation to Isle-sur-la-Sorgue

Although Isle-sur-la-Sorgue is renowned for its market days (Sun and Thu), it's an otherwise pleasant town with no important sights and a steady trickle of tourism. It's lively on weekends but calm most weeknights. The town revolves around its river and streams, the church square, and two pedestrian-only streets, Rue de la République and Rue Carnot.

TOURIST INFORMATION
The TI has an essential town map, hiking information (ask about trails accessible by short drives), biking itineraries, and a line on rooms in private homes, all of which are outside town (Mon-Sat 9:30-12:30 & 14:00-18:00, Oct-March until 17:30, Sun 9:30-12:30 year-round; in the town center right behind the church at 13 Place Ferdinand Buisson, +33 4 90 38 04 78, www.oti-delasorgue.fr).

ARRIVAL IN ISLE-SUR-LA-SORGUE
By Car: Traffic is a mess and parking is a headache on market days (all day Sun and Thu morning). Circle the ring road and look for

parking signs. There are several lots just west of the roundabout at Le Bassin. **Parking les Névons,** a pay lot, is closest and worth it for the convenience. You'll find free parking lots behind the train station and along Quai Clovis (see the map on the next page for locations). You'll also pass freestyle parking on roads leaving the city. Don't leave anything visible in your car.

By Train: Remember that the train station is called "L'Isle-Fontaine de Vaucluse." To reach my recommended hotels, walk straight out of the station and turn right on the ring road.

By Bus: The bus from Avignon drops you near the post office at the Robert Vasse stop (ask driver for "La Poste"), a block from the recommended Hôtel les Névons.

HELPFUL HINTS

Shop Hours: The antique shops this town is famous for are open Friday afternoon to Monday only.

Laundry: A *laverie automatique*, perhaps easier for drivers, is at the **Centre Commercial Super U** supermarket (daily 9:00-19:00, on the ring road at the roundabout, Cours Fernande Peyre).

Supermarkets: There's a handy **Casino** market at 12 Rue de la République and larger **Utile** market on the main ring road, near the train station at 225 Avenue de la Libération (Mon-Sat 8:30-20:00, Sun until 13:00).

Bike Rental: The TI has a good list. **Kvelo** is in the center of town (4 Rue de la République, +33 4 90 38 59 30). **Luberon Biking,** in the nearby village of Velleron, delivers electric or standard bikes (daily, +33 4 90 90 14 62, www.luberon-biking.fr).

Taxi: For a local cab call +33 6 43 54 15 48. **Luberon Taxi** is handy for tours but not based in Isle-sur-la-Sorgue (+33 4 90 76 70 08, mobile +33 6 08 49 40 57, www.luberontaxi.com).

Public WC: A WC is in the parking lot between the post office and the Hôtel les Névons.

Isle-sur-la-Sorgue Walk

LUBERON

The town has crystal-clear water babbling under pedestrian bridges stuffed with flower boxes, and its old-time carousel is always spinning. For this self-guided wander (shown on the "Isle-sur-la-Sorgue" map), navigate by the town's splintered streams and nine mossy waterwheels, which, while still turning, power only memories of the town's wool and silk industries.

• Start your tour at the church next to the TI—where all streets seem to converge—then make forays into the town from there.

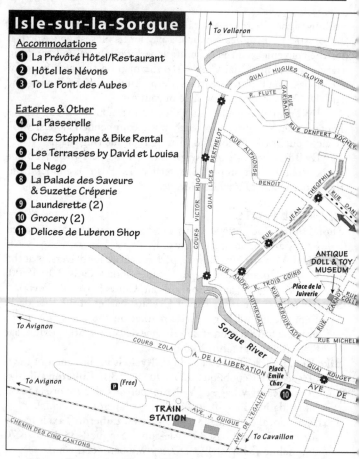

Isle-sur-la-Sorgue

Accommodations
1. La Prévôté Hôtel/Restaurant
2. Hôtel les Névons
3. To Le Pont des Aubes

Eateries & Other
4. La Passerelle
5. Chez Stéphane & Bike Rental
6. Les Terrasses by David et Louisa
7. Le Nego
8. La Balade des Saveurs & Suzette Créperie
9. Launderette (2)
10. Grocery (2)
11. Delices de Luberon Shop

Notre-Dame des Anges: This 12th-century church has a colorful Baroque interior and feels too big for today's town. Walk in. The curls and swirls and gilded statues date from an era that was all about Louis XIV, the Sun King. This is propagandist architecture, designed to wow the faithful into compliance. (It was made possible thanks to profits generated from the town's river-powered industries.) When you enter a church like this, the heavens should open up and assure you that whoever built it had celestial connections (daily 10:00-12:00 & 15:15-17:00, Mass on Sun at 10:30).

Turn right as you leave the church, then notice the buildings' faded facades around you, recalling their previous lives (*fabrique de chaussures* was a shoemaker; *meubles* means furniture; *3 étages d'exposition* means 3 showroom floors). Admire Fauque Beyret's antique storefront. Those big porches allowed goods to be sold outside, rain or shine. Isle-sur-la-Sorgue retains a connection to its past uncommon in this renovation-happy region.

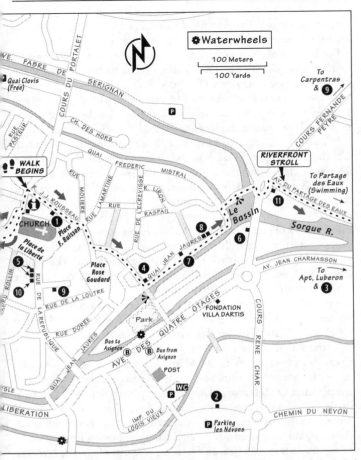

• *Wander down Rue Danton, the narrow street to the right of the faded* meubles *building, to lose the crowds. Keep going until you find...*

Three Waterwheels: These big, forgotten waterwheels have been in business here since the 1200s, when they were used for grinding flour. Paper, textile, silk, and woolen mills would later find their power from this river. At its peak, Isle-sur-la-Sorgue had 70 waterwheels thanks to the predictable flow of its spring-fed river. In the 1800s, the town competed with Avignon as Provence's cloth-dyeing

and textile center. Those stylish Provençal fabrics and patterns you see for sale everywhere were made possible by this river.

• *Double back to the church, turn left under the arcade, then find the small stream just past the TI. Breakaway streams like this run under the town like subways run under Paris. Take a right on the first street after the stream; it leads under a long arch (along Rue J. J. Rousseau). Look up for more faded advertisements* (bains, douches, *and* chambres meublées *means baths, showers, and furnished rooms). Follow this straight, and veer slightly right at Place F. Buisson onto Place Rose Goudard (likely crowded with parked cars), and walk to the main river. Then turn left and walk along the many café terraces until you come to...*

Le Bassin: Literally translated as a "pond," this is where the Sorgue River crashes into the town and separates into many branches. Track as many branches as you can see (the Franck Provost hair salon hides a big one), and then find the round lookout point for the best perspective (carefully placed lights make this a beautiful sight after dark). Fishing was the town's main industry until the waterwheels took over. In the 1300s, local fishermen provided the pope with his fresh-fish quota. They trapped them in nets and speared them while standing on skinny, flat-bottomed boats. Several streets are named after the fish they caught—including Rue de l'Aiguille ("Eel Street") and Rue des Ecrevisses ("Crayfish Street").

The sound of the rushing water reminds us of the power that rivers can generate. With its source (a spring) a mere five miles away, the Sorgue River never floods and has a constant flow and temperature in all seasons. Despite its exposed (flat) location, Isle-sur-la-Sorgue prospered in the Middle Ages, thanks to the natural protection this river provided. Walls with big moats once ran along the river, but they were destroyed during the French Revolution.

• *Cross the busy roundabout, and walk to the orange* **Delices de Luberon** *store. Find the small tasting table with scrumptious tapenades and olives. Turn right behind the store to find the river and take a refreshing...*

Riverfront Stroll: Follow the main river upstream, along the bike/pedestrian lane, as far as you like. The road meanders about a mile, following the serene course of the river, past waterfront homes and beneath swaying trees. It ends at the Hôtel le Pescador and a riverfront café. The wide and shallow Partage des Eaux, where the water divides before entering Isle-sur-la-Sorgue, is perfect for a cool swim on a hot day.

Activities and Sights in Isle-sur-la-Sorgue

▲▲Market Days

The town erupts into a carnival-like market frenzy each Sunday and Thursday, with hardy crafts and local produce. The Sunday market is astounding and famous for its antiques; the Thursday market is still impressive but focused more on produce and bric-a-brac than antiques (see market tips in the Shopping chapter).

Fondation Villa Dartis

Drop into this modern sculpture gallery to see what's on exhibit (free, Wed-Sun 11:00-18:30, closed Mon-Tue and likely Nov-April, on the river at 7 Avenue des Quatre Otages, +33 4 90 95 23 70, www.villadatris.com).

Antique Toy and Doll Museum
(Musée du Jouet et de la Poupée Ancienne)

The town's other main sight is a fun and funky toy museum with more than 300 dolls displayed in three small rooms. Most dolls date from 1880 to 1930.

Cost and Hours: €3.50, kids-€1.50, daily 10:30-17:30, shorter hours and closed Mon off-season, at 26 Rue Carnot down a short alley, +33 6 15 43 21 26, www.poupeesdelisle.com.

NEAR ISLE-SUR-LA-SORGUE

Fontaine-de-Vaucluse

You'll read and hear a lot about this overrun village, impressively located at the source of the Sorgue River, where the medieval Italian poet Petrarch mourned for his love, Laura. The river seems to magically appear from nowhere (the actual source is a murky, green waterhole) and flows through the town past a lineup of cafés, souvenir shops, and wall-to-river tourists. The setting is beautiful—with cliffs jutting to the sky and a ruined castle above—but the trip is worth it only if the spring is flowing (usually only after several days of hard rain or during early spring snow melt). *Sans* flowing spring, this may be the most overrated sight in France. Ask your hotelier if the spring is active (*Est-ce que la source diverse?*), and arrive early or late to avoid crowds. It's a 30-minute bike ride here from Isle-sur-la-Sorgue (about five miles).

Arriving by car, you'll pay to park (€5), and then walk about 20 minutes along the sparkling river to *la source* (the spring), located in a cave at the base of the cliff. (It's an uphill hike for the last part.) The spring itself is the very definition of anticlimactic, unless it's surging. At those times, it's among the most prolific water producers in the world, with a depth no one has yet been able to determine.

The path to the spring is lined with distractions. A worthwhile stop is at the **Moulin à Papier,** a reproduction of a 17th-century paper mill, where you'll see the value of harnessing the river's power. In the mill, a 22-foot-diameter paddle wheel turns five times a minute, driving hammers that pound paper for up to 36 hours (free, daily 9:00-19:00). As you watch the hammers pound away, imagine Isle-sur-la-Sorgue's waterwheels and the industries they once powered. The shop inside sells paper in every size. The best riverfront café seats are at **Philip's Café** (located after Moulin à Papier).

Canoe Trips on the Sorgue

If you're *really* on vacation, take the five-mile, two-hour canoe trip from Fontaine-de-Vaucluse down the river to Isle-sur-la-Sorgue. Guides escort small groups in canoes, or you can go it alone. You'll return to Fontaine-de-Vaucluse by shuttle bus (call for departure times; ask about shuttle service from Isle-sur-la-Sorgue). **Kayaks Verts** is a family operation (late April-mid-Oct, €22/person, +33 4 90 20 35 44, www.canoe-france.com/en/sorgue). To combine bike and boat, ask about shuttling your rental bikes back to Isle-sur-la-Sorgue while you float from Fontaine-de-Vaucluse (see suggested bike route below).

Biking

Isle-sur-la-Sorgue is ideally situated for short biking forays into the mostly level terrain. Pick up a biking itinerary at the TI, or ask your bike-rental shop for suggestions. These towns make easy biking destinations from Isle-sur-la-Sorgue: **Velleron** (5 flat miles north, a tiny version of Isle-sur-la-Sorgue with waterwheels, fountains, and an evening farmers market Mon-Sat 18:00-20:00); **Lagnes** (3 miles east, a pretty and well-restored hill town with views from its ruined château); and **Fontaine-de-Vaucluse** (5 gentle, uphill miles northeast, described earlier). Allow 30 miles and many hills for the round-trip ride to Roussillon.

Sleeping in and near Isle-sur-la-Sorgue

Pickings are slim for good sleeps in Isle-sur-la-Sorgue, though the few I've listed provide reliable values.

$$$ La Prévôté*** has the town's highest-priced digs. Its five meticulously decorated rooms—located above a classy and recommended restaurant—are adorned in earth tones, with high ceilings, a few exposed beams, and carefully selected furnishings. Antonia manages the hotel while her husband oversees the kitchen (includes breakfast, limited check-in/check-out times, no elevator, rooftop deck with hot tub, no parking, one block from the church at 4 Rue J. J. Rousseau, +33 4 90 38 57 29, www.la-prevote.fr, contact@la-prevote.fr).

$ Hôtel les Névons,*** two blocks from the center (behind the post office), is concrete motel-modern outside, with well-priced and comfortable-enough rooms within, a roof deck with a small pool, and quick access to the town center (family rooms, air-con, elevator, free and safe parking, 205 Chemin des Névons, +33 4 90 20 72 00, www.hotel-les-nevons.com, contact@hotel-les-nevons.fr).

$ Le Pont des Aubes is a nifty option, with six rooms for two people, each with full kitchens. Rooms are comfortable with modest bathrooms and face a large yard fronting the Sorgue River. It's a short hop to the town center by car or 15 minutes on foot. Sincere Martine is your host (3-night minimum, longer in high season, 189 Route d'Apt, +33 4 90 38 13 75, www.lepontdesaubes.com, lepontdesaubes@yahoo.fr).

Eating in Isle-sur-la-Sorgue

Cheap and mediocre restaurants are a dime a dozen in Isle-sur-la-Sorgue. You'll see several brasseries on the river, good for views and basic café fare. Dining on the river is a unique experience in this arid land, and shopping for the perfect table is half the fun. To assemble a riverside picnic, head to Rue de la République, which has bakeries, butchers, a *traiteur* (deli), cheesemongers, a wine shop, and a grocery store.

For a tasty riverside meal, find **$$ La Passerelle,** where charming Jennifer and Vincent serve salads, quiche, *plats du jour,* and more. Ask about their octopus dish (closed Wed, dinners served Fri-Sat only, 18 Quai Jean Jaurès, +33 6 62 18 23 57).

Begin your dinner with a glass of wine at the cozy wine and cheese shop **$ Chez Stéphane.** Or for a light meal, order a selection of cheeses from charming Stéphane (great to share) with your wine and call it good (wine barrel tables are outside or find the bar hiding in back; closed Sun evening and all day Mon, 12 Rue de la République, +33 4 90 20 70 25).

$$ Les Terrasses by David et Louisa is an appealing riverside wine-bar-bistro with a warm interior and ample choices (under a recommended hotel). The cuisine is a blend of French traditional and Provençal (daily, 2 Avenue du Général de Gaulle, +33 4 90 38 03 16).

$$ Le Nego is a relaxed place with generous outdoor seating and a large selection of reasonably priced, regional fare that works well for riverfront dining (daily, 12 Quai Jean Jaurès, +33 4 90 20 88 83).

$$$$ La Balade des Saveurs is a refreshing change from the many run-of-the-mill riverfront places. Here, the owners deliver fresh, well-presented Provençal and traditional French cuisine at riverside tables or in their elegantly sky-lit interior (closed Mon-Tue, 3 Quai Jean Jaurès, +33 4 90 95 27 85, www.balade-des-saveurs.com).

$$$$ La Prévôté is the place in town to do it up in the elegant French style. Its lovely dining room is country-classy but not stuffy, and the cuisine blends traditional French with regional specialties. A stream runs under the restaurant, visible through glass windows (€65 five-course *menu,* closed Tue-Wed in some seasons—check ahead, on narrow street that runs along left side of church as you face it, 4 Rue J. J. Rousseau, +33 4 90 38 57 29, www.la-prevote.fr). The owners also run a cool bistro where you can enjoy the same chef's talents for less in a more casual setting.

$ Suzette Créperie delivers tasty crêpes and a limited choice of other dishes at riverside tables or in their cozy interior. With friendly owners, it's the cheapest place to get a decent meal on the river (closed Sun evening and all day Mon-Tue, 6 Quai Jean Jaurès, +33 4 65 81 72 18).

The Heart of the Luberon

A 15-minute drive east of Isle-sur-la-Sorgue brings you to this protected area, where canyons and ridgelines rule, and land developers take a back seat. Still-proud hill towns guard access to winsome valleys, while carefully managed vineyards (producing inexpensive wines) play hopscotch with cherry groves, lavender fields, and cypress trees.

In the 1990s, Peter Mayle's *A Year in Provence* nudged tourism in this area into overdrive, and his quintessential Provence includes many of the popular villages and sights described in this chapter. While the hill towns can be seen as subtly different variations on the same theme, each has a distinct character. Look for differences: the color of shutters, the pattern of stones, the importance of flowers, or the number of tourist boutiques. Every village has something to offer—it's up to you to discover and celebrate it.

I like sleeping in or near Roussillon. By village standards, Roussillon is lively and struggles to manage its popularity. When restaurant hunting, read descriptions of the villages in this chapter—many good finds are embedded in the countryside. For aerial views high above this charmed land, consider a hot-air balloon trip.

LUBERON

PLANNING YOUR TIME

With a car and one full day, I'd linger in Roussillon in the morning (and explore its ochre cliffs), then admire the Julien Bridge before having lunch nearby in Lacoste or Bonnieux. After lunch, continue the joyride via Ménerbes to Oppède-le-Vieux, then return through Coustellet and Gordes. With a second full day, I'd start by climbing the Fort de Buoux and consider lunch at L'Auberge des Sequins near the fort. From Buoux, I'd continue to Saignon and Viens (good restaurant), then loop back via Le Colorado Provençal and St-Saturnin-lès-Apt.

I've described sights at each stop, but you'll need to be selective—you can't (and don't need to) see them all. Read through your options and choose the ones that appeal most. Slow down and get to know a few places well, rather than dashing between every stop you can cram in. The best sight is the dreamy landscape between the villages.

Roussillon

With all the trendy charm of Santa Fe on a hilltop, photogenic Roussillon requires serious camera and café time. Roussillon has been a protected village since 1943 and has benefited from a complete absence of modern development. An enormous deposit of ochre, which gives the earth and its buildings that distinctive reddish color, provided this village with its economic base until shortly after World War II. This place is popular; visit early before crowds arrive and while the rising sun highlights the ochre cliffs, or come late and stay for dinner.

Orientation to Roussillon

Roussillon sits atop Mont Rouge ("Red Mountain") at about 1,000 feet above sea level. The town's bell tower marks its center; exposed ochre cliffs form the village's southern limit. There's a small market on Thursdays near the TI.

Tourist Information: The little TI is in the center, across from the Chez David restaurant. Say bonjour to sweet Pascale. Walkers should get info on trails from Roussillon to nearby villages (TI hours are unreliable, usually Mon-Sat 8:30-12:30 & 14:00-18:00, Nov-March 14:00-17:30 only, closed

LUBERON

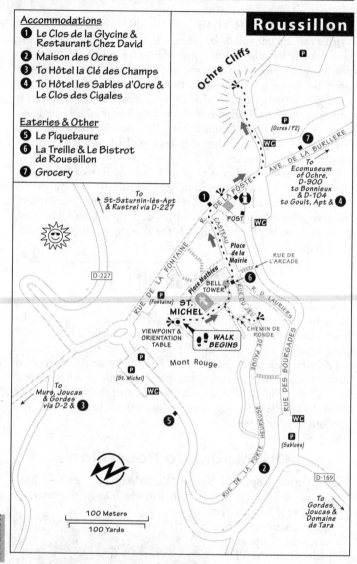

Roussillon

Accommodations
1. Le Clos de la Glycine & Restaurant Chez David
2. Maison des Ocres
3. To Hôtel la Clé des Champs
4. To Hôtel les Sables d'Ocre & Le Clos des Cigales

Eateries & Other
5. Le Piquebaure
6. La Treille & Le Bistrot de Roussillon
7. Grocery

Sun year-round, Place de la Poste, +33 4 90 05 60 25, http://otroussillon.pagesperso-orange.fr).

Parking: Parking areas are available at every entry to the village (free if you're staying overnight and have arranged it with your hotel). **Parking des Ocres** (also called "P2") is the largest lot on the hill and closest to the action. Day-trippers should head straight here, as spots are more available and the view of Roussillon is striking. Leave nothing of value visible in your car.

Parking Sablons is next to the recommended Maison des Ocres. **Parking St-Michel** is below the town on the way to Joucas and Gordes.

Sights in Roussillon

If you're here in the morning, walk the ochre cliffs first (before doing the village stroll). This is when colors are most vibrant and the cliffs are bathed in light.

▲▲Ochre Cliffs Trail (Le Sentier des Ocres)

Roussillon was Europe's capital for ochre production until World War II. A stroll to the south end of town, beyond the Parking des Ocres, shows you why: Roussillon sits on the world's largest known ochre deposit. Two radiant orange paths lead around the richly colored, Bryce Canyon-like cliffs—allow 35 minutes for the shorter path and 55 minutes for the longer one. If you choose the shorter route, follow the longer route for a few minutes uphill after the trails separate to a beautiful cliff view (then double back and pick up the shorter trail). Beware: Light-colored clothing (especially shoes) and orange powder don't mix.

Ochre is made of iron oxide and clay. When combined with sand, it creates the yellowish-red pigments you see in the town's buildings. Although ochre is also produced in the US and Italy, the quality of France's ochre is considered *le best*.

The value of Roussillon's ochre cliffs was known even in Roman times. Once excavated, the clay ochre was rinsed with water to separate it from sand, then bricks of the stuff were dried and baked for deeper hues. The procedure for extracting the ochre did not change much over 2,000 years, until ochre mining became industrialized in the late 1700s. Used primarily for wallpaper and linoleum, ochre use reached its zenith just before World War II. (After that, cheaper substitutes took over.)

Cost and Hours: €3; May-June and Sept 9:30-18:30, July-Aug 9:00-19:30, shorter hours off-season, closed Jan.

Village Stroll

To begin this walk, find the town's center, cross the cute square, and then climb under the bell tower and past the church to the summit of the village.

Find the orientation table and the **viewpoint,** often complete with a howling mistral wind. During the Middle Ages, a castle occupied this space on the top of the appropriately named Red Mountain (Mont Rouge), and watched over the village below. Although nothing remains of the castle today, the strategic advantage of this site is clear. Find naked Mont Ventoux and count how many villages you can identify, and then notice how little sprawl there is in the valley below. Because the Luberon has been declared a natural reserve (Parc Naturel Régional du Luberon), development is strictly controlled. This view has not changed in the many years I've been coming here. Nice.

Stroll back to the **church.** Duck into the pretty 11th-century Church of St. Michel, and appreciate the natural air-conditioning and the well-worn center aisle.

The white interior tells you that the stone came from elsewhere, and the WWI memorial plaque over the side door suggests a village devastated by the war (more than 40 people from little Roussillon died).

As you leave the church, look across the way to the **derelict building,** a reminder of Roussillon's humble roots. After World War II, when the demand for ochre faded, this was a dusty, desolate village with zero tourist appeal. Many residents fled for an easier life below, with fewer steps and modern conveniences. Abandoned buildings like this presented a serious problem (common throughout France)...until tourists discovered Roussillon, and folks began reinvesting in the village. Still, many of Roussillon's residents live very simply and could not imagine paying for the hotels we recommend. And that building across the way? It's still looking for a buyer. Detour behind the decrepit building to the left, down a small lane to find the **Chemin de Ronde,** with terrific views of the Luberon and Gordes from atop the medieval walls.

Return to the church and continue down to the village. Notice the clamped-iron beams that shore up old walls. Examine the different hues of yellow and orange. These lime-finished exteriors, called *chaux* (literally, "limes"), need to be redone about every 10 years. Locals choose their exact color...but in this town of ochre, it's never white. The church tower that you walk under once marked the entrance to the fortified town. Just before dropping down to the square, turn right and find the gigantic 150-year-old grapevine that decorates the recommended Restaurant la Treille. This is what you get when you don't prune.

LUBERON

Linger over *un café*, or—if it's later in the day—*un pastis*, in the picturesque **village square** (Place de la Mairie). Watch the stream of shoppers. Is anyone playing *boules* at the opposite end? You could paint the entire town without ever leaving the red-and-orange corner of your palette. Many do. While Roussillon receives scads of day-trippers, mornings and evenings are romantically peaceful on this square.

With the cafés on your right, drop downhill past the lineup of shops and turn right past the TI to find the small parking lot just beyond. Animals grazed here for centuries. It was later turned into a school playground. When cars outnumbered students, it became a parking lot. Walk past the parking lot and head left uphill, past picture-perfect views back to Roussillon. At the top, large displays on **metal easels** provide excellent background about ochre. If you haven't already strolled the cliffs, you can do so now (see listing, earlier).

NEAR ROUSSILLON
▲ Écomusée De L'ocre

For a good introduction to the history and uses of ochre, visit this intriguing reconstructed ochre factory. Grab a pamphlet to follow the well-done self-guided tour, which shows how ochre is converted from an ore to a pigment (allow 45 minutes). Your visit ends with a good bookshop and a chance to try your hand at ochre painting.

Cost and Hours: €7, daily 10:00-13:00 & 14:00-18:00, July-Aug until 19:00, shorter hours and closed some days in winter—check online, about a half-mile below Roussillon toward Apt on D-104, +33 4 90 05 66 69, www.okhra.com.

Domaine de Tara

Just below Roussillon, on the road to Joucas, this welcoming winery has been making excellent wines for about 15 years. Pascale runs the tasting room, and her husband makes wines to please every palate: red, white, rosé, sparkling, and sweet. Pop into the barrel room where they often exhibit local artists' work. They don't mind if you picnic on the property afterward.

Cost and Hours: Prices vary by wine though most under €15, Thu-Tue 10:00-18:00, closed Wed, +33 4 90 05 74 87, www.domainedetara.com.

LUBERON

Hot-Air Balloon Flight

Ply the calm morning air above the Luberon in a hot-air balloon. The **Vol-Terre** outfit offers a flight that includes a picnic and champagne (€230, around 1 hour in balloon, allow 3 hours total, maximum 4 passengers, reserve a few days ahead, mobile +33 6 03 54 10 92, www.montgolfiere-luberon.com).

Goult

Bigger than its sister hill towns, this surprisingly quiet village seems content to be away from the tourist path, though its good selection of restaurants is a draw for many. Climb the small lanes up the hill to the panoramic view and windmill. From there, drop back down through the arch and glide down, passing the old château. Notice how many of the historic buildings are built right on top of thick rock strata. Consider having a nice meal in one of Goult's several good restaurants—where you'll compete with locals rather than tourists for a table. **$$ Café de la Poste** is ideal for an outdoor lunch or dinner (+33 4 90 72 23 23). **$$$ La Bartavelle** is *the* place to settle in and enjoy an unhurried meal, with warm ambience and beautifully presented dishes (book a table a week in advance, closed Tue-Wed, 29 Rue du Cheval Blanc, +33 4 90 72 33 72). **$$ La Terrasse** serves regional dishes on a lovely rooftop deck or in their cozy dining room (Rue de la République, +33 4 90 72 20 20).

Sleeping in Roussillon

Parking is free if you sleep in Roussillon; arrange it with your hotelier. The village offers a couple of acceptable-value accommodations.

$$$ Le Clos de la Glycine*** delivers Roussillon's plushest accommodations with nine lovely rooms located dead-center in the village (some view rooms, air-con, parking options, located at the recommended restaurant Chez David—they prefer you pay for half-pension, across from the TI on Place de la Poste, +33 4 90 05 60 13, www.leclosdelaglycine.fr, contact@leclosdelaglycine.fr).

$$ Maison des Ocres,*** well located on the edge of the village center at the Sablons parking area, is a formal and stylish place with a spacious lounge, well-configured rooms (many with decks or balconies), a few good family rooms, a small bistro serving lunches and dinners, and a lovely pool (private parking, Route de Gordes, +33 4 90 05 60 50, www.lamaisondesocres-hotel.com, contact@lamaisondesocres-hotel.com). Coming from Gordes and Joucas, it's the first building you pass in Roussillon.

LUBERON

NEAR ROUSSILLON

These listings are for drivers only (for locations, see the "Luberon" map at the beginning of this chapter). The last two are most easily found by turning north off D-900 at the *Roussillon/Les Huguets* sign (the second turnoff to Roussillon coming from Avignon). Joucas and St-Saturnin-lès-Apt (both described later) also have good beds near Roussillon.

$$$ Hôtel la Clé des Champs,*** more like an elegant bed and breakfast, is a lovely nine-room Provençal splurge warmly run by René and Armelle in a peaceful, rural setting. Carefully appointed rooms are clustered about a heated pool, there's a hammam and hot tub, and dinners are available several days each week for €40 (between Roussillon and Joucas, off D-2 on Chemin du Garrigon, +33 4 90 05 63 22, www.hotelcledeschamps.com, contact@hotelcledeschamps.com).

$$ Hôtel les Sables d'Ocre** offers 22 spotless, motel-esque rooms, a big pool, the greenest grass around, air-conditioning, and fair rates (a half-mile from Roussillon toward Apt at intersection of D-108 and D-104, +33 4 90 05 55 55, www.sablesdocre.com, sablesdocre@orange.fr).

$ Le Clos des Cigales is a good forested refuge run by friendly Philippe. Of their five blue-shuttered, stylish bungalows, two are doubles and three are two-room family friendly suites with tiny kitchenettes; all have private patios facing a big pool (family rooms, includes breakfast, table tennis, hammock, 5 minutes from Roussillon toward Goult on D-104, +33 4 90 05 73 72, www.leclosdescigales.com, philippe.lherbeil@wanadoo.fr).

Eating in Roussillon

Restaurants change with the mistral here—what's good one year disappoints the next. But I have found a few reliable places that offer a good range of prices and cuisine. Consider my suggestions (or look over my recommendations in other Luberon villages, like Goult or Joucas, each just a few minutes away by car). The **Casino** grocery on Avenue de la Burlière has what you need to supply your ochre-view picnic (see the "Roussillon" map).

On Place de la Poste: A good place to splurge is at **$$$$ Chez David,** at the recommended hotel Le Clos de la Glycine. You can enjoy a fine meal on the terrace or from an interior window table with point-blank views over the ochre cliffs (closed Wed and Sun in off-season, Place de la Poste, +33 4 90 05 60 13).

$$$ Le Piquebaure—perched at the north side of town, a 10-minute walk from the center—delivers the best affordable "gourmet cuisine" in Roussillon. The food is delicious and beauti-

LUBERON

Luberon Restaurants Worth the Trip

The countryside near Roussillon yields a bushel of restaurants worthy of a detour. Refer to the list below, then flip to the full descriptions of those that appeal to you. All are within a 20-minute drive from Roussillon (locations for most can be found on the "Luberon" map at the beginning of this chapter).

Dinner

Chez David, in Roussillon, offers fine cuisine and views in a formal setting (see page 227).

Hôtel des Voyageurs, in St-Saturnin-lès-Apt, is a local favorite, with authentic decor and lovely hosts (see page 239).

La Bartavelle, in overlooked Goult, offers fine cuisine and draws a foodie crowd (see page 189).

La Terrasse, in peaceful Joucas, delivers grand views from a large terrace and tasty café cuisine at fair prices. This place works well for lunch too (see page 229).

Restaurant l'Arôme, in Bonnieux, is a dressy place with a warm dining room and refined Provençal cuisine (see page 236).

Lunch

Auzet Salon de Thé, in Ménerbes, serves luscious quiche and savory pies with salad, delicious baked goods, and more (see page 237).

Café de la Poste, in Goult, has a pleasant outdoor terrace and a traditional menu (see page 226).

Les Terrasses, in Bonnieux, serves café cuisine on an outside terrace with stunning vistas. This place works for dinner, too (see page 235).

Café de France, in Lacoste, is an easygoing eatery with sensational view tables (see page 236).

Le Petit Café, in Oppède-le-Vieux, has a charming setting facing Luberon cliffs and castle ruins (see page 238).

Le Petit Jardin, in remote Viens, offers an unpretentious lunch or dinner stop, with cozy interior tables and a garden terrace (see page 241).

LUBERON

fully presented. Eat in the stylish interior or on the covered terrace (closed Tue, 266 Avenue Dame Sirmonde, + 33 7 85 36 73 63).

$$ La Treille hangs just above the village square and serves good meals on a small terrace or under soft arches in an upstairs room (daily, Rue du Four, +33 4 90 05 64 47).

$ Le Bistrot de Roussillon is ideally situated on Roussillon's delightful square and serves simple café fare at good prices. Enjoy your meal at outdoor tables on the square (my favorite), inside the pleasant dining room, or on a small terrace out back with views to the ochre cliffs (open daily for lunch, may be open for dinner in high season, Place de la Mairie, +33 4 90 05 74 45).

Joucas

This understated, quiet, and largely overlooked village offers stone lanes with carefully arranged flowers, beautiful vistas, and well-restored homes. There's not much to do or see here, except eat, sleep, and just be. Joucas has a recommended view café/restaurant, one pharmacy, a small grocery, a good kids' play area, and one good-value accommodation option. Sleep here for a central location and utter silence. For views, walk past the little fountain in the center and up the steep lanes as high as you want.

Several **hiking** trails leave from Joucas. Gordes and Roussillon are each three miles away, uphill (allow 75 minutes at a steady pace to either). The three-mile hike up to the attractive village of Murs (which has several cafés/restaurants) is more scenic, though it's easier in the other direction (yellow signs point the way from the top of the village). You don't have to go far to enjoy the natural beauty on this trail.

Sleeping and Eating: Located in the center of lovely little Joucas, **$ Le Joucas**** has comfortable, good-value rooms and is kid-friendly, with a big pool and a sports field/play area next door. Ask for a south-facing room *(coté sud)* for the best views. All rooms have showers, air-conditioning, and mini fridges (above park at village entrance, +33 4 90 05 78 01, www.lescommandeurs.com, hostellerie@lescommandeurs.com). The traditional **$$ restaurant** offers Provençal cuisine at fair prices (closed Wed). Village kids like to hang out around the bar's pool table.

$ La Terrasse is the place to dine on a warm evening in Joucas. A generous deck gives way to vineyard and village views where diners enjoy simple but good dishes (pizza, salads, *plats du jour*) and a peaceful meal with a terrific backdrop at good prices (daily May-Sept, closed off-season, above the Hostellerie des Commandeurs, Rue Grande, +33 4 90 75 17 98).

LUBERON

More Luberon Towns

Le Luberon is packed with appealing villages and beautiful scenery, but it has only a handful of must-see sights. I've grouped them by area to make your sightseeing planning easier (see the "Luberon" map at the beginning of this chapter). The D-900 highway cuts the Luberon in half. The more popular and visited section lies above D-900 (with Roussillon and Gordes), while the villages to the south seem a bit less trampled.

Rambling the Luberon's spaghetti network of small roads is a joy, and getting lost comes with the territory—go with it. None of the sights listed below is a must-see, but all are close to each other. Pick up a good map (such as Michelin maps #332 and #527).

I'd make a loop through these villages and sights, doing them in the order described below (but start with the Abbey Notre-Dame de Sénaque). If you're sleeping in or near Roussillon, start there (mornings are peaceful, and the light is best on the ochre trails). Each town is about a 10-minute drive from the last.

Gordes

The Luberon's most impressively situated hill town is worth a quick stop to admire its setting. As you approach Gordes, veer right when you see the viewpoint icon. Get out, stroll along the road, and admire the sensational view. Now consider this: In the 1960s Gordes was a ghost town of derelict buildings with no economy, where locals led simple lives and had few ambitions. Then came the popularity of the theater festival in Avignon, bringing directors who wanted to re-create perfect Provençal villages on film. Parisians, Swiss, Brits, and a few Americans followed, willing to pay any price for their place in the Provençal sun.

Today Gordes is renovated top to bottom (notice how every stone seems perfectly placed) and filled with people who live in a world without calluses. Many Parisian big shots and moneyed foreigners invested heavily, restoring dream homes and putting property values and café prices out of sight for locals. Beyond its stunning views, the village has pretty lanes lined with trendy boutiques and restaurants but little else of interest.

SIGHTS NEAR GORDES

The first two sights—the Abbey Notre-Dame de Sénanque and the Village des Bories—are both well marked from Gordes.

Abbey Notre-Dame de Sénanque

This still-functioning and beautifully situated Cistercian abbey was built in 1148 as a back-to-basics reaction to the excesses of Benedictine abbeys. The Cistercians strove to be separate from the world and to recapture the simplicity, solitude, and poverty of the early Church. To succeed required industrious self-sufficiency—a skill these monks excelled at. Their movement spread and colonized Europe with a new form of Christianity. By 1200 there were more than 500 such monasteries and abbeys in Europe.

Visitors arriving as the abbey opens find a peaceful place; those arriving during high-season afternoons rub elbows with other visitors. Still, the interior, which doesn't measure up to the abbey's spectacular setting—is not why I come; it's worth the trip for its splendid and remote setting alone.

Cost and Hours: €8.50, includes multimedia guide, visits on the half hour, April-Nov Mon-Sat 9:30-11:00 & 13:00-17:00, Sun 14:00-17:30, +33 4 90 72 05 72, www.senanque.fr, visites@ndsenanque.net.

Dress Code: Modest dress is required for entry—shoulders and knees must be covered.

Visiting the Abbey: Come first thing and stop at a pullout for a bird's-eye view as you descend from Gordes, then wander the abbey's perimeter. The abbey church (closed for renovation through 2023) is usually open and free (except during Mass, but you're welcome to attend) and highlights the utter simplicity sought by these monks. In late June through much of July, the five hectares of lavender fields that surround the abbey make for breathtaking pictures and draw loads of visitors.

You can only visit the abbey on a 50-minute French-only guided tour, though handy "histopads" are free and allow you to make sense of the place. Abbey interior areas that you can visit include Sénanque's church (when open), the small cloisters, the refectory, and a *chauffoir,* a small heated room where monks could copy books year-round. I enjoy just wandering the grounds.

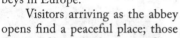

LUBERON

Medieval Monasteries

France is littered with medieval monasteries, and Provence is no exception. Most have virtually no furnishings (they never had many), which leaves the visitor with little to reconstruct what life must have been like in these cold stone buildings a thousand years ago. A little history can help breathe life into these important yet underappreciated monuments.

After the fall of the Roman Empire, monasteries arose as refuges of peace and order in a chaotic world. While the pope got rich and famous playing power politics, monasteries worked to keep the focus on simplicity and poverty. Throughout the Middle Ages, monasteries were mediators between Man and God. In these peacefully remote abbeys, Europe's best minds struggled with the interpretation of God's words. Every sentence needed to be understood and applied. Answers later debated in universities were once contemplated in monasteries.

St. Benedict established the Middle Ages' most influential monastic order (Benedictine) in Monte Cassino, Italy, in AD 529.

He scheduled a rigorous program of monastic duties that combined manual labor with intellectual tasks. His movement spread north and took firm root in France, where the abbey of Cluny (Burgundy) eventually controlled more than 2,000 dependent abbeys and vied with the pope for control of the Church.

Benedictine abbeys became rich, and with wealth came excess (king-size beds and saunas). Monks lost sight of their purpose and became soft and corrupt. In the late 1100s, the deter-

---

A small monastic community still resides here. For more on monasteries, see the sidebar.

Leaving the Abbey: Leave the abbey opposite the way you arrived, following signs to *Gordes*, then *Roussillon*, then follow *Murs* and *Joucas*...and enjoy the ride.

Village des Bories

A twisting, mile-long, stone-bordered dirt road sets the mood for this mildly entertaining open-air museum of stone huts *(bories)*. The vertical stones you see on the walls as you approach the site were used as counterweights to keep these mortar-free walls intact. The "village" you tour is made up of dry-laid stone structures, proving that there has always been more stone than wood in this rugged region. Stone villages like this predated the Romans—some say by 2,000 years. This one was inhabited for 200 years (from about 1600

LUBERON

mined and charismatic St. Bernard rallied the Cistercian order by going back to the original rule of St. Benedict. Cistercian abbeys thrived as centers of religious thought and exploration from the 13th through the 15th centuries.

Cistercian abbots ran their abbeys like little kingdoms, doling out punishment and food to the monks, and tools to peasant farmers. Abbeys were occupied by two groups: the favored monks from aristocratic families (such as St. Bernard) and a larger group of lay brothers from peasant stock, who were given the heaviest labor and could join only the Sunday services.

Monks' days were broken into three activities: prayer, reading holy texts, and labor. Monks lived in silence and poverty, with few amenities—meat was forbidden, as was cable TV. In summer, they ate two daily meals—in winter, just one. Monks slept together in a single room on threadbare mats covering solid-rock floors.

With their focus on work and discipline, Cistercian abbeys became leaders of the medieval industrial revolution. Among the few literate people in Europe, monks were keepers of technological knowledge—about clocks, waterwheels, accounting, foundries, gristmills, textiles, and agricultural techniques. Abbeys became economic engines that helped drive France out of its Middle Aged funk.

As France (and Europe) slowly got its act together in the late Middle Ages, cities reemerged as places to trade and thrive. Abbeys gradually lost their relevance in a brave new humanist world. Universities became the new center of intellectual development. Kings took over abbot selection, further degrading the abbeys' power, and Gutenberg's movable type made monks obsolete. The French Revolution closed the book on abbatial life, with troops occupying and destroying many abbeys. The still-functioning Abbey Notre-Dame de Sénanque, near Gordes, is a rare survivor.

to 1800). *Bories* can still be seen in fields throughout the Luberon; most are now used to store tools or hay.

The Village des Bories is composed of five "hamlets." Start with the short film (English subtitles) in the first building, then find the good English explanations upstairs that tell you all you need to know about *bories*. You'll duck into several homes and see animal pens, a community oven, and more (identified in English). Study the "beehive" stone-laying method and imagine the time it took to construct. The villagers had no scaffolds or support arches—just hammers and patience.

Cost and Hours: €6, daily 9:00-20:00, Oct-May until 17:30, +33 4 90 72 03 48, www.levillagedesbories.com.

LUBERON

St. Pantaléon

This postage-stamp-sized village feels lost in the valley below Gordes. It comes with two unusual sights. The adorable 12th-century **Romanesque church** has a remarkable necropolis around back, with tombs—many in the distinct shape of a human body, even one of a baby—carved right out of the rock on which the church was built. The **Musée des Boullions** is an ancient Roman olive mill displaying presses from the 1st and 16th centuries. Earnest Carole speaks excellent English and will take you on a short tour explaining how the Romans pressed olives, how the massive 16th-century press worked, and the many uses of olive oil over the millennia. Skip the stained-glass museum that's connected (€7.50, Wed-Mon 10:00-12:00 & 14:00-18:00, off-season until 17:00, closed Tue year-round).

Moulin Saint Augustin

Originally a 16th-century flour mill, this olive oil boutique is on the busy D-900 just east of Coustellet. Moulin Saint Augustin is a property with centuries of history, but you can only enter the shop. The charming owners do their best to explain the qualities of the native olive varieties in English—yes, just like grapes, there are specific olive varieties that fare better locally (daily 9:00-12:00 & 14:00-18:00, 2800 Route d'Apt, +33 4 90 72 43 66, www.moulin-saintaugustin.fr).

Villages and Sights South of Roussillon

These villages and sights below Roussillon and D-900 feel less visited than places north of this busy road. You'll need a good half-day to visit them all (see the "Luberon" map at the start of this chapter to get oriented). They work well in the order described next, with lunch in Bonnieux or Lacoste (for recommendations, see the "Luberon Restaurants Worth the Trip" sidebar, earlier). The first sight is situated south of Roussillon, where D-108 crosses D-900.

Julien Bridge (Pont Julien)

This delicate, three-arched bridge, named for Julius Caesar, survives as a testimony to Roman engineers—and to the importance of this rural area 2,000 years ago. It's the only surviving bridge on what was the main road from northern Italy to Provence—the primary route used by Roman armies. The 215-foot-long Roman bridge was under construction from

27 BC to AD 14. Mortar had not yet been invented, so (as with Pont du Gard) the stones were carefully set in place. Amazingly, the bridge survives today, having outlived Roman marches, hundreds of floods, and decades of automobile traffic. A new bridge finally rerouted traffic from this beautiful structure in 2005.

Walk below the bridge. Notice how thin the layer of stone seems between the arch tops and the road. Those open niches weren't for statues, but instead allowed water to pass through when the river ran high. (At its current trickle, that's hard to fathom.) Walk under an arch and examine the pockmarks in the side—medieval thieves in search of free bronze stole the clamps.

Château de la Canorgue Winery

Well signed halfway between the Julien Bridge and Bonnieux, this pretty winery was the setting for the film *A Good Year*, with Russell Crowe and French actress Marion Cotillard, but I come here for the good wines. A welcoming tasting room offers a full range of wines—from viognier and chardonnay whites to rosés and rich reds—with owner-in-waiting and winemaker Nathalie greeting guests on most weekdays. The range of taste in their reds is remarkable. Château de la Canorgue was one of the first wineries in the area to make organic wines, and their wines are now exported to many US states.

Cost and Hours: Average bottle costs €10, Mon-Sat 9:00-12:00 & 14:00-18:00, closed Sun, +33 4 90 75 81 01, www.chateaulacanorgue.com.

Bonnieux

Spectacular from a distance, this town lacks a pedestrian center, though the Friday-morning market briefly creates one. It's a welcoming place that doesn't get buried with tourists and is convenient for exploring the area. The main reason to visit here is to enjoy the views from a well-positioned restaurant or hotel.

Sleeping: Located in Bonnieux's center, **\$\$ Hôtel le Clos du Buis***** is a 10-room delight, run by eager-to-please Pierre and Céline. Rooms are lovingly decorated, some with private decks, their veranda allows fine views over the Luberon, and the garden pool is a peaceful retreat (includes breakfast, air-con, free parking, guest kitchen, in the middle of town on Rue Victor Hugo, +33 4 90 75 88 48, www.leclosdubuis.fr, contact@leclosdubuis.fr).

Eating: \$\$ Le Kosy is a fun place to eat well on a budget. This lighthearted place has good seating inside, but outside tables have views. The menu varies with the chef's fancy, creative hamburgers, and cleverly composed if not traditional dishes are the norm (closed Mon-Tue, +33 90 75 60 83).

Another option with a view, is **\$ Les Terrasses**, serving up basic café cuisine (pizza, etc.) on a sensational view terrace at the top of the village (lunch and dinner, closed Mon-Tue, Cours Elzéar Pin, +33 4 90 75 99 77).

To dine in Provence elegance *sans* view, find **$$$ Restaurant l'Arôme.** You'll sit under stone arches or on a streetside terrace in this formal-but-warm place, where every course feels carefully prepared and artfully presented (closed Wed, across from Hôtel le Clos du Buis at 2 Rue Lucien Blanc, +33 4 90 75 88 62).

Lacoste

Little Lacoste slumbers across the valley from Bonnieux in the shadow of its looming castle. Climb through this photogenic village of arches and stone paths, passing American art students (from the Savannah College of Art and Design) showing their work. Support an American artist, learn about the art, and then keep climbing and climbing to the ruined castle base. The view of Bonnieux from the base of Lacoste's castle is as good as it gets.

The Marquis de Sade (1740-1814) lived in this **castle** for more than 30 years. Author of pornographic novels, he was notorious for hosting orgies behind these walls, and for kidnapping peasants for scandalous purposes. He was eventually arrested and imprisoned for 30 years, and thanks to him, we have a word to describe his favorite hobby—sadism. Much later, fashion designer Pierre Cardin lived in the lower part of the castle, after spent a fortune shoring up its protective walls.

Eating: If it's time for lunch or dinner, find **$ Café de France** with its outdoor tables overlooking Bonnieux and savor the view (reasonably priced omelets, quiche, and *plats;* daily, lunch only off-season, +33 4 90 75 82 25).

Abbey St. Hilaire

A dirt road off D-103 between Lacoste and Ménerbes leads down to this long-forgotten and pint-size abbey (200-yard walk from parking area). There's not much to see here—it's more about the experience. The tranquility and isolation sought by monks 800 years ago are still palpable in the simple church and modest cloisters. Once a Cistercian outpost for the bigger abbey at Sénanque, Abbey St. Hilaire is now owned by Carmelite Friars. Make a small donation for use of the English translations. The rear terraces are picnic-ready. Leave nothing valuable in your car at this remote site.

Ménerbes

Ménerbes, still (in)famous as the village that drew author Peter Mayle's attention to this region, has an upscale but welcoming feel in its small center (small parking fee). Wine bars, cafés, and a smattering of galleries gather where key lanes intersect. To explore the linear rock-top village, follow *Eglise* signs.

At the east end of Rue Corneille you'll pass the **citadel,** built in 1584 (after the Protestants of Ménerbes were defeated in the religious wars of 1577)—and never tested. The citadel is privately owned today, but from the outside you can still enjoy the impressive facade, which spans the width of the rock. Nearby, the ancient stone prison tower is also worth a peek.

At the village's very western end, find the heavy Romanesque church and **graveyard** (good views in all directions). You're face-to-face with the Grand Luberon ridge. Notice the quarry carved into its side, where the stone for this village came from.

On the way back, foodies can duck into the snazzy **$$$$ Maison de la Truffe et du Vin,** which offers "truffle discovery workshops," fine meals, and wine tastings (Place de l'Horloge, +33 4 90 72 38 37, www.vin-truffe-luberon.com).

The **Corkscrew Museum** (Musée du Tire-Bouchon) is actually part of the **Domaine de la Citadelle** winery, a half-mile below Ménerbes. It's worth a stop if you're a corkscrew enthusiast or want to taste their very good wines. They have 1,200 corkscrews on display in glass cases and a well-stocked gift shop (small fee for the "museum," includes tasting, daily 9:00-12:00 & 14:00-18:00, shorter hours and closed Sun off-season, +33 4 90 72 41 58, www. domaine-citadelle.com).

Eating: A delicious lunch or snack awaits at the **$ Auzet Salon de Thé,** with a cozy interior or view tables from the small terrace. You'll find cheap homemade quiche and savory pies with salad, delicious baked goods, and more (Tue-Sun 8:00-19:00, closed Mon, 52 Rue du Portail Neuf, +33 4 90 72 37 53).

▲Oppède-le-Vieux

This windy barnacle of a town clings with all its might to its hill-side. There are a handful of businesses and a dusty little square at the base of a short, ankle-twisting climb to a pretty little church and ruined castle. This off-the-beaten-path fixer-upper of a village was completely abandoned in 1910, and today has a ghost town-like feel (it once housed 200 people). The barely inhabited village below has a rugged character and shows little inclination for boutiques and smart hotels. It's ideal for those looking to perish in Provence.

LUBERON

Getting There: To find Oppède-le-Vieux from D-900, follow signs to *Oppède* and *Oppède le Village*, then *Oppède-le-Vieux*, and drive toward le Petit Luberon massif. You'll follow a one-way loop and be forced to park in a remote lot several hundred yards from the village.

Sights: Even though the **castle ruins** are off limits, the Luberon views justify the climb up to them. To reach them from the parking lot, walk 10 minutes along the park path to the village (follow the stubby gray light fixtures, which will lead you through the "modern" village to the abandoned part). From the central arch (building across from Le Petit Café), climb the rugged 15-minute path up to the church and castle ruins (still following the gray light fixtures and occasional English info panels). After walking under the arch, look back to notice the handsome building it supports. At the fork, you can go either way (though the path to the right seems a bit easier). Find the little church terrace. From here, tiled rooftops paint a pretty picture with the grand panorama. Notice the flat plain of the Rhône delta off to the left. (After the climb, you'll understand why locals abandoned this spot for more level terrain.)

The colorful **Notre-Dame d'Alidon church** (1588) may be closed during renovation (peek in if open and grab the English text). There's been a church on this site for 1,000 years—imagine having to climb this distance at least every Sunday for your entire life. Notice the pride locals have for their church: You'll see new gold-leaf accents and other efforts to spruce up the long-abandoned building. The steps to chapels on the right were necessary thanks to the church's hillside setting.

Eating: Back down in the village center, consider a meal with views of the castle ruins at **$ Le Petit Café,** where all-business Laurent is in charge (closed Wed and mid-Dec-Feb, +33 4 90 76 74 01, www.lepetitcafedesjeanne.fr).

Villages and Sights East of Roussillon

Provence can be busy with tourists, but there are still plenty of less-discovered places to explore. The area east of Roussillon, deep in the heart of Provence *(la Provence profonde)*, feels overlooked. Come here to get a sense of how most villages were before they became "destinations." Here are the key sights in the order that you'll pass them coming from the west. Allow a full day to complete this loop.

St-Saturnin-lès-Apt

This pleasant town (with a lively Tuesday market) has a ruined castle with grand views and a funky budget hotel with a good restaurant.

Ditch your car below the main entry to
the town (just below the old city) and
walk up the main drag past the Hôtel
Saint Hubert (Rue de la République).
You'll come to a striking church that's
a fine example of Provençal Romanesque, with a tall, octagonal spire (the
interior is often closed) and a perfectly
situated plane tree.

From here, find the ramp with
Le Château signs (on the left) and
climb. The first castle was started
here a thousand years ago. Today's
ruins are mostly from the 1300s and
grow right out of the rock, making it difficult to tell the man-
made from the natural. Go left when you see the opening and
hike as high as the sun allows with no shade—faded green dots
sort of guide you along. It's a scamperer's paradise, with views
that rank among the best village-top vistas I've found in Provence.
Find your way through the small opening to the little dam. On
the opposite side of the reservoir, you'll discover fine views of the
castle reflected in the water and appreciate its original scale. The
small chapel at the very top is open only on Sunday mornings in
summer, but at any time you can take the path to the right of the
chapel back down the hill to the village, where you'll see a lovely
medieval gate.

Sleeping and Eating: For a warm welcome, stay at **$$ Mas
Perréal** just outside St-Saturnin-lès-Apt. American Kevin and his
Parisian wife, Elisabeth, left no stone unturned as they restored
their lovely farmhouse. This place features traditional rooms (a few
with kitchens, each with its own terrace), a pool, 360-degree views
(they own the vineyards and orchards around you), and no lan-
guage barrier (rooms without kitchens include elaborate American-
size breakfast; closed mid-Oct-March, +33 4 90 75 46 31, www.
masperreal.com, elisabeth-kevin@masperreal.com). Mas Perréal
is off D-943, between St-Saturnin-lès-Apt and D-900. Heading
north along D-943, turn left at Moulin à Huile Jullien, continue
three-quarters of a mile, cross one "major" road, and have faith
until you see the signs—it will be on your right.

¢ Hôtel/Restaurant des Voyageurs,* with amiable owners
Nadine and Alain (who speak no English), is a time warp that has
survived many Provençal trends without changing its look or prod-
uct. The basic accommodations gather around uneven floors and a
frumpy upstairs terrace that only an artist could love (rooms are just
comfortable enough, 2 Place Gambetta, +33 4 90 75 42 08, www.
voyageursenprovence.fr, must reserve by phone or fax +33 4 90 75

LUBERON

50 58—what's that?). The sweet Old World **$$ restaurant,** with vintage floor tiles and beams, serves big portions of traditional cuisine that locals adore (well-priced *menus* from about €25, best to book a day ahead, nice outdoor terrace). Both the hotel and the restaurant are closed all day Wednesday and Thursday

until 18:00. It's at the base of the old village, below the Spar store.

Le Colorado Provençal

This park has ochre cliffs similar to Roussillon's, but they're spread over a larger area, with well-signed trails. If hiking through soft, orange sand and Bryce Canyon-like rocks strikes your fancy—and you didn't get enough in Roussillon—make time for Le Colorado Provençal.

You'll be directed to a big dirt parking lot (WCs and a café) and given a map of the two trails. Parking attendants are available from about 9:00 until 17:00 or 18:00. Before or after those times, you can park for free (but get no map).

For the best walk, cross the little footbridge, turn right, and follow arrows leading to the Sahara trail. Do the loop counterclockwise. The first 15 minutes or so are uninspiring, though the scenery improves quickly after that. The two trails (Sahara and Belvédères) are color-coded. The shorter Sahara trail (signed in blue) offers a wide spectrum of colors and provides views of the chimney formations (allow 90 minutes round-trip from your car). You can extend your walk by 40 minutes and combine both trails. Forgo light-colored clothing.

Cost and Hours: The park is free, parking-€5, always open; located a half-mile below Rustrel off D-22, between Apt and Gignac—follow signs toward the village of *Rustrel*, the gateway to Le Colorado Provençal.

Viens

Located about 15 minutes uphill and east of Le Colorado Provençal, this village is where Luberon locals go to get away. With a setting like this, it's surprising that modest Viens is not more developed. The panoramas are higher and vaster than around Roussillon and Gordes (with some lavender fields), and the vegetation is more raw. Walk the streets of the old town (bigger than it first appears) and visit the few shops scattered about. Walk to the end of the village past the post office and enjoy a view over the unusual church tower and beyond.

Eating: Just below the town's only phone booth, **$$ Le Petit Jardin** fits perfectly in this unpretentious town where tourists are viewed as curiosities. Come for a drink and rub shoulders with locals or, better, have a meal. Dine in the small traditional interior or outside on a delightful garden terrace (good-value weekday *menu du jour,* more elaborate weekend *menu,* closed Mon, +33 4 90 75 20 05). A small **grocery store** (closed Sun afternoon and all day Mon) and a **bakery** (closed Wed) are a few blocks past the café, toward St. Martin de Castillon.

To reach the next village (Saignon), follow signs to *St. Martin de Castillon,* then turn right on D-900 toward Apt.

Saignon

Sitting high atop a rock spur, this village looks down onto Apt, a city of only 11,500—which from here looks like a megalopolis after all these tiny villages. You can peek into the too-big-for-this-village Romanesque church (Notre-Dame de la Pitié) and admire its wood doors and tympanum, then follow *Le Rocher* signs through the village up to the "ship's prow." If you need to see it all, climb to the Le Rocher Bellevue for grand views over lavender fields (about three stories of stairs to the top). There are a handful of cafés and a grocery store in the linear village's center. Parking is best just above the town (hike or drive farther above town for sensational views over Saignon).

Buoux

Buoux (pronounced "b-ewe-oox"), a way-off-the-beaten-path village, is home to a remote hotel/restaurant and one of Provence's best ruined castles. A trip to this far-flung corner rewards with rocky canyons, acres of lavender, and few tourists. Start early and climb to the castle before the heat rises, then have a long, well-earned lunch at the recommended L'Auberge des Sequins (see below). If you liked Les Baux but weren't so fond of the crowds and don't need an audioguide, you'll love it here. But you'll need good shoes, stamina, and balance because much of the footing is tricky.

Buoux is south of Apt on D-113 between Saignon and Lourmarin. Ambitious travelers can combine a visit to Buoux with Lourmarin and Bonnieux.

Sights in Buoux

▲Fort de Buoux

The remains of this remote ridgetop castle are a playground for energetic lovers of crumbled ruins and grand views. Allow an hour for this hike.

Cost and Hours: €5, daily 10:00-17:00, closed in bad weather (wind or rain) when it's slippery and dangerous, +33 4 90 74 25 75, www.lefortdebuoux.e-monsite.com.

Getting There: The fort is 10 minutes by car from the village of Buoux. To reach the fort from Apt and the north, drive through Buoux on D-113, drop down, and be on the lookout for small signs to *Fort de Buoux* (and *L'Auberge des Seguins*). Slow down and expect sharp turns. If coming from the south, follow signs to *Bonnieux*, then *L'Auberge des Seguins* and *Fort de Buoux*. You can use one of several dirt parking areas; you'll find the closest lot after passing two others. Once parked, walk through the gate and then about 15 easy minutes up a dirt road to the foot of the fort. From here the footing gets challenging.

Visiting the Fort: Floating like a cloud above the valleys below, the fort is easy to miss—it disappears beside the limestone rock cliffs that rule the landscape. The long, rocky outcrop has been inhabited since prehistoric times. In the Middle Ages, it had a population over 200, with a powerful castle that controlled a vast area. Like Les Baux, the fort was destroyed in the 1500s during the wars of religion (it was a Protestant base) and again in the 1600s by a paranoid King Louis XIII (see sidebar on page 196).

Monsieur le Gardien (the caretaker) greets you with tickets and a simple map of the sight with brief English explanations (picnic tables available and drinks sold at the entry). The map suggests a one-way route through the rocky ruins. You'll enter by the round tower and walk past what's left of the village, then scramble up and around rock piles along a stony spine to the castle remains, once home to hundreds of residents. You'll also climb around the remains of homes, a church, cisterns, and medieval storage silos. The castle keep stands at the highest point.

An unforgettable highlight of this castle is a three-story stone spiral staircase, which would never in a million years be open to the public in the US. Dating from the Bronze Age (experts think) and cut into the cliffs, it leads back down to the base. I'd skip this part (returning as you came) unless you are sure-footed and adventurous. To find the staircase, look for #36, near the grain silos (the many holes in the ground), then walk under the archway and follow the faded white arrows as you leave the ruins (you'll walk uphill for 10 minutes at first). The staircase is steep with no handrails and some really big steps.

Sleeping and Eating in Buoux

¢ **L'Auberge des Seguins** is a few stone's throws from the parking area for the fort and draws a hiking crowd. It's a modest, Shangri-la kind of place at the end of the valley, with confident young Amélie in charge. The rambling old farm is isolated and purposefully unmanicured—guests are encouraged to disconnect and appreciate the natural beauty and views of the fort. Come here for a light lunch (€10 salads and *plats*), dinner, or a drink (good local beer), or consider spending the night. The 27 rooms are simple though comfortable, clean, and squirreled about the place: Some require a dirt path to reach, and some are built into the rocky cliffs. Kids love it (there's also a big pool, but it's not heated). This place is a fine value for unpicky types—or for those on the lam (good half-pension with dinner-€70/person for a double room, €44/person if you sleep in the cool 20-bed dorm room; coming from Fort de Buoux, take your first possible right, which turns into a dirt road; +33 4 90 74 16 37, www.aubergedesseguins.com, aubergedesseguins@gmail.com).

Lourmarin

The southernmost Luberon village of Lourmarin has a good Friday market (and a smaller one Tue evenings), a beautiful Renaissance château on its fringe, and an enchanting town center. Lourmarin sits on a level plain and feels peaceful and happy, away from the more-visited villages in the heart of the Luberon. This self-assured, handsome town accommodates a healthy tourist demand without feeling

too overrun (though there is no lack of boutiques). It's among the best Luberon villages to enjoy in the off-season when other, better-known towns rattle about with few residents and little commercial activity.

Existentialist writer Albert Camus *(The Stranger)* lived in Lourmarin in the 1950s and is buried here, lending it a certain fame that persists today. Author Peter Mayle lived here as well, adding to the village's cachet...and now you're here, too. Lourmarin makes a good base for drivers touring the southern Luberon, Aix-en-Provence, and even Marseille and maybe Cassis. From here you can tour big cities, beaches, and castles, returning every night to the comfort of your village.

Getting There: Trans Vaucluse bus #9 links Lourmarin to Aix-en-Provence (3/day, 1.5 hours, more departures with a transfer in Cadenet, www.sudmobilite.fr).

Tourist Information: The TI is located on Place Henri Barthélémy (daily 10:00-12:30 & 13:30-18:00, closed Sun-Mon in off-season, +33 4 90 68 10 77, www.lourmarin.com). Free public WCs are located to the right as you exit the TI, down the stairs. Park centrally, and leave nothing of value visible in your car.

Sights in Lourmarin

Château de Lourmarin

This Renaissance château looks across a grassy meadow at the village. It's more impressive from outside than within; you'll visit a few well-furnished rooms, an intriguing kitchen and exterior galleries, and a slick double spiral staircase in stone.

Cost and Hours: €7.50, daily 10:00-18:45, Oct-April until 17:30 and closes for lunch, decent English handout and posted explanations, +33 4 90 68 15 23, www.chateau-de-lourmarin.com.

Market Day

Little Lourmarin hosts a terrific market every Friday until 13:00. Sleep here Thursday night and awake to the commotion, arrive early, or prepare for a good walk from your car.

Sleeping in Lourmarin

Try to stay here on a Thursday, so you can be here for Friday's market.

$$ Le Moulin de Lourmarin*** is a contemporary 18-room hotel in the old town with fair rates, bright and spacious rooms, and an elevator (Rue du Temple, +33 4 90 68 06 69, www.moulindelourmarin.com).

$ Les Chambres de la Cordière is a cool getaway. Charming owner Françoise's goal is to make you feel at home. Six cozy rooms are tucked into one of the village's oldest buildings (c. 1582), with a tiny courtyard and welcoming cats (family rooms, 4 rooms come with mini kitchens—the 3 *gîtes* with full kitchens are usually rented only by the week, cash only, some rooms have air-con, no Sun arrivals, Rue Albert Camus, +33 4 90 68 03 32, mobile +33 6 81 02 18 04, www.cordiere.com, cordiereluberon@aol.com).

Eating in Lourmarin

All roads seem to converge on the postcard-perfect Place de l'Ormeau. Several appealing places line the square, making comparison shopping easy. **$ Café Gaby** offers good-value fare (salads, omelets, *steak-frites*) with authentic decor inside and a good outside terrace (daily lunch and dinner, +33 4 90 68 38 42). **$$ Café l'Ormeau** serves mediocre cuisine but has a larger selection and an interior courtyard,  making it a calm retreat in the middle of the village bustle (daily, +33 4 90 68 02 11).

$ La Maison Café Bar draws a younger crowd and is best for a drink before or after dinner (till late) with a cool upstairs terrace and cozy bar inside (closed Mon-Tue, Rue du Galinier, +33 4 90 09 54 01).

At **$$ La Récréation,** owner Jean-Louis and his bright smile have been welcoming guests for more than 30 years. You'll find an inviting terrace and regional cuisine with vegetarian options (lunch and dinner, daily except closed Fri for dinner, below the TI on Avenue Philippe de Girard, +33 4 90 68 23 73).

LUBERON

MARSEILLE & NEARBY

Marseille • Cassis • Aix-en-Provence

In the rush to get between Avignon and the Riviera, most travelers zip through the eastern fringe of Provence. That's a shame, as this is a tight package of compelling cities separated by a rugged landscape and finished with a strikingly beautiful coastline. I cover three different-as-night-and-day places, each worth a visit. Marseille is an untouristy, semi-seedy-but-vibrant port city. The nearby coastal village of Cassis offers the perfect antidote to the big city. And just inland, polished Aix-en-Provence is the fancy yin to Marseille's working-class yang, with beautiful people to match its lovely architecture. Aix-en-Provence makes a good and easy first- or last-day stop for those using Marseille's airport.

For good regional guides who specialize in this area, see page 253.

Marseille

Marseille (mar-say) is both the Naples and the Barcelona of France. Big and gritty, it has all the color and pitfalls that come with being a major seaport. It's a place with a distinct culture, a proud spirit, and a populace determined to clean up its act. Historic buildings have been renovated, cultural centers opened, daringly modern buildings erected, a sleek new tram rolled out, and

Marseille & Nearby

To Luberon, Grand Canyon du Verdon & Nice

To Lourmarin & Southern Luberon

Mont Ste-Victoire

Aix-en-Provence

Etang de Berre

To Camargue & Arles

L'Estaque

Marseille

FRIOUL ISLANDS

CHATEAU D'IF

To Nice

Aubagne

CASSIS TRAIN STN.

Cassis

LES CALANQUES

Cap Canaille

LA ROUTE DES CRETES

La Ciotat

To Toulon

5 Kilometers

5 Miles

Mediterranean Sea

Paris FRANCE

100 Miles

the once rough-and-tumble harbor has blossomed into an inviting and fun-loving pedestrian zone.

France's oldest (600 BC) and second biggest city (and a leading European port) owns a history that goes back to ancient Greek times. Marseille is a world apart from France's other leading cities. Rather than offering blockbuster sights, it's a bustling, well-lived-in city whose happy-go-lucky residents make its ambience.

Marseille is Europe's gateway to Africa, with nearly two million people a year riding its ferries—most shuttling between it and Tunisia and Algeria. Immigrants from North Africa make up more than 25 percent of the city's population. In certain quarters you'll hear more Arabic than French. (This infuriates anti-immigrant French people who are certain that the rest of "their" country is destined to follow suit.)

Most tourists leave Marseille off their itinerary, as it doesn't fit their idea of the French Riviera or Provence. But it would be a shame to come to the south of France and not experience the region's leading city and namesake of the French national anthem. By train, it's made-to-order for a convenient day trip from Aix-en-Provence (45 minutes), Avignon (35 minutes by TGV), or even from Paris (just a little more than three hours by TGV).

PLANNING YOUR TIME

For a stimulating four-hour tour of Marseille, take my self-guided "Marseille City Walk." You'll head from the train station down a main boulevard (La Canebière), dip into the North African market, wander around the hilly old town (Le Panier) as you climb to the La Charité Museum, find the cathedral, and survey the Euro-méditerranée (Euromed) development, then return to the port and take the shuttle ferry across to the new town. Finally, take a bus, tourist train, or taxi up to Notre-Dame de la Garde before returning to the station.

Orientation to Marseille

Marseille is big, with 860,000 people. Keep your visit simple and focus on the area immediately around the Old Port (Vieux Port).

La Canebière boulevard meets the colorful Old Port. The Panier district is the old town, blanketing a hill that tumbles down to the port. The harborside is a lively, broad promenade lined with inviting eateries, amusements, and a morning fish market. Everything described here (except Notre-Dame de la Garde) is within a 30-minute walk of the train station.

TOURIST INFORMATION

The main TI is two blocks up from the Old Port on La Canebière (daily 9:00-18:00, 11 La Canebière, www.marseille-tourisme. com). There's also a TI kiosk at St. Charles train station (daily 9:00-18:00, closed Sun in winter), and in summer, they run a kiosk at the cruise port. Pick up the good city map, which has a self-guided walk through the old town, and information on museums and the weekly bus and walking tours—but pass on their city pass.

ARRIVAL IN MARSEILLE

For information on arriving in Marseille by plane or cruise ship, see "Marseille Connections," later.

By Train

St. Charles Station (Gare St. Charles) is busy, modern, and user-

Vive la Différence

Marseille is one of Europe's greatest cultural melting pots. An important trading center since ancient times, Marseille has long been defined by the waves of immigrant peoples who have called this beautiful setting home. Accessible by land and sea to North Africa, Spain, Italy, and Greece, Marseille once attracted Phoenicians, Greeks, and Romans. Today, Marseille houses France's largest concentration of immigrants: 200,000 of its 860,000 residents are Muslim; 80,000 are Jewish (Marseille has had a large Jewish population since the Jews were expelled from Spain in 1492); 80,000 are Armenian Orthodox (escaping Ottoman injustices); and there are 70,000 Comorans (from a group of islands in the Indian Ocean).

There's a spirit of cooperation among Marseille's immigrants, who understand that what benefits one group helps them all. Unlike in Paris, immigrants in Marseille live in the city center, not the suburbs, so they are more visible. And though unemployment is high among immigrants, it is not as high as in Parisian suburbs. The commercial port, a thriving high-tech industry, and tourism (mostly from cruise ships) fuel Marseille's economy. The city also has invested mightily in jobs programs and city-center renovation projects that have benefited its lower-income residents.

Marseille engenders a strong sense of identity apart from France (and the French language) that unites this city's diverse population. Locals see themselves as *Marseillais* (mar-say-ay) first and as French second (or third, after their native country). Locals' fierce pride is manifested in their passion for Olympique de Marseille, the city's soccer team. Since 1899 *Marseillais* have lived and died with the fate of their team. (A few years ago, I was here the day that 30,000 *Marseillais* fans were boarding trains to Paris for the France finals.) Olympique de Marseille has made a point of creating a team that looks like the city by recruiting players with North African backgrounds (Zinédine Zidane was the most famous example). The strategy seems to have worked—Marseille has played in the French Cup final more than any other team in France.

Immigrant populations are present in cities throughout Europe, challenging local governments to accommodate them. Many would do well to study Marseille.

friendly. Many services are along track A, including WCs and a grocery store. The TI kiosk, Métro access, and taxis are all down the escalator opposite track F. If you exit the station at track A to Square Narvik, you'll see Hôtel Ibis on your left (with car rental behind it); access to the old city by foot is to the right. Inside the station, with your back to the tracks, you'll find shops, lots of food

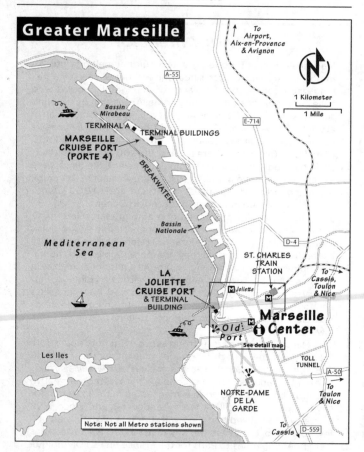

Greater Marseille

To Airport, Aix-en-Provence & Avignon

A-55

E-714

Bassin Mirabeau

TERMINAL A   TERMINAL BUILDINGS

MARSEILLE CRUISE PORT (PORTE 4)

BREAKWATER

Bassin Nationale

Mediterranean Sea

D-4

ST. CHARLES TRAIN STATION

To Cassis, Toulon & Nice

LA JOLIETTE CRUISE PORT & TERMINAL BUILDING

M Joliette

Marseille Center

Old Port

See detail map

TOLL TUNNEL   A-50

To Toulon & Nice

NOTRE-DAME DE LA GARDE

Les Iles

To Cassis   D-559

1 Kilometer

1 Mile

Note: Not all Metro stations shown

options, and the bus station and its ticket office (with airport buses and more) to the far right, past track N.

Getting from the Train Station to the Old Port: To reach the Old Port, you can walk, take the Métro, or catch a taxi. On **foot** it's a 15-minute downhill gaunt-let along grimy streets. Leave the station through the exit at track A (past the big departure board), veer right, and admire the view from atop the stairs. That's Notre-Dame de la Garde overlooking the city. Walk down the stairs and straight on Boule-vard d'Athènes, which becomes

Boulevard Dugommier. When you come to the trams, turn right

onto the grand boulevard, La Canebière. This leads to the main TI and the Old Port.

By **Métro** it's an easy subterranean trip from the train station to the Old Port: Go down the escalator opposite track E and then take a longer escalator to your left. Buy a ticket from the machines or ticket window (closed 12:40-13:40). Your ticket is good for one hour of travel on Métro or buses; an all-day pass costs about €5.50 (www.rtm.fr). Take blue line M1 (direction: La Fourragère) two stops to Vieux Port (Old Port). Following *Sortie* signs, then *la Canebière* exit signs, you'll pop out within sight of the TI. To return to the station from here, take blue line M1 (direction: La Rose) two stops and get off at Gare St. Charles.

Taxis are out the front doors opposite track E. Allow €16 to the port and €20 to Notre-Dame de la Garde—though train station cabbies may refuse these short trips (+33 4 91 02 20 20). Taxis elsewhere will take you on shorter rides.

By Car

Even drivers who are comfortable in big, crazy cities will be frustrated in Marseille. Traffic is bad except on Sundays and holidays. If coming from the east (Cassis and other Riviera destinations), opt for autoroute A-50, which leads to Marseille's 1.5-mile-long tunnel (toll about €4)—avoiding much of the city's traffic-ridden center streets—and pops you out under Fort St. Nicolas at the Old Port. After you leave the autoroute from any direction, signs to *Vieux Port* (not to *"port"*), *Centre-Ville*, and *Office du Tourisme* take you to the Old Port. At the Old Port, follow the blue *P* signs to the underground *Parking Charles de Gaulle-Canebière* lot. Locals claim pay lots are patrolled and safe, but I wouldn't leave anything in the car.

HELPFUL HINTS

Pickpockets: As in any big city, thieves thrive in crowds and target tourists. Wear your money belt, and assume any commotion is a smokescreen for theft. Marseille (while nowhere near as dangerous as many American cities) is one of the most dangerous cities in France. Use a little extra caution and don't venture into sketchy areas after dark.

Save on Bus Tickets: The same tickets work on buses and the Métro, but cost €1.70 at a Métro station and €2 on the bus. Marseille transit tickets are also valid on Cassis buses.

Bike Cabs: In summer, look for bicycle cabs that will zip you up and down the Old Port (€5/person, holds 1-3 people).

Taxi to Cassis or Aix-en-Provence: A taxi from Marseille to Cassis or Aix-en-Provence runs about €70.

Car Rental: All the major companies are represented at St. Charles Station (see "Arrival in Marseille," earlier).

Soccer Matches: *Le football* is to Marseille what American football is to Green Bay: Frenzied fans go crazy, and star worship is fickle. One of France's best-ever soccer players was raised here: Zinédine Zidane (notorious for his head-butt of an Italian opponent during the 2006 World Cup Final). If you're here during soccer season (end of July to mid-May), consider getting tickets to a match (every other Sat, from €30, ask at the TI). To get to the soccer stadium (Orange Vélodrome), take the Métro's red line M2 (direction: Ste. Marguerite-Dromel) to Rond-Point du Prado.

Tours in Marseille

Le Petit Train
These little tourist trains take two routes through town. Trains depart from the far northwest corner of the Old Port (a 15-minute walk from the TI) and have skimpy recorded information. The better Notre-Dame de la Garde route (#1) saves you the 30-minute climb to the basilica's fantastic view and runs along a nice section of Marseille's coastline (€9; allow 75 minutes for round-trip, including 20 minutes to visit the church; runs daily, about every 20 minutes 10:00-12:20 & 13:40-18:20; every 40 minutes and stops earlier Nov-March; +33 4 91 25 24 69, www.petit-train-marseille.com). The Vieux Marseille route (#2) toots you through the Panier district—best done on foot (€9, 65 min-

utes including one or two 30-minute stops, less frequent Nov-Dec, closed Jan-March).

The Colorbus
These double-decker buses, with open seating up top and recorded narration, offer two hop-on, hop-off routes similar to Le Petit Train's routes. The red line (14 stops, €19) is best as it connects the Old Port with Notre-Dame de la Garde, runs along a scenic stretch of coastline, and delivers nice views over the Old Port. The blue line (11 stops, €15) runs along the coast then heads inland to central Marseille. Buses depart from near the Petit Train stop and run every 30 minutes (45 minutes in off-season), leaving you too long at most stops (75 minutes round-trip, +33 4 91 91 05 82, www.colorbus.fr/en).

Marseille at a Glance

▲▲**Notre-Dame de la Garde** Marseille's landmark sight: a huge Neo-Romanesque/Neo-Byzantine basilica, towering above everything, with panoramic views. **Hours:** Daily 7:00-18:00. See page 262.

▲▲**Panier District** Marseille's answer to Paris' Montmartre, this charming tangle of lanes in the oldest part of town draws photographers and poets. See page 259.

▲**North African Market** Taste of North Africa in downtown Marseille. **Hours:** Open long hours except Sun. See page 256.

▲**Old Port (Vieux Port)** Economic heart of town, featuring lots of boats and a fish market, protected by two impressive fortresses. **Hours:** Fish market—nearly daily until 13:00. See page 257.

▲**La Charité Museum** Housed in a beautiful building with Celtic, Greek, Roman, and Egyptian artifacts. **Hours:** Tue-Sun 9:00-18:00, closed Mon. See page 259.

Local Guides
Pascale Benguigui is a smart and colorful guide for Marseille, Aix-en-Provence, Avignon, and anything in between (€180/half-day, €300/day, mobile +33 6 20 80 07 51, pascaleguide@gmail.com). **Dominique Barte** is also very good (generally €210/half-day, €320/full day, dominique_barte@hotmail.com).

Marseille City Walk

This self-guided walk strings together the main sights in the areas surrounding the Old Port (Vieux Port). I've listed the sights in roughly the order you'll come to them as you amble along La Canebière to the Old Port, from where you'll loop through the Panier district and ultimately wind up across the harbor in the new town (follow the route on the Marseille map in this chapter). This walk takes about four hours and is ideal for day-trippers arriving by train.
• *Start at the corner of La Canebière and Boulevard Dugommier (near the Noailles Métro stop), a five-minute walk from the train station or uphill from the Old Port.*

Boulevard La Canebière
The Boulevard La Canebière (pronounced "can-ah' bee-air"—or

Marseille

To
Cruise Port 4

Place
de la Joliette

Ⓜ Joliette

JETTY

BLVD. DES DAMES

AVE. ROBERT SCHUMAN

QUAI DE LA JOLIETTE

RUE DE LA

To Marseille Provence
Cruise Terminal

Bassin
de la
Grande
Joliette

❿ LA CHARITÉ
MUSEUM

R. DU
PETIT PUITS

R. PUITS
DU DENIER

R. DU
REFUGE

RUE PANIER

R. D. MOULINS R. D. BELLES
ÉCUELLES

LE
PANIER

CATHEDRALE
DE LA
NOUVELLE
MAJOR

LA JOLIETTE
CRUISE PORT

MUSEE
REGARDS DE
PROVENCE

RUE PANIER

RUE DES
REPENTIES

D. MUETTES

Place des
Moulins

R. D. POIRIER

INTER-
CONTINENTAL
HOTEL

RUE MERY

EUROMED

HHPR

QUAI DE LA TOURETTE

RUE JEAN GALLAND

MONTÉE DES ACCOULES

ALTERNATE
ROUTE

R. CAISSERIE

R. DE LA
PRISON

CITY
HALL

RUE DE LA

VILLA COSQUER
MEDITERRANEE

AVE. VAUDOYER

ESPLANADE DE LA TOURETTE

R. ST. LAURENT

RUE DE LA LOGE

RUE DE

AVE. ST. JEAN

MuCEM
MUSEUM

SKY-
BRIDGES

ST.
LAURENT

Ⓑ #60
& Color Bus
Tour

Ⓑ

Ⓣ

Ⓑ #60

PORT

Med.
Sea

Place de la
Tourette

Ⓑ❻Ⓑ

Ⓑ❺

#60

Ⓑ

FORT ST.
JEAN

WW II
MEMORIAL

Ⓑ

Ⓑ

#60

QUAI DU

Petit
Train
Stop

CHATEAU

#60

Old Port

Jardin
du Pharo

QUAI DE RIVE NEUVE

❼

BLVD. CHARLES LIVON

TOLL TUNNEL
TO A-50

RUE NEUVE STE. CATHERINE

NEW TOWN/
ARSENAL
QUARTER

FORT ST.
NICOLAS

Bassin
de
Carénage

RUE SAINTE

RUE ROBERT

RUE D'ENDOUME

BLVD. DE LA CORDERIE

AVE. DE LA CORSE

To
Notre-Dame
de la Garde

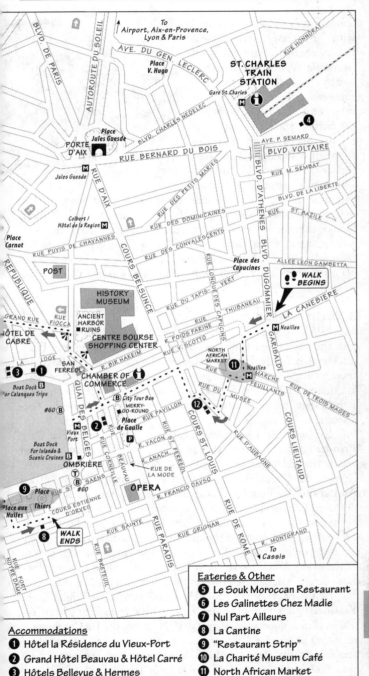

WALK BEGINS

WALK ENDS

Accommodations
1 Hôtel la Résidence du Vieux-Port
2 Grand Hôtel Beauvau & Hôtel Carré
3 Hôtels Bellevue & Hermes
4 Hôtel Ibis Marseille Gare St. Charles

Eateries & Other
5 Le Souk Moroccan Restaurant
6 Les Galinettes Chez Madie
7 Nul Part Ailleurs
8 La Cantine
9 "Restaurant Strip"
10 La Charité Museum Café
11 North African Market
12 Chez Yassine & Le Carthage

MARSEILLE & NEARBY

"can-o-beer" if you prefer)—
with its classy tramway—is
the celebrated main drag of
Marseille. While strolling this
stubby thoroughfare, you feel
surrounded by a teeming, diverse city. Two blocks before
the harbor, you'll find two museums, the TI, and a stylish
shopping district. The boulevard
dead-ends at the Old Port. La
Canebière's name comes from

the same root as cannabis—not the smoking kind but the rope-
making kind. Marseille was long the French kingdom's main naval
base, and hemp was a vital ingredient in the rope used by the fleet.
• *For a taste of Africa, walk a block down La Canebière (from the No-*
ailles Métro stop) to Rue Papère, and side-trip left another block to the
old tram station and the colorful North African market filling Place du
Marché.

▲North African Market

Marseille's huge Moroccan, Algerian, and Tunisian populations
give the city a special spice. Wander downhill the length of Place
du Marché. Suddenly you're immersed in an exotic, bustling, and
fragrant little medina—and no one's speaking French. The market thrives daily except Sunday with fresh and very cheap produce.
Labels show the price as well as the origin: *Maroc, Provence, Côte*
d'Ivoire, and so on.

Explore a bit. Linger over a coffee at an outside table at **Café**
Prinder (at the bottom of the square, on the right)—listen to and
watch the kaleidoscope of cultures. Next, venture left on Rue
Longue des Capucins. At #16 there's a big bright butcher called
Au Paradis des Viandes (Paradise of Meat), where all the meat is
prepared halal-style for Muslim consumption. Twenty or so steps
beyond on the right is a bakery/*rôtisserie*: **Warma.** Stop here and try
a *bourek* wrap (potato and ground round), a *pastilla* wrap (chicken,
almonds, onions, and egg), or the crêpe-like *mahjouba* (best hot out
of the oven). You'll see the busy kitchen behind the counter. They
also serve €5 paella to-go (makes for a very cheap lunch for two).

At the next corner, Rue d'Aubagne, take a hard right. **Chez**
Yassine at #8 is a thriving and inviting little restaurant (cheap Tunisian plates, good seating upstairs). Next door is **Le Carthage,** a
tempting bakery for Tunisian pastries and mint tea. You could assemble an assortment of baklava-like sweets, have them with mint
tea, crank up the music, and almost be in Tunisia.
• *Continue downhill. At the end of the block, jog left to the big street*

(dominated by tram lines), Cours St. Louis. The grand triumphal arch you see in the distance to the right celebrates the Revolution and French Republic. Cross to the north side of La Canebière, then turn left and continue downhill toward the Old Port. Two blocks before you hit the water, on the right side (just after the TI), you can't miss the grandiose building.

Chamber of Commerce (Le Palais de la Bourse)

Step inside and take in the grand 1860s interior (free, daily 10:00-18:00, handy public WC to the right as you enter). A relief on the ceiling shows great moments in Marseille's history. The grand hall is circled by a United Nations of plaques, reminding locals that their economy is based on trade from around the world.

• *Continue down the main boulevard, cross the busy street to the Old Port, and stop at the copper plaque in the pavement about 30 feet from the water.*

▲Old Port (Vieux Port)

This plaque marks a very central (and proud) point. The monument at your feet reads: "On this spot in 600 BC Greek sailors landed and founded Marseille from where Western civilization rose." From here, Greeks fanned out along the coast and as far inland as Vaison-la-Romaine, bringing grapevines, their alphabet, and technical know-how that the Romans would later capitalize on.

Protected by two impressive fortresses at its mouth, Marseille's Old Port has long been the economic heart of town. The citadels were built in the 17th century under Louis XIV, supposedly to protect the city. But their cannons pointed inland, and locals understood that the forts were actually designed to keep an eye on Marseille (a city that was essentially autonomous until 1660). They challenged Marseille to thoroughly incorporate into the growing and ever more centralized kingdom of France.

Today, the serious shipping is away from the center, and the Old Port is the happy domain of pleasure craft. The fish market along Quai des Belges—where you're standing—splashes and wiggles nearly every morning. (As fishermen don't make any money from gawking tourists, don't expect any smiles.) The stalls are gone by 13:00.

Looking out to sea from here, the Panier district (the old town) rises to your right. The harborfront below Le Panier was destroyed in 1943 by the Nazis, who didn't want a tangled refuge for resistance fighters so close to the harbor. It's now filled with modern condos and trendy restaurants. City Hall (see the flags) is in the middle on the harborfront.

Take a spin tour to the right. Farther along is the Jesuit church San Ferréol, a Gothic building with a bright and creamy Neo-Baroque facade slapped on in the 19th century. (You'll walk behind this church in a moment to find the ruins of Marseille's ancient harbor.) Spinning past the grand boulevard, La Canebière, you come to le Ombrière ("the shade-giver"), a modern mirror-ceilinged roof on the waterfront that provides both shade and lots of photo fun (it was designed by Norman Foster for the 2013 European Capital of Culture festivities). Behind that to the left is a neighborhood that used to be full of prostitutes and strip clubs—an area still considered unsafe late at night. Capping the hill beyond the mirror is the Notre-Dame de la Garde basilica (you'll see its golden Mary peeking above the roofline). Looking farther to the right (just across the Old Port from where you stand) is the new town and the Arsenal Quarter, with lots of fun restaurants and bars—the liveliest place in town after dark.

• *After you've had your fun under the shade-giver, walk back toward the Chamber of Commerce building and turn left onto Rue Reine Elisabeth, passing San Ferréol Church. Across the street from the church is the Bourse shopping center with a Galeries Lafayette department store, a Carrefour grocery store, and a food court for a fast cheap lunch. Continue up Rue Reine Elisabeth until you reach a view of an archaeological park.*

Ancient Harbor and Marseille History Museum

Look over the low fence into an archaeological park the size of a city block surrounded by ugly buildings from the 1960s and 1970s. It's an excavation site filled with Greek and Roman ruins cradled by the city's history museum. Below is the stony footprint of the harbor of ancient Marseille, the port Julius Caesar would have seen 2,000 years ago. Back in the 1960s, this land was slated for development, but the ruins were discovered and that was the end of that.

Overlooking the park is the **Marseille History Museum,** an impressive collection of artifacts from Julius Caesar to Louis XIV to the 20th century (free access to permanent collections, may include audioguide and access to archaeological park, Tue-Sun 10:00-18:00, closed Mon). While there are few English descriptions, the audioguide does a good job making sense of what you're seeing.

• *Continue walking up Rue Reine Elisabeth to the first crosswalk. Look right into the excavations and see the main road of ancient Marseille. Turn 180 degrees and follow that road uphill (Rue Henri Fiocca, follow signs to Le Panier), which later becomes Grand Rue.*

Grand Rue dates back to the 6th century BC. Notice three fine blocks of Second Empire (circa 1860) architecture (like the Haussmann style so elegant in Paris). After three blocks (at Rue Bonnéterie) you come to the oldest house in Marseille, **Hôtel de Cabre**, from 1535. This is a rare historic building in this neighborhood that survived the German bombs of 1943.

• *Continue up Grand Rue to the broad set of stairs. To the left is the harbor (and a nice view of Notre-Dame de la Garde capping the hill beyond), and to the right is the 18th-century Hôtel Dieu (formerly a hospital, now the luxurious Intercontinental Hotel, with its popular café view terrace). Continue straight, entering Le Panier.*

▲▲Panier District (Old Town)

Ahead of you rises the Panier district. Until the mid-19th century, Marseille was just this hill-capping old town and its fortified port. Today, that historic and tangled hilltop—the old sailor's quarter, Jewish quarter, and working-class district—is the best place to find the town's soul. It's a 15-minute hike to our next stop, La Charité Museum. But take your time. The city keeps the rent cheap here, so you'll find lots of artists and artisans working and lots of creative little commercial ventures.

• *Passing the Intercontinental Hotel, continue about a hundred yards, bear right onto the steps of Montée des Accoules at the traffic light, and weave your way uphill. At the crest of the hill, take a hard right up a stepped lane (Rue des Moulins) to the neighborhood square, **Place des Moulins**. This is called "Place of the Windmills" because 19 mills once churned here, catching the hilltop breeze and powering local industry. Today, under shade-giving plane trees, there's a relaxed neighborhood vibe. Look for the stairs left of the water fountain and head downhill to Rue des Muettes. Turn right, and after 100 yards, go left on Rue du Panier a few steps to a charming restaurant- and café-filled square, leading to the grand old La Charité. This was and remains the center of Le Panier.*

▲La Charité Museum (Centre de la Vieille Charité)

Now a museum, this was once a poorhouse. In 1674 the French king decided that all the poor people on the streets were bad news. He built a huge triple-arcaded home to take in a thousand needy subjects. In 1940 the famous architect Le Corbusier declared it a shame that such a fine building was so underappreciated. Today, the striking building—renovated and beautiful in its arcaded simplicity—is used as a collection of art galleries surrounding a Pantheon-esque church. You can

stroll around the courtyard for free. (Good WCs are in the far-left corner.)

Cost and Hours: Permanent collections are free, fee for temporary exhibits, Tue-Sun 9:00-18:00, closed Mon, idyllic café/bar, +33 4 91 14 58 80.

Visiting the Museum: The pediment of the church features the figure of Charity taking care of orphans (as the state did with this building). She's flanked by pelicans (symbolic of charity, for the way they were said to pick flesh from their own bosom to feed their hungry chicks, according to medieval legend). The ground floor outside the church houses temporary exhibits. On the upper levels of the complex you'll find rooms with interesting collections of Celtic (c. 300 BC), Greek, and Roman artifacts from this region. There's also a good Egyptian collection, along with masks from Africa and the South Pacific.

• *With your back to La Charité and facing the small cobbled square, look for the colorful wall murals, turn right, and follow the white stripe downhill on Rue du Petit Puits. At its end you'll run into a charming square with* **Le Bar des 13 Coins.** *This eclectic little bar was the inspiration for the main setting of France's most famous soap opera,* Plus Belle La Vie. *(* Pétanque *players enjoy the little shop opposite, with the best balls for sale and a small court for testing them.) Then descend Rue Sainte-Françoise a couple of blocks and turn right toward the harbor and a massive church.*

Cathédrale de la Nouvelle Major

Bam. This huge, striped cathedral seems lost out here, away from the action and above the nondescript port. The Neo-Byzantine cathedral was built in the late 1800s to replace the old cathedral (adjacent on the inland side) that the city had outgrown. Locals brag it's the largest church built in France during the 19th century. It certainly feels big.

Cost and Hours: Free, Wed-Mon 10:00-18:30, off-season until 17:30, closed Tue.

• *Outside the cathedral, enjoy the view from the terrace. Marseille's modern port sprawls off to the right. Cruise ships tie up in the distance across the bay.*

Great Maritime Port of Marseille (GPMM)

The economy of Marseille is driven by its modern commercial ports, which extend 30 miles west from here. Over 100 million tons of freight pass through this port each year (60 percent of which is petroleum), making this one of Europe's busiest ports. Container traffic is significant but is hampered by crippling strikes, for which the left-leaning city is famous. Meanwhile, cruise-ship tourism brings more than a million passengers to Marseille each year. And each year two million ferry passengers shuttle between here and Corsica, Sardinia, Algeria, and Tunisia. You're looking at Europe's gateway to Africa.

• *You now have a choice of two ways to return to the Old Port: Either take the grand staircase down from the cathedral and through the vast new Euromed harbor development (described next) or view it from above as you walk up the tree-lined Esplanade de la Tourette (directly to Place de la Tourette). Locals are proud of their Euromed complex, with its visually striking architecture. While its venues host temporary exhibits that are generally of little interest to tourists, buzz is building around a new permanent attraction that re-creates a trove of prehistoric cave paintings.*

Euroméditerranée Culture District

As Europe's Capital of Culture in 2013, Marseille gained several important cultural centers, including two impressive buildings standing side by side on the harbor. Euromed was a grand scheme with a big, politically correct vision to revitalize the old immigration port while tying together the great (and contentious) cultures of the Mediterranean.

The **Musée Regards de Provence** displays classical and modern art in the building where immigrants were inspected and their clothing was disinfected (€7.50, Tue-Sun 10:00-18:00, closed Mon, good rooftop café with view, www.museeregardsdeprovence.com).

The Villa Méditerranée building, with a cantilevered top floor, was designed by Milanese architect Stefano Boeri and highlights events that inspire peace, brotherhood, and understanding between Mediterranean cultures. Its evocative new **Cosquer Méditerranée** exhibit re-creates some of an undersea cave with more than 500 prehistoric paintings, as discovered by a scuba diver in a *calanque* near Cassis in 1985 (€16, daily 9:00-21:00, shorter hours off-season, www.grotte-cosquer.com).

The modern building next door, **Musée des Civilisations de l'Europe et de la Méditerranée** (MuCEM), has a tiny permanent collection about Mediterranean cultures and hosts more special exhibits (www.mucem.org). From its rooftop (free access), which has a fine café/restaurant, you can cross the skybridge to Fortress St. Jean, which contains additional exhibition space.

• *If you've explored Euromed and are coming from Fortress St. Jean, take the skybridge leading to Place de la Tourette. Otherwise, if you're coming directly from the cathedral, continue walking up Esplanade de la Tourette. From either direction, a fabulous view awaits you at the...*

Place de la Tourette View Terrace

Voilà! This is one of the best views of Marseille, with Notre-Dame de la Garde presiding above, and twin forts below protecting the entrance to the Old Port. The ugly, boxy building marked "Memorial" at the base of the fort (below and to your right) stands in tribute to those lost during the Nazi occupation of the city in World War II. The small church to your left is the Church of St. Laurent, which once served as a parish church for sailors and fishermen—no-

tice the lighthouse-like tower. The old-town portion of your walk is complete.

• *Continue down the steps back to the Old Port. From the bottom of the steps, you have several options.*

An entertaining covered arcade leads left along the harbor back to where this walk started.

If you want to continue from here to the new town or Notre-Dame de la Garde, you can hop on bus #60 (stop is across the street and a few steps left, €2, 20 minutes to new town, direction: Notre-Dame de la Garde), the Petit Train, or Colorbus (stop is a few steps farther along the promenade). All go to the new town and the basilica.

*Or you can stroll 10 minutes to the **ferry** stop and ride the boat across to the new town (€0.50, exact change, included in Métro day pass, every 10 minutes, generally 8:00-20:00). To reach the ferry, walk half-way along the promenade (Quai du Port) to City Hall and a bust of Louis XIV overlooking the harbor.*

New Town

Arriving in the new town aboard the ferry, you'll find popular bars and brasseries in front of the ferry dock and to the left toward the top of the harbor. These are good for a quick meal or a memorable drink. Wander in along Place aux Huiles, make your way left, and find a smart pedestrian zone crammed with cafés and restaurants.

• *You could end your walk here, but be sure to take a trip up to Notre-Dame de la Garde (30-minute walk or take a bus—see details below).*

▲▲Notre-Dame de la Garde

Crowning Marseille's highest point, 500 feet above the harbor, is the city's landmark sight. This massive Neo-Romanesque/Neo-Byzantine basilica, built in the 1850s during the reign of Napoleon III, is a radiant collection of domes, gold, and mosaics. The monumental statue of Mary and the Baby Jesus towers

above everything (Jesus' wrist alone is 42 inches around, and the statue weighs 9 tons). And although people come here mostly for the commanding city view, the interior (with its countless ex-voto messages of thanks to Mary) is unforgettable. This hilltop has served as a lookout, as well as a place of worship, since ancient times. Climb to the highest lookout for an orientation table and the best views. The islands straight ahead are the Iles du Frioul, including the island of If—where the Count of Monte Cristo spent time (reachable by a boat excursion).

Cost and Hours: Free, daily 7:00-18:00, last entry 45 minutes before closing, modest attire is expected, cafeteria and WCs are just below the view terrace.

Getting There: To reach the church, you can hike 30 minutes straight up from the harbor; catch a taxi (about €10); or ride bus #60, the hop-on, hop-off red Colorbus line, or the tourist train—all stop on the harborfront near City Hall and in the new town.

Boat Excursions from Marseille

Boats depart from the top of the Old Port to these destinations—look for the ticket kiosks. Get the latest schedules and info on route options at the TI or directly at the pier.

Château d'If and Islands of Frioul (Iles du Frioul)

A tourist ferry connects Château d'If (a former fortress and prison) and the Island of Frioul, with hiking and places to eat. The whole excursion takes about a half-day.

When King François I visited Marseille in the 16th century, he realized the potential strategic importance of a fort on the uninhabited island of If (one of the Islands of Frioul), just outside the harbor. His **château** was finished in 1531. The impregnable fortress, which never saw battle, became a prison—handy for locking up Protestants during the Counter-Reformation. Among its illustrious inmates was José Faria, a spiritualist priest who was the idol of Paris and whom Alexandre Dumas immortalized in *The Count of Monte Cristo*. Since 1890, when the prison was closed, the château has been open to the public (€6 entry).

The **Island of Frioul** (Iles du Frioul) is a more inviting isle, offering a nature break from the big city with a few hiking paths and cafés.

The tourist ferry makes the circuit in about an hour with these two stops (20 minutes to the château, then another 15 minutes to the island). You could make the round-trip with adequate time on both islands (and a lunch on Frioul) in about four hours. If it's windy, the boat doesn't stop at Château d'If.

Cost and Hours: €11 round-trip for one island (but this comes with big gaps in the schedule), €17 for both, boats usually depart daily and at least hourly 6:30-20:30, +33 4 96 11 03 50, https://lebateau-frioul-if.fr/en. Boats depart from the southeast corner of the Old Port.

Calanques Cruises

For those who won't get to Cassis, **Croisières Marseille Calanques** offers day trips to the dramatic fjord-like inlets known as *calanques* east of Marseille (€25/2.5 hours, €30/3.5 hours, +33 4 91 33 36 79, www.croisieres-marseille-calanques.com). The ride comes with French narration (and a printed English description). Boats depart from the northeast corner of the Old Port.

Short and Scenic Cruise to Pointe Rouge

To appreciate Marseille's remarkable setting (and enjoy some beach time), take a round-trip cruise on the *navette* boat south to the Pointe Rouge neighborhood (€5 each way, departs on the hour from the southeast corner of the Old Port, about 25 minutes each way).

Pointe Rouge is where the people of Marseille go for their beach fun. From the dock a strip of popular beaches stretches back toward the city (the first one sandy, the others made from fill excavated from Marseille Métro tunnels). These are fully equipped to handle the masses and are part of a well-developed, parklike people zone. (From here you can catch bus #19 back into the city.) The pebbly beaches to the right as you leave the boat are more intimate and remote.

Sleeping in Marseille

Stay in Marseille only if you want a true urban experience. The scene is more mellow 20 minutes away in Cassis (described later).

$$$$ Hôtel la Résidence du Vieux-Port**** is pricey, modern, and superbly located on the Old Port, offering bright and airy rooms done in primary colors. All rooms face the port. Many have balconies and are worth the extra euros (18 Quai du Port, +33 4 91 91 91 22, www.hotel-residence-marseille.com, info@hrvpm.com).

$$$$ Grand Hôtel Beauvau** overlooks the harbor and lets you buy away the gritty reality outside your door with business-class comfort (rates frequently reduced, pay parking, 4 Rue Beauvau, +33 4 91 54 91 00, www.accorhotels.com, h1293@accor.com).

$$$ Hôtel Bellevue** sits right on the port and comes with tasteful rooms mixing modern and slightly worn-out furniture; it's above a small restaurant/café with a view. All rooms have port views (34 Quai du Port, +33 4 96 17 05 40, www.hotelbellevuemarseille.com, info@hotelbellevuemarseille.com).

$$ Hôtel Carré,** a block off the port, has an arty lobby and offers modern comfort at fair rates (6 Rue Beauvau, +33 4 91 33 02 33, www.hotel-carre-vieux-port.com, carre@hvpm.fr).

$$ Hôtel Ibis Marseille Gare St. Charles,** with 170 rooms, is a worthwhile value because it's right at the train station—left as you exit—and has all the services, including a restaurant, café, and bar (pay parking, look for deals on website, Square Narvik, +33 4 91 95 62 09, www.ibis.com, h1390@accor.com).

$$ Hôtel Hermes,* barely off the port, houses 29 smallish, basic-but-bright rooms. The rooftop terrace delivers smashing views over the port (behind Hôtel Bellevue at 2 Rue Bonneterie, +33 4 96 11 63 63, www.hotelmarseille.com, hotel.hermes@orange.fr).

Near the Airport: For travelers needing to catch an early flight, the airport **$$ Holiday Inn** is handy and has easy train connections to Marseille (Impasse Pythagore, Z.I. de Couperigne, 13127 Vitrolles; +33 4 42 15 09 30, www.ihg.com, reception@himarseilleairport.com).

Eating in Marseille

For lunch I'd be adventurous, eating in the North African market area (see recommendations in my "Marseille City Walk," earlier) or up in the Panier district (around La Charité). Much more forgettable and certainly stress-free is the food court in the Bourse shopping center behind the TI and Chamber of Commerce Building.

For dinner, I've listed four choices: Moroccan, fancy fish, fun and basic on the harbor, and elegant in the touristy restaurant zone.

$$ Le Souk Moroccan Restaurant is a quality and authentic-feeling place facing the harbor under the old town (vegetarian options, lunch only on Sun, closed Mon, 98 Quai du Port, +33 4 91 91 29 29).

$$$ Les Galinettes Chez Madie is good for bouillabaisse (the local fish stew specialty) and is also on the harbor under the old town (daily, 138 Quai du Port, +33 4 91 90 40 87). For a "poor man's bouillabaisse" you can order the fish soup—*soupe de poissons de roche*.

$$ Nul Part Ailleurs, overlooking the harbor on the new-town side (near the little ferry dock), is a Corsican-run eatery with a fun and accessible menu of pizza and salads, plus a passion for steak tartare. Their *tarte tatin* (apple pie) is big enough to split and understandably popular. Find it just beyond the tourist zone, with great seating inside and out (daily, 18 Quai de Rive Neuve, +33 4 91 33 58 95).

$$ La Cantine, on the Cours Honoré d'Estiene d'Orves square at #27, is surrounded by tourist joints yet maintains its dignity. It's an intimate place—cozy inside and pleasant outside—that serves nicely presented Mediterranean dishes (daily, +33 4 91 33 37 08).

The Restaurant Strip: Rue Saint-Saëns and Place aux Huiles are lined with restaurants and littered with sandwich boards listing mostly similar menus. While these places are extremely touristy, their prices are reasonable, and they offer an enticing variety of cuisines. The area is a melting pot of international eateries.

Marseille Connections

BY TRAIN AND BUS
Marseille is well served by TGV and local trains and is the hub for many smaller stations in eastern Provence.

From Marseille by Train to: Cassis (2/hour, 25 minutes, Cassis train station far outside town so consider the bus—see below), **Aix-en-Provence Centre-Ville** (2/hour, 45 minutes), **Antibes** (hourly, 2.5 hours), **Nice** (18/day, 2.5 hours), **Arles** (1-2/hour, 1 hour), **Avignon TGV** (hourly, 35 minutes), **Paris** (hourly, 3.5 hours), **Isle-sur-la-Sorgue** (12/day, 1.5-3 hours), and **London** (8 hours by TGV and Eurostar).

From Marseille's Train Station by Bus to: **Marseille Airport** (3/hour, 25 minutes), **Aix-en-Provence** (5/hour, 35 minutes).

From Marseille's Castellane Métro Stop by Bus to: Cassis— bus #M8 gets you closer to Cassis center than train but is far less frequent (7/day Mon-Sat, 5/day Sun, 40 minutes, TI has schedule, beware of afternoon gaps in service, schedule also at www.ot-cassis.com/en/access.html). The stop in Cassis is labeled *Gendarmerie* (on Avenue du 11 Novembre), from which it's a five-minute walk to the port.

BY PLANE
Marseille's airport (Aéroport Marseille-Provence), about 16 miles north of the city center, is small and easy to navigate (code: MRS, www.marseille.aeroport.fr).

Getting from the Airport to Other Destinations: Frequent buses run to Marseille's St. Charles train station (€9, 3/hour, 25 minutes) and to Aix-en-Provence (stops at Aix-en-Provence's TGV station and its bus station, 5/hour, 35 minutes). A taxi to downtown Marseille takes 30 minutes and costs €65 (€80 if it's really early, late, or Sun).

A five-minute shuttle bus trip connects the airport to the nearby Vitrolles Aéroport train station, which is handy for direct service to cities west of Marseille, including Arles, Avignon, and Nîmes. (You can also take a train from this station into Marseille, but the bus described above is easier and more frequent.)

For destinations east of Marseille (such as Cassis, Nice, or Italy), take the bus to Marseille's St. Charles Station and connect by train from there. If you need to sleep near the airport, you'll find hotels in all price ranges.

BY CRUISE SHIP

If your cruise visits Provence, you'll arrive either at Marseille or at Toulon, about 40 miles east of Marseille.

Arrival at Marseille: The Marseille Provence Cruise Terminal (MPCT) sprawls beneath a bluff west of downtown. Cruise ships tuck themselves in between cargo vessels at the main port (Porte 4), which has several *postes* (piers).

Most cruise lines offer a convenient **shuttle bus** that takes you to downtown Marseille's Old Port in 15-20 minutes (skip the complicated public-transportation trip—it's worth springing for the shuttle). From the Old Port, you can walk to many of the sights in town or head up to the **train station** (20-minute walk or take Métro to St. Charles stop) to connect to outlying destinations, such as Aix-en-Provence or Cassis (see train connections, earlier).

Taxis meet arriving cruise ships, but rates are high (€25-29 to Old Port, Notre-Dame de la Garde, or train station; one-way to Aix-en-Provence-€65; all-day round-trip to Arles/Avignon area, including several stops-€350). Try to agree on a fixed rate up front, or make sure the meter is set to the correct rate.

Arrival at Toulon: Though the city of Toulon has a cruise terminal, most of the big cruise lines dock at La Seyne-sur-Mer, across the harbor from Toulon. From there you can take the cruise-line shuttle bus or a public ferry into Toulon, then connect to a train for Marseille (1 hour) or Cassis (30 minutes).

Cassis

Hunkered below impossibly high cliffs, Cassis (kah-see) is an unpretentious yet lively port town that gives travelers a sunny break from their busy vacation. Two hours away from the fray of the Côte d'Azur, Cassis is a prettier, poor man's St-Tropez. Outdoor cafés line the small port on three sides, where boaters polish their teak as they chat up café clients. Cassis is popular with the French and close enough to Marseille to be busy on weekends, April school holidays, and all summer. Come to Cassis to dine portside, swim in the glimmering-clear water, and explore its rocky *calanques* (inlets). The name Cassis has nothing to do with the liquor with which the popular *kir* aperitifs are made.

Orientation to Cassis

The Massif du Puget mountain hovers over little Cassis, with hills spilling down to the port. Cap Canaille cliff rises from the southeast, and the famous *calanques* inlets hide along the coast northwest of town. Hotels, restaurants, and boats line the attractive little port.

TOURIST INFORMATION

The TI is in the modern building in the middle of the port among the boats. They have good maps (some are free) and the latest on *calanques* conditions (daily 9:30-18:00 with midday closure, longer hours in summer, closed Sun in winter; Quai des Moulins, toll +33 8 92 39 01 03, www.ot-cassis.com). If you're going to Marseille, ask for a map here.

ARRIVAL IN CASSIS
By Train

Cassis' hills forced the train station to be built two miles away (a 50-minute walk). It's a small station with no baggage storage and very limited hours. If you need to buy tickets when the station is closed, use the machine. Bag storage is available in the town center in peak season (see "Helpful Hints," later).

Getting from the Station to Town: Marcouline **buses** link the station with the town center (€1, every hour, schedule posted at all stops—though bus schedules in southern France are approximate). Check TI website in advance to get the schedule and plan your arrival accordingly—and be ready to take a taxi. The bus drops you at the Casino stop in Cassis: From here, turn right on Rue de l'Arène and walk downhill five minutes to reach the port.

A **taxi** into town costs €14 with baggage and is well worth the expense unless a Marcouline bus is coming soon. If there's no taxi waiting, call +33 4 42 01 78 96. Electric **tuk-tuks** can shuttle you into town for €5 (see "Helpful Hints," later).

By Bus

Regional buses (including those from Marseille) run limited hours (check with the TI before taking one). The bus stop is a 10-minute walk from the port on Avenue du 11 Novembre (stop is labeled *Gendarmerie*).

By Car

There are two exits from the autoroute for Cassis; the second (coming from Aix-en-Provence, exit #8) saves you 10 minutes, provides easy access to La Route des Crêtes (described later, under "Experiences in and near Cassis"), and offers memorable views. The hills above Cassis can make it difficult to navigate. Hotels are signed, although the blue signs can be tricky to follow. Hotel parking is minimal (carefully read each hotel's listing in this book as some have more parking than others).

Parking: No matter where you park, leave nothing of value in your car and expect some uphill walking back to your car. Outside of summer, drivers arriving by 10:00 usually can find curbside parking (€2/hour, free 19:00-9:00); latecomers will likely need to park in one of the well-marked pay lots above the port (**Parking de la Viguerie** is closest but often full, and their *Abonnés* entrance is for locals only). Check the electronic signboards as you enter town to find available spaces. **Parking Daudet**, up the road from Parking de la Viguerie, usually has better availability, as does **Parking la Madie** up the road from the Casino bus stop. Another option nearby is **Parking les Mimosas**, which has a 400-car capacity.

If you're driving here on weekends, holidays, during school vacation periods (April), or any day in July and August, Cassis can be packed. If need be, take advantage of the free parking at **Les Gorguettes**, high above the town (well signed), and use the *navette* shuttle-bus service into town (€1.60 round-trip, every 30 minutes, can be slammed at the end of the day forcing you to wait longer, July-Aug daily until 24:00; April-June, Sept weekends, and school holidays 9:00-20:00). A second parking *navette* bypasses the town center with stops at Plage du Bestouan (with two of my recommended hotels) and goes straight to Calanque de Port-Miou, saving you a 30-minute walk (stop marked *Presqu'ile*, same schedule as above).

HELPFUL HINTS

Market Days: The market fills Place Baragnon on Wednesdays and Fridays until 12:30.

Beaches: Cassis' beaches are pebbly. The big beach behind the

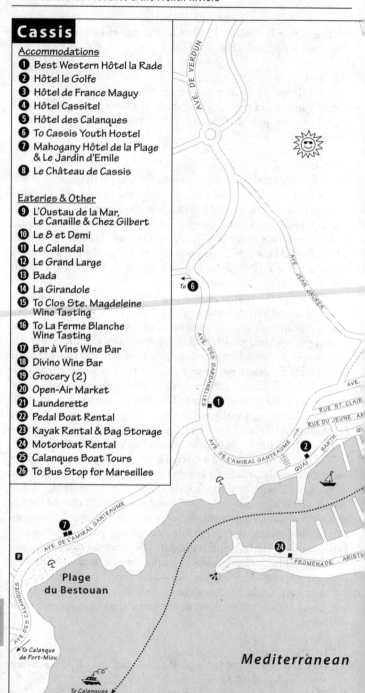

Cassis

Accommodations

1. Best Western Hôtel la Rade
2. Hôtel le Golfe
3. Hôtel de France Maguy
4. Hôtel Cassitel
5. Hôtel des Calanques
6. To Cassis Youth Hostel
7. Mahogany Hôtel de la Plage & Le Jardin d'Emile
8. Le Château de Cassis

Eateries & Other

9. L'Oustau de la Mar, Le Canaille & Chez Gilbert
10. Le 8 et Demi
11. Le Calendal
12. Le Grand Large
13. Bada
14. La Girandole
15. To Clos Ste. Magdeleine Wine Tasting
16. To La Ferme Blanche Wine Tasting
17. Bar à Vins Wine Bar
18. Divino Wine Bar
19. Grocery (2)
20. Open-Air Market
21. Launderette
22. Pedal Boat Rental
23. Kayak Rental & Bag Storage
24. Motorboat Rental
25. Calanques Boat Tours
26. To Bus Stop for Marseilles

AVE. DE VERDUN

AVE. JEAN JAURÈS

To **6**

AVE. DES DARDANELLES

AVE.

RUE ST. CLAIR

RUE DU JEUNE AN

AVE. DE L'AMIRAL GANTEAUME

QUAI BARTH

QU

1

2

24

PROMENADE ARIST

AVE. DE L'AMIRAL GANTEAUME

7

P

Plage du Bestouan

AVE. DES CALANQUES

To Calanque de Port-Miou

To Calanques

Mediterranean

MARSEILLE & NEARBY

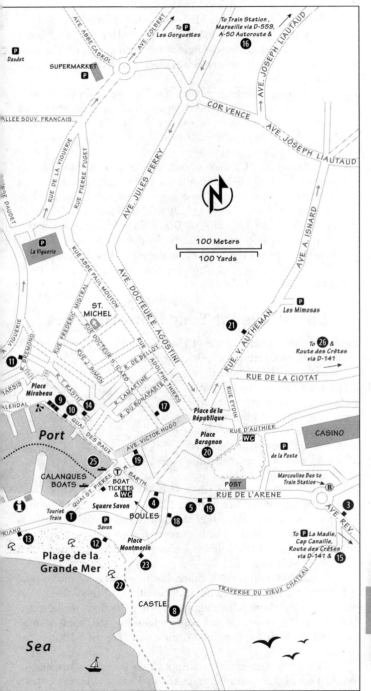

AVE. ABBE CABROL
AVE. COLBERT
To P Les Gorguettes
To Train Station, Marseille via D-559, A-50 Autoroute & 16
AVE. JOSEPH LIAUTAUD

P Daudet

SUPERMARKET P

ALLEE SOUV. FRANCAIS
COR VENCE
AVE. JOSEPH LIAUTAUD

RUE DE LA VIGUERIE
RUE PIERRE PUGET
AVE. JULES FERRY

GEORGE DAUDET

P La Viguerie

RUE ABBE PAUL MOUTON
AVE. DOCTEUR E. AGOSTINI

100 Meters
100 Yards

ST. MICHEL
RUE FREDERIC MISTRAL
RUE DOCTEUR S. ICARD
RUE DE BELLOY
RUE ADOLPHE THIERS

P Les Mimosas

AVE. V. AUTHEMAN
AVE. A. ISNARD

21

To 26 & Route des Crêtes via D-141

VIGUERIE
BREMOND
TAESIS
CALENDAL

11

Place Mirabeau

R. T. RASTIT
RUE J. SIMON
R. LAMARTINE
R. DUBONAPARTE

9
10
14
17

RUE DE LA CIOTAT

RUE E. EYDIN

Place de la République

Place Baragnon
20

RUE D'AUTHIER
WC

CASINO

Port

QUAI DES BAUX
AVE. VICTOR HUGO

19

25

P de la Poste

CALANQUES BOATS

QUAI ST. PIERRE
R. BARTH.

BOAT TICKETS & WC

T

POST

Marcouline Bus to Train Station B

RUE DE L'ARENE

AVE. REV.

3

i

Tourist Train T

Square Savon

BOULES

4

5
19

18

To P La Madie, Cap Canaille, Route des Crêtes via D-141 & 15

BRIAND

13

P Savon

12

Place Montmorin

23

Plage de la Grande Mer

22

CASTLE
8

TRAVERSE DU VIEUX CHATEAU

Sea

TI—Plage de la Grande Mer—is sandier than others. You can rent a mattress with a towel (about €16/day) and pedal boats (about €15/30 minutes). Underwater springs just off the Cassis shore make the water clean, clear, and a bit cooler than at other beaches.

Baggage Storage: In high season, **La Bagagerie de Cassis** will store your bags (€5/half-day, open April-Sept, in the kayak club on Place Montmorin, +33 4 42 01 80 01).

Laundry: A self-service *laverie automatique* is at 9 Rue Victor Autheman (daily 6:30-21:30).

Grocery Store: The **Casino** market is next door to Hôtel le Liautaud (daily 8:00-20:00, shorter hours and closed Wed in winter). There's a bigger **Spar** market just past Hôtel des Calanques on Rue de l'Arène (daily 8:00-20:00).

Taxi or Tuk-Tuk: Call +33 4 42 01 78 96 or find the main taxi stand across from Hôtel Cassitel by the *boules* court. Electric tuk-tuks can transport up to six people to key destinations in Cassis, including Cap Canaille, the train station, and Port-Miou (+33 4 84 48 58 68).

Cassis Visual Tour from the Port

Find a friendly bench in front of **Hôtel le Golfe**—or enjoy a drink at their café—and read this quick town intro.

Cassis was born more than 2,500 years ago on the hill with the castle ruins, across the harbor. Ligurians, Phoenicians, maybe Greeks, certainly Romans, and plenty of barbarians all found this spot to their liking. Parts of the castle date from the eighth century, and the **fortress walls** were constructed in the 13th century to defend against seaborne barbarian raids. The Michelin family sold the fortress to investors who turned it into a luxury five-suite *chambres d'hôte*, where celebrities often hole up looking for peace and quiet (see "Sleeping in Cassis," later).

In the 18th century, life became more secure, and people moved their homes back to the waterfront. Since then, Cassis has made its living through fishing, quarrying its famous white stone, and producing well-respected white wines—which, conveniently, pair well with the local seafood dishes, and *bien sûr*, with tourists like us.

With improvements in transportation following the end of World War II, tourism rose gradually in Cassis, although crowds remain sparse by Riviera standards. While foreigners overwhelm nearby resorts, Cassis is popular mostly with the French and still feels unspoiled. The town's protected status limits the height of the buildings along the waterfront. Cassis' port is home to some nice boats...but they're dinghies compared with those in the glitzier harbors farther east.

The big cliff towering above the castle hill is **Cap Canaille.** France's highest maritime cliff, it was sculpted by receding glaciers and today drops 1,200 feet straight down. You can—and should—drive or taxi along the top for staggering views (see "La Route des Crêtes Drive," later). Return to this bench at sunset, when the Cap glows a deep red.

Walk to the right past the small Bureau du Port. The rocky shore off to the right looks as if it were cut away just for sunbathers. But Cassis was once an important **quarry,** and stones were sliced right out of this beach for easy transport to ships. Locals say that the Statue of Liberty's base sits on this rock. Cassis stone remains highly valued throughout the world and today is used mostly for sinks and fireplaces...but yesterday's quarrymen have been replaced by today's sunbathers.

Experiences in and near Cassis

CALANQUES

Until you see these exotic Mediterranean fjords—with their translucent blue water, tiny intimate beaches, and stark cliffs plunging into the sea or forming rocky promontories—it's hard to understand what all the excitement is about.

Calanques (kah-lahnks) are narrow, steep-sided valleys partially flooded by the sea, surrounded by rugged white cliffs usually made of limestone (quarries along the *calanques* have provided building stone for centuries). The word comes from the Corsican word *calanca,* meaning

"inlet"—the island of Corsica also has *calanques.* These inlets began as underwater valleys carved by the seaward flow of water at river mouths and were later gouged deeper by glaciers. About 12,000 years ago, when the climate warmed and glaciers retreated at the end of the last Ice Age, the sea level rose partway up the steep rocky sides of the *calanques.* Today these cliffs harbor a unique habitat that includes rare plants and nesting sites for unusual raptors.

The most famous inlets are in the Massif des Calanques, which runs along a 13-mile stretch of the coast from Marseille to Cassis.

This area and part of the surrounding region became a national park in 2012. A visit here is worth ▲▲.

Visiting the *Calanques*

You can hike or cruise (by boat or kayak) to many *calanques*. Bring water, sunscreen, and anything else you need for the day, as there's nary a baguette for sale. Don't dawdle—to limit crowds and because of fire hazards, the most popular *calanques* can be closed to visitors in high season (June-Sept). When they are "closed," the only way to see the *calanques* is by boat or kayak. The TI can give you plenty of advice.

Cruising the *Calanques*

A lineup of boats near the TI offers trips of various lengths (three *calanques*-€17, 2/hour, 45 minutes; five *calanques*-€21, 5/day, 1 hour; eight or nine *calanques*-€24-29, 2-6/day, 1.5-2 hours, www. calanquesdecassis.com). The three-*calanques* tour is the most popular. Tickets are sold (and boats depart) from a small booth on the port opposite the Hôtel le Liautaud. *Prochain départ* means "next departure." Boats vary in size (some seat up to 75).

Hiking the *Calanques*

The trail lacing together *calanques* Port-Miou, Port-Pin, and d'En-Vau will warm a hiker's heart (and makes this a ▲▲▲ sight for them). Views are glorious, and the trail is manageable if you have decent shoes (though shade is minimal). For route information, see the directions below. Beware that the last sections of the trails—offering beach access—are steep, slippery, and not for everyone. These beaches also tend to be busy and noisy. Views from the trail above satisfy most.

The closest *calanque* is the linear, boat-lined **Calanque de Port-Miou**—about 30 minutes from Cassis. This works as a destination if time is short.

For most, the best *calanque* by foot is **Calanque Port-Pin**—40 minutes beyond Port-Miou and a little over an hour from Cassis. Calanque Port-Pin is well forested, with a precipitous final descent to a small, rocky beach that is relatively peaceful until early afternoon.

The most spectacular is **Calanque d'En-Vau,** a two-hour hike one-way from Cassis with an even more treacherous descent to the beach that's not for the faint of heart. In summer (June-Sept), access is strictly controlled depending on weather conditions.

Hiking Tips: The TI's free map of Cassis gives a general idea of the *calanques* trail; they also sell a more detailed IGN *calanques* map for €10. Most don't need a map for a basic hike.

For any hike, plan ahead. From June to September, many of the *calanques* are closed in certain weather conditions due to the high risk of brush fires. For information, check with the TI. Conditions and closures are announced starting at 18:00 the day before. Start your hike first thing in the morning to minimize crowds.

Hiking Directions: To reach the trailhead from Cassis, start along the road behind Hôtel le Golfe and walk past Plage du Bestouan (pay attention to your route for an easier return). At the fork in the road, go right up Traverse du Soleil, a narrow residential street. When you see a traffic sign prohibiting right turns, make a hard right up Avenue du Révérend Père Jayne, which turns into Avenue des Calanques. Walk about 10 minutes, following Avenue des Calanques as it makes a hard right, then find the trailhead on your left. Look for hiker signs as you go.

You'll eventually land at the foot of Calanque de Port-Miou, where the dirt trail begins. Follow signs to *Calanques Port-Pin* and *d'En-Vau*, walking 500 yards along a wide trail and passing through an old quarry.

You're now on the *GR (Grande Randonnée)* trail, indicated by red, white, and green markers painted on rocks, trees, and other landmarks. Follow those markers as they lead uphill (great views at the top). From here, there are two options: another 40 minutes to Calanque Port-Pin on a wide trail or 25 minutes on a shorter but challenging, jagged, and slippery stone trail—use caution (nice beach, good scampering). The trail continues from Calanque Port-Pin back up and on to Calanque d'En-Vau. *Bonne route!*

Tips for Drivers: The **Presqu'île** parking lot is close to the *calanques* and an easy, one-hour loop walk called "Petit Prince," with good views to Calanque de Port-Miou (skip in July-Aug when traffic clogs the road). This is a good option for those wanting a look at the *calanques* with less effort.

A better option for those with more energy is to park in the Les Gorguettes lot in Cassis and take the *navette* shuttle bus directly to Port-Miou—get off at the final stop (see "Arrival in Cassis, By Car," earlier). To find the hiking trail from the Presqu'île stop, exit the bus to the right; when you see the *calanque* water, swing right again to find the beginning of the path (verify with other walkers).

Other Ways to Reach the *Calanques*

From about mid-April to mid-October, you can rent a **kayak** in Cassis (try Club Sports Loisirs Nautiques on Place Montmorin, behind the merry-go-round, +33 4 42 01 80 01, www.cassis-kayak.com). The TI has brochures for more kayak companies. You can also take a **kayak tour** (€35/half-day, €55/day, €35/sunset tour, reservations smart, mobile +33 6 12 95 20 12, www.kayak-marseille.fr). If the hiking trails are closed, this is the only way you'll be able to get to the *calanque* beaches.

You can rent a small **motorboat** without a special boating license at JCF Boat Services, located behind the TI toward the lighthouse (about €150/3 hours, €250/3 hours for an electric boat, mobile +33 6 75 74 25 81, https://jcfboat.com).

You can also join a guided **electric mountain bike tour** to reach the *calanques* via the national park trails (about €45 for a 3-hour tour, book with the TI).

OTHER EXPERIENCES
▲▲La Route des Crêtes Drive

If you have a car, consider this sweeping 30-minute drive above Cassis (or spring for a taxi—about €35, 4 people per taxi). Ride straight up to the top of Cap Canaille and toward the next town, La Ciotat. It's a twisty road, providing access to numbingly high views over Cassis and the Mediterranean. From Cassis, follow signs to *La Ciotat/Toulon*, then *La Route des Crêtes*. The towns just east of Cassis (La Ciotat, Bandol, etc.) do not merit a detour. This road is occasionally closed (because of strong winds or the high risk of brush fires June-Sept), though you can usually get partway up. Check at the TI before investing time and money in this trip.

Wine Tasting

The following places give you the chance to taste the famous (mostly white) cassis wine.

In the Hills Behind Cassis: Here's your chance to sample the local wine with the folks who make it (remember, if it's a *free* tasting, it's polite to buy a bottle).

Easiest to reach without a car, the reputable **Clos Ste. Magdeleine** has good tastings (ask about English tours of the vineyard and cellar, winery open Tue-Sat 10:00-12:30 & 14:00-18:00, closed Sun-Mon; Avenue du Revestel, +33 4 42 01 70 28; confirm and book with the TI or through website, www.clossaintemagdeleine. fr, clos.sainte.magdeleine@gmail.com).

La Ferme Blanche offers tastings in a small shop right on the busy D-559 road above town. Their English-speaking staff enjoys revealing what makes cassis wine so special (Mon-Sat 9:00-12:00 & 14:00-19:00, until 17:30 in winter, Sun 9:00-12:00 year-round, +33 4 42 01 00 74).

In Town: The following places let you do some wine tasting without leaving town.

Bar à Vins is a wine bar with a good selection of regional wines offered by the glass (€7) or by the bottle, with nibbles. Cassis *blanc* and rosé wines are always available (Tue-Sun 10:00-13:00 & 16:00-24:00, 4 blocks from the port at 6 Rue Séverin Icard, +33 4 42 01 99 80).

Divino is a hole-in-the-wall wine bar with a good selection of local wines by the glass and simple dishes for a light meal (daily until late, 3 Rue Alexandre Rossat, +33 4 42 98 83 68).

Sleeping in Cassis

Cassis hotels are laid-back places with less polish but lower rates than those on the Riviera (rooms average about €100). Some close from November to March, but those that stay open offer good discounts. All are busy on weekends and in summer, when many can come with late-night noise (though most hotels have effective double-paned windows). Book early for sea views. A few offer parking spots that you can reserve when booking your room. None of the places I list has an elevator. Consider skipping your hotel breakfast and head to the port for café au lait with a view.

NEAR THE PORT OR IN TOWN

$$$ Best Western Hôtel la Rade,*** a 10-minute walk uphill from the port, has good views from its lovely poolside deck and welcoming lounge. It's a well-run place with tastefully designed but smallish rooms (pay garage parking, Route des Calanques, 1 Avenue de Dardanelles, +33 4 42 01 02 97, www.bestwestern-cassis. com, larade@hotel-cassis.com).

$$ Hôtel le Golfe,** over an easygoing (but not late-night) café, has good rates, small bathrooms with showers, and the best views of the port. Half its simple rooms come with views and small balconies—ask for a first-floor room for a bigger balcony—and are worth booking ahead. Sleep elsewhere if you can't get a view (family rooms, 3 pay parking spaces, nearby pay garage, 3 Place Grand Carnot, +33 4 42 01 00 21, www.hotel-legolfe-cassis.com, contact@legolfe-cassis.fr).

$$ Hôtel de France Maguy*** has been run by the same family for four generations. It's easy for drivers (plenty of parking), and a few blocks up from the port, so it's fairly quiet. There's a heated swimming pool, sauna, and hot tub. Rooms are well maintained and *très* modern. Several black-and-white contemporary apartments come with private terraces and a two-night minimum—longer stays required in July-Aug (parking included if you book directly with hotel, closed Nov-Feb, near the Casino on Avenue du Revestel, +33 4 42 01 72 21, www.hoteldefrancemaguy.com, hoteldefrancemaguy@gmail.com).

$$ Hôtel Cassitel,** located on the harbor over a lively café (noisy on weekends), has comfortable rooms and double-paned windows that block out most portside noise. In the more expensive rooms with balconies and sea views, the shower and sink are open to the room (family rooms, no parking—drop bags in load zone and head to Les Mimosas lot, Place Clemenceau, +33 4 42 01 83 44, www.cassitel.com, contact@cassitel.com).

$ Hôtel des Calanques** rents decent budget beds in small, simple, but clean rooms. Back rooms are quieter, and some have views of Le Château de Cassis (2 blocks off the port beyond Hôtel Cassitel at 8 Rue de l'Arène, reserve pay parking, +33 4 42 01 88 78, www.hoteldescalanquescassis.com, contact@hoteldescalanquescassis.com, friendly staff).

¢ Cassis Youth Hostel (Les Heures Claires) rents cheap beds in a classy villa with sea views, a pool, flowery gardens, and a handy location to the *calanques* trail. The dorms and private rooms are all well maintained—as are the relaxing public areas (book well in advance, common kitchen, 5-minute walk from the town center at 4 Avenue du Picouveau; +33 9 54 37 99 82, www.cassishostel.com, cassishostel@free.fr).

ON PLAGE DU BESTOUAN

The next two hotels are a 10-minute walk from the port on the next beach west, Plage du Bestouan. Easy parking makes them good for drivers.

$$$$ Mahogany Hôtel de la Plage*** faces the beach, with a concrete exterior and mod interior, generous public spaces, and a bar/restaurant facing the sea. Its 30 rooms are quite comfortable and mostly spacious, but pricey. Half the rooms offer decks and sea views (family rooms, air-con, pay parking—reserve ahead, closed in winter, +33 4 42 01 05 70, www.hotelmahogany.com, info@hotelmahogany.com).

$$ Le Jardin d'Emile,*** located below the Mahogany Hôtel de la Plage, feels like an intimate Italian villa. It's a charming little refuge with rich colors inside and out, cozy rooms, and a green garden. Five of the seven rooms have decks, four have sea views, and two are big suites (closed in winter, air-con, free and secure parking, +33 4 42 01 80 55, www.lejardindemile.fr, info@lejardindemile.fr).

HIGH ABOVE THE PORT

$$$$ Le Château de Cassis rents five luxurious suites as *chambres d'hôte*. Celebrities are often in residence, so access is strictly forbidden unless you have a reservation (spacious pool, gardens, views galore, all the amenities you can imagine, book well in advance, +33 4 42 01 63 20, www.chateaudecassis.com, contact@chateaudecassis.com).

Eating in Cassis

Peruse the lineup of tempting restaurants along the port, window shop the recommended places below, and then decide for yourself. You can have a ham-and-cheese crêpe or go all-out for bouillabaisse with the same great view. Arrive by 19:30 for the view tables. Picnickers can enjoy a beggars' banquet at the benches near Hôtel le Golfe or on the beach, or discover your own quiet places along the lanes away from the port (small grocery stores open until 19:30). Local wines are terrific: red from Bandol and whites/rosés from Cassis.

DINING PORTSIDE

These places are ideally situated along the port and offer seafood as their specialty.

$$ L'Oustau de la Mar has a loyal following, seating inside and out, and a good selection (closed Wed, 20 Quai des Baux, +33 4 42 01 78 22).

$$ Le Canaille specializes in fresh seafood platters, oysters, and other shellfish (closed Wed, 22 Quai des Baux, +33 4 42 01 72 36).

$$$ Chez Gilbert is a venerable place to dine well on Cassis' port. It has a formal feel and a more limited menu featuring lobster, shellfish, and bouillabaisse (daily, 19 Quai des Baux, +33 4 42 01 71 36).

$ Le 8 et Demi serves crêpes, pizza, salads, and ice cream on plastic tables with front-and-center portside views (daily, 8 Quai des Baux, +33 4 42 01 94 63).

DINING AWAY FROM THE PORT

$$$ Le Calendal serves up *menus* that feature local dishes in a warm, charming, and cozy setting with indoor or terrace seating. Don't be surprised if the chef visits your table. If you want bouillabaisse, you must order it a day ahead of time (dinner only, closed Wed, 3 Rue Brémond, +33 4 42 01 17 70).

$$$ Le Grand Large is indeed large and owns the scenic beachfront next to the TI. Come here for a quiet drink before dinner, or to dine on good quality seafood with a sea view (closed Wed-Thu, Plage de Cassis, +33 4 42 01 81 00).

$$ Bada is a cool beachfront place behind the TI, serving breakfast, salads, and fresh *plats* with the sounds of crashing waves (daily, dinner June-Sept only, Promenade Aristide Briand, +33 4 42 83 70 09).

$ La Girandole is an easy place for families to dine well and cheaply, with good pizza, pasta, *plats*, and salads. It's a block off the port (closed Tue, 1 Rue Thérèse Rastit, +33 4 42 01 13 39).

Cassis Connections

Cassis' train station is two miles from the port. Shuttle buses meet some trains on weekdays, and taxis and tuk-tuks are reasonable (for details, see "Arrival in Cassis," earlier). All destinations below require a transfer in Marseille.

From Cassis by Train to: Marseille (2/hour, 25 minutes), **Aix-en-Provence Centre-Ville** (hourly, 1.5 hours), **Arles** (hourly, 2 hours), **Avignon TGV** (10/day, 1.5 hours), **Nice** (hourly, 3 hours, transfer in Toulon), **Paris** (7/day, 4 hours).

From Cassis by Bus to: Marseille (#M8, 7/day Mon-Sat, 5/day Sun, 40 minutes, easier than train, TI has schedule—beware of afternoon gaps in service). Buses run from the stop labeled *Gendarmerie* on Avenue du 11 Novembre (a 10-minute walk from the port) to Marseille's Castellane Métro stop.

Aix-en-Provence

Aix-en-Provence is famous for its outdoor markets, handsome pedestrian lanes, and its cultivated residents who embrace the good life. Nowhere else in France is *l'art de vivre* (the art of living) so stylishly lived. It was that way when the French king made the town his administrative capital of Provence, and it's that way today. For a tourist, Aix-en-Provence (the "Aix" is pronounced "X") is happily free of any obligatory turnstiles. And there's not a single ancient site to see. It's just a wealthy town filled with 140,000 people—most of whom, it seems, know how to live well and look good. Aix-en-Provence's 40,000 well-dressed students (many from other countries) give the city a year-round youthful energy, and its numerous squares,  lined with cafés and fine shops, allow everyone a comfortable place to pose.

Orientation to Aix-en-Provence

With no "must-see" sights, Aix works well as a day trip, and is best on days when the markets thrive (Tue, Thu, and Sat). The city can be seen in a 1.5-hour stroll from the TI or Centre-Ville train station, though connoisseurs of southern French culture will want more time to savor it. Aix makes a handy base for day-tripping to

Marseille, Cassis, and southern villages of the Luberon (such as Lourmarin).

Cours Mirabeau (the grand central boulevard) divides the stately, quiet Mazarin Quarter from the lively old town, where the action is. In the old town, picturesque squares are connected by fine pedestrian shopping lanes, many of which lead to the cathedral. Right-angle intersections define the Mazarin Quarter but are rare in the old town—expect to get turned around regularly.

TOURIST INFORMATION

The TI, France's grandest, is located at La Rotonde traffic circle. Get the walking-tour brochure *In the Footsteps of Cézanne*, with an excellent city-center map and a good overview of excursions in the area. The TI also has maps covering areas beyond old Aix (Mon-Sat 8:30-19:00, Sun 10:00-13:00 & 14:00-18:00, shorter hours and closed Sun in winter, 300 Avenue Giuseppe Verdi, +33 4 42 16 11 61, www.aixenprovencetourism.com).

English-language **walking tours** (shown on monitors in the TI) of the old town are offered at 10:00 on Tuesdays and Saturdays; Cézanne walking tours leave at 10:00 on Thursdays (€10, two hours, depart from the TI).

Daily **excursions** into the countryside—Luberon villages, Pont du Gard, Les Baux, wineries, Mt. Ste. Victoire, and more—are also available from the TI (figure per-person costs of €60-80/half-day and €120-140/day).

ARRIVAL IN AIX-EN-PROVENCE

By Train: Aix-en-Provence has two train stations: Centre-Ville, near the city center, and the faraway TGV station. Neither has baggage storage.

Centre-Ville Station: It's a breezy 10-minute stroll to the TI and pedestrian area. Cross the boulevard in front of the station and walk up Avenue Victor Hugo; turn left at the first intersection (you're still on Victor Hugo). At the large fountain (La Rotonde), turn left and go about a quarter of the way around the fountain to find the TI.

Aix-en-Provence TGV Station: Bus #40 connects the TGV station with Aix-en-Provence's city-center bus station (€6, 4/hour, 20 minutes). From the tracks, follow signs for *Bus/Cars* to the end of the hall and downstairs (buses leave from an underpass below the tracks).

Aix-en-Provence

MARSEILLE & NEARBY

Accommodations
1. Hôtel Cézanne
2. Hôtel Cardinal
3. Hôtel des Quatre Dauphins
4. Hôtel le Concorde
5. Hôtel des Augustins

Eateries & Other
6. Le Papagayo
7. De l'Une à l'Autre
8. L'incontournable
9. Restaurant Mitch
10. Chez Charlotte
11. La Fromagerie du Passage
12. Drôle d'Endroit
13. La Tomate Verte
14. Le Grillon
15. Café du Temps
16. Mana Espresso
17. Pizza Capri (3)
18. Simply Food
19. Crêpes à Gogo
20. Patisserie Weibel
21. O'Shannon's Pub
22. Pub O'Sullivan's
23. La Brûlerie
24. Fromagerie Andre Savelli
25. Maison Béchard (Candy)
26. Maison Bremond (Candy)
27. Book In Bar
28. Launderette (3)
29. Grocery
30. To Car Rental

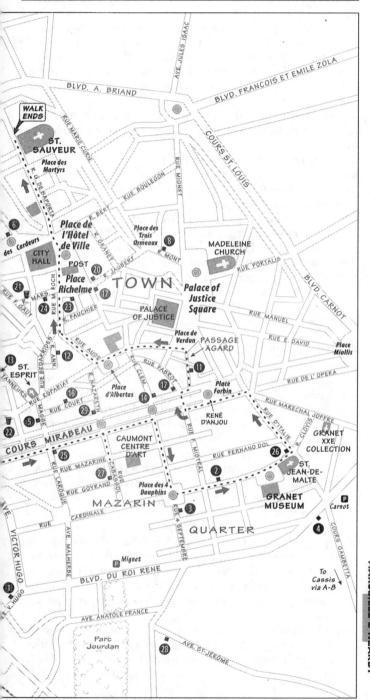

By Bus: Aix-en-Provence's looooong bus station *(gare routière)* is on Avenue de l'Europe near its intersection with Avenue des Belges. From the bus station, it's a 10-minute walk to the town center and the TI. Head slightly uphill to the flowery roundabout, turn left on Avenue des Belges, and walk to the splashing fountain (La Rotonde, the big traffic circle by the TI).

By Plane: Bus #40 links Marseille's airport with Aix's TGV station and its bus station (€10, 2/hour, 35 minutes to the bus station).

By Car: The city is well signed (yellow for hotels, green for parking). First, follow signs to *Centre-Ville,* then the yellow signs to find your hotel (GPS is handy). If your hotel has parking, use it. Otherwise, once you've spotted your hotel sign, follow green signs to park in the first pay lot you see (I've noted the closest parking to each hotel under "Sleeping in Aix-en-Provence," later). Day-trippers should look for **La Rotonde parking** (at 2 Rue Lapierre, below the TI) or **Mignet parking** (on Boulevard du Roi René), then walk to La Rotonde to start their visit (allow €18/day for parking). Those staying several days can park for cheap at the vast **Park and Ride Krypton** lot (about €3/day, just off A-8, exit 30). From here, you can take a frequent and free bus to La Rotonde (clearly marked).

HELPFUL HINTS

Markets: Aix-en-Provence bubbles over with photogenic open-air morning markets in several of its squares and streets: **Richelme** is my favorite (produce, daily). The following run Tuesdays, Thursdays, and Saturdays: **Palace of Justice/Rue Thiers** (food and crafts), **L'Hôtel de Ville** (flower market; book market first Sun of each month), and along **Cours Mirabeau** (textiles and fashion). One Sunday a month, Cours Mirabeau also hosts an antiques market—check at the TI. Most pack up at 13:00, except the book market, which runs all day. Saturday market days are the biggest. It's worth planning your visit for a market day, as these markets are the sightseeing highlights of the town.

Shopping: Signs at fancy bakeries advertise *calissons d'Aix,* the city's famous homemade candy. It's made with almond paste—kind of like a marzipan cake—and makes a pleasing souvenir.

Services: Public WCs, as they're not stylish, are rare in Aix. Take advantage of WCs in restaurants, museums, or at other stops you make.

English Bookstore: Located on the quiet side of Aix-en-Provence, the atmospheric **Book in Bar** has a fine collection of adult and children's books, a good selection of tourist guides (Cassis, Arles, Avignon, and so on), and an inviting café (Mon-Sat

10:00-19:00, closed Sun, 4 Rue Joseph Cabassol, where it crosses Rue Goyrand, +33 4 42 26 60 07).

Laundry: Launderettes are scattered throughout the city. **Ecolav'** is just behind the TI on Square Narvik at 3 Rue Lapierre (daily 7:00-21:00). Others are at 11 Rue des Bernardines (daily 8:00-20:00) and at 8 Avenue St-Jérôme (daily 7:00-21:00).

Supermarket: Find a grocery store in the basement of **Monoprix,** at 27 Cours Mirabeau, two long blocks up from La Rotonde (Mon-Sat 8:00-20:40, Sun 9:00-13:00), plus other small ones all over the city.

Taxi: Call +33 4 42 27 71 11. A taxi from your Aix-en-Provence hotel to Marseille costs about €70 and to Cassis about €115.

Car Rental: Renting is easiest at the TGV station outside of town where all major companies have offices that are open Sundays. Only **Europcar** is in the city center, near La Rotonde (Mon-Sat 9:00-12:00 & 13:00-17:00, closed Sun, 55 Boulevard de la République, +33 4 22 57 30 27).

Tours in Aix-en-Provence

Local Guides

Pascale Benguigui and **Dominique Barte** are good choices for this area (also recommended for Marseille; see "Tours in Marseille," earlier). Also consider **Catherine D'antuono** and **Sarah Pernet**, who runs Discover Provence tours (listed on page 41).

Food Tour

Tastes of Provence run walking tours and cooking classes, offering a unique "taste" of daily life and food in Aix-en-Provence. Mathilde or Jennifer lead small groups on a gourmet walking tour, during which you'll chat with locals in traditional food shops and the farmers market, taste sweet and savory regional specialties, and learn about the city's royal history and unique food culture while meeting the families whose businesses represent the best addresses in town (see their website for latest offerings and prices). You can also help prepare a three-course lunch at their cooking school, using fresh market ingredients (€115/person, 5 hours, includes wine; +33 6 72 83 98 28, www.tastesofprovence.com, info@tastesofprovence.com).

Electric Minibus Joyride

For a mere €1.40, take a joyride through the winding lanes of the old town center on a *Diabline*—a six-seater electric-powered minibus. Designed with local seniors in mind, the minibus provides a fun (and less glamorous) slice-of-life experience in Aix-en-Provence. It leaves every 10 minutes from the La Rotonde fountain, opposite the TI (Mon-Sat 8:30-19:30, none on Sun, 40 minutes round-trip). Just wave one down anywhere and hop on. There are three routes (A, B, and C); get route maps at the TI or ask the driver when you board. Line A gives you the best overview of the city and runs a route similar to the self-guided walk described later. It also gets you near Cézanne's studio.

Petit Train

Rest your feet and discover Aix-en-Provence's historic center with English commentary on a 45-minute tour on the little train (€10, departs hourly 10:00-18:00 from La Rotonde fountain near the TI).

Aix-en-Provence Walk

I've listed these streets, squares, and sights in the order of a handy, lazy orientation stroll. To follow the route, see the "Aix-en-Provence" map, earlier.

• *Start on Cours Mirabeau at La Rotonde, near the statues on either side of the street, and face...*

La Rotonde

In the 1600s, the roads from Paris and Marseille met just outside the Aix-en-Provence town wall at a huge roundabout called La Rotonde. From here locals enjoyed a sweeping view of open
countryside before entering the
town. As time passed, growing
Aix-en-Provence needed space
more than fortifications. The
wall was destroyed and replaced
by a grand boulevard (Cours
Mirabeau). A modern grid-plan
town, the Mazarin Quarter (to

the right as you look up Cours Mirabeau), arose across the boule-
vard from the medieval town (on the left). In 1860, to give residents water and shade, the town graced La Rotonde with a fountain and a grand boulevard lined with trees. The three figures on top of the fountain represent Justice, Agriculture, and Fine Arts. *Voilà:* The modern core of Aix-en-Provence was created. The Apple store facing La Rotonde is another feather in Aix's style cap.

• *Saunter slowly up the right side of Cours Mirabeau.*

Cours Mirabeau

This "Champs-Elysées of Provence" divides the higgledy-piggledy old town (left) and the stately Mazarin Quarter (right). Designed for the rich and famous to strut their fancy stuff, Cours Mirabeau

Aix-en-Provence History

Aix-en-Provence was founded in about 120 BC as a Roman military camp on the site of a thermal hot spring (in France, "Aix" refers to a city built over a hot spring). The Romans' mission: to defend the Greek merchants of Marseille against the local Celts.

Strategically situated, this was the first Roman base outside the Italian Peninsula—the first foreign holding of what would become a vast empire. (The name Provence comes from its status as the first Roman province.) But Rome eventually fell, and the barbarians destroyed Aix-en-Provence in the fourth century. Through the Dark Ages, the city's Roman buildings were robbed of their stones. No buildings from Roman Aix-en-Provence survive.

Aix-en-Provence was of no importance through the Middle Ages. Because the area was once owned by Barcelona, Provence has the same colors as Catalunya: gold and red. In 1481 the Count of Provence died. He was hairless (according to my guide). Without a hair, Provence was gobbled up by France. When Aix-en-Provence was made the district's administrative center, noble French families moved in, kicking off the city's beautiful age (belle époque). They built about 200 *hôtels particuliers* (private mansions), many of which survive today. As you wander, look up, peek in, and notice the stately architecture with its grandiose extra touches.

Aix-en-Provence thrived thanks to its aristocratic population. But when the Revolution made being rich dicey, the local aristocracy and clergy fled. Aix-en-Provence entered the next stage of its history as the "Sleeping Beauty city." Later in the 19th century, the town woke up and resumed its pretentious ways. Here, the custom of rich people being bobbed along in sedan chairs survived longer than anywhere else in France.

After the Revolution, you couldn't have servants do it—but you could hire pallbearers in their off-hours to give you a lift. If being ostentatious ever became the norm...it happened in Aix-en-Provence.

survives much as it was: a single lane for traffic and an extravagant pedestrian promenade, shaded by newly replanted plane trees, cafés on the sunny side, and lined by 17th- and 18th-century mansions for the aristocracy on its shady side. Rich folks lived on the right side (in the Mazarin Quarter); common folk lived on the left side (in the old town). Cross streets were gated to keep everyone in their place. Which side are you sleeping on?

The street follows a plan based on fours: 440 meters long, 44 meters wide, plane trees (originally elms) 4 meters apart, and decorated by 4 fountains. The "mossy fountains," overgrown by 200 years of neglect, trickle with water from the thermal spa that gave Aix its first name (and make steamy sights on cold winter days).

Cours Mirabeau was designed for showing off. Today, it remains a place for *tendance* (trendiness)—or even *hyper-tendance*. If French culture has a pretentious quality, it seems that such pretense was born right here. Show your stuff and strut the broad sidewalk. As you stroll up the boulevard, stop in front of Aix's oldest and most venerated *pâtisserie*, **Maison Béchard** (on the right side at 12 Cours Mirabeau), and get a whiff coming from the vent under the entry. They are famous for the candy called *calisson*. Like many local treats, these come with a history. The venerable delicacy of almond, melon, and orange rind draped in icing, whose name means "hug" in French, was concocted for a royal wedding here in the 14th century.

For a glimpse of the finest surviving mansion in the Mazarin Quarter (described next), take a side-trip from the next fountain one block right down Rue Joseph Cabassol to #3 (peek through the gate). The 17th-century Hôtel Caumont hosts the **Caumont Centre d'Art.** While it has two permanent rooms offering a feel for aristocratic luxury in the age of Louis XIV, its main attractions are its special exhibits, elegant café, and formal garden. Cézanne fans will enjoy the 30-minute movie (with English subtitles) about the artist in the center's theater—check showtimes as you enter (overpriced for most at €15, daily 10:00-19:00, Oct-April until 18:00).

• *Keep strutting up Cours Mirabeau. From the mossy fountain at Rue du 4 Septembre, turn right and walk three blocks into Aix-en-Provence's quiet side, stopping at the pleasing little Place des Quatre Dauphins. This marks the center of the...*

Mazarin Quarter (Quartier Mazarin)

Built in a grid plan during the reign of King Louis XIV, the Mazarin Quarter remains a peaceful, elegant residential neighborhood—although each of its mansions now houses several families rather than just one. Study the quarter's Baroque and Neoclassical architecture (from the 17th and 18th centuries). The square's Fountain of the Four Dolphins, inspired by Bernini's fountains in Rome, dates from an age when Italian culture set the Baroque standard across Europe. Appreciate how calm this half of the city feels.

Wander left up Rue Cardinale toward a 12th-century church facing a handsome square. (If you're inspired to buy or rent an apartment here, check out the prices in the display windows at the start of Rue Cardinale.) Follow the brass studs in the sidewalk (part of the TI's Cézanne trail) to the church.

St. Jean-de-Malte was built when this area was outside the town wall—500 years before the advent of the Mazarin Quarter. The adjacent **Musée Granet** features Aix's homegrown artists (including several "lesser" paintings by Cézanne). The museum is most popular for its selection of post-Impressionist works, including several by Picasso, some Van Gogh, and Braque. Most of its 20th century paintings are housed in the Granet XXE Collection in a nearby chapel. Check the website to learn about current exhibits, or ask at the TI (€6-9, open Tue-Sun 10:00-18:00, Oct-May from 12:00, closed Mon year-round, www.museegranet-aixenprovence. fr).

Walk behind St. Jean-de-Malte (on the left) to the next street, and look above the window of the **Maison Bremond** candy shop (on the left-hand corner) where a sweet mosaic of the Fountain of the Four Dolphins Square gives a fun glimpse of the sedan-chair elegance of this quarter back in its heyday. Maison Bremond has been making *calisson* since 1830 (my hunch is that's what the woman in the mosaic is after). Drop in and enjoy a sample.

• *Turn left on Rue d'Italie, lined by edible temptations. Pause and appreciate the kingly architecture mixed with the patina of age. (The king seems to be looking way down to the end of the boulevard to Lady Justice, Lady Agriculture, and Lady Fine Arts, where this walk began.) Walk along Rue d'Italie to Place Forbin, go left to the top of Cours Mirabeau, and find the statue. This is René d'Anjou, the last count of Provence, during whose rule this region joined France (c. 1450). He was nicknamed "Bon Vivant" for his cultured lifestyle and taste for the good life. Stroll down the right side of the street to #53, what was formerly...*

Les Deux Garçons

A café in this spot, once frequented by Paul Cézanne, was *the* hangout on the boulevard until a fire destroyed it in late 2019. The Cézanne family hat shop was next door (#55). Cézanne's dad parlayed that successful business into a bank, then into greater wealth, setting up his son to be free to enjoy his artistic pursuits.

• *From here we'll enter the lively old town, where pedestrian streets are filled with fine food stores, boutiques, and romantic street musicians. This is the place in Aix-en-Provence for shopping.*

Leave Cours Mirabeau at #55, through the tiny Passage Agard. (At the far end, notice the gate that was locked at night to keep the rich *safe from the poor.) The passage leads to a square dominated by the Palace of Justice, which hosts a bustling food and crafts market (Tue, Thu, and Sat mornings). If the market is on, take some time to explore the scene. Otherwise, head left along the first street you crossed as you came into the square, Rue Marius Reinaud, which hosts the top designer shops in town. Walk straight and pause several blocks down when you hear the gurgling of water at the peaceful courtyard called...*

Place d'Albertas

This sweet little square was created by the guy who lived across the street. He hated the medieval mess of buildings facing his mansion, so he drew up a har-monious facade with a fountain, and had his ideal vision built to mask the ugly neighborhood. The long-overdue restoration of this once run-down square hit a snag. Since only two-thirds of the property owners agreed to help fund the work, one-third remains undone.

With your back to the foun-tain, find the large wooden door on the building across the street. Look at the names on the door buzzers—the Albertas family still lives here (but their grand historic residence is now shared).

• *Turn right on Rue Aude, the main street of medieval Aix-en-Provence (which turns into Rue du Maréchal Foch). Continue uphill on Rue du Maréchal Foch to...*

Place Richelme

This inviting square hosts a lively market, as it has since the 1300s (daily 8:00-13:00). It's the perfect Provençal scene—lovely build-ings, plane trees, and farmers selling local produce. The goat-cheese merchants here add life to the market. The cafés at the downhill end of the square are ideal for savoring the market ambience. The square is ground zero for foodies. For perhaps the best coffee in Aix (or maybe a chocolate frappé), go local at **La Brûlerie**, then find the perfect pastry at Aix's venerable **Patisserie Weibel** (see "Eating in Aix-en-Provence," later). And if cheese would please, find **Fro-magerie Andre Savelli,** facing the square at 9 Rue des Marseillais.

• *One block uphill is the stately...*

Place de l'Hôtel de Ville

This square is anchored by a Roman column. Stand with your back to the column and face the Hôtel de Ville. The center niche of this 17th-century City Hall once featured a bust of Louis XIV. But since the Revolution, Marianne (the Lady of the Republic) has taken his place. As throughout Europe, the three flags represent the region (Provence), country (France), and the European Union. Provence's flag carries the red and yellow of Catalunya (the proud and semiautonomous re-  gion around Barcelona in Spain) because the counts of Provence originated there. Aix-en-Provence's coat of arms over the doorway combines the Catalan flag and the French fleur-de-lis.

The 18th-century building on your left was once the town's grain exchange (today it's a post office). Its exuberant pediment features figures representing the two rivers of Provence: old man Rhône and madame Durance. While the Durance River floods frequently (here depicted overflowing its frame), it also brings fertility to the fields (hence the cornucopia).

Back toward Hôtel de Ville, the 16th-century bell tower was built in part with stones scavenged from ancient Roman buildings—notice the lighter stones at the tower's base. The niche above the arch also once displayed the bust of the king. Since the Revolution, it has housed a funerary urn that symbolically honors all who gave their lives for French liberty. Under the arch notice a small plaque honoring the American 3rd Division that liberated the town in 1944 (with the participation of French troops; Aix-en-Provence got through World War II relatively unscathed).

History aside, the square is a delight for its vintage French storefronts and colorful morning markets, such as the flower market (Tue, Thu, and Sat). On nonmarket days and each afternoon, café tables replace the market stalls.

• *Stroll under the bell tower and uphill on Rue Gaston de Saporta, passing stately hôtels particuliers (private mansions, sometimes used for government purposes) until you reach the...*

Cathedral of the Holy Savior (Saint-Sauveur)

This church was built atop the Roman forum—likely on the site of a pagan temple. As the cathedral grew with the city, its interior became a parade of architectural styles. The many-faceted interior is at once confusing and fascinating, with three distinct sections: Standing outside, at the entrance, you face the Romanesque section; to the left are the Gothic and then the Baroque sections.

Cost and Hours: Free, daily 8:30-18:30.

Visiting the Cathedral: In the **Romanesque section** (to the

MARSEILLE & NEARBY

Paul Cézanne in Aix-en-Provence

Post-Impressionist artist Paul Cézanne (1839-1906) loved Aix-en-Provence. He studied law at the university (opposite the cathedral), and produced most of his paintings in and around Aix-en-Provence—even though at the time this conservative town was disinclined to understand him or his art. Today the city fathers milk anything remotely related to his years here. While there's almost no actual art by Cézanne in Aix, and certainly no masterpieces, fans of the artist will want to pick up the *In the Footsteps of Cézanne* self-guided-tour flier at the TI and follow the bronze pavement markers around town.

Atelier de Cézanne, the artist's last studio, has been preserved as it was when he died and is open to the public. Although there is no art here, his tools and personal belongings make it meaningful for enthusiasts.

Cost and Hours: €6.50, helpful audioguide €3, daily 9:30-18:00, shorter hours off-season, closed Sun-Mon in winter, reservations essential for 30-minute timed visit, best to book online (http://reservation.aixenprovencetourism.com) or through TI , +33 4 42 21 06 53, www.atelier-cezanne.com.

Getting There: It's a 30-minute, two-mile walk from the TI, but just 10 minutes from the end of my self-guided walk. Or you can ride electric minibus A or bus #5 from La Rotonde (9 Avenue Cézanne).

right as you enter) step down and into a different age. Find the modern baptistery (which stands upon a much older one), surrounded by ancient columns with original fourth-century capitals below a Renaissance cupola. The baptistery was located outside the church until the 14th century, when the church was expanded to encompass the baptistery.

Farther down is the door to the 12th-century cloister, with its delicate carved capitals (French-only tours on the hour and half-hour except 12:00-14:30). After passing a side chapel, find the closet-sized architectural footprint of the original Christian chapel from the Roman era (it's several feet below today's floor level). This too would have been outside the current church walls until the 14th century.

In the **Gothic section,** two organs flank the nave: One works, but the other is a prop, added for looks...an appropriately symmetrical Neoclassical touch, as was the style in the 18th century (notice the lack of depth in one of them). And the high altar is, like the city itself, a stately mix of old and new.

• *Your tour is over. It's all downhill from here to La Rotonde. Cézanne fans can walk to the workshop or "atelier" of Paul Cézanne (see the sidebar). Walk up Avenue Pasteur, following the brown signs, heading uphill for about 10 minutes.*

Sights near Aix-en-Provence

Site-Mémorial du Camp des Milles

Once a huge tile factory, this site was used as a French internment camp to lock up German aliens at the beginning of World War II, then as a prison for enemies of Vichy France and Nazi Germany, and finally as a deportation center sending thousands of French Jews to Auschwitz. The almost haunted old factory is the only French internment and deportation camp still intact. Its museum has a three-part focus: history, remembrance, and reflection. While there are few actual artifacts here, the lesson is clear: We must learn from history. For example, the exhibits explain the chilling steps from racism to outright genocide—and how people can resist such dangerous spirals. Its mission is important, but the site—while interesting and informative—is best for WWII aficionados.

Cost and Hours: €9.50, daily 10:00-19:00, last entry at 17:30, essential audioguide-€3.50, +33 4 42 39 17 11, www. campdesmilles.org.

Getting There: It's three miles from Aix. You can either take **bus** #4 from the La Rotonde stop or **drive** along A-51 toward Marseille (use exit #5 and follow the yellow signs to the memorial camp).

Sleeping in Aix-en-Provence

Hotel rooms, starting at about €75, are surprisingly reasonable in this highbrow city. Reserve ahead, particularly on weekends. Hotel stars have less meaning here. The best values are on the quiet side of Cours Mirabeau in the Mazarin Quarter.

$$$$ Hôtel Cézanne,**** a block up from the Centre-Ville train station, delivers top comfort and professional service. The lobby and 55 spacious rooms are modern and surround a generous patio (pay parking—must book ahead, 40 Avenue Victor Hugo, +33 4 42 91 11 11, https://boutiquehotelcezanne.com, boutiquehotelcezanne@hotelaix.com).

$ Hôtel Cardinal** is a top value in Aix-en-Provence's quiet and classy Mazarin Quarter. It's a creaky old mansion that literally shakes when people walk, with tilting floors, old-time bathrooms, and spacious, 19th-century elegance under chandeliers in each room. The paintings hanging in public spaces were done by the owner Nathalie's papa (RS%, closest parking is Mignet, 24 Rue Cardinale, +33 4 42 38 32 30, www.hotel-cardinal-aix.com, hotel.cardinal@wanadoo.fr).

$ Hôtel des Quatre Dauphins*** is a welcoming, cozy place in the quiet quarter with sharp rooms at great rates (no elevator, 3 floors, closest parking is Mignet, 54 Rue Roux Alphéran, +33 4 42 38 16 39, www.hotel-aix-lesquatredauphins.fr, lesquatredauphins@wanadoo.fr).

$ Hôtel le Concorde*** sits on the busy ring road, but most of its comfortable rooms face its quiet, convivial courtyard. Choose between larger rooms in the main building (best ones face the rear and have balconies) or the motel-esque rooms (with thinner walls) on the small courtyard (pay parking, 68 Boulevard du Roi René, +33 4 42 26 03 95, www.hotel-aixenprovence-concorde.com, contact@hotel-leconcorde.fr). Helpful Claire runs the place.

$$ Hôtel des Augustins*** has a restored 15th-century chapel serving as a cozy lobby. The 29 rooms spread over three floors offer simple and quiet comfort in this busier part of town, just north of Cours Mirabeau (elevator to second floor only, 3 Rue de la Masse, +33 4 42 27 28 59, https://hotel-augustins.com, contact@hotel-augustins.com).

Eating in Aix-en-Provence

In Aix-en-Provence, you can dine on bustling squares, along a grand boulevard, or on atmospheric side streets. To sit and enjoy the grand parade of life here, Cours Mirabeau is good for desserts and drinks, as are many of the outdoor places lining leafy squares. While I like to sleep in a quiet neighborhood, I love the commotion of table-lined squares and the romance of a tangled old town. My recommendations offer plenty of variety and are carefully reviewed by my friends at Tastes of Provence food tours (see "Tours in Aix-en-Provence," earlier). *Bon appétit!*

OLD TOWN
On Forum des Cardeurs

This big traffic-free esplanade is Aix's popular living room, with a festive variety of places to eat and drink (bars downhill, best food at the top). This is the high-energy place to be if you want to dine under the sky. Walk around, survey the scene, then decide.

$$ Friendly and welcoming **Le Papagayo** serves a range of Mediterranean cuisine, including a good selection of salads and plates to share. The tables are all outside, and while big umbrellas shade them in bad weather, the restaurant closes for lunch when it gets too hot (daily, weather permitting, +33 9 54 59 44 23).

If Forum des Cardeurs feels too busy, try peaceful $$ **De l'Une à l'Autre**, just off the big square. Trust smiling Sophie for a fine Provençal dining experience under the fig tree in the courtyard or in the cocooning interior (closed Sun-Mon, 12 Rue du Cancel, better to reserve in summer, +33 4 42 22 79 61).

On Romantic Place des Trois Ormeaux

This intimate square is a true *bijou* (gem), with tables under leafy trees crowding a small fountain. A candlelit, romantic alternative to the more boisterous Forum des Cardeurs, it's best for dining outdoors. $$$ **L'incontournable** offers good-value, high-end Provençal cuisine with a hint of Japanese flavor, reflecting the chef's world travels (closed Sun-Mon except in July-Aug, reservations essential, 14 Rue Montigny, +33 9 80 32 86 32, https://lincontournable-grill.eatbu.com).

Other Favorites Buried in the Old Town

$$$$ **Restaurant Mitch** is a dressy choice for a classic French dinner. Enjoy the seasonal, well-presented dishes, excellent wine list, modern flair, and top-notch service that Mitch, with a twinkle in his eye, assures. Tables on the traffic-free lane afford great people-watching (closed Sun, no lunch, 26 Rue des Tanneurs, +33 4 42 26 63 08).

$ **Chez Charlotte,** run by Laurent, is Aix's low-key diner where locals go for "grandma's cooking" at a good price. While they have indoor seating, I prefer the fun back garden (open from 20:00, closed Sun-Mon except in July-Aug, 32 Rue des Bernardines, +33 4 42 26 77 56).

$$ **La Fromagerie du Passage**, upstairs from its cheese shop, is fun for anyone who's hungry and likes French cheese. Study their menu and ask for your server's help—there's a world of good options. I like the €21 five-cheeses-bread-and-salad deal (open for lunch and dinner Tue-Sat, shop open same days plus on Sun morning, good wine options by the glass or bottle, big charcuterie plates, off 55 Cours Mirabeau in the Passage Agard, +33 4 42 22 90 00). The best seating is on the top-floor terrace.

WHERE THE LOCALS GO

$$ **Drôle d'Endroit** ("Funny Place") is down a tiny alley close to the Place Richelme daily market. Considered a cultural and gourmet destination, the colourful restaurant offers a happy atmosphere

where diners are treated to seasonal specialities. The place also features rotating art expositions (open for dinner Tue-Sat, also open for lunch Tue and Thu-Sat; closed Sun-Mon; reservations essential, 14 Rue Annonerie Vieille, +33 4 42 38 95 54, https://droledesite.fr).

$$ La Tomate Verte serves fresh and modern Mediterranean cuisine. The daily offerings—direct from the market—are written on a blackboard. Sit inside or outside on a typical car-free lane watching the world go by, while the owner-couple proudly serves you a memorable Aix-en-Provence meal (closed Sun-Mon, 15 Rue des Tanneurs, +33 4 42 60 04 58).

NEAR COURS MIRABEAU

If you're interested in a delicious view more than delicious food, eat with style on Cours Mirabeau. Try **$$ Le Grillon,** a boisterous choice and a rare all-day dining institution. Its bar is a hit with locals for the prime seating—front and center on the boulevard's strolling fashion show (daily, on the corner of Rue Clemenceau and Cours Mirabeau, +33 4 42 27 58 81).

Veggie/Vegan Options: $$ Café du Temps, often used in film sets, is a quintessential Aix-en-Provence scene. Appetizing and exclusively vegetarian cuisine features fresh market ingredients, served by the owners. Leafy plane trees and a peaceful fountain complete the picture-perfect square. It's popular with locals, so don't arrive too late at lunchtime (31 Rue de la Couronne, +33 9 52 01 25 89). **$ Mana Espresso** is a popular and bustling café serving fine roasted coffee, Turkish eggs for breakfast, a vegetarian burger topped with grilled halloumi cheese for lunch, and homemade carrot cake for an afternoon snack (daily, 14 Rue Courteissade, +33 4 86 22 44 44).

CHEAP EATS AND TAKEOUT

The town's multiple squares with benches call out to those who want to enjoy a quick to-go meal.

$ Pizza Capri is an institution in Aix, with several locations around town. The place offers a solid range of toppings—grab a slice or a whole pizza (daily 11:00–23:00, locations on Place Richelme and at the top and bottom of Cours Mirabeau, see map on page 282).

$ Simply Food is a modern and healthy fast-food place serving salads, sandwiches, and smoothies at simple outdoor tables. They also sell items to go (daily 8:00-19:00, on La Rotonde directly opposite the TI).

$ Crêpes à Gogo, located in a tunnel passage under La Rotonde traffic circle, slings sweet and savory crepes cooked to order—just follow your nose. For those renting apartments in the old town, you can also take away fresh crêpe batter to cook at home (Tue–Sat 11:00–19:00, closed Sun-Mon, 2 Avenue Victor Hugo).

$$ Patisserie Weibel, a bakery run for three generations, offers a plethora of choices for quick lunches, including spectacular pastries, sandwiches, and salads. The elegant tearoom is a great spot for people-watching—and the WC here makes a good pit-stop while sightseeing (daily 7:30–19:00, just off Place Richelme at 2 Rue Chabrier).

LE LATE-NIGHT

Bar Hopping: Elegant old Aix comes to life after dark in clusters of Irish pubs and sports bars buried in its old town. For the young—and young at heart—the best action centers on Rue de la Verrerie (start with **O'Shannon's Pub** at #30) and near La Rotonde, next to Hôtel de France on Place des Augustins (start with **Pub O'Sullivan's**).

Aix-en-Provence Connections

BY BUS

Most regional buses depart from the bus station on Avenue de l'Europe. The station has a helpful ticket office (Mon-Sat 6:30-19:30, Sun 7:30-18:30, +33 9 69 32 82 07, English spoken) and a good waiting room with WCs. Several companies operate buses from this station (www.lepilote.com). When connecting big cities (like Aix-en-Provence and Avignon or Lyon), check FlixBus and BlaBlaBus schedules as well as the local lines listed below (see the "Transportation" section of the Practicalities chapter for more on these bus companies).

From Aix-en-Provence by Bus to: Marseille (5/hour, 35 minutes), **Marseille Airport** (bus #40, 2/hour, 35 minutes), **Avignon** (6/day Mon-Sat, 3/day Sun, 75 minutes, faster and easier than train), **Arles** (requires transfer but faster than trains, 6/day Mon-Fri, 4/day Sat-Sun, 1.5 hours), **Lourmarin** (3/day Mon-Sat, 1/day Sun, 1.5 hours, bus departs 500 yards from the main bus station, ask at the station), **Nice** (3/day, direct takes 2 hours, cheaper and quicker option than taking the train).

BY TRAIN

Aix-en-Provence has two train stations: one in the center and one for TGV trains, outside of town. In some cases, destinations are served from both stations; I've listed the station with the best connection.

To reach the TGV station from the center, take bus #40, which runs from Aix-en-Provence's bus station (€6, 4/hour, 20 minutes; some of these buses continue to Marseille's airport). To reach the

TGV station by car from Aix-en-Provence, get on the A-51 auto-route toward *Marseille*, get off at the first exit (Les Milles), and follow signs for another 10 minutes. (A kiosk café is inside the TGV station, with sandwiches, drinks, and snacks.)

From Aix-en-Provence's Centre-Ville Station by Train to: Marseille (2/hour, 45 minutes). The following connections all require a transfer in Marseille: **Cassis** (hourly, 1.5 hours), **Arles** (hourly, 2 hours; train may separate midway—be sure you're in the section going to Arles), Avignon (hourly, 2.5 hours).

From Aix-en-Provence's TGV Station by Train to: Avignon TGV (hourly, 20 minutes), **Nice** (10/day, 3-4 hours, most change in Marseille), **Paris** (hourly, 3.5 hours, may require transfer in Lyon).

THE FRENCH RIVIERA

FRENCH RIVIERA

La Côte d'Azur

A hundred years ago, celebrities from London to Moscow flocked to the French Riviera to socialize, gamble, and escape the dreary weather at home. Today, budget vacationers and heat-seeking Europeans fill belle époque resorts at France's most sought-after fun-in-the-sun destination.

The region got its nickname from turn-of-the-20th-century vacationing Brits, who simply extended the Italian Riviera west to France to include Nice. Today, the Riviera label stretches even farther westward, running from the Italian border to St-Tropez. To the French, this summer fun zone is known for the dazzling azure color of the sea along this coast: La Côte d'Azur. All of my French Riviera destinations are on the sea, except for a few hill towns and the Grand Canyon du Verdon (Gorges du Verdon).

This sunny sliver of land has been inhabited for more than 3,000 years. Ligurians were first, then Greeks, then Romans—who, as usual, had the greatest impact. After the fall of Rome, Nice became an important city in the kingdom of Provence (along with Marseille and Arles). In the 14th century Nice's leaders voted to join the duke of Savoy's mountainous kingdom (also including several regions of northern Italy), which would later evolve into the kingdom of Sardinia. It was not until 1860 that Nice (and Savoy) became a part of France—the result of a plebiscite. (The "vote" was made possible because the king of Sardinia had to trade the region to France as a quid pro quo for Napoleon III's support of the Italian states that wanted to break away from Austria to create modern Italy).

Nice has world-class museums, a splendid beachfront promenade, a seductive old town, and all the drawbacks of a major city (traffic, crime, pollution, and so on). The day-trip possibilities are easy and exciting: Monaco offers a royal welcome and a fairy-tale

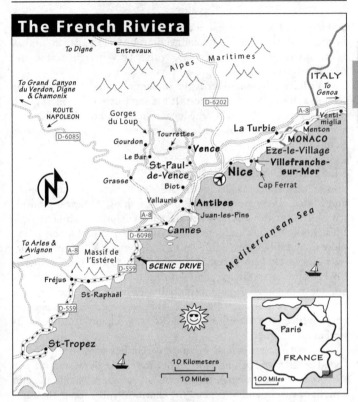

past; Antibes has a thriving port and silky sand beaches; and im-age-conscious Cannes is the Riviera's self-appointed queen, with an elegant veneer hiding...very little. Yacht-happy St-Tropez swims alone an hour west. The Riviera's overlooked yet right-there interior transports travelers to a world apart, with cliff-hanging villages, steep canyons, and alpine scenery—a refreshing alternative to the beach scene.

CHOOSING A HOME BASE

My favorite home bases are Nice, Antibes, and Villefranche-sur-Mer.

Nice is the region's capital and France's fifth-largest city. With convenient train and bus connections to most regional sights, this is the most practical base for train travelers. Urban Nice also has museums, a beach scene that rocks, the best selection of hotels in all price ranges, and good nightlife options. A car is a headache in Nice.

Nearby **Antibes** is smaller, with a bustling center, a lively night scene, great sandy beaches, grand vistas, good walking trails, and a stellar Picasso museum. Antibes has frequent train service to Nice and Monaco, and good connections by train or car to Grasse. It's a convenient base for drivers, with relatively light traffic and easy hotel parking.

Villefranche-sur-Mer is the romantic's choice, with a serene setting and small-town warmth. It has sand-pebble beaches; quick public transportation to Nice, Monaco, and Cap Ferrat; and a small selection of hotels, most with easy parking, and good restaurants in most price ranges.

PLANNING YOUR TIME

The French Riviera is best in the off-season, between late October and March. There are no crowds or cruise ships, no heat or humidity. Skies are clear, and views to the snowy Alps are exhilarating.

Ideally, allow a day and a half for Nice itself, an afternoon to explore inland hill towns, a full day for Italianesque Villefranche-sur-Mer and lovely Cap Ferrat, a day for Monaco and the Corniches (including Eze-le-Village), and—if time allows—a day for Antibes and maybe Cannes. If you must do distant St-Tropez, visit it while traveling to or from destinations farther west (such as Cassis, Aix-en-Provence, and Arles) and avoid it on weekend afternoons, as well as all summer.

Monaco is radiant at night, and Antibes works well by day (good beaches and hiking) and night (fine choice of restaurants and a lively after-hours scene). Hill-town-loving naturalists should add a night or two inland to explore the charming hill-capping hamlets near Vence.

Depending on the amount of time you have in the Riviera, here are my recommended priorities:

3 days:	Nice, Villefranche-sur-Mer with Cap Ferrat, and Monaco
5 days, add:	Antibes and hill towns near Vence
7 days, add:	Grand Canyon du Verdon and/or just slow down

HELPFUL HINTS

Sightseeing Tips: Mondays and Tuesdays can frustrate market lovers and museumgoers. Closed on Monday: Nice's Modern and Contemporary Art Museum, Fine Arts Museum, and Cours Saleya produce and flower market; Antibes' Picasso Museum and market hall (Sept-May). Closed on Tuesday: Chagall, Matisse, Masséna, and Archaeological museums in Nice; Renoir Museum in Cagnes-sur-Mer. Matisse's Chapel of the Rosary in Vence is closed Sunday and Monday and in the morning on Wednesday and Saturday.

The **French Riviera Pass** includes entry to many Riv-

FRENCH RIVIERA

iera sights and activities, including Nice's Chagall, Matisse, Fine Arts, and Masséna Museums; Monaco's Oceanography Museum; and Villa Ephrussi de Rothschild on Cap Ferrat (€28/24 hours, €40/48 hours, €59/72 hours, +33 4 92 14 46 14, http://en.frenchrivierapass.com). This pass also includes walking tours in several locations (such as Vieux Nice and Villefranche-sur-Mer), wine tastings, and a boat trip around Cap Ferrat. It's well worth the cost if you have an aggressive sightseeing plan or want to do some bigger-ticket items like the included Le Grand Tour Bus in Nice or the boat trip.

The €15 **All Museums Pass** for Nice covers entrance for three days to all of the city's museums, except the Chagall Museum (www.nice.fr/fr/culture—click *"Muées et Galeries"* then *"Préparer ma Visite"*).

Medical Help: Riviera Medical Services has a list of English-speaking physicians all along the Riviera. They can help you make an appointment or call an ambulance (+33 4 93 26 12 70, www.rivieramedical.com).

Events: The Riviera is famous for staging major events. Unless you're taking part in the festivities, these occasions give you only room shortages and traffic jams. Here are the three big-gies: **Nice Carnival** (two weeks in Feb, www.nicecarnaval. com), **Cannes Film Festival** (12 days in mid-May, www. festival-cannes.com), and the **Grand Prix of Monaco** (4 days in late May, www.acm.mc). To accommodate the busy sched-ules of the rich and famous (and really mess up a lot of normal people), the film festival and car race often overlap.

English Website: Travel writer and Riviera resident Jeanne Oliver runs FrenchRivieraTraveller.com, an extremely helpful web-site for visitors.

Cruise-Ship Sightseeing: The French Riviera is a popular cruise destination. Arriving ships are divided about evenly between Nice, Villefranche-sur-Mer, and Monaco (for arrival help, see the "Connections" section at the end of each of those chap-ters). Because these three ports line up conveniently along a 10-mile stretch of coast—easily connected by train or bus—those arriving by cruise from any of them have the Riviera by the tail. Hiring a local guide helps make the most of cruisers' limited time in port (see "Tours in the Riviera," later). For in-depth coverage, consider my guidebook, *Rick Steves Mediter-ranean Cruise Ports.*

GETTING AROUND THE RIVIERA

Trains and buses do a good job of connecting places along the coast, with fine views along many routes. Buses also provide reasonable service to some inland hill towns. Nice makes the most convenient base for train, bus, or boat day trips, though public transport also works well from Riviera towns such as Antibes and Villefranche-sur-Mer. Driving is a challenge in this congested region (traffic, parking, etc.).

By Public Transportation

In the Riviera, buses are often less expensive and more convenient while trains are faster and more expensive. For an overview of the most useful train and bus connections, see the "Public Transportation in the French Riviera" chart in this chapter (confirm all connections and last train/bus times locally). You'll also find details under each destination's "Connections" section. For a scenic inland train ride, take the narrow-gauge train into the Alps (see page 352).

If taking the train or bus, have coins handy. Ticket machines don't take some US credit cards or any euro bills, smaller train stations may be unstaffed, and bus drivers can't make change for large bills.

Buses: Most of the area's top destinations are connected by the Lignes d'Azur bus network (www.lignesdazur.com). Tickets are an amazing deal. For travel on Nice's city buses, **single tickets** cost just €1.50 and are good for 74 minutes of travel in one direction (including transfers). Or you can pay €5 for an **all-day pass**, €10 for a shareable **10-ride ticket**, or €15 for a **7-day pass.** These options are all valid for Nice and destinations near Nice

(such as Villefranche-sur-Mer, Cap Ferrat, and Eze-le-Village). Buy single bus tickets or a day pass from the driver (coins only), or from machines at stops, and validate on board; 10-ride tickets and 7-day passes are available only from machines or the Lignes d'Azur offices (see page 315).

For buses serving destinations farther from Nice, buy a **Ticket Azur** (€1.50, valid 2.5 hours). With this ticket, you can transfer from Nice's tram to regional buses (to Monaco, St-Paul-de-Vence, Vence, and anywhere west of Cagnes-sur-Mer, such as Antibes and Cannes). For an outbound journey, it's easy to buy your ticket at the tram station. And because Nice's trams are essential for reaching regional bus departure points at the edge of town, any ticket purchased on a tram is a Ticket Azur. On the way back, buy the Ticket Azur from the driver when you board the bus (ask for a *ticket correspondance*).

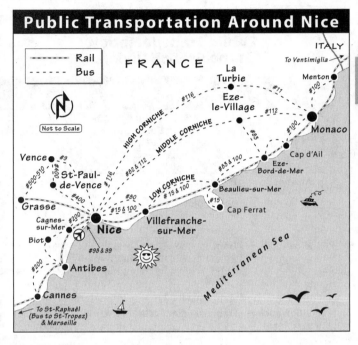

Public Transportation Around Nice

You'll be able to get around most of the Riviera on the following major bus routes:

- **Bus #100** runs eastbound from **Nice** along the Low Corniche (3-4/hour) stopping in **Villefranche-sur-Mer** (20 minutes), **Beaulieu-sur-Mer** (**Villa Kérylos**; 30 minutes), **Eze-Bord-de-Mer** (40 minutes, transfer to **#83** to Eze-le-Village), **Monaco** (1 hour), and **Menton** (1.5 hours).
- **Bus #15** runs eastbound from **Nice** (2-3/hour) to **Villefranche-sur-Mer** (15 minutes), **Beaulieu-sur-Mer** (**Villa Kérylos**; 20 minutes), and all **Cap Ferrat** stops, ending at **St-Jean-Cap-Ferrat** (30 minutes).
- **Buses #82** and **#112** run from **Nice** and upper **Villefranche-sur-Mer** to **Eze-le-Village** (together they depart about hourly; only #82 runs on Sunday; 30 minutes to reach Eze from Nice). **Bus #112,** which runs along the scenic Middle Corniche, continues from Eze-le-Village to **Monte Carlo** in Monaco (6/day, none on Sun, 20 minutes).

The following leave from the Parc Phoenix stop on the T-2 tram line, west of Nice before the airport:

- **Bus #200** goes from **Nice** westbound (4/hour Mon-Sat, 2/hour Sun) to **Cagnes-sur-Mer** (1 hour), **Antibes** (1.5 hours), and **Cannes** (2 hours).
- For the inland towns, **bus #400** runs from **Nice** (2/hour) to

FRENCH RIVIERA

Public Transportation in the French Riviera

From \ To	Cannes	Antibes	Nice
Cannes	N/A	**Train:** 2/hr, 15 min **Bus:** #200, 2-4/hr, 35 min	**Train:** 2/hr, 30 min **Bus:** #200, 2-4/hr, 2 hrs
Antibes	**Train:** 2/hr, 15 min **Bus:** #200, 2-4/hr, 35 min	N/A	**Train:** 2/hr, 20 min **Bus:** #200, 2-4/hr, 1.5 hrs
Nice	**Train:** 2/hr, 30 min **Bus:** #200, 2-4/hr, 2 hrs	**Train:** 2/hr, 20 min **Bus:** #200, 2-4/hr, 1.5 hrs	N/A
Villefranche-sur-Mer	**Train:** 2/hr, 50 min	**Train:** 2/hr, 40 min	**Train:** 2/hr, 10 min **Bus:** #100, 3-4/hr, 20 min; also #15, 2/hr, 15 min
Cap Ferrat	**Bus/Train:** #15 to Beaulieu-sur-Mer (2-3/hr, 10 min), then train to Cannes (2/hr, 1 hr)	**Bus/Train:** #15 to Beaulieu-sur-Mer (2-3/hr, 10 min), then train (2/hr, 40 min)	**Bus:** #15, 2-3/hr, 30 min
Eze-le-Village	**Bus/Train:** #83 to Eze-Bord-de-Mer (8/day, 15 min), then train (2/hr, 1 hour)	**Bus/Train:** #83 to Eze-Bord-de-Mer (8/day, 15 min), then train (2/hr, 45 min)	**Bus/Train:** #83 to Eze-Bord-de-Mer (8/day, 15 min), then train (2/hr, 15 min) **Bus:** #82/#112, hourly, 30 min
Monaco	**Train:** 2/hr, 70 min	**Train:** 2/hr, 50 min	**Train:** 2/hr, 20 min **Bus:** #100, 3-4/hr, 1 hour

Note: Bus frequencies are given for Monday-Saturday (Sunday often has limited or no bus service).

...efranche-sur-Mer	Cap Ferrat	Eze-le-Village	Monaco
...in: 2/hr, 50 min	**Train/Bus:** 2/hr, 1 hr to Beaulieu-sur-Mer, then bus #15 (2-3/hr, 10 min)	**Train/Bus:** 2/hr, 1 hr to Eze-Bord-de-Mer, then bus #83 (8/day, 15 min)	**Train:** 2/hr, 70 min
...in: 2/hr, 40 min	**Train/Bus:** 2/hr, 40 min to Beaulieu-sur-Mer, then bus #15 (2-3/hr, 10 min)	**Train/Bus:** 2/hr, 45 min to Eze-Bord-de-Mer, then bus #83 (8/day, 15 min)	**Train:** 2/hr, 50 min
...in: 2/hr, 10 min ...s: #100, 3-4/...0 min; also #15, ...hr, 15 min	**Bus:** #15, 2-3/hr, 30 min	**Train/Bus:** 2/hr, 15 min to Eze-Bord-de-Mer, then bus #83 (8/day, 15 min) **Bus:** #82/#112, hourly, 30 min	**Train:** 2/hr, 20 min **Bus:** #100, 3-4/hr, 1 hour
	Bus: #15, 2-3/hr, 15 min	**Train/Bus:** 2/hr, 5 min to Eze-Bord-de-Mer, then bus #83 (8/day, 15 min) **Bus:** #100 to Eze-Bord-de-Mer, then transfer to #83; also #82/#112 from upper Villefranche	**Train:** 2/hr, 10 min **Bus:** #100, 3-4/hr, 40 min
...: #15, 2-3/hr, ...in	N/A	**Bus:** 30-min walk or bus #15 to Beaulieu-sur-Mer (3-4/hr, 10 min), then #83 to Eze-le-Village (8/day, 20 min)	**Bus:** 30-min walk or bus #15 to #100 (3-4/hr, 20 min)
.../Train: #83 ...ze-Bord-de-Mer ...ay, 15 min), then ...(2/hr, 5 min) ...: #83 to Eze-...d-de-Mer, then ...sfer to #100; ...#82/#112 to ...er Villefranche	**Bus:** #83 to Beaulieu-sur-Mer (8/day, 20 min), then walk 30 min or transfer to #15	N/A	**Bus:** #112, 6/day, 20 min
...in: 2/hr, 10 min ...: #100, 3-4/hr, ...in	**Bus:** #100, 3-4/hr, 20 min (plus 30-min walk or transfer to #15)	**Bus:** #112, 6/day, 20 min	N/A

St-Paul-de-Vence (45 minutes) and **Vence** (1 hour); **bus #9** runs from **Nice** to **Vence** but not St-Paul (4/hour, 1 hour); and **buses #500/510** run between **Vence** and **Grasse** (6/day, 50 minutes).

Trains: These are more expensive (Nice to Monaco by train is about €4) but much faster and less jammed than the bus, and there's no quicker way to move about the Riviera (www.sncf-connect.com/en-en). Speedy trains link the Riviera's beachfront destinations—Cannes, Antibes, Nice, Villefranche-sur-Mer, Monaco, Menton, and the inland perfume town of Grasse. (Never board a train without a ticket or valid pass—fare inspectors accept no excuses. The minimum fine: €50.)

By Car

This is France's most challenging region to drive in. Beautifully distracting vistas (natural and human), loads of Sunday-driver tourists, and every hour being lush-hour in the summer make for a dangerous combination. Parking can be exasperating. Bring lots of coins and patience.

The Riviera is awash with scenic roads. To sample some of the Riviera's best scenery, connect Provence and the Riviera by driving the splendid coastal road between Cannes and Fréjus (D-6098 from Cannes/D-559 from Fréjus). Once in the Riviera, the most scenic and thrilling road trip is along the three coastal roads—called "corniches"—between Nice and Monaco (see page 384). Farther inland, take my recommended inland hill-towns drive (on page 463). Farther yet, explore the Grand Canyon du Verdon, with breathtaking gorges and alpine scenery. But for basic sightseeing between Monaco and Cannes, I'd ditch the car and use trains and buses.

By Boat

Trans Côte d'Azur offers seasonal boat service from Nice to Monaco or to St-Tropez, as well as between Cannes and St-Tropez. For details, see the "By Boat" section under Nice Connections (page 366).

TOURS IN THE RIVIERA

Most hotels and TIs have information on economical shared minivan excursions from Nice (per person: roughly €60-80/half-day, €90-140/day).

Local Guides with Cars

These two energetic and delightful women adore educating people about this area's culture and history, and have comfortable minibuses: **Sylvie Di Cristo** (€300/half-day, €600/day for up to 3

> ## Top Art Sights of the Riviera
>
> These are listed in order of importance.
>
> Chagall Museum (Nice)
> Picasso Museum (Antibes)
> Fondation Maeght (St-Paul-de-Vence)
> Matisse Museum (Nice)
> Chapel of the Rosary (Vence)
> Museum of the Annonciade (St-Tropez)
> Modern and Contemporary Art Museum (Nice)
> Renoir Museum (Cagnes-sur-Mer)
> Fine Arts Museum (Nice)

people; €400/half-day, €800/day for 4-8 people; +33 6 09 88 83 83, http://frenchrivieraguides.com) and **Ingrid Schmucker,** who drives a cushy Mercedes van (from €540/day for 2-4 people, €600/day for 5-6 people, €220/half-day to explore old Nice on foot, +33 6 14 83 03 33, https://bestfrenchriviera.tours). Their websites explain their programs well, and they are happy to adapt to your interests.

Charming Fouad Zarrou runs **France Azur Excursions** and offers a fun experience. His tours are more about exploring the region's natural beauty, food, and wine than its cultural history. He provides comfortable transportation in his minivan (figure €300/half-day, +33 6 20 68 10 70, http://franceazurexcursions.com).

Local Guides Without Cars

For a guided tour of Nice or the region using public transit or with a guide joining you in your rental car, **Boba Vukadinovic-Millet** is an effective and engaging teacher, ideal for those wanting to dive more deeply into the region's history and art. She can arrange chauffeur-driven rental options (car, minivan, bus) if needed (from €250/half-day and €400/day, +33 6 27 45 68 39, www.yourguideboba.com, boba@yourguideboba.com).

Food Tours

For food tours and cooking classes offered in Nice, see page 321.

THE RIVIERA'S ART SCENE

The list of artists who have painted the Riviera reads like a Who's Who of 20th-century art. Pierre-Auguste Renoir, Henri Matisse, Marc Chagall, Georges Braque, Raoul Dufy, Fernand Léger, and Pablo Picasso all lived and worked here—and raved about the region's wonderful light. Their simple, semi-abstract, and—most important—colorful works reflect the pleasurable atmosphere of the Riviera. You'll experience the same landscapes they painted in this bright, sun-drenched region, punctuated with views of the azure sea. Try to imagine the Riviera with a fraction of the people and development you see today.

But the artists were mostly drawn to the un-complicated lifestyle of fishermen and farmers that has reigned here for centuries. As the artists grew older, they retired in the sun, turned their backs on modern art's "isms," and painted with the wide-eyed wonder of children, using bright primary colors, basic outlines, and simple subjects.

A collection of modern- and contemporary-art museums (many described in this book) dot the Riviera, allowing art lovers to appreciate these masters' works while immersed in the same sun and culture that inspired them. Many of the mu-seums were designed to blend pieces with the surrounding views, gardens, and fountains, thus highlighting that modern art is not only stimulating, but sometimes simply beautiful.

Entire books have been written about the modern-art galleries of the Riviera. If you're a fan, do some studying before your visit to be sure you know about that far-out museum of your dreams. If you've never enjoyed modern art, the two best places to give it a try here are the Fondation Maeght in St-Paul-de-Vence and the Chagall Museum in Nice.

THE RIVIERA'S CUISINE SCENE

The Riviera adds an Italian-Mediterranean flair to the food of Provence. While many of the same dishes served in Provence are available in the Riviera (see "Provence's Cuisine Scene" on page 44), there are differences, especially if you look for anything Italian or from the sea. Proximity to the water and historic ties to Italy are clear in this region's dishes.

That said, memorable restaurants that showcase the Riviera's cuisine can be difficult to find. Because most visitors come more for the sun than the food, and because the clientele is predominantly international, many restaurants aim for the middle and are hard to distinguish from one another. Trust my recommendations.

A fresh and colorful *salade niçoise* makes the perfect introduc-tion to the Riviera's cuisine. The authentic version has lots of ripe tomatoes, raw vegetables (such as radishes, green peppers, cel-ery, and perhaps artichoke or fava beans), as well as tuna (usually canned), anchovy, hard-boiled egg, and olives (but no potatoes or green beans). This is my go-to salad for a tasty, healthy, cheap, and fast lunch. I like to spend a couple of extra euros and eat it in a place with a nice ambience and view.

For lunch on the go, look for a *pan bagnat* (like a *salade niçoise* stuffed into a crusty roll drizzled with olive oil and wine vinegar).

Other tasty bread treats include *pissaladière* (bread dough topped with caramelized onions, olives, and anchovies), *fougasse* (a spindly, lace-like bread sometimes flavored with nuts, herbs, olives, or ham), and *socca* (a thin chickpea-and-olive-oil crêpe, seasoned with pepper and often served in a paper cone by street vendors).

Said to have been invented in Nice, ravioli and potato gnocchi can be found on menus everywhere (ravioli can be stuffed with a variety of fillings, but the classic local version is made with beef and Swiss chard).

Bouillabaisse is the Riviera's most famous dish; you'll find it in seafront villages and cities. It's a spicy fish stew based on recipes handed down from sailors in Marseille. It must contain at least four types of fresh fish, though most have five to twelve kinds. A true bouillabaisse never has shellfish. The fish—cooked in a tomato and onion-based stock and flavored with saffron (and sometimes anise and orange)—is separated from the stock, and the two are served as separate courses. Diners then heighten the soup's flavor by adding toasted croutons slathered with *rouille* sauce (a thickened reddish mayonnaise heady with garlic and spicy peppers) and topped with grated parmesan or Emmental cheese. This dish often requires a minimum order of two and can cost up to €40-60 per person.

Far less pricey than bouillabaisse and worth trying is the local *soupe de poissons* (fish soup). It's a creamy soup flavored like bouillabaisse, with anise and orange, and served with croutons and *rouille* sauce (but has no chunks of fish). For a less colorful but still tasty soup, look for *bourride,* a creamy fish concoction thickened with an aioli sauce instead of the red *rouille.*

The Riviera specializes in all sorts of fish and shellfish. Options include *fruits de mer* (platters of seafood—including tiny shellfish, from which you get the edible part only by sucking really hard), herb-infused mussels, stuffed sardines, squid (slowly simmered with tomatoes and herbs), and tuna *(thon).* The popular *loup flambé au fenouil* is grilled sea bass, flavored with fennel and torched with *pastis* prior to serving.

For a truly local dessert, try the *Niçoise* specialty *tourte de blettes,* a sugar-dusted pie with a sweet filling of Swiss chard, rum-soaked raisins, pine nuts, and apple. In St-Tropez, the *tropézienne* is a brioche topped with sugar crystals and sandwiching an airy vanilla cream. Desserts on the Riviera make use of the abundant local fruits, especially citrus in winter, and regional flavors such as orange flower water.

For details on dining in France's restaurants, cafés, and brasseries, getting takeout, and assembling a picnic—as well as a rundown of French cuisine—see the "Eating" section in the Practicalities chapter.

WINES OF THE RIVIERA

Do as everyone else does: Drink wines from Provence. Bandol (red) and cassis (white) are popular and from a region nearly on the Riviera. The most popular wines made in the Riviera are Bellet rosé and white, the latter often found in fish-shaped bottles. For more on Provençal wines, see the Provence chapter.

NICE

Nice (sounds like "niece"), with its spectacular Alps-meets-Mediterranean surroundings, is the big-city highlight of the Riviera. Its traffic-free Vieux Nice—the old town—blends Italian and French flavors to create a spicy Mediterranean dressing, while its big squares, broad seaside walkways, and long beaches invite lounging and people-watching. Nice may be nice, but it's jammed from mid-May through August—reserve ahead and get a room with air-conditioning. Nice gets quiet and stays fairly mild from November to April. Everything you'll want to see in Nice is either within walking distance, or a short bike, bus, or tram ride away.

Orientation to Nice

Focus your time on the area between the beach and the train tracks (about 15 blocks apart). The city revolves around its grand Place Masséna, where pedestrian-friendly Avenue Jean Médecin meets Vieux Nice and the Promenade du Paillon parkway (with quick access to the beaches). It's a 20-minute walk from the train station to the beach, and a 20-minute stroll along the promenade from the fancy  Hôtel Negresco to the heart of Vieux Nice. Two handy-for-tourists tram lines run through the heart of Nice; see "Getting Around Nice," later, for details.

TOURIST INFORMATION

Nice has two helpful TIs, one at the **train station** and another at #5 **Promenade des Anglais** (both daily 9:00-18:00, July-Aug until 19:00, +33 8 92 70 74 07, www.explorenicecotedazur.com). Ask for day-trip information (including maps of Monaco, Antibes, and Cannes) and details on boat excursions, bus stop locations, and transit schedules.

ARRIVAL IN NICE

By Train: All trains stop at Nice's main station, called Nice-Ville. With your back to the tracks, car rentals are to the right. Bag storage is to the left inside the station; you can also stash your bags a short block away at the recommended Hôtel Belle Meunière. The TI is straight out the main doors. The region's primary bus company, Lignes d'Azur, has a ticket machine in the station (see "Helpful Hints," later).

The nearby T-1 tram zips you to the center in a few minutes (several blocks to the left as you leave the station, departs every few minutes, direction: Hôpital Pasteur; see "Getting Around Nice," later). To walk to the beach, Promenade des Anglais, or many of my recommended hotels, cross Avenue Thiers in front of the station, go down the steps by Hôtel Interlaken, and continue down Avenue Durante. A taxi to the beach is about €15.

By Car: To reach the city center from the autoroute, take the *Nice Centre* exit and follow signs. Ask your hotelier where to park (about €20-30/day in central garages; some hotels offer deals but space is limited—arrange ahead). The parking garage at the Nice Etoile shopping center on Avenue Jean Médecin is near many recommended hotels (ticket booth on third floor, 18:00-8:00). You can park for free on Nice streets any day from 20:00-9:00 and all day Sunday, otherwise street parking is strictly metered (usually a 2-hour limit).

Day-trippers can avoid driving in the center—and park for free during the day (no overnight parking)—by stashing their car at a parking lot at a remote tram or bus stop. Look for blue-on-white *Parcazur* signs (find locations at www.lignesdazur.com/en/parc-relais, French only), and ride the bus or tram into town (10/hour, 15 minutes, buy round-trip tram or bus ticket and keep it with you—you'll need it later to exit the parking lot; for tram details, see "Getting Around Nice," later). The easiest lot to use is Parcazur Henri Sappia, right off the *Nice Nord* autoroute exit. It always has room and saves you from navigating city streets (daily until 2:30 in the morning). As lots are not guarded, don't leave anything of value in your car.

By Plane or Cruise Ship: For information on Nice's airport and cruise-ship port, see "Nice Connections" at the end of this chapter.

HELPFUL HINTS

Theft Alert: Nice has its share of pickpockets (especially at the train station, on the tram, and trolling the beach). Stick to main streets in Vieux Nice after dark.

Sightseeing Tips: The Cours Saleya produce and flower market is closed Monday, and the Chagall and Matisse museums are closed Tuesday. All Nice museums—except the Chagall Museum—are covered by the €15 **All Museums Pass** (valid 3 days, buy at any participating museum). The separate **French Riviera Pass** also covers several Nice museums (Chagall, Matisse, Fine Arts, and Masséna) and varied activities such as bike rental, a boat cruise, and the hop-on, hop-off bus; see page 302.

Boutique Shopping: The chic streets where Rue Alphonse Karr meets Rue de la Liberté and then Rue de Paradis are known as the "Golden Square." If you need pricey stuff, shop here.

Baggage Storage: You can store your bags inside the train station (€5-10/bag per day), at the recommended **Hôtel Belle Meunière** (€5/bag per day), or at the **Bagguys** in Vieux Nice (€8/bag per day, daily 10:00-19:00, 34 Rue Centrale, +33 6 12 49 11 36, www.bagguys.fr).

Grocery Store: Small grocery shops are easy to find. The big **Monoprix** on Avenue Jean Médecin and Rue Biscarra has it all (open daily, see map on page 363).

Renting a Bike (and Other Wheels): Bike-rental shops are a breeze to find in Nice, and several companies offer bike tours of the city. Bikes *(vélos)* can be taken on trains. **Booking Bikes,** located near the main TI at 9 Rue Massenet, has electric bikes (www.loca-bike.fr). **Roller Station** is well situated near the sea and rents bikes, rollerblades, skateboards, and Razor-style scooters (bikes—€5/hour, €14/half-day, €18/day; leave ID as deposit, open daily, 49 Quai des Etats-Unis—see map on page 358, +33 4 93 62 99 05). The **Vélo Bleu** bike-sharing program has affordable bikes docked at many stations in the city for short-term use, but the French-only website makes it difficult for most travelers (www.velobleu.org).

Car Rental: Renting a car is easiest at Nice's airport, which has offices for all the major companies. Most companies are also represented at Nice's train station and near the southwest side of Albert I Park.

Lignes d'Azur Bus Tickets: You'll find the Lignes d'Azur office (Espace Mobilité) at 33 Boulevard Dubouchage, where you

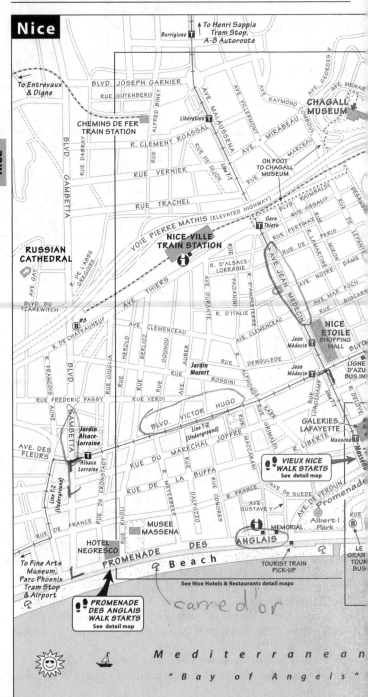

NICE

Nice

To Henri Sappia Tram Stop, A-8 Autoroute

Borriglione T

To Entrevaux & Digne

BLVD. JOSEPH GARNIER

RUE GUTENBERG

AVE. VILLERMONT

AVE. MALAUSSENA

AVE. RAYMOND COMBOUL

AVE. GEORGES V

AVE. MENAR

CHAGALL MUSEUM

AVE. MIRABEAU

RUE MARCEAU

Libération T

CHEMINS DE FER TRAIN STATION

RUE DABRAY

RUE ALFRED BINET

R. CLÉMENT ROASSAL

RUE DE DIJON

ON FOOT TO CHAGALL MUSEUM

Line T-1

RUE VERNIER

BLVD. GAMBETTA

RUE TRACHEL

BLVD. RAIMBALDI

RUE ASSALIT

RUE DE LEPANTE

VOIE PIERRE MATHIS (ELEVATED HIGHWAY)

Gare Thiers T

RUE PERTINAX

RUE LAMARTINE

RUE DE PARIS

RUSSIAN CATHEDRAL

R. DE L'ABBÉ GRÉGOIRE

NICE-VILLE TRAIN STATION ℹ

R. D'ALSACE-LORRAINE

PAGANINI

AVE. JEAN MÉDECIN

AVE. NOTRE DAME

AVE. MAR. FOCH

RUE BISCAR

AVE. GAY

BLVD. DU TZAREWITCH

AVE. THIERS

RUE DURANTE

R. D'ANGLETERRE

R. D'ITALIE

AVE. CLEMENCEAU

NICE ÉTOILE SHOPPING MALL

Ⓑ #8

R. DE CHATEAUNEUF

AVE. CLEMENCEAU

HÉROLD

BERLIOZ

GOUNOD

AUBER

RUE

DEROULEDE

Jean Médecin

BLVD

R. FRANÇOIS AUNE

BLVD. GAMBETTA

RUE GIUGLIA

RUE

RUE

AVE. VERDI

RUE VERDI

Jardin Mozart

ALPHONSE

ROSSINI

Jean Médecin T

LIGNE D'AZU BUS IN

Line T-1

RUE LONGCHAMP

R. DELOTE

RUE FRÉDÉRIC PASSY

BLVD. VICTOR HUGO

Line T-2 (Underground)

RUE GRIMALDI

RUE KIRK

GALERIES LAFAYETTE

AVE. DES FLEURS

Jardin Alsace-Lorraine

Alsace Lorraine T

RUE DU MARÉCHAL JOFFRE

RUE MACCARANI

R. LIBERTÉ

Masséna T

Masséna

Line T-2 (Underground)

RUE DE CRONSTADT

RUE DE LA BUFFA

RUE MEYERBEER

RUE DALPOZZO

R. FRANCE

AVE. DE SUEDE

VIEUX NICE WALK STARTS
See detail map

RUE DE FRANCE

RUE DE RIVOLI

RUE CONGRÈS

AVE. GUSTAVE V

AVE. DE VERDUN

Promenade

RUE

Ⓑ

MUSÉE MASSÉNA

ℹ MEMORIAL

Albert I Park

LE GRAN TOUR BUS

HOTEL NEGRESCO

PROMENADE

DES ANGLAIS

TOURIST TRAIN PICK-UP

To Fine Arts Museum, Parc Phoenix Tram Stop & Airport

Beach

See Nice Hotels & Restaurants detail maps

carré d'or

PROMENADE DES ANGLAIS WALK STARTS
See detail map

☀

⛵

M e d i t e r r a n e a n

"B a y   o f   A n g e l s"

NICE

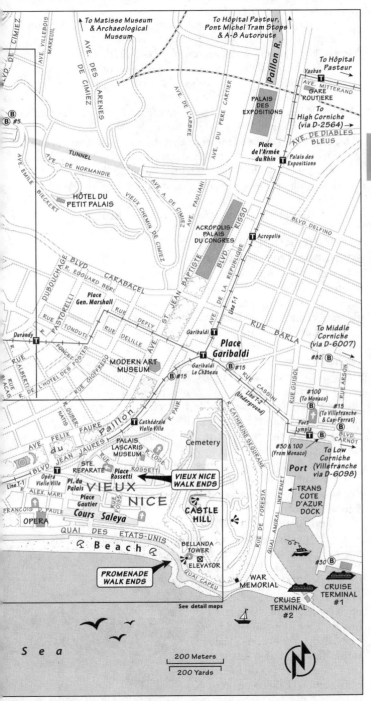

can buy tickets and passes (Mon-Fri 7:30-19:30, Sat until 15:00, closed Sun, www.lignesdazur.com).

Views: For panoramic views, climb Castle Hill (see "Sights in Nice," later), walk to the very eastern end of the Promenade des Anglais, or take a one-hour boat trip (see "Tours in Nice," later).

Hike to Villefranche-sur-Mer: Take the four-mile coastal trail to reach Villefranche-sur-Mer's port (see page 379).

Beach Tips: To make life tolerable on the rocks, swimmers should buy the cheap plastic beach shoes sold at many shops. Locals swim most of the year—except in July and August when the warming sea brings swarms of stinging jellyfish. Ask before you dip.

English Radio: Tune in to Riviera-Radio at FM 106.5.

GETTING AROUND NICE
By Public Transportation

Although you can walk to most attractions, smart travelers make good use of the buses and trams within Nice. The bus is especially handy for reaching the Chagall and Matisse museums and the Russian Cathedral (see listings under "Sights in Nice" for specifics).

Tickets: Buses and trams are covered by the same €1.50 single-ride ticket, or you can pay €10 for a 10-ride *Multi* ticket that can be shared (each use good for 74 minutes in one direction, including transfers between bus and tram). The €5 all-day pass is valid on city buses and trams, as well as buses to some nearby destinations. You must validate your ticket inside the tram on every trip—imitate how the locals do it. Buy single tickets or a day pass from the bus driver (coins only) or from the ticket machines on tram platforms (press the green button once to validate choice and twice at the end to get your ticket). The 7-day pass and 10-ride tickets are also available from machines at tram stops and from the Lignes d'Azur office (see "Helpful Hints," earlier), but not from drivers. Info: www.lignesdazur.com.

Trams: The L-shaped T-1 tram line runs every few minutes along Avenue Jean Médecin and Boulevard Jean Jaurès, and connects the main train station with Place Masséna and Vieux Nice (Opéra/Vieille Ville stop), the port (transfer at Place Garibaldi or Jean Médecin stops to T-2 line for Port Lympia), and buses east along the coast (Vauban stop). The tram also stops near the Chemins de Fer de Provence train station (Libération stop)—

the departure point for the scenic narrow-gauge rail journey. Boarding the tram in the direction of Hôpital Pasteur from the station takes you toward the beach and Vieux Nice (direction: Henri Sappia goes the other way).

The **T-2 tram** goes from the airport through the city center to Port Lympia in 30 minutes, starting at street level, then dipping underground through central Nice (from Centre Universitaire to Port Lympia stops). Central Nice stations are deep, but all have elevators and escalators. If using the tram to reach the airport, make sure the overhead signs read *Airport*—the line splits before the airport. Info: Tramway.nice.fr.

By Taxi or Uber

Taxis are useful for getting to Nice's less-central sights (figure €10 for shortest ride, up to €16-20 from Promenade des Anglais to the Chagall Museum). Cabbies normally pick up only at taxi stands *(tête de station)*, or you can call +33 4 93 13 78 78. **Uber** works here like it does at home, though the price may not be much cheaper than a taxi. Still, Uber drivers are often nicer and more flexible, and you usually get a car without much delay.

Tours in Nice

ON WHEELS
Hop-On, Hop-Off Bus

Le Grand Tour Bus provides a useful 16-stop, hop-on, hop-off service on an open-deck bus with good headphone commentary. The route includes the Promenade des Anglais, Port Lympia, Cap de Nice, the Chagall and Matisse museums and—best of all—Villefranche-sur-Mer (1-day pass-€23, 2-day pass-€26, buy tickets on bus, 2/hour, daily 10:00-19:00, 1.75-hour loop with Villefranche-sur-Mer, main stop near where Promenade des Anglais and Quai des Etats-Unis meet—across from the Albert I Park, +33 4 92 29 17 00, www.nicelegrandtour.fr/en-gb). While it's not the best way to get to the Chagall and Matisse museums, this bus is a good value if you're looking for a city overview and want to also visit these museums or spend time in Villefranche-sur-Mer (best seats are up top on the left as you face forward).

Tourist Train

For €10, you can spend 45 minutes on the tourist train tooting along the promenade, through the old city, and up to Castle Hill (2/hour, daily 9:40-16:40, until 17:40 in high season, recorded English commentary, meet train at the Monument du Centenaire statue at Albert I Park, across from the Promenade des Anglais, +33 6 20 38 09 00, www.francevoguette.fr).

NICE

Nice at a Glance

▲▲▲**Promenade des Anglais** Nice's four-mile sun-struck seafront promenade. See page 321.

▲▲▲**Chagall Museum** The world's largest collection of Marc Chagall's work, popular even with people who don't like modern art. **Hours:** Wed-Mon 10:00-18:00, Nov-April until 17:00, closed Tue year-round. See page 337.

▲▲**Vieux Nice** Charming old city quarter offering an enjoyable atmosphere and a look at Nice's French-Italian cultural blend. See page 328.

▲**Matisse Museum** Modest collection of Henri Matisse's paintings, sketches, and paper cutouts. **Hours:** Wed-Mon 10:00-18:00, Nov-April until 17:00, closed Tue year-round. See page 344.

▲**Russian Cathedral** Finest Orthodox church outside Russia. **Hours:** Daily 9:00-18:00. See page 350.

▲**Castle Hill** Site of an ancient fort boasting great views. **Hours:** Park closes at 20:00 in summer, earlier off-season. See page 351.

Modern and Contemporary Art Museum Enjoyable collection from the 1960s and '70s, including Warhol and Lichtenstein. **Hours:** Tue-Sun 10:00-18:00, Nov-April from 11:00, closed Mon year-round. See page 348.

Bike Tours

Tina Balter at **Lifesparkz Bike Tours** offers well-designed, customized bike tours for individuals or small groups of all abilities (+33 6 40 52 94 39, www.lifesparkz.net).

A Taste of Nice runs e-bike tours in Nice, into nearby vineyards, and around Monaco (€50 for Nice tour, €125 for others, +33 9 86 68 93 81, www.atasteofnice.com).

BY BOAT
▲Trans Côte d'Azur Cruise

To see Nice from the water, hop on this one-hour tour run by Trans Côte d'Azur. You'll cruise in a comfortable yacht-size vessel to Cap Ferrat and past Villefranche-sur-Mer, then return to Nice with a final lap along Promenade des Anglais.

Guides enjoy pointing out mansions owned by famous people, such as Elton John (€19; April-Oct Tue-Sun 2/day, usually at 11:00

and 15:00, no boats Mon or during off-season; verify schedule, arrive 30 minutes early to get best seats). The boats leave from Nice's port just below Castle Hill—look for the ticket booth *(billeterie)* on Quai de Lunel. The same company also runs boats to Monaco and St-Tropez (see "Nice Connections," later).

ON FOOT
Local Guides and Walking Tours

If interested in hiring a local guide for Nice and other regional destinations, see page 308 for suggestions.

The TI on Promenade des Anglais organizes weekly walking tours of Vieux Nice in French and English (€12, Sat morning at 9:30, 2.5 hours, reservations necessary, departs from TI, +33 8 92 70 74 07).

Food Tours and Cooking Classes

Charming Canadian Francophile **Rosa Jackson,** a food journalist, Cordon Bleu-trained cook, and longtime resident of France, runs Les Petits Farcis cooking school and offers a good street-food tour in Vieux Nice for small groups (€80-135/person based on group size). She also combines a morning shopping trip to the market on Cours Saleya with a cooking session and lunch for €195/person, and teaches a macaron or choux pastry class for €90/person (12 Rue St-Joseph, +33 6 81 67 41 22, www.petitsfarcis.com).

A Taste of Nice Food Tours runs daily scratch-and-taste tours in Vieux Nice that combine cultural history with today's food scene. You'll stop for 10 different tastings of classic Niçois products (€75/4 hours, +33 9 86 68 93 81, www.atasteofnice.com).

Walks in Nice

These two self-guided walks take you down an iconic seaside promenade ("Promenade des Anglais Walk") and through the colorful old town blending French and Italian cultures ("Vieux Nice Walk").

PROMENADE DES ANGLAIS WALK

Welcome to the Riviera. There's something for everyone along this four-mile promenade, worth ▲▲▲. Stroll like the belle époque English aristocrats for whom the promenade was paved. Watch Europeans at play, admire the azure Mediterranean, anchor yourself on a blue seat, and prop your feet up on the made-to-order guardrail. Later, you can come back to join the evening parade of tans along the promenade.

The broad sidewalks of the Promenade des Anglais ("Walkway of the English") were financed by upper-crust English tour-

NICE

Promenade des Anglais Walk

1 Hôtel Negresco
2 Villa Masséna
3 Bay of Angels
4 Palais de la Méditerranée
5 Albert I Park
6 Steel Girders Sculpture
7 Metal Winch

ists who wanted a clean and comfortable place to stroll and admire the view. The Brits originally came to Nice seeking relief from tuberculosis; both the warm climate and the salt air helped ease their suffering. It was an era when tanned bodies were frowned upon (aristocrats didn't want to resemble lower-class laborers who had to work outside).

Length of This Walk: Allow one hour at a promenade pace for this leisurely, level walk, which covers a straight one-mile stretch of this much-strolled beachfront, beginning near the landmark Hôtel Negresco and ending at the elevator to Castle Hill.

When to Go: While this walk is enjoyable at any time, the first half makes a great stroll before or after breakfast or dinner (meals served at some beach cafés). If you're doing the entire walk to Castle Hill, try to time it so you wind up on top of the hill at sunset.

Biking the Promenade: See page 335 for tips on cycling along the seafront.

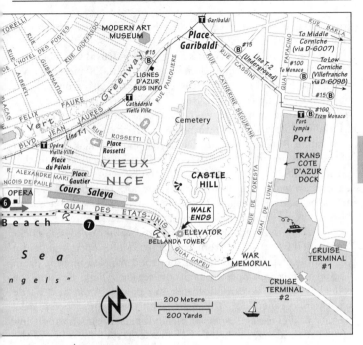

➔ Self-Guided Walk

• *Start at the pink-domed...*

❶ Hôtel Negresco

Built in 1913, Nice's finest hotel is also a historic monument, home to the city's most expensive beds and a museum-like interior.

If you wonder why such a grand hotel has such an understated entry, it's because today's front door was originally the back door. In the 19th century, elegant people avoided the sun, and any posh hotel that cared about its clientele would design its entry on the shady north side. If you walk around to today's "back" you'll see a grand but unused front door.

The hotel is technically off-limits if you're not a privileged guest, but if you're decently dressed and explain to the doorman that you'd like to get a drink at Negresco's classy-cozy 37 Prom bar, you'll be allowed past the registration desk. You could also book a table at Negresco's La Rotonde brasserie, which offers a reasonable weekday lunch menu (three courses for about €30), or explain that you want to shop at their store. *Bonne chance.*

If you get in, you can't miss a huge **Salon Royal** ballroom. The chandelier hanging from its dome is made of 16,000 pieces of crystal. It was built in France for the Russian czar's Moscow palace... but thanks to the Bolshevik Revolution in 1917, he couldn't take delivery. Bronze portrait busts of Czar Alexander III and his wife, Maria Feodorovna—who returned to her native Denmark after the Revolution—are to the right, facing the shops. Circle the interior of the ballroom and admire the soft light from the glass dome that Gustave Eiffel designed two decades after his more famous tower in Paris, then wander the perimeter to enjoy both historic and modern art. Fine portraits include Emperor Napoleon III (who acquired Nice for France from Italy in 1860) and his wife, Empress Eugénie.

Touring the outer hall that rings the ballroom counterclockwise, you'll first pass **37 Prom Bar.** If the door is open, wander up the marble steps for a look into the wood-paneled interior (from 11:30 in high season, from 14:30 off-season). Next, nip into the toilets for either an early 20th-century powder room or a Battle of Waterloo experience. The chairs with the high, scooped backs were typical of the age (cones of silence for an afternoon nap sitting up). Further along, the hotel's **Chantecler** restaurant is one of the Riviera's best (allow €100 per person before drinks).

Over 6,000 works of art decorate the hotel, as art was a passion of the hotel's former owner, Jeanne Augier. She died in 2019 and willed the Negresco to organizations that care for orphans and stray animals. Find the portrait of her as you leave the ballroom area on the right.

Peek into the **Salon Versailles** to the right of the entry lobby as you leave, with a grand fireplace and France's Sun King, Louis XIV, on the wall (English descriptions explain the room).

• *Across the street from the Hôtel Negresco (to the east) is...*

❷ Villa Masséna

When Nice became part of France, France invested heavily in what it expected to be the country's new high society retreat—an elite resort akin to Russia's Sochi on the Black Sea. This fine palace was built for Jean-Andre Masséna, a military hero of the Napoleonic age. Take a moment to stroll around the lovely garden. Immediately on your right, find a memorial to the 86 people who died in the 2016 terrorist attack on the Promenade des Anglais, with pictures, stuffed animals, and names engraved in granite (garden is free, open daily 10:00-18:00). The Masséna Museum inside the villa (described under "Sights in Nice") offers an interesting look at belle-époque Nice.

• *From Villa Masséna, head for the beach and begin your Promenade des Anglais stroll. But first, grab a blue chair and gaze out to the...*

❸ Bay of Angels (Baie des Anges)

Face the water. The body of Nice's patron saint, Réparate, was supposedly escorted into this bay by angels in the fourth century. To your right is where you might have been escorted into France—Nice's airport, built on a massive landfill. The tip of land beyond the runway is Cap d'Antibes. Until 1860, Antibes and Nice were in different countries—Antibes was French, but Nice was a protectorate of the Italian kingdom of

Savoy-Piedmont, a.k.a. the kingdom of Sardinia. During that period, the Var River—just west of Nice—was the geographic border between these two peoples (and to this day the river functions as a kind of cultural border). In 1850, the people here spoke Italian or Nissart (a local dialect) and ate pasta. As the story goes, the region was given a choice: Join newly united Italy or join France, which was enjoying prosperous times under the rule of Napoleon III. The majority voted in 1860 to go French...and *voilà!* This referendum was later revealed to have been falsified in a deal brokered between King Victor Emmanuel of Sardinia and Napoleon III—*oh là là*. But either way, France lent a helping hand to "Italy" and got the county of Nice in return.

The lower green hill to your left is Castle Hill (where this walk ends). Beyond that lie Villefranche-sur-Mer and Cap Ferrat (marked by the tower at land's end, and home to lots of millionaires), then Monaco (which you can't see, with more millionaires), then Italy. Behind you are the foothills of the Alps, which trap threatening clouds, ensuring that the Côte d'Azur enjoys sunshine more than 300 days each year. While 350,000 people live in Nice, pollution is carefully treated—the water is routinely tested and is very clean. But with the climate crisis, the warmer water is attracting jellyfish in the summer, making swimming a stinging memory.
• *With the sea on your right, begin strolling.*

The Promenade

This area was the favorite haunt of 19th-century British tourists, who wanted a place to stroll in their finery while admiring the sea views (locals called this area—between Boulevard Victor Hugo and the sea—"Little London"). Before the promenade was built, they had to venture into Vieux Nice and climb to the two-story gallery

NICE

walkway that lines the southern edge of the Cours Saleya (you'll see it on the "Vieux Nice Walk"). When first built, this promenade was a dusty path about six feet wide and about 10 blocks long. It's been widened and lengthened over the years to keep up with tourist demand,

Fit-bits, and increased bicycle use. As you walk, be careful to avoid the bike lanes.

Nearby sit two fine belle-époque establishments: the West End and Westminster hotels, both boasting English names to help those original guests feel at home. (The Westminster, one of the oldest hotels on the promenade, is now part of the Best Western group.) These hotels symbolize Nice's arrival as a tourist mecca in the 19th century, when the combination of leisure time and a stable economy allowed visitors to find the sun even in winter.

Just after Hôtel Le Royal, look out to the sea and imagine a grand casino built on piers over the water (you might see easels with paintings of it nearby). La Jetée Promenade, Nice's elegant pier and first casino, was built in 1883. Even then, there was sufficient tourism in Nice to justify constructing a palatial building with gaming rooms. La Jetée Promenade stood just offshore, until the Germans dismantled it during World War II to salvage its copper and iron. When La Jetée was thriving, it took gamblers two full days to get to the Riviera by train from Paris. In those days, the Promenade was all about dressing up, being seen, and struttin' your stuff.

Although La Jetée Promenade is gone, you can still see the striking 1927 Art Nouveau facade of the ❹ **Palais de la Méditerranée,** once a magnificent complex housing a casino, luxury hotel, and theater. It became one of the most famous destinations in all of Europe until a terrible fire left only the facade standing. It was destroyed in the 1980s to make room for a new hotel (the Hyatt Regency). The facade of the grand, old building was spared the wrecking ball, but the classy interior was lost forever.

The modern Casino Ruhl (with the most detested facade on the strip) disfigures the next block. In the spirit of modern efficiency, a lovely old hotel that resembled the Negresco was destroyed in the 1980s to make room for this...thing.

Despite the lack of sand, the pebble beaches here are still a popular draw, and every year tons of rocks are trucked in to shore them up. France has a strong ethic of public access when it comes to its beaches, including a 1980 law guaranteeing free public access to beaches like these. All along the Riviera you'll find public beaches (and public showers).

You can go local and rent gear—about €18 for a *chaise longue* (long chair) and a *transat* (mattress), €5-10 for an umbrella, and €5 for a towel. You'll also pass several beach restaurants, some serve breakfast, all serve lunch, some do dinner, and a few have beachy bars...tailor-made for a break from this walk.

❺ **Albert I Park**, on the left, is named after the Belgian king who defied a German ultimatum at the beginning of World War I. While the English came first, the Belgians and Russians arrived soon after and were also big fans of 19th-century Nice. The tall statue capped by an angel commemorates the 100-year anniversary of Nice's annexation to France. The happy statue features two beloved women embracing at its base—the idea of union (Marianne—Ms. Liberty, Equality, and Brotherhood, and the symbol of the Republic of France—and Catherine Ségurane, a 16th-century heroine who helped Nice against the Saracen pirates).

The park is part of a long, winding greenbelt called the Promenade du Paillon. The Paillon River flows under the park on its way to the sea. If it's been raining in the hills, you'll see the river flow into the sea on the beach opposite the statue. This is the historical divide between Vieux Nice and the new town. Before the river was covered, locals would do their laundry along its banks.

Continuing along the promenade you'll soon enter the **Quai des Etats-Unis** ("Quay of the United States"). This name was given as a tip-of-the-cap to the Americans for finally entering World War I in 1917. The big, blue chair statue celebrates the inviting symbol of this venerable walk and kicks off the best stretch of beach—quieter and with less traffic. Check out the laid-back couches at the **Plage Beau Rivage** lounge and consider a beachfront drink. The lovely hotel (not yet destroyed) that borders the beach was Henri Matisse's favorite when he first visited Nice. He loved it so much that he painted pictures of his hotel room at different times of day, creating masterpieces that are among his most recognized paintings.

Those tall, rusted ❻ **steel girders** reaching for the sky were erected in 2010 to celebrate the 150th anniversary of Nice's union with France. (The nine beams represent the nine valleys of the Nice region.) Done by the same artist who created the popular Arc of the Riviera sculpture in the parkway near Place Masséna, this "art" justifiably infuriates many locals as an ugly waste of money. But I know how to make it easier to appreciate the erection every local loves to hate: Stand directly under it, look straight up, and spin 720 degrees. Then look across the way to marvel at the 18th-century facades that line the Esplanade Georges Pompidou. Find the one that is entirely fake-painted on a flat stucco surface. Then, look down and notice the buried uplighting—a French forte. And then, give it another 720 degrees of spin and try to walk on.

At the next palm tree, look left (at the impressive back side of Apollo, a couple of blocks away), then angle right for a view of the beach action. Topless bathing is now out of fashion. Locals say that the awareness of skin cancer and the proliferation of North African and tourist lookie-loos have made it less appealing. Some say the only people still bathing topless are older ladies who remember fondly the liberation of 1968...and tourists.

A block ahead on the left, the elegant back side of Nice's opera house faces the sea. The tiny bronze Statue of Liberty (right in front of you as you face the opera) reminds all that this stretch of seafront promenade is named for the USA.

As you continue your stroll, you'll come to a long stretch of two-level galleries on the left, with a walkway on top (likely closed). This was British tourists' preferred place for a seaside stroll before the Promenade des Anglais was built. The ground floor served the city's fishermen, and the smell alone was motivation enough to find a new place to promenade. Behind the galleries bustles the **Cours Saleya Market**—long the heart and soul of Vieux Nice, with handy WCs under its arches.

Near the eastern end of those galleries, on the far-right side of the promenade, find the three-foot-tall white ❼ **metal winch** at the ramp to the beach. Long before tourism—and long before Nice dredged its harbor—hardworking fishing boats rather than vacationing tourists lined the beach. The boats were hauled in through the surf by winches like this and tied to the iron rings on either side.

• *You could end your walk here, but the view from the point just past the Hôtel la Pérouse is wonderful. Either way, you have several great options: Continue 15 minutes along the coast to Port Lympia, around the base of Castle Hill (fine views of the entire promenade and a monumental war memorial carved into the hillside); hike or ride the free elevator up to Castle Hill (catch the elevator next to Hôtel Suisse; see listing for Castle Hill in "Sights in Nice," later); head into Vieux Nice (you can follow my "Vieux Nice Walk," next); or grab a blue chair or piece of beach and just be on vacation—Riviera style.*

VIEUX NICE WALK

This self-guided walk through Nice's old town, worth ▲▲, gives you an introduction to the city's bicultural heritage and its most interesting neighborhoods.

Length of This Walk: Allow about one hour at a leisurely pace for this level walk from Place Masséna to Place Rossetti.

When to Go: It's best done in the morning while the outdoor market thrives on Cours Saleya—consider coffee or breakfast at a café there (suggestions later in this walk)—and preferably not on a Sunday, when things are quiet. This ramble is also a joy at night, when fountains glow and pedestrians rule the streets.

❍ Self-Guided Walk

• *Start where Avenue Jean Médecin hits the people-friendly Place Masséna—the successful result of a long, expensive city upgrade and the new center of Nice. Find a spot on the black-and-white checkerboard pavement for best views.*

❶ Place Masséna

The grand Place Masséna is Nice's drawing room, where old meets new, and where the tramway bends between Vieux Nice and the

train station. The square's black-and-white pavement feels like an elegant outdoor ballroom, with the sleek tram waltzing across its dance floor. While once congested with cars, today's square is crossed only by these trams, which swoosh silently by every couple of minutes. The men on pedestals sitting high above are modern-art additions that arrived with the tram. For a mood-altering experience, return after dark and watch the illuminated figures float yoga-like above. Place Masséna is at its sophisticated best after the sun goes down.

This vast square dates from 1848 and pays tribute to Jean-André Masséna, a French military leader during the Revolutionary and Napoleonic wars. Not just another pretty face in a long lineup of French military heroes, he's considered among the greatest commanders in history—anywhere, anytime. Napoleon called him "the greatest name of my military Empire." No wonder this city is proud of him.

Looking across Place Masséna with your back to the fountains, start a clockwise spin tour: Underneath you, unseen, Nice's historic Paillon River flows to the sea (it's been covered since the late 1800s). For centuries this river was Nice's natural defense to the north and west (the sea protected the south, and Castle Hill defended the east). A fortified wall once ran along the river's length to the sea. It's been covered since the late 1800s.

The **modern swoosh sculpture** at palm-tree height in the parkway is meant to represent the arc of Nice's beautiful bay. To the right stretches modern Nice, born with the arrival of tourism in the 1800s. **Avenue Jean Médecin,** Nice's Champs-Elysées, cuts from here through the new town to the train station. Looking up

NICE

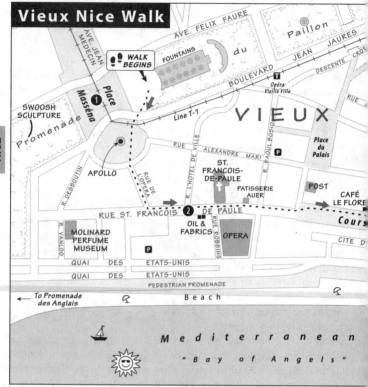

the avenue, you'll see the tracks, the freeway, and the Alps beyond. Once crammed with cars, buses, and delivery vehicles tangling with pedestrians, Avenue Jean Médecin was turned into a walking and cycling nirvana in 2007. I used to avoid this street. Now I can't get enough of it. Businesses along it flourish in the welcoming environment of generous sidewalks and no traffic.

Appreciate the city's Italian heritage—it feels more like Venice than Paris (though it was intended to resemble the city of Turin—then capital of Savoy, the Duchy that controlled Nice). The lovely portico flanking the beginning of Avenue Jean Médecin is Italian, not French. The rich colors of the buildings reflect the taste of previous Italian rulers, while the architecture past the porticos, along Avenue Jean Médecin, has a more French sensibility.

Now turn to face the fountains and look east to see Nice's ongoing effort to "put the human element into the heart of the town." An ugly concrete bus station and parking structures were demolished, and the **Promenade du Paillon** (named for the river which it covers) was created to fill the space. Today, this pedestrian-friendly parkway extends from the sea to the Museum of Modern Art—a

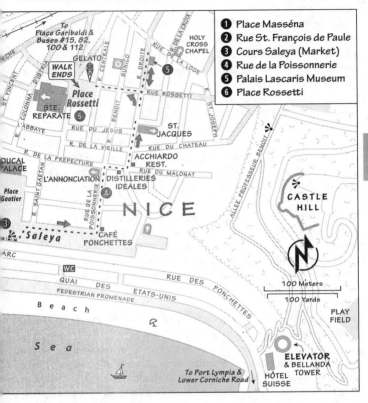

modern-day, green Promenade des Anglais. Forming a key spine for biking, walking, and kids at play, the Promenade du Paillon is a delight any time of day. Notice the fountain—its surprise geysers delight children by day and its night mood lighting fires up a romantic's heart. Past the fountain stands a bronze statue of the square's namesake, Masséna. The hills beyond separate Nice from Villefranche-sur-Mer.

To the right of the Promenade du Paillon lies **Vieux Nice,** with its jumbled and colorful facades below Castle Hill. Looking closer and farther to the right, the **statue of Apollo** has horsy hair and holds a beach towel (in the fountain) as if to say, "It's beer o'clock, let's go."

• *Walk past Apollo into Vieux Nice (careful of those trams). A block down Rue de l'Opéra you'll see a grouping of rusted steel girders (described earlier in my "Promenade des Anglais Walk"). Turn left onto...*

❷ Rue St. François de Paule

This colorful street leads into the heart of Vieux Nice. On the left is the Hôtel de Ville (City Hall). Peer into the **Alziari olive oil**

shop (at #14 on the right). Dating from 1868, the shop produces top-quality stone-ground olive oil. The proud and charming owner, Gilles Piot, claims that stone wheels create less acidity, since grinding with metal creates heat (see photo in back over the door). Locals fill their own containers from the huge vats.

A few awnings down, **La Couqueto** is a colorful shop filled with Provençal fabrics and crafts, including lovely folk characters *(santons)*. Walk in for a lavender smell sensation—is madame working the sewing machine upstairs? The **Jeannot** *boulangerie* next door is handy for a cheap lunch and has good outdoor seating.

Next door is Nice's grand **opera house,** built by a student of Charles Garnier (architect of Monte Carlo's casino and opera house). Imagine this opulent jewel back in the 19th century, buried deep in Vieux Nice. With all the fancy big-city folks wintering here, this rough-edged town needed some high-class entertainment. And Victorians needed an alternative to those "devilish" gambling houses. (Queen Victoria, so disgusted by casinos, would actually close the drapes on her train window when passing Monte Carlo.) The four statues on top represent theater, dance, music, and party poopers.

Across the street, **Pâtisserie Auer**'s grand old storefront would love to tempt you with chocolates and candied fruits. It's changed little over the centuries. The writing on the window says, "Since 1820 from father to son." Wander in for a whiff of chocolate and a dazzling interior. The twin gold royal shields on the mirrors partway back remind shoppers that Queen Victoria indulged her sweet tooth here.

• *Continue on, sifting your way through a cluttered block of tacky souvenir shops to the big market square.*

❸ Cours Saleya

Named for its broad exposure to the sun *(soleil)*, Cours Saleya (koor sah-lay-yuh)—a commotion of color, sights, smells, and people—has been Nice's main market square since the Middle Ages (flower market all day Tue-Sun, produce market Tue-Sun until 13:00, antiques on Mon). While you're greeted by the mouth of an underground parking lot, much of this square itself was a parking lot until 1980, when the mayor of Nice cleared away the  cars, and the lovely Cours Saleya was born. If you're early enough for coffee, pause for a break at **Café le Flore**'s outdoor tables in the heart of the market (a block up on the left).

The first section is devoted to the Riviera's largest **flower market.** In operation since the 19th century, this market offers plants and flowers that grow effortlessly in this climate, including the local favorites: carnations, roses, and jasmine. Locals know the season by what's on sale (mimosas in February, violets in March, and so on). Until the recent rise in imported flowers, this region supplied all of France with flowers. Still, fresh flowers are cheap here, the best value in this expensive city. The Riviera's three big industries are tourism, flowers, and perfume (made from these flowers... take a whiff).

The boisterous **produce section** trumpets the season with mushrooms, strawberries, white asparagus, zucchini flowers, and more—whatever's fresh gets top billing. What's in season today?

The market opens up at Place Pierre Gautier. It's also called Plassa dou Gouvernou—you'll see bilingual street signs here that include the old Niçois language, a Provençal dialect. This is where farmers set up stalls to sell their produce and herbs directly. It's also where Thérèse sets up her *socca* stand—treat yourself to this cheap and tasty flatbread/chickpea concoction.

For a great **rooftop view** over the market, climb the steps by Le Grand Bleu restaurant (along the gallery wall separating Cours Saleya from the sea). Check out the top level of the two-story buildings nearby; this is where the Brits strolled before their exclusive Promenade des Anglais was built.

Look up to the **hill** that dominates to the east. The city of Nice was first settled there by Greeks (circa 400 BC). In the Middle Ages, a massive castle stood there with soldiers at the ready. Over time, the city sprawled down to where you are now. With the river guarding one side (running under today's Promenade du Paillon parkway) and the sea the other, this mountain fortress seemed strong—until Louis XIV leveled it in 1706. Nice's medieval seawall ran along the line of two-story buildings where you're standing.

Now, look across Place Pierre Gautier to the large "palace." The **Ducal Palace** was where the kings of Sardinia, the city's Italian rulers until 1860, resided when in Nice. (For centuries, Nice was under the rule of the Italian capital of Turin.) Today, the palace is the local police headquarters. The land upon which the Cours Saleya sits was once the duke's gardens and became a market after Nice's union with France.

• *Continue down Cours Saleya. The golden building that seals the end of the square is where Henri Matisse spent 17 years on the top two floors. I imagine he was inspired by his view. Turn left a block before Matisse's home onto...*

❹ Rue de la Poissonnerie

Look up at the first floor of the first building on your right. **Adam**

and Eve are squaring off, each holding a zucchini-like gourd. This scene represents the annual rapprochement in Nice to make up for the sins of a too-much-fun Carnival (Mardi Gras, the pre-Lenten festival). Residents of Nice have partied hard during Carnival for more than 700 years. The **spice shop** below offers a fine selection of regional herbs.

As you continue down the street, look above the doors. The iron grills (like the one above #6) allow air to enter the buildings but keep out uninvited guests. You'll see lots of these open grills in Vieux Nice. They were part of a clever system that sucked in cool air from the sea, circulating it through homes and blowing it out through vents in the roof.

A few steps ahead, check out the small **Baroque church** (Notre-Dame de l'Annonciation, closed 12:00-14:30). It's dedicated to St. Rita, the patron saint of desperate causes and desperate people (see display in window). She holds a special place in locals' hearts, making this the most popular church in Nice. Drop in for a peek at the dazzling Baroque decor. The first chapel on the right is dedicated to St. Erasmus, protector of mariners.

• *Turn right on the next street, where you'll pass one of Vieux Nice's happening bars (the recommended Distilleries Ideales), with a swashbuckling interior that buzzes until the wee hours. Pause at the next corner and study the classic Vieux Nice scene in all directions. Now turn left on Rue Droite and enter an area that feels like Little Naples.*

Rue Droite

In the Middle Ages, this straight, skinny street provided the most direct route from river to sea within the old walled town. Donkeys carrying salt on their backs used this so-called salt road to reach Turin, then the county's capital. Pass the recommended restaurant Acchiardo. Notice stepped lanes leading uphill to the castle. Pop into the Jesuit **Eglise St-Jacques** (also called Eglise du Gésu) for an explosion of Baroque exuberance hidden behind that plain church facade. Its bell tower is crammed in at the rear making it almost impossible to see—peer down the lane to the left to see it. Inside the church, at the wooden pulpit, notice the crucifix held by a sculpted arm. This clever support allowed the priest to focus on his sermon while reminding the congregation that Christ died for their sins.

We're turning left onto Rue Rossetti...but if you continued another block along Rue Droite you'd find the ❺ **Palais Lascaris** (c. 1647), home of one of Nice's most prestigious families. Today it's a museum and worth a quick look (peek in the entry for free or take a tour, covered by All Museums Pass, Wed-Mon 10:00-18:00, from 11:00 off-season, closed Tue year-round). Inside you'll find a collection of antique musical instruments—harps, guitars, violins, and violas (good English explanations)—along with elaborate tapestries and a few well-furnished rooms. The palace has four levels—but only two are open to the public: The ground floor was used for storage, the first floor was devoted to reception rooms (and musical events), the owners lived a floor above that, and the servants lived at the top. Look up and make faces back at the guys under the balconies.

• *Shortly after making a left on Rue Rossetti, you'll cross Rue Benoît Bunico.*

In the 18th century, this street served as a **ghetto** for Nice's Jews. At sunset, gates would seal the street at either end, locking people in until daylight. To identify Jews as non-Christians, the men were required to wear yellow stars and the women to wear yellow scarves. The pastel facade at #18 was the synagogue until 1848, when revolution ended the notion of ghettos in France.

• *Continue down Rue Rossetti to...*

⑥ Place Rossetti

The most Italian of Nice's squares, Place Rossetti comes alive after dark—in part because of the **Fenocchio gelato shop,** popular for its many innovative flavors.

Check out the **Cathedral of Ste. Réparate**—an unassuming building for a big-city cathedral. It was relocated here in the 1500s, when Castle Hill was temporarily converted to military use. The name comes from Nice's patron saint, a teenage virgin named Réparate, whose martyred body floated to Nice in the fourth century accompanied by angels (remember the Bay of Angels?). The interior of the cathedral gushes Baroque, a response to the challenge of the Protestant Reformation in the 16th century. With the Catholic Church's Counter-Reformation, the theatrical energy of churches was cranked up with re-energized, high-powered saints and eye-popping decor.

• *This is the end of our walk. From here you can hike up Castle Hill (from Place Rossetti, take Rue Rossetti uphill; see Castle Hill listing under "Sights in Nice"). Or you can have an ice cream and browse the colorful lanes of Vieux Nice...or grab Apollo and hit the beach.*

Sights in Nice

PROMENADE DES ANGLAIS
▲▲▲Walking or Biking the Promenade

Enjoying Nice's four-mile seafront promenade on foot or by bike is an essential Riviera experience. Since the days when wealthy English tourists filled the grand seaside hotels, this stretch has been *the* place to be in Nice. (For a self-guided **walk,** see my "Promenade des Anglais Walk," earlier.)

To rev up the pace of your promenade saunter, rent a **bike** and glide along the coast in either or both directions (about 30 minutes each way; for rental info see "Helpful Hints," earlier). Both of the following paths start along Promenade des Anglais.

To the West: The path stops just before the airport at perhaps the most scenic *boules* courts in France. Pause here to watch the old-timers while away the afternoon tossing shiny metal balls (for more on this game, see page 52).

To the East: The path rounds the hill—passing a scenic promontory and the town's memorial to both world wars—to the harbor of Nice, and gives you a chance to survey some fancy yachts. Walk or pedal around the harbor and follow the coast past the Corsica ferry terminal to Coco Beach (you'll need to carry your bike up a flight of steps). From there the path leads to Boulevard Mont Bouron, an appealing tree-lined residential district.

Beach

Beaches are free to the public (by law). Settle in on the smooth rocks, or get more comfortable by renting a lounge chair or mat-

tress (*chaise longue* or *transat*- about €18, umbrella-€5-10, towel-€5). Have lunch in your bathing suit (€15 salads and pizzas in bars and restaurants all along the beach). I enjoy stopping here first thing in the morning (before the crowds hit) for a peaceful breakfast or café au lait on the Mediterranean. *Plage Publique* signs (with English translations) explain the 10 beach no-nos.

MUSEUMS

The Chagall and Matisse museums are a long walk northeast of Nice's city center. Because they're in the same direction and served by the same bus line (see "Getting There," next page), try to visit them on the same trip. From Place Masséna, the Chagall Museum is a 10-minute bus ride, and the Matisse Museum is several stops beyond that. It's a bracing 25-minute walk between them. For details on the two sightseeing passes covering Nice's museums, see "Helpful Hints" on page 315.

▲▲▲Chagall Museum
(Musée National Marc Chagall)

Even if you don't get modern art, this museum—with the world's largest collection of Marc Chagall's work in captivity—is a delight. For fans of Chagall, it's a can't-miss treat.

After World War II, Chagall returned from the United States to settle first in Vence and later in St-Paul-de-Vence, both not far from Nice. Between 1954 and 1967, he painted a cycle of 17 large murals designed for, and donated to, this museum. These paintings, inspired by the biblical books of Genesis, Exodus, and the Song of Songs, make up the "nave," or core, of what Chagall called the "House of Brotherhood." Combining his Russian and Jewish heritage with the Christian message, he hoped this would be a place where people of all faiths could come together and celebrate love.

Cost and Hours: €8, €2 more during frequent special exhibits, covered by French Riviera Pass; Wed-Mon 10:00-18:00, Nov-April until 17:00, closed Tue year-round; ticket includes helpful audioguide (though Chagall would suggest that you explore his art without guidance); must check daypacks, idyllic **$** garden café (salads and *plats*), +33 4 93 53 87 20, https://musees-nationaux-alpesmaritimes.fr/chagall

Getting There: The museum is located on Avenue Docteur Ménard. **Taxis** from the city center cost about €16-20. **Buses** connect the museum with downtown Nice. From downtown, catch bus #5 (Mon-Sat 6/hour, Sun 3/hour, 10 minutes). Catch the bus from the east end of the Galeries Lafayette department store, near the Masséna tram stop, on Rue Sacha Guitry (see "Nice" map near the beginning of this chapter). Watch for a *Musée Chagall* sign on the bus shelter where you'll get off (on Boulevard de Cimiez).

You can **walk** from the train station to the museum in 25 minutes. Walk to the station's tram stop, turn left, then make a right on the last street before the overpass—Boulevard Raimbaldi. Follow Boulevard Raimbaldi for several blocks until you see a Lidl grocery store. Turn left on Avenue Raymond Comboul, walk under the freeway, and then follow the signs.

Overview

This small museum consists of the main hall and Song of Songs room with the 17 murals, two rooms for special exhibits, an au-

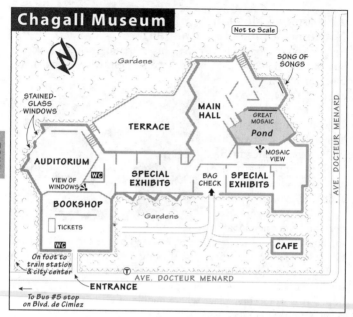

Chagall Museum

Not to Scale

SONG OF SONGS

Gardens

STAINED-GLASS WINDOWS

MAIN HALL

GREAT MOSAIC

TERRACE

Pond

MOSAIC VIEW

AUDITORIUM

WC

VIEW OF WINDOWS

SPECIAL EXHIBITS

BAG CHECK

SPECIAL EXHIBITS

BOOKSHOP

Gardens

TICKETS

WC

CAFE

On foot to train station & city center

AVE. DOCTEUR MENARD

ENTRANCE

AVE. DOCTEUR MENARD

To Bus #5 stop on Blvd. de Cimiez

ditorium with stained-glass windows, and a mosaic-lined pond (viewed from inside). It takes about one hour to see the whole thing. The core of the collection (Genesis and Exodus scenes) is in the main hall. The adjacent octagonal Song of Songs room houses five more paintings.

At the end of this tour, in the auditorium, you can see a wonderful film about Chagall (52 minutes), which plays at the top of each hour (alternately in French and English—ask about showtimes when you arrive—you may want to see the movie first, then tour the museum; no showings during special exhibits). You can enter the auditorium at any point during the movie and find it worthwhile. Even the French version offers a fascinating look at old clips of the master and a chance to see the creative energy and charisma in his eyes.

❷ Self-Guided Tour

• *Buy your ticket, pass through the garden, and enter the museum at the baggage-check counter. Pick up your included audioguide and step into the main hall.*

Old Testament Scenes

Each painting is a lighter-than-air collage of images that draws from Chagall's Russian folk-village youth, his Jewish heritage, the

Bible, and his feeling that he existed somewhere between heaven and earth. He believed that the Bible was a synonym for nature, and that both color and biblical themes were key for understanding God's love for his creation. Chagall's brilliant blues and reds celebrate nature, as do his spiritual and folk themes. Notice the focus on couples. To Chagall, humans loving each other mirrored God's love of creation.

The paintings are described in the order you should see them, going counterclockwise around the room.

Abraham and the Three Angels: In the heat of the day, Abraham looked up and saw three men. He said, "Let a little food and water be brought, so you can be refreshed..." (Genesis 18:1-5)

Abraham refreshes God's angels on this red-hot day and, in return, they promise Abraham a son (in the bubble, at right), thus making him the father of the future Israelite nation.

The Sacrifice of Isaac: Abraham bound his son Isaac and laid him on the altar. Then he took the knife to slay his son. But the angel of the Lord called out to him from heaven, "Abraham!" (Genesis 22:9-11)

Tested by God, Abraham prepares to kill his only son, but the angel stops him in time. Notice that Isaac is posed exactly as Adam is in *The Creation* (described next). Abraham's sacrifice echoes three others: the sacrifice all men must make (Adam, the everyman), the sacrifice of atonement (the goat tied to a tree at left), and even God's sacrifice of his own son (Christ carrying the cross, upper right).

The Creation: God said, "Let us make man in our image, in our likeness..." (Genesis 1:26)

A pure-white angel descends through the blue sky and carries a still-sleeping Adam from radiant red-yellow heaven to earth. Heaven is a whirling dervish of activity, spinning out all the events of future history, from the tablets of the Ten Commandments to the Crucifixion—an overture of many images that we'll see in later paintings. (Though not a Christian, Chagall saw the Crucifixion as a universal symbol of man's suffering.)

Moses Receives the Ten Commandments: The Lord gave him the two tablets of the Law, the tablets of stone inscribed by the finger of God... (Exodus 31:18)

An astonished Moses stretches toward heaven, where God reaches out from a cloud to hand him the Ten Commandments. While Moses tilts one way, Mount Sinai slants the other, lead-

Chagall's Style

Chagall uses a deceptively simple, almost childlike style to paint a world that's hidden to the eye—the magical, mystical world below the surface. Here are some of the characteristics of his paintings:

Deep, radiant colors, inspired by Expressionism and Fauvism (an art movement pioneered by Matisse and other French painters).

Personal imagery, particularly from his childhood in Russia—smiling barnyard animals, fiddlers on the roof, flower bouquets, huts, and blissful sweethearts.

A Hasidic Jewish perspective, the idea that God is everywhere, appearing in everyday things like nature, animals, and humdrum activities.

A fragmented Cubist style, multifaceted and multidimensional, a perfect style to mirror the complexity of God's creation.

Overlapping images, like double-exposure photography, with faint imagery that bleeds through, suggesting there's more to life under the surface.

Stained-glass-esque technique of dark, deep, earthy, "potent" colors, and simplified, iconic, symbolic figures.

Gravity-defying compositions, with lovers, animals, and angels twirling blissfully in midair.

Happy (not tragic) mood depicting a world of personal joy, despite the violence and turmoil of world wars and revolution.

Childlike simplicity, drawn with simple, heavy outlines, filled in with Crayola colors that often spill over the lines. Major characters in a scene are bigger than the lesser characters. The grinning barnyard animals, the bright colors, the magical events presented as literal truth...Was Chagall a lightweight? Or a lighter-than-air-weight?

ing our eye up to the left, where a golden calf is being worshipped by the wayward Children of Israel. But down to the right, Aaron and the menorah assure us that Moses will set things right. In this radiant final panel, the Jewish tradition—after a long struggle—is finally established.

• *Skip around the corner to...*

Driven from Paradise: So God banished him from the Garden of Eden...and placed cherubim and a flaming sword to guard the way... (Genesis 3:23-24)

An angel drives them out with a fire hose of blue (there's

Adam still cradling his flaming-red *coq*), while a sparkling yellow, flower-filled tree stands like a wall preventing them from ever returning. Deep in the green colors, the painting offers us glimpses of the future—Eve giving birth (lower-right corner) and the yellow sacrificial goat of atonement (top right).

Paradise: God put him in the Garden of Eden...and said, "You must not eat from the tree of the knowledge of good and evil..." (Genesis 2:15-17)

Paradise is a rich, earth-as-seen-from-space pool of blue, green, and white. On the left, amoebic, still-evolving animals float around Adam (celibately practicing yoga) and Eve (with lusty-red hair). On the right, an angel guards the tempting tree, but Eve offers an apple and Adam reaches around to sample the forbidden fruit while the snake gawks knowingly.

The Rainbow: God said, "I have set my rainbow in the clouds as a sign of the covenant between me and the earth." (Genesis 9:13)

A flaming angel sets the rainbow in the sky, while Noah rests beneath it and his family offers a sacrifice of thanks. The pure-white rainbow's missing colors are found radiating from the features of the survivors.

Jacob's Ladder: He had a dream in which he saw a ladder resting on the earth with its top reaching to heaven, and the angels of God were ascending and descending on it... (Genesis 28:12)

In the left half, Jacob (Abraham's grandson, in red) slumps asleep and dreams of a ladder between heaven and earth. On the right, a lofty angel with a menorah represents how heaven and earth are bridged by the rituals of the Jewish tradition.

Jacob Wrestles with an Angel: So Jacob wrestled with him till daybreak. Jacob said, "I will not let you go unless you bless me..." (Genesis 32: 24, 26)

Jacob holds on while the angel blesses him with descendants (the Children of Israel) and sends out rays from his hands. On the right are scenes from Jacob's life, including his son Joseph being stripped of his bright-red coat and sold into slavery by his brothers.

Noah's Ark: Then he sent out a dove to see if the water had receded... (Genesis 8:8)

Adam and Eve's descendants have become so wicked that God destroys the earth with a flood, engulfing the sad crowd on the right. Only righteous Noah (center), his family (lower right), and the animals (including our yellow goat) are spared inside an ark. Here Noah opens the ark's window and sends out a dove to test the waters.

Moses Brings Water from the Rock: The Lord said, "Strike the rock, and water will come out of it for the people to drink..." (Exodus 17:5-6)

In the brown desert, Moses nourishes his thirsty people with

Marc Chagall (1887-1985)

1887-1910: Russia

Chagall is born in the small town of Vitebsk, Belarus. He's the oldest of nine children in a traditional Russian Hasidic Jewish family. He studies realistic art in his hometown. In St. Petersburg, he is first exposed to the Modernist work of Paul Cézanne and the Fauves.

1910-1914: Paris

A patron finances a four-year stay in Paris. Chagall hobnobs with the avant-garde and learns technique from the Cubists, but he never abandons painting recognizable figures or his own personal fantasies. (Some say his relative poverty forced him to paint over used canvases, which gave him the idea of overlapping images that bleed through. Hmm...)

1914-1922: Russia

Returning to his hometown, Chagall marries Bella Rosenfeld (1915), whose love will inspire him for decades. He paints happy scenes despite the turmoil of wars and the Communist Revolution. Moving to Moscow (1920), he paints his first large-scale works, sets for the New Jewish Theater. These would inspire many of his later large-scale works.

water miraculously spouting from a rock. From the (red-yellow) divine source, it rains down actual (blue) water, but also a gush of spiritual yellow light.

Moses and the Burning Bush: The angel of the Lord appeared to him in flames of fire from within a bush... (Exodus 3:2)

Horned Moses—Chagall depicts him according to a medieval tradition—kneels awestruck before the burning bush, the event that calls him to God's service. On the left, we see Moses after the call, his face radiant, leading the Israelites out of captivity across the Red Sea, while Pharaoh's men drown (lower half of Moses' robe). The Ten Commandments loom ahead.

• *Return to Moses Receives the Ten Commandments, then walk past a window into a room with five red paintings.*

Song of Songs

Chagall wrote, "I've been fascinated by the Bible ever since my earliest childhood. I have always thought of it as the most extraordinary source of poetic inspiration imaginable. As far as I am concerned, perfection in art and in life has its source in the Bible, and

1923-1941: France and Palestine

Chagall returns to France. In 1931 he travels to Palestine, where the bright sun and his Jewish roots inspire a series of gouaches (opaque watercolor paintings). These gouaches would later inspire 105 etchings to illustrate the Bible (1931-1952), which would eventually influence the 17 large canvases of biblical scenes in the Chagall Museum (1954-1967).

1941-1947: United States/World War II

Fearing persecution for his Jewish faith, Chagall emigrates to New York, where he spends the war years. The Crucifixion starts to appear in his paintings—not as a Christian symbol, but as a representation of the violence mankind perpetrates on itself. In 1944 his beloved Bella dies, and he stops painting for months.

1947-1985: South of France

After the war, Chagall returns to France, eventually settling in St-Paul-de-Vence. In 1952 he remarries. His new love, Valentina Brodsky, plus the southern sunshine, brings Chagall a revived creativity—he is extremely prolific for the rest of his life. He experiments with new techniques and media—ceramics, sculpture, book illustrations, tapestry, and mosaic. In 1956 he's commissioned for his first stained-glass project. Eventually he does windows for cathedrals in Metz and Reims, and a synagogue in Jerusalem (1960). The Chagall Museum opens in 1973.

exercises in the mechanics of the merely rational are fruitless. In art as well as in life, anything is possible, provided there is love."

The paintings in this room were inspired by the Old Testament Song of Songs. Chagall cherished verses such as: I sleep, but my heart is awake (5:2). Until the day breaks and the shadows flee, turn, my lover, and be like a gazelle or like a young stag on the rugged hills (2:17). Your stature is like that of the palm, and your breasts like clusters of fruit (7:7). Chagall, who dedicated this room to his wife Valentina (Vava), saw divine love and physical love as a natural mix.

Chagall enjoyed the love of two women in his long life—his first wife, Bella, then Valentina, who gave him a second wind as he was painting these late works. Chagall was one of the few "serious" 20th-century artists to portray unabashed love. Where the Bible uses the metaphor of earthly, physical, sexual love to describe God's love for humans, Chagall uses unearthly colors and a mystical ambience to celebrate human love. These red-toned canvases are hard to interpret literally, but they capture the rosy spirit of a man in love with life.

• *Head back toward the entry and turn left at The Sacrifice of Isaac to find the...*

Pond

The great mosaic evokes the prophet Elijah in his chariot of fire (from the Second Book of Kings)—with Chagall's addition of the 12 signs of the zodiac, which he used to symbolize Time.

• *Return to the main hall, veer left, and exit the hall to the right. Pass through the exhibition room with temporary displays. At the end, you'll find the...*

Auditorium

This room, where the Chagall documentary film shows (see "Overview," earlier), is worth a peaceful moment to enjoy three Chagall stained-glass windows depicting the seven days of creation (right to left): the creation of light, elements, and planets (a visual big bang that's four "days" wide); the creation of animals, plants, man and woman, and the ordering of the solar system (two "days" wide, complete with fish and birds still figuring out where they belong); and the day of rest (the narrowest—only one "day" wide, imagine angels singing to the glory of God).

• *Our tour is over. From here, you can return to downtown Nice or head to the Matisse Museum. Taxis usually wait in front of the museum. For the bus back to downtown Nice, turn right out of the museum, then make another right down Boulevard de Cimiez, and ride bus #5 heading downhill. To continue to the Matisse Museum, catch #5 using the uphill stop located across the street, or enjoy a 20-minute walk uphill passing belle-époque villas at every turn.*

To walk to the train station area from the museum (25 minutes), turn right out of the museum grounds and follow the first street to the right (hugging the museum). Drop down ramps and staircases, turn left at the bottom under the freeway and train tracks, then turn right on Boulevard Raimbaldi.

▲Matisse Museum (Musée Matisse)

This small, underachieving museum fills an old mansion in a park surrounded by scant Roman ruins; it houses a limited sampling of works from Henri Matisse's artistic career. (Matisse was first recognized as a master by American and Russian collectors who bought up most of his masterpieces, leaving little of his best work for French museums.) The museum offers an introduction to the artist's many styles and materials, both shaped by Mediterranean light and by fellow Côte d'Azur artists Picasso and Renoir.

Cost and Hours: Covered by €15 All Museums Pass; Wed-

Mon 10:00-18:00, Nov-April until 17:00, closed Tue year-round; 164 Avenue des Arènes de Cimiez, +33 4 93 81 08 08, www.musee-matisse-nice.org.

Getting There: Take a cab (€20 from Promenade des Anglais). These buses serve the Matisse Museum: bus #5, direction: Rimiez, from the east end of Galeries Lafayette just off Place Masséna or from the Chagall Museum; or bus #33 from Port Lympia, direction: Cimiez Hôpital. Get off at the Arènes-Matisse bus stop (look for the crumbling Roman arena that once held 10,000 spectators), then walk 50 yards into the park to find the pink villa.

Background: Henri Matisse, the master of leaving things out, could suggest a woman's body with a single curvy line—letting the viewer's mind fill in the rest. Ignoring traditional 3-D perspective, he expressed his passion for life through simplified but recognizable scenes in which dark outlines and saturated, bright blocks of color create an overall decorative pattern.

Matisse understood how colors and shapes affect us emotionally. He could create either shocking, clashing works (early Fauvism) or geometrical, balanced, harmonious ones (later cutouts). Whereas other modern artists reveled in purely abstract design, Matisse (almost) always kept the subject matter at least vaguely recognizable. He used unreal colors and distorted lines not just to portray what an object looks like, but to express its inner nature (even inanimate objects). Meditating on his paintings helps you connect with life—or so Matisse hoped.

As you tour the museum, look for Matisse's favorite motifs—including fruit, flowers, wallpaper, and sunny rooms—often with a window opening onto a sunny landscape. Another favorite subject is the *odalisque* (harem concubine), usually shown sprawled in a seductive pose and with a simplified, masklike face. You'll also see a few souvenirs from his travels to places like Morocco, which much influenced his work.

Visiting the Museum: The museum is in a constant state of flux, so expect changes from this description. Enter on the basement floor and find Matisse's colorful paper cutout *Flowers and Fruits* hanging from the wall. This piece makes a fine introduction to his decorative art, shouting "Riviera!" The basement also has a room devoted to two 25-foot-long watery ceramic works for an uncompleted pool project *(La Piscine)* for the city of Nice, which shows his abiding love of deep blue.

Henri Matisse (1869-1954)

Here's an outline of Henri Matisse's busy life:

1880s and 1890s: At age 20, Matisse, a budding lawyer, is struck down with appendicitis. Bedridden for a year, he turns to paint-ing as a healing escape from pain and bore-dom. After recovering, he studies art in Paris and produces dark-colored, realistic still lifes and landscapes. His work is exhib-ited at the Salons of 1896 and 1897.

1897-1905: Influenced by the Impression-ists, he experiments with sunnier scenes and brighter colors. He travels to southern France, including Collioure (on the coast near Spain), and seeks still more light-filled scenes to paint. His experiments are influ-enced by Vincent van Gogh's bright, surre-alistic colors and thick outlines, and by Paul Gauguin's primitive visions of a Tahitian par-adise. From Paul Cézanne, he learns how to simplify objects into their basic geometric shapes. He also experiments (like Cézanne) with creating the illusion of 3-D not by traditional means, but by using contrasting colors for the foreground and background.

1905: Back in Paris, Matisse and his colleagues (André Derain and Maurice de Vlaminck) shock the art world with an exhibition of their experimental paintings. The thick outlines, simple forms, flattened perspective, and—most of all—bright, clashing, unreal-istic colors seem to be the work of "wild animals" (*fauves*). Fau-vism is hot, and Matisse is instantly famous. (Though notorious as a "wild animal," Matisse himself was a gentle, introspective man.)

1906-1910: After just a year, Fauvism is out, and African masks are in. This "primitive" art form inspires Matisse to simplify and distort his figures further, making them less realistic but more ex-pressive.

1910-1917: Matisse creates his masterpiece paintings. Cubism is the rage, pioneered by Matisse's friend and rival for the World's Best Painter award, Pablo Picasso. Matisse dabbles in Cubism, simplifying forms, emphasizing outline, and muting his colors. But

On the mezzanine above, leaf through discarded cutouts from various papier-mâché works and find black-and-white photos of the artist at work and play.

Rooms on the street level usually contain paintings from Matisse's formative years as a student (1890s) and are the high-light of the museum for me. Notice how quickly his work evolves: from dark still lifes *(nature mortes)*, to colorful Impressionist scenes, to more abstract works, all in the matter of a few years. Find the translation of his "Découverte de la Lumière" (discovery of light),

ultimately it proves to be too austere and analytical for his deeply sensory nature. The Cubist style is most evident in his sculpture.

1920s: Burned out from years of intense experimentation, Matisse moves to Nice (spending winters there from 1917, settling permanently in 1921). Luxuriating under the bright sun, he's reborn, and he paints colorful, sensual, highly decorative works. Harem concubines lounging in their sunny, flowery apartments epitomize the lush life.

1930s: A visit to Tahiti inspires more scenes of life as a sunny paradise. Matisse experiments with bolder lines, swirling arabesques, and decorative patterns.

1940s: Duodenal cancer (in 1941) requires Matisse to undergo two operations and confines him to a wheelchair for the rest of his life. Working at an easel becomes a struggle for him, and he largely stops painting in 1941. But as World War II ends, Matisse emerges with renewed energy. Now in his 70s, he explores a new medium: paper cutouts pasted onto a watercolored surface (découpage on gouache-prepared surface). The technique plays to his strengths—the cutouts are essentially blocks of bright color (mostly blue) with a strong outline. Scissors in hand, Matisse says, "I draw straight into the color." (His doctor advises him to wear dark glasses to protect his weak eyes against the bright colors he chooses.) In 1947, Matisse's book *Jazz* is published, featuring the artist's joyful cutouts of simple figures. Like jazz music, the book is a celebration of artistic spontaneity. And like music in general, Matisse's works balance different tones and colors to create a mood.

1947-1951: Matisse's nurse becomes a Dominican nun in Vence. To thank her for her care, he spends his later years designing a chapel there. He oversees every aspect of the Chapel of the Rosary (Chapelle du Rosaire) at Vence, from the stained glass to the altar to the colors of the priest's robe. Though Matisse is not a strong Christian, the church exudes his spirit of celebrating life and sums up his work.

1954: Matisse dies.

which the Riviera (and his various travels to sun-soaked places like Corsica, Collioure, and Tahiti) brought to his art. To appreciate the speed of change in his painting, notice the dramatic differences in his portraits of Madame Matisse, painted just a few years apart.

Other rooms on this floor (or nearby) highlight Matisse's fascination with dance and the female body. You'll see pencil and charcoal drawings, and a handful of bronze busts; he was fascinated by sculpture. *The Acrobat*—painted only two years before Matisse's death—shows the artist at his minimalist best.

The floor above features sketches and models of Matisse's famous Chapel of the Rosary in nearby Vence (described in the Inland Riviera chapter) and related religious works. On the same floor, you might find paper cutouts from his *Jazz* or *Dance* series, more bronze sculptures, various personal objects, and linen embroideries inspired by his travels to Polynesia.

Leaving the Museum: Before leaving the park, consider visiting the Franciscan **Monastery of Cimiez** (turn right out of the museum and cross the olive orchard). Enter its church to find two beautiful altarpieces by Louis Bréa and savor the flowery gardens and sublime views. Otherwise, turn left from the museum into the park, exiting at the Archaeological Museum, and turn right at the street. The bus stop across the street is for bus #33, which heads to Port Lympia. For bus #5 (frequent service to downtown and the Chagall Museum), continue walking—with the Roman ruins on your right—to the small roundabout, and find the shelter (facing downhill).

Modern and Contemporary Art Museum
(Musée d'Art Moderne et d'Art Contemporain)

This ultramodern museum features an explosively colorful, far-out, yet manageable collection focused on American and European American artists from the 1960s and 1970s (Pop Art and New Realism are highlighted. The exhibits cover three floors, one of which is devoted to temporary shows. The permanent collection includes a few works by Andy Warhol, Roy Lichtenstein, and Jean Tinguely. You should also find rooms dedicated to Yves Klein and Niki de Saint Phalle. English explanations are posted in some rooms, and there's a good timeline of Riviera artists from 1947 to 1977. The temporary exhibits can be as appealing to modern-art lovers as the permanent collection: Check the museum website for what's playing. Don't leave without exploring the views from the rooftop terrace.

Cost and Hours: Covered by All Museums Pass; Tue-Sun 10:00-18:00, Nov-April from 11:00, closed Mon year-round; near Vieux Nice on Promenade des Arts, +33 4 93 62 61 62, www.mamac-nice.org.

Fine Arts Museum (Musée des Beaux-Arts)

Housed in a sumptuous Riviera villa with lovely gardens, this museum lacks a compelling collection but holds 6,000 artworks from the 17th to 20th century. Start on the first floor and work your way up to enjoy paintings by Sisley, Bonnard, and Raoul Dufy, as well as a few sculptures by Rodin and Carpeaux.

Cost and Hours: Covered by All Museums Pass; Tue-Sun 10:00-18:00, Nov-April from 11:00, closed Mon year-round; at the western end of Nice—take T-2 tram to the Centre Universitaire

Méditerranéen and follow sign up the big stairs; 33 Avenue des Baumettes; +33 4 92 15 28 28, www.musee-beaux-arts-nice.org.

Archaeological Museum (Musée Archéologique)

This museum displays various objects from the Romans' occupation of this region. It's convenient if you're visiting the Matisse Museum—but is of little interest except to ancient Rome aficionados. Entry includes access to the poorly maintained Roman bath ruins (find the English handouts).

Cost and Hours: Covered by All Museums Pass, daily 10:00-18:00, Nov-April until 17:00 and closed Tue, near Matisse Museum at 160 Avenue des Arènes de Cimiez, +33 4 93 81 59 57.

NICE

Masséna Museum (Musée Masséna)

Like Nice's main square, this museum was named in honor of Jean-André Masséna (born in Antibes), a highly regarded commander during France's Revolutionary and Napoleonic wars. The beachfront mansion is worth a look for its lavish decor and lovely gardens alone (for English explanations, try the QR code at the ticket desk).

Cost and Hours: Covered by All Museums Pass, gardens always free, Wed-Mon 10:00-18:00, Nov-April from 11:00, closed Tue year-round, 35 Promenade des Anglais, +33 4 93 91 19 10.

Visiting the Museum: There are three levels. The elaborate reception rooms on the ground floor host occasional exhibits and give the best feeling for aristocratic Nice from 1860, when it joined France, until World War I (find Masséna's portrait to the right).

The first floor up, offering a folk-museum-like look at Nice through the years, deserves most of your time. Start in a small room dedicated to the museum's namesake, Jean-André Masséna, then find Napoleonic paraphernalia, including the emperor's vest and sword, and Josephine's impressive cape and tiara. Moving counterclockwise around the floor, find bric-a-brac of the aristocracy and antique posters promoting vacations in Nice—look for the model and photos of the long-gone La Jetée Promenade and its casino, Nice's first. You'll see paintings of some of the Russian and British nobility who appreciated Nice's climate (including imperious Queen Victoria, who single-handedly transformed the region from a backwater to a destination resort for the rich and noble, igniting tourism in Nice for all classes). You'll eventually see a dashing painting honoring Italian patriot and Nice favorite Giuseppe Garibaldi, then find a room with images of Nice before the Promenade des Anglais was built and before the town's river was covered over by Place Masséna. The top floor is a painting gallery with temporary exhibits.

The gardens on the seaward side of the museum house a memorial to the 86 people who died in the terrorist attack on the Promenade des Anglais in 2016.

OTHER SIGHTS IN NICE
▲Russian Cathedral (Cathédrale Russe)

Nice's Russian Orthodox church—claimed by some to be the finest outside Russia—is worth a visit. Five hundred rich Russian fami-

lies wintered in Nice in the late 19th century, and they needed a worthy Orthodox house of worship. Dowager Czarina Maria Feodorovna and her son, Nicholas II, offered the land and construction began in 1903. Nicholas underwrote much of the project and gave this church to the Russian community in 1912. (A few years later, Russian comrades who *didn't* winter on the Riviera assassinated him.) Here in the land of olives and anchovies, these proud onion domes seem odd. But, I imagine, so did those old Russians.

Cost and Hours: Free; daily 9:00-18:00, no visits during services (often 12:00-14:00), chanted services Sat at 18:00, Sun at 10:00; free guided tours in the afternoon with the French Riviera Pass; no shorts or bare shoulders (shawls available), Avenue Nicolas II, +33 4 93 96 88 02, www.sobor.fr.

Getting There: It's a 15-minute walk from the train station, or ride the T-2 tram to the Alsace-Lorraine stop. You'll approach the church from Avenue Gambetta and walk under the train tracks, then follow signs leading immediately to the left. Or take bus #8 from Place Masséna (northwest corner of Galleries Lafayette) and get off at the Thiers-Gambetta stop.

Visiting the Cathedral: Before entering, enjoy the exterior done in the "old Russian" style, inspired by 16th- and 17th-century Russian religious architecture. Russian President Vladimir Putin funded the fine restoration of the facade. The park around the church stays open at lunch and makes a nice setting for picnics. There's also clean (pay) WC.

Step inside. The one-room interior is filled with icons and candles, and traditional Russian music adds to the ambience. The wall of icons (iconostasis) divides the spiritual realm from the temporal world of the worshippers. Only the priest can walk between the two worlds, by using the "Royal Door."

Get close to the altar and take a look at items lining the front. In the left corner, look for the icon of St. Nicholas, the most venerated one in the cathedral. On the right, find a striking icon of Our Lady of Kazan, painted on wood and set in an array of silver and precious stones. The Archangel Michael with red boots and wings—the protector of the Romanov family—stands over a symbolic tomb of Christ a little right of center (on the doors used only by the priests).

The tall, black, hammered-copper cross commemorates the massacre of Nicholas II and his family in 1918. Notice the Jesus icon to the right of the Royal Door. According to a priest here, as worshippers meditate, staring deep into the eyes of Jesus, they enter a lake where they find their souls. Surrounded by incense, chanting, and your entire community...it could happen. Closer in on the right on the easel, the icon of the Virgin and Child is decorated with semiprecious stones from the Ural Mountains. Artists worked a triangle into each iconic face—symbolic of the Trinity.

▲Castle Hill (Colline du Château)

This hill—in an otherwise flat city center—offers sensational views over Nice, the port (to the east, created for trade and military use in the 15th century), the foothills of the Alps, and the Mediterranean. The views are best early, at sunset, or whenever the weather's clear.

Nice was founded on this hill. Residents were crammed onto the hilltop until the 12th century as life in the flatlands below was too risky. Today you'll find a tower (Tour Bellanda, where the elevator is), playground, two cafés, ruins of Nice's first cathedral, and two intriguing cemeteries (one Jewish and one Christian)—but no castle—on Castle Hill.

Cost and Hours: Park is free and closes at 20:00 in summer, earlier off-season.

Getting There: You can get to the top by foot, by elevator (free, daily 9:00-19:00, until 20:00 in summer, Oct-March 10:00-18:00, next to beachfront Hôtel Suisse), or by pricey tourist train (see "Tours in Nice," earlier).

See the "Promenade des Anglais Walk" for a pleasant stroll that ends near Castle Hill.

Leaving Castle Hill: After enjoying the views and hilltop fun, you can walk via the cemetery directly down into Vieux Nice (just follow the signs), descend to the beach (via the elevator or a stepped lane next to it), or hike down the back side to Nice's port (departure point for boat trips and buses to Monaco and Villefranche-sur-Mer).

NICE

EXCURSION FROM NICE
Narrow-Gauge Train into the Alps
(Chemins de Fer de Provence)

Leave the tourists behind and take the scenic train-bus-train combination that runs between Nice and Digne through canyons, along whitewater rivers, and through tempting villages (4/day, departs Nice from Chemins de Fer de Provence station, two blocks from the Libération T-1 tram stop, 4 Rue Alfred Binet, +33 4 97 03 80 80, www.cpzou.fr/train-des-pignes-vapeur).

An appealing stop on the scenic railway is little **Entrevaux,** a good destination that feels forgotten and still stuck in its medieval shell (about €25 round-trip, rail passes not accepted, 1.5 scenic hours from Nice). Cross the bridge, meet someone friendly, and consider the steep hike up to the town citadel.

Nightlife in Nice

The city is a walker's delight after dark. I can't get enough of the night scene on Place Masséna or the fountains lining Promenade du Paillon. Promenade des Anglais, Cours Saleya, and Vieux Nice are also worth an evening wander.

Nice's bars play host to a happening late-night scene, filled with jazz, rock, and trolling singles. Most activity focuses on Vieux Nice. Rue de la Préfecture and Place du Palais are ground zero for bar life, though Place Rossetti and Rue Droite are also good targets. **Distilleries Ideales** is a good place to start or end your evening, with a lively international crowd, a Pirates of the Caribbean interior, and a *Cheers* vibe (lots of beers on tap, 24 Rue de la Préfecture, where it meets Rue de la Poissonnerie—see "Vieux Nice Hotels & Restaurants" map, happy hour 18:00-21:00). **Wayne's Bar** and others nearby are happening spots for the younger, Franco-Anglo backpacker crowd (15 Rue Préfecture). Along the Promenade des Anglais, the classy 37 Prom bar at the recommended **Hôtel Negresco** is fancy-cigar old English with frequent live jazz.

To savor fine views over Nice, find the **Hôtel Aston La Scala**: Its sixth-floor "club" lounge has comfy seats with grand views over old Nice, but the seventh-floor outdoor bar/terrace wins for a drink any night, and offers jazz and blues on many Thursdays, Fridays, and Saturdays (daily, sixth floor open 11:00-late, seventh floor open from 18:00, on the Promenade du Paillon at 12 Avenue Félix Faure, +33 4 92 22 20 06).

Sleeping in Nice

Don't look for charm in Nice. Seek out a good location and modern, reliable amenities (like air-conditioning). Prices generally drop considerably November through March and sometimes in April, but go sky-high during the Nice Carnival (February), the Cannes Film Festival (May), and Monaco's Grand Prix (late May). Between the film festival and the Grand Prix, the second half of May is slammed. Nice is also one of Europe's top convention cities, and June is convention month here.

I've focused my sleeping recommendations on three areas: city center, Vieux Nice, and near the Promenade des Anglais. Those in the city center are between the train station and Place Masséna (easy access to the train station and Vieux Nice via the T-1 tram, 15-minute walk to Promenade des Anglais). Those in Vieux Nice are between Place Masséna and the sea (below the Promenade du Paillon, good access to the sea at Quai des Etats-Unis). And those near the Promenade des Anglais are farther west, between Boulevard Victor Hugo and the sea (a classier and quieter area easily reached by the T-2 tram, offering better access to the sea but longer walks to the train station and Vieux Nice). For parking, ask your hotelier, or see "Arrival in Nice—By Car" on page 314.

IN THE CITY CENTER

The train station area offers Nice's cheapest sleeps, but the neighborhood feels sketchy after dark. The cheapest places are older, well worn, and come with some street noise. Places closer to Avenue Jean Médecin are more expensive and in a more comfortable area.

$$$ Hôtel du Petit Palais** is a little belle-époque jewel with 25 handsome rooms tucked neatly into a residential area on the hill several blocks from the Chagall Museum. It's bird-chirping peaceful and plush, with tastefully designed rooms, a garden terrace, and small pool. You'll walk 15 minutes down to Vieux Nice (or use bus #5). Free street parking is usually easy to find (17 Avenue Emile Bieckert, +33 4 93 62 19 11, www.petitpalaisnice.com, reservation@petitpalaisnice.com).

$$ Hôtel Vendôme* gives you a whiff of the belle époque, with pastel pinks, high ceilings, and grand staircases in a mansion set off the street. The modern rooms come in all sizes; many have balconies (limited pay parking—book ahead, 26 Rue Pastorelli at the corner of Rue Alberti, +33 4 93 62 00 77, www.hotel-vendome-nice.com, contact@hotel-vendome-nice.com).

$ Hôtel Durante* rents quiet rooms in a happy orange

NICE

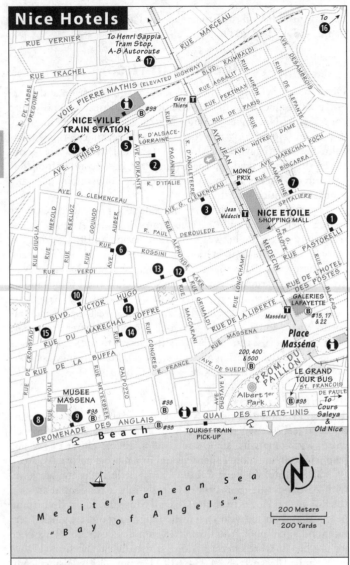

Nice Hotels

1. Hôtel Vendôme
2. Hôtel Durante
3. Hôtel St. Georges
4. Hôtel Ibis Nice Centre Gare
5. Hôtel Belle Meunière
6. B&B Nice Home Sweet Home
7. Auberge de Jeunesse les Camélias Hostel
8. Hôtel Negresco
9. Hôtel West End
10. Hôtels Splendid & Gounod
11. Hôtel Villa Victoria
12. Hôtel Le Grimaldi
13. Hôtel Carlton
14. Hôtel les Cigales
15. Hôtel Victor Hugo
16. To Hôtel du Petit Palais
17. To Chemins de Fer Station

building with rooms wrapped around a flowery courtyard. The rooms have adequate comfort (mostly modern decor), and all but two overlook the well-maintained patio. The price is right, and the parking is free on a first-come, first-served basis (family rooms, 16 Avenue Durante, +33 4 93 88 84 40, www.durante.nice. hotelescotedazur.com, info@hotel-durante.com).

$ Hôtel Ibis Nice Centre Gare,*** 100 yards to the right as you leave the station, provides a secure refuge in this seedy area. It's big (200 rooms), modern, has well-configured rooms and a pool, and is next to a handy parking garage (bar, café, 14 Avenue Thiers, +33 4 93 88 85 55, www.ibis.com, h1396@accor.com).

$ Hôtel Belle Meunière,* a block below the train station, in an old mansion built for Napoleon III's mistress, attracts budget-minded travelers with cheap rates. Simple but well kept, the place has adequate rooms and charismatic Mademoiselle Marie-Pierre presiding with her perfect English (family rooms, air-con, no elevator but just 3 floors, laundry service, limited pay parking, 21 Avenue Durante, +33 4 93 88 66 15, www.bellemeuniere.com, hotel. belle.meuniere@cegetel.net).

Hostel: The fun, good-value ¢ **Auberge de Jeunesse les Camélias** has a handy location, modern facilities, and lively evening atmosphere. Rooms accommodate four to eight people and come with showers and sinks—WCs are down the hall; private rooms for up to three people are available (includes breakfast, rooms closed 11:00-15:00 but can leave bags, laundry, kitchen, safes, bar, 3 Rue Spitalieri, +33 4 93 62 15 54, www.hihostels.com, nice-les-camelias@hifrance.org.).

NEAR THE PROMENADE DES ANGLAIS

These hotels are close to the beach. The Negresco and West End are big, vintage Nice hotels that open onto the sea from the heart of the Promenade des Anglais.

$$$$ Hôtel Negresco***** owns Nice's most prestigious address on the Promenade des Anglais and knows it. Still, it's the kind of place that if you were to splurge just once in your life... Rooms are opulent (see my "Promenade des Anglais Walk" for more description), tips are expected, and the clientele looks spendy (some view rooms, *très* classy bar, 37 Promenade des Anglais, +33 4 93 16 64 00, www.hotel-negresco-nice.com, reservations@ lenegresco.com).

$$$$ Hôtel West End**** opens onto the Promenade des Anglais with formal service and decor, classy public spaces, and high prices (some view rooms, 31 Promenade des Anglais, +33 4 92 14 44 00, www.westendnice.com, reservation@westendnice.com).

$$$ Hôtel Splendid**** is a worthwhile splurge if you miss your Marriott. The panoramic rooftop pool, bar/restaurant, and breakfast room almost justify the cost...but throw in plush rooms, a free gym, and spa services, and you're as good as at home (pay parking, 50 Boulevard Victor Hugo, +33 4 93 16 41 00, www.splendid-nice.com, info@splendid-nice.com).

$$$ Hôtel Villa Victoria** is a service-oriented place managed by cheery and efficient Marlena and her staff, who welcome travelers into a classy old building with a spacious lobby overlooking a sprawling and wonderful rear garden-courtyard. Rooms are comfortable and well kept, but those facing the street come with some noise (limited pay parking, 33 Boulevard Victor Hugo, +33 4 93 88 39 60, www.villa-victoria.com, contact@villa-victoria.com).

$$$ Le Grimaldi** is a lovely place with a beautiful lobby and 48 spacious rooms with high ceilings and tasteful decor (big breakfast extra, a few suites and connecting rooms ideal for families, 15 Rue Grimaldi, +33 4 93 16 00 24, www.le-grimaldi.com, info@le-grimaldi.com).

$$ Hôtel Gounod* is a fine value behind Hôtel Splendid. Because the two share the same owners, Gounod's guests are allowed free access to Splendid's pool, hot tub, and other amenities. Most rooms are quiet, with high ceilings and traditional decor (family rooms, pay parking, 3 Rue Gounod, +33 4 93 16 42 00, www.gounod-nice.com, info@gounod-nice.com).

$$ Hôtel Carlton* is a good deal. It's a well-run, unpretentious, and comfortable place with spacious, simply decorated rooms, many with decks (26 Boulevard Victor Hugo, +33 4 93 88 87 83, www.hotel-carlton-nice.com, info@hotel-carlton-nice.com, helpful Lionel at reception).

$$ Hôtel les Cigales,* a few blocks from the Promenade des Anglais, is a sweet little place with 19 richly colored rooms and a cool upstairs terrace, all well managed by friendly Veronique and Eliane (RS%, 16 Rue Dalpozzo, +33 4 97 03 10 70, www.hotel-les-cigales.fr, www.hotel-lescigales.com, infos@hotel-lescigales.com).

$ Hôtel Victor Hugo, a traditional and spotless seven-room hotel, is an adorable time-warp place where Gilles warmly welcomes guests. All rooms are on the ground floor and come with kitchenettes and air-conditioning. While it's a short walk from the Promenade des Anglais, it's a hefty walk from Vieux Nice (RS%, includes breakfast, 59 Boulevard Victor Hugo, +33 4 93 88 12 39, www.hotel-victor-hugo-nice.com, contact@hotel-victor-hugo-nice.com).

IN OR NEAR VIEUX NICE

Most of these hotels are either on the sea or within an easy walk of it. (Hôtel Lafayette and the Villa Saint Exupéry Beach hostel are more central).

$$$$ Hôtel la Perouse,** built into the rock of Castle Hill at the east end of the bay, is a fine splurge. This refuge-hotel is top-to-bottom flawless in every detail—from its elegant rooms (satin curtains, velour headboards) and attentive staff to its rooftop terrace with hot tub, sleek pool, and lovely **$$$$** garden restaurant. Sleep here to be spoiled and escape the big city (good family options, 11 Quai Rauba Capeu, +33 4 93 62 34 63, www.hotel-la-perouse.com, lp@hotel-la-perouse.com).

$$$$ Hôtel Suisse,**** below Castle Hill, has brilliant sea and city views—for a price. It's surprisingly quiet given the busy street below (most view rooms have balconies, 15 Quai Rauba Capeu, +33 4 92 17 39 00, www.hotels-ocre-azur.com, suisse@hoa-hotels.com).

$$$ Hôtel Albert 1er*** is a fair deal in a central, busy location on Albert I Park, two blocks from the beach and Place Masséna. The staff is formal and the rooms are well appointed and spotless, with heavy brown tones. Some have views of the bay, while others overlook the park or a quiet interior courtyard (4 Avenue des Phocéens, +33 4 93 85 74 01, www.hotel-albert-1er.com, info@hotel-albert1er.com).

$$$ Hôtel Mercure Marché aux Fleurs**** is ideally situated near the sea and Cours Saleya. Rooms are sharp and prices can be either reasonable or exorbitant (superior rooms worth the extra euros—especially those with views, standard doubles are tight, some beds in a loft set-up; 91 Quai des Etats-Unis, +33 4 93 85 74 19, www.hotelmercure.com, h0962@accor.com).

$$ Room With a Vue rents four well-designed rooms (several with small balconies) right on Cours Saleya above the Pain et Cie bakery/café where you check in (3 Louis Gassin, +33 4 93 62 94 32, roomwithavue@gmail.com, enthusiastic manager Fred).

$$ Hôtel Lafayette,*** located a block behind the Galeries Lafayette department store, is a modest place with 17 mostly spacious, well-configured, and good-value rooms. All rooms are one floor up from the street—some traffic noise sneaks in (RS%, 32 Rue de l'Hôtel des Postes, +33 4 93 85 17 84, www.hotellafayettenice.com, info@hotellafayettenice.com).

Hostel: ¢ Villa Saint Exupéry Beach is a sprawling place with more than 200 beds, split between a building with private rooms (figure **$**) and the hostel next door (dorms with 4-8 beds). The owners and many staff are English so communication is easy. The vibe is young and fun, with a bar, cheap restaurant, community kitchen, air-con, elevator, and *beaucoup* services including laundry, yoga classes, free walking tour of Vieux Nice, and scuba diving (no curfew, 6 Rue Sacha Guitry, +33 4 93 16 13 45, www.villahostels.com, info@villahostels.com).

NICE

Vieux Nice Hotels & Restaurants

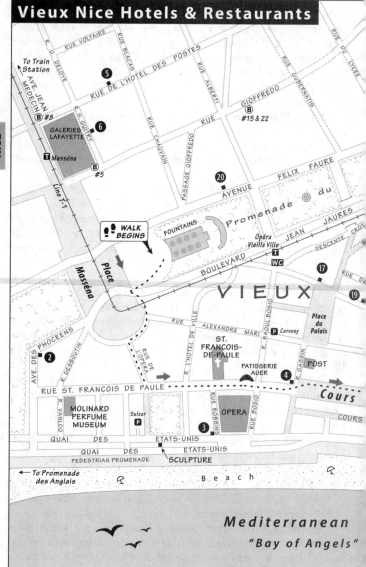

Accommodations

1. Hôtel la Perouse & Hôtel Suisse
2. Hôtel Albert 1er
3. Hôtel Mercure Marché aux Fleurs
4. Room With a Vue & Pain et Cie Bakery
5. Hôtel Lafayette
6. Villa Saint Exupéry Beach Hostel

Eateries, Nightlife & Other

7. Le Safari
8. Acchiardo
9. Le Panier
10. Citrus & Olive et Artichaut
11. Lavomatique
12. Peppino

NICE

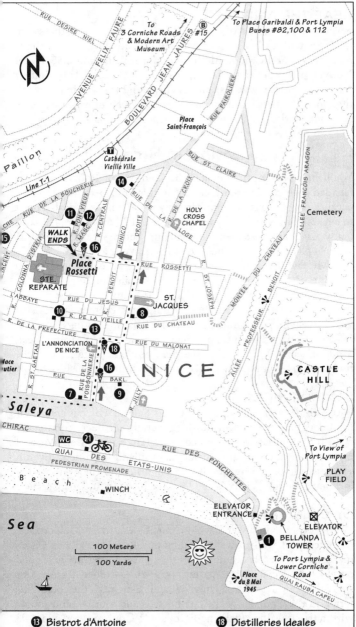

⑬ Bistrot d'Antoine	⑱ Distilleries Ideales
⑭ Oliviera	⑲ Wayne's Bar
⑮ Comptoir du Marché	⑳ Hôtel Aston La Scala Bar
⑯ Fenocchio Gelato (2)	㉑ Bike Rental
⑰ Oui, Jelato	

NEAR THE AIRPORT

Several airport hotels offer a handy and cheap port-in-the-storm for those with early flights or who are just stopping in for a single night: **$$ Hôtel Campanile** (www.campanile.fr) and **$$$ Hôtel Nouvel** (www.novotel.com) are closest; **$$ Hôtel Ibis Budget Nice Aéroport** (www.ibis.com) is cheap and a few minutes away, though two other Ibis hotels are closer and a bit pricier. Free shuttles connect these hotels with both airport terminals.

Eating in Nice

You'll find plenty of regional dishes and lots of Italian influence blended with classic French cuisine in this Franco-Italian city. Just because you're in a resort, don't lower your standards. Locals expect to eat well and so should you. Sundays and Mondays are tricky as many places are closed—check the hours before you get your heart set on a place and always be ready to book a day ahead.

My favorite dining spots are in Vieux Nice. It's well worth booking ahead for these places (think about booking in person while you take the "Vieux Nice Walk"). If Vieux Nice is too far, I've listed some great places handier to your hotel. Promenade des Anglais is ideal for picnic dinners on warm, languid evenings or a meal at a beachside restaurant. For a more romantic and peaceful meal, head for nearby Villefranche-sur-Mer (see next chapter). Avoid the fun-to-peruse but terribly touristy eateries lining Rue Masséna.

IN VIEUX NICE

Nice's dinner scene converges on Cours Saleya, which is entertaining enough in itself to make the generally mediocre food a fair deal. It's a fun, festive spot to compare tans and mussels. Most of my recommendations are on side lanes inland from here. Even if you're eating elsewhere, wander through here in the evening. For locations, see the "Vieux Nice Hotels & Restaurants" map, earlier.

On Cours Saleya

While local foodies would avoid Cours Saleya like a McDonald's, the energy of wall-to-wall restaurants taking over Vieux Nice's market square each evening is enticing. **$$ Le Safari** is a good option for Niçois cuisine, pasta, pizza, and outdoor dining. This sprawling café-restaurant, convivial and rustic with the coolest interior on the Cours, is packed with locals and tourists, and staffed with hurried waiters (daily noon to late, 1 Cours Saleya, +33 4 93 80 18 44, www.restaurantsafari.fr).

Characteristic Places in Vieux Nice

$$ Acchiardo is a homey but lively eatery that mixes loyal clientele with hungry tourists. As soon as you sit down you know this is a treat. It's a family affair overseen by Jean-François and Raphael Acchiardo. A small plaque under the menu outside says the restaurant has been run by father and son since 1927. The food is delicious and copious, and the house wine is good and reasonable (Mon-Fri 19:00 until late, closed Sat-Sun and Aug, often a line out the door, reservations smart, indoor seating only, 38 Rue Droite, +33 4 93 85 51 16).

$$ Le Panier, a short block off Cours Saleya but a world apart, is a sweet place that greets you with a few outdoor tables and a soft white dining room in a mezzanine above an open kitchen. The chef offers refined seafood dishes from octopus to sea bream, and a few tasty meat options (closed Tue-Wed, 5 Rue Barillerie, +33 4 89 97 14 37).

Near the Cathedral of Ste. Réparate

The next few places sit a stone's throw from the Cathedral of Ste. Réparate in the very thick of old Nice, each offering a different yet equally enticing dining experience. You're smart to arrive right when they open or, better, book ahead (a day or two is usually fine) for these top places. All are welcoming and easy to work with.

$$ Citrus is an oasis of calm in this lively area with soft lighting, a warm interior, and comfortable seating. The cuisine mixes refined classic French and Niçois French cuisine with creative touches. The outside chalkboard menu is translated in English so you know what you're getting into (closed Mon-Tue, 7 Rue Sainte-Réparate, +33 4 93 16 27 93).

$$$ Olive et Artichaut is a sharp bistro-diner with a small counter, black-meets-white floor tiles, and a foodie vibe. You'll find carefully prepared Mediterranean dishes with tasty twists. Owner Aurelie works the front of the house while her husband Thomas works *la cuisine* (book several days ahead, closed Sun-Mon, 6 Rue Sainte-Réparate, +33 4 89 14 97 51, www.oliveartichaut.com).

$ Lavomatique, named for the launderette that once thrived here, is a top choice for a fun meal of cleverly composed "small plates" that are a joy to share. There's a lively commotion to the place where you'll rub shoulders with (generally younger) locals while the chefs prepare dishes in front of you in an open kitchen. Come early, land a spot at the counter, and put yourself in owner Gregoire's capable hands (closed Sat-Sun, 11 Rue du Pont Vieux, +33 4 93 55 54 18).

$ Peppino, run by one French owner and one Italian owner, has to be the friendliest place in town. There are a few tables outside, but the fun lies inside where you'll dine in what feels like a funky antique shop with simple tables and chairs. The cuisine favors mama's Italian recipes (the lasagnas are amazing), though you'll find some classic French dishes as well (good charcuterie plates). Arrive right at 6:30 when it opens or book a few days ahead for later times (closed Tue-Wed, 8 Rue du Pont Vieux, +33 4 93 80 41 12).

$$ Bistrot d'Antoine has appeal inside and out. It's a warm, vine-draped place whose menu emphasizes affordable Niçois cuisine and good grilled selections. It's popular, so call a day or two ahead to reserve a table. The upstairs room is quieter than the outdoor tables and ground-floor room (closed Sun-Mon, 27 Rue de la Préfecture, +33 4 93 85 29 57).

Lunch and Olive Oil Tasting

$$ Oliviera venerates the French olive. This fun shop/restaurant offers olive oil tastings and a menu of Mediterranean dishes paired with specific oils (like a wine pairing). Adorable owner Nadim speaks excellent English, knows all of his producers, and provides animated "Olive Oil 101" explanations with your meal. It's a good place for vegetarians—try his guacamole-and-apple dish; the pesto is also excellent (lunch only, closed Sun-Mon, cash only, 8 bis Rue du Collet, +33 4 93 13 06 45).

And for Dessert...

Gelato lovers should save room for the tempting ice-cream stands in Vieux Nice (open daily until late). **Fenocchio** is the city's favorite, with mouthwatering displays of dozens of flavors ranging from lavender to avocado (two locations: 2 Place Rossetti and 6 Rue de la Poissonnerie). Gelato connoisseurs should head for **Oui, Jelato,** where quality is the priority rather than selection (5 Rue de la Préfecture, on Place du Palais).

IN THE CITY CENTER
Near Nice Etoile, on Rue Biscarra

An appealing lineup of bistros overflowing with outdoor tables stretches along the broad sidewalk on Rue Biscarra (just east of Avenue Jean Médecin behind Nice Etoile). Come here to dine with area residents away from most tourists. Peruse the choices—they're all different and reservations are normally not needed.

Near Place Masséna

$ L'Ovale takes its name from the shape of a rugby ball. Come here for an unpretentious and local café-bistro experience. Animated owner David serves traditional dishes from southwestern France (rich and meaty). Dining is inside only. Consider the *cassoulet* or the hearty *salade de manchons* with duck and walnuts (daily, 29 Rue Pastorelli, +33 4 93 80 31 65).

$$$ Les Sens ("The Senses") is a handsome restaurant with

NICE

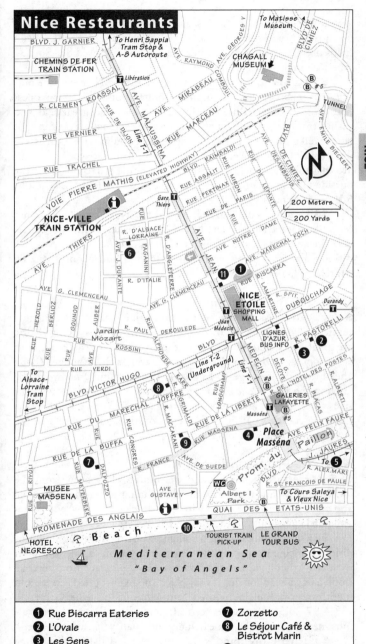

Nice Restaurants

1. Rue Biscarra Eateries
2. L'Ovale
3. Les Sens
4. La Maison de Marie
5. To Comptoir du Marché
6. Voyageur Nissart
7. Zorzetto
8. Le Séjour Café & Bistrot Marin
9. Crêperie Bretonne
10. Restaurant Le Galet
11. Grocery

a wine-bar-meets-bistro feel, serving classic French fare at reasonable prices (good three-course *menus*). Welcoming owner Gauvain helps non-French speaking diners feel at home (closed Sat-Sun, 37 Rue Pastorelli, +33 9 81 06 57 00).

$$ La Maison de Marie is a rare find in Nice—a welcoming, reasonably priced restaurant that offers something for modest and gourmet diners alike. The fixed-price *menu* is a great deal, and dishes from *la carte* offer a good choice of regional specialties that come well garnished. It's a bustling place, popular with locals seeking a special experience, but don't let that intimidate you—the staff are easygoing and helpful. It's worth booking a day ahead for the outside tables though the interior tables are candlelit-classy (daily, 5 Rue Masséna, +33 4 93 82 15 93).

$$ Comptoir du Marché, named for its red wooden counter, feels like a wine shop-meets-bistro-meets-bakery with cozy ambience in and out. It's at a busy pedestrian corner and serves traditional French cuisine with a smile (closed Sun-Mon, 8 Rue du Marché, +33 4 93 13 45 01).

Near the Train Station

$ Voyageur Nissart has blended good-value cuisine with friendly service since 1908. Kind owner Max and his able assistant Cédric are great hosts, and the quality of their food makes this place both very popular and a good choice for travelers on a budget (book ahead, leave a message in English). Try anything *à la niçoise,* including the fine *salade niçoise* (good three-course *menus,* inexpensive wines, indoor and outdoor seating, closed Mon, a block below the train station at 19 Rue d'Alsace-Lorraine, +33 4 93 82 19 60, www.voyageurnissart.com).

Near the Promenade des Anglais

$$$ Zorzetto is a relaxed and welcoming place away from the tourist fray. While the name sounds Italian, the cuisine is regional and creative, with a focus on what's fresh (closed Tue-Wed, indoor and outdoor seating, 3 Rue Dalpozzo, +33 4 89 24 83 14).

$$$ Le Séjour Café is a romantic bistro delivering fine, traditional cuisine to appreciative diners in a warm, candlelit interior with rich colors and fine glassware, or on a pleasant front terrace. Book a day ahead for this dressy place and expect good service and mouthwatering cuisine (closed Sun-Mon, 11 bis Rue Grimaldi, +33 4 97 20 55 36, www.sejourcafe.com). The **Bistrot Marin** almost next door has the same owners and quality (closed Tue-Wed).

$ Crêperie Bretonne is the only *crêperie* I list in Nice. Dine on the broad terrace or inside, with relaxed service and jukebox-meets-gramophone ambience. Their top-end, house-special crêpes are creative and enticing. Split a salad to start—try the goat cheese salad with honey (closed Sun, on Place Grimaldi, +33 4 93 82 28 47).

Dining on the Beach

$$$ Restaurant Le Galet is your best eat-on-the-beach option. The city vanishes as you step down to the beach. The food is nicely presented, and the tables feel elegant, even at the edge of the sand. Arrive for the sunset and you'll have an unforgettable meal (open for dinner May-mid-Sept, 3 Promenade des Anglais, +33 4 93 88 17 23). Sunbathers can rent beach chairs and have drinks and meals served literally on the beach (lounge chairs-€16/half-day, €19/day).

NICE

Nice Connections

GETTING AROUND THE RIVIERA

Nice is perfectly situated for exploring the Riviera by public transport. Monaco, Eze-le-Village, Villefranche-sur-Mer, Antibes, Vence, and St-Paul-de-Vence are all within about a one-hour bus or train ride. With a little planning, you can link key destinations in an all-day circuit (for example: Nice, Monaco, and Eze-le-Village or La Turbie, then loop back to Nice). For a comparison of train and bus connections from Nice to nearby coastal towns, see the "Public Transportation in the French Riviera" sidebar on page 306. It's also possible to take a boat to several destinations in the Riviera.

By Train

From Nice-Ville Station to: Cannes (2/hour, 30 minutes), **Antibes** (2/hour, 20 minutes), **Villefranche-sur-Mer** (2/hour, 10 minutes), **Eze-le-Village** (2/hour, 15 minutes to Eze-Bord-de-Mer, then infrequent bus #83 to Eze, 8/day, 15 minutes), **Monaco** (2/hour, 20 minutes), **Menton** (2/hour, 35 minutes), **Grasse** (15/day, 1 hour).

By Bus

To connect to regional destinations, use the following bus lines and stops. Most buses to regional destinations depart from tram stops at the edges of town (see the "Nice" map for tram-stop locations). A Nice bus ticket, all-day pass, or 10-ride pass is good for some nearby destinations (such as Villefranche-sur-Mer, Cap Ferrat, and Eze-le-Village); for destinations farther from Nice, you'll need a different ticket called a Ticket Azur. For more info on buses in the Riviera, see page 304 and www.lignesdazur.com.

Eastbound Buses: Trams T-1 and/or T-2 will get you close to these stops.

Bus #100 runs from Nice's Port Lympia through **Villefranche-sur-Mer** (3-4/hour, 20 minutes), **Monaco** (1 hour), and **Menton**

(1.5 hours). To find the #100 bus stop from the Port Lympia T-2 station, cross the tracks and climb the steps, then cross the busy street and keep straight along Rue Pacho for a short block.

Bus #15 runs to **Villefranche-sur-Mer** (2-3/hour, 15 minutes) and around **Cap Ferrat** (30 minutes to **St-Jean-Cap-Ferrat**). Catch the bus at the Promenade des Arts bus stop (near the Modern and Contemporary Art Museum) or Port Lympia tram stop. To find the #15 bus stop at Port Lympia, cross the tram tracks, climb the steps and cross the busy street, then turn right. The stop is around the first corner to the left.

These buses leave from the Gare Routière at the Vauban T-1 tram stop (turn right off the tram and take your first left): Buses #82 and #112 to **Eze-le-Village** (about hourly, only #82 runs on Sun, 30 minutes). For **La Turbie,** bus #116 runs 4/day (40 minutes, Sun leaves from Pont Michel T-1 tram stop).

Westbound Buses: Take the T-2 tram to the Parc Phoenix stop to catch these buses (bus stops are parallel to the tram stop). Bus #200 goes to **Antibes** (4/hour Mon-Sat, 2/hour Sun, 1.5 hours) and **Cannes** (2 hours). Bus #400 heads to **St-Paul-de-Vence** (2/hour, 45 minutes) and **Vence** (1 hour). Bus #9 also serves **Vence** (4/hour, 1 hour). Bus #500 goes to **Grasse** (2/hour, 1 hour).

By Boat

In summer, Trans Côte d'Azur offers scenic trips several days a week from Nice to Monaco and Nice to St-Tropez. Boats leave in the morning and return in the evening, giving you all day to explore your destination. Drinks and WCs are available on board.

Boats to **Monaco** depart at 9:30 and 16:00, and return at 11:00 and 18:00. The morning departure can be combined with the late-afternoon return from Monaco, allowing you a full day with Prince Albert II (€40 round-trip, €30 if you don't get off in Monaco, 45 minutes each way, June-Sept Tue, Thu, and Sat only).

Boats to **St-Tropez** depart at 9:00 and return at 16:30 (€70 round-trip, 2.5 hours each way; early July-Aug daily; late May-early July and Sept Tue, Thu, and Sat-Sun only).

Reservations are required for both boats, and tickets for St-Tropez should be booked in advance (+33 4 92 98 71 30, www.trans-cote-azur.com). The same company also runs one-hour round-trip cruises along the coast to Cap Ferrat (see listing under "Tours in Nice," earlier).

GETTING TO DESTINATIONS BEYOND THE RIVIERA
By Long-Distance Bus and Train

Blablabus and Flixbus run long-distance bus service from Nice; see

"Transportation" in the Practicalities chapter. Compare schedules and fares with trains.

Most long-distance train connections from Nice to other French cities require a change in Marseille. The Intercité train to Bordeaux (serving Antibes, Cannes, Toulon, and Marseille—and connecting from there to Arles, Nîmes, and Carcassonne) requires a reservation.

From Nice by Train to: Marseille (18/day, 2.5 hours), **Cassis** (hourly, 3 hours, one transfer), **Arles** (11/day, 4-5 hours, most require transfer in Marseille or Avignon), **Avignon** (10/day, most by TGV, 4 hours, many require transfer in Marseille), **Lyon** (hourly, 4.5 hours, may require change, night train available), **Paris** Gare de Lyon (hourly, 6.5 hours, may require change), **Aix-en-Provence** TGV Station (10/day, 3-4 hours, usually changes in Marseille), **Chamonix** (4/day, 11 hours, requires multiple changes), **Beaune** (7/day, 7 hours, 1-2 transfers), **Florence** (6/day, 8 hours, 1-3 transfers), **Milan** (hourly, 6 hours, several transfers), **Venice** (7/day, 9-13 hours, 1-3 transfers), **Barcelona** (2/day via Montpellier or Valence, 9 hours, more with multiple changes).

By Plane

Nice's easy-to-navigate airport (Aéroport de Nice Côte d'Azur, code: NCE, www.nice.aeroport.fr) is 30 minutes west of the city center and literally in the Mediterranean, with landfill runways. The two terminals are far apart, but linked by frequent shuttle buses and the T-2 tram (both free for this connection). Both terminals have airport info desks, banks, ATMs, and trams and buses to seaside destinations. Terminal 2 has car rental and a bus station across from the main entry (see below for destinations served). Planes leave roughly hourly for Paris (one-hour flight, about the same price as a train ticket).

Linking the Airport and City Center

By Taxi/Uber: There's a flat-rate taxi fee of €32 to the center of Nice, but Nice's airport taxis are notorious for overcharging—consider Uber as it should be cheaper. Otherwise, by taxi allow €60 to Villefranche-sur-Mer, €70 to Antibes, and about €5 more at night and on weekends (small fee for bags). Before riding, confirm your fare. It's always a good idea to ask for a receipt *(reçu)*. There's no designated Uber pickup zone; arrange a pickup location with your driver.

By Tram: The T-2 tram serves both airport terminals and runs frequently into Nice (allow 30 minutes), and at €1.50 it's a swinging deal. The tram is handy for those sleeping at hotels near the Promenade des Anglais and Place Masséna. If you're heading to the airport from Nice, make sure the tram reads *Airport* since the line splits—don't take one heading to *Cadam*.

By Airport Shuttle: These services vary in reliability but can be cost-effective for families or small groups. Airport shuttles are better for trips from your hotel to the airport, since they require you to book a precise pickup time in advance. Shuttle vans offer a fixed price (about €30 for one person, a little more for additional people or to Villefranche-sur-Mer). Your hotel can arrange this, and I would trust their choice of company.

Linking the Airport and Nearby Destinations by Tram/Bus
To get to **Villefranche-sur-Mer** from the airport, take the T-2 tram to the last stop (Port Lympia). There, you can use the same ticket to transfer to buses #15 or #100 (see "Nice Connections—By Bus," earlier).

To reach **Antibes,** take bus #250 from either terminal (about 2/hour, 40 minutes, €11). For **Cannes,** take bus #210 from either terminal (1-2/hour, 50 minutes on freeway, €22). Express bus #110 runs from the airport directly to **Monaco** (2/hour, 50 minutes, €22). **Flixbus** and **Blablabus** serve destinations farther afield and stop at Terminal 2.

By Cruise Ship
Nice's port is at the eastern edge of the town center, below Castle Hill; the main promenade and Vieux Nice are on the other side of the hill. Cruise ships dock at either side of the mouth of this port: Terminal 1 to the east or Terminal 2 to the west.

Getting into the City Center: The T-2 tram connects Port Lympia to the city center and airport. To reach the start of my "Vieux Nice Walk" or to catch a bus to the Chagall or Matisse museums (#5), take the tram to the Jean Médecin stop, then transfer to the T-1 tram to Place Masséna.

If arriving at Terminal 2 and heading to Vieux Nice, you can stroll directly there by heading around the base of the castle-topped hill, with the sea on your left (10-15 minutes).

A **taxi** from the terminals is about €25 to points within Nice; the **hop-on, hop-off bus** has a stop at the top of the port (see page 319).

Getting to Nearby Destinations: To visit Villefranche-sur-Mer or Monaco, it's best to take **bus #100** (the train is faster, but the bus stop is much closer to Nice's port). The bus stops along the top of the port at 9 Rue Fodéré (see "Nice" map at the beginning of this chapter).

To take the **train** to Villefranche-sur-Mer, Monaco, Antibes, Cannes, or elsewhere, ride the T-2 tram to the Jean Médecin stop, transfer to the T-1 line, and ride it to the Gare Thiers stop (one long block to the main train station). You can also take a **taxi** to these destinations.

EAST OF NICE

Villefranche-sur-Mer •
The Three Corniches •
Cap Ferrat • Eze-le-Village

Between Nice and Monaco lies the Riviera's richest stretch of real estate, paved with famously scenic roads (called the Three Corniches) and dotted with cliff-hanging villages, million-dollar vistas, and sea-splashed walking trails connecting beach towns. Fifteen minutes east of Nice, little Villefranche-sur-Mer stares across the bay to woodsy and exclusive Cap Ferrat. The eagle's-nest Eze-le-Village and the Corniche-topping Le Trophée des Alpes survey the scene from high above.

PLANNING YOUR TIME

I'd spend one day in Villefranche-sur-Mer and Cap Ferrat, and a second day in Monaco and either Eze-le-Village or La Turbie (or both if you're efficient).

If you only have one day, spend it in Villefranche-sur-Mer and Monaco: Those using Nice or Villefranche-sur-Mer as a home base can take the bus and follow my self-guided bus tour to Monaco (see the end of this chapter), arriving in Monaco in time for a quick tour of the casino when it's quieter, then witness the changing of the guard at 11:55. If you're returning to Nice, take the train or bus back to Villefranche-sur-Mer and follow my self-guided walk (then consider having an early dinner there before returning to Nice). If you're sleeping in Villefranche-sur-Mer, return from Monaco by bus via Eze-le-Village, spend the late afternoon there, then take a bus or taxi back to Villefranche.

Drivers can connect these destinations with some scenic driving along the Corniche roads.

Villefranche-sur-Mer

In the glitzy world of the Riviera, Villefranche-sur-Mer offers travelers an easygoing slice of small-town Mediterranean life. From

here, convenient day trips let you gamble in Monaco, saunter the Promenade des Anglais in Nice, indulge in seaside walks and glorious gardens in Cap Ferrat, and savor views from Eze-le-Village and the Grande Corniche.

Villefranche-sur-Mer feels more Italian than French—pastel orange buildings line steep, narrow lanes that spill into the sea, and linguine is on most menus. Luxury yachts glisten in the bay, while cruise ships make regular calls to Villefranche-sur-Mer's deep harbor, creating periodic rush hours of frenetic shoppers and bucket-listers. Sand-pebble beaches, a handful of interesting sights, and quick access to Cap Ferrat keep other visitors just busy enough.

Originally a Roman port, Villefranche-sur-Mer was overtaken by fifth-century barbarians. Villagers fled into the hills, where they stayed and farmed their olives. In 1295 the Duke of Provence—like many in coastal Europe—needed to stand up to the Saracen Turks. He enticed the olive farmers to move from the hills down to the water and establish a front line against the invaders, thus denying the enemy a base from which to attack Nice. In return for tax-free status, they stopped farming, took up fishing, and established a *Ville-* (town) *franche* (without taxes). Since there were many such towns, this one was specifically "Tax-free town on the sea" *(sur Mer)*. In about 1560, the Duke of Savoy built an immense, sprawling citadel in the town. And today, while the town has an international following, two-thirds of its 8,000 people call it their primary residence. That makes Villefranche-sur-Mer feel more like a real community than neighboring Riviera towns.

Orientation to Villefranche-sur-Mer

TOURIST INFORMATION

The TI is just off the road that runs between Nice and Monaco, located in a park (Jardin François Binon) below the Nice/Monaco bus stop, labeled *Octroi* (July-Aug daily 9:00-18:00; Sept-June Mon-Sat 9:00-12:00 & 13:00-17:00, closed Sun; +33 4 93 01 73

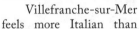

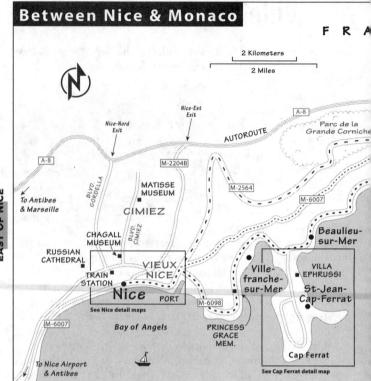

Between Nice & Monaco

F R A

EAST OF NICE

2 Kilometers
2 Miles

Parc de la Grande Corniche

A-8

Nice-Nord Exit

Nice-Est Exit

AUTOROUTE

M-2204B

M-2564

M-6007

MATISSE MUSEUM

CIMIEZ

CHAGALL MUSEUM

RUSSIAN CATHEDRAL

BLVD. GORBELLA

BLVD. CIMIEZ

To Antibes & Marseille

A-8

TRAIN STATION

Nice

VIEUX NICE

PORT

See Nice detail maps

Bay of Angels

M-6098

PRINCESS GRACE MEM.

Ville-franche-sur-Mer

Beaulieu-sur-Mer

VILLA EPHRUSSI

St-Jean-Cap-Ferrat

Cap Ferrat

See Cap Ferrat detail map

M-6007

To Nice Airport & Antibes

68, www.villefranche-sur-mer.com). Pick up bus schedules and info on sightseeing boat rides. The TI has brochure-maps showing seaside walks around Villefranche and neighboring Cap Ferrat and information on the Villa Ephrussi de Rothschild.

ARRIVAL IN VILLEFRANCHE-SUR-MER

By Bus: Get off at the Octroi stop. To reach the old town, walk past the TI along Avenue Général de Gaulle, take the first stairway on the left, turn right at the street's end, then make a sharp left to U-turn down the long ramp just after the crosswalk. The hop-on, hop-off bus from Nice stops at the citadel (see page 319).

By Train: Not all trains stop in Villefranche-sur-Mer (you may need to transfer to a local train in Nice or Monaco). Ville-franche-sur-Mer's train station is just above the beach, a 15-minute stroll from the old town and most of my recommended hotels (taxis usually won't take such a short trip).

By Car: From Nice's port, follow signs for *Menton, Monaco,* and *Basse Corniche.* In Villefranche-sur-Mer, turn right at the TI (first signal after Hôtel la Flore) for parking and hotels. For a quick visit to the TI, park at the pay lot just below the TI. You'll pay to

park in all public parking areas except from 12:00 to 14:00 and 19:00 to 9:00. Street parking around the citadel is reasonable (about €1.50/hour) but the lot at the harbor is pricey (Parking Wilson, €26/day). Some hotels have their own parking, but most charge.

By Plane: Allow an hour to connect from Nice's airport to Villefranche-sur-Mer (for details, see page 367).

By Cruise Ship: See "Villefranche-sur-Mer Connections," later.

HELPFUL HINTS

Market Days: A fun bric-a-brac market enlivens Villefranche-sur-Mer on Sundays (on Place Amélie Pollonnais by Hôtel Welcome, and in Jardin François Binon by the TI). On Saturday and Wednesday mornings, a market sets up in Jardin François Binon. A small trinket market springs to action on Place Amélie Pollonnais whenever cruise ships grace the harbor.

E-Bike Rental: The adventurous can try **Eco-Loc** e-bikes as an alternative to taking the bus to Cap Ferrat, Eze-le-Village, or even Nice. You get about 25 miles on a fully charged battery (after that you're pedaling; €25/half-day, €35/day, mid-April-

Sept daily 9:00-17:00, deposit and ID required, best to reserve 24 hours in advance; helmets, locks, and baskets available; pick up bike by the cruise terminal entrance at the port, +33 6 66 92 72 41, www.ecoloc06.fr).

Hop-On, Hop-Off Bus Tour: Le Grand Tour Bus provides a 16-stop hop-on, hop-off service that connects Villefranche-sur-Mer with Nice (see page 319).

Spectator Sports: Lively *boules* action takes place each evening just below the TI and the huge soccer field.

GETTING AROUND VILLEFRANCHE-SUR-MER

By Bus: Electric **minibus #80** runs from the waterfront up the main drag along the Low Corniche road *(Basse Corniche)* to upper Villefranche on the Middle Corniche road *(Moyenne Corniche)*. At best it only goes once per hour but saves you the sweat of walking uphill (and gets you within a 15-minute walk of the fort, described later); handy stops are Place Amélie Pollonnais (by the cruise terminal), the Octroi stop on the Low Corniche road (Avenue Foch), and at the Col de Villefranche stop, near Hôtel la Fiancée du Pirate (for buses to Eze-le-Village). The bus continues to the outlying suburban Nice Riquier train station (€1.50, runs daily 7:00-19:00, schedule posted at stops and available at TI).

By Taxi/Uber: Taxis wait between the cruise terminal and Place Amélie Pollonnais. Beware of taxi drivers who overcharge. Normal weekday, daytime rates to outside destinations should be about €22 to Cap Ferrat, €40 to central Nice or Eze-le-Village, and €70 to the airport or Monaco. For a reliable taxi, call **Didier** (+33 6 15 15 39 15). General taxi +33 4 93 55 55 55. Uber is less present here than in Nice so you may wait a bit longer.

Villefranche-sur-Mer Town Walk

For tourists, Villefranche is a tiny, easy-to-cover town that snuggles around its harbor under its citadel. This quick self-guided walk laces together everything of importance, starting at the waterfront near where cruise-ship tenders land and finishing at the citadel.

• *If arriving by bus or train, you'll walk five minutes to the starting point. Go to the end of the short pier directly in front of Hôtel Welcome, where we'll start with a spin tour (spin to the right) to get oriented.*

The Harbor: Look out to sea. Cap Ferrat, across the bay, is a landscaped paradise where the 1 percent of the 1 percent compete for the best view. The Rothschild's once-pink, now soft-orange mansion, Villa

Ephrussi (roughly straight across, hugging the top) is the most worthwhile sight to visit in the area (local officials recently required it be painted orange to match local color tones even though its original color was pink—the baroness' favorite). To its right, in the saddle of the hill, the next big home, with the red-tiled roof, belongs to Paul Allen. Geologically, Cap Ferrat is the southern tip of the Alps. The range emerges from the sea here and arcs all across Europe, over 700 miles, to Vienna.

Today, ships bring tourists rather than pirates. The bay is generally filled with beautiful yachts. (In the evenings, you might see well-coiffed captains being ferried in by dutiful mates to pick up statuesque call girls.) Local guides keep a list of the world's 100 biggest yachts and talk about some of them as if they're part of the neighborhood.

At 2,000 feet, this is the deepest natural harbor on the Riviera and was the region's most important port until Nice built its own in the 18th century. Greek, Roman, and American naval ships appreciated the setting. In fact, the United States Sixth Fleet called Villefranche-sur-Mer's port home for almost 20 years. The biggest cruise ships drop their hooks here rather than in Nice or Monaco. The tiny jetty is the landing point for the cruise-ship tenders that come ashore each morning in season.

Close on the hill to the right, the 16th-century citadel (where this walk ends) is marked by flags. Much closer, the yellow fisherman's chapel (with the little-toe bell tower) has an interior painted by Jean Cocteau. Hôtel Welcome offers the balconies of dreams. Peer up the skinny lane just right of the hotel for a glimpse of the baroque facade of St. Michael's Church and bell tower. The waterfront, lined by fancy fish restaurants, curves right, to the town beach. Fifty yards above the beach stands the train station and above that, supported by arches on the right, is the Low Corniche road *(Basse Corniche)*, which leads to Monaco. Until that road was built in the 1860s, those hills were free of any development all the way to Monaco. The big yellow building just above can be rented for €300,000 a month (as Madonna did once for a birthday).

• *Leave the pier and walk left 20 yards past the last couple of fishing boats surviving from the town's once-prominent fishing community to find a small bronze bust of Jean Cocteau, the artist who said, "When I look at Villefranche, I see my youth." A few more steps take you to the little chapel he painted.*

Chapel of St. Pierre (Chapelle Cocteau): This chapel is the town's cultural highlight. Cocteau, who decorated the place, was a Parisian transplant who adored little Villefranche-sur-Mer and whose career was distinguished by his work as an artist, poet, novelist, playwright, and filmmaker. Influenced by his pals Marcel Proust, André Gide, Edith Piaf, and Pablo Picasso, Cocteau was a

Villefranche-sur-Mer

EAST OF NICE

To Eze-Le-Village & Monaco via Middle Corniche Road

BLVD. DE LA CORNE D'OR

To Nice

BLVD. LAZARE SETTIMELLI

AVE. DE LA BARMASSA

AVE. DES OEILLETS

To B #80 & 3

AVE. BARMASSA

CAMPO QUADRO STAIRS

R. VICTOIRE

100 Meters
100 Yards

AVE. ALBERT 1ER

AVE. SADI CARNOT

7

POST

AVE. DE GEN. LECLERC

AVE. M. JOFFRE

AVE. VERDUN

AVE. DE GRANDE BRETAGNE

T

15 B Octroi

B 14

i WC

AVE. DE GAULLE

AVE. FOCH

Jardin Binon

P

ALLEE DU DUVAL

P

PLAY AREA

RUE DE LA CITADELLE

P

AVE. DE SAINT-ESTEVE

BLVD. PRINCESSE GRACE DE MONACO

AVE. D. L. MALMAISON

2

PETANQUE COURTS

AVE. DE GAULLE

Jardin Narvick

Sainte-Estève

Sainte-Estève

AVENUE DE GAULLE

To Mont-Alban Fort (on foot) & Nice via Low Corniche Road

To Sentier du Littoral

9

4

QUAI P. L. CORDERIE

PLAY AREA

Port de la Darse

To Beaulieu-sur-Mer, Eze-Bord-de-Mer & Monaco via Low Corniche Road

AVE. ALBERT 1ER

AVE. GEORGES CLEMENCEAU

RUE CONTESSO

R. VOLTI

R. MAY

BARON DE BRES

RUE DU POILU

CHEMIN DE LA FOÂN

AVE CLEM

TRAIN STATION

DES MARINIÈRES

Beach

To Cap Ferrat on foot

BEACH WALK

#80 ⑧

PROMENADE

QUAI COURBET

Place du Conseil

Bay of Villefranche-sur-Mer (Mediterranean Sea)

OLD

ST. MICHAEL'S

Place Poullan

Pl. de l'Eglise

RUE OBSCURE

QUAI

TOWN

❻

VALLON

ALBINI

SADI-CARNOT

GAMBETTA

Place Rep.

❺

❿

L'EGLISE

❶

❽

⓫

WALK BEGINS

AVE. M. JOFFRE

RUE BLAIS

QUAI COURBET

Place Pollonais

⓭

Port

B #80

CHAPEL OF ST. PIERRE

Ⓣ

⓬

P Wilson

GARE MARITIME (CRUISE TENDER DOCK)

Hop-On, Hop-Off B

WALK ENDS

CITADEL

CHEMIN DES DOUANIERS

SCENIC WALKWAY

Accommodations
❶ Hôtel Welcome
❷ Hôtel La Flore
❸ To Hôtel la Fiancée du Pirate
❹ Hôtel de la Darse

Eateries
❺ La Grignotière
❻ La Belle Etoile & Le Serre
❼ La Cantine de Tiflo
❽ La Mère Germaine
❾ La Trinquette
❿ Le Cosmo
⓫ Grocery

Other
⓬ Boat Rides & E-Bike Rental
⓭ Motor Boat Rental
⓮ Octroi Bus Stop (from Nice; to Monaco & Cap Ferrat)
⓯ Octroi Bus Stop (to Nice; from Monaco & Cap Ferrat)

leader among 20th-century avant-garde intellectuals. At the door, Marie-France—who is passionate about Cocteau's art—collects a €3 donation for a fishermen's charity. She then sets you free to enjoy the chapel's small but intriguing interior. She's delighted to give you a small tour if you ask (Wed-Sun 9:30-12:30 & 14:00-18:00, usually closed Mon-Tue, hours vary with cruise-ship traffic and season).

In 1955 Cocteau tattooed the barrel-vaulted chapel with heavy black lines and pastels. Each of Cocteau's Surrealist works—the Roma (Gypsies) of Stes-Maries-de-la-Mer who dance and sing to honor the Virgin, girls wearing traditional outfits, and three scenes from the life of St. Peter—is explained in English. Is that Ville-franche-sur-Mer's citadel in the scene above the altar?

• *From the chapel, turn right and stroll the harbor promenade 100 yards past romantic harborside tables.* **Restaurant La Mère Germaine** *is named for Mother Germaine, who famously took care of US Navy troops in World War II (step inside to see sketches and old photos on the wall). Immediately after the restaurant, a lane leads up into the old town. Walk up a few steps until you reach a long tunnel-like street.*

Rue Obscure, the Old Town, and St. Michael's Church: Here, under these 13th-century vaults, you're in another age. Turn right and walk to the end of Rue Obscure (which means "dark street"). Watch your head as the ceiling gets low. Wind up to the sunlight past a tiny fountain at Place du Conseil, and a few steps beyond that to a viewpoint overlooking the harbor.

Turn around and stroll back along the open lane past the fountain, and walk gently downhill. Notice the homes built over heavy arches. At Place des Deux Garçons (the square with a namesake restaurant), turn right on Rue May and climb the stepped lane. Take your first left at the recommended La Belle Etoile and La Serre restaurants to find St. Michael's Church, facing a delightful square with a single magnolia tree (Place de l'Eglise). The deceptively large church features an 18th-century organ, a particularly engaging crucifix at the high altar, and (to the left) a fine statue of a recumbent Christ—carved, they say, from a fig tree by a galley slave in the 1600s.

• *Leaving St. Michael's, go downhill halfway to the water, where you hit the little commercial street (Rue du Poilu) and turn right. Find your way through a sweet little square, then climb the pedestrian ramp on the left (browsing a real-estate window if you'd like to move here) and walk up to the...*

Citadel: The town's mammoth castle was built in the 1500s by the Duke of Savoy to defend against the French. When the region joined France in 1860, the castle became just a barracks. Since the 20th century, it's housed the police station, City Hall, a summer outdoor theater, and art galleries. The single fortified entry—originally a drawbridge over a dry moat (a.k.a. kill zone)—still leads into this huge complex.

The exterior walls slope thickly at the base, indicating that they were built in the "Age of Black Powder"—the 16th century—when the advent of gunpowder made thicker, cannonball-deflecting walls a necessity for any effective fortification. The bastions are designed for smarter crossfire during an attack. The inside feels vast and empty. If you wander around, you'll find a memorial garden for victims of World War II, five free and empty museums and galleries, a garden in the bastion, and the City Hall (which offers a free WC, as all City Halls in France are required to by law).

• *And that concludes our introductory walk. For a brilliant seaside stroll (described next), drop back down below the citadel to the harbor parking lot (Parking Wilson) and find the stone path that leads to the right.*

Activities in Villefranche-sur-Mer

▲▲Seafront Walks

Chemin des Douaniers: This seaside walkway, originally used by customs agents to patrol the harbor, leads under the citadel and connects the old town with the workaday harbor (Port de la Darse). At the port you'll find a few cafés, France's Institute of Oceanography (an outpost for the University of Paris oceanographic studies), and an 18th-century dry dock. This scenic walk turns downright romantic after dark.

Sentier du Littoral: Ambitious walkers can go all the way from Port de la Darse to Nice's Port Lympia. Figure two hours for this roughly cobbled, sea-swept, and sporty four-mile trail. While you could hike all the way into Nice and bus back, I wouldn't—the closer you get to Nice, the more stairs you'll find and there's a sizeable stretch along the main road with a narrow sidewalk; it's better to walk as far as you want then double back. To reach the trail, walk 15 minutes through the very long Port de la Darse, veering left at the little kiosk café. Following signs to *Plage de la Darse,* you'll pass a section of apartments before reaching the trail.

Beach Walk: You can also wander along the waterfront past the train station and along the beach. Especially in the early morning, this short walk yields postcard-perfect views back to Villefranche-sur-Mer (go before breakfast). You can even extend your walk to Cap Ferrat (see "Getting to Cap Ferrat," later).

Hike to Mont-Alban Fort

This fort, with a remarkable setting on the high ridge that separates Nice and Villefranche-sur-Mer, is a good destination for hikers (also accessible by car and bus; info at TI, fort interior closed to tourists). From the TI, gaze up at your destination hugging the hill high above, then walk on the main road toward Nice about 10 minutes past Hôtel La Flore (stay on the sidewalk on the left side of the road). Look on the right for wooden trail signs labeled *Escalier de Verre* and climb about 45 minutes as the trail makes long switchbacks through the woods up to the ridge. When you reach the paved lane, veer right to reach the fort and its sensational view terrace over Villefranche-sur Mer and Cap Ferrat. To visit with a much shorter hike, minibus #80 drops you a 15-minute walk away at the Col de Villefranche stop; bus #33 takes you within a few minutes of the fort (catch it at the Vauban T-1 tram stop in Nice).

Boat Rides (Promenades en Mer)

To view this beautiful coastline from the sea, consider taking a quick **sightseeing cruise** with AMV (€15-25, some stay in the bay, others go as far as Monaco, select days June-Sept, departs across from Hôtel Welcome, +33 4 93 76 65 65, www.amv-sirenes.com). You can also rent your own **motorboat** through Glisse Evasion (€65/hour for a small boat, larger boats available, www.location-bateaux-villefranche.fr).

Sleeping in Villefranche-sur-Mer

You have a handful of great hotels in all price ranges to choose from in Villefranche-sur-Mer. The ones I list have sea views from at least half of their rooms—well worth paying extra for.

$$$$ Hôtel Welcome** has the best location in Ville-franche-sur-Mer, and charges for it. Anchored seaside in the old town, with all of its 35 plush, balconied rooms overlooking the harbor and a lounge/wine bar that opens to the water, this place lowers my pulse and empties my wallet (pricey garage—must reserve, 3 Quai de l'Amiral Courbet, +33 4 93 76 27 62, www.welcomehotel.com, contact@welcomehotel.com).

$$ Hôtel La Flore** is a fine value—particularly if your idea of sightseeing is to enjoy a panoramic view from your spacious bedroom balcony (even street-facing rooms have nice decks). The hotel is warmly run and good for families. Several rooms in the annex sleep four and come with kitchenettes, views, and private hot tubs. It's a 10-minute uphill hike from the old town but parking is easy and secure (€10/day), and the bus stops for Nice and Monaco are close by (use the St. Estève stop; hotel on the main road at 5 Boulevard Princesse Grace de Monaco, +33 4 93 76 30 30, www.hotellaflore.fr, infos@hotellaflore.fr).

$$ Hôtel la Fiancée du Pirate** is a family-friendly view refuge high above Villefranche-sur-Mer on the Middle Corniche and a 15-minute walk to Mont-Alban Fort views (best for drivers, although it is on bus lines #80, #82, and #112 to Eze-le-Village and

Nice). Don't be fooled by the modest facade—Eric and Laurence offer 15 lovely and comfortable rooms, a large pool, a hot tub, a nice garden, and a terrific view lounge area. The big breakfast features homemade crêpes (RS%, laundry service, free parking, 8 Boulevard de la Corne d'Or, Moyenne Corniche/N-7, +33 4 93 76 67 40, www.fianceedupirate.com, info@fianceedupirate.com).

$ Hôtel de la Darse** is a shy little hotel burrowed in the shadow of its highbrow neighbors and the only budget option in Villefranche. It's a great value with handsome rooms, but isn't central—figure 10 scenic minutes of level walking to the harbor and a steep 15-minute walk up to the main road (minibus #80 stops in front; handy for drivers, free parking usually available close by). Seaview rooms are easily worth the extra euros (no elevator, +33 4 93 01 72 54, www.hoteldeladarse.com, info@hoteldeladarse.com). From the TI, walk or drive down Avenue Général de Gaulle (walkers should turn left on Allée du Colonel Duval into the Jardins de Narvik and follow steps to the bottom).

Eating in Villefranche-sur-Mer

Locals don't come here in search of refined cuisine and nor should you. For me, dining in Villefranche-sur-Mer is about comfort food, attitude, and ambience. Comparison-shopping is half the fun—make an event out of a predinner stroll through the old city. Saunter past the string of pricey candlelit places lining the waterfront and consider the smaller, less expensive eateries embed-

ded in the old town. For dessert, pop into a *gelateria,* and then enjoy a floodlit, after-dinner walk along the sea.

$$$ La Grignotière, hiding in the back lanes, features Mediterranean comfort food. Servings are generous and the food is good. Consider the giant helping of spaghetti and *gambas* (prawns) or the chef's personal-recipe bouillabaisse, all served by gentle Chantal (cozy seating inside, a few tables outside, daily, 3 Rue du Poilu, +33 4 93 76 79 83).

$$ La Belle Etoile is the romantic's choice, with a charming interior graced with white tablecloths and soft lighting. This intimate place, serving fine Mediterranean cuisine, is a few blocks above the harbor on a small lane (closed Tue-Wed, 1 Rue Baron de Brès, +33 4 97 08 09 41).

$ Le Serre, nestled in the old town near St. Michael's Church, is a simple, cozy place. Hardworking owners Mary and mama Sylvie serve well-priced dinners to a loyal local clientele and greets all clients with equal enthusiasm. Choose from the many thin crust pizzas (named after US states), salads, and meats. Try the *daube niçoise* meat stew or the great-value, three-course *menu* (open evenings only from 18:00, closed Mon, cheap house wine, 16 Rue de May, +33 4 93 76 79 91).

$$ La Cantine de Tiflo sits above the tourist fray behind St. Michael's Church, a few flights of stairs above the previous two listings. It merits the extra climb from the waterfront (though it's closer to the main road) for its delicious blend of Franco-Italo cuisine and friendly owners. You'll rub shoulders with locals here (good outside terrace, closed Sun-Mon, 2 Placce Charles II d'Anjou, +33 4 93 16 24 23).

$$$$ La Mère Germaine, right on the harbor, is the only place in town classy enough to lure a yachter ashore. It's dressy, with formal service and high prices. The name commemorates the current owner's grandmother, who fed hungry GIs during World War II (daily, reserve for harborfront table, 9 Quai de l'Amiral Courbet, +33 4 93 01 71 39).

$ La Trinquette is a relaxed, low-key place away from the fray on the "other port," next to the recommended Hôtel de la Darse (a lovely 10-minute walk from the other recommended restaurants). Gentle Jean-Charles runs the place with charm, delivering reliable cuisine, friendly vibes at good prices, and a cool live-music scene on weekends (daily in summer, closed Wed off-season, 30 Avenue Général de Gaulle, +33 4 93 16 92 48).

$$ Le Cosmo serves a broad range of brasserie fare on the town's appealing main square (daily, Place Amélie Pollonnais, +33 4 93 01 84 05).

Grocery Store: A handy **Casino** is a few blocks above Hôtel Welcome at 12 Rue du Poilu (Thu-Tue 8:00-12:30 & 15:30-19:30 except closed Sun afternoon and all day Wed).

Dinner Options for Drivers: If you have a car and are staying a few nights, take a short drive to Eze-le-Village or La Turbie for a late stroll, an early dinner, or a sunset drink (dining suggestions later in this chapter). If it's summer (June-Sept), the best option of all is to go across to a restaurant on one of Cap Ferrat's beaches, such as **$$$ Restaurant de la Plage de Passable** or **$$$ Plage de la Paloma** (see page 391) for a before-dinner drink or a dinner you won't soon forget.

Villefranche-sur-Mer Connections

For a comparison of connections by train and bus, see the "Public Transportation in the French Riviera" sidebar on page 306. If you're going to Nice's airport, take a cab or an airport shuttle van (see "Nice Connections," on page 367). Because buses are infrequent, make good use of taxis or Uber for a return trip.

BY TRAIN

Trains are faster and run later than buses (until 24:00). It's a level, 10-minute walk from the port to the train station.

From Villefranche-sur-Mer by Train to: Monaco (2/hour, 10 minutes), **Nice** (2/hour, 10 minutes), **Antibes** (2/hour, 40 minutes), **Eze-Bord-de-Mer** (2/hour, 5 minutes) then transfer to bus #83 for Eze-le-Village (see "Getting to Eze-le-Village," later).

BY BUS

In Villefranche-sur-Mer, the most convenient bus stop is Octroi, just above the TI.

Bus #15 runs from Villefranche-sur-Mer in one direction to **Nice** (15 minutes) and in the other direction through **Beaulieu-sur-Mer** (5 minutes) to **Cap Ferrat,** ending at the port in the village of **St-Jean** (15 minutes; for other transportation options, see "Getting to Cap Ferrat," later). The last bus departs from Nice around 20:15, and from St-Jean around 20:50.

Bus #100 runs along the coastal road from Villefranche-sur-Mer westbound to **Nice** (3-4/hour, 20 minutes) and eastbound to **Beaulieu-sur-Mer** (10 minutes), **Monaco** (40 minutes), and **Menton** (1.25 hours). The last bus from Nice to Villefranche leaves at about 21:00 and from Villefranche to Nice at about 22:00.

To reach **Eze-le-Village** by bus you have two choices: Walk or take bus #80 to the Col de Villefranche stop on the Middle Corniche (see "Villefranche-sur-Mer" map, earlier), then catch bus #82 or #112, which together provide about hourly service to Eze-le-Village (only #82 runs on Sun). You can also take bus #100 or #15 to the Baie du Fourmis stop in nearby Beaulieu-sur-Mer, then catch bus #83 to Eze-le-Village (8/day).

For more on these buses, including ticket info, routes, and frequencies, see page 304.

BY CRUISE SHIP

Tenders deposit passengers at a slick terminal building (Gare Maritime) at the Port de la Santé, right in front of Villefranche-sur-Mer's old town.

Getting into Town: It's easy to **walk** to various points in Villefranche-sur-Mer. The town's charming, restaurant-lined square is a straight walk ahead from the terminal, the main road (with the TI and bus stop) is a steep hike above, and the train station is a short stroll along the beach. **Minibus #80,** which departs from in front of the cruise terminal, saves you some hiking up to the main road and bus stop (described earlier).

Getting to Nearby Towns: To connect to other towns, choose between the **bus** or **train.** Leaving the terminal, you'll see directional sights pointing left, to *Town center/bus* (a 10-15 minute, steeply uphill walk to the Octroi bus stop with connections west to Nice or east to Monaco); and right, to *Gare SNCF/train station* (a 10-minute, level stroll with some stairs at the end). See train and bus connections earlier.

Taxis wait in front of the cruise terminal and charge exorbitant rates (minimum €15 charge to train station, though most will refuse such a short ride). For farther-flung trips, see the price estimates on page 374.

The Three Corniches

Nice, Villefranche-sur-Mer, and Monaco are linked by three coastal routes: the Low, Middle, and High Corniches. The roads are named for the decorative frieze that runs along the top of a building (cornice). Each Corniche (kor-neesh) offers sensational views and a different perspective. The villages and sights in this section are listed from west to east in the order you'll reach them when traveling from Villefranche-sur-Mer to Monaco.

The corniches are peppered with impressive villas such as La Leopolda, a sprawling estate with a particularly grand entry that's named for its 1930s owner, King Leopold II of Belgium (who owned most of the peninsula of Cap Ferrat in addition to this estate). Those driving up to the Middle Corniche from Villefranche-sur-Mer can look down on this yellow mansion and its lush garden, which fill an entire hilltop. The property was later owned by the Agnelli family (of Fiat fame and fortune), and then by the Safra family (Syrian and Brazilian bankers). Its current value is more than a half-billion dollars.

THE CORNICHE ROADS

For an overview of these three roads, see the "Between Nice & Monaco" map.

Low Corniche: The Basse Corniche (also called "Corniche Inférieure") strings ports, beaches, and seaside villages together for a traffic-filled ground-floor view. It was built in the 1860s (along with the train line) to bring people to the casino in Monte Carlo.

When this Low Corniche was finished, many hill-town villagers descended to the shore and started the communities that now line the sea. Before 1860, the population of the coast between Ville-franche-sur-Mer and Monte Carlo was zero. Think about that as you make the congested trip today.

Middle Corniche: The Moyenne Corniche is higher, quieter, and far more impressive. It runs through Eze-le-Village and provides breathtaking views over the Mediterranean, with several scenic pullouts.

High Corniche: Napoleon's crowning road-construction achievement, the Grande Corniche caps the cliffs with staggering views from almost 1,600 feet above the sea. Two thousand years ago, this was called the Via Aurelia, used by the Romans to conquer the West.

By Car

Drivers can find the three routes from Nice by driving up Boulevard Jean Jaurès, past Vieux Nice and the port. For the Low Corniche (to Villefranche-sur-Mer and Cap Ferrat), follow signs to *Monaco par la Basse Corniche,* which leads past Nice's port. The turnoff for the Middle Corniche *(Moyenne Corniche)* is shortly after the turnoff to the Low Corniche (follow *autoroute* signs). Signs for the High *(Grande)* Corniche appear a bit after that; follow D-2564 to *Col des 4 Chemins* and the *Grande Corniche.*

The Best Route from Nice to Monaco: This breathtaking drive, worth ▲▲▲, takes the Middle Corniche from Nice or Villefranche-sur-Mer to Eze-le-Village, then uphill for cloud-piercing, 360-degree views. Across from across Eze-le-Village's parking lot, follow *Parc de la Grande Corniche* signs uphill. Cross the Grande Corniche at the top and follow *Fort de la Revère* signs, where you'll find jaw-dropping views north to the Alps, straight down to the village, and along the Riviera from Naples to Barcelona (well, almost). Bring a picnic, as benches and tables are plentiful. Continue east from here back along the Grande Corniche to La Turbie, keeping an eye out for brilliant views back over Eze-le-Village, then finish by dropping down into Monaco.

By Bus

Buses travel along each Corniche; the higher the route, the less frequent the buses (see the "Between Nice & Monaco" map in this chapter). **Bus #100** runs along the **Low Corniche** from Nice to Monaco (3-4/hour). **Bus #112** provides the single best route to enjoy this area as it connects Monaco and Nice via Eze-le-Village along the **Middle Corniche** (6/day, none on Sun). **Bus #116** connects Nice with La Turbie along the **High Corniche** (4/day), and **bus #11** does the same from Monaco (6/day). There are no buses between Eze-le-Village and La Turbie (45-minute walk), though buses do connect Nice and Monaco with La Turbie.

If traveling by bus, follow my self-guided bus tour to Monaco (at the end of this chapter), then consider returning to Nice or Villefranche-sur-Mer by bus via Eze-le-Village, or to Nice via La Turbie (see "Monaco Connections" on page 416).

Cap Ferrat

This exclusive peninsula, rated ▲▲, decorates Villefranche-sur-Mer's views. Cap Ferrat is a peaceful eddy off the busy Nice-Monaco route (Low Corniche). You could spend a leisurely day on this peninsula, wandering the sleepy port village of St-Jean-Cap-Ferrat (usually called "St-Jean"), touring the Villa Ephrussi de Rothschild mansion and gardens, and walking on sections of the beautiful trails that follow the coast. If you owned a house here, some of the richest people on the planet would be your neighbors.

Tourist Information: The TI is at the harbor in St-Jean (Mon-Sat 9:30-18:00, Sun 10:00-17:30; Oct-April Mon-Sat 9:00-17:00, closed Sun; +33 4 93 76 08 90, www.saintjeancapferrat-tourisme.fr).

PLANNING YOUR TIME

Here's how I'd spend a day on the Cap: From Nice or Villefranche-sur-Mer, take bus #15 to the Villa Ephrussi de Rothschild stop (called Passable/Rothschild), then visit the villa. Walk 30 minutes, mostly downhill, to St-Jean for lunch (many options, including grocery shops for picnic supplies) and poke around the village. Take the 45-minute walk on the Plage de la Paloma trail (ideal for picnics). After lunch, take bus #15 or walk the beautiful 30-minute trail to the Villa Kérylos in Beaulieu-sur-Mer and maybe tour that villa. Return to Villefranche-sur-Mer, Nice, or points beyond by train or bus. (If you have a car, skip the loop drive around the peninsula; there's nothing to see from the road except the walls in front of homes owned by people whose challenge in life is keeping the public out.)

You can add Eze-le-Village to this day by taking bus #15 or walking the seaside trail from St-Jean-Cap-Ferrat to Beaulieu-sur-Mer (Plage Beaulieu stop), and transferring to bus #83 to Eze-le-Village (skip Villa Kérylos). Bus #83 only runs eight times day so check the schedule (www.lignedazur.com).

Here's an **alternative plan** for the star-gazing, nature-loving beach bum: Visit Villa Ephrussi, then walk to St-Jean for lunch, hike six miles clockwise around the entirety of Cap Ferrat (2-3 hours), and enjoy the late afternoon on the beach at Plage de Pass-

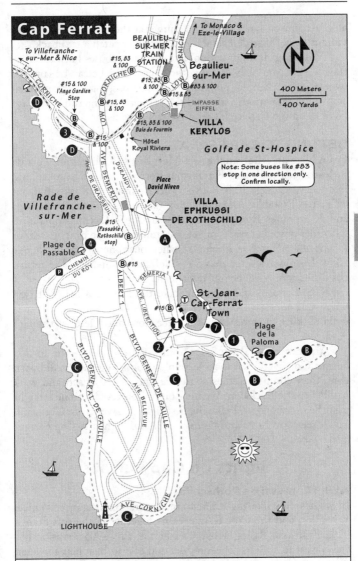

EAST OF NICE

Cap Ferrat

Accommodations & Eateries

1. Hôtel Brise Marine
2. Hôtel Oursin
3. Hôtel Patricia
4. Restaurant de la Plage de Passable
5. Plage de la Paloma Restaurant
6. Restaurant La Cabane de l'Ecailler & Grocery
7. Capitaine Cook Restaurant

Trails

A. St-Jean to Beaulieu-sur-Mer (30 minutes)
B. Plage de la Paloma Loop (45 minutes)
C. Plage de Passable to St-Jean (2-3 hours)
D. Walk to Villefranche-sur-Mer (1 hour)

able. At sunset, have a drink or dinner at the recommended Restaurant de la Plage de Passable, then walk or catch a taxi back.

Warning: In high season, late-afternoon buses back to Villefranche-sur-Mer or Nice along the Low Corniche can be jammed (worse on weekends), potentially leaving passengers stranded at stops for long periods. To avoid this, either take the train or board bus #15 on the Cap itself (before it gets crowded).

GETTING TO CAP FERRAT

From Nice or Villefranche-sur-Mer: Bus #15 (direction: Port de St-Jean) runs to all Cap Ferrat stops (for info on tickets, route, and frequency, see page 304). For the Villa Ephrussi de Rothschild, get off at the Passable/Rothschild stop (allow 30 minutes from Nice and 10 minutes from Villefranche-sur-Mer's Octroi stop). Find schedules posted at stops, or get one from a TI. The times listed for *Direction Le Port/Cap Ferrat* are when buses depart from Nice—allow 15 minutes after that for Villefranche-sur-Mer. The return bus (direction: Nice) begins in St-Jean.

Cap Ferrat is quick by **car** (take the Low Corniche) or **taxi** (allow €22 one-way from Villefranche-sur-Mer). You'll pay for metered parking in summer, but it's free from mid-October through April.

You can also **walk** an hour from Villefranche-sur-Mer to Cap Ferrat: Go past Villefranche's train station along the small beach lane, then climb the steps at the far end of the beach and walk parallel to the tracks on Avenue Louise Bordes. Continue straight past the mansions, and take the first right on Avenue de Grasseuil. You'll see signs to *Villa Ephrussi de Rothschild*, then to Cap Ferrat's port.

Sights on Cap Ferrat

▲Villa Ephrussi de Rothschild

In what seems like the ultimate in Riviera extravagance, Venice, Versailles, and the Côte d'Azur come together in the soft orange Villa Ephrussi. Rising above Cap Ferrat, this 1905 mansion has views west to Villefranche-sur-Mer and east to Beaulieu-sur-Mer. As you enter the grounds, look back and see the neighboring Villa Maryland, on an equally prominent high point surrounded by a private forest.

Cost and Hours: Palace and gardens-€16, includes excellent audioguide; daily 10:00-18:00, until 19:00 in summer, Nov-Jan Mon-Fri 14:00-18:00, Sat-Sun from 10:00; +33 4 93 01 33 09, www.villa-ephrussi.com.

Getting There: With luck, drivers can find a free spot to park along the entry road just inside the gate. The nearest bus stop is

Passable, just a few minutes after the bus turns onto Cap Ferrat (bus #15, 5-minute walk uphill to the villa). If returning to Nice or Villefranche-sur-Mer by bus, check the posted schedule, and keep in mind that you're only a minute from the time-point listed for Port de St-Jean.

Visiting the Villa: Buy your ticket at the side of the building with the gift shop and get the small map of the gardens, then walk to the main entrance and pick up an audioguide (which does not cover the gardens). Start with the well-furnished ground floor, where you'll see a variety of personal possessions, including those belonging to Béatrice, Baroness de Rothschild, the French banking heiress who built and furnished the place (such as her bathroom case for cruises). Upstairs, a 20-minute film (with English subtitles) describes life on the Riviera during the belle époque and gives good background on the life of the rich and eccentric baroness.

As you stroll through the upstairs rooms, you'll pass royal furnishings, the baroness' porcelain collection, and more. Her bedroom, sensibly, has views to the sea on both the port and starboard sides, and toward the bow, stretching like the prow of a vast cruise ship, is her garden. Don't miss the view from her private terrace.

The gorgeous **gardens** are why most come here. The ship-shaped gardens were inspired by Béatrice's many ocean-liner trips. She even dressed her small army of gardeners like sailors. Behind the mansion, stroll through the nine lush gardens re-created from locations all over the world—and with maximum sea views. Don't miss the Jardin Exotique's wild cactus, the rose garden at the far end, and the view back to the house from the "Temple of Love" gazebo. Cross the stepping-stone bridge by the playful fountains, if you dare.

An appropriately classy **$$ garden-tearoom** serves drinks and lunches with a view (12:00-17:30).

Walks from the Villa Ephrussi: It's a lovely 30-minute stroll, mostly downhill and east, from the Villa Ephrussi to the Villa Kérylos in Beaulieu-sur-Mer (described later) or to the port of St-Jean. To get to either, make a U-turn left at the stop sign below the Villa Ephrussi and follow signs along a small road toward the Hôtel Royal Riviera on Avenue Henri Honoré Sauvan (see "Cap Ferrat" map). Walk about five minutes down; when the road comes to a T, keep straight, passing a brown gate down a pedestrian path, which ends at the seafront trail (on Place David Niven)—go left to reach the Villa Kérylos, or head right to get to St-Jean. It's about 15 minutes to either destination once you join this seaside path.

To get to Plage de Passable from the Villa Ephrussi, turn left on the main road just below the villa (Avenue Denis Séméria); after 50 yards you'll find signs leading down to the beach.

St-Jean-Cap-Ferrat

This quiet harbor town lies in Cap Ferrat's center, yet is off most tourist itineraries and feels overlooked. St-Jean houses yachts, boardwalks, views, and bou-tiques packaged in a "take your time, darling" atmosphere. It's a few miles off the busy Nice-to-Monaco road—convenient for drivers. A string of restaurants lines the port, with just enough visitors and locals to keep them in business. St-Jean is especially peaceful at night. Sit on a whale-tail bench, enjoy the giant clam-shell flowerboxes, and work on your Cyrillic (as many signs come in Russian to cater to the needs of the town's wealthiest guests).

The stop for the bus back to Villefranche-sur-Mer is a half-block above the village center on Avenue Dénis Séméria and the taxi stand is next to the bus stop (+33 4 93 76 86 00). The hiking trail to Beaulieu-sur-Mer (with access to the Villa Ephrussi and Villefranche-sur-Mer for hard-core walkers) begins past the beach, to the left of the port as you look out to the water (details follow). If it's lunchtime, you'll find plenty of good options.

Eating in St-Jean: For picnics, the short pedestrian street in St-Jean has all you need (grocery store, bakery, charcuterie, and pizza to go), and you'll have no trouble finding portside or seaside seating. There's a big **Casino grocery** on the port below the main drag. Plage de la Paloma, described later, is a 10-minute walk away. Easygoing cafés and pizza joints with views over the port are easy to find.

$$$ Restaurant La Cabane de l'Ecailler, right on the har-bor, with fancy yachts for a view, is elegant and expensive but of-fers a reasonable two-course lunch on weekdays (Nouveau Port de Plaisance, +33 4 93 87 39 31).

$$ Capitaine Cook is a sweet little mom-and-pop place that takes its fish seriously yet seems to turn its back on the harbor (no views). There's a small patio out back and a cozy interior (good three-course *menu*, tasty *soupe de poisons* and bouillabaisse, closed Wed, a block uphill from the port toward Plage de la Paloma at 11 Avenue Jean Mermoz, +33 4 93 76 02 66).

Activities on Cap Ferrat

BEACHES
Plage de Passable
This pebbly little beach, located below the Villa Ephrussi, comes with great views of Villefranche-sur-Mer. It's a peaceful place, popular with families. One half is public (steps down are to the right of the Plage de Passable steps; free, snack bar, shower, WC), and the other is run by a small restaurant (€40-55—varies by how close you are to the sea, includes changing locker, lounge chair, and shower; reserve ahead in summer or on weekends as this is a prime spot, +33 4 93 76 06 17). If you want to experience the French Riviera rent-a-beach ritual, this is the place.

Parking near the beach (curbside or in a nearby lot) is tricky; plan on a healthy walk from your car to the beach and figure about €14/day in metered spots (free mid-Oct-April). Bus #15 stops a 10-minute walk uphill from the beach, near Villa Ephrussi.

For me, the best reason to come here is dinner. Arrive before sunset, then watch as darkness descends and lights flicker over Villefranche-sur-Mer's heavenly setting. **$$$ Restaurant de la Plage de Passable** is your chance to dine on the beach with romance and class (with good-enough food) while enjoying terrific views and the sounds of children still at play (daily late May-early Sept, always make a reservation, +33 4 93 76 06 17).

Plage de la Paloma
This half-private, half-public beach (described next) is a 10-minute walk from St-Jean-Cap-Ferrat. For €40 you get a lounge chair and the freedom to relax on the elegant side. Or enjoy the pebbly free beach (with shower and WC).

$$$ Plage de la Paloma Restaurant is inviting for dining on the beach, with salads for lunch and delicious, elegant dinners (daily from 12:00 and from 20:00, closed late Sept-Easter, +33 4 93 01 64 71, www.paloma-beach.com).

WALKS AROUND CAP FERRAT
The Cap is perfect for a walk; you'll find well-maintained and well-marked foot trails covering most of its length with three easy, mostly level options of varying lengths (worth ▲▲). The TIs in Villefranche-sur-Mer and St-Jean have maps of Cap Ferrat showing the walking paths, or you can use the following itineraries with this book's map.

Between St-Jean and Beaulieu-sur-Mer (30 minutes)
A level walk takes you past sumptuous villas, great views, and fun swimming opportunities. From St-Jean's port, walk along the harbor and past the beach with the water on your right. Head up the

steps to Promenade Maurice Rouvier and continue; before long you'll see smashing views of the whitewashed Villa Kérylos. You'll pass Gustave Eiffel's former home just before arriving at Villa Kérylos (look for the small sign).

To get from Beaulieu-sur-Mer to St-Jean or the Villa Ephrussi, start at the Villa Kérylos (with the sea on your left), walk toward the Hôtel Royal Riviera, and find the trail. If going to St-Jean, stay left at the Villa Sonja Rello (about halfway down); if going to the Villa Ephrussi, after about 20 minutes look for signs leading uphill at Place David Niven (walk up the path to Avenue Henri Honoré Sauvan, then keep going). If you're walking from St-Jean to the Villa Ephrussi, turn left off the trail at Place David Niven.

Plage de la Paloma Loop Trail (45 minutes)

A few blocks east of St-Jean's port, a scenic trail offers an easy sampling of Cap Ferrat's beauty. From the port, walk or drive about a quarter-mile east (with the port on your left, passing Hôtel La Voile d'Or); parking is available at the port or (if you're lucky) on streets near Plage de la Paloma. You'll find the trailhead where the road comes to a T. Cross the small gravel park *(Jardin de la Paix)* to start the trail, and do the walk counterclockwise. The trail is level and paved, yet uneven enough that good shoes are helpful. Plunk your picnic on one of the benches along the trail, or eat at the restaurant on Plage de la Paloma at the end of the walk (described earlier).

Plage de Passable Around the Cape to St-Jean (2-3 hours)

For a longer hike that circles the cape, follow the signs below the Villa Ephrussi marked *Plage Passable* (10 minutes downhill on foot from the villa, parking available nearby). Walk down to the beach (you'll pass the recommended Restaurant de la Plage de Passable—ideal for lunch), turn left, and cross the beach. Go along a paved road behind the apartment building, and after about 60 yards, take the steps down to the trail *(Sentier Littoral)*. Walk as far as you want and double back, or do the whole enchilada—it's about six miles (10 kilometers) around the cape. Near the end of the trail, you'll pass through the port of St-Jean, where you can take bus #15 back to the Plage de Passable/Villa Ephrussi stop, or ride to Villefranche-sur-Mer or to Nice.

Sleeping on Cap Ferrat

In St-Jean: While St-Jean is the main town serving the notoriously wealthy community of Cap Ferrat, it does have some affordable hotels.

$$$ Hôtel Brise Marine,*** graced with gardens and a sea-view terrace, is a peaceful retreat. Warmly run by Monsieur Maître-Henri, this aged mansion—with Old World character—feels lost in time. Most of its 16 comfortable rooms come with simple furnishings but fine views, and some have balconies—worth requesting (secure pay parking with reservation, between the port and Plage de la Paloma at 58 Avenue Jean Mermoz, +33 4 93 76 04 36, www.hotel-brisemarine.com, info@hotel-brisemarine.com).

$ Hôtel Oursin** is central in the village, with 13 well-priced rooms all on one floor. Run by quirky mother-and-son team Chantal and Aubrey, it's a humble place with white walls that feels more like a B&B than a hotel, though it does have air-con (1 Avenue Denis Séméria, +33 4 93 76 04 65, www.hoteloursin.com, reception@hoteloursin.com).

Between St-Jean and Villefranche-sur-Mer: Sitting across from Villefranche, at the start of Cap Ferrat, **$ Hôtel Patricia*** is a 20-minute walk to Villefranche or the Villa Ephrussi, and 10 minutes to Beaulieu-sur-Mer. Helpful owners Joelle and Franck provide 11 simple and homey rooms with eclectic decor (no elevator, air-con in some rooms, pay parking, near bus #100's l'Ange Gardien stop at 310 Avenue de l'Ange Gardien, +33 4 93 01 06 70, www.hotel-patricia.riviera.fr, hotel.lavillapatricia@gmail.com).

Villa Kérylos

The village of Beaulieu-sur-Mer, right on the Low Corniche road (just after Cap Ferrat), is busy with traffic and tourists. It's a good

place to pick up the hiking trail to Cap Ferrat sights and to visit the unusual Villa Kérylos. In 1902, an eccentric millionaire modeled his mansion after a 200-BC Greek villa from the island of Delos. No expense was spared in re-creating this Greek fantasy, from the floor mosaics to Carrara marble columns to exquisite wood furnishings modeled on discoveries made in Pompeii. The rain-powered shower is fun (but from a later time), and the included audioguide will increase your Greek

IQ. The mosaic workshop—open only high season and weekend afternoons—offers a chance to test your talents.

Cost and Hours: €12, includes audioguide; daily 10:00-19:00, Oct-May until 17:00; +33 4 93 01 47 29, www.villakerylos.fr.

Getting There: Drivers should park near the casino in Beaulieu-sur-Mer, not on the villa's access road. **Buses** #15 and #100 drop you at the Villa Kérylos stop at the villa's access road (for details on these buses, see page 305). **Trains** (2/hour, 10 minutes from Nice or Monaco) leave you a 10-minute walk away: Turn left out of the train station and left again down the main drag, then follow signs. The **walking trail** from Villa Kérylos to Cap Ferrat and the Villa Ephrussi de Rothschild begins on the other side of the bay, beneath Hôtel Royal Riviera.

Eze-le-Village

Capping a peak high above the sea, flowery and flawless Eze-le-Village (pronounced "ehz"; don't confuse it with the seafront town of Eze-Bord-de-Mer) is entirely consumed by tourism. This *village d'art et de gastronomie* (as it calls itself) is home to perfume outlets, stylish boutiques, steep cobbled lanes, and magnificent views. Touristy as it Eze, its stony state of preservation and magnificent hilltop setting over the Mediterranean affords a fine  memory. Day-tripping by bus to Eze-le-Village from Nice, Monaco, or Villefranche-sur-Mer works well. While Eze-le-Village can be tranquil early and late, during the day it is mobbed by cruise-ship and tour-bus groups. Come very early or late in the day.

GETTING TO EZE-LE-VILLAGE

There are two Ezes: Eze-le-Village (the spectacular hill town on the Middle Corniche) and Eze-Bord-de-Mer (a modern beach resort far below the "village" of Eze). Parking in Eze-le-Village may be a headache as construction is underway for a new underground garage, during which you may be directed to a remote lot with a free shuttle bus.

From Nice and upper Villefranche-sur-Mer, buses #82 and #112 together provide about hourly service to Eze-le-Village (only #82 runs on Sun, 30 minutes from Nice).

From Nice, Villefranche-sur-Mer, or Monaco, you can also take the train or the Nice-Monaco bus (#100) to Eze-Bord-de-Mer, getting off at the Gare d'Eze stop. From there, take the infrequent #83 shuttle bus straight up to Eze-le-Village (8/day, daily about 9:00-18:00, schedule posted at stop, 15 minutes). Those coming from Villefranche-sur-Mer can also take buses #15 or #100 and transfer to bus #83 at the Plage Beaulieu stop in Beaulieu-sur-Mer.

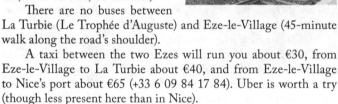

To connect Eze-le-Village directly with Monte Carlo in Monaco, take bus #112 (6/day Mon-Sat, none on Sun, 20 minutes).

There are no buses between La Turbie (Le Trophée d'Auguste) and Eze-le-Village (45-minute walk along the road's shoulder).

A taxi between the two Ezes will run you about €30, from Eze-le-Village to La Turbie about €40, and from Eze-le-Village to Nice's port about €65 (+33 6 09 84 17 84). Uber is worth a try (though less present here than in Nice).

Orientation to Eze-le-Village

Tourist Information: The helpful TI is adjacent to Eze-le-Village's main parking lot, just below the town's entry. Ask here for bus schedules. Call at least a week in advance to arrange a €12, one-hour English-language tour of the village that includes its gardens (TI open daily 9:00-12:00 & 13:00-18:00, July-Aug until 19:00, Nov-March until 17:00 and closed Sun, Place de Gaulle, +33 4 93 41 26 00, www.eze-tourisme.com).

Helpful Hints: The stop for **buses** to Nice is across the road by the Avia gas station, and the stops for buses to Eze-Bord-de-Mer and Monaco are on the village side of the main road, near the Casino grocery. Public **WCs** are just behind the TI and in the village behind the church.

Eze-le-Village Walk

This self-guided walk gives you a quick orientation to the village.

• *From the TI, hike uphill into the town. You'll come to an exclusive hotel gate and the start of the Nietzsche Path, a steep trail down to the beach, marked* Eze/Mer. *For a panoramic view and an ideal picnic perch, side-trip 90 steps down this path (for details, see "Hike to Eze-Bord-de-Mer," later). Continuing up into the village, find the steps immediately after the ritzy hotel gate and climb to...*

Place du Centenaire: In this minuscule square, a stone plaque in the flower bed (behind the candy stand) celebrates the 100th anniversary of the 1860 plebiscite, the time when all 133 Eze residents voted to leave the Italian Duchy of Savoy and join France. A town map here helps you get oriented.

• *Now pass through the once-formidable town gate and climb into the 14th-century village.*

As you walk, stop to read the few information plaques (in English) and contemplate the change this village has witnessed in the last 90 years. Eze-le-Village was off any traveler's radar until well after World War II (running water was made available only in the 1950s), yet today hotel rooms outnumber local residents two to one (66 to 29).

• *Wandering the narrow lanes, consider a detour to* **Château de la Chèvre d'Or** *for its elegant bar-lounge and sprawling view terrace (high prices but high views). Continue on following signs to the...*

Château Eza: This was the winter getaway of the Swedish royal family from 1923 until 1953; today it's a 15-room hotel. The château's tearoom (Salon de Thé), on a cliff  overlooking the jagged Riviera and sea, offers another scenic coffee or beer break—for a price. The view terrace is also home to an expensive-but-excellent **$$$$** restaurant (open daily, +33 4 93 41 12 24).

• *Backtrack a bit and continue uphill (follow signs to* Jardin Exotique*). The lane ends at the hilltop castle ruins—now blanketed by the...*

Jardin d'Eze: You'll find this prickly festival of cactus and exotic plants suspended between the sea and sky at the top of Eze-le-Village. Since 1949, the ruins of an old château have been home to 400 different plants 1,400 feet above the sea (€6, daily 9:00-18:30, July-Sept until 19:30, Nov-March until 16:30, well described in English, +33 4 93 41 10 30). At the top, you'll be treated to a commanding 360-degree view, with a helpful *table d'orientation*. On a clear day (they say...) you can see Corsica. The castle was demolished by Louis XIV in 1706. Louis destroyed castles like this all over Europe (most notably along the Rhine), because he didn't want to risk having to do battle with their owners at some future date.

• *As you descend, follow the pastel bell tower and* Eglise *signs and drop by the...*

Eze Church: Though built during Napoleonic times, this church has an uncharacteristic Baroque fanciness—a reminder that 300 years of Savoy rule left the townsfolk with an Italian savoir faire and a sensibility for decor. Notice the pulpit with the arm holding a crucifix, reminding the faithful that Christ died for their sins.

Sights in Eze-le-Village

Fragonard Perfume Factory (Parfumerie Fragonard)

This factory, with its huge tour-bus parking lot, lies on the Middle Corniche, 100 yards below Eze-le-Village. Designed for tour groups, it cranks them through all day long. If you've never seen mass tourism in action, this place will open your eyes. (The gravel is littered with the color-coded stickers each tourist wears so that salespeople know which guide gets the kickback.) Drop in for an informative and free tour (2/hour, 15 minutes). You'll see how the perfume and scented soaps are made before being herded into the gift shop.

Cost and Hours: Daily 9:30-18:00, but best Mon-Fri 9:00-11:00 & 14:00-15:30 when people are actually working in the "factory," +33 4 93 41 05 05, https://usines-parfum.fragonard.com.

Nearby: For a more intimate (but unguided) look at perfume, cross the main road in Eze-le-Village to visit the **Gallimard** shop. Explore the small museum (no English) and let the lovely ladies show you their scents (daily 9:00-18:00, across from Eze parking lot). They can give you a short tour if you ask.

Hike to Eze-Bord-de-Mer

A steep trail leaves Eze-le-Village from the foot of the hill-town entry, near the fancy hotel gate (100 yards up from the main road), and descends 1,300 feet to the sea along a no-shade, all-view trail. The trail is easy to follow but uneven in a few sections—allow 45 minutes (good walking shoes are essential; expect to be on all fours in certain sections). Once in Eze-Bord-de-Mer, you can catch a bus or train to all destinations between Nice and Monaco. In the late 1800s while walking this trail—now named for him—German philosopher Friedrich Nietzsche was moved to write his unconventionally spiritual novel, *Thus Spoke Zarathustra*.

Eating in Eze-le-Village

There's a handy **Casino** grocery at the foot of the village by the bus stop (daily 8:00-19:30) and an excellent bakery across the main road from that. Take your feast to the sensational picnic spot at the beginning of the trail to Eze-Bord-de-Mer or see my driving directions under "The Corniche Roads" (described earlier) to get to an eagle's-nest picnic site. **$ Le Cactus** serves crêpes, salads, and sandwiches at outdoor tables near the entry to the old town and inside their cozy, vaulted dining room (daily 10:00-18:30, later in summer, +33 4 93 41 19 02). For a real splurge, dine at

$$$$ Château de la Chèvre d'Or (described earlier, on my "Eze-le-Village Walk").

Le Trophée des Alpes

High above Monaco, on the Grande Corniche in the overlooked village of La Turbie, lies the ancient Roman "Trophy of the Alps," one of this region's most evocative historical sights (with dramatic views over the entire country of Monaco as a bonus). Rising well above all other buildings, this massive monument, worth ▲, commemorates Augustus Caesar's conquest of the Alps and its 44 hostile tribes. It's exciting to think that, in a way, Le Trophée des Alpes (also called "Le Trophée d'Auguste" for the emperor who built it) celebrates a victory that kicked off the Pax Romana—joining Gaul and Germania, freeing up the main artery of the Roman Empire, and linking Spain and Italy.

GETTING THERE

By Car: Take the High Corniche to La Turbie, ideally from Eze-le-Village (La Turbie is 10 minutes east of, and above, Eze-le-Village), then look for signs to *Le Trophée d'Auguste*. Once in La Turbie, drive to the site by turning right in front of the La Régence café. Those coming from farther afield can take the efficient A-8 to the La Turbie exit. To reach Eze-le-Village from La Turbie, follow signs to *Nice,* and then look for signs to *Eze-le-Village.*

By Bus: From Nice, you can get here on bus #116 (4/day, Mon-Sat departs from Gare Routière at the Vauban T-1 tram stop, Sun departs from Pont Michel T-1 tram stop). From Monaco, bus #11 connects to La Turbie (8/day Mon-Sat, 5/day Sun, 30 minutes). La Turbie's bus stop is near the post office (La Poste) on Place Neuve. Parking is tight in this compact town.

On Foot: Eze-le-Village is a 45-minute roadside walk downhill from La Turbie (no buses). There's a bike lane for half of the trip, but the rest is along a fairly quiet road with no shoulder. Follow D-2564 from La Turbie to Eze-le-Village, and don't miss the turnoff for D-45. The views of Eze-le-Village are magnificent as you get close.

ORIENTATION TO LE TROPHEE DES ALPES

Cost and Hours: €6, Tue-Sun 9:30-13:00 & 14:30-18:30, mid-Sept-mid-May from 10:00 and until 16:30, closed Mon year-round.

Information: +33 4 93 41 20 84, www.la-turbie.monuments-nationaux.fr

Tours: The €3 audioguide may be overkill, as English explanations are posted throughout the site.

VISITING THE MONUMENT

You'll enter through a small park that delivers grand views over Monaco and allows you to appreciate the remarkable setting selected by the Romans for this monument.

Circumnavigate the hulking structure. Notice how the Romans built a fine stone exterior using 24 massive columns that held together a towering cylinder filled with rubble and coarse concrete. Find the huge inscription on the back side of the monument. Flanked by the vanquished in chains, the towering inscription (one of the longest such inscriptions surviving from ancient times) tells the story: It was erected "by the senate and the people to honor the emperor."

The structure served no military purpose when built except to intimidate local tribes. The monument was fortified a thousand years later in the Middle Ages (like the Roman Arena in Arles) as a safe haven for villagers. When Louis XIV ordered the destruction of the area's fortresses in the early 18th century, he sadly included this one. The monument later became a quarry for homes in La Turbie before being restored in the 1930s and 1940s with money from the Tuck family of New Hampshire.

A guardian will escort you halfway up the monument and give you a detailed explanation in English if you ask.

The good little one-room **museum** shows a model of the monument, a video, and information about its history and reconstruction. There's also a translation of the dramatic inscription, which lists all the feisty alpine tribes that put up such a fight.

NEAR THE MONUMENT: LA TURBIE

The sweet old village of La Turbie sees almost no tourists, but it has plenty of cafés and restaurants. To stroll the old village, walk behind the post office and find brick footpaths that lead through the peaceful back lanes of the village.

Eating in La Turbie: Your best bet is the bustling **$$ Brasserie Pampérigouste,** with big views and tables under umbrellas. The menu offers excellent pizza, pasta, salads, and *plats du jour* for very fair prices (daily for lunch and dinner, near the post office at the main parking lot, 17 Place Neuve, +33 4 93 83 00 56). **$$ Café de la Fontaine**, popular with cyclists, is another good choice (daily, 4 Avenue du Général de Gaulle, +33 4 93 28 52 79).

EAST OF NICE

Quickie Riviera Bus Tour

The Riviera from Nice to Monaco is so easy to tour by bus and train that those with a car should leave it parked. While the train laces together the charms of this dramatic stretch of Mediterranean coast as if on a scenic bracelet, the public bus affords a far better view of the crags, dreamy villas, and much-loved beaches that make it Europe's coast with the most.

Planning Your Ride

This tour is designed for those riding the bus from Nice to Monaco and back. You could also ride the entire route to Menton (1.5 hours), enjoy Menton (see the end of the next chapter), and then see Monaco on the way back to Nice. Get an early start. Keep in mind that afternoon buses back to Nice are often crammed and agonizingly slow after Villefranche-sur-Mer—at these times, take the train.

Bus Tips: Bus #100 runs frequently along the Low Corniche (3-4/hour). The first stop in Nice is at the city's port—see map on page 316. One €1.50 ticket is good for 74 minutes, no matter how far you go (one-way only). Pay the driver as you get on.

Riding from Nice toward Monaco, grab a seat on the right and start before 9:00. Stops are announced on most buses and shown on a screen at the front. The last bus leaves Monaco for Nice at about 21:30 (always verify last times).

Since bus fares are cheap, consider hopping on and off at great viewpoints (the next bus is always 15-20 minutes away). All stops have names that are usually posted on the shelter or bus stop sign— I'll use the bus stop names to orient you as we go.

Some bus drivers on this line are in training for the Grand Prix of Monaco—hold on tight.

From Nice to Monaco

This route along the Low Corniche was inaugurated with the opening of the Monte Carlo Casino in 1863. It was designed to provide easy and safe access from Nice (and the rest of France) to the gambling fun in Monaco. Here's what you'll see along the way:

Nice Harbor: This harbor—dredged by 400 convicts—was finished in the mid-1800s. Before then, boats littered Nice's beaches. You'll see some yachts, an occasional cruise ship, and maybe the ferry to Corsica. The one-hour boat tour along Cap Ferrat and Villefranche-sur-Mer leaves from the right side, about halfway down (see page 320). If you return by bus #100, it's a pleasant 35-minute walk around the distant point to or from the Promenade des Anglais and Nice's old town.

From Nice to Villefranche-sur-Mer: As you glide away

from Nice, look back for views of the harbor, Castle Hill, and the sweeping Bay of Angels. Imagine the views from the homes below, and imagine 007 on his deck admiring a sunset (the soft, yellow, rounded tower straight ahead near the top of the hill was part of Sean Connery's property). Elton John's home is higher up the hill (and out of view). Imagine his neighbor, Tina Turner, dropping by for a glass of wine.

You'll soon pass the Palais Maerterlinck, one of several luxury hotels to go belly-up in recent years and be converted to luxury condos. Next, you'll come to the yacht-studded bay of Villefranche-sur-Mer and the peninsula called Cap Ferrat—retreat of the rich and famous, marked by its lighthouse on the point just across the bay. This bay is a rare natural harbor along the Riviera. Since it's deeper than Nice's, it hosts many cruise ships, which drop anchor and tender passengers in.

Villefranche-sur-Mer: To visit Villefranche-sur-Mer, get off at the stop labeled *Octroi*.

After passing through Villefranche-sur-Mer, look for sensational views back over the town (best from the Madonne-Noire stop). Spot the small point of land on the water with umbrella pine trees as the road arcs to the right—the Rolling Stones recorded 1972's *Exile on Main Street* in the basement of the Villa Nellcôte, the mansion below the l'Ange Gardien stop. The Baroness Rothschild's pink Villa Ephrussi, with its red-tiled roof, breaks the horizon on Cap Ferrat's peninsula.

Cap Ferrat: This peninsula is home to the Villa Ephrussi de Rothschild, the port town of St-Jean, and some lovely seaside paths. To visit Cap Ferrat, get off at l'Ange Gardien stop. As you move on, remember that this road was built in the 1860s to bring customers to Monaco. Before then, there was nothing along this route—no one even lived here—all the way to Monaco.

Beaulieu-sur-Mer: To take the seaside walk to St-Jean on Cap Ferrat get off at Plage Beaulieu. To visit the Villa Kérylos, get off at the next stop (Kérylos).

Just after the town of Beaulieu-sur-Mer, the cliffs create a microclimate and a zone nicknamed "Little Africa." (The bus stop is labeled *Petite Afrique*.) Exotic vegetation (including the only bananas on the Riviera) grows among private, elegant villas that made Beaulieu-sur-Mer *the* place to be in the 19th century.

Eze-Bord-de-Mer: Soon after leaving Beaulieu-sur-Mer,

EAST OF NICE

be ready for quickie views way up to the fortified town of Eze-le-Village. After passing through a rock arch, you'll swing around a big bend going left: Eze-le-Village crowns the ridge toward the right. To reach Eze-le-Village by bus, the #83 shuttle bus makes the climb from the Gare d'Eze stop in Eze-Bord-de-Mer—see page 394. U2's Bono owns a villa on the beach below.

Cap d'Ail: After passing through several short tunnels, you emerge at Cap d'Ail. Near the Deux Tunnels stop, you can't miss the huge, yellowish, hospital-like building below that once thrived as a luxury hotel popular with the Russian aristocracy. Now it's luxury condos. At the next stop (Cap d'Ail-Edmonds), try to look left and above at the switchbacks halfway up the barren hillside (visible from the left side of the bus). It was at the bend connecting these two switchbacks that Princess Grace Kelly (the American movie star who married into the royal family of Monaco) was killed in a car crash in 1982.

Monaco (three bus stops): Cap d'Ail borders Monaco—you're about to leave France. You'll pass by some junky development along this no-man's-land stretch. Eventually, to the right, just before the castle-topped hill (Monaco-Ville), is Monaco's Fontvieille district, featuring tall, modern apartments all built on land reclaimed from the Mediterranean. The first Monaco stop (Place d'Armes) is best for visiting the palace and other old-town sights in Monaco-Ville.

If you stay on the bus, you'll pass through the tunnel, then emerge to follow the road that Grand Prix racers speed along. In late May you'll see blue bleachers and barriers set up for the big race.

You'll pass the second Monaco stop (on the port, named Princesse Antoinette), then enjoy the harbor and city views as you climb to the last Monaco stop (Casino), near the TI. Get off here for the casino. For information on Monaco, see the next chapter. If you stay on the bus for a few more minutes, you'll be back in France, and in 15 more minutes you'll reach the end of the line, **Menton** (described in the following chapter).

Bonne route!

MONACO

Despite high prices, wall-to-wall daytime tourists, and a Disney-esque atmosphere, Monaco is a Riviera must. Monaco is on the go. Since 1929, cars have raced around the port and in front of the casino in one of the world's most famous auto races, the Grand Prix de Monaco. The modern breakwater—constructed elsewhere and towed in by sea—enables big cruise ships to dock here, and the district of Fontvieille, reclaimed from the sea, bristles with luxury high-rise condos. But don't look for anything too deep in this glittering tax haven. Many of its 36,000 residents live here because there's no income tax—there are only about 6,000 true Monegasques.

This minuscule principality (0.75 square mile) borders only France and the Mediterranean. The country has always been tiny, but it used to be...less tiny.

In an 1860 plebiscite, Monaco lost two-thirds of its territory when the region of Menton voted to join France. To compensate, France suggested that Monaco build a fancy casino and promised to connect it to the world with a road (the Low Corniche) and a train line. This started a high-class tourist boom that has yet to let up.

Although "independent," Monaco is run as a part of France. A French civil servant appointed by the French president—with the blessing of Monaco's prince—serves as state minister and manages the place. Monaco's phone system, electricity, water, and so on, are all French.

The glamorous romance and marriage of the American actress Grace Kelly to Prince Rainier added to Monaco's fairy-tale mystique. Princess Grace first came to Monaco to star in the 1955 Alfred Hitchcock movie *To Catch a Thief*, in which she was filmed racing along the Corniches. She married the prince in 1956 and adopted the country, but tragically, the much-loved princess died in 1982 after suffering a stroke while driving on one of those same scenic roads. She was just 52 years old.

The death of Prince Rainier in 2005 ended his 56-year-long enlightened reign. Today, Monaco is ruled by Prince Albert Alexandre Louis Pierre, Marquis of Baux—son of Prince Rainier and Princess Grace. Prince Albert was long considered Europe's most eligible bachelor—until he finally married on July 2, 2011, at age 53. His bride, known as Princess Charlene, is a South African commoner 20 years his junior.

A graduate of Amherst College, Albert is a bobsled enthusiast who raced in several Olympics, and an avid environmentalist who seems determined to clean up Monaco's tarnished tax-haven, money-laundering image. (Monaco is infamously known as a "sunny place for shady people.") Monaco is big business, and Prince Albert is its CEO. Its famous casino contributes only 5 percent of the state's revenue, whereas its many banks—which offer a hard-to-resist way to hide your money—are hugely profitable. The prince also makes money for Monaco with a value-added tax (20 percent, same as in France), plus real estate and corporate taxes.

Monaco is a special place: There are more people in Monaco's philharmonic orchestra (about 100) than in its army (about 80). Yet the princedom is well guarded, with police and cameras on every corner. (They say you could win a million dollars at the casino and walk to the train station in the wee hours without a worry.) Stamps are printed in small quantities and increase in value almost as soon as they're available. And collectors snapped up the rare Monaco versions of euro coins (with Prince Rainier's portrait) so quickly that many Monegasques have never even seen one.

Orientation to Monaco

The principality of Monaco has three tourist areas: Monaco-Ville, Monte Carlo, and La Condamine. **Monaco-Ville** fills the rock high above everything else and is referred to by locals as Le Rocher ("The Rock"). This is the oldest part of Monaco, home to the Prince's Palace and all the key sights except the casino. **Monte Carlo** is the area around the casino. **La Condamine** is the port, which lies between Monaco-Ville and Monte Carlo. From here it's a 20-minute walk up to the Prince's Palace or to the casino, or a few minutes by frequent bus to either (see "Getting Around Monaco," later).

Most travelers will want to organize their trip around the changing of the guard at the palace (at 11:55) and touring the casino. The surgical-strike plan is to start at Monaco-Ville (where you'll spend the most time and see the changing of the guard), then wander down along the port area, and finish by gambling away whatever you have left in Monte Carlo (the casino's high-roller game rooms don't

open until 14:00, but the rest of the joint opens at 9:00). If you don't care to gamble and can get started early, consider reversing this route: Tour the casino first, then visit Monaco-Ville in time to see the changing of the guard. You can walk the entire route in about 1.5 hours, or take three bus trips and do it in 15 minutes.

TOURIST INFORMATION
The main TI is at the top of the park above the casino (Mon-Sat 9:30-18:00, Oct-May until 17:30, closed Sun except July-Aug, 2 Boulevard des Moulins, +377 92 16 61 16 or +377 92 16 61 66, www.visitmonaco.com). Another TI is at the train station (Mon-Sat 9:00-17:00, closed Sun; July-Aug daily until 18:30).

ARRIVAL IN MONACO
By Bus #100 from Nice and Villefranche-sur-Mer: See my "Quickie Riviera Bus Tour" on page 400 to plan your route. Bus riders need to pay attention to the monitor showing the next stop. Cap d'Ail is the town before Monaco, so be on the lookout after that (the last stop before Monaco is called "Cimetière"). You'll enter Monaco through the modern cityscape of high-rises in the Fontvieille district. When you see the rocky outcrop of old Monaco, be ready to get off.

There are three stops in Monaco. In order from Nice, they are: Place d'Armes (at the base of Monaco-Ville), Princesse Antoinette (on the port), and Monte Carlo-Casino (in front of the TI on Boulevard des Moulins).

Most riders will get off at **Place d'Armes** to visit Monaco-Ville first. Use the crosswalk in front of the tunnel, then keep right and find bus stops #1 and #2 and the ramp to the palace. Casino-first types wait for the *Monte Carlo-Casino* stop. There's no reason to exit at the port stop.

MONACO

Monaco

FRANCE

MIDDLE CORNICHE

To Menton

To Nice

MONEGHETTI

T — ACCESS TO TRAIN STATION

B — BUS STOP

BLVD. PRINCESSE

#2
TRAIN STATION
(UNDERGROUND)

MONA

B #100 to Nice

AUTOMOBILE
CLUB DE MONACO

1 & 2 and
#100 from Nice

RUE GRIMALDI

R. PRIN. ANT.

BLVD. ALBERT I

LA CONDAMINE

BLVD. DU JARDIN EXOTIQUE

R. SUFFREN-REYMOND

BLVD. RAINIER III

R. BARON

Jardin
Exotique

2   3

RUE DE LA TURBIE

R. PRINCESSE CAROLINE

LOTSA
YACHTS!

1

Place d'Armes
(Local Buses)

B

#100
to Nice

B

WC B #1 & 2

LOW CORNICHE

B
#100 from Nice

RAMPE
MAJOR

GRIMALDI
STATUE

B #1 & 2

AVE. DE FONTVIELLE

WALK
BEGINS

AVE. DE L.

To
Nice

PRINCE'S
PALACE

Place du
Palais

RUE DES REMPARTS

R. COMTE GASTALDI

BASSE

4

AVE. ALBERT II

5

R. EMILE DE LOTH

POST

R. CTE BEL.
DE CASTO

CATHEDRAL

LOUIS II
SOCCER
STADIUM

Port du
Fontvielle

WC

AVE. SAINT

Jardins de
Saint-Martin

FONTVIELLE

BEAUSOLEIL

BLVD. DES MOULINS

To Villa Sauber & Menton via Low Corniche

BLVD. LARVOTTO

#100 from Nice, #11 to La Turbie, #112 to Eze-le-Village & Nice

CHARLOTTE

#1 & 2 and #100 to Nice

Casino Gardens

AVE. SPEL

AMERICAN-STYLE CASINO

AVE. DE LA COSTA

#1 & 2

Place du Casino

CASINO

MONTE CARLO

AVE. D'OSTENDE

PALAIS DES CONGRES & "Le Casino"

MONACO

Port

LOTSA YACHTS!

BATEAU BUS

CRUISE TENDER DOCK

TERMINAL

MONACO-VILLE

AVE. QUARANTINE

FORT ANTOINE

Mediterranean Sea

ORTE NEUVE

Place de la Visitation

RUE EMILE DE LOTH

#1 & 2 Tourist Train Stop

WALK ENDS

ARTIN

"Le Palais"

OCEANOGRAPHY MUSEUM

300 Meters

300 Yards

Accommodation
1 Hotel de France

Eateries
2 Huit et Demi
3 Bella Vita
4 Boulangerie
5 U Cavagnetu

By Train from Nice: The long, entirely underground train station is in the center of Monaco. From here, it's a 15-minute walk to the casino or the port, and about 15 minutes to the base of the palace (and frequent local buses). The station has no baggage storage.

The TI, train-ticket windows, and WCs are up the escalator at the Italy end of the station. There are three exits from the train platform level (one at each end and one in the middle).

To reach Monaco-Ville and the palace, take the exit at the Nice end of the tracks (signed *Sortie Fontvieille/Le Rocher*), which leads through a long tunnel and along a pedestrian plaza to the base of Monaco-Ville at Place d'Armes (turn left when you reach the busy street). From here, it's about a 15-minute hike up to the palace, or five minutes by bus (#1 or #2) plus a short walk.

To reach Monaco's port and the casino, take the middle exit, following *Sortie Port Hercule* signs down the steps and escalators, and then *Accès Port* signs until you pop out at the port, where you'll see the stop for buses #1 and #2 across the busy street. From here, it's a 20-minute walk to the casino (up Avenue d'Ostende to your left), or a short trip via bus #1 or #2.

To return to Nice by train in the evening (after ticket windows close), buy your return tickets on arrival or use the ticket machines (about €4, coins or credit card).

By Car: Follow *Centre-Ville* signs into Monaco (warning: traffic can be heavy), then watch for the signs to parking garages at *Le Casino* (for Monte Carlo) or *Le Palais* (for Monaco-Ville). You'll pay about €4/hour.

By Cruise Ship: See "Monaco Connections," near the end of this chapter.

HELPFUL HINTS

Grand Prix Prep: From early April through May, visitors will encounter construction detours as the country prepares for its largest event of the year, the Grand Prix de Monaco.

Combo-Tickets: If you plan to see both of Monaco's big sights (Prince's Palace and Oceanography Museum), buy the €24 combo-ticket. Another combo-ticket includes the prince's private car collection in Fontvieille (not covered in this book).

Changing of the Guard: This popular event takes place daily (in good weather) at 11:55 at the Prince's Palace. Arrive by 11:30 to get a good viewing spot.

Local Guides: Catherine and Cecilia at **Tour Prestige** offer local expertise in and around Monaco (+33 4 93 41 31 98, www.traveltourprestige.com).

Loop Trip by Bus or Train: From Nice, you can get to Monaco by bus or train, then take a bus from Monaco to Eze-le-Village or La Turbie, and return to Nice from there by bus. For bus numbers, frequencies, and stop locations, see "Monaco Connections," near the end of this chapter.

Evening Events: Monaco's cultural highlights include its **Philharmonic Orchestra** and the **Monte Carlo Ballet** (+377 98 06 28 28, www.opmc.mc).

Souvenirs: For a memento of your visit, you can get a souvenir Monaco passport at the TI.

Post Office: The handiest post office for local stamps is in Monaco-Ville (described on my self-guided walk; Mon-Fri 8:00-19:00, Sat until 13:00, closed Sun).

GETTING AROUND MONACO

By Local Bus: Buses #1 and #2 link all areas with frequent service (10/hour, fewer on Sun, buses run until 21:00). If you pay the driver, a single ticket is €2, 15 tickets €20, and a day pass €5.50; save by using red curbside machines, where you get 10 tickets for €10. You can split a 10- or 15-ride ticket with your travel partners. Bus tickets are good for a free transfer if used within 30 minutes.

For a **cheap and scenic loop ride** through Monaco, ride bus #2 from one end to the other and back (25 minutes each way). You'll need two tickets and must get off the bus at the last stop and then get on again.

By Tour Bus: You could pay €25 for a hop-on, hop-off open-deck bus tour that makes 12 stops in Monaco, but I wouldn't. Local bus #2 (see above) offers the same scenic tour of the principality and includes its best views—for much less.

By Tourist Train: An efficient way to enjoy a scenic blitz tour, **Monaco Tours** tourist trains begin at the Oceanography Museum and pass by the port, casino, and palace (€10, 2/hour, 30 minutes, recorded English commentary).

By Taxi: If you've lost all track of time at the casino, you can call the 24-hour taxi service (+377 93 15 01 01)...assuming you still have enough money to pay for the cab home.

Monaco-Ville Walk

All of Monaco's major sights (except the casino) are in Monaco-Ville, packed within a few Disneyesque blocks. This self-guided walk connects these sights in a tight little loop, starting from the palace square.

• *To get from anywhere in Monaco to the palace square (Monaco-Ville's sightseeing center and home of the palace), take bus #1 or #2 to the end of the line at Place de la Visitation. Turn right as you step off the bus and walk five minutes down Rue Emile de Loth. You'll pass the post office, a worthwhile stop for its collection of valuable Monegasque stamps (we'll go there later—to visit it now, see the end of this walk).*

Palace Square (Place du Palais)

This square is the best place to get oriented to Monaco. Facing the palace, walk to the right and look out over the city (er...principality). This rock gave birth to the little pastel Hong Kong look-alike in 1215, and it's managed to remain an independent country for most of its 800 years. Looking beyond the glitzy port, notice the faded green dome roof: It belongs to the casino that put Monaco on the map in the 1800s. The casino was located away from Monaco-Ville because Prince Charles III (r. 1856-1889) wanted to shield his people from low-life gamblers.

The modern buildings just past the casino mark the eastern limit of Monaco. The famous Grand Prix runs along the port and then up the ramp to the casino (at top speeds of 180 mph). Italy is so close, you can almost smell the pesto. Just beyond the casino is France again (it flanks Monaco on both sides)—you could walk one-way from France to France, passing through Monaco, in about an hour.

The odd statue of a woman with a fishing net is dedicated to the glorious reign of **Prince Albert I** (1889-1922). The son of Charles III (who built the casino), Albert I was a true Renaissance man. He had a Jacques Cousteau-like fascination with the sea (and built Monaco's famous aquarium, the Oceanography Museum) and was a determined pacifist who made many attempts to dissuade Germany's Kaiser Wilhelm II from becoming involved in World War I.

Keeping the view on your left, escape the crowds for a moment with a short detour 50 yards up the street. Gawk at the houses lining this street and imagine waking up to that view every day.

• *Head toward the palace, passing electric car chargers (Prince Albert is an environmentalist), and find a statue of a monk grasping a sword.*

Meet François Grimaldi, a renegade sword-carrying Italian dressed as a monk, who captured Monaco in 1297 and began the dynasty that still rules the principality. Prince Albert is his great-great-great...grandson, which gives Monaco's royal family the distinction of being the longest-lasting dynasty in Europe.

• *Now walk to the...*

Prince's Palace (Palais Princier)

A medieval castle once sat where the palace is today. Its strategic setting has had a lot to do with Monaco's ability to resist at-

tackers. Today, Prince Albert and his wife live in the palace, while Princesses Stephanie and Caroline live down the street. The palace guards protect the prince 24/7 and still stage a **changing of the guard** ceremony with all the pageantry of an important nation (daily at 11:55 in good weather, fun to watch but jam-packed, arrive by 11:30).

An audioguide takes you through part of the prince's lavish palace in 30 minutes. The rooms are well furnished and impressive, but interesting only if you haven't seen a château lately. Even if you don't tour the palace, get close enough to check out the photos in the palace entry of the last three princes.

Cost and Hours: €10, includes audioguide, €24 combo-ticket includes Oceanography Museum; hours vary but generally daily 10:00-18:00, July-Aug until 19:00, closed Nov-March; buy ticket at the *Billeterie* at the souvenir stand 75 yards opposite the palace entrance; +377 93 25 18 31, www.palais.mc.

• *Head to the west end of the palace square. Below the cannonballs is the district known as...*

Fontvieille

Monaco's newest, reclaimed-from-the-sea area has seen much of Monaco's post-WWII growth (residential and commercial—notice the lushly planted building tops). Prince Rainier continued—some say, was obsessed with—Monaco's economic growth, creating landfills (topped with apartments, such as in Fontvieille), flashy ports, more beaches, a big sports stadium marked by tall arches, and a rail station. (An ambitious new landfill project is in the works and would add still more prime real estate to Monaco's portfolio.) Today, thanks to Prince Rainier's past efforts, tiny Monaco is a member of the United Nations. (If you have kids with you, check out the nifty play area just below.)

• *With your back to the palace, leave the square through the arch at the far right (onto Rue Colonel Bellando de Castro) and find the...*

Cathedral of Monaco (Cathédrale de Monaco)

The somber but beautifully lit cathedral, rebuilt in 1878, shows that Monaco cared for more than just its new casino. It's where centuries of Grimaldis are buried, and where Princess Grace and Prince Rainier were married. Inside, circle slowly behind the altar (counterclockwise). The second tomb is that of Albert I, who did much to put Monaco on the world stage. The second-to-last tomb—inscribed *"Gratia Patricia, MCMLXXXII"* and displaying the 1956 wedding photo of Princess Grace and Prince Rainier—is where the princess was buried in 1982. Prince Rainier's tomb lies next to hers (cathedral open daily 8:30-19:15).

• *Leave the cathedral and dip into the immaculately maintained **Jardins de Saint-Martin**, with more fine views. In the gardens, turn left. Eventually you'll find the impressive building housing the...*

Oceanography Museum (Musée Océanographique)

Prince Albert I had this cliff-hanging museum built in 1910 as a monument to his enthusiasm for things from the sea. The museum's aquarium, which Jacques Cousteau captained for 32 years, has 2,000 different specimens, representing 250 species. You'll find Mediterranean fish and colorful tropical species (all well described in English). Rotating exhibits occupy the entry floor. Upstairs, the fancy Albert I Hall is filled with ship models, whale skeletons, oceanographic instruments and tools, and scenes of Albert and his beachcombers hard at work (with good English information). Don't miss the elevator to the rooftop terrace view café.

Cost and Hours: €18, €12 for kids under 18, €24 combo-ticket includes Prince's Palace; daily 10:00-19:00, longer hours July-Aug, Oct-March until 18:00; down the steps from Monaco-Ville bus stop, at the opposite end of Monaco-Ville from the palace; +377 93 15 36 00, www.oceano.mc.

• *The red-brick steps across from the Oceanography Museum lead up to stops for buses #1 and #2, both of which run to the port, the casino, and the train station. To walk back to the palace and through the old city, turn left at the top of the brick steps. If you're into stamps, walk down Rue Emile de Loth to find the **post office**, where philatelists and postcard writers with panache can buy—or just gaze in awe at—the impressive collection of Monegasque stamps.*

Sights in Monaco

Jardin Exotique

This cliffside municipal garden (which may be closed when you visit), located above Monaco-Ville, has eye-popping views from France to Italy. It's home to more than a thousand species of cacti (some giant) and other succulent plants, but worth the entry only for view-loving botanists (some posted English explanations provided). Your ticket includes entry to a skippable natural cave, an anthropological museum, and a view snack bar/café. You can get similar views over Monaco for free from behind the souvenir stand at the Jardin's bus stop; or, for even grander vistas, cross the street and hike toward La Turbie.

Cost and Hours: €7.50, daily 9:00-19:00, Oct-April until about dusk, take bus #2 from any stop in Monaco or take the elevator up from the Nice end of the train station and follow signs, +377 93 15 29 80, www.jardin-exotique.com.

▲Monte Carlo Casino (Casino de Monte-Carlo)

Monte Carlo, which means "Charles' Hill" in Spanish, is named for Charles III, the prince who presided over Monaco's 19th-century makeover. In the mid-1800s, olive groves stood here. Then, with the construction of casino and spas, and easy road and train access (thanks to France), one of Europe's poorest countries was on the Grand Tour map—*the* place for the vacationing aristocracy to play. Today, Monaco has the world's highest per-capita income.

Count the counts and Rolls-Royces in front of the casino and **Hôtel de Paris**. The hotel was built at the same time as the casino to house gamblers— transportation back to Nice was not as fast as it is today (visitors allowed in the hotel, no shorts). Ignore the tacky American-style casino that hides behind the outdoor café across from the hotel.

The Monte Carlo casino is intended to make you feel elegant while losing your shorts. Charles Garnier designed the place (with an opera house inside) in 1878, in part to thank the prince for his financial help in completing Paris' Opéra Garnier (which the architect also designed). The central doors provide access to slot machines, gaming rooms, and the opera house. The gaming rooms occupy the left wing of the building. Cruise ship visitors can jam the entry during afternoons.

Cost and Hours: Tightwads can view the atrium entry and slot-machine room for free; daily 10:00-late. Touring the casino costs €17 (includes a €10 voucher to use on games or at the bar); you'll see the atrium area and inner-sanctum gaming rooms with an audioguide, take photos, and have your run of the joint (daily 14:00 until the wee hours, must be 18 and show ID; no shorts, T-shirts, hoodies, tennis shoes, or torn jeans). Whether you gamble or not, expect lines at the entrance from May through September (+377 92 16 20 00, www.montecarlocasinos.com).

Le Grand Prix Automobile de Monaco

The Grand Prix de Monaco focuses the world's attention on this little country. The race started as an enthusiasts' car rally by the Automobile Club de Monaco (and is still run by the same group, more than 80 years later). The first race, held in 1929, was won by a Bugatti at a screaming average speed of...48 mph (today's cars triple that speed). To this day, drivers consider this one of the most important races on their circuits. The race takes place every year toward the end of May (www.acm.mc).

By Grand Prix standards, it's an unusual course, running through the streets of this tiny principality, sardined between mountains and sea. The hilly landscape means that the streets are narrow, with tight curves, steep climbs, and extremely short straightaways. Each lap is about two miles, beginning and ending at the port. Cars climb along the sea from the port, pass in front of the casino, race through the commercial district, and do a few dandy turns back to the port. The race lasts 78 laps, and whoever is still rolling at the end wins (most don't finish).

The Formula 1 cars look like overgrown toys that kids might pedal up and down their neighborhood street (if you're here a week or so before the race, feel free to browse the parking structure below Monaco-Ville, where many race cars are kept). Time trials to establish pole position begin three days before the race, which is always on a Sunday. More than 150,000 people attend the gala event; like the nearby film festival in Cannes, it's an excuse for yacht parties, restaurant splurges, and four-digit bar tabs at luxury hotels. During this event, hotel rates in Nice and beyond rocket up (even for budget places).

Fans wanting to touch the storied past of this race can window-shop the Automobile Club de Monaco's headquarters and patronize its boutique next door (on the port at 23 Boulevard Albert 1; see "Monaco" map in this chapter).

Visiting the Casino: Enter through sumptuous **atrium**. This is the lobby for the 520-seat opera house (open Nov-April only for performances). A model of the opera house is at the far-right side of the room, near the bar-café. The **first gambling rooms** (Salle Europe and Salle des Amériques) offer slot machines, European and English roulette, blackjack, Punto Banco—a version of baccarat—and slot machines. The more glamorous **game rooms** (Salons Touzet and Salle Medecin) have those same games and Ultimate

Texas Hold 'em poker, but you play against the cashier with higher stakes (the exclusive Salle Blanche is off-limits to you).

The scene, flooded with camera-toting tourists during the day, is great at night—and downright James Bond-like in the private rooms. This is your chance to rub elbows with some high rollers.

The **park** behind the casino is a peaceful place with a good view of the building's rear facade and of Monaco-Ville.

Eating: The casino has two dining options. The **$$$$ Train Bleu** restaurant is for deep pockets for whom price is no object and elegance is everything. **$$$ Le Salon Rose** offers brasserie food—big salads and pasta dishes in a classy setting. If you paid to tour the casino or to gamble, show your ticket for a discount.

Take the Money and Run: The stop for buses returning to Nice and Villefranche-sur-Mer, and for local buses #1 and #2, is on Avenue de la Costa, at the top of the park above the casino (at the small shopping mall; for location, see the "Monaco" map). To reach the train station from the casino, take bus #1 or #2 from this stop, or find Boulevard Princesse Charlotte (parallels Avenue de la Costa one block above) and walk 15 minutes.

Sleeping and Eating in Monaco

Sleeping: Centrally located in Monaco-Ville, **$$ Hôtel de France**** is comfortable, well run by friendly Sylvie and Christoph, and reasonably priced—for Monaco (includes breakfast, air-con, no elevator; exit west from train station, 10-minute walk to 6 Rue de la Turbie, +377 93 30 24 64, www.hoteldefrance.mc, hoteldefrance@monaco.mc).

Eating on the Port: Several cafés serve basic, inexpensive fare (day and night) on the port. Troll the places that line the flowery and traffic-free Rue Princesse Caroline between Rue Grimaldi and the port. **$$$ Huit et Demi** is a reliable choice, with a white-table-cloth-meets-director's-chair ambience and good outdoor seating (closed Sun, 7 Rue Princesse Caroline, +377 93 50 97 02). A few blocks below, **$$ Bella Vita**—an easygoing place for salads, Italian fare, and classic French dishes—has a large terrace and modern interior (daily, serves nonstop from 7:00 to late, 21 Rue Princesse Caroline, +377 93 50 42 02).

Eating in Monaco-Ville: You'll find sandwiches—including the massive *pan bagnat*, basically *salade niçoise* on country bread—and quiche at the yellow-bannered **$ Boulangerie** (daily until 19:00, near Place du Palais at 8 Rue Basse). At **$$ U Cavagnetu**, just a block from Albert's palace, you'll dine cheaply on specialties from Monaco—pizza and such (daily, serves nonstop 11:00-23:00, 14 Rue Comte Félix Gastaldi, +377 97 98 20 40). Monaco-Ville has other pizzerias, *créperies,* and sandwich stands, but the neighborhood is dead at night.

Monaco Connections

BY TRAIN

For a comparison of train and bus connections, see the "Public Transportation in the French Riviera" sidebar on page 306. Most trains heading west will stop in Villefranche-sur-Mer, Nice, and Antibes (ask). The last train leaves Monaco for Villefranche-sur-Mer and Nice at about 23:30.

From Monaco by Train to: Villefranche-sur-Mer, Nice, Antibes, or **Cannes** (2/hour).

BY BUS

Frequent **bus #100,** which runs along the Low Corniche back to **Nice** (1 hour), and **Villefranche-sur–Mer** (40 minutes) is often slammed. For a better chance of securing a seat, board at the stop near the TI on Avenue de la Costa (see the "Monaco" map in this chapter) rather than the stop near Place d'Armes. The last bus leaves Monaco for Nice at about 21:30. In the other direction bus #100 goes to **Menton** (30 minutes). For bus details, including tickets, routes, frequencies, and travel times, see the "Getting Around the Riviera" section in the French Riviera chapter.

Bus #112, which goes along the scenic Middle Corniche to **Eze-le-Village** then on to Nice (6/day Mon-Sat, none on Sun, 20 minutes to Eze), departs Monaco from in front of the main TI near the casino.

Bus #11 to **La Turbie** (9/day Mon-Sat, 5/day Sun, 30 minutes) stops in front of the TI (same side of street).

Bus #110 express takes the freeway from the Place d'Armes stop to **Nice Airport** (2/hour, 50 minutes, €22).

BY CRUISE SHIP

Cruise ships tender passengers to the end of Monaco's yacht harbor, a short walk from downtown. It's a long walk or a short bus ride to most sights in town. To reach other towns, such as Villefranche-sur-Mer or Nice, you can take public transportation. To summon a taxi (assuming none are waiting when you disembark), look for the gray taxi call box near the tender dock—just press the button and wait for your cab to arrive.

Getting into Town: To reach **Monaco-Ville,** which towers high over the cruise terminal, you can either hike steeply and scenically up to the top of the hill, or walk to Place d'Armes and hop on bus #1 or #2, which will take you up sweat-free. It's a 15-minute, level walk to the bus stop from the port: Cross Boulevard Albert

I, follow green *Gare S.N.C.F./Ferroviare* signs, and take the public elevator to Place d'Armes.

The ritzy skyscraper zone of **Monte Carlo** is across the harbor from the tender dock, about a 25-minute walk. You can also ride the little electric "bateau bus" shuttle boat across the mouth of the harbor (works with a bus ticket). To reach the upper part of Monte Carlo—with the TI and handy bus stops (including for Eze-le-Village and La Turbie)—catch bus #1 or #2 at the top of the yacht harbor, along Boulevard Albert I.

Getting to Sights Beyond Monaco: Monaco is connected to most nearby sights by both train and bus. See the "Arrival in Monaco" section early in this chapter as well as the bus and train connection information in this section for details.

The train station is about a 20-minute walk from the tender harbor—first walk to Place d'Armes (directions earlier, under "Getting into Town"), then follow Rue Grimaldi to find stairs and an elevator to the station. For buses, see earlier for bus stop locations and frequencies. If taking bus #112 to Eze-le-Village or bus #11 to La Turbie, first ride bus #1 or #2 to the TI and casino, then follow the directions above.

MONACO

Menton

If you wish the Riviera were less glitzy and more like a place where locals take their families to lick ice cream and make sand castles, visit Menton (east of Monaco). Menton feels like a poor man's Nice. It's unrefined and unpretentious, with lower prices, fewer rentable umbrellas, and lots of Italians day-tripping in from right over the border (five miles away). There's not an American in sight.

Getting There: While trains serve Menton regularly (35 minutes from Nice, 10 minutes from Monaco), the station is a 15-minute walk from the action. Buses are much slower (1.5 hours from Nice, 30 minutes from Monaco) but they drop visitors right on the beach promenade (bus #100; see the "Getting Around the Riviera" section in the French Riviera chapter for details). If coming from a day trip via Monaco, take the bus here and train back to your home base.

Visiting Menton: Menton's TI is at 8 Avenue Boyer (+33 4 92 41 76 76, www.tourisme-menton.fr). Though a bit rough, the Menton waterfront is a joy. An inviting promenade lines the beach, and seaside cafés serve light meals and salads at good prices. A snooze or stroll here is a fine Riviera experience. From the promenade, a pedestrian street leads through town. Small squares are alive with jazz bands playing crowd-pleasers under palm trees.

Stepping into the old town—which blankets a hill capped by a fascinating cemetery—you're immersed in a pastel-painted, yet dark and tangled Old World scene with (strangely) almost no commerce. A few elegant restaurants dig in at the base of the towering centuries-old apartment flats. The richly decorated Baroque St. Michael's Church (midway up the hill, closed to visitors Sat-Sun) is a reminder that, until 1860, Menton was a thriving part of the larger state of Monaco. Climbing past sun-grabbing flower boxes and people who don't get out much anymore, the steep stepped lanes finally deposit you at the ornate gate of a grand cemetery that fills the old castle walls. Explore the cemetery, which is the final resting place of many aristocratic Russians (buried here in the early 1900s) and offers breathtaking Mediterranean views.

MONACO

ANTIBES & NEARBY

Antibes • Cannes • St-Tropez

The Riviera opens up west of Nice with bigger, sandier beaches and an overabundance of tasteless beachfront development. Ancient Antibes and superficial Cannes buck the slap-it-up high-rise trend, both with thriving centers busy with pedestrians and yachts. Glamorous St-Tropez, a scenic 1.5-hour drive from Antibes, marks the western edge of the French Riviera.

PLANNING YOUR TIME

Antibes works well by car, bus, or train. You can day-trip in from Nice or, better, sleep here (hotels outside the town center have easier parking than in Nice or Villefranche-sur-Mer, and train/bus service to nearby destinations is efficient). Allow a full day for Antibes sights (two nights is good). Antibes also works as a base for day trips: Cannes is a short hop away by bus, train, or car (train is best); the Inland Riviera hill towns of St-Paul-de-Vence, Vence, and Grasse (all covered in the next chapter) are also easy by car and doable by bus and/or train—but Grasse is the only inland destination with train service. St-Tropez—a 1.5-hour drive from Antibes—is best visited on your way in or out of the Riviera.

Antibes

West of Nice, Antibes has a down-to-earth, easygoing ambience. Its old town is a warren of narrow streets and red-tile roofs rising above the blue Med, protected by twin medieval towers and wrapped in medieval ramparts. Visitors making the short trip from Nice can browse Europe's biggest yacht harbor, snooze on a sandy beach, loiter through an enjoyable old town, and hike along a sea-

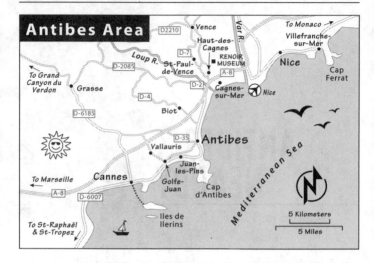

Antibes Area

swept trail. The town's cultural claim to fame, the Picasso Museum (closed on Mondays), shows off its appealing collection in a fine old building.

Though much smaller than Nice, Antibes has a history that dates back just as far. Both towns were founded by Greek traders in the fifth century BC. To the Greeks, Antibes was "Antipolis" —the town *(polis)* opposite *(anti)* Nice. For the next several centuries, Antibes remained in the shadow of its neighbor. By the turn of the 20th century, the town was a military base so the rich and famous partied elsewhere. But when the army checked out after World War I, Antibes was "discovered" and enjoyed a particularly roaring '20s with the help of party animals like Rudolph Valentino, F. Scott Fitzgerald and his wife, Zelda, and the rowdy (yet silent) Charlie Chaplin. Fun seekers even invented water-skiing right here in the 1920s.

Orientation to Antibes

Antibes' old town lies between the port and Boulevard Albert I and Avenue Robert Soleau. Place Nationale is the old town's hub of activity. Stroll above the sea between the old port and Place Albert I (where Boulevard Albert I meets the water). Good beaches lie just beyond Place Albert I, and the walk there continues to fine views. Fun play areas for children are along this

path and on Place des Martyrs de la Résistance (close to recommended Hôtel Relais du Postillon).

TOURIST INFORMATION

The TI on Place Guynemer may have moved to a new complex near Place des Martyrs de la Résistance by the time you visit (July-Aug daily 9:00-19:00; Sept-June Mon-Sat 9:30-12:30 & 14:00-18:00, Sun 9:00-13:00; shorter hours and closed Sun in winter; +33 4 22 10 60 10, www.antibesjuanlespins.com). Hikers should get the free tourist map of the Sentier Touristique de Tirepoil hike (see "Sights in Antibes," later).

ARRIVAL IN ANTIBES

By Train: Bus #14 runs from below the train station and along Avenue Robert Soleau to the city center (near several recommended hotels and the old town), then continues to the fine Plage de la Salis, with quick access to the Phare de la Garoupe trail (hourly, runs 10:00-16:00, none on Sun, bus stop 100 yards to right as you exit train station). **Taxis** usually wait in front of the station.

Day-trippers can store bags at **Luggage Storage** (daily 9:00-20:00, 14 Avenue Robert Soleau, +33 6 11 96 09 12, www. luggagestorage-antibes.com).

To **walk** from the station to the port, the old town, and the Picasso Museum (15 minutes), cross the street in front of the station, skirting left of the café, and follow Avenue de la Libération downhill as it bends left. At the end of the street, head to the right along the port. If you walk on the water's edge, you'll see the yachts get bigger as you go.

To walk directly to the baggage storage, TI, and recommended hotels in the old town, turn right out of the station and walk down Avenue Robert Soleau.

The last train back to Nice leaves at about midnight.

By Bus: Antibes' **regional bus station** (called the *Pôle d'Echange* and serving buses #200 & #250) is behind the train station; take the pedestrian overpass from behind the train station to reach it. Buses to and from Nice stop at the far right/east end (info office open Mon-Fri 7:00-19:00, Sat 9:00-12:30 & 14:00-17:00, closed Sun). Bus #200 to Nice also stops in the center near Place Général de Gaulle on Boulevard Dugommier.

Some **city buses** (like handy bus #2) use the *Pôle d'Echange* regional bus station, but most stop on Place Guynemer, a block below Place Général de Gaulle (info at TI, www.envibus.fr).

By Car: Day-trippers follow signs to *Centre-Ville*, then *Port Vauban*. The easiest place to park is a convenient but pricey underground parking lot located outside the ramparts near the archway leading into the old town (about €13/4 hours, €23/12 hours, just

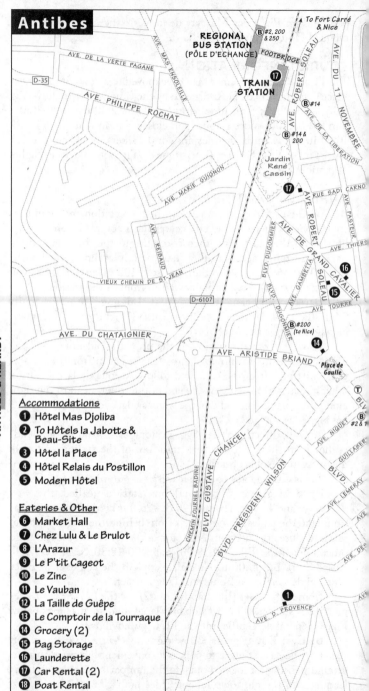

Antibes

Accommodations

1. Hôtel Mas Djoliba
2. To Hôtels la Jabotte & Beau-Site
3. Hôtel la Place
4. Hôtel Relais du Postillon
5. Modern Hôtel

Eateries & Other

6. Market Hall
7. Chez Lulu & Le Brulot
8. L'Arazur
9. Le P'tit Cageot
10. Le Zinc
11. Le Vauban
12. La Taille de Guêpe
13. Le Comptoir de la Tourraque
14. Grocery (2)
15. Bag Storage
16. Launderette
17. Car Rental (2)
18. Boat Rental

ANTIBES & NEARBY

Port Vauban

"QUAI DES MILLIARDAIRES"

Vieux Port

NOMADE

BASTION ST. JAUME

MEDIEVAL WALL

AVE. DE VERDUN

AVE. MISTRAL

Best Parking

WC

WALK BEGINS

18

ARCH

WC

RAMPARTS DETOUR

BLVD. D'AGUILLON

RUE D'ANDREOSSY

RUE D'AGUILLON

THURET

RUE AUBERNON

QUAI H. RAMBAUD

Plage de la Gravette

AVE. MIRABEAU

OLD

11

8

R. VAUBAN

AV. DOUZER

RUE LACAN

RUE FERSAN

PALMIERS

RUE PALMIERS

Place du Revely

POST

9

DE LA REPUBLIQUE

MARKET HALL

Place Nationale

Antibes Books

7

6

R. SADE

CHURCH OF THE IMMACULATE CONCEPTION

Place des Martyrs de la Résistance

Tourist Train

PICASSO MUSEUM

CHATEAU GRIMALDI

4

i

5

14

ABSINTHE BAR

COURS MASSENA

RUE GUILL

RUE BATEAU

B #14

R. FOUR

RUE DE FERSEN

12

10

13

RUE DE GRASSE

3

TOWN

16

R. VANDENBERG

TOURRAQUE

PROM. AMIRAL DE GRASSE

SAFRANIER

Place du Safranier

R. VIAL

RUE CLOSE

CANNET

ALBERT I

RUE HAUT CASTELET

Mediterranean

Sea

GAZAN

FRERES ROUSTAN

AVE. MARECHAL REILLE

BARQUIER

MEDIEVAL WALL

MARECHAL FOCH

HISTORY & ARCHAEOLOGY MUSEUM

BOURGEOIS

BLVD. M. LECLERC

Place Albert I

WC

PLAY AREA

Plage de l'Ilette

Pointe de l'Ilette

WALK ENDS

To Plage Ponteil & Plage Salis, Cap d'Antibes, Hikes &

2

100 Meters

100 Yards

south of Port Vauban—see the "Antibes" map in this chapter). A free lot is available opposite Fort Carré (north of the port). Take bus #14 or the free *navette* (every 15 minutes) to the harbor and the beginning of my walk, or walk 15 level-but-unappealing minutes to the old town. Street parking is free Monday through Friday (12:00-14:00 & 19:00-8:00), and all day Saturday and Sunday.

If you're sleeping in Antibes, follow *Centre-Ville* signs, then signs to your hotel. The most appealing hotels in Antibes are best by car, and Antibes works well for drivers—compared with Nice, parking is easy, traffic is minimal, and it's a convenient springboard for the Inland Riviera. Pay parking is available at Antibes' train station, so drivers can ditch their cars here and day-trip from Antibes by train.

HELPFUL HINTS

Markets: Antibes' old-time market hall (Marché Provençal) hosts a vibrant produce market in the morning (daily until 13:00, closed Mon Sept-May) and handicrafts in the afternoon (from 15:00 mid-June-Sept Tue-Sun, Oct-mid-June Fri-Sun only). A lively antiques/flea market fills Place Nationale and Place Audiberti, next to the port (Thu and Sat 7:00-18:00). A clothing market unfolds on Boulevard Albert I (Thu 8:00-13:00).

English Bookstore: With a welcoming vibe, **Antibes Books** has a good selection of new and used books—normally including mine (daily 10:00-19:00, 13 Rue Georges Clemenceau, +33 4 93 61 96 47, www.antibesbooks.com).

Laundry: The Lav'Matic launderette is at 19 Avenue du Grand Cavalier (daily 6:00-21:00). There's another *laverie* on Place des Gendarmes d'Ouvéa, close to my recommended hotels (daily 7:00-20:00).

Bike Rental: The TI has a list of places where you can rent bikes (including e-bikes)—a good way for nondrivers to reach the hikes described later in this chapter.

Taxi: +33 4 93 67 67 67.

Car Rental: The big-name agencies have offices in Antibes. The most central are **Avis/Budget** (at the train station, daily 9:00-12:00 & 13:00-17:00, +33 4 93 34 65 15) and **Hertz** (a few blocks from the train station at 31 Avenue Robert Soleau, Mon-Sat 8:00-12:00 & 14:00-18:00, closed Sun, +33 4 92 91 28 00).

Boat Rental: You can motor your own seven-person yacht thanks to **Antibes Bateaux Services** (€100/half-day, at the small fish market on the port, +33 6 15 75 44 36, www.antibes-bateaux.com).

GETTING AROUND ANTIBES

Local buses (Envibus) cost €1 if you buy a ticket from a machine or at the bus station (€1.50 from driver, cash only). They're handiest for carless travelers wanting access to Cap d'Antibes. Get schedules online (www.envibus.fr/en/bus-routes) or at the bus station. **Bus #14** links the train station, city center, old town, and Plage de la Salis (Mon-Sat 10:00-16:00, hourly). It also takes you to Fort Carré, where free parking is available. **Bus #2** provides access to the best beaches, the path to La Phare de la Garoupe, and the Cap d'Antibes trail. It runs from the Pôle d'Echange bus station (behind the train station) through the city center and down Boulevard Albert I (daily 7:00-19:00, every 40-60 minutes).

Antibes Walk

This 40-minute self-guided walk will help you get your bearings, and works well day or night.

• *Begin at the old port (Vieux Port) at the southern end of Avenue de Verdun. Stand at the port, across from the archway with the clock.*

Old Port: Locals claim that this is Europe's first and biggest pleasure-boat harbor, with 1,600 stalls. That star-shaped stone

structure crowning the opposite end of the port is **Fort Carré,** which protected Antibes from foreigners for more than 500 years.

The pathetic remains of a once-hearty **fishing fleet** are moored in front of you. The Mediterranean is pretty much fished out. Most of the seafood you'll eat here comes from fish farms or the Atlantic.

• *With the port on your left, walk a block past the sorry fleet and duck under the first open arch to the shell-shaped...*

Plage de la Gravette: This normally quiet public beach is tucked right in the middle of old Antibes. Walk out onto the paved area. Appreciate the scale of the ramparts that protected this town. Because Antibes was the last fort before the Italian border, the French king made sure the ramparts were top-notch. The twin towers crowning

ANTIBES & NEARBY

the old town are the church's bell tower and the tower topping Château Grimaldi (today's Picasso Museum). As you face the old town, forested Cap d'Antibes is the point of land in the distance to the left. Is anyone swimming? Locals don't swim much in July and August because of jellyfish—common now in warmer water. Throughout the Mediterranean, you'll see red flags warning of dangerous storms or tides. Many beaches now also have white flags with jellyfish symbols warning that swimming might be a stinging experience.

• *For a close-up look at the megayachts and a walk along the ramparts, follow this fun detour. Otherwise, skip ahead to the "Old Antibes" directions.*

Antibes' Megayacht Harbor: Take a three-block detour to the right as you leave Plage de la Gravette for a glimpse at the epitome of conspicuous consumption. You'll walk along the harbor under the ramparts known as Bastion St. Jaume.

You'll eventually reach a restricted area harboring massive yachts. Climb the ramparts on your right and make your way to the **modern white sculpture.** *Nomade*—a man of letters looking pensively out to sea—was created in 2010 by the Spanish artist Jaume Plensa (find the posted English explanations nearby). Have a seat inside the sculpture and ponder how human communication forms who we are and links all people. Looking north, the Alps make a beautiful backdrop when it's clear.

Browse the line of huge pleasure craft stern-tied to the pier (which was built in the 1970s with financial aid from mostly Saudi Arabian yacht owners, who wanted a decent place to tie up). Locals call this the *Quai des Milliardaires* ("billionaire's dock"). The Union Jacks fluttering above most of the boats signal that they're registered in the Cayman Islands (can you say tax dodge?). The crews you see keep these toys shipshape all year long—even though many of them are used for just a few days a year. Today, Antibes is the haunt of a large community of English, Irish, and Aussie boaters who help crew these giant yachts. (That explains the Irish pubs and English bookstores.)

Old Antibes: Return along the ramparts, then enter Antibes' old town through the arch under the clock.

• *You can walk directly up the main street to get to our next stop, but here's a more scenic option: Passing through the gate, turn immediately left, and then walk up the steps in the small square. Walk straight through the arch at #14 and into picturesque Place du Revely. Cross Place du Revely to the right, and go down the ramp under several arches, then turn left when you reach the main drag into the old town and Antibes' market hall, Le Marché Provençal.*

Market Hall: Antibes' market hall bustles under a 19th-century canopy, with flowers, produce, Provençal products, and beach accessories. The market wears many hats: fresh produce until 13:00 and varied handicrafts from 15:00. The market hall also offers fun outdoor dining options in the evenings.

On the right (at the corner of Rue Sade), a pretty shop hides an atmospheric **absinthe bar** in its ninth-century vaulted cellar. You're welcome to go through the shop (or enter via Rue Sade) and descend to find an amazing collection of absinthe fountains, the oldest dating from the 1860s. The owner will gladly show you his memorabilia. You can even taste the now-legal drink to better understand Picasso's paintings. On Friday and Saturday nights (and daily in July-Aug), the basement is transformed into an absinthe-infused jazz bar lounge with 1920s ambience.

• *Double back to where you first entered the market and exit the hall, and find Rue Christian Chessel leading uphill to the pretty pastel...*

Church of the Immaculate Conception: Built on the site of a Greek temple, this is worth a peek inside. A church has stood on this site since the 12th century. This one served as the area's cathedral until the mid-1200s. The stone bell tower standing in front of the church predates it by 600 years, when it was part of the city's defenses. Many of those heavy stones were pillaged from Antibes' Roman monuments.

• *Looming above the church on prime real estate is the white-stone...*

Château Grimaldi: This site was home to the acropolis of the Greek city of Antipolis and later a Roman fort. Later still, the château was the residence of the Grimaldi family (a branch of which still rules Monaco). Today it houses Antibes' Picasso Museum. Its proximity to the cathedral symbolized the sometimes too-cozy relationship between society's two dominant landowning classes: the Church and the nobility. (In 1789, the French Revolution changed all that.)

• *After visiting the **Picasso Museum** (see "Sights in Antibes," next), work your way through the warren of pretty lanes, then head out to the water, turn right along the ramparts, and find a sweeping sea view. As you walk, you'll pass a charming neighborhood (La Commune Libre du Safranier) on your right, making a lovely return route. As you wander, look for forested **Cap d'Antibes** (to the south), crowned by its lighthouse and studded with mansions (a proposed hike here is described later).*

The Cap was long the refuge of Antibes' rich and famous, and a favorite haunt of F. Scott Fitzgerald and Ernest Hemingway.

*The rampart walk leads to the **History and Archaeology Museum**. After taking a quick spin through its galleries (see "Sights in Antibes," next), continue hugging the shore past Place Albert I until you see the smashing views back to old Antibes. Benches and soft sand await. You're on your own from here—energetic walkers can continue on the trail, which leads to the lighthouse (see "Hikes," later in this chapter); others can return to old Antibes and wander around in its peaceful back lanes.*

Sights in Antibes

▲▲Picasso Museum (Musée Picasso)

Sitting serenely where the old town meets the sea, this compact three-floor museum offers a manageable collection of Picasso's paintings, sketches, and ceram-ics. Picasso lived in this castle for part of 1946, when he cranked out an amazing amount of art (most of the paintings you'll see are from this short but prolific stretch of his long and varied ca-reer). He was elated by the end of World War II, and his works show a celebration of color and

a rediscovery of light after France's long nightmare of war. Picasso was also reenergized by his young and lovely companion, Françoise Gilot (with whom he would father two children). The resulting col-lection (donated by Picasso) put Antibes on the tourist map. For more on Picasso's life, see the sidebar.

Cost and Hours: €8; Tue-Sun 10:00-18:00 (mid-Sept-mid-June closed at lunchtime), closed Mon year-round; +33 4 92 90 54 20.

Visiting the Museum: After buying your ticket, go through the glass door. Before heading inside, pause in the sculpture garden to appreciate Picasso's working environment (and wonder why he spent only a few months here).

The museum's interior is a calm place of white walls, soft arches, and ample natural light—a great space for exhibiting art. Tour the museum clockwise, noticing the focus on sea creatures, tridents, and other marine themes (*oursin* is a sea urchin, *poulpe* is an octopus, and *poisson* is, well, fishy). *Nature morte* means still life, and you'll see many of these in the collection. Each room has helpful English explanations posted. Expect some changes to these descriptions as the collection is shuffled periodically.

The **ground floor** houses a cool collection of paintings by Norwegian artist Ann-Eva Bergmen and her husband, Hans Hartung, who spent their last years in Antibes. The **first floor** up holds temporary exhibitions (usually related to Picasso) and a small collection of intriguing paintings by Nicholas de Stael, whose style was greatly influenced by southern France and artists such as Henri Matisse (the painting of Antibes' Fort Carré is mood altering).

The museum's highlight is on the **top floor,** where you'll find the permanent collection of Picasso's works. Visitors are greeted by a large image of Picasso and a display of photographs of the artist at work and play during his time in Antibes. Times were tough in 1946. Artists had to improvise. Picasso experimented with materials and surfaces like industrial paint on recycled canvases, random pieces of plywood, and even concrete. Try not to analyze too much. He's happy and in the French Riviera. Remember: The war's over and he's in love—this is pure happiness.

The first gallery room (up the small staircase to your left) houses several famous works, including the lively, frolicking, and big-breasted *La Joie de Vivre* painting (from 1946). This Greek bacchanal sums up the newfound freedom in a just-liberated France and sets the tone for the rest of the collection. You'll also see several ceramic creations and the colorless, three-paneled *Satyr, Faun, and Centaur with Trident.* As you leave this room don't miss the adorable (pregnant?) goat.

Throughout, you'll see both black-and-white and colorful ink sketches that challenge the imagination—these show off Picasso's drawing skills as a cartoonist and caricaturist. Look also for the cute Basque fishermen (*Pêcheur attablé*) and several Cubist-style nudes *(nus couchés),* one painted on plywood.

Near the end, don't miss the wall devoted to Picasso's ceramic plates. In 1947, inspired by a visit to a ceramics factory in nearby Vallauris, Picasso discovered the joy of this medium. He was smitten by the texture of soft clay and devoted a great deal of time to exploring how to work with it—producing over 2,000 pieces in one year. In the same room, the wall-sized painting *Ulysses and the Sirens* screams action and anxiety. Lashed to the ship mast, Ulysses survives the temptation of the sirens.

History and Archaeology Museum
(Musée d'Histoire et d'Archéologie)

More than 2,000 years ago, Antibes was the center of a thriving maritime culture. It was an important Roman commercial port with aqueducts, theaters, baths, and so on. This museum—the only place to get a sense of the city's ancient roots—displays Greek, Roman, and Etruscan odds and ends in two simple halls but sadly, no English descriptions—yet. Your visit starts at an 1894 model of Antibes and continues past displays of Roman coins, cups, plates,

Pablo Picasso (1881-1973)

Pablo Picasso was the most famous and, for me, the greatest artist of the 20th century. Always exploring, he became the master of many styles (Cubism, Surrealism, Expressionism) and of many media (painting, sculpture, prints, ceramics, assemblages). Still, he could make anything he touched look unmistakably like "a Picasso."

Born in Málaga, Spain, Picasso was the son of an art teacher. At a very young age, he quickly advanced beyond his teachers. Picasso's teenage works are stunningly realistic and capture the inner complexities of the people he painted. As a youth in Barcelona, he fell in with a bohemian crowd that mixed wine, women, and art.

In 1900, at age 19, Picasso started making trips to Paris, and he moved there four years later. He absorbed the styles of many painters (especially Henri de Toulouse-Lautrec) while searching for his own artist's voice. His paintings of beggars and other social outcasts show the empathy of a man who was himself a poor, homesick foreigner. When his best friend, Spanish artist Carlos Casagemas, committed suicide, Picasso plunged into a **Blue Period** (1901-1904)—so called because the dominant color in these paintings matches their melancholy mood and subject matter (emaciated beggars, hard-eyed pimps).

In 1904, Picasso got a steady girlfriend (Fernande Olivier) and suddenly saw the world through rose-colored glasses—the **Rose Period.** He was further jolted out of his Blue Period by the "flat" look of the Fauve paintings being made around him. Not satisfied with their take on 3-D, Picasso played with the "building blocks" of line and color to find new ways to reconstruct the real world on canvas.

At his studio in Montmartre, Picasso and his neighbor Georges Braque worked together in poverty so dire they often didn't know where their next bottle of wine was coming from. And then, at age 25, Picasso reinvented painting. Fascinated by the primitive power of African tribal masks, he sketched human faces with simple outlines and almond eyes. Intrigued by his girlfriend's body, he sketched Fernande from every angle, then experimented with showing several different views on the same canvas. A hundred paintings and nine months later, Picasso gave birth to a monstrous canvas of five nude, fragmented prostitutes with mask-like faces—*Les Demoiselles d'Avignon* (1907).

This bold new style was called **Cubism.** With Cubism, Picasso shattered the Old World and put it back together in a new way. The subjects are somewhat recognizable (with the help of the titles), but they're built with geometric shards (let's call them "cubes")—it's like viewing the world through a kaleidoscope of brown and gray. Cubism presents several different angles of the subject at once—say, a woman seen from the front and side simultaneously, resulting in two eyes on the same side of the nose. Cubism showed the traditional three dimensions, plus Einstein's new fourth dimension—the time it takes to walk around the subject to see other angles.

In 1918, Picasso married his first wife, Olga Kokhlova. He then traveled to Rome and entered a **Classical Period** (1920s) of more realistic, full-bodied women and children, inspired by the three-dimensional sturdiness of ancient statues. While he flirted with abstraction, throughout his life Picasso always kept a grip on "reality." His favorite subject was people. The anatomy might be jumbled, but it's all there.

Though he lived in France and Italy, Picasso remained a Spaniard at heart, incorporating Spanish motifs into his work. Unrepentantly macho, he loved bullfights, seeing them as a metaphor for the timeless human interaction between the genders. The horse—clad with blinders and pummeled by the bull—is just a pawn in the battle between bull and matador. To Picasso, the horse symbolizes the feminine, and the bull, the masculine. Spanish imagery—bulls, screaming horses, a Madonna—appears in Picasso's most famous work, *Guernica* (1937). The monumental canvas of a bombed village summed up the pain of Spain's brutal civil war (1936-1939) and foreshadowed the onslaught of World War II.

At war's end, Picasso left Paris, his wife, and his emotional baggage behind, finding fun in the **south of France.** Sun! Color! Water! Freedom! Senior citizen Pablo Picasso was reborn, enjoying worldwide fame. He lived at first with the beautiful young painter Françoise Gilot, mother of two of his children, but it was another young beauty, Jacqueline Roque, who became his second wife. Dressed in rolled-up white pants and a striped sailor's shirt, bursting with pent-up creativity, Picasso often cranked out a painting a day. Picasso's Riviera works set the tone for the rest of his life. They're sunny, lighthearted, and childlike; filled with motifs of the sea, Greek mythology (fauns, centaurs), and animals; and freely experimental in their use of new media. The simple drawing of a dove holding an olive branch became an international symbol of peace.

Picasso made collages, built "statues" out of wood, wire, ceramics, papier-mâché, or whatever, and even turned everyday household objects into statues (like his famous bull's head made of a bicycle seat with handlebar horns). **Multimedia** works like these have become so standard today that we forget how revolutionary they once were. His last works have the playfulness of someone much younger. As it is often said of Picasso, "When he was a child, he painted like a man. When he was old, he painted like a child."

and scads of amphorae. The lanky lead pipe connected to a center box was used as a bilge pump; nearby is a good display of Roman anchors made of lead. In a later exhibit, the orange stones hanging from strings are from a Roman loom.

Cost and Hours: €3; Tue-Sun 10:00-12:30 & 14:00-18:00, shorter hours off-season, closed Mon year-round, on the water between Picasso Museum and Place Albert I, +33 4 92 95 85 98.

Fort Carré

This impressively situated, mid-16th-century citadel, on the headland overlooking the harbor, protected Antibes from Nice (which until 1860 wasn't part of France). You can tour this unusual star-shaped fort for the fantastic views over Antibes, but there's little to see inside (€3, Tue-Sun 10:00-18:00, mid-Sept-mid-June until 17:00, closed Mon year-round).

▲Beaches (Plages)

Good beaches stretch from the south end of Antibes toward Cap d'Antibes. They're busy but manageable in summer and on weekends, with cheap snack stands and good views of the old town. The closest beach to the old town is at the port (Plage de la Gravette), which seems calm in any season.

HIKES

I list two good hikes below. Orient yourself from the seaside rampart walk below the Picasso Museum or from the bottom of Boulevard Albert I (where it meets the beach). That tower on the hill is your destination for the first hike. The longer Cap d'Antibes hike begins over that hill, a few miles farther away. The two hikes are easy to combine by bus, bike, or car.

▲▲Chapelle et Phare de la Garoupe Hike

The territorial views—best in the morning, skippable if it's hazy—from this viewpoint more than merit the 20-minute uphill climb from Plage de la Salis (a few blocks after Maupassant Apartments, where the road curves left, follow signs and the rough, cobbled Chemin du Calvaire up to lighthouse tower). An orientation table explains that you can see from Nice to Cannes and up to the Alps. The peaceful **$$ Le Bistrot du Curé** has drinks and light snacks (Tue-Sun 11:00-18:00, closed Mon, in winter open Thu-Sun only).

Getting There: Take bus #2 or bus #14 to the Plage de la Salis stop and find the trail a block ahead. By car or bike, follow signs for *Cap d'Antibes*, then look for *Chapelle et Phare de la Garoupe* signs.

▲▲Cap d'Antibes Hike (Sentier Touristique de Tirepoil)

Cap d'Antibes is filled with exclusive villas and mansions protected by high walls. Roads are just lanes, bounded on both sides by the

high and greedy walls in this home of some of the most expensive real estate in France (and where "public" seems like a necessary evil). But all the money in the world can't buy you the beach in France, so a thin strip of rocky coastline forms a two-mile long, parklike zone with an extremely scenic, mostly paved but often rocky trail (Sentier Touristique de Tirepoil).

As you walk, you'll have fancy fences with security cameras on one side and dramatic sea views on the other. The public space is rarely more than 50 yards wide and often extremely rocky—impassible if not for the paved trail carved out of it for the delight of hikers.

At a fast clip you can walk the entire circle in just over an hour. Don't do the hike without the tourist map (available at hotels or the TI). You can do it in either direction (or in partial segments; see "Getting There," below). I've described the walk starting at its western end going counterclockwise).

From the La Fontaine bus stop walk five minutes down Avenue Mrs. L. D. Beaumont to the gate of the Villa Eilenroc. Enter through the gate to the trail skirting the villa on your left, and walk five more minutes to the rocky coastal trail. Now turn left and follow the trail for nearly an hour around Cap Gros. There's no way to get lost without jumping into the sea or scaling villa security walls. You return to civilization at a tiny resort (Plage de la Garoupe), with an expensive restaurant, a fine beach (both public and private), and a fun and inexpensive beachside bar/café. From here it's a 10-minute walk up Avenue André Sella to your starting point and the bus stop. With a car (or bike), you could start and end at Plage de la Garoupe.

Getting There: Drivers will find parking easier at the trail's eastern end (Plage de la Garoupe), though some street parking is also available a few blocks from the trail's other end (look near Hôtel Beau-Site). Pedestrians should start at the trail's western end. Take bus #2 from Antibes for about 15 minutes to the La

Fontaine stop at Rond-Point A Meiland (next to the recommended Hôtel Beau-Site, see "Getting Around Antibes," earlier), then follow the route described earlier.

NEAR ANTIBES

Juan-les-Pins Town

The low-rise town of Juan-les-Pins, sprawling across the Cap d'Antibes isthmus from Antibes, is where the action is...after hours. It's a modern waterfront resort with good beaches, plenty of lively bars and restaurants, and a popular jazz festival in July. The town is also known for its clothing boutiques that stay open until midnight (people are too busy getting tanned to shop at normal hours). As locals say, "Party, sleep in, shop late, party more."

Getting There: Frequent buses and trains (see "Getting Around Antibes," earlier) make the 10-minute trip to and from Antibes.

Renoir Museum (Musée Renoir)

Halfway between Antibes and Nice, above Cagnes-sur-Mer, Pierre-Auguste Renoir found his Giverny. Here, the artist spent

the last 12 years of his life (1907-1919) tending his gardens, painting, and even dabbling in sculpture (despite suffering from rheumatoid arthritis). In fact, there are more sculptures than paintings here. His home was later converted into a small museum. Visitors get a personal look into Renoir's later years but very little art. You'll see his studio, wheelchair, and bedroom; take a stroll in his gardens; and enjoy several of his and other artists' paintings of people and places around Cagnes-sur-Mer. It's a pleasant place and an enjoyable pilgrimage for his fans.

Cost and Hours: €6, Wed-Mon 10:00-12:00 & 14:00-18:00, Oct-April until 17:00, closed Tue year-round, Chemin des Collettes, +33 4 93 20 61 07.

Getting There: It's complicated by public transport (and not worth the trouble for most), but manageable by car: Go to Cagnes-sur-Mer (on the A-8 autoroute, take exit 47 if coming from the west, exit 48 if coming from the east), then follow *Centre-Ville* and brown *Musée Renoir* signs.

Biot Village

The artsy pottery and glassblowing village of Biot is popular with aesthetic types and home to the Fernand Léger Museum.

Getting There: Biot is easy to reach on bus #10 from the Antibes city bus station (2/hour Mon-Sat, hourly Sun). Parking des Bâchettes is free and allows quick access to its pretty pedestrian street.

Sleeping in Antibes

Several sleepable options are available in the town center, but my favorite Antibes hotels are farther out and most convenient for drivers.

OUTSIDE THE TOWN CENTER

$$$ Hôtel Mas Djoliba*** is a traditional manor house with chirping birds and a flower-filled moat. While convenient for drivers, it's workable for walkers (10-minute walk to Plage de la Salis, 15 minutes to old Antibes). Bigger rooms are worth the additional cost, and several rooms come with small decks (several good family rooms, no elevator but just three floors, *boules* court and loaner balls; 29 Avenue de Provence—from Boulevard Albert I, look for gray signs two blocks before the sea, turn right onto Boulevard Général Maizière, and follow signs; +33 4 93 34 02 48, www.hotel-djoliba.com, contact@hotel-djoliba.com, Delphine).

$$$ Hôtel la Jabotte** is a cozy little hotel hidden along an ignored alley a block from the best beaches and a 20-minute walk from the old town. Run with panache by Nathalie and Pierre (and dog Hush), the hotel's rich colors and decor show a personal touch. The immaculate rooms have smallish bathrooms and individual terraces facing a cute, central garden where you'll get to know your neighbor (no TVs, 3-night minimum in high season, free breakfast for Rick Steves readers with current guidebook; sauna, bikes, kayaks, and paddleboards available; 13 Avenue Max Maurey, take the third right after passing Hôtel Josse, +33 4 93 61 45 89, www.jabotte.com, info@jabotte.com). The hotel can shuttle clients to hiking trails, restaurants, etc. in their small tuk-tuk vehicle for a small fee. They also offer transport to the train station or the airport in their electric car.

$$ Hôtel Beau-Site,*** my only listing on Cap d'Antibes, is a 10-minute drive from town. It's a terrific value if you want to get away...but not *too* far away. (Without a car, you'll feel isolated.) Helpful Nathalie welcomes you with a pool, a comfy patio garden, and secure pay parking. Rooms are spacious and comfortable, and several have balconies (electric bikes available, 141 Boulevard Kennedy, +33 4 93 61 53 43, www.hotelbeausite.net, contact@hotelbeausite.net). The hotel is a 10-minute walk from Plage de la Garoupe on the Cap d'Antibes loop hike (described earlier).

IN THE TOWN CENTER

$$$ **Hôtel la Place***** is central, pricey, and comfortable. It overlooks the ugly old bus station with tastefully designed rooms and a comfy lounge (no elevator, 1 Avenue 24 Août, +33 4 97 21 03 11, www.la-place-hotel.com, contact@la-place-hotel.com).

$ **Hôtel Relais du Postillon,**** is a mellow, central place above a cozy café with 16 impeccable rooms at very fair rates. The furnishings are tasteful, and several rooms have small balconies or terraces (tiny elevator, pay parking, 8 Rue Championnet, +33 4 93 34 20 77, www.relaisdupostillon.com, relais@relaisdupostillon.com).

$ **Modern Hôtel,**** in the pedestrian zone behind the city bus station, is suitable for budget-conscious travelers. The 17 standard-size rooms are simple and spick-and-span (no elevator, 1 Rue Fourmillière, +33 4 92 90 59 05, www.modernhotel06.com, modern-hotel@wanadoo.fr).

Eating in Antibes

Antibes is a fun and relaxed place to dine out. But there are precious few really good options (particularly on Mon—book ahead), and those get booked up on weekends in particular (when you're smart to book a day ahead). All but one of my recommendations are within a few blocks of each other, so it's easy to comparison shop.

Antibes' **Market Hall** (Marché Provençal) has great ambience and is popular with budget-minded diners each evening after the market stalls close. It's not *haute cuisine*, but prices are usually reasonable, and slurping mussels under a classic 19th-century canopy can make for a great memory. To start your soirée, consider a glass of wine from one of several wine bars that call the market hall home.

Try $$ **Chez Lulu** for an ultimate family-style dining adventure that seems utterly out of place on the Riviera. Diners fork over €28 and settle in, while charismatic owner Frank (who speaks flawless English), his wife Alice, and—when they're busy—their granddaughter dish out charcuterie, salads, soups, a main course, and desserts to be shared. Tables seat 6-10, and the setting is warm and convivial. Don't come for a romantic meal. You'll be on a first-name basis with your neighbors, cut your own bread, and serve your own soup (fun!). Book a day ahead or arrive early (from 19:00, closed Sun-Tue, +33 4 89 89 08 92, 5 Rue Frédéric Isnard).

$$$$ **L'Arazur** is the love child of a young couple who both worked as chefs at Michelin-starred restaurants and wanted a quieter life in the south. Lucas does the cooking while Jeanne runs the restaurant. The setting is relaxed yet elegant, and the attention to quality is obvious (book ahead, dinner only, closed Mon, 8 Rue des Palmiers, +33 4 93 34 75 60, www.larazur.fr).

$$ Le P'tit Cageot is a find. The chef makes delicious Mediterranean cuisine affordable. The place is tiny, just 25 seats inside and out, so book ahead (closed Sun-Mon, 5 Rue du Docteur Rostan, +33 4 89 68 48 66).

$$ Le Zinc is a cool little wine-bar bistro at the upper end of the market hall serving a limited selection of tasty cuisine. Book ahead or arrive early for an outside table (closed Sun evening and all day Mon, 15 Cours Masséna, +33 4 83 14 69 20).

$$$ Le Vauban is a traditional and dressy place with red-velvet chairs and serious service. It's popular with locals for special events and its seafood (closed Mon-Tue, opposite 4 Rue Thuret, +33 4 93 34 33 05, www.levauban.fr).

$$$ Le Brulot, an institution in Antibes, is known for its Provençal cuisine and meat dishes (most cooked over an open fire). It's a small, rustic place with tables crammed every which way (big, splittable portions, come early or book ahead, closed Sun, 2 Rue Frédéric Isnard, +33 4 93 34 17 76, www.brulot.fr).

$$$ La Taille de Guêpe is family-run by Olivier in the kitchen and Katy in the relaxing garden-like dining room. The chef has worked for several years with flowers; the colorful varieties you find on your plate are all edible and add a twist to the fresh, fine, and light food. The *moëlleux au chocolat* is a perfect way to end your meal. *Menus,* enjoyed with cheap and good local wine, are a good deal (reservations recommended, closed Sun-Mon, 24 Rue de Fersen, +33 4 93 74 03 58).

$$$ Le Comptoir de la Tourraque offers reliably delicious Mediterranean cuisine in a warm setting with a good-value fixed-price *menu*. As this is one of the few restaurants open on Monday, reserve ahead (dinner only, closed Wed, 1 Rue de la Tourraque, +33 4 93 95 24 86).

Picnic on the Beach or Ramparts: Romantics on a shoestring can find grocery stores open until late in Antibes and assemble their own picnic dinner to enjoy on the beach or ramparts. There's a good **Carrefour City** market at 44 Rue de la République and a **Monoprix** on Place Général de Gaulle—both open late.

ANTIBES & NEARBY

Antibes Connections

For a comparison of train and bus connections, see the "Public Transportation in the French Riviera" sidebar on page 306.

From Antibes by Train: TGV and local trains deliver great service to Antibes' little station. Trains go to **Cannes** (2/hour, 15 minutes), **Nice** (2/hour, 20 minutes), **Grasse** (1/hour, 40 minutes), **Villefranche-sur-Mer** (2/hour, 40 minutes), **Monaco** (2/hour, 50 minutes), and **Marseille** (hourly, 2.5 hours).

By Bus: All the buses listed below serve the Pôle d'Echange regional bus station (behind the train station). Handy **bus #200** ties everything together from Cannes to Nice, but runs at a snail's pace when traffic is bad. It goes west to **Cannes** (35 minutes) and east to near **Biot** village (15 minutes—bus #10 is better, see the Biot village listing under "Near Antibes," earlier), **Cagnes-sur-Mer** (25 minutes), and **Nice** (1.5 hours). For bus details, including info on tickets, routes, and frequencies, see the "Getting Around the Riviera" section in the French Riviera chapter. **Bus #250** runs to **Nice Airport** (2/hour, 40 minutes).

Cannes

Cannes (pronounced "can"), famous for its May film festival, is the sister city of Beverly Hills. That says it all. When I asked at the TI for a list of museums and sights, they just smiled. Cannes—with big, exclusive hotels lining mostly private stretches of perfect, sandy beach—is for strolling, shopping, dreaming of meeting a movie star, and lounging on the seafront. Cannes has little that's unique to offer the traveler...except a mostly off-limits film festival and quick access to two undeveloped islands. You

can buy an ice-cream cone at the train station and see everything before you've had your last lick. Money is what Cannes has always been about—wealthy people come here to make the scene, and there's always enough *scandale* to go around. The king of Saudi Arabia purchased a serious slice of waterfront just east of town and built his compound with no regard to local zoning regulations. Money talks on the Riviera...and always has.

Handy Cannes and St-Tropez Phrases

English	French
Where is a movie star?	*Où est une vedette?*
I am a movie star.	*Je suis une vedette.*
I am rich and single.	*Je suis riche et célibataire.*
Are you rich and single?	*Etes-vous riche et célibataire?*
Are those real?	*Ils sont des vrais?*
How long is your yacht?	*Quelle est la longeur de votre yacht?*
How much did that cost?	*Combien coûtait-il?*
You can always dream...	*On peut toujours rêver...*

GETTING TO CANNES

Don't sleep or drive in Cannes. Day-trip here by train or bus. It's a breeze, as frequent trains and buses link to Cannes from seafront cities like Antibes (15 minutes by train) and Nice (30 minutes; longer by bus). For details, see the transportation chart in the "Getting Around the Riviera" section in the French Riviera chapter. From Grasse, you can take a direct train or bus to Cannes. Buses stop next to the train station. A car is a headache best avoided in Cannes, though there's a darn scenic drive just west of Cannes (from Fréjus on D-6098).

Orientation to Cannes

Buses stop in front of the train station, where you'll find a TI (to the left as you exit the train station), baggage storage (to the right as you exit), and a handy train-information desk with maps of the city. If you must drive, store your car at the parking garage next to the train station.

Tourist Information: Cannes' main TI is located in the Film Festival Hall at 1 Boulevard de la Croisette (daily July-Aug 9:00-20:00, Sept-June 10:00-19:00, +33 4 92 99 84 22, www.cannes-destination.fr). Another TI is next to the train station (same hours, 4 Place de la Gare).

Cannes Walk

This self-guided cancan will take you to Cannes' sights in a level, one-hour walk at a movie-star pace.

• *Walk straight out of the train station, crossing the bus station/street in front and turn left. Make a quick right on Rue des Serbes, and stroll for five unglamorous minutes to the beachfront. Cross the busy Boulevard de*

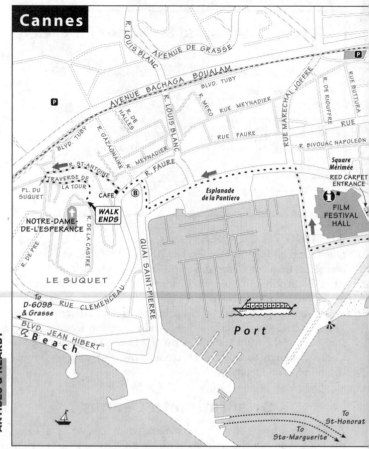

Cannes

la Croisette, turn left on the promenade, and walk a few blocks down until you're about opposite the Marriot Casino. Now get familiar with...

The Lay of the Land: Cannes feels different from its neighbors to the east. You won't find the pastel oranges and pinks of Old Nice and Villefranche-sur-Mer. Cannes was never part of Italy—and its architecture and cuisine remind me more of Paris than Nice.

Face the water. The land jutting into the sea on your left is actually two islands, St-Honorat and Ste-Marguerite. St-Honorat has been the property of monks for over 500 years; today its abbey, vineyards, trails, and gardens can be visited by peace-seeking travelers. Ste-Marguerite, which you also can visit, is famous for the stone prison that housed the 17th-century Man in the Iron

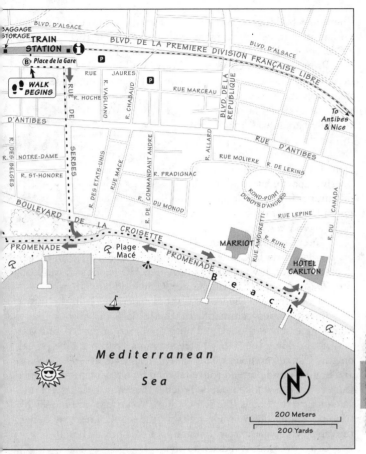

Mask (whose true identity remains unknown). For more on visiting these islands, see the boat excursions listed under "Activities in Cannes," later.

Now look far to your right. Those striking mountains sweeping down to the sea are the Massif de l'Estérel. Their red-rock outcrops oversee spectacular car and train routes (see "Cannes Connections," later). Closer in, the hill with the medieval tower caps Cannes' old town (Le Suquet). This hilltop offers grand views and pretty lanes—and the only place in Cannes where you feel its medieval past. Below the old town, the port welcomes yachts of all sizes...provided they're really big.

Face inland. Closer, on the left, find the unexceptional, cream-colored building with the tinted windows overlooking the sea. That convention-center-like structure is home of the famous film festival (we'll visit there soon). Back the other way, gaze up the boulevard.

That classy building with twin black-domed roofs is Hôtel Carlton, our eventual target and as far as we'll go together in that direction.

• *Continue with the sea on your right and stroll the...*

Promenade (La Croisette): You're walking along Boulevard de la Croisette—Cannes' famed two-mile-long promenade. First popular with kings who wintered here after Napoleon fell, the elite parade was later joined by British aristocracy. Today, Boulevard de la Croisette is fronted by some of the most expensive apartments and hotels in Europe. If it's lunchtime, you might try one of the beach cafés.

• *Stop when you get to...*

Hôtel Carlton: Built in 1911, this is the most famous address on Boulevard de la Croisette (small double room—€1,500, bigger double—€7,000). It was featured in Alfred Hitchcock's classic 1955 film *To Catch a Thief* (starring Grace Kelly and Cary Grant).

Face the beach. The iconic Cannes experience is to slip into a robe (ideally, monogrammed with your initials), out of your luxury hotel (preferably this one), and onto the beach or pier. While you may not be doing the "fancy hotel and monogrammed robe" ritual on this Cannes excursion, you can—for about €30—rent a chair and umbrella and pretend you're tanning for a red-carpet premiere. Cannes has a few token public beaches, but most beaches are private and run by hotels like the Carlton. You could save money by sunning among the common folk, but the real Cannes way to flee the rabble and paparazzi is to rent a spot on a private beach.

Cross over and wander into the hotel—you're welcome to browse (harder during the festival). Ask for a hotel brochure, verify room rates, check for availability. How do people afford this? Groupon? Imagine the scene here during the film festival. An affordable café (considering the cost of a room) lies just beyond the champagne lounge.

• *You can continue your stroll down La Croisette, but I'm doubling back to the cream-colored building that is Cannes'...*

Film Festival Hall: Cannes' film festival (Festival de Cannes), staged since 1946, completes the "Big Three" of Riviera events (with Monaco's Grand Prix and Nice's Carnival). The hall where the festival takes place—a busy-but-nondescript convention center that also hosts the town TI—sits plump on the beach. You'll recognize the formal grand entryway (most likely without the famed red carpet). Find the famous (Hollywood-style) handprints in the sidewalk nearby (also by the entry to the TI). To get inside during the festival, you have to be a star (or a photographer—some 3,000 paparazzi attend  the gala event, and most bring their own ladders to get above the crowds). It's an amazing scene.

The festival originated in part as an anti-fascist response to Mussolini's Venice Film Festival. Cannes' first festival was due to open in 1939, on the very day Hitler invaded Poland. Because of World War II, the opening was delayed until 1946. The first movie screened was American, The Hunchback of Notre Dame, starring Charles Laughton and Maureen O'Hara. Cannes' film festival is also famous as the first festival to give one vote per country on the jury (giving films from smaller countries a better chance).

Though generally off-limits to curious tourists, the festival is everything around here—and is worth a day trip to Cannes if you happen to be in the region when it's on. The town buzzes with megastar energy, press passes, and revealing dresses. Locals claim that it's the world's third-biggest media event, after the Olympics and the World Cup (soccer). The festival prize is the Palme d'Or (like the Oscar for Best Picture). The French press can't cover the event enough, and the average Jean in France follows it as Joe would the World Series in the States.

• *Around the other side of the festival hall is the port (Gare Maritime).*

The Port and Old Town (Le Suquet): The megayachts line up closest to the Film Festival Hall. After seeing these amazing boats, everything else looks like a dinghy. Boat service to St-Tropez and the nearby islands of St-Honorat and Ste-Marguerite depart from the far side of the port (at Quai Laubeuf; for boat info, see "Activities in Cannes," later).

Cannes' oldest neighborhood, Le Suquet, crowns the hill past the port. Locals refer to it as their Montmartre. Artsy and charming, it's a steep 15-minute walk above the port, with little of interest except the panoramic views from its ancient church, Notre-Dame-de-l'Espérance (Our Lady of Hope).

• *To find the views in Le Suquet, aim for its clock tower and start by passing the bus station at the northwest corner of the port, then make your way up cobbled Rue Saint-Antoine (next to the Café St. Antoine).*

Yachters' Itinerary

If you're visiting Cannes on your private yacht, here's a suggested itinerary:

1. Take in the Festival de Cannes and the accompanying social scene. Organize an evening party on your boat.
2. Motor over to Monte Carlo for the Grand Prix, scheduled—conveniently for yachters—just after the film festival.
3. On your way back west to St-Tropez, deconstruct events from the film festival and Grand Prix with Brigitte Bardot.
4. Drop down to Porto Chervo on Sardinia, one of the few places in the world where your yacht is "just average."
5. Head west to Ibiza and Marbella in Spain, where your friends are moored for the big party scene.

Turn left on Place du Suquet, and then follow signs to Traverse de la Tour *for the final leg.*

Cue music. Roll end credits. Our film is over. For further exploration, look for Cannes' "underbelly" between Le Suquet and the train station—narrow lanes with inexpensive cafés and shops that regular folks can afford.

Activities in Cannes

Shopping

Cannes is made for window shopping (the best streets are between the station and the waterfront). For the trendiest boutiques, stroll down handsome Rue d'Antibes (parallel to the sea about three blocks inland). Rue Meynadier anchors a pedestrian zone with more affordable shops closer to the port. To bring home a real surprise, why not consider cosmetic surgery? Cannes is well known as *the* place on the Riviera to have your face (or other parts) realigned.

Boat Excursions to St-Honorat and Ste-Marguerite Islands

Two boat companies ferry tourists 15 minutes from the Quai Laubeuf dock in Cannes' port to twin islands just offshore: St-Honorat and Ste-Marguerite. Both outfits charge the same (€15.50 round-trip) and run every half hour (daily 9:00-18:00). There's no ferry between the two islands. For the Ste-Marguerite schedule, go to www.trans-cote-azur.com; for St-Honorat hours, it's www.cannes-ilesdelerins.com.

The islands offer a refreshing change from the town scene, with almost no development, good swimming, and peaceful walking paths. On Ste-Marguerite you can hike, visit the castle (part of which is now a youth hostel) and the cell where the mysterious Man in the Iron Mask was imprisoned (with a good little museum with decent English explanations featuring cargo from a sunken

Roman vessel), and tour the Musée de la Mer's ancient collection and underwater exhibits. On St-Honorat you can hike seafront trails and visit the abbey where monks have lived and prayed for 16 centuries. Today they make fine wines in their free time. St-Honorat also has a few shops and a restaurant.

Cannes Connections

From Cannes by Train to: Antibes (2/hour, 15 minutes), **Nice** (2/hour, 30 minutes), **Monaco** (2/hour, 70 minutes), **Grasse** (hourly, 30 minutes).

By Bus: Bus #200 heads east from Cannes along the Riviera, stopping at **Antibes** (35 minutes) and **Nice** (2 hours; trip duration depends on traffic; for bus details, see the "Getting Around the Riviera" section in the French Riviera chapter). **Bus #210** runs from the train station express on the freeway to **Nice Airport** (1-2/hour, 50 minutes on freeway, €22). Both buses stop at the Cannes train station.

By Boat: Trans Côte d'Azur runs boat excursions from Cannes to **St-Tropez** (€55 round-trip, 1 hour each way with 5 hours in St-Tropez; July-Aug daily 1/day; June and Sept 1/day Tue, Thu, and Sat-Sun only; no service Oct-May; +33 4 92 98 71 30, www.transcote-azur.com). This boat trip is popular—book a few days ahead from June to September.

By Cruise Ship: Ships tender passengers to the west side of Cannes' port. From here, it's an easy walk into town: Head inland, with the port on your right-hand side. Note that the tender dock is near the end of my "Cannes Walk"; if planning to follow it, you can either start the walk here and do it in reverse or stroll about 10 minutes around the port to the walk's starting point (see "Cannes Walk," earlier). If heading to points beyond Cannes, it takes about 15 minutes to walk from the tender dock to the train station, where you can catch a train for Antibes, Nice, or Villefranche-sur-Mer.

St-Tropez

St-Tropez is a busy, charming, and traffic-free port town smothered with fashion boutiques, elegant restaurants, and luxury boats. If you came here for history or quaintness, you caught the wrong yacht. But if you have more money than you know what to do with, you're home. There are 5,700 year-round residents...and more than 100,000 visitors daily in the summer. If St-Tropez is on your must-visit list, hit it on your way to or from Provence—and skip it altogether in summer and on weekend afternoons.

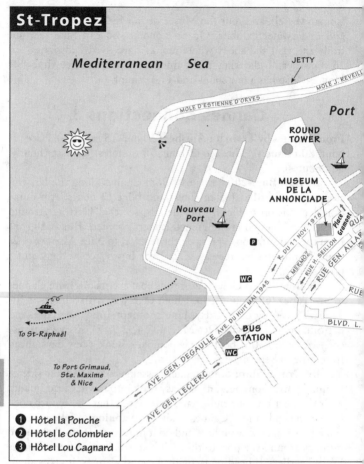

St-Tropez

Mediterranean Sea

JETTY

MOLE J. KEVEILL

MOLE D'ESTIENNE D'ORVES

Port

ROUND TOWER

MUSEUM DE LA ANNONCIADE

Nouveau Port

R. DU 11 NOV. 1918

Place Grammt

QUA

R. MERMOZ

RUE H. SEILLON

RUE GEN. ALLAR

WC

RUE

To St-Raphaël

AVE. DU HUIT MAI 1945

BLVD. L.

BUS STATION

WC

To Port Grimaud, Ste. Maxime & Nice

AVE. GEN. DEGAULLE

AVE. GEN. LECLERC

AVE. GEN. DEGAULLE

❶ Hôtel la Ponche
❷ Hôtel le Colombier
❸ Hôtel Lou Cagnard

ANTIBES & NEARBY

As with lots of now-famous villages in southern France, St-Tropez was "found" by artists. Painter Paul Signac brought several of his friends to St-Tropez in the late 1800s, giving the village its first whiff of popularity (get rid of the yachts filling the harbor, and the town would resemble what it looked like then). But it wasn't until Brigitte Bardot made the scene here in the 1956 film...*And God Created Woman* that St-Tropez became synonymous with Riviera glamour. Since then, it's the first place that comes to mind when people think of the jet set luxuriating on Mediterranean beaches. For many, the French Riviera begins here and runs east to Menton, on the Italian border.

The village is the attraction here; the nearest big beach is miles away. Window shopping, people-watching, tan maintenance, and savoring slow meals fill people's days, weeks, and, in some cases, lives. Here, people dress up, size up one another's

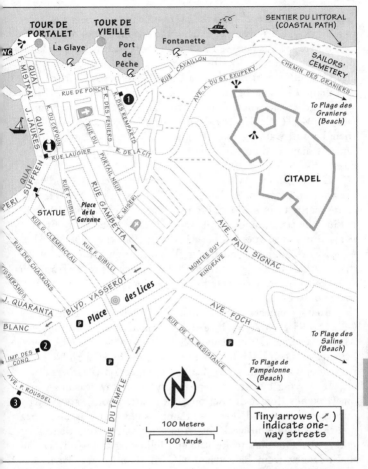

yachts or cars, and troll for a partner. While the only models you'll see are in the shop windows, Brigitte Bardot still hangs out on a bench in front of the TI signing autographs (Thu 15:00-17:30, and if you believe that...).

Wander the harborfront, where fancy yachts moor stern-in, their carefully coiffed captains and first mates enjoying *pu-pus* for happy hour—they're seeing and being seen. Take time to stroll the back streets (the small lanes below La Citadelle are St-Tropez's most appealing) while nibbling a chocolate-and-

Grand Marnier crêpe. Find the big local hangout, Place des Lices (good cafés), where you can catch some serious games of *pétanque*.

St-Tropez lies between its famous port and the hilltop Citadelle (with great views). The network of lanes between the port and Citadelle are strollable in a Carmel-by-the-Sea sort of way. The main **TI** is on the starboard side of the port (to the right as you face the sea), where Quai Suffren and Quai Jean Jaurès meet (+33 4 94 97 45 21, www.sainttropeztourisme.com). Pick up their helpful walking tour brochure, ask about events in town, and get maps and bus information if you plan to hike along the coast.

Getting There: With no trains to St-Tropez, buses and boats are your only options without a car. **Buses** connect to St-Tropez from nearby train stations. From the east, catch bus #7601 from behind the train station in St-Raphaël (closest station to St-Tropez, 70 minutes, goes via Ste-Maxime); from the west, take bus #7801 or #7802, 1.5 hours from Toulon's train station (if arriving at either station by train, check bus schedules to St-Tropez in advance to ensure you make the connection; https://services-zou.maregionsud.fr).

Boats connect to St-Tropez from St-Raphaël twice daily (+33 4 94 95 17 46, www.bateauxsaintraphael.com) and from Ste-Maxime or Port Grimaud about hourly (+33 4 94 49 29 39, www.bateauxverts.com). For boats connecting St-Tropez with Nice, see page 366; with Cannes, see "Cannes Connections," earlier.

If arriving by **car,** prepare for traffic in any season—worse on weekends (forget driving on Sunday afternoons), always ugly during summer, and downright impossible between St-Tropez and Ste-Maxime on weekends. You can avoid this bottleneck by taking the autoroute to Le Luc and following the windy D-558 to St-Tropez from here (via La Garde-Freinet and Port Grimaud). The last few miles to St-Tropez are along a too-long, two-lane road with one way in, one way out, and too many people going exactly where you're going. There are two main parking lots: Parking des Lices (near recommended hotels) and Parking du Nouveau Port (best for day-trippers).

Visiting St-Tropez: Use the TI's self-guided walking tour brochure to connect the following highlights.

The **port** has been a key player in St-Tropez's economy since the 18th century, when it saw a brisk trade in wine, cork, and lumber. St-Tropez's shipyards were famous for their three-mast ships, which could carry more than 1,000 barrels of wine. Today's port is famous for its big boats. There's something bizarre about the size of those boats, stern-tied tightly in such a small harbor. While strolling around, you'll see busy deckhands (hustling before their captains arrive) and artists competing for room.

The red-tabled **Le Sénéquier,** by the TI, is one of the town's most venerated cafés—and has long attracted celebrities, including the philosopher Jean-Paul Sartre. High-end cafés and restaurants line the port from here to the jetty—it doesn't seem to matter that you can't see the sea for the big yachts. The bulky **Tour du Portalet** tower at the port's end has views across the bay to the town of Ste-Maxime and out to sea. A plaque honors the American, British, and French troops who liberated Provence on August 15, 1944. Climb the jetty for great views over the port.

The **Museum of the Annonciade,** though generally ignored, houses an enchanting collection of works from the Post-Impressionist and Fauvist artists who decorated St-Tropez before Brigitte. Almost all canvases feature St-Tropez sights and landscapes. You'll see colorful paintings by Paul Signac, Henri Matisse, Georges Braque, Pierre Bonnard, Maurice de Vlaminck, and more. Gaze out the windows and notice how the port has changed since they were here daily (+33 4 94 17 84 10).

The scenic **Sentier du Littoral coastal path,** originally patrolled by customs agents, runs past the 1558 Citadelle fortress (which houses a maritime museum) and continues for 12 miles along the coast. The trail is marked with yellow dashes on the pavement, walls, and trees. Leave St-Tropez along the road below the Citadelle, pass the Sailors' Cemetery, and you'll join the path before long.

Several companies offer mildly interesting **boat tours** of the surrounding coastline. You'll learn a smidgen about St-Tropez's history and a lot about the villas of the rich and famous (details at TI).

The vast *pétanque (boules)* **court** on Place des Lices is worth your attention. Have a drink at Le Café and take in the action.

Nearby: Although more modern than St-Tropez, **Port Grimaud** (located a few miles toward Ste-Maxime) is no less attractive or upscale. This "Venice of Provence" was reclaimed from a murky lagoon about 40 years ago and is now lined with four miles of canals, lovely homes, and moorage for thousands of yachts. It's a fascinating look at what clever minds can produce from a swamp. Park at the lot across from the town entry (TI next to the parking lot, www.grimaud-provence.com), and cross the barrier and bridge into a beautiful world of privilege. Climb the church bell tower for a good panorama view.

Sleeping in St-Tropez: If you're spending the night here, remember that high season in St-Tropez runs from June through September, and weekends are busy year-round. Hotels worth considering include: **$$$$ Hôtel la Ponche****** (central and luxurious with a restaurant to match, 3 Rue des Remparts, +33 4 94

97 02 53, www.laponche.com; **$$ Hôtel le Colombier**** (small, adorable, and on a quiet street—Impasse des Conquêtes, reservations by phone only, +33 4 94 97 05 31, http://lecolombierhotel. free.fr); and **$$ Hôtel Lou Cagnard**** (pretty courtyard garden, 18 Avenue Paul Roussel, +33 4 94 97 04 24, www.hotel-lou-cagnard.com).

INLAND RIVIERA

St-Paul-de-Vence • Vence •
Grasse • Inland Riviera Drive •
Grand Canyon du Verdon

For a verdant, rocky, fresh escape from the beaches, head inland and upward. Some perfectly perched hill towns and splendid scenery hang overlooked in this region more famous for beaches and bikinis. A short car or bus ride away from the Mediterranean reaps big rewards: lush forests, deep canyons, and swirling hilltop villages. It's easy to link the main sights and towns of this region in a day's drive from Nice. A longer drive brings you to Europe's greatest canyon, the Grand Canyon du Verdon (also known as the Gorges du Verdon).

PLANNING YOUR TIME

With one full day, rent a car and do my Inland Riviera Drive (described later in this chapter). Start in Nice (or Antibes) and arrive in St-Paul-de-Vence as early as you can to minimize crowds (or just skip it). Visit the Fondation Maeght, then head to nearby Vence for lunch, then take an ice cream stroll through unspoiled Tourrettes-sur-Loup. End your day with a visit to the perfume city of Grasse. (This same trip can be done by bus if you depart early in the morning and forgo Grasse.)

With two days (and a car), conclude your driving tour with an overnight in Vence, then spend your second day visiting the Grand Canyon du Verdon (ideally ending in the Luberon, Cassis, or Aix-en-Provence).

GETTING AROUND THE INLAND RIVIERA

By Car: Driving is the best way to tour this area, though weekend traffic and parking challenges will test your patience. You can rent a car for a day from Nice or Antibes.

By Bus: Buses get you to many of the places in this chapter. Vence, St-Paul-de-Vence, and Grasse are well served by bus from

Inland Riviera

To Gorges du Verdon — D-2 — Gréolières — D-8 — D-6202

Loup — Courségoules — Col de Vence

PONT DU BRAMAFEN — Waterfall — D-2 — D-2210

Gorges du Loup — D-6 — TRAILHEAD — St-Jeannet — A-8

Gourdon — PONT-DU-LOUP — **Vence** — To Monaco

To Gorges du Verdon — D-3 — D-2210 — Tourrettes-sur-Loup — D-36 — **Nice**

Le Bar-sur-Loup — D-7 — St-Paul-de-Vence — Haut-de-Cagnes — Villefranche-sur-Mer

D-6085 — D-2085 — Cap Ferrat

Grasse — D-4 — Cagnes-sur-Mer — Nice Airport

D-6185 — Biot — A-8

D-35 — Antibes — Mediterranean Sea

To Marseille — Vallauris — To Cannes

5 Kilometers / 5 Miles

INLAND RIVIERA

Nice. From there, take the T-2 tram to the Parc Phoenix station (just before the Nice airport) to catch these buses: to Vence, bus #9; to St-Paul-de-Vence and Vence, bus #400; and to Grasse, bus #500. These buses all run about twice an hour.

Note that Grasse is also connected by trains from Nice, Antibes, and Cannes (there's also a bus connection between Grasse and Cannes, bus #600). Within the area, bus #510/511 runs from Vence to Grasse via Tourrettes-sur-Loup and Le Bar-sur-Loup (6/day, 50 minutes, buy tickets in these towns at *tabacs,* not from drivers). Bus connections for the Gorges du Loup, the village of Gourdon, or the Gorges du Verdon are either too complicated or nonexistent. For schedules, see www.lignesdazur.com or www. frenchrivieratraveller.com.

With a Local Guide: See page 308 for guides with cars who can get you to places you would not find on your own.

St-Paul-de-Vence

This most famous of Riviera hill towns is said to be the most-visited village in France—and I believe it. This incredibly situated hamlet, with views to the sea and the Alps, is understandably popular. Every cobble and flower seem just so, and the setting is postcard-perfect. But it can also

feel like an overrun and over-restored artist's shopping mall. Avoid visiting between 11:00 and 18:00, particularly on weekends. Beat the crowds by skipping breakfast at your hotel to get here early, or come for dinner and experience the village at its tranquil best.

Orientation to St-Paul-de-Vence

Tourist Information: The helpful TI, just through the gate into the old town on Rue Grande, has maps with minimal explanations of key buildings, and cheap rental *boules* for *pétanque* on the square. Ask about their lantern-led evening tours in English (daily 10:00-18:00, June-Sept until 19:00, closes for lunch on weekends, +33 4 93 32 86 95, www.saint-pauldevence.com). Fill your water bottle at the stone tap across the lane.

Arrival in St-Paul-de-Vence: Pay to park close to the village, or park for free higher up on the road to Fondation Maeght (look for *Parking Conseillé* signs) and walk down to the village. Free parking is also available at the entry to Fondation Maeght (a 20-minute walk to town but takes longer going back). Bus #400 (connecting Nice and Vence) stops on the main road, just above the village. Regardless of how you arrive, if the pedestrian lane leading into the old town is jammed, walk along the road that veers up and left after Café de la Place, and enter the town through its side door.

Sights in St-Paul-de-Vence

Old Town

St-Paul's old town has no essential sights, though its perfectly cobbled lanes and peekaboo views delight most who come. You'll pass two vintage eateries before piercing the walls of the old town. The recommended **La Colombe d'Or** is a memorable place for a meal. Back when the town was teeming with artists, this historic hotel/restaurant served as their clubhouse. Its walls are covered with paintings by Picasso, Miró, Braque, Chagall, and others who traded their art for free meals. **Café de la Place** is *the* spot to have a coffee and croissant while watching waves of tourists crash into town and the intense *pétanque* competition. Find the cool *boules* sculpture.

After entering the walls of St-Paul, meander deep to find its quieter streets and panoramic views. How many art galleries can this village support? Imagine the time it took to create the intricate stone patterns in the street you're walking along. Visit **Marc Chagall's grave** in the cemetery at the opposite end of town (easy to find with TI map), a 10-minute walk keeping straight along the main drag (from the cemetery entrance, turn right, then left to find Chagall). Walk up the stairs to the **view platform** above the

INLAND RIVIERA

cemetery and try to locate the hill town of Vence at the foot of an impressive mountain. Is the sea out there—somewhere?

▲Fondation Maeght

This inviting, pricey, and far-out private museum is situated a steep walk or short drive above St-Paul-de-Vence. Fondation Maeght (fohn-dah-shown mahg) offers a memorable introduction to modern Mediterranean art by gathering many of the Riviera's most famous artists under one roof.

Cost and Hours: €16, daily 10:00-18:00, July-Aug until 19:00, great gift shop and cafeteria, 623 Chemin des Gardettes, +33 4 93 32 81 63, www.fondation-maeght.com.

Getting There: The museum is a steep uphill 20-minute walk from St-Paul-de-Vence. Parking is usually available (and free) at the sight and in lower lots, signed *Parking Conseillé*. Bus #400 stops below the museum (from the stop, walk on the main road with St-Paul village on your left, then find the road up and up on the right).

Visiting the Museum: The founder, Aimé Maeght, long envisioned the perfect exhibition space for the artists he supported and befriended as an art dealer. He purchased this arid hilltop, planted 35,000 trees and shrubs, and hired the Catalan architect José Luis Sert to enact his vision.

A sweeping lawn laced with lighthearted sculptures and bending pine trees greets visitors. On the right, a chapel designed by Georges Braque—in memory of the Maeghts' young son, who died of leukemia—features a moving purple stained-glass work over the altar. The unusual museum building is purposely low profile to let its world-class modern art collection take center stage. Works by Fernand Léger, Joan Miró, Alexander Calder, Georges Braque, Marc Chagall, and many others are thoughtfully arranged in well-lit rooms (the permanent collection is sometimes replaced by special thematic shows). Outside, in the back, you'll find a Gaudí-esque sculpture labyrinth by Miró and a courtyard filled with the wispy works of Alberto Giacometti—both designed by the artists for these spaces.

Eating in St-Paul-de-Vence

$$ Le Tilleul (Linden Tree) is my choice for dining well in St-Paul, either at inviting tables on the broad terrace or in its comfy interior (daily, across from the TI on Place du Tilleul, +33 4 93 32 80 36, www.restaurant-letilleul.com).

Book well ahead for **$$$$ La Colombe d'Or,** a veritable institution in St-Paul where the menu hasn't changed in 50 years (see description earlier). Dine on good-enough cuisine inside by the fire to best feel its pulse (closed Nov-Dec, +33 4 93 32 80 02, www. la-colombe-dor.com).

Vence

Vence, an appealing town set high above the Riviera, sees a fraction of the crowds that you'll find in St-Paul. While growth has sprawled beyond Vence's old walls and cars jam its roundabouts, the traffic-free lanes of the old city are a delight, the mountains are front and center, and the breeze is fresh. Vence bubbles with workaday life—and ample tourist activity in the day, focused on its artistic claim to fame—Matisse's Chapel of the Rosary—but it's quiet at night. With far fewer visitors and cooler temperatures, you'll feel a distinct difference from the resorts lining the coast. You'll also find terrific choices for affordable hotels and restaurants. Vence makes a handy base for travelers wanting the best of both worlds: a hill-town refuge near the sea. Some enjoy the Grand Canyon du Verdon as a long day trip from Vence (see the route described at the end of this chapter).

INLAND RIVIERA

Orientation to Vence

Tourist Information: Vence's helpful TI is at the southwest corner of the main square, Place du Grand Jardin (in the Villa Alexandrine; Mon-Sat 9:00-12:00 & 14:00-18:00, closed Sun except 10:00-14:00 in July-Aug, shorter hours in winter; +33 4 93 58 06 38, www.vence-tourisme.fr). Pick up the artistic city map and a list of art galleries and bus schedules.

Arrival in Vence: Bus #9 (fastest bus from Nice, about an hour) or #400 (from Nice, Cagnes-sur-Mer, and St-Paul-de-Vence) drop you at the Ara bus stop/plaza just off the roundabout at Place Maréchal Juin, a 10-minute walk to the town center (along Avenue Henri Isnard or Avenue de la Résistance). If returning to Nice, your bus ticket is good for the tram as well. If arriving by **car,** follow signs to *cité historique* and park in the underground Parking

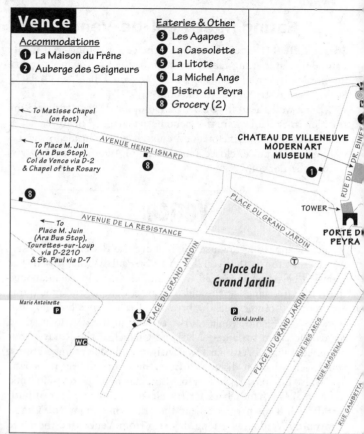

Vence

Accommodations

1. La Maison du Frêne
2. Auberge des Seigneurs

Eateries & Other

3. Les Agapes
4. La Cassolette
5. La Litote
6. La Michel Ange
7. Bistro du Peyra
8. Grocery (2)

← To Matisse Chapel (on foot)

← To Place M. Juin (Ara Bus Stop), Col de Vence via D-2 & Chapel of the Rosary

AVENUE HENRI ISNARD

← To Place M. Juin (Ara Bus Stop), Tourettes-sur-Loup via D-2210 & St. Paul via D-7

AVENUE DE LA RESISTANCE

CHATEAU DE VILLENEUVE MODERN ART MUSEUM

RUE DU DR. BINF...

PLACE DU GRAND JARDIN

TOWER →

PORTE DE PEYRA

Place du Grand Jardin

Marie Antoinette P

WC

P Grand Jardin

RUE DES ARCS

RUE MASSENA

RUE GAMBETTA

Grand Jardin, near the TI. For a **taxi,** call +33 4 93 58 11 14, or have the TI call for you.

Helpful Hints: Market days are Tuesdays and Fridays until 13:00 on the Place du Grand Jardin and in the *cité historique* around Place Clemenceau. A big all-day antiques market is on Place du Grand Jardin every Wednesday. If you miss market day, Monoprix **supermarkets** are at 12 Avenue de la Résistance, across from the entrance to the Marie Antoinette parking lot (grocery store upstairs, Mon-Sat 8:30-19:00, Sun 9:00-13:00), and at 41 Avenue Henri Isnard (same hours).

Sights in Vence

Explore the narrow lanes of the old town using the TI's worthwhile self-guided tour map. Connect the picturesque streets, enjoy a drink on a quiet square, inspect an art gallery, and find the small 11th-century cathedral with its colorful Chagall mosaic of Moses.

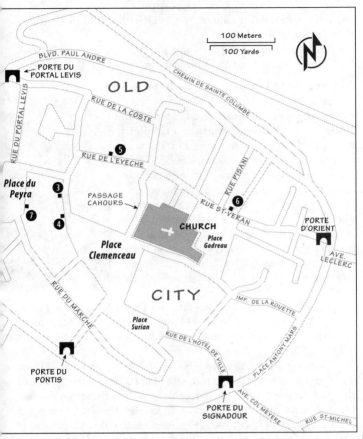

And, of course, visit Matisse's Chapel of the Rosary. If you're in Vence later in the day, enjoy the *boules* action across from the TI.

Old City

Vence's old city is a delight to wander using the TI map and the information plaques (in English) scattered through town. Find the lookout to the left of the Auberge des Seigneurs hotel to get perspective on Vence's setting. Try to visit during market days and don't miss the 11th-century church—the third to be built on this site—with a colorful Chagall mosaic. The proud guardian hands out English explanations and will explain the history (in limited English) if you show interest. Pick your favorite café and stop to appreciate where you are.

Château de Villeneuve

This 17th-century mansion, adjoining an imposing 12th-century watchtower, bills itself as one of the Riviera's high temples of modern art, with a rotating collection. Check with the TI to see what's showing in the temple.

Cost and Hours: €7, Tue-Sun 11:00-18:00, closed Mon, ask for loaner guide in English, 2 Place du Frêne, +33 4 93 58 15 78.

▲Chapel of the Rosary (Chapelle du Rosaire)

The chapel—a short drive or 20-minute walk from town—was designed by an elderly and ailing Henri Matisse as thanks to a Dominican nun who had taken care of him (he was 81 when the chapel was completed). While the chapel is the ultimate pilgrimage for his fans, the experience may underwhelm others. (Picasso thought it looked like a bathroom.) The chapel's design seems basic—white porcelain tiles, simple black designs, and floor-to-ceiling windows—but it's a space of light and calm that many claim only a master could have created. (For helpful background about Matisse, see the sidebar on page 346.)

Cost and Hours: €7; Tue, Thu, and Fri 10:00-12:00 & 14:00-18:00, Wed and Sat 14:00-18:00 (Nov-March until 17:00), closed Sun-Mon and mid-Nov-mid-Dec, 466 Avenue Henri Matisse, +33 4 93 58 03 26.

Getting There: On foot, it's a 20-minute walk from Place du Grand Jardin. Walk down Avenue Henri Isnard all the way to the traffic circle. Turn right across the one-lane bridge on Avenue Henri Matisse, following signs to *St-Jeannet*. **By car,** follow signs toward *St-Jeannet*, cross the bridge, and start looking for curbside parking—the chapel is about 400 yards after the bridge toward St-Jeannet.

Visiting the Chapel: The modest chapel holds a simple series of charcoal black-on-white tile sketches and uses three symbolic colors as accents: yellow (sunlight and the light of God), green (nature), and blue (the Mediterranean sky). Bright sunlight filters through the stained-glass windows and does a cheery dance across the sketches.

Your entry ticket includes a 20-minute tour from one of the kind nuns who speak English. In the little museum, you'll find pictures of the artist, displays of the vestments Matisse designed for the priests, his models of the chapel, and sketches. Outside, there's a terrace with terrific views toward Vence.

Matisse was the master of leaving things

out. Decide for yourself whether Matisse met the goal he set for himself: "Creating a religious space in an enclosed area of reduced proportions and to give it, solely by the play of colors and lines, the dimensions of infinity."

Sleeping in and near Vence

These places tend to close their reception desks between 12:00 and 16:00. Make arrangements in advance if you plan to arrive during this time.

$$ La Maison du Frêne, centrally located behind the TI, is a modern, art-packed B&B with thoughtful touches everywhere and four sumptuous suites at great rates. Energetic and art-crazy Thierry and Guy make fine hosts (RS%, includes good breakfast, kids under 12 free; next to the Château de Villeneuve at 1 Place du Frêne; +33 6 88 90 49 69, www.lamaisondufrene.com, contact@lamaisondufrene.com).

$ Auberge des Seigneurs is a modest Old World place located in a 17th-century building over a restaurant that merits a visit. There are six spacious and spotless rooms, some with bathrooms in need of upgrades, but all with good character (no air-con, no elevator, 1 Rue du Docteur Binet, +33 4 93 58 04 24, http://auberge-seigneurs.fr, sandrine.rodi@wanadoo.fr).

Eating in Vence

Tempting outdoor eateries litter the old town. Lights embedded in the cobbles illuminate the way after dark. The restaurants I list have similar prices and quality, and all have outside dining options.

At **$$ Les Agapes,** Chef Jean-Philippe goes beyond the standard fare with lavish presentations, creative food combinations, and moderate (for the Riviera) prices. Try the *sphere chocolat* dessert to round out your meal (small outside terrace, closed Mon year-round and Sun off-season, reservations smart, 4 Place Clemenceau, +33 4 93 58 50 64, www.les-agapes.net).

$$$ La Cassolette is an intimate place with a fine reputation and romantic tables across from the floodlit church (closed Tue-Wed except in July-Aug, 10 Place Clemenceau, +33 4 93 58 84 15).

$$ La Litote is a favorite, with outdoor tables on a quiet, hidden square, a cozy interior, and traditional cuisine (closed Wed-Thu off-season, 7 Rue de l'Evêché, +33 4 93 24 27 82).

$ Le Michel Ange is a sweet, kid-friendly place on an adorable square serving excellent-value cuisine from pizza to pasta, as well as tasty, well-presented *plats du jour* (open for lunch Tue-Sun, dinner Fri-Sat, closed Mon, 1 Place Godeau, +33 4 93 58 32 56).

For inexpensive, casual dining, head to Place du Peyra, where

INLAND RIVIERA

you'll find ample outdoor seating and early dinner service. At the basic **$$ Bistro du Peyra,** enjoy a relaxed dinner salad or pasta dish outdoors to the sound of the town's main fountain (closed Sun-Mon off-season, 13 Place du Peyra, +33 4 93 58 67 63).

Grasse

The historic and contemporary capital of perfume, Grasse offers a contrast to the dolled-up hill towns above the Riviera. Though famous for its pricey product, Grasse is an unpolished but intriguing collection of walking lanes, peekaboo squares, and vertical staircases. Its urban center feels in need of a graffiti facelift and a jobs program for its large immigrant population. For me, Grasse is refreshingly real. Its historic alliance with Genoa explains the Italian-esque look of the old city. Still, the only good reasons to visit Grasse are if you care about perfume, or if you're heading to or from the Grand Canyon du Verdon.

Orientation to Grasse

All sights in Grasse cluster near the Cours Honoré Cresp, also referred to as Place du Cours.

Tourist Information: The TI is a 10-minute walk from the center on Place de la Buanderie, where buses from Nice and Cannes stop (daily 9:00-18:00, Oct-April Mon-Sat 9:00-13:00 & 14:00-17:00, closed Sun), +33 4 93 36 66 66, www.ville-grasse.fr). Pick up a map with a simple, self-guided tour of the old city. If heading to the Grand Canyon du Verdon, get specifics here.

Arrival in Grasse: Buses from Cannes (#600) and Nice (#500) are better than trains, as they are cheap and run directly to the town center (stopping at the TI and the *gare routière*).

To reach the town center from the TI, walk out to Avenue Thiers, turn left, and merge onto Boulevard du Jeu de Ballon (where you'll soon find the stop for bus #510/511 to Vence).

Trains (15/day) connect Grasse with Nice (1 hour), Antibes (40 minutes), and Cannes (30 minutes). Taxis usually wait at the station and are the best option to reach the town center. From the train station, bus #5 runs to the TI; buses #A, #B, and #C take you to the old town center (€1.50 round-trip, daily service but less frequent on Sun, schedules at www.sillages.paysdegrasse.fr).

Those arriving by **car** are confounded by Grasse's size, hilly terrain, and inconsistent signage. Follow signs to *Centre-Ville*, then *Office de Tourisme*, and park at Parking Notre Dame des Fleurs (under the TI, direct access to the old town) or at Parking Honoré Cresp (follow *Sortie Parfumerie* signs directly to the Fragonard Perfume Factory).

Sights in Grasse

▲International Museum of Perfume
(Musée International de la Parfumerie, MIP)

This city museum is a magnificent—if overwhelming—tribute to perfume, providing a thorough examination of its history and production from ancient Greece until today. The well-designed museum, with excellent English explanations, a good audioguide, and impressive multimedia exhibits, could keep a perfume fan busy for days. Start in the Sensorial Room, where you'll get mellow while preparing your senses for the visit. The three floors below—organized chronologically—teach you everything there is to know about perfume. Your visit ends with a cool display of perfume packaging for every year since 1900 and a chance to sniff 32 key perfume ingredients. Allow at least one hour to see everything.

Cost and Hours: €6, keep ticket for 50 percent off at the gardens (see next); daily 10:00-19:00, Oct-April until 17:30, audioguide-€1, two blocks above Fragonard Perfume at 2 Rue Jeu de Ballon, +33 4 97 05 58 00, www.museesdegrasse.com.

Perfume Gardens (Les Jardins du MIP): The museum's terraced gardens, about five miles from Grasse, display acres of plants and flowers used in perfume production (€4, 50 percent off with perfume museum ticket, includes multimedia guide, same hours as museum, see website or ask at museum for location).

Fragonard Perfume Factory (Parfumerie Fragonard)

This historic but still-functioning factory, located dead-center in Grasse, provides frequent, fragrant, informative 20-minute tours and an interesting "museum" to explore while you wait. Pick up the English brochure describing what's in the museum cases, then drop down to where the tour begins. You'll learn the difference between perfume, eau de toilette, and cologne (it's only a matter of perfume percentages); how the product is made today; and how it was made in the old days (by pressing flowers in animal fat). The tour ends with a whiff in the elegant gift shop.

Cost and Hours: Free guided tour, daily 9:00-19:00, closes for lunch Nov-Jan, just off Cours Honoré Cresp at 20 Boulevard Fragonard, +33 4 93 36 44 65, https://usines-parfum.fragonard.com.

Museum of Provençal Costume and Jewelry
(Musée Provençal du Costume et du Bijou)

This small, dimly lit museum, a few steps from the Fragonard factory, displays traditional dresses and jewelry from the 18th and

INLAND RIVIERA

Fragrant Grasse

Grasse has been at the center of the fragrance industry since the 1500s, when it was known for its scented leather gloves. The cultivation of aromatic plants around Grasse slowly evolved to produce ingredients for soaps and perfumes, and by the 1800s, Grasse was recognized as the center for perfume—thanks largely to its flower-friendly climate.

It can take a ton of carefully picked petals—that's about 10,000 flowers—to make about two pounds of essence. A damaged flower petal is bad news. Today, perfumes are made from as many as 500 different scents; most are imported to Grasse from countries around the world. The "blender" of these scents and the perfume mastermind is called the "nose" (who nose best). The five master "noses" who work here must study their profession longer than a doctor goes to med school (seven years). They must show that they have the gift before entering "nose school" (in Versailles), and they cannot drink alcohol, ever. What?

Skip the outlying perfumeries with French-only tours. Only three factories out of forty open their doors to visitors, and only one is worth visiting: Fragonard Perfume in Grasse.

19th centuries, giving a sense of the lives of the high- and low-born women of Grasse.

Cost and Hours: Free, daily 10:00-13:00 & 14:00-18:30, closed Sun in winter, a block above the *parfumerie* on the pedestrian street at 2 Rue Jean Ossola, +33 4 93 36 44 65.

Fragonard Museum (Musée Fragonard)

This free, air-conditioned museum houses paintings by three of Grasse's most famous artists: Jean-Honoré Fragonard, Marguerite Gérard, and Jean-Baptiste Mallet. Ask for the English explanations at the welcome desk.

Cost and Hours: Free, daily 10:00-18:00, just a few doors down from the costume museum, 14 Rue Jean Ossola, +33 4 93 36 02 07.

Old Grasse

Just above Fragonard Perfume, Rue Jean Ossola leads into the labyrinthine ancient streets that form an intriguing pedestrian area. To sample old Grasse, you can follow the TI's minimalist self-guided tour with your map (takes an hour at a brisk pace, read the posted information plaques as you go) or, better, wander at will and read the plaques when you see them.

I'd start by strolling up Rue Jean Ossola (just above Boulevard Fragonard), then turn right down Rue Gazan to find the Romanesque cathedral opposite an unusual WWI monument (it's worth peering into the cathedral to see its tree-trunk columns and austere decor). Find the view terrace behind the cathedral. Double back to Rue Jean Ossola, turn right, then make a left up bohemian Rue de l'Oratoire and pop out onto a terrific square, making a left just after 27 Place aux Aires (with good eating options).

Inland Riviera Drive

NICE TO GRASSE LOOP

This splendid loop drive takes you from the Riviera up to inland villages and through a rocky gorge before returning you to the coast. The basic route connects Nice (or Antibes) to St-Paul-de-Vence, Vence, Tourrettes-sur-Loup, and Grasse.

Planning Your Drive: This route adds up to about 2.5 hours of driving and 70 zigzagging round-trip miles, but be sure to add plenty of extra time for stops along the way. Allow 45 minutes to drive from Nice (or Antibes) to the first village, St-Paul-de-Vence. Once you are inland, each stop is only minutes away from the next. Start early to see St-Paul-de-Vence without the mobs. Be prepared for twisty mountain roads, and be aware of bicyclists sharing the road, particularly on weekends.

Route Options: With more time (or if you are staying in Vence), consider taking the beautiful long way around from Vence via the Col de Vence (see the alternate route outlined below). Hardy day-trippers or those leaving the Riviera altogether can extend the drive through the Grand Canyon du Verdon to reach Provence (see "Grand Canyon du Verdon Drive" at the end of this chapter).

Nice to Grasse (via Tourrettes-sur-Loup)

The major towns—St-Paul-de-Vence, Vence, and Grasse—on this drive are described earlier in this chapter. The remaining inland villages and sights you'll see are described later, under "Inland Riviera Towns and Sights."

Leaving Nice, you'll drive west, through Cagnes-sur-Mer (passing the Renoir Museum—see page 434), then follow *Vence* and *St-Paul-de-Vence* signs into the village of **St-Paul-de-Vence.** Consider having breakfast there (at the Café de la Place just before the town walls), then explore the village and visit the Fondation Maeght.

From St-Paul-de-Vence, continue a few miles to **Vence,** with many good lunch options and Matisse's famous **Chapel of the Rosary** (closed Sun-Mon, sparse parking). The best views of Vence are a mile beyond the chapel, where there's a turnaround.

Next, from Vence, follow D-2210 through slippery-sloped **Tourrettes-sur-Loup** (great views of Tourrettes-sur-Loup a quarter-mile after you pass through the town). Before long, you'll see views of Le Bar-sur-Loup, clinging to its hillside in the distance. (Sugar addicts can detour quickly down to Pont-du-Loup and visit the small candied-fruit factory of Confiseries Florian).

Follow *Gourdon* and *Gorges du Loup* signs to the right along D-6 and climb into the teeth of a rocky canyon, the **Gorges du Loup.** It's a mostly low-gear road that winds between severe rock faces above a surging stream. Several miles into the gorge, stop by the Cascades du Saut du Loup **waterfall,** which may have you thinking you've made a wrong turn onto Hawaii (€1, easy walk down).

The drive passes all too quickly to where the road hooks back, crossing Pont du Bramafen and around toward Gourdon on D-3. As you climb above the canyon you just drove through, you'll watch the world below miniaturize. At the top, the Shangri-La village of **Gourdon**—known as the "Eagle's Nest" (2,400 feet)—waits for tourists with shops, good lunch options, and grand panoramas.

From Gourdon, slide downhill (stopping at pullouts for views back and up to Gourdon) toward **Grasse.** Enjoy sensational views down to (literally) overlooked Le Bar-sur-Loup. Follow signs to *Grasse,* then *Centre-Ville,* then *Office de Tourisme* (park under the TI at Parking Notre Dame des Fleurs).

After mastering your scent in Grasse—the capital of perfume—return to your Riviera home base (allow 45 minutes back to Nice or 30 minutes to Antibes), or continue to the Grand Canyon du Verdon (see the end of this chapter).

Nice to Grasse (Col de Vence Alternate)

This dilly of a route is ideal if you're staying in Vence (it adds about 25 miles and an hour of driving time to the basic route): Follow the route described above until **Vence,** then find D-2 just before the bridge that leads to St-Jeannet, and follow signs for *Col de Vence* (the Vence pass) and *Coursegoules.* The road rises beyond the tree line into a barren landscape to the pass in about 15 minutes. From the pass (3,000 feet), continue on D-2, trading rocky slabs for lush forests, pastures, and vast canyons.

You'll soon pass the postcard-perfect village of **Coursegoules** (worth a photo but not a detour), then follow signs to *Gréolières.* At a roundabout just before Gréolières, find D-3, which leads to Nice, Gorges du Loup, and Gourdon. But first, continue a few minutes past **Gréolières** to the pullout barely above the village, with stirring views of its ruined castle. Consider a coffee break in Gréolières before backtracking to the roundabout, following signs to *Gourdon*. After visiting **Gourdon,** you can continue to Grasse, or return to Nice or Antibes.

INLAND RIVIERA TOWNS AND SIGHTS
Tourrettes-sur-Loup

This unspoiled and picturesque town, hemmed in·by forests, looks like it's ready to skid down its hill. Stroll the beautifully preserved, narrow medieval lanes, admire the wall-to-wall homes (built for defense, not the view), have an ice cream, and finish with a view drink. Many prefer this peaceful hill town to St-Paul-de-Vence. Known as the *Cité des Violettes*, this small village grows more violets, most of which end up in perfume, than anywhere else in France. In early March, Tourrettes-sur-Loop fills with almost 10,000 visitors (hard to imagine) for the annual Violet Festival.

Park in the village center lot, on Place de la Libération, where you'll also find the **TI** (Mon-Sat 9:30-13:00 & 14:00-18:00, closed Sun, +33 4 89 87 73 33, www.tourrettessurloup.com). Wednesday is **market day** on Place de la Libération (you'll be forced to park elsewhere if you arrive before 13:30).

If it's lunchtime, consider sitting outside at the **Les Gourmandises** *pâtisserie* on the square, which has delicious *pissaladière* (pizza-like dough topped with onions, olives, and anchovies) and the filling *tourte de Blettes* (Swiss chard tart).

Enter the medieval village under the clock tower (just off the square's right corner) onto Grande Rue. Stroll in a counterclockwise direction, ending up back at the parking lot. Along the way, you'll find a smattering of arts and crafts boutiques as well as a handful of other places to eat or take a break.

Tom's Ice Cream may entice you with its violet-flavored scoops or tasty coffee (daily from 12:00, 25 Grand Rue, +33 4 93 24 12 12). Or finish your walk with a glass of wine on the tiny back terrace at **La Cave de Tourrettes.** This small wine bar serves salads and quiches, with a daily by-the-glass selection from its vast cellar. The sliver-sized balcony has panoramic views (daily, near St. Grégoire church and the parking lot, 8 Rue de la Bourgade, +33 4 93 24 10 12).

Confiseries Florian in Pont-du-Loup

This candied-fruit factory hides between trees down in Pont-du-Loup (though their big, bright sign is hard to miss). Frequent 10-minute tours of the factory cover the candied-fruit process and explain the use of flower petals (like violets and jasmine) in their products. Everything they make is fruit-filled—even their chocolate (with oranges). The tour ends with a tasting of the *confiture* in the dazzling gift shop.

Cost and Hours: Tours are free, daily 9:00-12:00 & 14:00-18:30, gift shop stays open during lunch in summer, +33 4 93 59 32 91, www.confiserieflorian.com.

Gorges du Loup

The Inland Riviera is crawling with spectacular canyons only miles from the sea. Slotted between Grasse and Vence, the Gorges du Loup is the easiest to reach and works well on a day trip from the Nice area. You can drive about five miles right up into the canyon (on D-6)—passing numerous waterfalls, deep pools, and sheer rock walls. Circling back on the gorge's rooftop (on D-3) to the village of Gourdon gives magnificent vistas and a complete change of scenery.

Gourdon

This 2,400-foot-high, cliff-topping hamlet features grassy picnic areas, a short lineup of tourist shops, and a few good lunch options

(there's an upper parking lot that reduces some of the uphill walk). The village's most famous building is its château, which is best enjoyed from the outside. Walk out to the broad terrace for the splendid view (TI in the far corner). Facing the view, a trail (Chemin du Paradis) leads down those cliffs from the far left side of the village to Le Bar-sur-Loup (1 hour)—now *that's* steep (you'll pass the trailhead as your enter the village). This part of the village features fabulous vistas, a tiny Romanesque church, and a nice option for lunch with a view, **$$ La Taverne Provençale,** which boasts a popular spread of outdoor tables for pizza, pasta, and salads (daily, +33 4 93 09 68 22). The building below on the left, Le Nid de l'Aigle ("The Eagle's Nest"), was until a few years ago the region's greatest view restaurant (now closed).

Grand Canyon du Verdon Drive

Two hours north of Nice and three hours east of Avignon lies the Parc Naturel Régional du Verdon. This immense area of natural beauty is worth ▲▲▲—even to Arizonans. The park, far more than just its famous canyon, is a vast area mixing alpine scenery with misty villages, meandering streams, and seas of gentle meadows.

The Grand Canyon du Verdon (a.k.a. Gorges du Verdon) is the heart of the park, where colossal slabs of white and salmon-colored limestone plunge impossible distances to the snaking Verdon River.

For millions of years, this region was covered by the sea. Over time, sediments and the remains of marine animals were deposited here, becoming thick layers of limestone as they were buried. Later, plate tectonics uplifted the limestone and erosion exposed it, and the Verdon River—with help from Ice Age glaciers—carved out the gorges and its side canyons. At their deepest points, the gorges drop 2,200 feet to the river. At the bottom, the canyons narrow to as little as 26 feet across, while at the top, the canyon walls spread as far as 4,700 feet apart.

The Verdon River is named for its turquoise-green hue (derived from *vert*, the French word for green). The striking color comes from very fine particles of rock suspended in the water, pulverized by glaciers high at the river's source. It's a sight that has inspired visitors since Ligurian Celts ruled the region.

PLANNING YOUR DRIVE

The Grand Canyon du Verdon offers a magnificent drive between the Riviera and Provence. You'll need a car, ample time, and a lack of vertigo to enjoy this area.

The canyon itself is located between the villages of Moustiers-Ste-Marie and Aiguines to the west and Castellane to the east. Roads crawl along both sides of the canyon. The most scenic driving segments are along the south side (Rive Gauche), between Aiguines and the Balcon de la Mescla, and the north side (Rive Droite) between Moustiers-Ste-Marie and the Point Sublime overlook. The Rive Gauche works best for most, though both sides are spectacular. Thrill seekers head for the Castellane area, where the whitewater rafting, climbing, and serious hiking trails are best.

When to Go: The canyon can be overrun with cars in summer and on weekends, but is quiet most other days. If you are traveling in summer or on holiday weekends, go really early or skip it.

The Basic Route: You'll drive from the coast through Grasse and toward Castellane, then turn off to join the canyon at the Balcon de la Mescla. After seeing the canyon's most scenic stretch, you can either split off (after Aiguines) to return to the Riviera, or continue through Moustiers-Ste-Marie and on to Provence. (For drivers coming *from* Provence, this tour works in reverse, west to

INLAND RIVIERA

east; see "Approaching the Canyon from Provence," at the end of the tour.)

Length of This Drive: Figure seven hours and about 150 miles with modest canyon time between Nice and the Luberon or Aix-en-Provence.

Here are some rough driving times: Riviera to Grasse—1 hour, Grasse to Balcon de la Mescla—1.5 hours, Balcon de la Mescla to Aiguines—1.5 hours with photo stops, Aiguines to Moustiers-Ste-Marie—25 minutes, Moustiers-Ste-Marie to Manosque (en route to Provence)—1.5 hours.

Driving Tips: Fill your tank before leaving Grasse or Moustiers-Ste-Marie. Don't expect US national park-style conditions—you won't see a ranger, signage is minimal, and the road rarely has a shoulder.

There are fewer pullouts and viewpoints than you'd expect, but picnickers will find some good choices for the perfect lunch stop. Just be sure to stock up on provisions—stores are scarce on this route.

Hiking in the Canyon: Hikes into the canyon are long and pretty steep. Most visitors are better off walking along the main road for a bit, or detouring down some of the short paths scattered alongside the road. Your best bet for a true canyon hike is the **Cavaliers trail,** which leads down to the river from a spot near the Hôtel-Restaurant Grand Canyon du Verdon (details later, under "Along the Canyon, from Balcon de la Mescla to Aiguines").

Overnighting in the Canyon: If you get a late start or just want to savor the canyon, overnighting en route works well (see suggestions later in this chapter).

Round-Trip Option from Nice: You can reach the canyon on a very long round-trip drive from the Nice area if you leave early. From Nice, figure on five hours of driving without stops and about 175 miles round-trip (easier if staying in Vence or Antibes). To do this, take the most direct route to or from the canyon and make it a one-way loop (from Nice take the route via Grasse to Balcon de la Mescla, as outlined later, tour the canyon in the westbound direction, leave the route just before the Lac de Ste-Croix, and connect to the autoroute back to Nice; details later, under "Aiguines").

FROM THE RIVIERA TO PROVENCE

For drivers connecting the Riviera with Provence via the canyon, this self-guided drive along the Rive Gauche offers the most accessible and most scenic tour of the gorges. You'll be driving the canyon from east to west in the outside lane, which is best for views, but a challenge if you suffer from acrophobia.

Cannes to Balcon de la Mescla

The most direct route from the Riviera follows D-6185, which starts near Cannes (A-8 autoroute from Nice to Cannes saves time) and passes through Grasse, changing to D-6085 and continuing north toward Digne and Castellane. You'll turn left off D-6085 about 25 kilometers before Castellane, following signs to the *Gorges du Verdon* and *Draguignan* (an impressive medieval bridge stands just north of the road, about 3 kilometers before Comps-sur-Artuby, signed *La Souche*). Turn right onto D-71 at Comps-sur-Artuby, following signs to *Gorges du Verdon, Rive Gauche* (not *Rive Droite*). In a few minutes, you'll reach a pullout with a good view of the village of Trigance.

Driving along D-71, you'll soon arrive at the canyon rim at the Balcon de la Mescla. Park just below **Le Relais de Balcon** café/gift shop, and find the steps down to a memorable lookout above the river bend. The café/gift shop has a small selection of maps and books, and a big selection of drinks.

Along the Canyon, from Balcon de la Mescla to Aiguines

From here, follow the canyon lip for about 90 serpentine minutes (which includes ample time for stops). You'll drive at an escargot's pace, navigating hairpin turns while enjoying views of rocky masses and vanishing-point views up the canyon. There are small pullouts along the route that come without warning.

A little beyond the Balcon de la Mescla, you can amble across Europe's second-highest bridge, the **Pont de l'Artuby,** and imagine working on its construction crew. There's a large parking lot at the far end of the bridge; get out and breathe here. About 3 kilometers past the bridge, you'll find a dirt road and pullout on the north side of the road; drive down 50 yards and you can park easily. A five-minute stroll along the dirt road (push straight through some bushes at end) leads to good views of the canyon and acres of limestone to scramble over—and no car noise. It's a rare chance to lose the road and be alone with the canyon.

About 10 minutes beyond the bridge, you'll reach the recommended cliffhanger **Hôtel-Restaurant Grand Canyon du Verdon.** This funky, concrete place looks slapped together, but the café terrace has tables with stupendous views (drinks, snacks, and meals available at fair prices). If your driver feels cheated about missing the views, make sure you stop here for a break. Just beyond and below the hotel, the **Cavaliers trail** (signposted) is your best chance to hike into the canyon. For those in reasonable shape, it's a 90-minute round-trip hike on a well-maintained path to the river and back. For those with more time and expertise, the trail joins the spectacular but technical **Imbut trail** at the river (see details at www.alltrails.com).

Back along the main road, you'll pass some of the canyon's most stunning views along the next stretch. Notice small red and white markers along the guardrails at pullouts. These are trail markers, where you can hop over the guardrail, if you dare, for better views. The **Col d'Illoire**—the last pass before leaving the canyon—provides sweeping views from the western portal, including your first peek at **Lac de Ste-Croix.** Park in the large pullout, where you'll find a few picnic tables scattered above and some good rock-scampering just below.

Aiguines

Just west of the canyon, the small village of Aiguines squats below waves of limestone and overlooks the long turquoise Lac de Ste-Croix. This unspoiled village has a handful of shops, recommended hotels, and cafés. It's an outdoorsy, popular-with-hikers place that most canyon visitors cruise right through. Detour onto the grounds of the 15th-century château for the view over Aiguines (with picnic benches and a play area for kids; château  interior closed to the public). Aiguines' **TI** is on the main drag (July-Aug Mon-Sat 8:30-18:00, Sun 10:00-13:00; Sept-June Mon-Fri 9:00-12:00 & 14:00-17:00, closed Sat-Sun and all afternoons in winter; Allée des Tilleuls, +33 4 94 70 21 64, www.lacs-gorges-verdon.com). Have lunch at the recommended **Hôtel du Vieux-**

Château's café on charming Place de la Fontaine (described later under "Sleeping and Eating near the Grand Canyon du Verdon").

For more views over Aiguines and the lake, stroll north of Place de la Fontaine, then head right and up one of the staircases to find the small **Chapelle St. Pierre.** From here, you can walk up the small road five minutes to the campground café, with nice tables on its broad view terrace (ideal for a predinner drink or morning coffee).

Returning to the Riviera: If you're day-tripping from the Riviera rather than continuing to Provence, this is your turnaround point: Follow signs for *Aups* (D-957) as you leave Aiguines, then *Draguignan,* then *Nice* via A-8.

Aiguines to Moustiers-Ste-Marie

Barely 50 years old, the man-made **Lac de Ste-Croix** is about six miles long and is the last stop for water flowing out of the Gorges du Verdon. For a fun lake/river experience, rent a canoe or a pedal boat at either side of the low bridge halfway between Moustiers and Aiguines (no motor boats are allowed). You can paddle under the bridge, then follow the aquamarine inlet upstream as far as 2.5 miles, tracing the river's route up the gorge on its final journey to the lake.

Moustiers-Ste-Marie

Here's another pretty Provençal face lined with boutiques and visitors—though this one comes with an impressive setting, strad-

dling a small stream at the base of the limestone cliffs of the Grand Canyon du Verdon. The town is busy, as tourists clamoring for the locally famous china compete with hikers. Parking can be difficult, especially in high season (use one of the signed lots, and expect a fair walk to the village center). The **TI** is in the center, next to the church (daily 10:00-12:30 & 14:00-18:00, no midday break July-Aug, Place de l'Eglise, +33 4 92 74 67 84, www. moustiers.fr).

You can escape some of the crowds by climbing 20 minutes on a steep, ankle-twisting path (262 steps) to the **Chapelle Notre-Dame de Beauvoir**—a simple chapel that has attracted pilgrims for centuries. A notebook in the chapel allows travelers to pen a request for a miracle for a loved one. For most, the chapel does not warrant the effort, though you'll get great views over the village by walking a short way up the path.

Moustiers-Ste-Marie to Provence

From here it's another 1.5 to 2 hours to most Provençal destinations. From Moustiers-Ste-Marie, head for Riez, then Gréoux-les-Bains. From Gréoux-les-Bains, follow signs for *Manosque*, then *Apt* for the Luberon and Avignon; or use A-51 south to reach Aix-en-Provence, Lourmarin in the Luberon, Cassis, Marseille, or Arles.

APPROACHING THE CANYON FROM PROVENCE

Drivers coming from Provence can reverse the above tour, traveling from west to east (Moustiers-Ste-Marie to the Balcon de la Mescla).

All roads from Provence pass through Gréoux-les-Bains, an hour northeast of Aix-en-Provence. Those coming from Cassis, Aix-en-Provence, the southern Luberon, and Arles will find A-51 north the fastest path; those coming from the central Luberon and Avignon should take D-900 via Apt (turns into D-4100), then follow signs for *Manosque*. From Gréoux-les-Bains, everyone follows signs to *Riez*, *Moustiers-Ste-Marie*, and *Aiguines* before entering the Grand Canyon du Verdon (Rive Gauche). Ignore the *Grand Canyon du Verdon* signs as you leave Moustiers-Ste-Marie—they lead to the Rive Droite. Follow the *Aiguines* signs instead to make sure you are going to the Rive Gauche.

Leave the canyon after the Balcon de la Mescla. To get to Nice, follow signs for *Comps-sur-Artuby* (and *Draguignan* for a short distance), then *Grasse* and *Nice*. The fastest way from Grasse to Nice is via Cannes and A-8.

SLEEPING AND EATING NEAR THE GRAND CANYON DU VERDON

These places are listed in the order you'll reach them on the self-guided driving tour from east to west. Most hotels in this area want you to take half-pension, but it is rarely required outside of high season. Budget-minded travelers will find lots of places to picnic, but bring groceries with you as stores are scarce (grocery stores and bakeries are in Gréoux and Moustiers if coming from the west, but there's not much if coming from the east—stock up before you head out).

Midway Through the Canyon

$ **Hôtel-Restaurant Grand Canyon du Verdon**** is housed in a funky structure that must have been grandfathered-in to own such an unbelievable location—2,500 feet high on the Corniche Sublime. The hotel rents 14 basic, simple, but sleepable rooms—half on the canyon side and many with decks (the best are rooms 8 and 10, well worth reserving ahead, easy parking, good-value restaurant, closed Oct-early April, +33 4 94 76 91 31, www.hotel-canyon-verdon.com, hotel.gd.canyon.verdon@wanadoo.fr).

In Aiguines

$ Hôtel du Vieux-Château** has been in business for 200 years and is Aiguines' most characteristic hotel. Its 10 snug rooms are red-tiled, spotless, and tastefully appointed. The hotel's good restaurant has hearty fare (great goat-cheese salad and fresh trout, no air-con, no elevator, Place de la Fontaine, closed mid-Oct-March, +33 4 94 70 22 95, www.hotelchateauverdon.fr, contact@hotelchateauverdon.fr).

$ Hôtel Altitude 823,** around the bend below the town, offers a fair deal with good rooms, big public spaces, and quirky owners (no air-con, no elevator, open all year, +33 4 98 10 22 17, www.altitude823-verdon.com, altitude823@gmail.com).

In Moustiers-Ste-Marie

$ Le Mas du Loup is a fine-value *chambre d'hôte,* a scenic 10-minute walk below town. Charming Julie welcomes guests to her five-bedroom *bastide,* where rooms are spacious, tastefully decorated, and come with private patios (cash only, includes breakfast, free parking, +33 4 92 74 65 61, www.le-mas-du-loup.fr, masduloup7@hotmail.fr).

Eating: There is no shortage of dining options in Moustiers-Ste-Marie. The simple **$ Restaurant Clerissy** offers inexpensive and simple meals (crêpes and pizza) and appealing indoor and outdoor tables (cash only, Place du Chevalier de Blacas, in the village center across from the left transept of the church, +33 4 92 74 62 67). **$$$ Côté Jardin** is a quiet haven a few steps south of the old town, with a pleasing garden setting, great views, and good cuisine at fair prices (closed Wed, +33 4 92 74 68 91). **$$$ La Treille Muscate** hangs above the stream and is the place to enjoy a romantic Provençal meal in a lovely atrium room (closed Tue-Wed, across from the TI on Place de l'Eglise, +33 4 92 74 64 31).

TRAVELING WITH CHILDREN

With relatively few must-see museums, plenty of outdoor activities, and cooperative weather, Provence and the French Riviera are practically made for kids. This part of France has beaches, fun canoeing on safe rivers, good biking, Roman ruins to scramble over, abundant sunshine, and swimming pools everywhere. Teenagers love the seaside resorts (Cassis and Antibes are best) and enjoy the hustle and bustle of cities like Avignon, Arles, Aix-en-Provence, and Nice. Younger kids tend to prefer the rural areas, which offer more swimming pools, open spaces, and parks.

Trip Tips

PLAN AHEAD

Involve your kids in trip planning. Have them read about the places that you may include in your itinerary (including the accommodations you're considering), and let them help with your decisions.

Where to Stay

- Hotel selection is critical. In my recommendations, I've identified hotels that seem particularly kid-friendly (pools, table tennis, grassy areas, easygoing owners, etc.). Most hotels have some sort of crib you can use.
- Minimize hotel changes by planning three-day stays.
- Aim for hotels with restaurants, so older kids can go back to the room while you finish a pleasant dinner.
- If you're staying for a week or more in one place, a great option is to rent an apartment, a house, or a *gîte* (for more on these options, see the "Sleeping" section in the Practicalities chapter).

Parenting French-Style

Famous for their topless tanning, French women are equally comfortable with public breastfeeding of their babies: No need for shawls or "hooter hiders" here. Changing tables are nonexistent, so bring a roll-up changing mat and get comfortable changing your baby on your knees, on a bench, or wherever you find enough space.

French grandmothers take their role as community elders seriously and won't hesitate to recommend that you put more sunscreen on your child in the summer or add a layer of clothing if it's breezy.

Rather than saying *bonjour* to French children, say *coucou* (coo-coo) if they are young and *salut* (sal-oo) if they are pre-teens or older.

What to Bring (or Not)

- Don't bother bringing a car seat—car-rental agencies usually rent them, though you must reserve one in advance.
- Bring your own drawing supplies and English-language picture books, as these supplies are pricey in France.
- If your kids love peanut butter, bring it from home (hard to find in France).

EATING

Provence offers plenty of food options for children.

What to Eat (and Drink)

- Kid-friendly foods that are commonly available and easy to order include crêpes (available at many takeout stands), *croque monsieurs* (grilled ham and cheese sandwiches), and *tartines* (open-faced sandwiches). Plain pasta is available at many cafés and some bistros (ask for *pâtes nature*). Carry a baguette to snack on. In the south of France, pizza is omnipresent.
- For breakfast, try a *pain au chocolat* (chocolate-filled pastry) or dip your baguette in a *chocolat chaud* (hot chocolate). Fruit, cereals, and yogurt are usually available.
- Help your kids acquire a taste for Nutella, the tasty hazelnut-chocolate spread available everywhere. Look for organic *(bio)* stores in cities, where you can find numerous nut butters and *Chocolade,* a less-sugary version of Nutella.
- For a refreshing drink, kids enjoy *Sirop de Provence,* a concentrated syrup that comes in many flavors like grenadine, violet, rose, lavender, and strawberry, and is mixed with sparkling water.
- For older kids, be aware that the drinking age is 16: Your

CHILDREN

Books and Films for Kids

Get your kids into the traveling spirit with books and movies about France, Provence, and the French Riviera. For longer drives, audio books can be fun for the whole family (if carefully chosen)—I recommend Peter Mayle's *A Year in Provence.* (Also see "Books and Films," including some good choices for teenagers, in the appendix.)

Anatole (Eve Titus, 1956). This Caldecott Honor Book introduces young readers to the great world of French food via a rat who finds work in a cheese factory.

Anni's Diary of France (Anni Axworthy, 2000). This fun, picture-filled book about a young girl's trip will inspire your little ones.

Camille and the Sunflowers (Laurence Anholt, 1994). In a tale based on a true story, the postman's son Camille befriends his town's new resident, Vincent van Gogh.

The Cat Who Walked Across France (Kate Banks, 2004). Beautiful illustrations accompany the marvelous journey of a cat through France—including a stop at Pont du Gard near Avignon.

Discovering Great Artists: Hands-On Art for Children in the Styles of the Great Masters (MaryAnn Kohl and Kim Solga, 1997). Get to know your favorite artists, from the Renaissance to the present day, by learning their techniques through various art activities.

Getting to Know France and French (Nicola Wright, 1993). This illustrated guide is a fun crash course for younger travelers,

waiter will assume that your teen will have wine with you at dinner. Teens are also welcome in most bars and lounges.

When and Where to Eat
- Eat dinner early (restaurants open for dinner at 19:00-19:30, cafés open earlier).
- Skip romantic eateries. Try relaxed cafés (or fast-food restaurants) where kids can move around without bothering others.
- Picnics work well. *Boulangeries* are good places to grab off-hour snacks when restaurants aren't serving. (For picnic tips, see the "Eating" section of the Practicalities chapter.)

SIGHTSEEING
The key to a successful Provence family vacation is to slow down. Tackle one or two key sights each day, mix in a healthy dose of pure fun at a park or square, and take extended breaks when needed.

featuring history, school life, food, festivals, and language.

Henri's Scissors (Jeanette Winter, 2013). This beautiful picture book illustrates how Matisse found new inspiration in paper cutouts as he lay in bed near the end of his life.

How Would You Survive in the Middle Ages? (Fiona MacDonald, 1995). MacDonald makes history fun for kids and adults alike in this engaging guide to life in the Middle Ages.

The Lady and the Squire (Terry Jones, 2000). In this fun read by a former Monty Python member, the Duke of Lancaster's squire, Tom, makes a fantastical visit to 19th-century Avignon.

Madeline (Ludwig Bemelmans, 1939). Kids love the *Madeline* series, which follows the adventures of a Parisian girl and her boarding-school pals. A live-action 1998 film brings the stories to life.

Picasso and the Girl with a Ponytail (Laurence Anholt, 2002). This picture book relates the story of Sylvette, who models for Picasso and then eventually becomes a painter herself.

Ratatouille (2007). In this animated film named for the famous Provençal dish, a mouse becomes a chef at a fine French restaurant.

The Red Balloon (1956). A small boy chases his balloon through the streets of Paris in this classic of French cinema.

When Pigasso Met Mootisse (Nina Laden, 1998). A silly picture-book take on the tempestuous relationship between Picasso and Matisse, which ultimately ended in friendship.

Planning Your Time

- Lower your sightseeing ambitions and let kids help choose daily activities. Plan longer stays at fewer stops—you won't regret it.
- To make your trip fun for everyone in the family, mix heavy-duty sights with kids' activities, such as playing mini-golf or *pétanque*, renting bikes or canoes, and riding the little tourist trains popular in many towns.
- Older kids and teens can help plan the details of a museum visit, such as what to see, how to get there, and ticketing details.

Successful Sightseeing

- Museum audioguides are great for older children (some have kid-friendly versions). For younger children, hit the gift shop first so they can buy postcards and have a scavenger hunt to find the pictured artwork. When boredom sets in, try "I spy"

CHILDREN

games or have them count how many babies or dogs they can spot in all the paintings in the room.

- Bring a sketchbook to a museum and encourage kids to select a painting or statue to draw. It's a great way for them to slow down and observe.
- If you're in France near Bastille Day, remember that fireworks stands pop up everywhere on the days leading up to July 14. Putting on their own fireworks show can be a highlight for teenagers.

Making or Finding Quality Souvenirs

- Buy your kids a trip journal, where they can record observations, thoughts, and favorite sights and memories. This journal could end up being your child's favorite souvenir.
- For a group project, keep a family journal. Pack a small diary and a glue stick. While relaxing at a café over a *citron-pressé* (lemonade), take turns writing about the day's events and include mementos such as ticket stubs from museums, postcards, or stalks of lavender.
- Let kids pick out some toys and books. The best and cheapest toy selections are usually in department stores, like Monoprix and Galeries Lafayette. Note that Legos are sometimes different in Europe than in the US, and the French have wonderful doll clothes with a much wider selection than typically found in the US. Kids like the French adventure comics Astérix and Tintin (both available in English, sold in bigger bookstores with English sections).

MONEY, SAFETY, AND STAYING CONNECTED

Before your trip gets underway, talk to your kids about safety and money.

- Give your child a money belt and an expanded allowance; you are on vacation, after all. Let your kids budget their funds by comparing and contrasting the dollar and euro.
- If you allow older kids to explore a museum or neighborhood on their own, be sure to establish a clear meeting time and place.
- Have a "what if" procedure in place in case something goes wrong. If you child has a mobile phone, enable the "Find My Phone" feature in case you get separated. Give your kids your hotel's business card, your phone number, and emergency taxi fare. Let them know to ask to use the phone at a hotel if they are lost. And if they have mobile phones, show them how to make calls in France (see page 537).
- Most parents find it worth the peace of mind to buy supplemental messaging and data plans for the whole family. Adults

can stay connected to teenagers while allowing them maximum independence, and teens can keep in touch with friends via apps such as FaceTime, WhatsApp, Facebook Messenger, Snapchat, Google Chat, or Skype. Wi-Fi is readily available at TIs, train stations, hotels, some cafés, and all Starbucks and McDonald's.

Top Kids' Sights and Activities

ATTRACTIONS

These are listed in no particular order (and all described in more detail elsewhere in this book):

- Pont du Gard. An entire wing of the museum is dedicated to kids, who can also swim or take a canoe trip on the river nearby.
- Cassis. Boat trip to the *calanques,* or the port and beaches for teenagers.
- Monaco. Changing of the Guard in Monaco, Oceanography Museum, and the casino scene.
- Pedal boats on the Mediterranean (in Cassis) and into the Grand Canyon du Verdon (from Lac de St-Croix).
- Biking or in-line skating on the Promenade des Anglais in Nice.
- Biking through vineyards to small villages, from Vaison-la-Romaine.
- Les Baux's castle ruins, with medieval weaponry and great walls to climb.
- Canoeing on the Ardèche River or the Sorgue River.
- Boat trips from Nice, Villefranche-sur-Mer, or St-Tropez.

Honorable mention goes to Arles' Ancient History Museum, horseback riding and public beaches in the Camargue, Roman arenas in Nîmes and Arles, the beaches of Antibes, and the narrow-gauge train ride from Nice.

ACTIVITIES
Movies

It's fun to take kids to movies (even if not in English) just to see how theaters work elsewhere. Movies shown in their original language—usually with subtitles—are listed as *v.o.* at the box office. (One showing could be *v.o.* and the next could be dubbed in French, labeled *v.f.;* be aware that *v.o.* movies are hard to find outside major cities.) *Dessin animé* means "cartoon." While many live-action movies can be found in their original language with French subtitles, cartoons and kids' movies (intended for an audience that doesn't read so well yet) are almost always dubbed.

CHILDREN

Swimming

I've listed swimming pools in many places. But be warned: Public pools in France commonly require a small, tight-fitting bathing suit for boys and men; most pools sell these (baggy, American-style swim trunks won't do, as they want to avoid people wearing the shorts they may have worn elsewhere during the day). At hotel pools, any type of swimsuit will do.

Rides

You'll find old-style merry-go-rounds in many cities, perfect for young travelers (when my daughter was young, her goal was to ride a merry-go-round in every town...she came close). There are also little tourist trains in nearly every city.

Farms

Visits to local goat-cheese makers are possible in early spring (look for *fromage fermier de chèvre* signs along the country roads). Goats are social animals and goat-cheese makers will usually let your child hold or pet one. You can also pick up some superb fresh cheese for your picnic.

Boules

Consider buying a set of *boules* (a.k.a. *pétanque*, a form of outdoor bowling—for the rules, see sidebar on page 52). Play *boules* before dinner, side by side with real players on the village court. Get your *boules de pétanque* at sporting-goods stores or larger department stores. Some hotels have *pétanque* areas and balls, but you can play anywhere level with dirt or light gravel. Since they're heavy, buy a set only if you'll be driving. The *boules* also make fun, if weighty, souvenirs, and are just as enjoyable to play back at home.

CHILDREN

SHOPPING

Provence and the Riviera offer France's best shopping outside of Paris, with a great range of reasonably priced items ideal for souvenirs and gifts. If approached thoughtfully, shopping in the south of France can even be a culturally enlightening experience. There's no better way to mix serious shopping business with travel pleasure than at the weekly markets *(marchés)* in towns and villages throughout the region. These traditional market days offer far more than fresh produce and fish; in many cases, about half the market is devoted to durable goods (baskets, tablecloths, pottery, and fabrics). If you miss market day, most Provençal towns have more than enough small shops that sell local products—and more than enough kitschy souvenirs. If you crave French fashion, several destinations in this book have a good selection of clothing boutiques.

In this chapter, you'll find information about shopping for souvenirs, navigating market days, and browsing shops and boutiques.

WHAT TO BUY

Here's a shopping list of locally made goods in Provence and the Riviera. You'll find most of these items in tourist-oriented boutiques, though many of them are cheaper on market days. If you buy more expensive, nonperishable goods, most stores will work with you to send them home.

- **Jams** *(confiture)* containing lush and often exotic fruits, such as *fruit de la passion* (passion fruit), *figues* (figs), and *pastèque* or *citre* (different types of watermelon).
- **Honey** *(miel)*, particularly lavender *(lavande)* or rosemary *(romarin)*. Stronger palates should try the chestnut *(châtaigne)* or even oak-flavored *(chêne)* honey.
- Tins of **tapenade** (olive paste) and all kinds of **olives**: black, green, and stuffed with garlic or anchovies.

- **Soaps and lotions,** particularly those perfumed with local plants such as lavender, rosemary, or linden *(tilleul)*. You'll also find colorful **sachets** containing the same fragrances.
- **Olive-wood products,** such as utensils and bowls. Olives are not just for nibbling; in Provence, the entire tree is used.
- Canned **pâtés,** including the buttery, rich foie gras (its "home" is Périgord, but you'll also find it in the markets of Provence). Canned goose, duck, and pork pâté can be imported to the US, but not beef.
- Packets of **herbs** (including the famous *herbes de Provence*), **salt** from the Camargue (look for *Fleur de Sel* for the best, and use sparingly), and bottles or tins of **olive oil** from local trees (Nyons is France's olive capital, though Les Baux is rightly proud of its olives as well). Most of these items can be found in attractive packaging that can be saved and enjoyed long after the product itself is gone.
- Sweets, including the famous ***nougat de Montélimar*** (a rich, chewy confection made with nuts and honey, sometimes flavored with lavender or other fragrances), *calissons* (orange-and-almond-flavored candy, shaped like the nut and originally from Aix-en-Provence), and **chocolates** from the Provençal producer Puyricard.
- Brightly colored **table linens.** Souleiado and Les Olivades are the most famous local manufacturers, but good-quality knockoffs can be found in most any market or store. Waterproof versions are great for outdoor use.
- **Cloth bags** with French designs for grocery shopping (can be packed easily and cost pennies).
- Local **pottery** (*poterie; faïence* is hand-painted pottery). Terre Provence is a well-known (and pricey) brand, but many other producers offer excellent quality, usually for less. Serious potters can plan ahead to visit a pottery fair featuring the best of the regions' potters.
- *Santons,* the tiny, brightly adorned clay or wood Provençal figurines. Originally designed for traditional Christmas crèche scenes, today's *santons* ("little saints") represent all walks of life—from the local *boulanger* to the woman sewing bright Provençal cloth to the village doctor. The most famous *santon* makers are in Séguret and Aubagne. All santon makers belong to the *santon*-maker guild (think medieval stonecutters or woodworkers), and each *santon* is handmade and signed.

SHOPPING

MARKET DAY

Market day *(jour de marché)* is a big deal throughout France, and in no other region is it more celebrated than in Provence and the Riviera. Markets have been a central feature of life in rural areas and cities since the Middle Ages. Many locals mark their calendars with the arrival of fresh produce.

Provence is a Mediterranean melting pot where Italy, Spain, and North Africa intersect with France to do business. Notice the ethnic mix of the vendors (and the products they sell). Spices from Morocco and

Tunisia, fresh pasta from Italy, saffron from Spain, and tapenade from Provence compete for your attention at Provence's *marchés*. For the best overview of this region's amazing market scene, pick up a copy of *Markets of Provence* by Marjorie R. Williams.

Types of Markets: There are two kinds of weekly open-air markets—*les marchés* and *les marchés brocantes*.

Les marchés are more general in scope, more common, and more colorful, featuring products from area farmers and artisans. These markets can offer a mind-boggling array of choices, including produce, meats, cheeses, breads, pastries, kitchen wares, inexpensive clothing, brightly colored linens, pottery, and more.

Les marchés brocantes specialize in quasi-antiques and flea market bric-a-brac (think rummage sale). *Brocantes* markets began in the Middle Ages, when middlemen would gather to set up small stalls and sell old, flea-infested clothes and the discarded possessions of the wealthy at bargain prices to eager peasants. Buyers were allowed to rummage through piles of aristocratic garbage.

Many *marchés* have good selections of produce and some *brocantes*. The best of all market worlds may rest in the unassuming town of Isle-sur-la-Sorgue, where on Sunday mornings, a festive food *marché* tangles with an active flea market and a good selection of antiques.

I've listed days and locations for both market types throughout this book. Notice the signs as you enter towns indicating the *jours de marché* (essential information to any civilized soul, and a reminder not to park on the streets the night before—be on the lookout for *stationnement interdit* signs that mark "no parking" areas). Most *marchés* take place once a week in the town's main square; larger *marchés* spill into nearby streets.

Usually, the bigger the market, the greater the overall selection, particularly of nonperishable goods. In big towns, market day may be twice a week; the larger offering is typically on a weekend day. In the largest cities (such as Avignon and Nîmes), fun modern market halls that are open daily until about 18:00 mix produce stands and meat counters selling fresh goods with small restaurants and bars. While the modern, interior setting is not as characteristic as the town square, these market halls are alive with authentic French action and offer good lunch options.

Market Day Tips: Markets begin at about 8:00, with setup commencing in the predawn hours (for some, a reason not to stay in a main-square hotel the night before market day). They usually end by 13:00. Savoring a relaxed lunch at an outdoor café amid the hustle and bustle of market day is a joy—but be aware that cafés and restaurants are slammed at lunch on market days; book ahead or arrive by noon to secure a table.

At the root of a good market experience is a sturdy shopping basket or bag. (Bring or buy your own bag—small plastic ones are no longer legal in France.) Find the vendor selling baskets and other wicker items and go local (*osier* is the French name for wicker, *cade* is the Provençal name—from the basket-making Luberon village of Cadenet); you can also find plastic and nylon versions. Most baskets are inexpensive, make for fun and colorful souvenirs, and come in handy for holding odd-shaped or breakable carry-on items on the plane trip home. With bag or basket in hand, shop for your heaviest items first. (You don't want to put a kilo of fresh apples on top of bread.)

It's bad form to be in a hurry on market day. Allow the crowd to set your pace. Observe the interaction between vendor and client. Notice the joy they can find in chatting each other up. Wares are displayed with pride. Remember, the French use metric weight. Ask for *un kilo* (about 2 pounds), *un demi-kilo* (about 1 pound—also called *une livre*), or *un quart de kilo* (pronounced "car-kilo," about half a pound). Your total price will be hand-tallied on scraps of paper and given to you. Vendors are normally honest and speak enough English to work out your transaction. If you're struggling to find the correct change, just hold out your hand and they will take only what is needed. (Still, you're wise to double-check the amount you just paid for that olive tree.)

What to Look For: Markets change seasonally. In April and May, look for asparagus (green, purple, or the prized white—after being cooked, these are dipped in vinegar or homemade mayonnaise and eaten by hand). In late spring, shop for strawberries, including the best: *fraises des bois* (wild strawberries). Almost equally prized are the strawberries called *gariguettes* and *maras des bois*. In early summer, look for cherries and other stone fruits, plus the famously sweet Cavaillon melons (resembling tiny cantaloupes, often served cut in half with a spoonful or two of the sweet Rhône white wine Beaumes-de-Venise). Don't worry if these are split open (*fendu*)—the abundance of sugar and sunshine are the cause (*fendus*

Key Shopping Phrases

English	French
Just looking.	*Je regarde.* (zhuh ruh-gard)
How much is it?	*Combien?* (kohn-bee-an)
Too big/small/expensive	*Trop grand/petit/cher* (troh grahn/puh-tee/shehr)
May I try it on?	*Je peux l'essayer?* (zhuh puh lay-say-yay)
Can I see more?	*Je peux en voir d'autres?* (zhuh puh ahn vwar d'otruh)
I'd like this.	*Je voudrais ça.* (zhuh voo-dray sah)
On sale	*Solde* (sohld)
Discounted price	*Prix réduit* (pree ray-dwee)
Big discounts	*Prix choc* (pree shohk)

melons are considered the sweetest). In late June and early September, watch for figs *(figues)*. From July through September, essential vegetables for the Provençal dish ratatouille—including eggplant, tomatoes, zucchinis, and peppers—come straight from the open fields. In the fall, you'll see stands selling game birds, other beasts of the hunt, and a glorious array of wild mushrooms.

Truffles preserved and sealed in jars can safely be brought back to the United States. The Luberon is one of Provence's largest truffle-producing areas. The town of Carpentras hosts a truffles-only market on Friday mornings in winter (mid-Nov to March, located near the TI). The size and hours of the market depends on how successful the sellers were at finding the black gold. Listen carefully and you might hear the Provençal language being spoken between some vendors and buyers. Little Richerenches—Northern Provence's truffle capital—holds its own winter truffle market on Saturday mornings; during its annual truffle-themed Mass, some parishioners give a truffle as a small offering instead of money. *Vive la France.*

Look for local cheeses in any town (cow, called *vache;* sheep or ewe, called *brebis;* or the Provençal favorite: goat cheese, or chèvre, named *picodons*). Cheeses come in many shapes (round, logs, pyramids) and various sizes (from single-bite mouthfuls to wheels that will last several meals). Some are adorned with herbs or spices; others are rolled in ash *(à la cendre)* or wrapped in leaves *(banon)*. Watch for the locally produced *banon de banon,* a goat cheese soaked in *eau-de-vie* (the alcoholic "water of life"), then wrapped in chestnut leaves and tied with string—*oh là là.*

Be on the lookout for sausages and locally produced wines

and ciders (free tastings are standard). Find samples of foie gras (available in take-it-home tins), good with the sweet white wine of Beaumes-de-Venise.

You may pass vendors selling paella made *sur place* (on the spot) in huge traditional round pans. Paella varies by area and chef, but most recipes include the traditional ingredients of fresh shellfish, chicken, and sausages mixed into saffron-infused rice. And throughout France, you'll see vans selling sizzling, spit-roasted chicken (perfectly bagged for carrying out) or pizza (made to your liking on the spot). *Bon appétit!*

For more on shopping in a French market, see the sidebar on page 7.

TIPS ON SHOPPING IN SHOPS AND BOUTIQUES

Those who prefer fashion over food will be happy to learn they don't have to go to Paris to enjoy the latest trends. Stylish boutiques line the shopping streets of Avignon, Nîmes, Aix-en-Provence, St-Rémy, Uzès, Nice, Cannes, and the ultra-trendy Juan-les-Pins. While many shopkeepers speak some English, an effort to speak even a minimum of French earns better service. These tips should get you off on the right track:

- In small stores, always say, *"Bonjour, Madame/Monsieur"* when entering and *"Au revoir, Madame/Monsieur"* when leaving.
- The customer is not always right; in fact, some clerks figure they're doing you a favor by waiting on you.
- Except in department stores, it's not normal for the customer to handle clothing. Ask first before you pick up an item: *"Je peux?"* (zhuh puh), meaning, "Can I?"
- By law, the price of items in a window display must be visible, often written on a slip of paper set on the floor or framed on the wall—a good indication of the shop's general price range.
- For clothing-size comparisons between the US and France, see the appendix.
- Forget returns (and don't count on exchanges).
- Observe French shoppers, then imitate them.
- Saturday afternoons are *très* busy.
- Stores are closed on Sunday and usually on Monday mornings.
- Smaller shops may close for lunch.
- Don't feel obliged to buy. If a shopkeeper offers assistance, just say, *"Je regarde, merci"* meaning, "Just looking, thanks."
- For information on VAT refunds and customs regulations, see page 505.

FRANCE: PAST & PRESENT

FRENCH HISTORY IN AN ESCARGOT SHELL

About the time of Christ, Romans "Latinized" the land of the Gauls. With the fifth-century AD fall of Rome, the barbarian Franks and Burgundians invaded. Today's France evolved from this unique mix of Latin and Celtic cultures.

While France wallowed with the rest of Europe in medieval darkness, it got a head start in its development as a nation-state. In 507, Clovis, the king of the Franks, established Paris as the capital of his Christian Merovingian dynasty. Clovis and the Franks would eventually become Louis and the French. The Frankish military leader Charles Martel stopped the spread of Islam by beating the Spanish Moors at the Battle of Poitiers in 732. And Charlemagne, the most important of the "Dark Age" Frankish kings, was crowned Holy Roman Emperor by the pope in 800. Charles the Great presided over the "Carolingian Renaissance" and effectively ruled an empire that was vast for its time.

The Treaty of Verdun (843), which divided Charlemagne's empire among his grandsons, marks what could be considered the birth of Europe. For the first time, a treaty was signed in vernacular languages (French and German), rather than in Latin. This split established a Franco-Germanic divide and heralded an age of fragmentation. While petty princes took the reigns, the Frankish king ruled only Ile de France, a small region around Paris.

Vikings, or Norsemen, settled in what became Normandy. Later, in 1066, these "Normans" invaded England. The Norman king, William the Conqueror, consolidated his English domain, accelerating the formation of modern England. But his rule also muddied the political waters between England and France, kicking off a centuries-long struggle between the two nations.

In the 12th century, Eleanor of Aquitaine (a separate country

Provence & the French Riviera Almanac

Official Name: Provence and the French Riviera are part of the Provence-Alpes-Côte-d'Azur (PACA), one of 13 administrative regions of France.

Regional Population: Over 4.9 million.

Main Cities: Marseille (860,000), Nice (345,000), Aix-en-Provence (143,000), Avignon (90,000), Antibes (77,000), Cannes (74,000), Arles (52,000), St-Tropez (5,600).

Language: French is the official language. More than 1.5 million people in the south of France speak one of two lesser-known dialects: Occitan, and specifically in the Provence region, Provençal (both dialects are closely related to Catalan).

Geography: Located in the southeast of France, the Provence-Alpes-Côte-d'Azur region spans over 71 miles of Mediterranean coastline.

Climate: The Alps shield the region from severe weather and give Provence and the Riviera the highest average temperatures in France. Locals enjoy more than 300 days of sun per year.

Economy: The Provence-Alpes-Côte-d'Azur region is the third wealthiest in France and annually contributes nearly $158 billion (7%) to France's GDP. Tourism and service industries account for 80 percent of jobs, but the region is also a leading center for agriculture, biotechnology, and microelectronics.

Agriculture: Provence is known for its herbs (such as oregano, thyme, and rosemary), vegetables, and olives—the region pro-

in southwest France) married Louis VII, king of France, bringing Aquitaine under French rule. They divorced, and she married Henry of Normandy, soon to be Henry II of England. This marital union gave England control of a huge swath of land, from the English Channel to the Pyrenees. For 300 years, France and England would struggle for control of Aquitaine. Any enemy of the French king would find a natural ally in the English king.

In 1328, the French king Charles IV died without a son. The English king (Edward III), Charles IV's nephew, was interested in the throne, but the French resisted. This quandary pitted France, the biggest and richest country in Europe, against England, which had the largest army. They fought from 1337 to 1453 in what was modestly called the Hundred Years' War.

Regional powers from within France actually sided with England. Burgundy took Paris, captured the royal family, and recognized the English king as heir to the French throne. England controlled France from the Loire north, and things looked bleak for the French king.

Enter Joan of Arc, a 16-year-old peasant girl driven by reli-

duces nearly two-thirds of France's olive oil. These ingredients, combined with elements of French, Spanish, and Italian cooking, make Provence's cuisine fresh, colorful, and flavorful.

Crafts: In the 17th century, Marseille began manufacturing expensive and colorful printed linens called "Indiennes," inspired by fabrics imported from India. Though most traditional textile factories are closed today, Provence still produces cotton fabrics (scarves, shawls) using original "Indienne" techniques and featuring the local cicada (*cigale*) in their designs.

Tourism: The region welcomes over 34 million tourists every year. Celebrities and wealthy Brits have vacationed on the French Riviera since the 19th century (giving the Promenade des Anglais in Nice its name). Nowadays, the Riviera attracts more than just celebrities: More than 5 million tourists visit every summer, with Nice at the center of the tourist commotion.

Famous Residents: The rich and famous have homes throughout Provence and the Riviera, including actors Brigitte Bardot, Johnny Depp, Mel Gibson, and Brad Pitt; musicians Bono, Tina Turner, Elton John, and Rod Stewart; and billionaire Bill Gates.

gious voices. France's national heroine left home to support Charles VII, the dauphin (boy prince, heir to the throne but too young to rule). Joan rallied the French, ultimately inspiring them to throw out the English. In 1430, Joan was captured by the Burgundians, who sold her to the English, who then convicted her of heresy and burned her at the stake in Rouen. But the inspiration of Joan of Arc lived on, and by 1453 English holdings on the Continent had dwindled to the port of Calais.

By 1500 a strong, centralized France had emerged, with borders similar to those of today. Its kings (from the Renaissance François I through the Henrys and all those Louises) were model divine monarchs, setting the standard for absolute rule in Europe.

Outrage over the power plays and spending sprees of the kings—coupled with the modern thinking of the Enlightenment (whose leaders were the French *philosophes*)—led to the French Revolution in 1789. In France, it was the end of the *ancien régime*, as well as its notion that some are born to rule, while others are born to be ruled.

The excesses of the Revolution in turn led to the rise of Na-

PAST & PRESENT

Typical Church Architecture

History comes to life when you visit a centuries-old church. Even if you wouldn't know your apse from a hole in the ground, learning a few simple terms will enrich your experience. Note that not every church has every feature, and a "cathedral" isn't a type of church architecture, but rather a designation for a church that's a governing center for a local bishop.

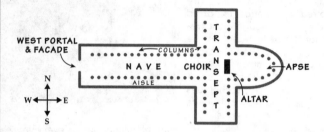

Aisles: Long, generally low-ceilinged arcades that flank the nave

Altar: Raised area with a ceremonial table (often adorned with candles or a crucifix), where the priest prepares and serves the bread and wine for Communion

Apse: Space behind the altar, sometimes bordered with small chapels

Barrel Vault: Continuous round-arched ceiling that resembles an extended upside-down U

Choir: Intimate space reserved for clergy and choir, located within the nave near the high altar and often screened off

Cloister: Covered hallways bordering a square or rectangular open-air courtyard, traditionally where monks and nuns got fresh air

Facade: Exterior of the church's main (west) entrance, usually highly decorated

Groin Vault: Arched ceiling formed where two equal barrel vaults meet at right angles

Narthex: Area (portico or foyer) between the main entry and the nave

Nave: Long central section of the church (running west to east, from the entrance to the altar) where the congregation sits or stands during the service

Transept: One of the two parts forming the "arms" of the cross in a traditional cross-shaped floor plan; runs north-south, perpendicularly crossing the east-west nave

West Portal: Main entry to the church (on the west end, opposite the main altar)

poleon, who ruled the French empire as a dictator. Eventually, *his* excesses ushered him into a South Atlantic exile, and after another half-century of monarchy and empire, the French settled on a compromise role for their leader. The modern French "king" is ruled by a constitution. Rather than dress in leotards and powdered wigs, the president goes to work in a suit and carries a briefcase.

The 20th century spelled the end of France's reign as a military and political superpower. Devastating wars with Germany in 1870, 1914, and 1940—and the loss of her colonial holdings—left France with not quite enough land, people, or production to be a top player on a global scale. But the 21st century may see France rise again: Paris is a cultural capital of Europe, and France—under the EU banner—is a key player in unifying Europe as a single economic power. And when Europe becomes a superpower, Paris may yet be its capital.

CONTEMPORARY POLITICS IN FRANCE

Today, the sociopolitical issues in France are—as in many countries—the economy, terrorism, relationship with the European Union, immigration, and managing Covid.

French unemployment remains high (just under 10 percent, even higher for youth) and growth has flatlined. France hasn't balanced its books since 1974, and public spending, at over half of GDP, chews up a bigger chunk of output than in any other eurozone country. The overwhelming challenge for French leadership is to address its economic problems while maintaining the high level of social services that French people have come to expect. The French want to continue the benefits of their generous social system, but are they willing to work to an older age (the current retirement age is 62) and pay the taxes required?

France also has its economic strengths: a well-educated workforce, an especially robust service sector and high-end manufacturing industry, and more firms big enough to rank in the global Fortune 500 than any other European country. Ironically, while France's economy may be one of the world's largest—and the French want all the creature comforts of a consumer economy—they remain skeptical about the virtues of capitalism and the work ethic. Globalization conflicts in a fundamental way with French values—many fear losing what makes their society unique in the quest for a bland, globalized world. Business conversation outside the office is generally avoided, as it implies a fascination with money that the French find vulgar. It's considered gauche even to ask what someone does for a living (in part because they think there's much more to a person than their occupation). In France, CEOs are not glorified as celebrities—chefs are.

The French believe that the economy should support social

Top French Notables in History

Madame and Monsieur Cro-Magnon: Prehistoric hunter-gatherers who moved to France (c. 30,000 BC), painted cave walls at Lascaux and Font-de-Gaume, and eventually settled down as farmers (c. 10,000 BC).

Vercingétorix (72-46 BC): This long-haired warrior rallied the Gauls against Julius Caesar's invading Roman legions (52 BC). Defeated by Caesar, France fell under Roman domination, resulting in 500 years of peace and prosperity. During that time, the Romans established cities, built roads, taught in Latin, and converted people to Christianity.

Charlemagne (742-814): For Christmas in 800, the pope gave King Charlemagne the title of Emperor, thus uniting much of Europe under the leadership of the Franks ("France"). Charlemagne stabilized France amid centuries of barbarian invasions. After his death, the empire was split, carving the outlines of modern France and Germany.

Eleanor of Aquitaine (c. 1122-1204): The beautiful, sophisticated ex-wife of the King of France married the King of England, creating an uneasy union between the two countries. During her lifetime, French culture was spread across Europe by roving troubadours, theological scholars, and skilled architects pioneering "the French style"—a.k.a. Gothic.

Joan of Arc (1412-1431): When France and England fought the Hundred Years' War (1337-1453), this teen—guided by voices in her head—rallied the French troops. Though Joan was captured and burned as a heretic, the French eventually drove England out for good, establishing the current borders. Over the centuries, the church upgraded Joan's status from heretic to saint (canonized in 1920).

François I (1494-1547): This Renaissance king ruled a united, modern nation, making it a cultural center that hosted the Italian Leonardo da Vinci. François set the tone for future absolute monarchs, punctuating his commands with the phrase, "For such is our pleasure."

Louis XIV (1638-1715): Charismatic and cunning, the "Sun King" ruled Europe's richest, most populous, most powerful nation-state. Every educated European spoke French, dressed in Louis-style leotards and powdered wigs, and built Versailles-like palaces. Though Louis ruled as an absolute monarch (distracting the nobility with courtly games), his reign also fostered the arts and philosophy, sowing the seeds of democracy and revolution.

Marie Antoinette (1755-1793): The Austrian-born wife of Louis XVI came to symbolize (probably unfairly) the decadence of France's ruling class. When the Revolution broke out (1789), she was arrested, imprisoned, and executed—one of thousands guillotined on Paris' Place de la Concorde as an enemy of the people.

Napoleon Bonaparte (1769-1821): This daring young military man became a hero during the Revolution, fighting Europe's royalty. He went on to conquer much of the Continent, become leader of France, and, eventually, rule as a dictator with the title of Emperor. In 1815, an allied Europe defeated and exiled Napoleon, reinstating the French monarchy—though future kings and emperors (including Napoleon's nephew, who ruled as Napoleon III) were somewhat subject to democratic constraints.

Claude Monet (1840-1926): His Impressionist paintings captured the soft-focus beauty of the belle époque—middle-class folk enjoying drinks in cafés, walks in gardens, and picnics along the Seine. At the turn of the 20th century, French culture reigned supreme while its economic and political clout was fading, and was soon shattered by World War I.

Charles de Gaulle (1890-1970): This career military man helped France survive occupation by Nazi Germany with his rousing radio broadcasts and unbending faith in his countrymen. He left politics after World War II, but following France's divisive wars in Vietnam and Algeria, he became president of the Fifth Republic in 1959. De Gaulle shocked allies by granting Algeria independence, blocking Britain's entry into the Common Market, and withdrawing from the military wing of NATO. Student riots in the late 1960s eventually led to his resignation in 1969.

Recent French Notables: Which French personalities of the last century will history remember? Marcel Marceau (1923-2007), world-famous mime? Brigitte Bardot (b. 1934), film actress, crusader for animal rights, and popularizer of the bikini? President François Mitterrand (1916-1996), the driving force behind Paris' La Grande Arche and Opéra Bastille? Chef Paul Bocuse (1926-2018), inventor of nouvelle cuisine? Yves Saint Laurent (1936-2008), the great fashion designer? Jean-Marie Le Pen (b. 1928), father of the far-right National Rally party...and 2022 presidential runner-up Marine Le Pen? Bernard Kouchner (b. 1939), co-founder of Doctors Without Borders? Zinédine Zidane (b. 1972), star soccer player, whose Algerian roots helped raise the status of Arabs in France? Or will it be actress Catherine Deneuve (b. 1943), retired NBA star Tony Parker (b. 1982), or wrestler-turned-actor Andre the Giant (1946-1993)? (Giants all.)

good, not vice versa, and that people are entitled to secure jobs from which they cannot be fired easily. This has produced a cradle-to-grave social security system of which the French are proud. But if you're considering starting a business in France, you're on the wrong track—taxes are *formidable* (figure a total small-business tax rate of around 66 percent—and likely to increase). And this job-security entitlement makes it difficult for employers to find motivated staff. You'll feel this impact in small hotels and restaurants where owners run themselves ragged trying to do everything themselves.

As part of the 27-member European Union, the "United States of Europe" that has successfully dissolved borders, France's governments have been decidedly pro-EU and critical to the EU's success. But many French are Euroskeptics, afraid that EU meddling threatens their job security and social benefits. The Brexit vote in 2016 focused attention on France. Would a Frexit follow? The EU can survive sans Britain but probably not sans France. For now, that possibility seems to have been shelved with President Macron, who is pro-EU.

French voters are notorious for their belief in the free market's heartless cruelty. France is routinely plagued with strikes, demonstrations, and slowdowns as workers try to preserve their rights in the face of a competitive global economy.

Meanwhile, immigration is shifting the country's ethnic and cultural makeup in ways that challenge French society. Ten percent of France's population is now of North African descent—mainly immigrants from former colonies. Many immigrants are Muslim, raising cultural questions in this heavily Catholic society with a history of official state secularism. In 2011 the government (quite controversially) made it illegal for women to wear a full, face-covering veil *(niqāb)* in public. Debates continue about whether banning the veil enforces democracy—or squelches diversity.

In 2015, Paris was hit with a double-whammy of Islamist terrorist attacks—at the offices of the satirical magazine *Charlie Hebdo,* and then at the Bataclan theater. In 2016, an attack in Nice shook the entire country. Armed soldiers now patrol rail stations and streets. The French have had to come to grips with the realization that many of the attackers were French citizens as well as immigrants. These attacks raised serious questions about immigration, policing, class divisions, and what it means to be French.

France is governed by a president elected by popular vote every five years. The president then selects the prime minister, who in turn chooses the cabinet ministers. Collectively, this executive branch is known as the *gouvernement.* The parliament consists of a Senate (348 seats) and Assemblée Nationale (577 seats).

In France, voters have an array of political parties to choose

Trouble in Paradise: Population Growth in Southern France

Life is not as perfect as it may appear amid the breezy, sun-kissed beaches, cities, and villages of Provence and the French Riviera. The south of France has become a bouillabaisse of people in search of their Provençal paradise. While some say the influx into this region has invigorated the culture, many residents are feeling growing pains. Two major trends are fueling the population boom in the south: northern Europeans looking for their place in the sun and North African immigrants looking for a better life. These trends collide in southern France.

Cheap flights and lightning-fast train service have enabled northern Europeans to experience the south of France as a weekend getaway...and a growing number are choosing to stay. Thanks to its sunny climate, relatively inexpensive homes (compared to northern Europe), and plentiful transportation options, this region is an understandably big draw. Unfortunately, as wealthy northerners pick off local homes and inflate prices, the average Jean loses out.

France has long looked across the Mediterranean to its old colonies for cheap sources of manual labor. When these workers came, they brought their families, who stayed in France and had families of their own.

Five million North Africans legally reside in France—and many more illegally. Around 100,000 illegal immigrants arrive in France each year, about half of whom are North African. Most live in the south (more than a quarter of Marseille's population is North African). This concentration of immigrants among a very Catholic French population, combined with high unemployment, has led to the rise of racist politics.

This anti-immigrant movement has been spearheaded by the National Rally party (formerly the National Front), which wants to keep "France for the French." National Rally leader Marine Le Pen carried the anti-immigrant torch and added populist policies in the latest elections. Although popular, she has failed to overcome centrist Emmanuel Macron, proving—for now—that the National Rally is still a minority.

from, making compromise and coalition-building essential to keeping power. Even the biggest parties rarely get more than one-third of the seats in parliament. And, because the parliament can force the *gouvernement* to resign at any time, it's essential that the *gouvernement* work with them.

To understand the current political landscape and the most recent election, it's helpful to consider the 2012 and 2017 elections. (French elections last only several months, with just a few TV debates.)

In 2012, socialist François Hollande defeated center-right

incumbent Nicolas Sarkozy. But when Hollande's term became fraught with scandal, rocked by terrorist events, and weighed down by a flat economy, Hollande opted against running for reelection in 2017. That left the field wide open.

The 2017 election was a wild ride, with events never seen before in France. Eleven candidates competed in the French version of a primary, reducing the field to two for the final vote. For the first time since de Gaulle, neither of the two finalists were from the traditional right and left parties. (Imagine a US presidential election sans Republican or Democratic candidates.) Emmanuel Macron, a centrist businessman, had no party affiliation and had never held elected office. Marine Le Pen represented the far-right National Front party, once a pariah party tarnished by accusations of anti-Semitism.

Le Pen rallied support by proposing to limit immigration and step back from the EU. Macron proposed a moderate stay-the-course plan that attracted both liberals and moderate conservatives. The tone of the debates was uncharacteristically nasty for genteel France. In the end, the French overwhelmingly chose the moderate path. Macron won with a whopping 66 percent of the vote. Still, Le Pen's result was the best yet for a National Front candidate.

Elected at 39 (and looking even younger), Macron became France's youngest leader since Napoleon Bonaparte. His success was completely unpredicted. He won as an outsider, representing a change from traditional party politics. (Sound familiar?)

After an almost flawless first year in office, Macron's second year was a different story. While he was internationally respected for his commitment to multilateralism and for combating climate change, his popularity among the French dropped from 64 percent to below 30 percent in 2018. The working class felt abandoned by Macron, calling him "the president of the rich" (thanks to more business-friendly policies). His proposal to fund climate change initiatives by raising the tax on gasoline led to the first true crisis of his presidency: "yellow vest" anti-government protests. In late 2019 and early 2020, a four-month transportation strike created havoc throughout France. Shortly after, the Covid-19 pandemic shut down the country—and most of Europe. Macron's measures to combat Covid—including tough restrictions on residents leaving their homes, and severe limits on travel—did not increase his popularity, but he seems to have emerged as well as any nation's leader.

Macron approached the 2022 presidential election with a strong lead in the polls, running against a broad range of candidates. Once again, Macron and Le Pen emerged as the two finalists—a repeat of the 2017 election. Voters were faced with the same sharp contrasts in policies and personalities: calm and steady Macron, middle-of-the-road but leaning left and all-in for the EU;

and rabble-rousing right-wing Le Pen, fashioning herself a bit after Donald Trump and wanting France out of the EU and NATO—and immigrants out of France (her role model: Viktor Orbán of Hungary).

The second and final vote happened on April 24, 2022. Macron was favored to win, as a majority of the other candidates put their support behind him, but the margin was close enough—and the stakes seemingly high enough—to make the election a nail-biter. In an eerily quiet city, with the lowest voter turnout in 50 years, Macron emerged again as the clear winner, with 58 percent of the vote. He's the first president to be reelected in 20 years.

For more about French history, consider Europe 101: History and Art for the Traveler *by Rick Steves and Gene Openshaw, available at RickSteves.com.*

PRACTICALITIES

This chapter covers the practical skills of European travel: how to get tourist information, pay for things, sightsee efficiently, find good-value accommodations, eat affordably but well, use technology wisely, and get between destinations smoothly. For more information on these topics, see RickSteves.com/travel-tips.

Travel Tips

Travel Advisories: Before traveling, check updated health and safety conditions, including restrictions for your destination, on the travel pages of the US State Department (www.travel.state.gov) and Centers for Disease Control and Prevention (www.cdc.gov/travel). The US embassy website for France is another good source of information (see next page).

Covid Vaccine/Test Requirements: It's possible you'll need to present proof of vaccination against the coronavirus and/or a negative Covid-19 test result to board a plane to Europe or back to the US. Carefully check requirements for each country you'll visit well before you depart, and again a few days before your trip. See the websites listed above for current requirements.

ETIAS Registration: The European Union may soon require US and Canadian citizens to register online with the European Travel Information and Authorization System (ETIAS) before entering France and other Schengen Zone countries (quick and easy process). For the latest, check www.etiasvisa.com.

Tourist Information: The French national tourist office is a wealth of information. Before your trip, scan their website—http://us.france.fr. It has particularly good resources for special-interest travel and plenty of free-to-download brochures.

In France, a good first stop is generally the tourist information office (abbreviated **TI** in this book). TIs are in business to help you spend money in their town—which can color their advice—but I still swing by to pick up a city map and get info on public transit, walking tours, special events, and nightlife. Some TIs have information on the entire country or at least the region, so you can pick up maps and other info for destinations you'll be visiting later in your trip. Towns with a lot of tourism generally have English-speaking guides available for private hire through the TI (about €100-150 for a 2-hour guided town walk).

The French call TIs by different names: *Office de Tourisme* and *Bureau de Tourisme* are used in cities; *Syndicat d'Initiative* and *Information Touristique* are used in small towns. Also look for *Accueil* signs in airports and at popular sights. These information booths are staffed with seasonal helpers who provide tourists with limited, though generally sufficient, information. Smaller TIs are often closed from 12:00 to 14:00 and on Sundays.

Emergency and Medical Help: For any emergency service—ambulance, police, or fire—call **112** from a mobile phone or landline (operators typically speak English). For hearing-assisted help for all services, dial 114. If you get sick, do as the French do and go to a pharmacist for advice. Or ask at your hotel for help—they'll know the nearest medical and emergency services.

Riviera Medical Services has a list of English-speaking physicians in the Riviera region and can help make an appointment or call an ambulance (+33 4 93 26 12 70, www.rivieramedical.com).

Theft or Loss: To replace a passport, you'll need to go in person to an embassy or consulate (see next). If your credit and debit cards disappear, cancel and replace them (see "Damage Control for Lost Cards" on page 504). File a police report, either on the spot or within a day or two; you'll need it to submit an insurance claim for lost or stolen items, and it can help with replacing your passport or credit and debit cards. For more information, see RickSteves.com/help.

US Consulates and Embassies: Appointment required, http://fr.usembassy.gov. Paris—dial +33 1 43 12 22 22 (2 Avenue Gabriel, to the left as you face Hôtel Crillon, Mo: Concorde).

Lyon—dial +33 1 43 12 48 60 (2 Rue Président Carnot). Marseille—dial +33 1 43 12 47 54 (Place Varian Fry).

Canadian Consulate and Embassy: Appointment required, www.canadainternational.gc.ca/france. Paris—dial +33 1 44 43 29 00 (130 Rue du Faubourg Saint-Honoré, Mo: Saint-Philippe-du-Roule). Lyon—dial +33 4 78 84 39 19 (3 Place de la Bourse). Nice—dial +33 4 93 13 17 19 (37 Boulevard Dubouchage).

Time Zones: France, like most of continental Europe, is generally six/nine hours ahead of the East/West Coasts of the US. The exceptions are the beginning and end of Daylight Saving Time: Europe "springs forward" the last Sunday in March (two weeks after most of North America), and "falls back" the last Sunday in October (one week before North America). For a handy time converter, use the world clock app on your phone or download one (see www.timeanddate.com).

Business Hours: You'll find much of rural France closed weekdays from 12:00 to 14:00 (lunch is sacred). On Sunday, most businesses are closed (family is sacred), though some small shops such as *boulangeries* (bakeries) are open until noon, special events and weekly markets pop up, and museums are open all day (but public transportation options are limited). On Mondays, some businesses are closed until 14:00 and possibly all day. Smaller towns are often quiet and downright boring on Sundays and Mondays, unless it's market day.

Watt's Up? Europe's electrical system is 220 volts, instead of North America's 110 volts. Most electronics (laptops, phones, cameras) and appliances (newer hair dryers, CPAP machines) convert automatically, so you won't need a converter, but you will need an adapter plug with two round prongs, sold inexpensively at travel stores in the US.

Discounts: Discounts for sights are generally not listed in this book. However, youths under 18 and students and teachers with proper identification cards (www.isic.org) can get discounts at many sights—always ask. Seniors age 65 and over may get the odd discount, but don't get your hopes up. To inquire about a senior discount, ask, *"Réduction troisième âge?"* (ray-dewk-see-ohn trwah-zee-ehm ahzh). Some discounts are available only to European citizens.

Online Translation Tips: Google's Chrome browser instantly translates websites; Translate.google.com and DeepL.com are also handy. The Google Translate app converts spoken or typed English into most European languages (and vice versa) and can also translate text it "reads" with your phone's camera.

Going Green: There's plenty you can do to reduce your environmental footprint when traveling. When practical, take a train

PRACTICALITIES

Exchange Rate

1 euro (€) = about $1.10

To convert prices in euros to dollars, add about 10 percent: €20 = about $22, €50 = about $55. Like the dollar, one euro is broken into 100 cents. Coins range from €0.01 to €2, and bills from €5 to €200.

Check www.oanda.com for the latest exchange rates.

---

instead of a flight within Europe, and use public transportation within cities. In hotels, use the "Do Not Disturb" sign to avoid daily linen and towel changes (or hang up your towels to signal you'll reuse them). Bring a reusable shopping tote and refillable water bottle (Europe's tap water is safe to drink). Skip printed brochures, maps, or other materials that you don't plan to keep—get your info online instead. To find out how Rick Steves' Europe is offsetting carbon emissions with a self-imposed carbon tax, see RickSteves.com/about-us/climate-smart.

Money

Here's my basic strategy for using money wisely in Europe. I pack the following and keep it all safe in my money belt.

Credit Card: You'll use your credit card for purchases both big (hotels, advance tickets) and small (little shops, food stands). Some European businesses have gone cashless, making a card your only payment option. A "tap-to-pay" or "contactless" card is the most widely accepted and simplest to use.

Debit Card: Use this at ATMs to withdraw a small amount of local cash. Wait until you arrive to get euros (European airports have plenty of ATMs); if you buy euros before your trip, you'll pay bad stateside exchange rates. While most transactions are by card these days, cash can help you out of a jam if your card randomly doesn't work, and can be useful to pay for things like tips and local guides.

Backup Card: Some travelers carry a third card (debit or credit; ideally from a different bank) in case one gets lost or simply doesn't work.

Stash of Cash: For an emergency reserve, in most of Europe bring dollars. But in France, consider bringing €200 (bring euros, as dollars can be hard to change in France).

BEFORE YOU GO

Know your cards. For credit cards, Visa and MasterCard are universal while American Express and Discover are less common. US debit cards with a Visa or MasterCard logo will work in any European ATM.

Go "contactless." Get comfortable using contactless pay options. Check to see if you already have—or can get—a tap-to-pay version of your credit card (look on the card for the tap-to-pay symbol—four curvy lines) and consider setting up your smartphone for contactless payment (see next section for details). Both options are widely used in Europe and are more secure than a physical credit card: Instead of recording your credit card number, a one-time encrypted "token" enables the purchase and expires shortly afterward.

Know your PIN. Make sure you know the numeric, four-digit PIN for each of your cards, both debit and credit. Request it if you don't have one, as it may be required for some purchases. Allow time to receive the information by mail—it's not always possible to obtain your PIN online or by phone.

Report your travel dates. Let your bank know that you'll be using your debit and credit cards in Europe, and when and where you're headed.

Adjust your ATM withdrawal limit. Find out how much you can withdraw daily and ask for a higher daily limit if you want to get more cash at once. Note that European ATMs will withdraw funds only from checking accounts, not savings accounts.

Find out about fees. For any purchase or withdrawal made with a card, you may be charged a currency conversion fee (1-3 percent) and/or a Visa or MasterCard international transaction fee (less than 1 percent). If you're getting a bad deal, consider getting a new card. Reputable no-fee cards include those from Capital One, as well as Charles Schwab debit cards. Most credit unions and some airline loyalty cards have low or no international transaction fees.

IN EUROPE
Using Credit Cards and Payment Apps

Tap-to-Pay or **Contactless Cards:** These cards have the usual chip and/or magnetic stripe, but with the addition of a contactless symbol. Simply tap your card against a contactless reader to complete a transaction—no PIN or signature is required. This is by far the easiest way to pay and has become the standard in much of Europe.

Payment Apps: Just like at home, you can pay with your smartphone or smartwatch by linking a credit card to an app such as Apple Pay or Google Pay. To pay, hold your phone near a contactless reader; you may need to verify the transaction with a face scan, fingerprint scan, or passcode. If you've arrived in Europe without a tap-to-pay card, you can easily set up your phone to work in this way.

Other Card Types: Chip-and-PIN cards have a visible chip embedded in them; rather than swiping, you insert the card into the payment machine, then enter your PIN on a keypad. In Europe, these cards have largely been supplanted by tap-to-pay cards, but you may be asked to use chip-and-PIN for certain purchases. **Swipe-and-sign** credit cards—with a swipeable magnetic stripe, and a receipt you have to sign—are increasingly rare.

Will My US Card Work? Usually, yes. On rare occasions, at self-service payment machines (such as transit-ticket kiosks, toll-booths, or fuel pumps), some US cards may not work. Usually a tap-to-pay card does the trick in these situations. Just in case, carry cash as a backup and look for a cashier who can process your payment if your card is rejected. Drivers should be prepared to move on to the next gas station if necessary. (In some countries, gas stations sell prepaid gas cards, which you can purchase with any US card). When approaching a toll plaza or ferry ticket line, use the "cash" lane.

Using Cash

Cash Machines: European cash machines work just like they do at home—except they spit out local currency instead of dollars, calculated at the day's standard bank-to-bank rate. In most places, ATMs are easy to locate—in France ask for a *distributeur* (dee-stree-bew-tur). When possible, withdraw cash from a bank-run ATM located just outside that bank.

If your debit card doesn't work, try a lower amount—your request may have exceeded your withdrawal limit or the ATM's limit. If you still have a problem, try a different ATM or come back later.

Avoid "independent" ATMs, such as Travelex, Euronet, Moneybox, Your Cash, Cardpoint, and Cashzone. These have high fees, can be less secure, and may try to trick users with "dynamic currency conversion" (see next).

Dynamic Currency Conversion: When withdrawing cash at an ATM or paying with a credit card, you'll often be asked whether you want the transaction processed in dollars or in the local currency. Always refuse the conversion and *choose the local currency*. While DCC offers the illusion of convenience, it comes with a poor exchange rate, and you'll wind up losing money.

Exchanging Cash: Minimize exchanging money in Europe; it's expensive (you'll generally lose 5 to 10 percent). In a pinch you can find exchange desks at major train stations or airports. Banks generally do not exchange money unless you have an account with them.

Security Tips

Pickpockets target tourists. Keep your cash, credit cards, and passport secure in your money belt, and carry only a day's spending money in your front pocket or wallet.

Before inserting your card into an ATM, inspect the front. If anything looks crooked, loose, or damaged, it could be a sign of a card-skimming device. When entering your PIN, carefully block other people's view of the keypad.

Avoid using a debit card for purchases. Because a debit card pulls funds directly from your bank account, potential charges incurred by a thief will stay on your account while your bank investigates.

To access your accounts online while traveling, be sure to use a secure connection (see the "Tips on Internet Security" sidebar, later).

Damage Control for Lost Cards

If you lose your credit or debit card, report the loss immediately to the respective global customer-assistance centers. With a mobile phone, call these 24-hour US numbers: Visa (+1 303 967 1096), MasterCard (+1 636 722 7111), and American Express (+1 336 393 1111). From a landline, you can call these US numbers collect by going through a local operator.

You'll need to provide the primary cardholder's identification-verification details (such as birth date, mother's maiden name, or Social Security number). You can generally receive a temporary card within two or three business days in Europe (see RickSteves.com/help for more).

If you report your loss within two days, you typically won't be responsible for unauthorized transactions on your account, although many banks charge a liability fee.

TIPPING

Tipping *(donner un pourboire)* in France isn't as automatic and generous as it is in the US. For special service, tips are appreciated, but not expected. As in the US, the proper amount depends on your resources, tipping philosophy, and the circumstances, but some general guidelines apply.

Restaurants: At cafés and restaurants, a service charge is included in the price of what you order, and it's unnecessary to tip extra, though you can for helpful service. If paying with a credit card, be prepared to tip separately with cash or coins; credit card receipts sometimes don't have a tip line. For details on tipping in restaurants, see "Eating," later.

Taxis: For a typical ride, round up your fare a bit (for instance, if the fare is €13, pay €14). If the cabbie hauls your bags and zips you to the airport to help you catch your flight, you might want to toss in a little more.

Services: In general, if someone in the tourism or service industry does a super job for you, a small tip of a euro or two is appropriate...but not required. If you're not sure whether (or how much) to tip, ask a local for advice.

GETTING A VAT REFUND

Wrapped into the purchase price of your French souvenirs is a value-added tax (VAT) of about 20 percent. You're entitled to get most of that tax back if you purchase more than €175 worth of goods at a store that participates in the VAT-refund scheme. Typically, you must ring up the minimum at a single retailer—you can't add up your purchases from various shops to reach the required amount. (If the store ships the goods to your US home, VAT is not assessed on your purchase.)

Getting your refund is straightforward...and worthwhile if you spend a significant amount.

At the Merchant: Have the merchant completely fill out the refund document, called a *bordereau de détaxe* (they'll ask for your passport; a photo of your passport usually works). Keep track of the paperwork and your original sales receipt. Note that you're not supposed to use your purchased goods before you leave Europe.

At the Border or Airport: Process your VAT document at your last stop in the European Union (such as at the airport) with the customs agent who deals with VAT refunds (allow plenty of extra time to deal with this process). At some airports, you'll have to go to a customs office to get your documents stamped and then to a separate VAT refund service (such as Global Blue or Planet) to process the refund. At other airports, a single VAT desk handles the whole thing. (Note that refund services typically extract a 4 percent fee, but you're paying for the convenience of receiving your money in cash immediately or as a credit to your card.) Otherwise, you'll need to mail the stamped refund documents to the address given by the merchant.

CUSTOMS FOR AMERICAN SHOPPERS

You can take home $800 worth of items per person duty-free, once every 31 days. Many processed and packaged foods are allowed, including cheeses, dried herbs, jams, baked goods, candy, chocolate, oil, vinegar, condiments, and honey. Fresh fruits and vegetables and most meats are not allowed, with exceptions for some canned items. As for alcohol, you can bring in one liter duty-free (it can be packed securely in your checked luggage, along with any other liquid-containing items).

To bring alcohol (or liquid-packed foods) in your carry-on bag on your flight home, buy it at a duty-free shop at the airport. You'll increase your odds of getting it onto a connecting flight if it's packaged in a "STEB"—a secure, tamper-evident bag. But stay away from liquids in opaque, ceramic, or metallic containers, which usually cannot be successfully screened (STEB or no STEB).

For details on allowable goods, customs rules, and duty rates, visit http://help.cbp.gov.

Sightseeing

Sightseeing can be hard work. Use these tips to make your visits to Provence and the Riviera's finest sights meaningful, fun, efficient, and painless.

MAPS AND NAVIGATION TOOLS

A good map is essential for efficient navigation while sightseeing. The maps in this book are concise and simple, designed to help you locate recommended destinations, sights, hotels, restaurants, and local TIs, where you can pick up more in-depth maps. More detailed maps are sold at newsstands and bookstores.

You can also use a mapping app on your mobile device, which provides turn-by-turn directions for walking, driving, and taking public transit. Google Maps, Apple Maps, and City-Maps2Go allow you to download maps for offline use; ideally, download the areas you'll need before your trip. For certain features, you'll need to be online—either using Wi-Fi or an international data plan.

PLAN AHEAD

Set up an itinerary that allows you to fit in all your must-see sights. For a one-stop look at opening hours in the bigger cities, see the "At a Glance" sidebars for Arles, Avignon, Marseille, and Nice. Since the Covid-19 pandemic, hours for museums and sights have been unstable. Both before and during your trip, confirm the latest opening days and times with the TI or on a museum or sight's official website (listed throughout this book).

Don't put off visiting a must-see sight—you never know when a place will close unexpectedly for a holiday, strike, or restoration. Many museums are closed or have reduced hours at least a few days a year, especially on holidays such as Christmas, New Year's, and Labor Day (May 1). A list of holidays is in the appendix; check for possible closures during your trip. In summer, some sights may stay open late. Off-season hours may be shorter.

Going at the right time helps avoid crowds. This book offers tips on the best times to see specific sights. Evening visits (when possible) are usually more peaceful, with fewer crowds. Late morning is usually the worst time to visit a popular sight.

If you plan to hire a local guide (recommended in this book and at local TIs), reserve ahead by email. Popular guides can get booked up.

Study up. To get the most out of the self-guided tours and sight descriptions in this book, read them before you visit.

RESERVATIONS, ADVANCE TICKETS, AND PASSES

Many popular sights in Europe come with long lines—not to get in, but to buy a ticket. Visitors who buy tickets online in advance (or who have a museum pass covering these key sights) can skip the line and waltz right in. Advance tickets are generally timed-entry, meaning you're guaranteed admission on a certain date and time.

For some sights, buying ahead is required (tickets aren't sold at the sight and it's the only way to get in). At other sights, buying ahead is recommended to skip the line and save time. And for many sights, advance tickets are available but unnecessary: At these uncrowded sights you can simply arrive, buy a ticket, and go in.

Don't confuse the reservation options: available, recommended, and required. Use my advice in this book as a guide. Note any must-see sights that sell out long in advance and be prepared to buy tickets early. If you do your research, you'll know the smart strategy.

Given how precious your vacation time is, I'd book in advance both where it's required (as soon as your dates are firm) and where it will save time in a long line (in some cases, you can do this even on the day you plan to visit).

You'll generally be emailed an eticket with a QR or bar code that you'll store on your phone to scan at the entrance (if you prefer, you can print it out). Look for the ticket-holders line rather than the ticket-buying line; you may still have to wait in a security line.

Several cities offer sightseeing passes (listed in this book) that can be worthwhile values.

AT SIGHTS

Here's what you can typically expect:

Entering: You may not be allowed to enter if you arrive too close to closing time. And guards start ushering people out well before the actual closing time, so don't save the best for last.

Many sights have a security check. Allow extra time for these lines. Some sights require you to check day packs and coats. (If you'd rather not check your day pack, try carrying it tucked under your arm like a purse as you enter.)

At churches—which often offer interesting art (usually free) and a cool, welcome seat—a modest dress code (no bare shoulders or shorts) is encouraged though rarely enforced.

Photography: If the museum's photo policy isn't clearly posted, ask a guard. Generally, taking photos without a flash or tripod is allowed. Some sights ban selfie sticks; others ban photos altogether.

Audioguides and Apps: Some sights offer audioguides with worthwhile recorded descriptions in English. In some cases, you'll rent a device to carry around (if you bring your own plug-in earbuds, you'll enjoy better sound). Increasingly, museums and sights instead offer an app you can download with their audioguide (often free; check websites from home and consider downloading in advance as not all sights offer free Wi-Fi).

Temporary Exhibits: Museums may show special exhibits in addition to their permanent collection. Some exhibits are included in the entry price, while others come at an extra cost (which you may have to pay even if you don't want to see the exhibit).

Expect Changes: Artwork can be on tour, on loan, out sick, or shifted at the whim of the curator. Pick up a floor plan as you enter and ask museum staff if you can't find a particular item. Say the title or artist's name, or point to the photograph in this book and ask for its location by saying, *"Où est?"* (oo ay).

Services: Important sights usually have a reasonably priced on-site café or cafeteria (handy and air-conditioned places to rejuvenate during a long visit). The WCs at sights are free and generally clean.

Before Leaving: At the gift shop, scan the postcard rack or thumb through a guidebook to be sure you haven't overlooked something that you'd like to see. Every sight or museum offers more than what is covered in this book. Use the information I provide as an introduction—not the final word.

Sleeping

Good-value accommodations in Provence and the Riviera are generally easy to find, if you book far enough ahead. Choose from one- to five-star hotels (two and three stars are my mainstays), bed-and-breakfasts (*chambres d'hôtes*, usually cheaper than hotels), hostels, campgrounds, and vacation homes (*gîtes*, rented by the week).

Extensive and opinionated listings of good-value rooms are a major feature of this book's Sleeping section. Rather than list accommodations scattered throughout a town, I choose hotels in my favorite neighborhoods that are convenient to your sightseeing.

My recommendations run the gamut, from dorm beds to luxurious rooms with all the comforts. I like places that are clean, central, relatively quiet at night, reasonably priced, friendly, small enough to have a hands-on owner or manager, and run with a respect for French traditions. I'm more impressed by a handy location and a fun-loving philosophy than oversized TVs and a spa. Most of my recommendations fall short of perfection. But if I can find a place with most of these features, it's a keeper.

Book your accommodations as soon as your itinerary is set, especially if you want to stay at one of my top listings or if you'll be traveling during busy times. Wherever you're staying, be ready for larger crowds in May and September and during these holiday periods: Easter weekend, Labor Day, Ascension weekend, Pentecost weekend, Bastille Day and the week during which it falls, and the winter holidays (mid-Dec-early Jan). Note that many holiday weekends fall in May, jamming French hotels. Check hotel websites for the best deals. See the appendix for a list of major holidays and festivals in France.

RATES AND DEALS

I've categorized my recommended accommodations based on price, indicated with a dollar-sign rating (see sidebar). Room prices can fluctuate significantly with demand and amenities (size, views, room class, and so on), but relative price categories remain constant.

Booking Direct: Once your dates are set, compare prices at several hotels. You can do this by checking hotel websites and booking sites such as Hotels.com or Booking.com. After you've zeroed in on your choice, book directly with the hotel itself. This increases the chances that the hotelier will be able to accommodate special needs or requests (such as shifting your reservation). And when you book on the hotel's website, by email, or by phone, the owner avoids the commission paid to booking sites, giving them wiggle room to offer you a discount, a nicer room, or a free breakfast. French hotels recently won the right to undercut Booking.com and Hotels.com

PRACTICALITIES

PRACTICALITIES

Sleep Code

Hotels in this book are categorized according to the average price of a standard double room without breakfast in high season.

$$$$	**Splurge:** Most rooms over €300
$$$	**Pricier:** €200-300
$$	**Moderate:** €130-200
$	**Budget:** €70-130
¢	**Backpacker:** Under €70
RS%	**Rick Steves discount**
*	**French hotel rating system** (0-5 stars)

Unless otherwise noted, credit cards are accepted, hotel staff speak basic English, and free Wi-Fi is available. Comparison-shop by checking prices at several hotels (on each hotel's own website, on a booking site, or by email). For the best deal, *book directly with the hotel.* Ask for a discount if paying in cash; if the listing includes **RS%,** request a Rick Steves discount.

prices on their websites; virtually all offer lower rates if you book direct. If the price they quote is higher than the offer on a booking site, let the hotel know, and they'll usually adjust the rate.

Getting a Discount: Some hotels extend a discount to those who pay cash or stay longer than three nights. And some accommodations offer a special discount for Rick Steves readers, indicated in this guidebook by the abbreviation "**RS%**." Discounts vary: Ask for details when you reserve. Generally, to qualify for this discount, you must book direct (not through a booking site), mention this book when you reserve, show it upon arrival, and sometimes stay a certain number of nights. In some cases, you may need to enter a discount code (which I've provided in the listing) in the booking form on the hotel's website. Rick Steves discounts apply to readers with either print or digital books. Understandably, discounts do not apply to promotional rates.

Room Taxes: Hotels in France must charge a daily tax *(taxe du séjour)* of about €1-4 per person per day (based on the number of stars the hotel has). Some hotels include it in their prices, but most add it to your bill.

TYPES OF ACCOMMODATIONS
Hotels

In this book, the price for a double room will normally range from €70 (very simple; toilet and shower down the hall) to €400 (grand lobbies, maximum plumbing, and the works), with most clustering around €100-150 (with private bathrooms).

Most hotels also offer single and triple rooms, and some offer larger rooms for four or more people (I call these "family rooms" in the listings). Some hotels can add an extra bed (for a small charge) to turn a double into a triple. A triple room is cheaper than the cost of a double and a single. Three or four people can economize by requesting one big room.

The French have a simple hotel rating system based on amenities and rated by stars (indicated in this book by asterisks, from * through *****). One star is modest, two has most of the comforts, and three is generally a two-star with a fancier lobby and more elaborately designed rooms. Four-star places give a bit more comfort than those with three. Five stars probably offer more luxury than you'll have time to appreciate. Two-star-and-above hotels are required to have an English-speaking staff, though nearly all hotels I recommend have someone who speaks English.

The number of stars does not always reflect room size or guarantee quality. One- and two-star hotels are less expensive, but some three-star (and even a few four-star) hotels offer good value, justifying the extra cost. Unclassified hotels (no stars) can be bargains...or depressing dumps.

Within each hotel, prices vary depending on the size of the room, whether it has a tub or shower, and the bed type (tubs and twins usually cost more than showers and double beds). If you have a preference, ask for it. Hotels often have more rooms with tubs (which the French prefer) and are inclined to give you one by default. You can save lots by finding the rare room without a private shower or toilet.

Most French hotels have queen-size beds in double rooms—to confirm, ask, *"Avez-vous des lits queen-size?"* (ah-vay-voo day lee queen-size). Some hotels push two twins together under king-size sheets and blankets to make *le king-size*. If you'll take either twins or a double, ask for a generic *une chambre pour deux* (room for two) to avoid being needlessly turned away. Some hotels have a few family-friendly rooms that open up to each other *(chambres communiquantes)*.

Arrival and Check-In: Hotels and B&Bs are sometimes located on the higher floors of a multipurpose building with a secured door. In that case, look for your hotel's name on the buttons by the main entrance. When you ring the bell, you'll be buzzed in.

Hotel elevators are common, though small, and some older buildings still lack them. You may have to climb a flight of stairs to

Using Online Services to Your Advantage

From booking services to user reviews, online businesses play a greater role in travelers' planning than ever before. Take advantage of their pluses—and be wise to their downsides.

Booking Sites

Booking websites such as Booking.com and Hotels.com offer one-stop shopping for hotels. While convenient for travelers, they're both a blessing and a curse for small, independent, family-run hotels. Without a presence on these sites, small hotels become almost invisible. But to be listed, a hotel must pay a sizable commission.

Here's the work-around: Use the big sites to research what's out there, then book directly with the hotel by email or phone, in which case hotel owners are free to give you whatever price they like. Ask for a room without the commission markup (or ask for a free breakfast if not included, or a free upgrade). If you do book online, be sure to use the hotel's own website. French hotels now have the right to offer room rates on their site below those listed on third-party websites; most will give you lower rates by booking direct.

As a savvy consumer, remember: When you book with an online service, you're adding a middleman who takes a cut. To support small, family-run hotels whose world is more difficult than ever, book direct.

Short-Term Rental Sites

Rental juggernaut Airbnb (along with other short-term rental sites) allows travelers to rent rooms and apartments, often providing more value, space, and amenities than a cookie-cutter hotel. Airbnb fans appreciate feeling part of a real neighborhood and getting into a daily routine as "temporary Europeans." Depending on the host, Airbnb can provide an opportunity to get to know a local person and keep your money in the community; but beware: others are impersonally managed by large, absentee agencies.

reach the elevator (if so, you can ask the front desk for help carrying your bags up).

The EU requires hotels to collect your name, nationality, and ID number. At check-in, the receptionist will normally ask for your passport and may keep it for several hours. If you're not comfortable leaving your passport at the desk, bring a copy to give them instead.

If you're arriving in the morning, your room probably won't be ready. Check your bag safely at the hotel and dive right into sightseeing.

In Your Room: Most hotel rooms have a TV and free Wi-Fi,

Critics of Airbnb see it as a threat to "traditional Europe." Landlords can make more money renting to short-stay travelers, driving rents up—and local residents out. Traditional businesses are replaced by ones that cater to tourists. And the character and charm that made those neighborhoods desirable to tourists in the first place goes too. Some cities have cracked down, requiring owners to obtain a license and to occupy rental properties part of the year (and staging disruptive "inspections" that inconvenience guests).

As a lover of Europe, I share the worry of those who see residents nudged aside by tourists. But as an advocate for travelers, I appreciate the value Airbnb can provide in offering the chance to stay in a local building or neighborhood with potentially fewer tourists.

User Reviews

User-generated review sites and apps such as Yelp and TripAdvisor can give you a consensus of opinions about everything from hotels and restaurants to sights and nightlife. If you scan reviews of a restaurant or hotel and see several complaints about noise or a rotten location, you've gained insight that can help in your decision-making.

As a guidebook writer, my sense is that there is a big difference between the uncurated information on a review site and the vetted listings in a guidebook. A user review is based on the limited experience of one person, who stayed at just one hotel in a given city and ate at a few restaurants there. A guidebook is the work of a trained researcher who forms a well-developed basis for comparison by visiting many restaurants and hotels year after year.

Both types of information have their place, and in many ways, they're complementary. If something is well reviewed in a guidebook and it also gets good online reviews, it's likely a winner.

which can vary in strength and quality. Room phones are fast becoming extinct.

Some places provide quilts as the only bed covering. While comfortable, they're warm in summers (forcing me to use air-conditioning)—ask the hotel for a sheet *(uhn drah)* for cooler sleeping.

Breakfast and Meals: Most hotels offer breakfast, but it's rarely included in the room rates—pay attention when comparing rates between hotels (though some offer free breakfast to Rick Steves readers or with direct booking—ask). The price of breakfast correlates with the price of the room: The more expensive the room, the more expensive the breakfast. This per-person charge rises with

PRACTICALITIES

French Hotel-Room Lingo

Know your options. Hoteliers often don't mention the cheaper rooms—they assume you want a private bathroom or a bigger room. Here are the types of rooms and beds:

French	English
une chambre avec douche et WC	room with private shower and toilet
une chambre avec bain et WC	room with private bathtub and toilet
une chambre avec cabinet de toilette	room with a toilet (shower down the hall)
une chambre sans douche ni WC	room without a private shower or toilet
chambres communiquantes	connecting rooms (ideal for families)
une chambre simple, une single	a true single room
un grand lit	double bed (55 in. wide)
deux petits lits	twin beds (30-36 in. wide)
un lit queen-size	queen-size bed (63 in. wide)
un king size	king-size bed (usually two twins pushed together)
un lit pliant	folding bed
un berceau	baby crib
un lit d'enfant	child's bed

the number of stars the hotel has and can add up, particularly for families. While hotels hope you'll buy their breakfast, it's optional unless otherwise noted; to save money, head to a bakery or café instead.

Some hoteliers, especially in resort towns, strongly encourage their peak-season guests to take *demi-pension* (half-pension)—that is, breakfast and either lunch or dinner. By law, they can't require you to take half-pension unless you are staying three or more nights, but, in practice, some do during high season. And though the food is usually good, it limits your ability to shop around. I've indicated where I think *demi-pension* is a good value.

Hoteliers uniformly detest it when people bring food into bedrooms. Dinner picnics are particularly frowned upon: Hoteliers worry about cleanliness, smells, and attracting insects. Be tidy and considerate.

Checking Out: While it's customary to pay for your room upon departure, it can be a good idea to settle your bill the day before, when you're not in a hurry and while the manager's in. Some

Keep Cool

If you're visiting France in the summer, you'll want an air-conditioned room. Most hotel air-conditioners come with a remote control that generally has similar symbols and features: fan icon (click to toggle through wind power, from light to gale); temperature (20 degrees Celsius is comfortable); louver icon (choose steady airflow or waves); snowflake and sunshine icons (cold air or heat, depending on season); and clock ("O" setting: run X hours before turning off; "I" setting: wait X hours to start). When you leave your room for the day, do as the environmentally conscious Europeans do, and turn off the air-conditioning.

hoteliers will ask you to sign their *Livre d'Or* (literally "Golden Book," for client comments). They take this seriously and enjoy reading your remarks.

Hotelier Help: Hoteliers can be a good source of advice. Most know their city well and can assist you with everything from public transit and airport connections to calling an English-speaking doctor, or finding a good restaurant, a late-night pharmacy, or a self-service launderette (*laverie automatique*, lah-veh-ree oh-to-mah-teek).

Hotel Hassles: Even at the best places, mechanical breakdowns occur: sinks leak, hot water turns cold, toilets may gurgle or smell, the Wi-Fi goes out, or the air-conditioning dies when you need it most. Report your concerns clearly and calmly at the front desk.

If you find that night noise is a problem (if, for instance, your room is over a nightclub or facing a busy street), ask for a quieter room in the back or on an upper floor. To guard against theft in your room, keep valuables out of sight. Some rooms come with a safe, and other hotels have safes at the front desk. I've never bothered using one and in a lifetime of travel, I've never had anything stolen from my room.

For more complicated problems, don't expect instant results. Above all, keep a positive attitude. Remember, you're on vacation. If your hotel is a disappointment, spend more time out enjoying the place you came to see.

Modern Hotel Chains: France is littered with ultramodern hotels, providing drivers with low-stress accommodations and often located on cheap land just outside town. The clean and inexpensive Ibis Budget chain (about €55/room for up to three people), the more attractive and spacious standard Ibis hotels (€100-150 for a double), and the cushier Mercure and Novotel hotels (€150-300 for a double) are all run by the same company, Accor (www.

Making Hotel Reservations

Reserve your rooms as soon as you've pinned down your travel dates. For busy national holidays, it's wise to reserve far in advance (see the appendix).

Requesting a Reservation: For family-run hotels, it's generally best to book your room directly via email or phone. For business-class and chain hotels, or if you'd rather book online, reserve directly through the hotel's official website (not a booking website). Almost all of my recommended hotels take reservations in English.

Here's what the hotelier wants to know:

- Type(s) of room(s) you want and number of guests
- Number of nights you'll stay
- Arrival and departure dates, written European-style as day/month/year (for example, 18/06/23 or 18 June 2023)
- Special requests (en suite bathroom, cheapest room, twin beds vs. double bed, quiet room)
- Applicable discounts (such as a Rick Steves discount, cash discount, or promotional rate)

Confirming a Reservation: Most places will request a credit-card number to hold your room. If the hotel's website doesn't have a secure form where you can enter the number directly, share this info via a phone call.

Canceling a Reservation: If you must cancel, it's courteous—and smart—to do so with as much notice as possible, especially for smaller family-run places. Cancellation policies can be strict; read

---

accorhotels.com). Though hardly quaint, these can be a good value (look for deals on their websites), particularly when they're centrally located; I list several in this book. Other chains to consider are Kyriad, with moderate prices and good quality (www.kyriad.com) and the familiar-to-Americans Best Western (www.bestwestern. com). Château and Hotels Collection has more cushy digs (www. chateauxhotels.com).

Bed & Breakfasts

B&Bs (*chambres d'hôte,* abbreviated "CH") generally are found in smaller towns and rural areas. They're usually family-run and a good deal, offering double the cultural intimacy for less than most hotels. While you may lose some hotel conveniences—such as lounges, TVs, daily bed-sheet changes, and credit-card payments— I happily make the trade-off for the personal touch and lower rates. It's always OK to ask to see the room before you commit. And though some CHs post small *Chambres* or *Chambres d'hôte* signs in

From:	rick@ricksteves.com
Sent:	Today
To:	info@hotelcentral.com
Subject:	Reservation request for 19-22 July

Dear Hotel Central,

I would like to stay at your hotel. Please let me know if you have a room available and the price for:
- 2 people
- Double bed and en suite bathroom in a quiet room
- Arriving 19 July, departing 22 July (3 nights)

Thank you!
Rick Steves

the fine print before you book (many hotels require 48 hour cancellation minimum for refunds). Many discount deals require pre-payment and can be expensive to change or cancel.

Reconfirming a Reservation: Always call or email to reconfirm your room reservation a few days in advance. For *chambres d'hôtes* or very small hotels, I call again on my arrival day to tell my host what time to expect me (especially important if arriving late—after 17:00).

Phoning: For tips on calling hotels overseas, see page 538.

their front windows, many are found only through the local tourist office.

I recommend reliable CHs that offer a good value and/or unique experience (such as CHs in renovated mills, châteaux, and wine *domaines*). For a list of over 21,000 *chambres d'hôte* throughout France, check www.chambres-hotes.fr. You can see images of places to stay, make a reservation, and get directions for any listing on the website. While *chambres d'hôte* have their own star-rating system, it doesn't correspond to the hotels' rating system. To avoid confusion, I haven't listed these stars for CHs. But virtually all of my recommended CHs have private in-room bathrooms and Wi-Fi, and some have common rooms with refrigerators and kitchenettes. Doubles generally cost €60-90; fancier places are about €100-130. Breakfast is usually included, but not always—ask. *Tables d'hôte* are CHs that offer an optional home-cooked dinner (usually a great value, must be requested in advance). And though your hosts may not speak English, they will almost always be enthusiastic and pleasant.

Gîtes

Countryside *gîtes* (pronounced "zheet") are usually urbanites' second, countryside homes, rentable by the week, from Saturday to Saturday.

Gîtes are best for drivers (they're usually rural, with little public-transport access) and ideal for families and small groups (since they can sleep many for the same price). Homes range in comfort from simple cottages and farmhouses to restored châteaux (BYO soap, shampoo, etc.). Sheets or linens may be included or provided for a bit extra. Like hotels, all *gîtes* are rated for comfort from one to four *épis* (ears of corn). Two or three *épis* generally indicate sufficient quality, but I'd look for three for more comfort. Prices generally range from €500 to €1,500 per week, depending on house size and amenities such as pools. Some owners may not speak English, so be prepared to do business in French.

For more information on *gîtes,* visit www.gites-de-france.com (with the most rentals) or www.gite.com. Also check sites like Airbnb and HomeAway/VRBO (see next).

Short-Term Rentals

A short-term rental—whether an apartment, a house, or a room in a private residence—is a popular alternative, especially if you plan to settle in one location for several nights. For stays longer than a few days, you can usually find a rental that's comparable to—and cheaper than—a hotel room with similar amenities. Plus, you'll get a behind-the-scenes peek into how locals live.

Many places require a minimum stay and have strict cancellation policies. And you're generally on your own: There's no reception desk, breakfast, or daily cleaning service. Apartments are available in larger towns such as Avignon, Aix-en-Provence, and Nice. It's usually more expensive to stay in an apartment than in a *gîte.*

Finding Accommodations: Websites such as Airbnb, FlipKey, Booking.com, and VRBO let you browse a wide range of properties. Alternatively, rental agencies such as InterhomeUSA. com and RentaVilla.com can provide more personalized service (their curated listings are also more expensive).

To find a place, try the resources listed above, or one of these: **France Homestyle,** which handpicks every home and apartment they list (US +1 206 325 0132, www.francehomestyle.com, info@ francehomestyle.com), or **Ville et Village,** which has a bigger selection of higher-end places (US +1 510 559 8080, www.villeetvillage. com).

Before you commit, be clear on the location. I like to virtually "explore" the neighborhood using Google Street View. Also consider the proximity to public transportation, and how well connected the property is with the rest of the city. Ask about amenities (elevator, air-conditioning, laundry, Wi-Fi, parking, etc.). Reviews from previous guests can help identify trouble spots.

Think about the kind of experience you want: Just a key and an affordable bed...or a chance to get to know a local? Some hosts offer self check-in and minimal contact; others enjoy interacting with you. Read the description and reviews to help shape your decision.

Confirming and Paying: Many places require payment in full before your trip, usually through the listing site. Be wary of owners who want to conduct your transaction offline; this gives you no recourse if things go awry. Never agree to wire money (a key indicator of a fraudulent transaction).

Apartments or Houses: If you're staying in one place for several nights, it's worth considering an apartment or house. Apartment or house rentals can be especially cost-effective for groups and families. European apartments, like hotel rooms, tend to be small by US standards. But they often come with laundry facilities and small, equipped kitchens, making it easier and cheaper to dine in.

Rooms in Private Homes: Renting a room in someone's home is a good option for those traveling alone, as you're more likely to find true single rooms—with just one single bed, and a price to match. These can range from air-mattress-in-living-room basic to plush-B&B-suite posh. While you can't expect your host to also be your tour guide—or even to provide you with much info—some are interested in getting to know the travelers who pass through their home.

Other Options: Swapping homes with a local works for people with an appealing place to offer (don't assume where you live is not interesting to Europeans). Good places to start are HomeExchange.com and LoveHomeSwap.com. To sleep for free, Couchsurfing.com is a vagabond's alternative to Airbnb. It lists millions of outgoing members who host fellow "surfers" in their homes.

Hostels

A hostel *(auberge de jeunesse)* provides cheap beds in dorms where you sleep alongside strangers for about €35 per night. Travelers of any age are welcome if they don't mind dorm-style accommodations and meeting other travelers. Most hostels offer kitchen facilities, guest computers, Wi-Fi, and a self-service laundry. Hostels almost always provide bedding, but the towel's up to you (though you can usually rent one). Family and private rooms are often available.

Independent hostels tend to be easygoing, colorful, and informal (no membership required; www.hostelworld.com). You may pay slightly less by booking directly with the hostel. **Official hostels** are part of Hostelling International (HI) and share an online booking site (www.hihostels.com). HI hostels typically require that you be a member or else pay a bit more per night.

Camping

In Europe, camping is more of a social than an environmental experience. It's a great way for American travelers to make European friends. Camping sites average about €25 per night, and almost every destination recommended in this book has a campground within a reasonable walk or bus ride from the town center and train station. A tent, pillow, and sleeping bag are all you need. Some campgrounds have small grocery stores and washing machines, and some even come with cafés and miniature golf. Local TIs have camping information. You'll find more detailed information in the annually updated *Michelin Camping France,* available in the United States and at most French bookstores.

Eating

The French eat long and well. Relaxed and tree-shaded lunches with a chilled rosé, three-hour dinners, and endless hours of sitting in outdoor cafés are the norm. Here, celebrated restaurateurs are as famous as great athletes, and mamas hope their babies will grow up to be great chefs. Cafés, cuisine, and wines should become a highlight of any French adventure: It's sightseeing for your palate. Even if the rest of you is sleeping in a cheap  hotel, let your taste buds travel first-class in France.

You can eat well without going broke—but choose carefully: You're just as likely to blow a small fortune on a mediocre meal as you are to dine wonderfully for €25. Read the information that follows and consider my restaurant suggestions in this book.

For listings in this guidebook, I look for restaurants that are convenient to your hotel and sightseeing. When restaurant-hunting, choose a spot filled with locals, not the place with the big neon signs boasting, "We Speak English and Accept Credit Cards."

RESTAURANT PRICING

I've categorized my recommended eateries based on the average price of a typical main course, indicated with a dollar-sign rating (see sidebar). Expensive specialties, fine wine, appetizers, and dessert can significantly increase your final bill.

The categories also indicate the personality of a place: **Budget**

Restaurant Code

Eateries in this book are categorized according to the average cost of a typical main course. Drinks, desserts, and splurge items can raise the price considerably.

$$$$	**Splurge:** Most main courses over €40
$$$	**Pricier:** €30-40
$$	**Moderate:** €20-30
$	**Budget:** Under €20

In France, a crêpe stand or other takeout spot is **$**; a sit-down brasserie, café, or bistro with affordable *plats du jour* range from **$** to **$$**; a casual but more upscale restaurant is **$$$**; and a swanky splurge is **$$$$**.

---

eateries include street food, takeaway, order-at-the-counter shops, basic cafeterias, and bakeries selling sandwiches. **Moderate** eateries are nice (but not fancy) sit-down restaurants, ideal for a pleasant meal with good-quality food. Most of my listings fall in this category—great for a taste of the local cuisine at a reasonable price.

Pricier eateries are a notch up, with more attention paid to the setting, presentation, and (often inventive) cuisine. **Splurge** eateries are dress-up-for-a-special-occasion-swanky—typically with an elegant setting, polished service, and pricey and refined cuisine.

BREAKFAST

Most hotels serve an optional breakfast, which is usually pleasant and convenient (generally €10-20, price rises proportionally with room cost). They almost all offer a buffet breakfast (cereal, yogurt, fruit, cheese, ham, croissants, juice, and hard-boiled eggs). Some add scrambled eggs and sausage. Before committing to breakfast, check to see if it's included in your room rate; if not, scan the offerings to be sure it's to your liking. Once committed, it's self-service and as much as you want. Coffee is often self-serve as well. If there's no coffee machine and you want to make your own *café au lait*, find the hot milk and mix it with your coffee. If your hotelier serves your coffee, ask for *café avec du lait*. For your basic American-style coffee (black and not too strong), ask for *café Américain*.

Breakfast is a great time to try the country's delightful array of breads, pastries, jams, and more. Many hotels and B&Bs take pride in serving these extremely fresh—often with a different selection each day.

If all you want is coffee or tea and a croissant, the corner café or bakery offers more atmosphere and is less expensive (though you get more coffee at your hotel). Go local at a café and ask for *une tartine* (ewn tart-een), a baguette slathered with butter or jam. If you crave eggs for breakfast, order *une omelette* or *œufs sur le plat* (fried eggs). Some cafés and bakeries offer worthwhile breakfast deals with juice, croissant, and coffee or tea for about €8-12 (for more on coffee and tea drinks, see the "Beverages" section, later).

To keep it cheap, pick up some fruit at a grocery store and pastries at your favorite *boulangerie* and have a picnic breakfast, then savor your coffee at a café bar *(comptoir)* while standing, like the French do.

PICNIC DINING AND FOOD TO GO

Whether going all out on a perfect French picnic or simply grabbing a sandwich to eat on an atmospheric square, dining with the town as your backdrop can be one of your most memorable meals.

Picnics

Great for lunch or dinner, French picnics can be first-class affairs and adventures in high cuisine. Be daring. Try the smelly cheeses, strange-looking pâtés, and minuscule yogurts. You'll find tasty €5 sandwiches, to-go salads, quiches, crêpes, and high-quality takeout at bakeries, charcuteries, and market stands (see "Assembling a Picnic," below).

Shopkeepers are accustomed to selling small quantities of produce. Get a succulent takeaway salad and ask for a fork. While single-use plastic cups and silverware are no longer allowed in France, biodegradable ones should be available at grocery stores. Plastic bags may not be available at markets; bring or buy your own bag (cheap at stores) or day pack for carrying items.

If you need a knife or corkscrew, buy it cheap at a grocery shop or borrow one from your hotelier (but please don't picnic in your room, as French hoteliers uniformly detest this). Though drinking wine in public places is taboo in the US, it's *pas de problème* in France. Wine merchants sell chilled, picnic-friendly bottles that they'll happily open for you. Scenic picnic sites are everywhere.

Assembling a Picnic: Visit several small stores to put together a complete meal. Shop early, as many shops close from 12:00 or 13:00 to 15:00 for their lunch break. Say *"Bonjour madame/monsieur"* as you enter, then point to what you want and say, *"S'il vous plaît."* For other terminology you might need while shopping, see the sidebar.

At the *boulangerie* (bakery), buy some bread. A baguette usually does the trick, or choose from the many loaves of bread on display: *pain aux céréales* (whole grain with seeds), *pain de campagne* (country bread, made with unbleached bread flour), *pain complet* (wheat bread), or *pain de seigle* (rye bread). To ask for it sliced, say *"Tranché, s'il vous plaît."*

At the *pâtisserie* (pastry shop, which is often the same place

PRACTICALITIES

Picnic Vocabulary

English	French
please	*s'il vous plaît* (see voo play)
a fork	*une fourchette* (ewn foor-sheht)
a cup	*un gobelet* (uhn goh-blay)
a paper plate	*une assiette en carton* (ewn ah-see-eht ahn kar-toh<u>n</u>)
napkins	*les serviettes* (lay sehr-vee-eht)
a small container	*une barquette* (ewn bar-keht)
a knife	*un couteau* (uhn koo-toh)
a corkscrew	*un tire-bouchon* (uhn teer-boo-shoh<u>n</u>)
sliced	*tranché* (trahn-shay)
a slice	*une tranche* (ewn trah<u>n</u>sh)
a small slice	*une petite tranche* (ewn puh-teet trah<u>n</u>sh)
more	*plus* (plew)
less	*moins* (mwa<u>n</u>)
It's just right.	*C'est bon.* (say boh<u>n</u>)
That'll be all.	*C'est tout.* (say too)
Thank you.	*Merci.* (mehr-see)

you bought the bread), choose a dessert that's easy to eat with your hands. My favorites are *éclairs* (*chocolat* or *café* flavored), individual fruit *tartes* (*framboise* is raspberry, *fraise* is strawberry, *citron* is lemon), and *macarons* (made of flavored cream sandwiched between two meringues).

At the *crémerie* or *fromagerie* (cheese shop), choose a sampling of cheeses *(un assortiment)*. I usually get one hard cheese (like Comté, Cantal, or Beaufort), one soft cow's milk cheese (like Brie or Camembert), one goat's milk cheese (anything that says chèvre), and one blue cheese (Roquefort or Bleu d'Auvergne). Goat cheese usually comes in individual portions. For all other large cheeses, point to the cheese you want and ask for *une petite tranche* (a small slice). The shopkeeper will show you the size of the slice about to be cut, then look at you for approval. If you'd like more, say, *"Plus."* If you'd like less, say *"Moins."* If it's just right, say *"C'est bon!"*

At the **charcuterie** or **trait-eur** (for deli items, prepared salads, meats, and pâtés), I like a slice of *pâté de campagne* (country pâté made of pork) and *saucissons secs* (dried sausages, some with pepper crust or garlic—you can ask to have it sliced thin like salami). I get a fresh salad, too. Typical options are *carottes râpées*

(shredded carrots in a tangy vinaigrette), *salade de betteraves* (beets in vinaigrette), and *céleri rémoulade* (celery root with a mayonnaise sauce). The food comes in takeout containers, and they may supply a biodegradable fork.

At a **cave à vin** you can buy chilled wines that the merchant is usually happy to open and recork for you.

At a **supermarché, épicerie,** or **magasin d'alimentation** (grocery store or minimart), you'll find biodegradable cutlery and glasses, paper plates, napkins, plus drinks, chips, and a display of produce. Daily Monop' and Carrefour City stores—offering fresh salads, wraps, juices, and more at reasonable prices—are everywhere and convenient one-stop places for assembling a picnic.

The best shopping option is to visit an **open-air market** *(marché)*. These are fun and photogenic, but shut down around 13:00 (many are listed in this book; local TIs have complete lists). There's more information about these wonderful experiences in the Shopping chapter (see "Market Day" on page 482).

To-Go Food

You'll find plenty of to-go options at *crêperies*, bakeries, and small stands. Baguette sandwiches, quiches, and pizza-like items are tasty, filling, and budget-friendly (about €5). Most grocery shops sell good and cheap packaged salads, wraps, sandwiches, and plastic containers of *carottes râpées* (shredded carrots), *salade de betteraves* (beets), and *céleri rémoulade* (celery root slaw).

Sandwiches: Anything served *à la provençale* has marinated peppers, tomatoes, and eggplant. A sandwich *à l'italienne* is a grilled *panini* (usually referred to as *pannini*). Here are some common sandwiches:

Fromage (froh-mahzh): Cheese only

Jambon beurre (zhahn-bohn bur): Ham and butter (a tasty, true French classic)

Jambon crudités (zhahn-bohn krew-dee-tay): Ham with tomatoes, lettuce, cucumbers, and mayonnaise

Fougasse (foo-gahs): Bread rolled up with salty bits of bacon, cheese, or olives

Poulet crudités (poo-lay krew-dee-tay): Chicken with tomatoes, lettuce, maybe cucumbers, and always mayonnaise

Saucisson beurre (soh-see-sohn bur): Thinly sliced sausage and butter

Thon crudités (tohn krew-dee-tay): Tuna with tomatoes, lettuce, and maybe cucumbers, but definitely mayonnaise

Quiche: Typical quiches you'll see at shops and bakeries are *lorraine* (ham and cheese), *fromage* (cheese only), *aux oignons* (with onions), *aux poireaux* (with leeks—my favorite), *aux champignons* (with mushrooms), *au saumon* (salmon), or *au thon* (tuna).

Crêpes: The quintessentially French thin pancake called a crêpe (rhymes with "step," not "grape") is filling, usually inexpensive, and generally quick. Place your order at the *crêperie* window or kiosk, and watch the chef in action. But don't be surprised if they don't make the crêpe for you from scratch; at some *crêperies*, they might premake a stack of crêpes and reheat them when they fill your order.

Crêpes generally are *sucrée* (sweet) or *salée* (savory). Technically, a savory crêpe should be made with a heartier buckwheat batter, and is called a *galette*. However, many cheap and lazy *crêperies* use the same sweet batter *(de froment)* for both their sweet-topped and savory-topped crêpes. A *socca* is a chickpea crêpe.

Standard crêpe toppings include cheese (*fromage;* usually Swiss-style Gruyère or Emmental), ham *(jambon)*, egg *(œuf)*, mushrooms *(champignons)*, chocolate, Nutella, jam *(confiture)*, whipped cream *(chantilly)*, apple jam *(compote de pommes)*, chestnut cream *(crème de marrons)*, and Grand Marnier.

RESTAURANT AND CAFE DINING

To get the most out of dining out in France, slow down. Give yourself time to dine at a French pace, engage the waiter, show you care about food, and enjoy the experience as much as the food itself. If you want a full meal, head to a restaurant or bistro, where you can choose from a two- to four-course set *menu* or order *à la carte*. If all you want is a salad, crêpe, bowl of soup, or other simple,

quick meal, go to a café, a crêperie, or a takeout joint.

French waiters probably won't overwhelm you with friendliness. As their tip is already included in the bill (see "Tipping," later), there's less schmoozing than we're used to at home. Notice how hard they work. They almost never stop. Cozying up to clients (French or foreign) is probably the last thing on their minds.

They're often stuck with client overload, too, because the French rarely hire part-time employees, even to help with peak times. To get a waiter's attention, try to make meaningful eye contact, which is a signal that you need something. If this doesn't work, raise your hand and simply say, *"S'il vous plaît"* (see voo play)—"please."

This phrase also works when you want to ask for the check. In French eateries, a waiter will rarely bring you the check unless you request it. To the French, having the bill dropped off before asking for it is *gauche*. But busy travelers are often ready for the check sooner rather than later. If you're in a hurry, ask for the bill when your server comes to clear your plates or checks in to see if you want dessert or coffee. To request your bill, say, *"L'addition, s'il vous plaît."* If you don't ask now, the wait staff may become scarce as they leave you to digest in peace. (For a list of other restaurant survival phrases, see the appendix.)

Note that all café and restaurant interiors are smoke-free. Today the only smokers you'll find are at outside tables, which—unfortunately—may be exactly where you want to sit.

Tipping: At cafés and restaurants, a 12-15 percent service charge is always included in the price of what you order (*service compris* or *prix net*), but you won't see it listed on your bill. Unlike in the US, France pays servers a decent wage (a favorite café owner told me that his waiters earn more than some high school teachers). Because of this, most locals only tip a little, or not at all. When dining, expect reasonable, efficient service. If you don't get it, skip the tip. If you feel the service was good, tip a little—about 5 percent; maybe 10 percent for terrific service. To tell the waiter to keep the change when you pay, say *"C'est bon"* (say bohn), meaning "It's good." If you are using a credit card, consider leaving your tip in cash; some credit-card receipts don't have space to add a tip. Never feel guilty if you don't leave a tip. Still, be aware that some waiters in areas popular with Americans may ask for a tip (knowing that Americans are accustomed to tipping generously). Don't feel pressured to tip in these circumstances. If you choose to, tip 10 percent or less.

Cafés and Brasseries

French cafés and brasseries provide user-friendly meals and a relief from sightseeing overload. They're not necessarily cheaper than many restaurants and bistros, and famous cafés on popular squares can be pricey affairs. Their key advantage is flexibility: They offer long serving hours, and you're welcome to order just a salad, a sandwich, or a bowl of soup, even for dinner. It's also OK to share starters and desserts, though not main courses.

Cafés and brasseries usually open by 7:00, but closing hours vary. Unlike some restaurants, which open only for dinner and

PRACTICALITIES

Vegetarians, Allergies, and Other Dietary Restrictions

Many French people think "vegetarian" means "no red meat" or "not much meat." If you're a strict vegetarian, be specific: Tell your server what you don't eat—and it can be helpful to clarify what you do eat. Write it out on a card and keep it handy.

But be reasonable. Think of your meal (as the French do) as if it's a finely crafted creation by a trained artist. The chef knows what goes well together, and substitutions are considered an insult to his training. Picky eaters should try their best to just take it or leave it.

However, French restaurants are willing to accommodate genuine dietary restrictions and other special concerns, or at least point you to an appropriate choice on the menu. These phrases might help:

French	English
Je suis végétarien/végétarienne. (zhuh swee vay-zhay-tah-ree-an/vay-zhay-tah-ree-ehn)	I am vegetarian.
Je ne peux pas manger de _____. (zhuh nuh puh pah mahn-zhay duh _____)	I cannot eat _____.
Je suis allergique à _____. (zhuh sweez ah-lehr-zheek ah _____)	I am allergic to _____.
Pas de _____, s'il vous plaît. (pah duh _____, see voo play)	No _____, please.

sometimes for lunch, many cafés and all brasseries serve food throughout the day (usually with a limited menu during off hours), making them the best option for a late lunch or an early dinner. *Service Continu* or *Service Non-Stop* signs indicate continued service throughout the day. Small-town cafés often close their kitchens from about 14:00 until 18:00.

Check the price list first, which by law should be posted. There are two sets of prices: You'll pay more for the same drink if you're seated at a table *(salle)* than if you're seated or standing at the bar or counter *(comptoir)*. (For tips on ordering coffee and tea, see the "Beverages" section, later.)

At a café or a brasserie, if the table is not set, it's fine to seat yourself and just have a drink. However, if it's set with a placemat and cutlery, you should ask to be seated and plan to order a meal. If you're unsure, ask the server before sitting down.

Ordering: A salad, crêpe, *croque monsieur,* or omelet is a fairly cheap way to fill up. Omelets come lonely on a plate with a basket

of bread. Sandwiches, generally served day and night, are inexpensive, but most are very plain (*boulangeries* serve better ones). To get more than a piece of ham *(jambon)* on a baguette, order a *sandwich jambon crudités* (garnished with veggies). Popular sandwiches are the *croque monsieur* (grilled ham-and-cheese) and *croque madame* (*monsieur* with a fried egg on top).

Salads are typically meal size and often can be ordered with warm ingredients mixed in, such as melted goat cheese, fried gizzards, or roasted potatoes. One salad is perfect for lunch or a light dinner. See the "French Cuisine" section later for a list of classic salads.

The daily special—*plat du jour* (plah dew zhoor)—is your fast, hearty, and garnished hot plate for about €15-25. At most cafés, feel free to order only *entrées* (which in French means the starter course); some find these lighter and more to their taste than a main course. A vegetarian can enjoy a tasty, filling meal by ordering two *entrées*.

Regardless of what you order, bread is free but almost never comes with butter; to get more bread, just hold up your basket and ask, *"Encore, s'il vous plaît?"*

Restaurants

Choose restaurants filled with locals. Consider my suggestions and your hotelier's opinion, but trust your instincts. If a restaurant doesn't post its prices outside, move along.

Restaurants open for dinner around 19:00 and are most crowded about 20:30. The early bird gets the table. Last seating is usually about 21:00 (22:00 in cities and on the French Riviera).

Tune into the quiet, relaxed pace of French dining. The French don't do dinner and a movie on date nights; they just do dinner. The table is yours for the night. Notice how quietly French diners speak in restaurants and how few mobile phones you see during a meal, and how this improves your overall experience. Go local.

Ordering: In French restaurants, you can choose something off the menu *(la carte),* or you can order a multicourse, fixed-price meal (confusingly, called a *menu*). If you ask for *un menu* (instead of *la carte*), you'll get a fixed-price meal.

Ordering **à la carte** gives you the best selection. I enjoy going à la carte especially when traveling with others and eating family style (waiters are usually happy to accommodate this approach and will bring small extra plates). It's traditional to order an *entrée* (a starter—not a main dish) and a *plat principal* (main course), though it's becoming common to order only a *plat principal*—and maybe a dessert. *Plats* are generally more meat-based, while *entrées* usually include veggies. Multiple-course meals, while time-consuming (a positive thing in France), create the appropriate balance of veggies to meat. Elaborate meals may also have *entremets*—tiny dishes served between courses. Wherever you dine, consider the waiter's recommendations and anything *de la maison* (of the house), as long as it's not an organ meat (tripe, *rognons*, or andouillette).

Two people can split an *entrée* or a big salad (small-size dinner salads are usually not offered á la carte) and then each get a *plat principal*. At restaurants, it's inappropriate for two diners to share one main course. If all you want is a salad or soup, go to a café or brasserie.

Fixed-price *menus*—which usually include two, three, or four courses—are always a better deal than eating à la carte, providing you want several courses. At most restaurants offering fixed-price *menus*, the price for a two- or three-course *menu* is only slightly higher than a single main course from the à la carte list (though the main course is usually larger than the one you get with the fixed-price *menu*). With a three-course *menu* you'll choose a starter of soup, appetizer, or salad; select from three or four main courses with vegeta-

Restaurant La Mer
18, rue de la Galette, Paris
MENU TOURISTIQUE €22

Entrée au choix (FIRST COURSE CHOICES)
• SOUPE DE POISSONS (FISH SOUP)
• 12 ESCARGOTS EN COQUILLE (SNAILS IN SHELL)
• SALADE NIÇOISE
• SUGGESTION DU CHEF

Plat au choix (SECOND COURSE CHOICES)
• PLATEAU FRUITS DU MER (PLATTER OF MIXED COLD SEAFOOD)
• POISSON DU MARCHE (FISH FROM THE MARKET)
• POULET BASQUAISE (CHICKEN BASQUE STYLE)
• STEAK-FRITES, SAUCE A L'ECHALOTE (STEAK W/FRIES +SHALLOT SAUCE)

Dessert au choix (DESSERT CHOICES)
• FROMAGE (CHEESE)
• PATISSERIE DU JOUR (PASTRY OF THE DAY)
• GLACE OU SORBET (ICE CREAM OR SHERBET)
• CREME BRULEE

~SERVICE COMPRIS~ (SERVICE INCLUDED)

Merci et Bon Appetit !

bles; and finish up with a cheese course and/or a choice of desserts. It sounds like a lot of food, but portions are a bit smaller with fixed-price *menus*, and what we cram onto one large plate they spread out over several courses. If you're dining with a friend, one person can get the full *menu* while the other can order just a *plat* (and share the *menu* courses). Also, many restaurants offer less expensive and less filling two-course *menus*, sometimes called **formules**, featuring an *entrée et plat*, or *plat et dessert*. Many restaurants have a reasonable *menu-enfant* (kid's meal).

Wine and other drinks are extra, and certain premium items add a few euros, clearly noted on the menu (*supplément* or *sup.*).

Lunch: If a restaurant serves lunch, it generally begins at

12:00 and goes until 14:00, with last orders taken at about 13:30. If you're hungry when restaurants are closed (late afternoon), go to a *boulangerie,* brasserie, or café (see previous section). Even fancy places usually have affordable lunch *menus* (often called *formules* or *plat de midi*), allowing you to sample the same gourmet cooking for a lot less than the price of dinner.

In the south, I usually order *une entrée* and *un plat* from *la carte* (often as a two-course *menu* or *formule*), then find an ice-cream or crêpe stand and take a dessert stroll. If that sounds like too much, just order *un plat* (but don't skip the dessert stroll!).

FRENCH CUISINE

General styles of French cooking include ***cuisine gastronomique*** (classic, elaborately prepared, multicourse meals); ***cuisine semi-gastronomique*** or ***bistronomie*** (the finest-quality home cooking); ***cuisine des provinces*** (traditional dishes of specific regions); and ***nouvelle cuisine*** (a focus on smaller portions and closer attention to the texture and color of the ingredients). Sauces are a huge part of French cooking. In the early 20th century, the legendary French chef Auguste Escoffier identified five French "mother sauces" from which all others are derived: *béchamel* (milk-based white sauce), *espagnole* (veal-based brown sauce), *velouté* (stock-based white sauce), *hollandaise* (egg yolk-based white sauce), and *tomate* (tomato-based red sauce).

The following list of items should help you navigate a typical French menu. Galloping gourmets should bring a menu translator. The most complete (and priciest) menu reader around is *A to Z of French Food* by G. de Temmerman (look for the cheaper app). The *Marling Menu-Master* is also good. The *Rick Steves French Phrase Book,* with a menu decoder, works well for most travelers. For dishes specific to each region, see the "Cuisine Scene" sections in both the Provence and the French Riviera intro chapters.

First Course (Entrée)

Crudités: A mix of raw and lightly cooked fresh vegetables, usually including grated carrots, celery root, tomatoes, and beets, often with a hefty dose of vinaigrette dressing. If you want the dressing on the side, say, *"La sauce à côté, s'il vous plaît"* (lah sohs ah koh-tay, see voo play).

Escargots: Snails cooked in parsley-garlic butter. You don't even have to like the snail itself. Just dipping your bread in garlic butter is more than satisfying. Prepared a variety of ways, the classic is *à la bourguignonne* (served in their shells).

Foie gras: Rich and buttery in consistency—and hefty in price—this pâté is made from the swollen livers of force-fed geese (or ducks, in *foie gras de canard*). Put small chunks on bread—don't spread it, and never add mustard. For a real French experience, try this dish with a sweet white wine (such as a Muscat).

Huîtres: Oysters, served raw any month, are particularly popular at Christmas and on New Year's Eve, when every café seems to have overflowing baskets in their window.

Œuf mayo: A simple hard-boiled egg topped with a dollop of flavorful mayonnaise

Pâtés and **terrines:** Slowly cooked ground meat (usually pork, though game, poultry liver, and rabbit are also common) that is highly seasoned and served in slices with mustard and *cornichons* (little pickles). Pâtés are smoother than the similarly prepared but chunkier *terrines*.

Soupe à l'oignon: Hot, salty, filling, and easiest to find at cafés, French onion soup is a beef broth served with a baked cheese-and-bread crust over the top.

Salads (Salades)

With the exception of a *salade mixte* (simple green salad, often difficult to find), the French get creative with their *salades*. Here are some classics:

Salade de chèvre chaud: This mixed-green salad is topped with warm goat cheese on small pieces of toast.

Salade de gésiers: Though it may not sound appetizing, this salad with chicken gizzards (and often slices of duck) is worth a try.

Salade composée: "Composed" of any number of ingredients, this salad might have *lardons* (bacon), Comté (a Swiss-style cheese), Roquefort (blue cheese), *œuf* (egg), *noix* (walnuts), and *jambon* (ham, generally thinly sliced).

Salade gourmande: The "gourmet" salad varies by region and restaurant but usually features cured and poached meats served on salad greens with a mustard vinaigrette.

Salade niçoise: A specialty from Nice, this tasty salad usually includes greens topped with ripe tomatoes, raw vegetables (such as radishes, green peppers, celery, and perhaps artichoke or fava beans), tuna (usually canned), anchovy, hard-boiled egg, and olives.

Salade paysanne: You'll usually find potatoes *(pommes de terre)*, walnuts *(noix)*, tomatoes, ham, and egg in this salad.

Main Course (Plat Principal)

Duck, lamb, and rabbit are popular in France, and each is prepared in a variety of ways. You'll also encounter various stew-like dishes that vary by region. The most common regional specialties are described here.

Bœuf bourguignon: A Burgundian specialty, this classy beef stew is

PRACTICALITIES

cooked slowly in red wine, then served with onions, potatoes, and mushrooms.

Cabillaud: Cod is France's favorite fish, and you'll find it on French menus. It's cooked in many ways that vary by region, but most commonly with butter, white wine, and herbs.

Confit de canard: A favorite from the southwest Dordogne region is duck that has been preserved in its own fat, then cooked in its fat, and often served with potatoes (cooked in the same fat). Not for dieters. (Note that *magret de canard* is sliced duck breast and very different in taste.)

Coq au vin: This Burgundian dish is rooster marinated ever so slowly in red wine, then cooked until it melts in your mouth. It's served (often family-style) with vegetables.

Daube: Generally made with beef, but sometimes lamb, this is a long and slowly simmered dish, typically paired with noodles or other pasta.

Escalope normande: This specialty of Normandy features turkey or veal in a cream sauce.

Gigot d'agneau: A specialty of Provence, this is a leg of lamb often grilled and served with white beans. The best lamb is *pré salé*, which means the lamb has been raised in salt-marsh lands (like at Mont St-Michel).

Le hamburger: This American import is all the rage in France. Cafés and restaurants serve it using local sauces, breads, and cheeses. It's fun to see their interpretation of this classic American dish.

Poulet rôti: Roasted chicken on the bone—French comfort food

Saumon and **truite:** You'll see salmon and trout *(truite)* dishes served in various styles. The salmon usually comes from the North Sea and is always served with sauce, most commonly a sorrel *(oseille)* sauce.

Steak: Referred to as *pavé* (thick hunk of prime steak), *bavette* (skirt steak), *faux filet* (sirloin), or *entrecôte* (rib steak), French steak is usually thinner and tougher than American steak and is always served with sauces (*au poivre* is a pepper sauce, *une sauce roquefort* is a blue-cheese sauce). Because steak is usually better in North America, I generally avoid it in France (unless the sauce sounds good). You will also see *steak haché*, which is a lean, gourmet hamburger patty served *sans* bun. When it's served as *steak haché à cheval*, it comes with a fried egg on top.

By American standards, the French undercook meats: Their version of rare, *saignant* (seh-nyahn), means "bloody" and is close to raw. What they consider medium, *à point* (ah pwan), is what an American would call rare. Their term for well-done, or *bien cuit* (bee-yehn kwee), would translate as medium for Americans (and overdone for the French).

Steak tartare: This wonderfully French dish is for adventurous types only. It's very lean, raw hamburger served with savory seasonings (usually Tabasco, capers, raw onions, salt, and pepper on the side) and topped with a raw egg yolk. This is not hamburger as we know it, but freshly ground beef.

Cheese Course (Le Fromage)

The cheese course is served just before (or instead of) dessert. It not only helps with digestion, it gives you a great opportunity to sample the tasty regional cheeses—and time to finish up your wine. Between cow, goat, and sheep cheeses, there are more than 350 different ones to try in France. Some restaurants will offer a cheese platter *(plateau de fromages),* from which you select a few different kinds. A good platter has at least four cheeses: a hard cheese (such as Cantal), a flowery cheese (such as Brie or Camembert), a blue or Roquefort cheese, and a goat cheese.

To sample several types of cheese from the cheese plate, say, *"Un assortiment, s'il vous plaît"* (uhn ah-sor-tee-mahn, see voo play). You'll either be served a selection of several cheeses or choose from a large selection offered on a cheese tray. If you serve yourself from the cheese tray, observe French etiquette and keep the shape of the cheese: Shave off a slice from the side or cut small wedges.

A glass of good red wine is a heavenly complement to your cheese course—but if you're eating goat cheese, do as the French do and opt for white wine.

Dessert (Le Dessert)

If you order espresso, it will always come after dessert. To have coffee with dessert, ask for *"café avec le dessert"* (kah-fay ah-vehk luh day-sayr). See the list of coffee terms next. Here are the types of treats you'll see:

Baba au rhum: Pound cake drenched in rum, served with whipped cream

Café gourmand: An assortment of small desserts selected by the restaurant, served with an espresso—a great way to sample several desserts

Crème brûlée: A rich, creamy, dense, caramelized custard

Crème caramel: Flan in a caramel sauce

Fondant au chocolat: A molten chocolate cake with a runny (not totally cooked) center. Also known as *moelleux* (meh-leh) *au chocolat.*

Fromage blanc: A light dessert similar to plain yogurt (yet different), served with sugar or herbs

Glace: Ice cream—typically vanilla, chocolate, or strawberry

Ile flottante: A light dessert consisting of islands of meringue floating on a pond of custard sauce

Mousse au chocolat: Chocolate mousse

Profiteroles: Cream puffs filled with vanilla ice cream, smothered in warm chocolate sauce

Riz au lait: Rice pudding

Sorbets: Light, flavorful, and fruity ices, sometimes laced with brandy

Tartes: Open-face pie, often filled with fruit

Tarte tatin: Apple pie like grandma never made, with caramelized apples, cooked upside down, but served upright

BEVERAGES

In stores, unrefrigerated soft drinks, bottled water, and beer are cheaper than cold drinks. Bottled water and boxed fruit juice are the cheapest drinks. Avoid buying drinks to-go at streetside stands; you'll pay far less in a shop.

In bars and at eateries, be clear when ordering drinks—you can easily pay €10 for an oversized Coke and €15 for a supersized beer at some cafés. When you order a drink, state the size in centiliters (don't say "small," "medium," or "large," because the waiter might bring a bigger drink than you want). For something small, ask for 25 *centilitres* (vant-sank sahn-tee-lee-truh; about 8 ounces); for a medium drink, order 33 cl (trahnte-trwah; about 12 ounces—a normal can of soda); a large is 50 cl (san-kahnt; about 16 ounces); and a super-size is one liter (lee-truh; about a quart—which is more than I would ever order in France). The ice cubes melted after the last Yankee tour group left.

Water, Juice, and Soft Drinks

The French are willing to pay for bottled water with their meal (*eau minérale;* oh mee-nay-rahl) because they prefer the taste over tap water. Badoit is my favorite carbonated water (*l'eau gazeuse;* loh gah-zuhz) and is commonly available. To get a free pitcher of tap water, ask for *une carafe d'eau* (ewn kah-rahf doh). Otherwise, you may unwittingly buy bottled water.

In France *limonade* (lee-moh-nahd) is Sprite or 7-Up. For a fun, bright, nonalcoholic drink of 7-Up with mint syrup, order *un diabolo menthe* (uhn dee-ah-boh-loh mahnt). For 7-Up with fruit syrup, order *un diabolo grenadine* (think Shirley Temple). Kids love the local orange drink, Orangina, a carbonated orange juice with pulp. They also like *sirop à l'eau* (see-roh ah loh), flavored syrup mixed with carbonated water.

For keeping hydrated on the go, hang on to your store-bought water bottle and refill. I drink tap water throughout France, filling up my bottle in hotel rooms.

Coffee and Tea

The French define various types of espresso drinks by how much milk is added. To the French, milk is a delicate form of nutrition: You need it in the morning, but as the day goes on, too much can upset your digestion. Therefore, the amount of milk that's added to coffee decreases as the day goes on. The average French person thinks a *café au lait* is exclusively for breakfast, and a *café crème* is only appropriate through midday. You're welcome to order a milkier coffee drink later in the day, but don't be surprised if you get a funny look.

In cafés, stand at the bar to sip your drink and get the lowest prices. Before ordering at a table, check out the price list *(les prix de consommation)*, which should be prominently displayed. This shows the price of the most commonly ordered drinks *au comptoir* (at the counter) and *en salle* (seated at a table). I use the price of *un café* (shot of espresso) at the counter as a reference—if the price is about €2 or less, the place is likely to be reasonable. If given a choice between a small, medium, or large beverage, be aware that small is usually the norm and larger drinks can be crazy pricey.

Provence is known for its herbal and fruit teas. Look for *tilleul* (linden), *verveine* (verbena), or interesting blends such as *poire-vanille* (pear-vanilla).

By law, a waiter must give you a glass of tap water with your coffee or tea if you request it; ask for *"un verre d'eau, s'il vous plaît"* (uhn vehr doh, see voo play).

Here are some common coffee and tea drinks:

Café (kah-fay): Shot of espresso

Café allongé, a.k.a. *café long* (kah-fay ah-lohn-zhay; kah-fay lohn): Espresso topped up with hot water—like an Americano

Noisette (nwah-zeht): Espresso with a dollop of milk (best value for adding milk to your coffee)

Café au lait (kah-fay oh lay): Espresso mixed with lots of warm milk (used mostly for coffee made at home; in a café, order *café crème*)

Café crème (kah-fay krehm): Espresso with a sizable pour of steamed milk (closest thing you'll get to an American-style latte)

Grand crème (grahn krehm): Double shot of espresso with a bit more steamed milk (and often twice the price)

Décaféiné (day-kah-fee-nay): Decaf—available for any of the above

Thé nature (tay nah-tour): Plain tea

Thé au lait (tay oh lay): Tea with milk
Thé citron (tay see-trohn): Tea with lemon
Infusion (an-few-see-yohn): Herbal tea

Alcoholic Beverages

The legal drinking age is 16 for beer and wine (18 for hard liquor)—at restaurants it's normal for wine to be served with dinner to teens.

Wine: Wines are often listed in a separate *carte des vins*. House wine is generally cheap and good enough (about €5/glass). Finer wines are harder to find by the glass. At a café, a carafe of house wine costs around €15. To order less expensive wine, ask for table wine *(vin de table)*. For specifics on Provençal wines, see page 47.

Here are some important wine terms:

Vin de table (van duh tah-bluh): House wine
Verre de vin rouge (vehr duh van roozh): Glass of red wine
Verre de vin blanc (vehr duh van blahn): Glass of white wine
Pichet (pee-shay) or *carafe* (kah-rahf): Pitcher or carafe
Demi-pichet (duh-mee pee-shay): Half-carafe
Quart (kar): Quarter-carafe (ideal for one)
Bouteille (boo-teh-ee): Bottle
Demi-bouteille (duh-mee boo-teh-ee): Half-bottle

Beer: Local *bière* (bee-ehr) costs about €6 at a restaurant and is cheaper on tap *(une pression;* ewn pres-yohn) than in the bottle. France's best-known beers are Alsatian; try Kronenbourg or the heavier Pelfort (one of your author's favorites). Craft beers *(bière artisanale)* are very popular—Brittany produces some of the best, though many regions are making craft beers these days.

Aperitifs: Champagne is a popular way to start your evening in France. For a refreshing before-dinner drink, order a *kir* (pronounced "keer")—a thumb's level of *crème de cassis* (black currant liqueur) topped with white wine (upgrade to a *kir royal* if you'd like it made with champagne). Also consider a glass of Lillet, a sweet, flowery fortified wine from Bordeaux. *Pastis,* the standard southern France aperitif, is a sweet anise (licorice) drink that comes on the rocks with a glass of water (cut it with water to taste). *Un Monaco* is a red drink made with beer, grenadine, and lemonade.

In Provence, try sweet wines *(vins doux naturel)* such as Muscat de Beaumes-de-Venise or Rasteau. Both should be served chilled (from the fridge, never with ice cubes) and are enjoyable before dinner or with certain desserts; they're terrific with foie gras, melons, peaches, or Roquefort cheese. Look also for sparkling wines, usually inexpensive versions of pricey champagne.

After Dinner: If you like brandy, try a *marc* (regional brandy—e.g., *marc de Bourgogne*) or an Armagnac, cognac's cheaper twin brother.

Staying Connected

One of the most common questions I hear from travelers is, "How can I stay connected in Europe?" The short answer? More easily and affordably than you might think.

The simplest solution is to bring your own device—phone, tablet, or laptop—and use it much as you would at home, following the money-saving tips below, such as getting an international plan or connecting to free Wi-Fi whenever possible. Another option is to buy a European SIM card for your mobile phone. Or you can use European landlines and computers to connect. More details are at RickSteves.com/phoning.

USING YOUR PHONE IN EUROPE

Here are some budget tips and options.

Sign up for an international plan. To stay connected at a lower cost, sign up for an international service plan through your carrier. Most providers offer a simple bundle that includes calling, messaging, and data. Your normal plan may already include international coverage (for example, T-Mobile's covers data and text, but not voice calls).

Before your trip, research your provider's international rates. Activate the plan a day or two before you leave, then remember to cancel it when your trip's over.

Use free Wi-Fi whenever possible. Unless you have an unlimited-data plan, save most of your online tasks for Wi-Fi (pronounced *wee-fee* in French). Most accommodations in Europe offer free Wi-Fi. Many cafés (including Starbucks and McDonald's) offer hotspots for customers; ask for the password when you buy something. You may also find Wi-Fi at TIs, city squares, major museums, public-transit hubs, important train stations, airports, aboard trains and buses, and at some autoroute (highway) rest stops.

Minimize the use of your cellular network. The best way to make sure you're not accidentally burning through data is to put your device in "airplane" mode (which also disables phone calls and texts) and connect to Wi-Fi as needed. When you need to get online but can't find Wi-Fi, simply turn on your cellular network (or turn off airplane mode) just long enough for the task at hand.

Even with an international data plan, wait until you're on Wi-Fi to Skype or FaceTime, download apps, stream videos, or do other megabyte-greedy tasks. Using a navigation app such as Google Maps over a cellular network can require lots of data, so download maps when you're on Wi-Fi, then use the app offline.

Limit automatic updates. By default, your device constantly checks for a data connection and updates app content. Check your device's settings menu for ways to turn this off, and change your

PRACTICALITIES

How to Dial

Here's how to dial from anywhere in the US or Europe, using the phone number of one of my recommended Paris hotels as an example (01 47 05 25 45). If a number starts with 0, drop it when dialing internationally (except when calling Italy).

From a US Mobile Phone

Phone numbers in this book are presented exactly as you would dial them from a US mobile phone. For international access, press and hold 0 (zero) to get a + sign, then dial the country code (33 for France) and phone number.

▶ To call the Paris hotel from any location, dial +33 1 47 05 25 45.

From a US Landline

Replace + with 011 (US/Canada access code), then dial the country code (33 for France) and phone number.

▶ To call the Paris hotel from your home landline, dial 011 33 1 47 05 25 45.

From a European Landline

Replace + with 00 (Europe access code), then dial the country code (33 for France, 1 for the US) and phone number.

▶ To call the Paris hotel from a Spanish landline, dial 00 33 1 47 05 25 45.

▶ To call my US office from a French landline, dial 00 1 425 771 8303.

From One French Phone to Another

To place a domestic call (from a French landline or mobile), drop +33 and dial the phone number (including the initial 0).

▶ To call the Paris hotel from Nice, dial 01 47 05 25 45.

More Dialing Tips

Local Numbers: European phone numbers and area codes can vary in length and spacing, even within the same country. Mobile phones use separate prefixes (for instance, in France, Paris landline numbers begin with 01, and mobile numbers begin with 06 or 07).

Toll and Toll-Free Calls: It's generally not possible to dial European toll or toll-free numbers from a US mobile or landline (although you can sometimes get through using Skype). Look for a direct-dial number instead.

Calling the US from a US Mobile Phone, While Abroad: Dial +1, area code, and number.

More Phoning Help: See HowToCallAbroad.com.

email settings from "auto-retrieve" to "manual" (or from "push" to "fetch").

Use Wi-Fi calling and messaging apps. Skype, WhatsApp, FaceTime, and Google Meet are great for making free or low-cost voice calls or sending texts over Wi-Fi worldwide. Just log on to a Wi-Fi network, then connect with friends, family members, or local contacts who use the same service.

Buy a European SIM card. If you anticipate making a lot of

Tips on Internet Security

Make sure that your device is running the latest versions of its operating system, security software, and apps. Next, ensure that your device and key programs (like email) are password-protected. On the road, use only secure, password-protected Wi-Fi. Ask the hotel or café staff for the specific name of their network, and make sure you log on to that exact one.

If you must access your financial info online, use a banking app rather than accessing your account via a browser, and use a cellular connection, not Wi-Fi. Never log on to personal finance sites on a public computer. If you're very concerned, consider subscribing to a VPN (virtual private network).

local calls, need a local phone number, or your provider's international data rates are expensive, consider buying a SIM card in Europe to replace the one in your (unlocked) US phone or tablet. SIM cards are sold at department-store electronics counters, some newsstands (you may need to show your passport), and vending machines. If you need help setting it up, buy one at a mobile-phone shop. There are generally no roaming charges when using a European SIM card in other EU countries, but confirm when you buy.

WITHOUT A MOBILE PHONE

It's less convenient but possible to travel in Europe without a mobile device. You can make calls from your hotel and check email or get online using public computers.

Most **hotels** charge a fee for placing calls. Prepaid international phone cards *(cartes international)* are not widely used in France, but can be found at some newsstands, tobacco shops, and train stations.

Public computers are not always easy to find. Some hotels have one in their lobby for guests to use; otherwise you may find one at a public library (ask your hotelier or the TI for the nearest location). On a European keyboard, use the "Alt Gr" key to the right of the space bar to insert the extra symbol that appears on some keys. If you can't locate a special character (such as @), simply copy and paste it from a Web page.

MAIL

You can mail one package per day to yourself worth up to $200 duty-free from Europe to the US (mark it "personal purchases"). If you're sending a gift to someone, mark it "unsolicited gift." For details, visit www.cbp.gov, select "Travel," and search for "Know Before You Go."

The French postal service works fine, but for quick transatlantic delivery (in either direction), consider services such as DHL (DHL.com). French post offices are referred to as *La Poste* or sometimes the old-fashioned PTT, for "Post, Telegraph, and Telephone." Hours vary, though most are open weekdays 8:00-19:00 and Saturday morning 8:00-12:00. Stamps are also sold at *tabacs*. It costs about €1 to mail a postcard to the US. One convenient, if expensive, way to send packages home is to use the post office's Colissimo XL postage-paid mailing box. It costs €50-90 to ship boxes weighing 5-7 kilos (about 11-15 pounds).

Transportation

Figuring out how to get around in Europe is one of your biggest trip decisions. **Cars** work well for two or more traveling together (especially families with small kids), those packing heavy, and those delving into the countryside. **Trains** and **buses** are best for solo travelers, blitz tourists, city-to-city travelers, and those who want to leave the driving to others. Short-hop **flights** within Europe can creatively connect the dots. Be aware of the potential downside of each option: A car is an expensive headache in any major city; with trains and buses you're at the mercy of a timetable; flying entails a trek to and from a usually distant airport and leaves a larger carbon footprint.

If your itinerary mixes cities and countryside, my advice is to connect cities by train (or bus) and to explore rural areas by rental car. Arrange to pick up your car in the last big city you'll visit, then use it to lace together small towns and explore the countryside. For more detailed information on transportation throughout Europe, see RickSteves.com/transportation.

I've included two sample itineraries—by car and by public transportation—to help you explore Provence and the French Riviera smoothly; you'll find these on pages 20 and 23.

TRAINS

France's SNCF rail system, short for Société Nationale Chemins de Fer, sets the pace in Europe (www.sncf.com). Its high-speed trains (TGV, tay zhay vay; *Train à Grande Vitesse*—also called "InOui") have inspired bullet trains throughout the world. The TGV, which requires a reservation, runs at 170-220 mph. Its rails are fused into one long, continuous track for a faster and smoother ride. The TGV has changed commuting patterns throughout France by putting most of the country within day-trip distance of Paris.

TGV trains serve these cities in Provence and the Riviera: Avignon, Arles (very few trains), Nîmes, Marseille, Orange, Aix-en-Provence, Antibes, Cannes, and Nice. Avignon and Aix-en-Provence have separate TGV stations on their outskirts (with bus

French Train Terms and Abbreviations

SNCF (Société Nationale des Chemins de Fer): This is the Amtrak of France, operating all national train lines that link cities and towns.

TGV (*Train à Grande Vitesse;* also called "InOui"): SNCF's network of high-speed trains (twice as fast as regular trains) that connect major cities in France. These trains always require a reservation.

Intercité: These trains are the next best to the TGV in terms of speed and comfort and, like TGV trains, they require a reservation.

TER (Transport Express Régional): These trains serve smaller stops within a region. For example, you'll find trains called TER Provence (Provence-only trains) and TER de Bourgogne (trains operating only in Burgundy). No reservations are needed.

International Trains Operating in France

Eurostar: Connects French cities of Paris, Lille, and Calais with London via the Chunnel.

ICE (Intercity Express): High-speed German-run trains connecting major cities in Europe.

Thalys: High-speed trains linking Paris with cities in Belgium, the Netherlands, and Germany.

TGV Lyria: High-speed trains connecting France and Switzerland.

connections into the town center)—note carefully which station your train serves (either "Centre-Ville" or "TGV"; if it's not specified, it's the central station).

The SNCF app is a great tool for looking up schedules and buying tickets (you'll receive a QR code for your trip, which the conductor will scan onboard). Any staffed train station also has schedule information, can make reservations, and can sell tickets for any destination. For more on train travel, see RickSteves.com/rail.

Schedules

Schedules change by season, weekday, and weekend. Verify train times and frequencies shown in this book—use the SNCF app, go to Bahn.com (Germany's excellent all-Europe schedule site), or check locally at train stations.

In France, bigger stations may have helpful information agents roaming the station (usually in bright red or blue vests) and at *Accueil* or *Information* offices or booths. Make use of their help; don't

PRACTICALITIES

Public Transportation in Provence

To Lyon & Paris

Montélimar

Rhône

Nyons

Buis-les-Baronnies

Vaison-la-Romaine

P R O V E N C E

Orange

COTES DU RHONE

Châteauneuf-du-Pape

Uzès

PONT DU GARD

Avignon

Isle-sur-la-Sorgue

Roussillon

To Grenoble

Avignon TGV

Cavaillon

Apt

L U B E R O N

Nîmes

Tarascon

Lourmarin

Rhône

St-Rémy

To Montpellier, Carcassonne & Barcelona (Spain)

Arles

Les Baux

Rhône

Aigues-Mortes

C A M A R G U E

Aix-en-Provence

To Nice

Petit Rhône

Aix TGV

Toulon

Stes-Maries-de-la-Mer

Marseille

Les Calanques

Cassis Stn.

La Ciotat

Cassis

Mediterranean Sea

Not to Scale

- - - - Rail
===== TGV High Speed Rail
- - - Bus
.... Boat
✈ Airports (Not All Shown)

Note: In some cases regular train lines and TGV lines share the same track

Some TGV trains also stop in Avignon city center & Orange stations

stand in a ticket line if all you need is a train schedule or to confirm a departure time.

Rail Passes

The single-country Eurail France Pass can be a good value for long-distance train travelers. Each day of use of your France Pass allows you to take as many trips as you want on one calendar day (you could go from Paris to Beaune in Burgundy, enjoy a wine tasting, then continue to Avignon, stay a few hours, and end in Nice—though I wouldn't recommend it).

Rail passes are delivered electronically via email and must be

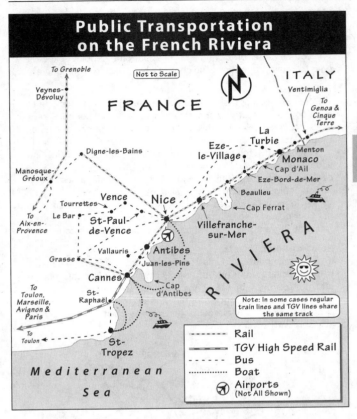

Public Transportation on the French Riviera

Not to Scale

FRANCE

ITALY

To Grenoble

Veynes-Dévoluy

Ventimiglia

To Genoa & Cinque Terre

Digne-les-Bains

Manosque-Gréoux

Eze-le-Village

La Turbie

Menton

Monaco

Cap d'Ail

Eze-Bord-de-Mer

Beaulieu

To Aix-en-Provence

Tourrettes

Vence

Nice

Cap Ferrat

Le Bar

St-Paul-de-Vence

Villefranche-sur-Mer

Vallauris

Grasse

Antibes

Juan-les-Pins

R I V I E R A

Cannes

Cap d'Antibes

To Toulon, Marseille, Avignon & Paris

St-Raphaël

Note: In some cases regular train lines and TGV lines share the same track

To Toulon

St-Tropez

Mediterranean

Sea

PRACTICALITIES

Rail

TGV High Speed Rail

Bus

Boat

✈ Airports (Not All Shown)

activated through the Eurail Rail Planner app. Download the app before you leave home. To activate your pass, enter the following in the app: the pass number (provided in the rail pass email), your passport number, and pass activation date (your first day of travel using the pass). Before boarding any train with a digital pass, open the app and "register" the specific journey you're taking (regardless of whether the train requires seat reservations). The app then generates a bar code (or QR code) that the ticket inspector will scan.

Be aware that France's fast TGV and international trains require paid seat reservations (starting at €12). Particularly on international trains, places for rail-pass holders can be limited—which means trains may "sell out" for pass holders well before they've sold out for ticket buyers. Reserving these fast trains at least several weeks in advance is recommended (for strategies, see "Reservations," later).

You'll save money with the second-class version of the France Pass, but first class gives you more options when reserving popular TGV routes. A first-class pass also grants you access to "Salon

Rail Pass or Point-to-Point Tickets?

Will you be better off buying a rail pass or point-to-point tickets? It pays to know your options and choose what's best for your itinerary.

Rail Passes

A Eurail France Pass lets you travel by train in France for one to eight days (consecutively or not) within a one-month period. France is also covered (along with most of Europe) by the classic Eurail Global Pass.

Discounted rates are offered for seniors (age 60 and up) and youths (ages 12-27). Up to two kids (ages 4-11) can travel free with each adult-rate pass (but not with senior rates). All passes offer a choice of first or second class for all ages.

While most rail passes are delivered electronically, it's smart to get your pass sorted before leaving home. For more on rail passes, including current prices and purchasing, visit RickSteves.com/rail.

Point-to-Point Tickets

If you're taking just a couple of train rides, buying individual point-to-point tickets may save you money over a pass. Use this map to add up approximate pay-as-you-go fares for your itinerary, and compare that to the price of a rail pass plus reservations. Keep in mind that significant discounts on point-to-point tickets may be available with advance purchase.

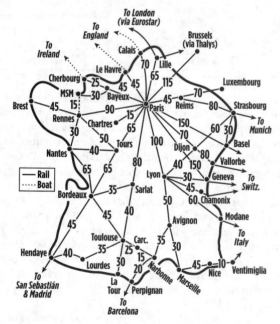

Map shows approximate costs, in US dollars, for one-way, second-class tickets on faster trains.

des Grand Voyageurs" lounges in many bigger-city stations. These first-class lounges are more basic than airport lounges—but they often offer free coffee and water, Wi-Fi, WCs, and a place to charge your phone.

For most trips in France, buy second-class point-to-point tickets. Long-distance trips are where you can really save money with either a rail pass or advance-purchase ticket discounts.

If your trip extends beyond France, consider the **Eurail Global Pass,** covering most of Europe. If you buy two separate passes for neighboring countries, note that you'll use a travel day on each when crossing the border. For more detailed advice on figuring out the smartest rail-pass options for your train trip, visit RickSteves.com/rail.

Buying Tickets

Online: You can buy tickets from home or on-the-go in France at SNCF's online sales site (http://oui.sncf.com) or through the SNCF app.

While there's no deadline to buy any train ticket, the fast, reserved TGV trains get booked up. Buy well ahead for any TGV you cannot afford to miss. Tickets go on sale four months in advance, with a wide range of prices. The cheapest tickets sell out early and reservations for rail-pass holders also get more expensive as seats fill up.

To buy the cheapest advance-discount tickets (up to 60 percent less than full fare), check the app or visit http://oui.sncf.com three to four months ahead of your travel date. (A pop-up window may ask you to choose between being sent to the Rail Europe website or staying on the SNCF page—select "Stay.") Choose your train carefully, noting the departure and arrival stations and number of connections.

Some of the cheapest rates you'll see are for a no-frills version of TGV called OUIGO (www.ouigo.com). These run equally fast but have all second-class seating, luggage limits, seats assigned just a few days before departure—and early check-in is required. They sometimes use alternate stations (such as Marne-la-Vallée outside central Paris), and they don't accept rail passes. Most tickets are delivered electronically, and the site is easy to use.

Note that with either site, many US credit cards won't work unless your bank has certain security protocols set up, such as the "Verified by Visa," "MasterCard SecureCode," or "American Express SafeKey" programs. PayPal is accepted for just a few (nonrefundable) ticket types, not including OUIGO.

Aside from those two websites and the SNCF app, US customers can order through a US agency, such as at RickSteves.com/rail, which does not sell OUIGO tickets; or Trainline (www.trainline.

Coping with Strikes

Going on strike (en grève) is a popular pastime in this revolution-happy country. Because bargaining between management and employees is not standard procedure, workers strike to get attention. Trucks and tractors block main roads and autoroutes (they call it Opération Escargot—"Operation Snail's Pace"), baggage handlers bring airports to their knees, and museum workers make artwork off-limits to tourists. Métro and train personnel seem to strike every year—probably during your trip. What does the traveler do? You could jeter l'éponge (throw in the sponge) and go somewhere less strike-prone (Switzerland's nice), or learn to accept certain events as out of your control. Strikes in France have become unpredictable in length, but if you're aware of them, you can usually plan around them. Your hotelier will know the latest (or can find out). Make a habit of asking your hotel receptionist about strikes. For a list of ongoing and upcoming strikes in France, check www.cestlagreve.fr.

eu), which includes OUIGO departures (and accepts PayPal and Apple Pay). Both charge about the same rates (in euros or dollars).

In France: You can buy train tickets in person at any train station, either from a staffed ticket window or from a machine. You can buy tickets on regional trains for a €10-60 surcharge depending on the length of your trip, but you must find the conductor immediately upon boarding; otherwise it's a €50 minimum charge.

The ticket machines available at most stations are great time-savers when other lines are long. While most machines accept American credit cards if you know your PIN, be prepared with euro coins and bills just in case. Some machines have English instructions, but for those that don't, here are the prompts. (Turn the dial or move the cursor to your choice, and press "Validez" to agree to each step.)

1. *Quelle est votre destination?* (What's your destination?)
2. *Billet Plein Tarif* (Full-fare ticket—yes for most.)
3. *1ère ou 2ème* (First or second class; normally second is fine.)
4. *Aller simple ou aller-retour?* (One-way or round-trip?)
5. *Prix en Euro* (The price should be shown if you get this far.)

Reservations

Reservations are required for any TGV or Intercité train, *couchettes* (sleeping berths) on night trains, and some other trains where indicated in timetables. You can reserve any train at any station any time before your departure. If you're buying a point-to-point ticket

---

Train-Ticket French

Hello, madam/sir, do you speak English?
Bonjour, madame/monsieur, parlez-vous anglais?
(bohn-zhoor, mah-dahm/muhs-yur, par-lay-voo ahn-glay)

I would like a departure for Avignon, on 10 May, about 9:00, the most direct way possible.
Je voudrais un train pour Avignon, pour le 10 Mai, vers 9:00, le plus direct possible.
(zhuh voo-dray uhn tran poor ah-veen-yohn, poor luh dees may, vehr nuhf, luh plew dee-rehk poh-see-bluh)

---

for a TGV or Intercité train, you'll reserve your seat when you purchase your ticket.

Popular TGV routes can fill up quickly. It's wise to book well ahead for any TGV, especially on the busy Paris-Avignon-Nice line. If the TGV trains you want are fully booked, ask about slower TER trains serving the same destination, as these don't require reservations.

If you're using a rail pass, reservations cost €12-20 for domestic travel, depending on the kind of train they're for and when you buy them. Seat reservations on international trains including Thalys, Eurostar, and international TGV routes usually range from €10 to €38, with the price depending on destination and class of service (and can cost up to €60 in first class on TGV Lyria trains to Swiss cities). These international routes allocate a very limited number of seats for rail-pass holders and accept only the Eurail Global Pass (no single-country passes).

Rail-pass holders can book TGV reservations directly at French stations up to departure, if still available, or book on Eurail's website (your account is linked with your pass in the Rail Planner app, though it's helpful to print your reservation as a backup). Given the possible difficulty of getting TGV reservations with a rail pass, I recommend making those reservations online before you leave home.

For trains other than the TGV and Intercité, reservations are generally unnecessary, but are advisable during busy times (for example, Friday and Sunday afternoons, Saturday mornings, weekday rush hours, and holiday weekends; see "Holidays and Festivals" in the appendix).

Baggage Check

While baggage check (*Consigne* or *Espaces Bagages*) is not available at most train stations, you can usually find a place to stash your bag for a small fee near a station. I list baggage check places throughout this book, but new places pop up every year—ask at the TI.

Several online sources allow travelers to arrange baggage storage in advance at shops near train stations in select towns and major cities. Check these websites to see which service might work best for your destinations: www.eelway.com and www.nannybag.com/en.

Major museums and monuments often have free baggage check for visitors. Even if the sight is not particularly interesting to you, the entry fee may be worth it if you need to stow your bags for a few hours.

For security reasons, all baggage should carry a tag with the traveler's first and last name and current address (though it's not enforced). This applies to hand luggage as well as bigger bags that are stowed. Free tags are available at many train stations.

Train Tips
At the Station

- Arrive at the station at least 30 minutes before your departure, when platform numbers are typically posted. Large stations have separate information *(accueil)* windows; at small stations the ticket office gives information. Remember that Avignon and Aix-en-Provence have separate TGV stations that are outside the town center.
- Small stations are minimally staffed; if there is no agent at the station, go directly to the tracks and look for the overhead sign that confirms your train stops at that track.
- Larger stations have platforms with monitors showing TGV layouts (numbered forward or backward) so you can figure out where your car *(voiture)* will stop on the long platform and where to board each car.
- Travelers with first-class tickets or rail passes can gain access to lounges at some stations (see "Rail Passes" earlier).

Validating Tickets, Reservations, and Rail Passes

- At major stations (including all Paris stations) you'll need to scan your ticket at turnstiles to access the tracks. Smaller stations without turnstiles continue to use the old system of validating your ticket in yellow machines near the platform or waiting area. Print-at-home tickets and etickets don't require

validation—just show your QR code to the conductor on the train.

- If you have a rail pass and your train requires a reservation, you may need to present your reservation QR code (in your Rail Planner app) for scanning before boarding the train. For all other trains, conductors will scan your code on board. Having a printed back-up or screenshot of your reservation code is helpful (in case Wi-Fi is spotty at the station and you can't use the app).

PRACTICALITIES

On the Train

- Before getting on a train, confirm that it's going where you think it is. For example, if you want to go to Antibes, ask the conductor or any local passenger, *"À Antibes?"* (ah ahn-teeb; "To Antibes?").
- Some longer trains split off cars en route. Make sure your train car is continuing to your destination by asking, for example, *"Cette voiture va à Avignon?"* (seht vwah-toor vah ah ah-veen-yohn; "This car goes to Avignon?").
- If a non-TGV train seat is reserved, it'll likely be labeled *réservé*, with the cities to and from which it is reserved.
- If you don't understand an announcement, ask your neighbor to explain: *"Pardon madame/monsieur, qu'est-ce qui se passe?"* (kehs kee suh pahs; "Excuse me, what's going on?").
- Verify with the conductor all the transfers you must make: *"Correspondance à Lyon?"* ("Must I transfer to get to Lyon?")
- To guard against theft, keep your bags in sight (directly overhead is ideal but rarely available—the early boarder gets the best storage space). If you must store them in the lower racks by the doors (available in most cars), pay attention at stops. Your bags are most vulnerable to theft before the train takes off and whenever it stops.
- Note your arrival time, so you'll be ready to get off.
- Use the train's free WCs before you get off.

Low-Cost TGV Trains

A TGV train called OUIGO (pronounced "we go") offers rock-bottom fares and no-frills service to select French cities also served by regular TGV trains. You must print your ticket within four days of departure (or download it to your phone), arrive 30 minutes before departure, and activate your ticket. Rail passes are not accepted, and you can only bring one carry-on-size bag plus one handbag for free (children's tickets allow you to bring a stroller). Larger or extra luggage is €5/bag if you pay when you buy your ticket. If you show up without paying in advance, it's €20/bag on the train. There's no food service on the train (BYO), but children under age 12 pay only €8 for a seat. The website explains it all in easy-to-understand English (https://en.oui.sncf/en/ouigo).

BUSES

Buses usually provide the cheapest transportation between European cities. (They're also the cheapest way to cross the English Channel; book at least two days in advance for the best fares.)

Eurolines is the old standby, but two relative newcomers—Blablabus and FlixBus—are cutting prices drastically while offering speedy service, snacks for purchase, Wi-Fi, easy booking, and lots of destinations in France. All of these companies usually provide service between train stations or between train stations and airports within France, as well as to international destinations. The bus is also a handy way to connect Parisian airports with other destinations in France, such as Blois, Rouen, and Caen, for example.

BlaBlaCar buses have routes mostly within France but serve some other European cities as well (www.blablacar.fr). German-run **FlixBus** connects key cities within France and throughout Europe, often from secondary airports and train stations (handy eticket system and easy-to-use app, www.flixbus.com).

A few bus lines are run by the SNCF rail system and are covered by your rail pass (show rail pass at station to get free bus ticket), but most bus lines are not covered. Bus stations *(gare routière)* are usually located next to train stations. Train stations usually have bus information where train-to-bus connections are important—and vice versa for bus companies.

Regional Bus Tips

These tips apply to buses you'll use to get to smaller towns, and for day trips to sights (like Pont du Gard from Avignon or Nîmes).

- Read the train tips described earlier—many also apply to buses (check schedules in advance, arrive at the station early, confirm the destination before you board, find out if you need to transfer, etc.).
- The bus company websites I've listed in this book are usually in French only. Here are some key phrases you'll see: *horaires* (schedules), *en semaine* (usually Monday through Friday or Saturday), *samedi* (Saturday), *dimanche* (Sunday), *jours fériés* (holidays), *LMMJV (Monday, Tuesday, Wednesday, Thursday, Friday), année* (bus runs all year on the days listed), *vac* (runs only during summer vacations), *scol/scolaire* (runs only when school is in session), *ligne* (route or bus line), and *réseau* (network—usually all routes).
- Use TIs to help plan your trip and verify times (TIs have regional bus schedules).
- Be aware that service is sparse or nonexistent on Sunday.

Wednesday bus schedules often are different during the school year, because school is out this day (and regional buses generally operate school service).

- Confirm a bus stop's location in advance (rural stops are often not signed) and be at bus stops at least five minutes early.

TAXIS AND RIDE-BOOKING SERVICES

Most European **taxis** are reliable and reasonable. In many cities, two people can travel short distances by cab for little more than the cost of bus or subway tickets. If you like ride-booking services such as **Uber,** their apps usually work in Europe just like they do in the US: Request a car on your mobile phone (connected to Wi-Fi or data), and the fare is automatically charged to your credit card. In France, Uber services generally work in only the largest cities and are not much cheaper than taxis.

BlaBlaCar offers both nearby and long-distance ride-sharing, connecting drivers with riders who can share the cost of gas, freeway tolls, and other expenses (www.blablacar.in). It's the cheapest way to get around France.

RENTING A CAR

It's cheaper to arrange most car rentals from the US, so research and compare rates before you go. Most of the major US rental agencies (including Avis, Budget, Enterprise, Hertz, and Thrifty) have offices throughout Europe. Also consider the two major Europe-based agencies, Europcar and Sixt, and the French agency, ADA (www.ada.fr). Consolidators such as Auto Europe (AutoEurope.com—or the sometimes cheaper AutoEurope.eu), compare rates at several companies to get you the best deal.

Wherever you book, always read the fine print. Check for add-on charges—such as one-way drop-off fees, airport surcharges, or mandatory insurance policies—that aren't included in the "total price."

Rental Costs and Considerations

If you book well in advance, expect to pay $350-500 for a one-week rental for a basic compact car. Allow extra for supplemental insurance, fuel, tolls, and parking.

Manual vs. Automatic: Many rental cars in Europe are manual—and cars with a stick shift are generally cheaper. If you need an automatic, reserve one specifically. When selecting a car, don't be tempted by a larger model, as it won't be as maneuverable on narrow, winding roads or when squeezing into tight parking lots.

Age Restrictions: Some rental companies impose minimum and maximum age limits. Young drivers (25 and under) and seniors (69 and up) should check the rental policies and rules section of car rental websites. If you're considered too young or too old, look into leasing (covered later), which has less stringent age restrictions.

Choosing Pickup/Drop-off Locations: Always check the hours of the locations you choose. Except at airports and major train stations, most rental offices close from midday Saturday until Monday morning and, in smaller towns, at lunchtime.

When selecting an office, confirm the location on a map. A downtown site might seem more convenient than the airport but could actually be in the suburbs or buried deep in big-city streets. Pedestrianized and one-way streets can make navigation tricky when returning a car at a big-city office or urban train station. Wherever you select, get precise details on the location and allow ample time to find it.

If you want a car for only a day or two (e.g., for the Côtes du Rhône wine route or Luberon villages), you'll likely find it easy to rent on the spot just about anywhere in France. In many cases, this is a worthwhile splurge. All you need is your American driver's license and a major credit card (figure €60-90/day; some include unlimited mileage, others give you 100 kilometers—about 60 miles—for free).

Picking Up Your Car: Before driving off in your rental car, check it thoroughly and make sure any damage is noted on your rental agreement. Rental agencies in Europe tend to charge for even minor damage, so be sure to mark everything. Find out how your car's gearshift, lights, turn signals, wipers, radio, and fuel cap function, and know what kind of fuel the car takes (diesel is common in Europe). When you return the car, make sure the agent verifies its condition with you.

Car Insurance Options

When you rent a car in Europe, the price typically includes liability insurance, which covers harm to other cars or motorists—but not the rental car itself. To limit your financial risk in case of damage to the rental, choose one of these options: Buy a Collision Damage Waiver (CDW; also called "loss damage waiver" or LDW by some firms) with a low or zero deductible from the car-rental company (roughly 30-40 percent extra), get coverage through your credit card (free, but more complicated), or get collision insurance as part of a larger travel-insurance policy.

Basic **CDW** costs $15-30 a day and typically comes with a $1,000-2,000 deductible, reducing but not eliminating your financial responsibility. When you reserve or pick up the car, you'll be offered the chance to "buy down" the basic deductible to zero (for an additional $10-30/day; this is sometimes called "super CDW" or "zero-deductible coverage").

If you opt for **credit-card coverage,** you must decline all coverage offered by the car-rental company, which means they can place a hold on your card to cover the deductible. In case of damage, it can be time-consuming to resolve the charges. Before relying on this option, quiz your credit-card company about how it works.

If you're already purchasing a **travel-insurance policy** for your trip, adding collision coverage can be an economical option. For example, Travel Guard (TravelGuard.com) sells affordable renter's collision insurance as an add-on to its other policies; it's valid everywhere in Europe except the Republic of Ireland, and some Italian car-rental companies refuse to honor it, as it doesn't cover you in case of theft.

For more on car-rental insurance, see RickSteves.com/cdw.

Leasing

For trips of three weeks or more, consider leasing (which automatically includes zero-deductible collision and theft insurance). By technically buying and then selling back the car, you save money on taxes and insurance. Leasing provides you a brand-new car with unlimited mileage and a 24-hour emergency assistance program. You can lease for as little as 21 days to as long as five and a half months; Idea Merge offers two-week leases. Car leases must be arranged from the US. One of several companies offering affordable lease packages is Auto Europe.

These reliable companies offer 21-day lease packages: **Auto France** (Peugeot cars only, +1 800 572 9655, www.autofrance.net); **Idea Merge** (ask about two-week leases; Citroën only, +1 503 715 5810, www.ideamerge.com); and **Kemwel** (Peugeot only, +1 877 820 0668, www.kemwel.com).

RV and Campervan Rental

Even given the extra fuel costs, renting your own rolling hotel can be a great way to save money, especially if you're sticking mainly to rural areas. Keep in mind that RVs in France are much smaller than those you see at home. Consider: **Van It** (rents pop-top VW Eurovan campers that are easy to maneuver on small roads, +33 06 95 99 61 46, www.van-it.com) and **Idea Merge** (best resource for small RV rental, see contact info above).

Navigation Options

If you'll be navigating using your phone or a GPS unit from home, remember to bring a car charger and device mount.

Your Mobile Phone: The mapping app on your phone works fine for navigating Europe's roads. To save on data, most apps allow you to download maps for offline use (do this before you need them, when you have a strong Wi-Fi signal). Some apps—including Google Maps—also have offline route directions, but you'll need mobile data access for current traffic. For more on using a mapping app without burning through data, see "Using Your Phone in Europe," earlier.

GPS Devices: If you want a dedicated GPS unit, consider renting one with your car (about $20/day, or sometimes included—ask). These units offer real-time turn-by-turn directions and traffic without the data requirements of an app. The unit may come loaded only with maps for its home country; if you need additional maps, ask. Make sure you know how to use the device—and that the language is set to English—before you drive off.

Paper Maps and Atlases: Even when navigating primarily with a mobile app or GPS, I always have a paper map, ideally a big, detailed regional road map. It's invaluable for getting the big picture, understanding alternate routes, and filling in if my phone runs out of juice. The free maps you get from your car-rental company usually don't have enough detail. It's smart to buy a better map before you go, or pick one up at a local gas station, bookshop, newsstand, or tourist shop.

Michelin maps are available throughout France at bookstores, newsstands, and gas stations (about €6 each, cheaper than in the US). The orange Michelin map #527 (1:275,000 scale) covers this book's destinations with good detail for drivers. Michelin map #332 is good for the Luberon and the Côtes du Rhône, and map #340 is best for the Bouches-du-Rhône (the southern area around Arles). Drivers going beyond Provence and the Riviera should consider the soft-cover Michelin France atlas (the entire country at 1:200,000, well-organized in a €20 book with an index and maps of major cities). Spend a few minutes learning the Michelin key to get the most sightseeing value out of these maps.

DRIVING

It's a pleasure to explore France by car, but you need to know the rules.

Road Rules: Seat belts are mandatory for all, and children under age 10 must be in the back with a special seat. In city and town centers, traffic merging from the right (even from tiny side streets) may have the right-of-way (*priorité à droite*). So even when you're driving on a major road, pay attention to cars merging from the right. In contrast, cars entering the countless suburban roundabouts must yield (*cédez le passage*). You can't turn right on a red light, U-turns are illegal, and on expressways it's illegal to pass drivers on the right.

When navigating France's narrow village lanes, you'll likely

STOP AND LEARN THESE ROAD SIGNS

 Speed Limit (km/hr)   Yield   No Passing   End of No Passing Zone

One Way   Intersection   Main Road   Expressway

Roundabout Ahead   Danger   No Entry   All Vehicles Prohibited

No Through Road   Restrictions No Longer Apply   Traffic on right has priority   No Stopping

Parking   No Parking   Customs or Toll Road   Peace

encounter short sections where cars must pass single file, one direction at a time (to control speeds). At those spots, you'll see a sign with thick and thin arrows pointing up and down. A thick (white) arrow pointing up in the direction you're traveling means you have priority to pass through the section; a red arrow indicates you must yield to cars coming the other way.

Be aware of typical European road rules; for example, many countries require headlights to be turned on at all times (in France, they must be used in any case of poor visibility), and nearly all forbid handheld mobile-phone use. Ask your car-rental company about these rules, or check the "International Travel" section of the US State Department website (www.travel.state.gov, search for your country in the "Learn About Your Destination" box, then click "Travel and Transportation").

Speed Limits: Because speed limits are by road type, they typically aren't posted, so it's best to memorize them:
- Two-lane D and N routes outside cities and towns: 80 or 90 km/hour, varies by region
- Two-lane roads in villages: 50 km/hour (unless posted at 30 km/hour)
- Divided highways outside cities and towns: 90-110 km/hour
- Autoroutes (toll roads): 130 km/hour (unless otherwise posted)

If it's raining, subtract 10 km/hour on D and N routes and 20 km/hour on divided highways and autoroutes. Speed-limit signs are a red circle around a number; when you see that same number again in gray with a broken line diagonally across it, this means that limit no longer applies. Speed limits drop to 30-50 km/hour in villages (always posted) and must be respected.

Road speeds are monitored regularly with cameras—a mere two kilometers over the limit yields a pricey ticket (a minimum of about €70). The good news is that signs warn drivers a few hun-

PRACTICALITIES

Driving in Provence & the French Riviera

To Paris 400m • 5.5h
To Lyon 120m • 1.5h

Vallon Pont d'Arc (Ardèche Gorges)

P R O V E N C E

Grignan
15m • .5h
Nyons
20m • .75h
30m • 1h
Brantes
30m • 1h
10m • .25h
20m • .5h
Vaison-la-Romaine
Bollène
20m • .5h
20m • .5h
15m • .5h Mont Ventoux
35m • 1.25h
35m • 1h
20m • .75h
35m • 1.5h
Orange
20m • .5h
25m • .75h
Isle-sur-la-Sorgue
Uzès
PONT DU GARD
Avignon
10m • .5h
15m • .5h
15m • .5h
16m • .5h
Roussillon
70m • 2h
Nîmes
15m • .5h
30m • .75h
30m • .75h
St-Rémy
55m • 1h
Lourmarin
15m • .75h
To Carcassonne 120m • 1.5h
20m • .75h
25m • .75h
LES BAUX
10m • .25h
25m • .75h
65m • 1.5h
Arles
55m • .75h
Aigues-Mortes
30m • .75h
30m • .5h
30m • .75h
Phare de la Gacholle
50m • .75h
Aix
95m • 2h (to Cannes)
20m • .5h
Marseille-Provence
20m • .5h
20m • .5h
Stes-Maries-de-la-Mer
20m • .5h
Marseille
20m • .5h
Mediterranean Sea
Cassis
25m • .5h
La Ciotat
Toulon
10m • .5h (via Route des Crêtes)

m = miles
h = hours

20 Kilometers
20 Miles

---

dred yards before the camera and show the proper speed (see image on this page). Look for a sign with a radar graphic that says *Pour votre sécurité, contrôles automatiques*. The French use these cameras not to make money but to slow down traffic—and it works.

Tire Pressure: In Europe, tire pressure is measured in *bars* of pressure. To convert to PSI (pounds per square inch) the formula is: *bar* × 14.5 = PSI (so 2 *bars* would be 2 × 14.5, or 29 PSI). To convert to *bar* pressures from PSI, the formula is: PSI × 0.07 = *bar* (so 30 PSI × 0.07 would

be 2.1 *bar*). Your car's recommended tire pressure is usually found on a sticker mounted on the driver-side doorframe.

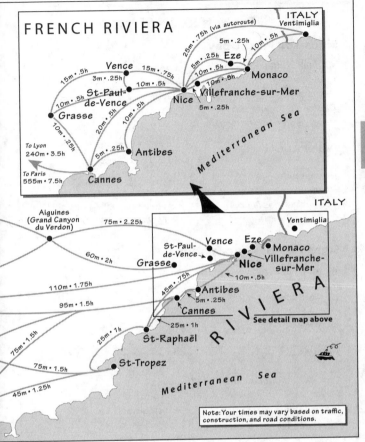

Pulling to the Side of the Road: All rental cars are equipped with a yellow safety vest and triangle. You must wear the vest and display the triangle whenever you pull over on the side of the road (say, to fix a flat tire). If you don't, you could be fined.

Fuel: Gas *(essence)* is expensive—normally about $7 per gallon. Know what type of fuel your car takes before you fill up. Many Americans get marooned by filling with unleaded in a diesel car (many rentals are diesel). Some pumps are color-coded: Unleaded pumps are green and labeled "E" while diesel pumps (often yellow or black) are labeled "B."

Fuel is most expensive on autoroutes and cheapest at big supermarkets. Your US credit and debit cards may not work at self-serve pumps—so you may need to find gas stations with attendants (all autoroute stations have them, as do most countryside stations during business hours)—and be sure to know your card's PIN (explained earlier, under "Money").

PRACTICALITIES

French Road Signs

Signs You Must Obey

Allumez vos feux	Turn on your lights
Cédez le Passage	Yield
Déviation	Detour
Dépassement Interdit	No passing
Parking Interdit/Stationnement Interdit	No parking
Priorité à Droite	Right-of-way is for cars coming from the right
Ralentissez	Slow down
Rappel	Remember to obey the sign
Vous n'avez pas la priorité	You don't have the right of way (when merging)

Signs for Your Information

Autres Directions	Other directions (follow when leaving a city)
Centre Commercial	Shopping center (not city center)
Centre-Ville	City center
Feux	Traffic signal
Horodateur	Ticket-vending machine for parking
Parc de Stationnement/Parking	Parking lot
Route Barrée	Road blocked
Rue Piétonne	Pedestrian-only street
Sauf Riverains	Local access only
Sens Unique	One-way street
Sortie des Camions	Work truck exit
Suivre... (e.g., Pont du Gard, suivre Nîmes)	Follow... (e.g., for Pont du Gard, follow signs for Nîmes)
Toutes Directions	All directions (follow when leaving a city)

Signs Unique to Autoroutes

Aire	Rest stop with WCs, telephones, and sometimes gas stations
Bouchon	Traffic jam ahead
Fluide	No traffic ahead
Péage	Toll
Par Temps de Pluie	When raining (modifies speed limit signs)
Télépéage	Automated tollbooths

Plan ahead for Sundays, as most staffed gas stations in town are closed. I fill my tank every Saturday. If stuck on a Sunday, use an autoroute, where the gas stations are always staffed.

Autoroutes and Tolls: Autoroute tolls are pricey, but the alternative to these super-"feeways" usually means being marooned in countryside traffic—especially near the Riviera. Autoroutes save enough time, gas, and nausea to justify the cost. Mix high-speed "autorouting" with scenic country-road rambling.

You'll usually take a ticket when entering an autoroute and pay when you leave. Figure roughly €1 in tolls for every 15 kilometers driven on the autoroute (or about €15 for two hours). Cash (coins or bills under €50) is your best payment option as some US credit cards won't work (for more on paying at tollbooths, see the sidebar). Estimate your distance and toll costs, then make sure that you have enough cash before entering the autoroute.

Autoroute gas stations are open on Sundays and usually come with well-stocked minimarts, clean restrooms, sandwiches, maps, local products, cheap vending-machine coffee, and Wi-Fi. Many have small cafés or more elaborate cafeterias with reasonable prices. For more information, see www.autoroutes.fr.

Highways: Roads are classified into departmental (D), national (N), and autoroutes (A). D routes (usually yellow lines on maps) are often slower but the most scenic. N routes and important D routes (red lines) are the fastest after autoroutes (orange lines on maps). Green road signs are for national routes; blue are for autoroutes. Some roads in France have had route-number changes (mostly N roads converting to D roads). If you're using an older map, the actual route name may differ from what's on your map. Navigate by destination rather than road name...or buy a new map. There are plenty of good facilities, gas stations (most closed Sun), and rest stops along most French roads.

Parking: Finding a parking place can be a headache in larger cities. Ask your hotelier for ideas, and pay to park at well-patrolled lots (blue *P* signs direct you to parking lots in French cities). Parking garages require that you take a ticket with you and pay at a machine (called a *caisse*) on your way back to the car or at a machine at the exit. American chip cards should work in these machines; otherwise, use euro coins (some accept bills, too). If your credit card does not work and you don't have enough coins, find the garage's *accueil* office, where the attendant can help or direct you to a nearby shop where you can change bills into coins. Overnight parking in garages (usually 19:00-8:00) is generally reasonable (priciest in cities).

Metered parking is strictly monitored in France. At parking machines, prepare to enter your car's license-plate number and the amount of time you need. You may be required to place the receipt

French Tollbooths

For American drivers, getting through the toll payment stations on France's autoroutes is mostly about knowing which lanes to avoid—and having cash and a credit card on hand. Don't assume that your US credit card will work even if it has a chip—have cash as a backup.

When approaching the tollbooths, slow down to study your options (and pull off to the side if you need time to consider your choices). Skip lanes marked only with an orange lowercase "t"—they're reserved for cars using the automatic Télépéage payment system. Follow green arrows to get a ticket (green-arrow lanes are sometimes combined with Télépéage lanes).

When exiting the autoroute, follow the coins icon (usually in white), meaning cash or cards are accepted. If you don't see these icons, take the green-arrow lane. Avoid the orange "t"-only (Télépéage) lane or the credit-card-only lane. Tollbooths are entirely automated (if you have a problem at the tollbooth, press the red button for help). Even machines that take cash usually have a credit card slot—give it a try (know your PIN). Have smaller bills ready (payment machines won't accept €50 bills). Shorter autoroute sections have periodic tollbooths, where you can pay by dropping coins into a basket (change is given for bills, but keep a good supply of coins handy to avoid waiting for an attendant).

To estimate how much cash to have on hand for tolls, use the planning tool at ViaMichelin.com.

on your dash. While the first 30 minutes is often free, you still need to input your license number and get a ticket. Metered parking is sometimes free 12:00-14:00 and usually free 19:00-9:00 and on Sunday (varies by city and parking area). Look for a small machine selling time (called an *horodateur*, usually one per block), and plug in a few coins or your credit card. Avoid spaces outlined in blue, as they require a special permit.

Theft: Theft is a problem, particularly in southern France. Thieves easily recognize rental cars and assume they are filled with a tourist's gear. Try to make your car look locally owned by hiding the "tourist-owned" rental-company decals and putting a French newspaper in your back window. Be sure all of your valuables are out of sight and locked in the trunk—or, even better, with you or in your room. And don't assume that just because you're parked on a main street that you'll be fine. Thieves work fast.

Driving Tips

- France is riddled with roundabouts—navigating them is an art. The key is to know your direction and be ready for your

PRACTICALITIES

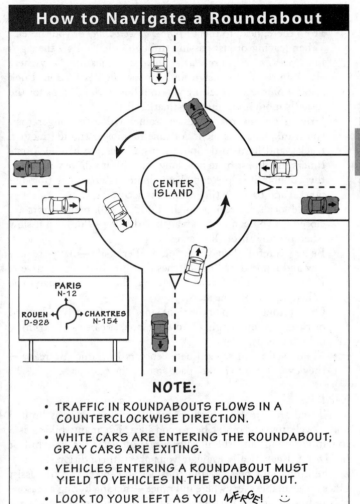

How to Navigate a Roundabout

CENTER ISLAND

PARIS
N-12

ROUEN ←
D-928

→ CHARTRES
N-154

NOTE:

- TRAFFIC IN ROUNDABOUTS FLOWS IN A COUNTERCLOCKWISE DIRECTION.
- WHITE CARS ARE ENTERING THE ROUNDABOUT; GRAY CARS ARE EXITING.
- VEHICLES ENTERING A ROUNDABOUT MUST YIELD TO VEHICLES IN THE ROUNDABOUT.
- LOOK TO YOUR LEFT AS YOU MERGE! ☺

turnoff. If you miss it, take another lap (or two). See the diagram above.

- At intersections and roundabouts, French road signs use the name of an upcoming destination for directions—the highway number is usually missing. That upcoming destination could be a major city, or it could be the next minor town up the road. Check your map ahead of time and get familiar with the names of towns and cities along your route—and even major cities on the same road beyond your destination.
- When navigating into cities, approach intersections cautiously,

stow the map, and follow the signs to *Centre-Ville* (city center). From there, head to the TI *(Office de Tourisme)* or your hotel.

- When leaving or just passing through cities, follow the signs for *Toutes Directions* or *Autres Directions* (meaning "anywhere else") until you see a sign for your specific destination. Look also for *Suivre* signs telling you to follow *(suivre)* signs for the (usually more important) destination listed.

- Driving on any roads but autoroutes will take longer than you think, so allow plenty of time for slower traffic (tractors, trucks, and hard-to-decipher signs all deserve blame). First-timers should estimate how long they think a drive will take... then double it. I pretend that kilometers are miles (for distances) and base my time estimates accordingly.

- While locals are eating lunch (12:00-14:00), many sights are closed, so you can make great time driving—but keep it slow when passing through villages.

- Be very careful when driving on smaller roads—many are narrow and flanked by little ditches that lure inattentive drivers. I've met several readers who "ditched" their cars (and had to be pulled out by local farmers).

- On autoroutes, keep to the right lanes to let fast drivers by, and be careful when merging into a left lane, as cars can be coming at high speeds.

- Motorcycles will scream between cars in traffic. Be ready— they expect you to make space so that they can pass.

BIKING

You'll find areas in France where public transportation is limited and bicycle touring might be a good idea. For many, biking is a romantic notion, and the novelty wears off after the first hill or headwind. Realistically evaluate your physical condition, be clear on the limitations present, and consider an e-bike. Electric-assist bikes are available everywhere in France—making biking a reasonable option for many. For a good touring bike, figure about €15 for a half-day and €20 for a full day (double that for e-bikes). You'll pay more for better equipment; generally the best bikes are available through bike shops, not at train stations or other outlets.

Whether on a standard bike or e-bike, start with an easy pedal, then decide how ambitious you feel. Most find that one hour on a narrow, hard seat is enough. I've listed bike-rental shops where appropriate (TIs can also guide you) and suggested a few of my favorite rides. French cyclists often do not wear helmets, though most rental outfits have them (for a small fee).

FLIGHTS

To compare flights, begin with an online travel search engine: Kayak is the top site for flights to and within Europe, easy-to-use Google Flights has price alerts, and Skyscanner includes many inexpensive flights within Europe. To avoid unpleasant surprises, before you book be sure to read the small print about refunds, changes, and the costs for "extras" such as reserving a seat, checking a bag, or printing a boarding pass.

Flights to Europe: Start looking for international flights about four to six months before your trip, especially for peak-season travel. Depending on your itinerary, it can be efficient and no more expensive to fly into one city and out of another. If your flight requires a connection in Europe, see our hints on navigating Europe's top hub airports at RickSteves.com/hub-airports.

Flights Within Europe: Flying between European cities is surprisingly affordable. If you're visiting one or more French cities on a longer European trip—or linking up far-flung French cities (such as Paris and Nice)—a flight can save both time and money. Before buying a long-distance train or bus ticket, first check the cost of a flight on one of Europe's airlines, whether a major carrier or a no-frills outfit like EasyJet, Vueling, or Ryanair. Also check Air France for specials. Be aware that flying with a discount airline can have drawbacks, such as minimal customer service, time-consuming treks to secondary airports, and a larger carbon footprint than a train or bus.

Flying to the US and Canada: Because security is extra tight for flights to the US, be sure to give yourself plenty of time at the airport (see www.tsa.gov for the latest rules).

Resources from Rick Steves

Begin Your Trip at RickSteves.com

My mobile-friendly **website** is *the* place to explore Europe in preparation for your trip. You'll find thousands of fun articles, videos, and radio interviews; a wealth of money-saving tips for planning your dream trip; travel news dispatches; a video library of travel talks; my travel blog; our latest guidebook updates (RickSteves. com/update); and the free Rick Steves Audio Europe app. You can also follow me on Facebook, Instagram, and Twitter.

Our **Travel Forum** is a well-groomed collection of message boards where our travel-savvy community answers questions and shares their personal travel experiences—and our well-traveled staff chimes in when they can be helpful (RickSteves.com/forums).

Our **online Travel Store** offers bags and accessories that I've designed to help you travel smarter and lighter. These include my popular carry-on bags (which I live out of four months a year), money belts, totes, toiletries kits, adapters, guidebooks, and planning maps (RickSteves.com/shop).

Our website can also help you find the perfect **rail pass** for your itinerary and your budget, with easy, one-stop shopping for rail passes, seat reservations, and point-to-point tickets (RickSteves.com/rail).

Rick Steves' Tours, Guidebooks, TV Shows, and More

Small Group Tours: Want to travel with greater efficiency and less stress? We offer more than 40 itineraries reaching the best destinations in this book...and beyond. Each year about 30,000 travelers join us on about 1,000 Rick Steves bus tours. You'll enjoy great guides and a fun bunch of travel partners (with small groups of around 24 to 28 travelers). You'll find European adventures to fit every vacation length. For all the details, and to get our tour catalog, visit RickSteves.com/tours or call us at +1 425 608 4217.

Books: This book is just one of many books in my series on European travel, which includes country and city guidebooks, Snapshots (excerpted chapters from bigger guides), Pocket Guides (full-color little books on big cities), "Best Of" guidebooks (condensed, full-color country guides), and my budget-travel skills handbook, *Rick Steves Europe Through the Back Door*. A complete list of my titles—including phrase books, cruising guides, and travelogues on European art, history, and culture—appears near the end of this book.

TV Shows and Travel Talks: My public television series, *Rick Steves' Europe*, covers Europe from top to bottom with over 100 half-hour episodes—and we're working on new shows every year (watch full episodes on my website for free). My free online video library, Rick Steves Classroom Europe, offers a searchable database of short video clips on European history, culture, and geography (Classroom.RickSteves.com). And to raise your travel I.Q., check out the video versions of our popular classes (covering most European countries as well as travel skills, packing smart, cruising, tech for travelers, European art, and travel as a political act—RickSteves.com/travel-talks).

Audio Tours on My Free App: I've produced dozens of free, self-guided audio tours of the top sights in Europe. For those tours and other audio content, get my free **Rick Steves Audio Europe app,** an extensive online library organized by destination. For more on my app, see page 28.

Radio: My weekly public radio show, *Travel with Rick Steves,* features interviews with travel experts from around the world. It airs on 400 public radio stations across the US. An archive of programs is available at RickSteves.com/radio.

Podcasts: You can enjoy my travel content via several free podcasts. The podcast version of my radio show brings you a weekly, hour-long travel conversation. My other podcasts include a weekly selection of video clips from my public television show, my audio tours of Europe's top sights, and live recordings of my travel classes (RickSteves.com/watch-read-listen/audio/podcasts).

APPENDIX

Holidays and Festivals

This list includes selected festivals in the Provence and French Riviera region, plus national holidays observed throughout France. Many sights and banks close on national holidays—keep this in mind when planning your itinerary. Before planning a trip around a festival, verify the dates with the festival website, France's tourist office (http://us.france.fr), or my "Upcoming Holidays and Festivals in France" web page at RickSteves.com/europe/france/festivals. Hotels get booked up on Easter weekend, Labor Day, Ascension Day, Pentecost, Bastille Day, and the winter holidays.

Jan 1	New Year's Day
Jan 6	Epiphany
Feb-March	Carnival (Mardi Gras) parades and fireworks, Nice (www.nicecarnaval.com)
March/April	Easter weekend (Good Friday-Easter Monday): April 7-10, 2023; March 29-April 1, 2024
March/April	Feria de Pâques, Arles (bullfights; coincides with Easter weekend)

May 1	Labor Day
May 8	V-E (Victory in Europe) Day
Mid-May	Cannes Film Festival (www.festival-cannes.com)
May	Ascension: May 18, 2023, May 9, 2024
Late May	Monaco Grand Prix auto race (www.acm.mc)
May/June	Pentecost and Whit Monday: May 28-29, 2023, May 19-20, 2024
July 14	Bastille Day (fireworks, dancing, and revelry)
Mid-July	Nice Jazz Festival (www.nicejazzfestival.fr)
July	Aix Festival (classical music and opera; www.festival-aix.com)
July	Avignon Festival (theater, dance, and music; www.festival-avignon.com)
July	Tour de France, national bicycle race culminating in Paris (www.letour.fr)
July	Jazz à Juan International Jazz Festival, Antibes/Juan-les-Pins (www.jazzajuan.com)
July-Aug	Festival of Pyrotechnic Art, Cannes (fireworks, www.festival-pyrotechnique-cannes.com)
Aug 15	Assumption of Mary
Mid-Sept	Féria du Riz, Arles (bullfights)
Nov 1	All Saints' Day
Nov 11	Armistice Day
Dec 25	Christmas Day
Dec 31	New Year's Eve

Books and Films

To learn more about France past and present, and specifically Provence and the French Riviera, check out a few of these books or films. To learn what's making news in France, you'll find *France 24 News* online at France24.com/en. See the Traveling with Children chapter for recommendations for kids.

Nonfiction

A to Z of French Food, a French to English Dictionary of Culinary Terms (G. de Temmerman, 1995). The most complete (and priciest) menu reader around is beloved by foodies.

At Home in France (Ann Barry, 1996). An American author describes her visits to her country house.

The Course of French History (Pierre Goubert, 1988). Goubert provides a basic summary of French history.

A Distant Mirror (Barbara Tuchman, 1987). Respected historian Barbara Tuchman paints a portrait of 14th-century France.

French or Foe? (Polly Platt, 1994). This best seller, along with its follow-up, *Savoir-Flair!* is an essential aid for interacting with the French and navigating the intricacies of their culture.

A Goose in Toulouse and Other Culinary Adventures in France (Mort Rosenblum, 2000). This series of essays provides keen insights on rural France through its focus on cuisine.

La Seduction: How the French Play the Game of Life (Elaine Sciolino, 2011). Sciolino, former Paris bureau chief of the *New York Times*, gives travelers a fun, insightful, and tantalizing peek into how seduction is used in all aspects of French life—from small villages to the halls of national government.

Markets of Provence (Marjorie R. Williams, 2016). This is the definitive guide to Provence's wondrous outdoor markets.

Portraits of France (Robert Daley, 1991). Part memoir, part travelogue, this is a charming reminiscence of the writer's lifelong relationship with France, including marrying a French girl on his first trip there.

Postcards from France (Megan McNeill Libby, 1997). This perceptive account tells the adventures of an American exchange student adjusting to life in France.

The Road from the Past: Traveling Through History in France (Ina Caro, 1994). Caro's enjoyable travel essays take you on a chronological journey through France's historical sights.

Sixty Million Frenchmen Can't Be Wrong (Jean-Benoît Nadeau and Julie Barlow, 2003). This is a must-read for anyone serious about understanding French culture, contemporary politics, and what makes the French tick.

Travelers' Tales: Paris and *Travelers' Tales: France* (edited by James O'Reilly, Larry Habegger, and Sean O'Reilly, 2002). Notable writers explore Parisian and French culture.

Two Towns in Provence (M. F. K. Fisher, 1964). Aix-en-Provence and Marseille are the subjects of these two stories by the celebrated American food writer. She also writes about her life in France in *Long Ago in France: The Years in Dijon* (1929).

A Year in Provence and *Toujours Provence* (Peter Mayle, 1989/1991). Mayle's memoirs include humorous anecdotes about restoring and living in a 200-year-old farmhouse in a remote area of the Luberon.

The Yellow House: Van Gogh, Gauguin, and Nine Turbulent Weeks in

Arles (Martin Gayford, 2006). This historical account vividly chronicles Van Gogh and Gauguin's tumultuous stay in Arles.

Fiction

The Fly-Truffler (Gustaf Sobin, 1999). After the death of his young wife, a Provençal man stays in touch with her spirit through intimate dream visions.

Hotel Pastis (Peter Mayle, 1993). Mayle, whose nonfiction books are recommended earlier, also wrote fiction set in Provence, including this book and *A Good Year.*

Joy of Man's Desiring (Jean Giono, 1935). Giano captures the charm of rural France. (The author also wrote the Johnny Appleseed eco-fable set in Provence, *The Man Who Planted Trees.*)

Film and TV

The Chorus (2004). Filled with angelic choir music, this touching film tells the story of a schoolteacher and the boys he brings together.

Cyrano de Bergerac (1990). A homely, romantic poet woos his love with the help of another, better-looking man (look for scenes filmed at the Abbaye de Fontenay).

Dirty Rotten Scoundrels (1988). Steve Martin and Michael Caine star in this comedy filmed in and around Villefranche-sur-Mer.

French Kiss (1995). This romantic comedy includes scenes in the French countryside and Cannes, as well as Paris.

A Good Year (2006). This British-American romantic comedy, starring Russell Crowe and Marion Cotillard, is loosely based on the novel by Peter Mayle and filmed at a Luberon winery recommended in this book.

The Horseman on the Roof (1995). The beautiful Juliette Binoche seeks her missing husband in this romance-drama set in 1830s southern France.

Jean de Florette (1986). This marvelous tale of greed and intolerance follows a hunchback as he fights for the property he inherited in rural France. Its sequel, *Manon of the Spring* (1986), continues with his daughter's story.

My Father's Glory and *My Mother's Castle* (1991). These companion films, based on the memoirs of writer/filmmaker Marcel Pagnol, depict his early life in Provence.

The Return of Martin Guerre (1982). A man returns to his village in southwestern France from the Hundred Years' War—but is he really who he claims to be?

Ronin (1998). Robert De Niro stars in this crime caper, which includes a car chase through Paris and scenes filmed in Nice, Villefranche-sur-Mer, and Arles.

To Catch a Thief (1955). Alfred Hitchcock's thriller showcases the French Riviera and crackling performances by Grace Kelly and Cary Grant.

Conversions and Climate

Numbers and Stumblers
- Europeans write a few of their numbers differently than we do. 1 = 1, 4 = 4, 7 = 7.
- In Europe, dates appear as day/month/year, so Christmas 2023 is 25/12/23.
- Commas are decimal points and decimals are commas. A dollar and a half is $1,50, one thousand is 1.000, and there are 5.280 feet in a mile.
- When counting with fingers, start with your thumb. If you hold up your first finger to request one item, you'll probably get two.
- What Americans call the second floor of a building is the first floor in Europe.
- On escalators and moving sidewalks, Europeans keep the left "lane" open for passing. Keep to the right.

Metric Conversions
A **kilogram** equals 1,000 grams (about 2.2 pounds). One hundred **grams** (a common unit at markets) is about a quarter-pound. One **liter** is about a quart, or almost four to a gallon.

A **kilometer** is six-tenths of a mile. To convert kilometers to miles, cut the kilometers in half and add back 10 percent of the original (120 km: 60 + 12 = 72 miles). One **meter** is 39 inches—just over a yard.

1 foot = 0.3 meter	1 square yard = 0.8 square meter
1 yard = 0.9 meter	1 square mile = 2.6 square kilometers
1 mile = 1.6 kilometers	1 hectare = 2.47 acres
1 centimeter = 0.4 inch	1 ounce = 28 grams
1 meter = 39.4 inches	1 quart = 0.95 liter
1 kilometer = 0.62 mile	1 kilogram = 2.2 pounds
32°F = 0°C	

Clothing Sizes
When shopping for clothing, use these US-to-European comparisons as general guidelines (but note that no conversion is perfect).

Women: For pants and dresses, add 32 in France (US 10 = French 42). For blouses and sweaters, add 8 for most of Europe (US 32 = European 40). For shoes, add 30-31 (US 7 = European 37/38).

Men: For shirts, multiply by 2 and add about 8 (US 15 = European 38). For jackets and suits, add 10. For shoes, add 32-34.

Children: Clothing is sized by height—in centimeters (2.5 cm = 1 inch), so a US size 8 roughly equates to 132-140. For shoes up to size 13, add 16-18, and for sizes 1 and up, add 30-32.

Nice's Climate

First line, average daily high; second line, average daily low; third line, average days without rain. For more detailed weather statistics for destinations in this book (as well as the rest of the world), check Wunderground.com.

J	F	M	A	M	J	J	A	S	O	N	D
50°	53°	59°	64°	71°	79°	84°	83°	77°	68°	58°	52°
35°	36°	41°	46°	52°	58°	63°	63°	58°	51°	43°	37°
23	22	24	23	23	26	29	26	24	23	21	21

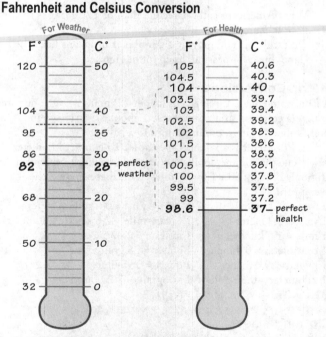

Fahrenheit and Celsius Conversion

Europe takes its temperature using the Celsius scale, while we opt for Fahrenheit. For a rough conversion from Celsius to Fahrenheit, double the number and add 30. For weather, remember that 28°C is 82°F—perfect. For health, 37°C is just right. At a launderette, 30°C is cold, 40°C is warm (usually the default setting), 60°C is hot, and 95°C is boiling. Your air-conditioner should be set at about 20°C.

APPENDIX

Packing Checklist

Whether you're traveling for five days or five weeks, you won't need more than this. Pack light to enjoy the sweet freedom of true mobility.

Clothing

- ☐ 5 shirts: long- & short-sleeve
- ☐ 2 pairs pants (or skirts/capris)
- ☐ 1 pair shorts
- ☐ 5 pairs underwear & socks
- ☐ 1 pair walking shoes
- ☐ Sweater or warm layer
- ☐ Rainproof jacket with hood
- ☐ Tie, scarf, belt, and/or hat
- ☐ Swimsuit
- ☐ Sleepwear/loungewear

Money

- ☐ Debit card(s)
- ☐ Credit card(s)
- ☐ Hard cash (US $100-200)
- ☐ Money belt

Documents

- ☐ Passport
- ☐ Other required ID: Vaccine card/Covid test, entry visa, etc.
- ☐ Driver's license, student ID, hostel card, etc.
- ☐ Tickets & confirmations: flights, hotels, trains, rail pass, car rental, sight entries
- ☐ Photocopies of important documents
- ☐ Insurance details
- ☐ Guidebooks & maps

Electronics

- ☐ Mobile phone
- ☐ Camera & related gear
- ☐ Tablet/ebook reader/laptop
- ☐ Headphones/earbuds
- ☐ Chargers & batteries
- ☐ Phone car charger & mount (or GPS device)
- ☐ Plug adapters

Toiletries

- ☐ Basics: soap, shampoo, toothbrush, toothpaste, floss, deodorant, sunscreen, brush/comb, etc.
- ☐ Medicines & vitamins
- ☐ First-aid kit
- ☐ Glasses/contacts/sunglasses
- ☐ Face masks & hand sanitizer
- ☐ Sewing kit
- ☐ Packet of tissues (for WC)
- ☐ Earplugs

Miscellaneous

- ☐ Daypack
- ☐ Sealable plastic baggies
- ☐ Laundry supplies: soap, laundry bag, clothesline, spot remover
- ☐ Small umbrella
- ☐ Travel alarm/watch
- ☐ Notepad & pen
- ☐ Journal

Optional Extras

- ☐ Second pair of shoes (flip-flops, sandals, tennis shoes, boots)
- ☐ Travel hairdryer
- ☐ Picnic supplies
- ☐ Disinfecting wipes
- ☐ Water bottle
- ☐ Fold-up tote bag
- ☐ Small flashlight
- ☐ Mini binoculars
- ☐ Small towel or washcloth
- ☐ Inflatable pillow/neck rest
- ☐ Tiny lock
- ☐ Address list (to mail postcards)
- ☐ Extra passport photos

Pronunciation Guide for Place Names

When using the phonetics: Try to nasalize the n sound (let the sound come through your nose). Note that the "ahn" combination uses the "ah" sound in "father," but the "an" combination uses the "a" sound in "sack." Pronounce the "ī" as the long "i" in "light." If your best attempt at pronunciation meets with a puzzled look, just point to the place name on the list.

Aigues-Mortes	ayg-mort
Aiguines	ayg-ween
Aix-en-Provence	ehks ahn proh-vahns
Antibes	ahn-teeb
Ardèche Gorges	ar-dehsh gorzh
Arles	arl
Avignon	ah-veen-yohn
Balazuc	bah-lah-zewk
Bedoin	buh-dwan
Biot	bee-oht
Bonnieux	bohn-yuh
Brantes	brahnt
Buis-les-Baronnies	bwee-lay-bah-roh-nee
Buoux	byoo
Cairanne	kay-rahn
Camargue	kah-marg
Cannes	kan
Cap Ferrat	kahp feh-rah
Cassis	kah-see
Cavaillon	kah-vī-yohn
Châteauneuf-du-Pape	shah-toh-nuhf-dew-pahp
Côte du Rhône	koht dew rohn
Crestet	kruh-stay
Eze-Bord-de-Mer	ehz-bor-duh-mehr
Eze-le-Village	ehz-luh-vee-lahzh
Gigondas	zhee-gohn-dahs
Gordes	gord
Gourdon	goor-dohn
Grasse	grahs
Grignan	green-yahn
Isle-sur-la-Sorgue	eel-sewr-lah-sorg
Joucas	zhoo-kahs
Juan-les-Pins	zhwahn-lay-pan
Le Trophée des Alpes	luh troh-fay dayz ahlp
La Turbie	lah tewr-bee

Pronunciation Guide for Place Names
(continued)

Lacoste	lah-kohst
Le Bar-sur-Loup	luh bar-sewr-loo
Les Baux	lay boh
Lourmarin	loor-mah-ran
Luberon	lew-buh-rohn
Marseille	mar-say
Ménerbes	may-nehrb
Menton	mahn-tohn
Monaco	moh-nah-koh
Monte Carlo	mohn-tay kar-loh
Mont Ventoux	mohn vahn-too
Moustier-Ste-Marie	moost-yay-sahnt-mah-ree
Nice	nees
Nîmes	neem
Nyons	nee-yohns
Oppède-le-Vieux	oh-pehd-luh-vee-uh
Orange	oh-rahnzh
Pont du Gard	pohn dew gar
Port Grimaud	por gree-moh
Provence	proh-vahns
Roussillon	roo-see-yohn
Saignon	sayn-yohn
Séguret	say-gew-ray
Ste-Jalles	san-zhahl
St-Jean	san-zhahn
St-Paul-de-Vence	san-pohl-duh-vahns
St-Rémy-de-Provence	san-ray-mee-duh-pro-vahns
St-Saturnin-lès-Apt	san-sah-tewr-nan-lehz-ahpt
St-Tropez	san-troh-pay
Stes-Maries-de-la-Mer	sahnt-mah-ree-duh-lah-mehr
Suzette	sew-zeht
Tourrettes-sur-Loup	too-reht-sewr-loo
Uzès	ew-zehs
Vaison-la-Romaine	vay-zohn lah roh-mehn
Vallauris	vah-loh-rees
Vence	vahns
Viens	vee-ahn
Villa Kérylos	vee-lah kay-ree-lohs
Villefranche-sur-Mer	veel-frahnsh-sewr-mehr

French Survival Phrases

When using the phonetics, try to nasalize the n sound.

Good day.	Bonjour.	bohn-zhoor
Mrs. / Mr.	Madame / Monsieur	mah-dahm / muhs-yuh
Do you speak English?	Parlez-vous anglais?	par-lay-voo ahn-glay
Yes. / No.	Oui. / Non.	wee / nohn
I understand.	Je comprends.	zhuh kohn-prahn
I don't understand.	Je ne comprends pas.	zhuh nuh kohn-prahn pah
Please.	S'il vous plaît.	see voo play
Thank you.	Merci.	mehr-see
I'm sorry.	Désolé.	day-zoh-lay
Excuse me.	Pardon.	par-dohn
No problem.	Pas de problème.	pah duh proh-blehm
It's good.	C'est bon.	say bohn
Goodbye.	Au revoir.	oh ruh-vwahr
one / two / three	un / deux / trois	uhn / duh / trwah
four / five / six	quatre / cinq / six	kah-truh / sank / sees
seven / eight	sept / huit	seht / weet
nine / ten	neuf / dix	nuhf / dees
How much is it?	C'est combien?	say kohn-bee-an
Write it?	Ecrivez?	ay-kree-vay
Is it free?	C'est gratuit?	say grah-twee
Included?	Inclus?	an-klew
Where can I buy / find...?	Où puis-je acheter / trouver...?	oo pwee-zhuh ah-shuh-tay / troo-vay
I'd like / We'd like...	Je voudrais... / Nous voudrions...	zhuh voo-dray / noo voo-dree-ohn
...a room.	...une chambre.	ewn shahn-bruh
...a ticket to ___.	...un billet pour ___.	uhn bee-yay poor ___
Is it possible?	C'est possible?	say poh-see-bluh
Where is...?	Où est...?	oo ay
...the train station	...la gare	lah gar
...the bus station	...la gare routière	lah gar root-yehr
...tourist information	...l'office du tourisme	loh-fees dew too-reez-muh
Where are the toilets?	Où sont les toilettes?	oo sohn lay twah-leht
men / women	hommes / dames	ohm / dahm
left / right	à gauche / à droite	ah gohsh / ah drwaht
straight	tout droit	too drwah
pull / push	tirez / poussez	tee-ray / poo-say
When does this open / close?	Ça ouvre / ferme à quelle heure?	sah oo-vruh / fehrm ah kehl ur
At what time?	À quelle heure?	ah kehl ur
Just a moment.	Un moment.	uhn moh-mahn
now / soon / later	maintenant / bientôt / plus tard	man-tuh-nahn / bee-an-toh / plew tar
today / tomorrow	aujourd'hui / demain	oh-zhoor-dwee / duh-man

In a French Restaurant

I'd like / We'd like...	Je voudrais / Nous voudrions... zhuh voo-dray / noo voo-dree-ohn
...to reserve...	...réserver... ray-zehr-vay
...a table for one / two.	...une table pour un / deux. ewn tah-bluh poor uhn / duh
Is this seat free?	C'est libre? say lee-bruh
The menu (in English), please.	La carte (en anglais), s'il vous plaît. lah kart (ahn ahn-glay) see voo play
service (not) included	service (non) compris sehr-vees (nohn) kohn-pree
to go	à emporter ah ahn-por-tay
with / without	avec / sans ah-vehk / sahn
and / or	et / ou ay / oo
breakfast / lunch / dinner	petit déjeuner / déjeuner / dîner puh-tee day-zhuh-nay / day-zhuh-nay / dee-nay
special of the day	plat du jour plah dew zhoor
specialty of the house	spécialité de la maison spay-see-ah-lee-tay duh lah may-zohn
appetizers	hors d'œuvre or duh-vruh
first course (soup, salad)	entrée ahn-tray
main course (meat, fish)	plat principal plah pran-see-pahl
bread / cheese	pain / fromage pan / froh-mahzh
sandwich / soup	sandwich / soupe sahnd-weech / soop
salad	salade sah-lahd
meat / chicken	viande / poulet vee-ahnd / poo-lay
fish / seafood	poisson / fruits de mer pwah-sohn / frwee duh mehr
fruit / vegetables	fruit / légumes frwee / lay-gewm
dessert	dessert day-sehr
mineral water	eau minérale oh mee-nay-rahl
tap water	l'eau du robinet loh dew roh-bee-nay
(orange) juice	jus (d'orange) zhew (doh-rahnzh)
coffee / tea / milk	café / thé / lait kah-fay / tay / lay
wine / beer	vin / bière van / bee-ehr
red / white	rouge / blanc roozh / blahn
glass / bottle	verre / bouteille vehr / boo-tay
Cheers!	Santé! sahn-tay
More. / Another.	Plus. / Un autre. plew / uhn oh-truh
The same.	La même chose. lah mehm shohz
The bill, please.	L'addition, s'il vous plaît. lah-dee-see-ohn see voo play
Do you accept credit cards?	Vous prenez les cartes? voo pruh-nay lay kart
tip	pourboire poor-bwahr
Delicious!	Délicieux! day-lees-yuh

For more user-friendly French phrases, check out *Rick Steves' French Phrase Book* or *Rick Steves' French, Italian & German Phrase Book*.

INDEX

INDEX

MAP INDEX

Explore Europe

At ricksteves.com you can browse through thousands of articles, videos, photos and radio interviews, plus find a wealth of money-saving travel tips for planning your dream trip. And with our mobile-friendly website, you can easily access all this great travel information anywhere you go.

TV Shows

Preview the places you'll visit by watching entire half-hour episodes of *Rick Steves' Europe* (choose from all 100 shows) on-demand, for free.

your travel dreams into affordable reality

Radio Interviews

Enjoy ready access to Rick's vast library of radio interviews covering travel tips and cultural insights that relate specifically to your Europe travel plans.

Travel Forums

Learn, ask, share! Our online community of savvy travelers is a great resource for first-time travelers to Europe, as well as seasoned pros.

Travel News

Subscribe to our free Travel News e-newsletter, and get monthly updates from Rick on what's happening in Europe.

Classroom Europe®

Check out our free resource for educators with 500 short video clips from the *Rick Steves' Europe* TV show.

Rick's Free Travel App

Get your FREE **Rick Steves Audio Europe**™ app to enjoy…

- Dozens of self-guided tours of Europe's top museums, sights and historic walks

- Hundreds of tracks filled with cultural insights and sightseeing tips from Rick's radio interviews

- All organized into handy geographic playlists

- For Apple and Android

With Rick whispering in your ear, Europe gets even better.

Find out more at ricksteves.com

Gear up for your next adventure at ricksteves.com

Light Luggage

Pack light and right with Rick Steves' affordable, custom-designed rolling carry-on bags, backpacks, day packs and shoulder bags.

Accessories

From packing cubes to moneybelts and beyond, Rick has personally selected the travel goodies that will help your trip go smoother.

Shop at ricksteves.com

Save time and energy

This guidebook is your independent-travel toolkit. But for all it delivers, it's still up to you to devote the time and energy it takes to manage the preparation and logistics that are essential for a happy trip. If that's a hassle, there's a solution.

Rick Steves Tours

A Rick Steves tour takes you to Europe's most interesting places with great

guides and small groups. We follow Rick's favorite itineraries, ride in comfy buses, stay in family-run hotels, and bring you intimately close to the Europe you've traveled so far to see. Most importantly, we take away the logistical headaches so you can focus on the fun.

Join the fun

This year we'll take thousands of free-spirited travelers—nearly half of them repeat customers— along with us on 50 different itineraries, from Athens to Istanbul. Is a Rick Steves tour the right fit for your travel dreams?

Find out at ricksteves.com, where you can also check seat availability and sign up. Europe is best experienced with happy travel partners. We hope you can join us.

See our itineraries at ricksteves.com

Rick Steves
BEST OF ITALY

Rick Steves
BEST OF SPAIN

Rick Steves
FRANCE

Rick Steves
LONDO

BEST OF GUIDES

Full-color guides in an easy-to-scan
format. Focused on top sights
and experiences in the most
popular European destinations

Best of England
Best of Europe
Best of France
Best of Germany
Best of Ireland
Best of Italy
Best of Scotland
Best of Spain

COMPREHENSIVE GUIDES

City, country, and regional guide
printed on Bible-thin paper. Pack
with detailed coverage for a mul
week trip exploring iconic sights
and venturing off the beaten pat

Amsterdam & the Netherlands
Barcelona
Belgium: Bruges, Brussels,
   Antwerp & Ghent
Berlin
Budapest
Croatia & Slovenia
Eastern Europe
England
Florence & Tuscany
France
Germany
Great Britain
Greece: Athens & the Peloponne
Iceland
Ireland
Istanbul
Italy
London
Paris
Portugal
Prague & the Czech Republic
Provence & the French Riviera
Rome
Scandinavia
Scotland
Sicily
Spain
Switzerland
Venice
Vienna, Salzburg & Tirol

HE BEST OF ROME

e, Italy's capital, is studded with
an remnants and floodlit-fountain
es. From the Vatican to the Colos-
with crazy traffic in between, Rome
derful, huge, and exhausting. The
s, the heat, and the weighty history

of the Eternal City where Caesars walked
can make tourists wilt. Recharge by taking siestas, gelato breaks, and after-dark
walks, strolling from one atmospheric
square to another in the refreshing evening air.

f Pantheon—which
t dome until the
2,000 years old
over 1,500).

Athens in the Vat-
es the humanistic
,.

adiators fought
other, entertaining

Rome ristorante,

Rick Steves books are available from your favorite booksel[f]
Many guides are available as ebooks.

POCKET GUIDES
Compact color guides for shorter trips

Amsterdam
Athens
Barcelona
Florence
Italy's Cinque Terre
London
Munich & Salzburg

Paris
Prague
Rome
Venice
Vienna

SNAPSHOT GUIDES
Focused single-destination coverage

Basque Country: Spain & France
Copenhagen & the Best of Denmark
Dublin
Dubrovnik
Edinburgh
Hill Towns of Central Italy
Krakow, Warsaw & Gdansk
Lisbon
Loire Valley
Madrid & Toledo
Milan & the Italian Lakes District
Naples & the Amalfi Coast
Nice & the French Riviera
Normandy
Northern Ireland
Norway
Reykjavík
Rothenburg & the Rhine
Sevilla, Granada & Southern Spain
St. Petersburg, Helsinki & Tallinn
Stockholm

CRUISE PORTS GUIDES
Reference for cruise ports of call

Mediterranean Cruise Ports
Scandinavian & Northern European
  Cruise Ports

Complete your library with...

TRAVEL SKILLS & CULTURE
Study up on travel skills and gain insight on history and culture

Europe 101
Europe Through the Back Door
Europe's Top 100 Masterpieces
European Christmas
European Easter
European Festivals
For the Love of Europe
Italy for Food Lovers
Travel as a Political Act

PHRASE BOOKS & DICTIONARIES
French
French, Italian & German
German
Italian
Portuguese
Spanish

PLANNING MAPS
Britain, Ireland & London
Europe
France & Paris
Germany, Austria & Switzerland
Iceland
Ireland
Italy
Scotland
Spain & Portugal

Credits

CONTRIBUTOR
Gene Openshaw

Gene has co-authored more than a dozen books with Rick, specializing in Europe's art, history, and culture. In particular, their *Europe 101: History and Art for the Traveler* and *Europe's Top 100 Masterpieces* have helped bring European art to life. Gene also writes for Rick's television shows, produces the audio tours, and is a regular guest on Rick's radio show. For public TV, Gene has co-authored *Rick Steves Fascism in Europe* and the ambitious six-hour series *Rick Steves Art of Europe*. Outside of the travel world, Gene has composed an opera called *Matter*, a violin sonata, and dozens of songs. His latest book is *Michelangelo at Midlife*. Gene lives near Seattle, where he roots for the Mariners in good times and bad.

RESEARCHER
For help with this edition, Rick and Steve relied on...

Virginie Moré

After living for 10 years in Los Angeles, Montana, and Florida, Virginie has been back in France for a few years. Originally from Brittany, she now lives in southern Burgundy with her husband Olivier, where they run an eco-friendly guesthouse. Along with doing book research, she teaches Americans about French culture and history while leading Rick Steves' Europe tours and guiding small private groups in this beautiful, off-the-beaten-path wine region.

ACKNOWLEDGMENTS
The co-authors would like to first thank ace researcher, Virginie Moré, for her fine work and helpful insights into French culture. We'd also like to thank David Price, who lives in Avignon and is a valuable source of information about key sights in Provence, and Boba Vukadinovic-Millet, who lives in Nice and keeps us up-to-date on sightseeing in the French Riviera. And thank you to Risa Laib for her 25-plus years of dedication to the Rick Steves guidebook series.

PHOTO CREDITS

Avalon Travel
Hachette Book Group
1700 Fourth Street
Berkeley, CA 94710

Printed in Canada by Friesens.
15th Edition. First printing November 2022.

ISBN 978-1-64171-477-8

For the latest on Rick's talks, guidebooks, tours, public television series, and public radio show, contact Rick Steves' Europe, 130 Fourth Avenue North, Edmonds, WA 98020, +1 425 771 8303, RickSteves.com, rick@ricksteves.com.

Rick Steves' Europe
Managing Editor: Jennifer Madison Davis
Assistant Managing Editor: Cathy Lu
Editors: Glenn Eriksen, Suzanne Kotz, Rosie Leutzinger, Teresa Nemeth, Jessica Shaw, Carrie Shepherd
Editorial & Production Assistant: Megan Simms
Contributor: Gene Openshaw
Researcher: Virginie Moré
Graphic Content Director: Sandra Hundacker
Maps & Graphics: Orin Dubrow, David C. Hoerlein, Lauren Mills, Mary Rostad, Laura Terrenzio

Avalon Travel
Senior Editor and Series Manager: Madhu Prasher
Associate Managing Editor: Jamie Andrade
Editor: Rachael Sablik
Proofreader: Kelly Lydick
Indexer: Stephen Callahan
Production & Typesetting: Lisi Baldwin, Rue Flaherty, Jane Musser, Ravina Schneider
Maps & Graphics: Kat Bennett
Cover Design: Kimberly Glyder Design

COLOR MAPS

Provence & The Riviera • Provence • The Riviera
• Arles • Nice

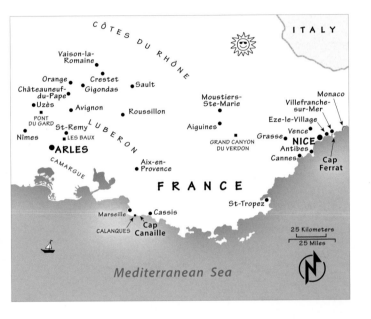

Provence & the Riviera

To Grenoble

To Valence & Lyon

A-7

D-93

Rhône

• Aubenas

• Montélimar

• Balazuc

Grignan

Ardèche Gorges

Valréas

• Nyons

St-Martin

A-7

COTES DU RHONE

Vaison-la-Romaine

Mont ▲ Ventoux

Sis

D-7

P R O V E N C E

Orange

Sault •

D-950

Carpentras

Châteauneuf-du-Pape

D-942

D-49

D-4

Le Colorado Provençal

Uzès •

PONT DU GARD

Avignon

Isle-sur-la-Sorgue

D-2

Roussillon

Viens

D-900

Apt

M

Nîmes

TGV STN.

Tarascon

St-Rémy

Cavaillon

L U B E R O N

N-570

• Lourmarin

A-9

Fontvieille

LES BAUX

Cadenet

Pertuis

To Montpellier

A-54

D-17

Maussane-les-Alpilles

A-7

Durance

I

Arles

D-113

• Salon

AIGUES-MORTES

D-37

C A M A R G U E

Rhône

D-568

Istres

Etang de Berre

AIX TGV STN.

Aix-en-Provence

A-8

St-Max

Petit Rhône

Salin de Giraud

Fos-sur-Mer

Marseille-Provence ✈

A-52

D-56(

Stes-Maries-de-la-Mer

Martigues

A-55

Marseille

• Aubagne

A

Les Calanques ♠ •

Cassis ↙

La Ciotat

D-141 (La Route des Crêtes)

La s

See Provence detail map

To Ajacc Corsic

M e d i t e r r e

LEGEND

▬ A-7 ▬	Freeway/Autoroute
───	Rail Line
━━━	TGV Rail (High-speed)
··········	Ferry Line
✈	Airport
♠	National Park/Natural Wonder
■	Ruin, Museum, Other Point of Interest

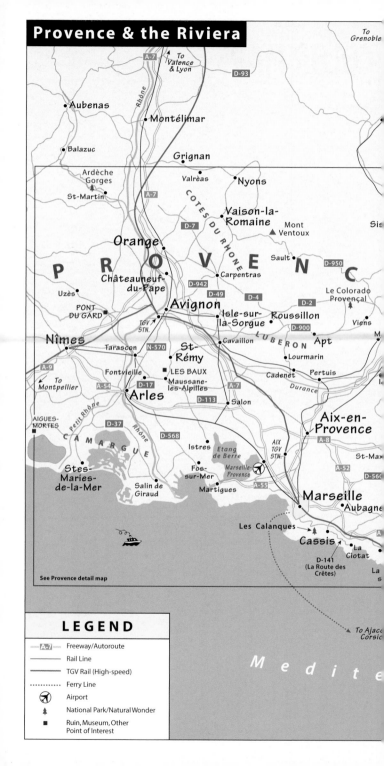

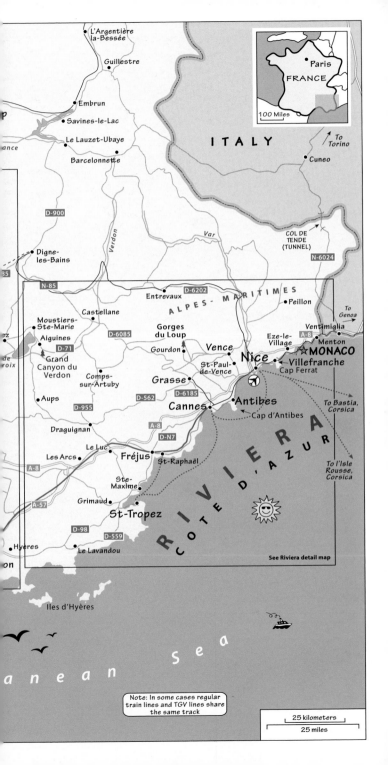

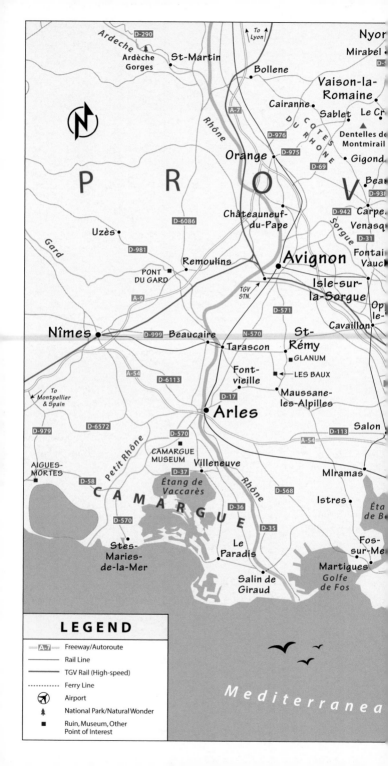

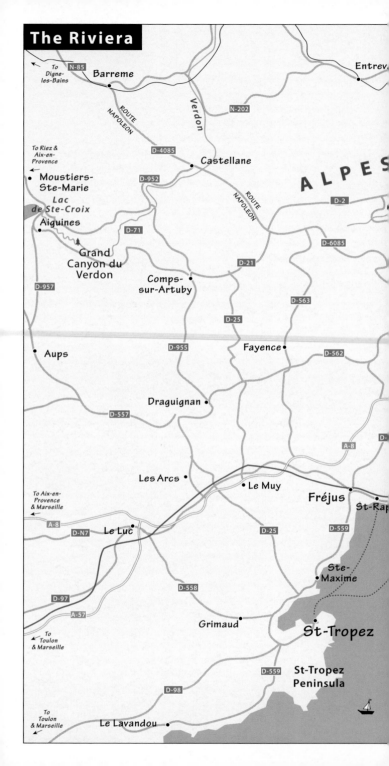

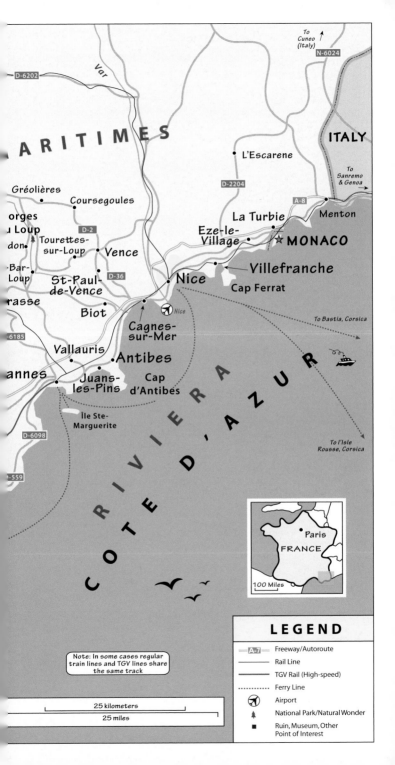

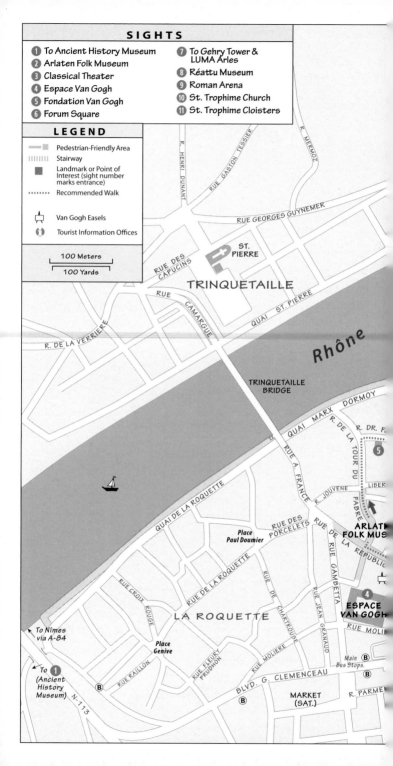

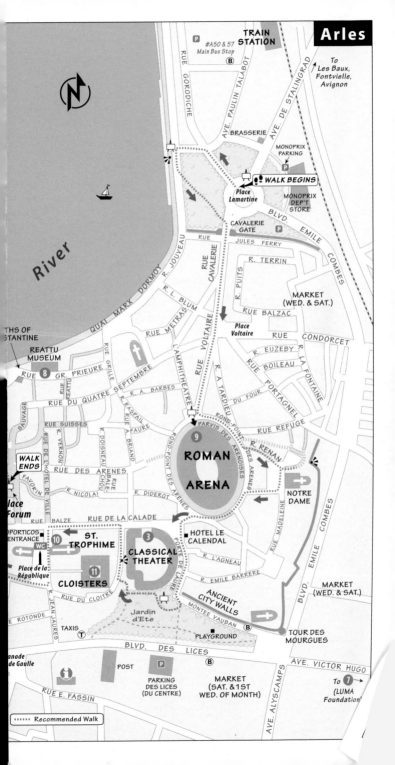

Arles

TRAIN STATION

P #A50 & 57 Main Bus Stop B

To Les Baux, Fontvielle, Avignon

RUE GORODICHE

AVE. PAULIN TALABOT

AVE. DE STALINGRAD

BRASSERIE

MONOPRIX PARKING P

WALK BEGINS

Place Lamartine

MONOPRIX DEP'T STORE

CAVALERIE GATE P

BLVD. EMILE COMBES

JULES FERRY

RUE CAVALERIE

R. TERRIN

R. PUITS

MARKET (WED. & SAT.)

QUAI MARX DORMOY

R. JOUVEAU

RUE METRAS

RUE BALZAC

Place Voltaire

RUE VOLTAIRE

RUE CONDORCET

R. EUZEBY

R. BOILEAU

LA FONTAINE

R. L. BLUM

BATHS OF CONSTANTINE

REATTU MUSEUM

RUE 8 GR. PRIEURE

RUE GRILLE

RUE DU QUATRE SEPTEMBRE

L'AMPHITHEATRE

R. A. TARDIEU

DU FOUR

RUE PORTAGNEL

RUE SAUVAGE

RUE REATTU

R. A. BARBES

ROND-POINT

RUE REFUGE

RUE SUISSES

R. RASPAIL

RUE FAURE

PARVIS DES ARENOISES

R. VERNON

R. DOISNEAU

R. BRIAND

9

ROMAN

R. RENAN

WALK ENDS

R. DE L'HOTEL DE VILLE

RUE DES ARENES

ARENA

NOTRE DAME

FAVORIN

R. NICOLAI

R. DIDEROT

Place Forum

RUE BALZE

RUE DE LA CALADE

PORTE DE LAURE

RUE MADELEINE

BLVD. EMILE COMBES

PORTICOS ENTRANCE

WC

10 ST. TROPHIME

3 CLASSICAL THEATER

HOTEL LE CALENDAL

R. L'AGNEAU

MARKET (WED. & SAT.)

Place de la République

11 CLOISTERS

RUE DU CLOITRE

R. EMILE BARRERE

ANCIENT CITY WALLS

R. JEAN JAURES

MONTEE VAUBAN B

TOUR DES MOURGUES

E. ROTONDE

TAXIS T

Jardin d'Ete

PLAYGROUND

AVE. VICTOR HUGO

Esplanade de Gaulle

RUE E. FASSIN

i

POST

P PARKING DES LICES (DU CENTRE)

BLVD. DES LICES B

MARKET (SAT. & 1ST WED. OF MONTH)

AVE. ALYSCAMPS

To 7 (LUMA Foundation)

······ Recommended Walk

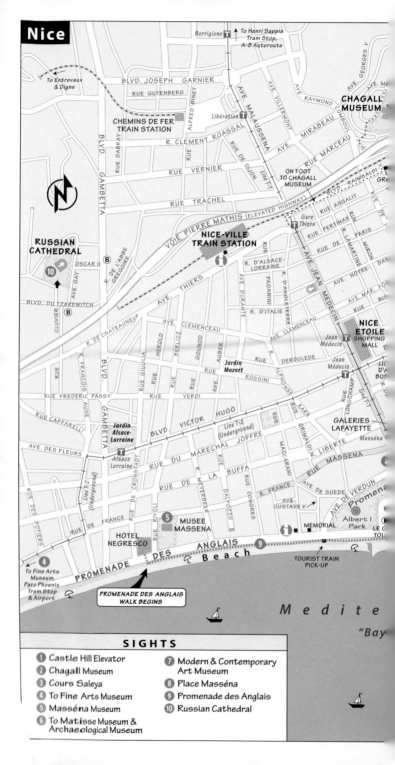

Nice

SIGHTS

1 Castle Hill Elevator
2 Chagall Museum
3 Cours Saleya
4 To Fine Arts Museum
5 Masséna Museum
6 To Matisse Museum & Archaeological Museum
7 Modern & Contemporary Art Museum
8 Place Masséna
9 Promenade des Anglais
10 Russian Cathedral

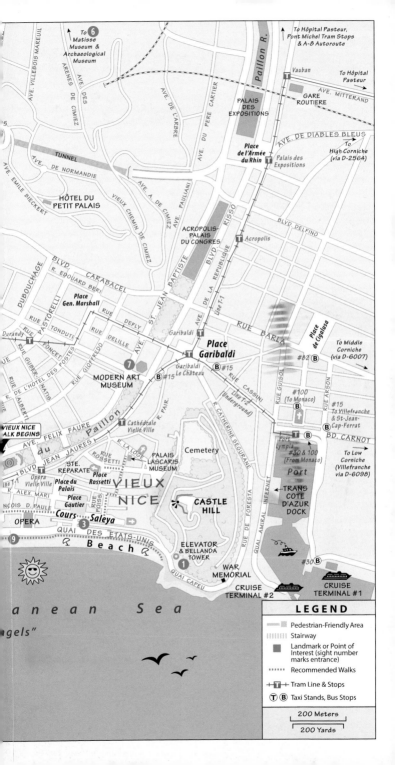

To **6** Matisse Museum & Archaeological Museum

To Hôpital Pasteur, Pont Michel Tram Stops & A-8 Autoroute

Paillon R.

Vauban

To Hôpital Pasteur

AVE. MAREUIL

AVE. VILLEBOIS MAREUIL

ARÈNES DE CIMIEZ

AVE. DES

AVE. DE CIMIEZ

AVE. DE L'ARBRE

AVE. DU PÈRE CARTIER

GARE ROUTIÈRE

AVE. MITTERAND

PALAIS DES EXPOSITIONS

Place de l'Armée du Rhin

AVE. DE DIABLES BLEUS

To High Corniche (via D-2564)

Palais des Expositions

AVE. EMILE BIECKERT

TUNNEL

AVE. DE NORMANDIE

AVE. A. DE CIMIEZ

AVE. PAULIANI

VIEUX CHEMIN DE CIMIEZ

BLVD. DELFINO

HÔTEL DU PETIT PALAIS

ACROPOLIS-PALAIS DU CONGRES

BLVD. RISSO

Acropolis

DUBOUCHAGE

BLVD. CARABACEL

R. EDOUARD BÉRI

ST. JEAN BAPTISTE

AVE. DE LA RÉPUBLIQUE

RUE BARLA

Place de Cigalusa

To Middle Corniche (via D-6007)

Place Gen. Marshall

RUE PASTORELLI

RUE

DEFLY

RUE

Line T-1

Garibaldi

Place Garibaldi

#62 B

RUE

DELILLE

AVE.

B #15

Durandy

RUE TONDUTI

RUE GUBER NATIS

RUE

GOFFREDO

MODERN ART MUSEUM

7

B #15

Garibaldi Le Château

B #15

RUE CASSINI

Line T-2 (Underground)

RUE GUSOL

#100 (To Monaco)

B

#15 To Villefranche & St-Jean-Cap-Ferrat

RUE DE L'HÔTEL DES POSTES

RUE AKSON

RUE ALBERTI

Cathédrale Vieille Ville

R. PAIR.

R. CATHERINE SÉGURANE

B

VIEUX NICE WALK BEGINS

AVE. FELIX FAURE

Paillon du

BLVD. JEAN JAURÈS

RUE ROSSETTI

PALAIS LASCARIS MUSEUM

Cemetery

Port Lympia

T B

BD. CARNOT

To Low Corniche (Villefranche via D-6098)

STE. RÉPARATE

Place Rossetti

#30 & 100 (From Monaco)

B

Line T-1

Opera Vieille Ville

ALEX. MARI

Place du Palais

VIEUX NICE

CASTLE HILL

RUE DE FORESTA

Port

NCOIS D. PAULE

Place Gautier

RUE DROITE

TRANS CÔTE D'AZUR DOCK

OPERA

9

Cours Saleya **3**

QUAI DES ETATS-UNIS

RUE AMIRAL INFERNET

QUAI AMIRAL INFERNET

Beach

ELEVATOR & BELLANDA TOWER

1

#30 B

WAR MEMORIAL

QUAI CAFEU

CRUISE TERMINAL #2

CRUISE TERMINAL #1

anean Sea

gels"

LEGEND

- Pedestrian-Friendly Area
- Stairway
- Landmark or Point of Interest (sight number marks entrance)
- Recommended Walks
- ┼Ⓣ┼ Tram Line & Stops
- Ⓣ Ⓑ Taxi Stands, Bus Stops

200 Meters

200 Yards

Let's Keep on Travelin'

Your trip doesn't need to end.

Follow Rick on social media!